CW01214214

The Gentle Civilizer of Nations
The Rise and Fall of International Law 1870–1960

Modern international law was born from the impulse to "civilize" late nineteenth-century attitudes towards race and society, argues Martti Koskenniemi in this highly readable study of the rise and fall of classical international law. In a work of wide-ranging intellectual scope, Koskenniemi traces the emergence of a liberal sensibility relating to international matters in the late nineteenth century, and its subsequent decline after the Second World War. He combines legal analysis, historical and political critique and semi-biographical studies of key figures (including Hans Kelsen, Hersch Lauterpacht, Carl Schmitt, and Hans Morgenthau); he also considers the role of crucial institutions (such as the *Institut de droit international* and the League of Nations). His discussion of legal and political realism at American law schools ends in a critique of post-1960 "instrumentalism." Along with the book's other chapters, this provides a unique reflection on the possibility of critical international law today.

MARTTI KOSKENNIEMI is Professor of International Law at the University of Helsinki and member of the Global Law School Faculty at New York University. He was a member of the Finnish Ministry for Foreign Affairs from 1978 to 1995, serving, among other assignments, as head of the International Law Division. He has also served as Finland's representative at a number of international bodies and meetings, including numerous sessions of the UN General Assembly; he was legal adviser to the Finnish delegation at the UN Security Council in 1989–1990. His main publications are *From Apology to Utopia. The Structure of International Legal Argument* (1989), *International Law Aspects of the European Union* (edited, 1997) and *State Succession: Codification Tested Against the Facts* (co-edited, with Pierre Michel Eisemann, 1999).

Available titles in the series

MARTTI KOSKENNIEMI
The Gentle Civilizer of Nations
The Rise and Fall of International Law 1870–1960
0 521 62311 1

ANTONIO CASSESE
Self-Determination of Peoples
A Legal Appraisal
0 521 63752 X

ARTHUR WATTS
International Law and the Antarctic Treaty System
0 521 46311 4

ELIHU LAUTERPACHT
Aspects of the Administration of International Justice
0 521 46312 2

CHRISTOPH H. SCHREUER
State Immunity
Some Recent Developments
0 521 46319 X

IAN SINCLAIR
The International Law Commission
0 521 46320 3

IGNAZ SEIDL-HOHENVELDERN
Corporations in and under International Law
0 521 46324 6

The Gentle Civilizer of Nations:

The Rise and Fall of International Law 1870–1960

MARTTI KOSKENNIEMI

CAMBRIDGE UNIVERSITY PRESS

PUBLISHED BY THE PRESS SYNDICATE OF THE UNIVERSITY OF CAMBRIDGE
The Pitt Building, Trumpington Street, Cambridge, United Kingdom

CAMBRIDGE UNIVERSITY PRESS
The Edinburgh Building, Cambridge CB2 2RU, UK
40 West 20th Street, New York NY 10011-4211, USA
477 Williamstown Road, Port Melbourne, VIC 3207, Australia
Ruiz de Alarcón 13, 28014 Madrid, Spain
Dock House, The Waterfront, Cape Town 8001, South Africa

http://www.cambridge.org

© Martti Koskenniemi 2001

This book is in copyright. Subject to statutory exception
and to the provisions of relevant collective licensing agreements,
no reproduction of any part may take place without
the written permission of Cambridge University Press.

First published 2002
Reprinted 2002

Printed in the United Kingdom at the University Press, Cambridge

Typeface Monotype Baskerville 11/13 pt.   *System* QuarkXPress™   [SE]

A catalogue record for this book is available from the British Library

Library of Congress Cataloguing in Publication data

Koskenniemi, Martti.
The gentle civilizer of nations: the rise and fall of international law, 1870–1960
/ Martti Koskenniemi.
p.   cm. – (Hersch Lauterpacht memorial lectures)
Includes bibliographical references and index.
ISBN 0-521-62311-1
1. International law–History.   I. Title.   II. Series.

KZ1242.K67   2001
341′.09–dc21   2001035099

ISBN 0 521 62311 1 hardback

I cannot resist the thought that if we were able to . . . refrain from constant attempts at moral appraisal – if, in other words, instead of making ourselves slaves of the concepts of international law and morality, we would confine these concepts to the unobtrusive, almost feminine, function of the gentle civilizer of national self-interest in which they find their true value – if we were able to do these things . . . then, I think, posterity might look back upon our efforts with fewer and less troubled questions.
                George Kennan, *American Diplomacy* (Expanded edn., University of Chicago Press, 1984) pp. 53–54.

To the memory of Vieno Koskenniemi (1897–1989),
the gentlest of civilizers

Contents

Preface	page xi
List of abbreviations	xiv
Introduction	1

1 "The legal conscience of the civilized world"   11
- A manifesto   12
- An old-fashioned tradition   19
- A transitional critic: Kaltenborn von Stachau   24
- An amateur science   28
- A time of danger   35
- A meeting in Ghent, 1873   39
- A romantic profession: Bluntschli   42
- A social conception of law   47
- Method: enlightened inwardness   51
- Towards a culture of human rights: Fiore   54
- Advancing the liberal project   57
- Limits of liberalism   67
- Cultural consciousness   70
- Culture as character   76
- The elusive sensibility   88

2 Sovereignty: a gift of civilization: international lawyers and imperialism 1870–1914   98
- Ambivalent attitudes   99
- Informal empire 1815–1870: *hic sunt leones*   110
- The lawyers 1815–1870   112
- The demise of informal empire in Africa   116
- The Berlin Conference 1884–1885   121

Contents

The myth of civilization: a logic of exclusion–inclusion	127
Looking for a standard	132
Between universality and relativism: colonial treaties	136
The myth of sovereignty: a beneficent empire	143
The limits of sovereignty: civilization betrayed	149
Occupation is nothing – Fashoda	152
Sovereignty as terror – the Congo	155
From sovereignty to internationalization	166

3 International law as philosophy: Germany 1871–1933 — 179

1871: law as the science of the legal form	182
From form to substance: the doctrine of the rational will	188
Between the dangerous and the illusory State	194
Rechtsstaat – domestic and international: Georg Jellinek	198
Rationalism and politics: a difficulty	206
Drawing lines in the profession	209
Public law and the Hague Treaties	210
A pacifist profession? Kohler, Schücking, and the First World War	213
The internationalists: between sociology and formalism	222
1914	228
Getting organized	231
Beyond Versailles: the end of German internationalism	236
Ways of escape – I: Hans Kelsen and liberalism as science	238
Ways of escape – II: Erich Kaufmann and the conservative reaction	249
Break: the end of philosophy	261

4 International law as sociology: French "solidarism" 1871–1950 — 266

Internationalism as nationalism: the idea of France	270
From civilists to functionalists 1874–1918: Renault to Pillet	274
Solidarity at the Hague: Léon Bourgeois	284
The theory of solidarism	288
The war of 1914–1918 and solidarism	291
Scientific solidarism: Durkheim and Duguit	297
International solidarity . . . almost: Alvarez and Politis	302
Meanwhile in Paris . . .	309
L'affaire Scelle	316
Solidarity with tradition: Louis Le Fur	317

Contents

The solidarity of fact: Georges Scelle	327
Which solidarity? Whose tradition? The Spanish Civil War	338
The European Union	342
The twilight of the idea of France: between politics and pragmatism	348

5 Lauterpacht: the Victorian tradition in international law — 353

Tradition in modernity	353
A complete system	361
Between Zionism and assimilation	369
A political commitment	376
Nuremberg and human rights	388
The birth of pragmatism	399
A Grotian tradition?	406
Coda	411

6 Out of Europe: Carl Schmitt, Hans Morgenthau, and the turn to "international relations" — 413

A 1950 retrospective	415
Vision of a new order	418
The ambivalences of a *Katechon* (restrainer)	422
A discipline transforms itself: Schmitt on Scelle and Lauterpacht	424
Against liberal neutralizations and depoliticizations	426
"Whoever invokes humanity wants to cheat"	432
Schmitt and Morgenthau: the primacy of the political	436
Another retrospective	437
International law and politics: an asymmetrical relationship	440
The formation of a German thinker: between law and desire	445
The guardian of international law: sanctions	455
Schmitt and Morgenthau: the pedigree of anti-formalism	459
From international law to international relations	465
The heritage of realism in American international law	474
Empire's law	480
A culture of formalism?	494

Epilogue	510
Bibliography	518
Index	558

Preface

The essays in this book are inspired by many sources and reflect various conversations I have had with international lawyers in the course of the past four years or so. The initiator of the idea of the book was Professor Sir Elihu Lauterpacht, who kindly invited me to give the Sir Hersch Lauterpacht Memorial Lectures at the University of Cambridge in 1998, and in that connection pointed out that this privilege also involved a commitment to prepare the lectures for publication. Eli's hospitality in Cambridge in 1997 and the discussions I had with him also underlie my interpretation of his father's work in chapter 5. As always, I am indebted to Professor David Kennedy from the Harvard Law School for innumerable conversations and collaborative projects, Dighton weeks and weekends, shorter and longer periods together and in wider company in the Boston area, Helsinki and other places, at various stages of writing of these essays. But the only person to have read the whole of this work, and whose comments and criticisms are reflected on every page, as in everything about its author, is Tiina Astola. This book would not exist without them.

Many other friends and colleagues have been involved. The comments and work of Dr. Outi Korhonen are reflected in the description of the culture of late nineteenth-century internationalists. The account of international lawyers and imperialism (chapter 2) draws on the important work of Professors Antony Anghie and Nathaniel Berman, and from discussions I have had with them over the years. That section owes much to the invitation I received from Dr. Surya Subedi to give the Josephine Onoh Memorial Lecture at the University of Hull in February 1999. I also want to thank the participants in the international legal history project under Professor Michael Stolleis at the Max Planck

Institute for Legal History in Frankfurt for the debate on persons and problems relating to my German story (chapter 3), among them particularly Dr. Betsy Roeben, whose work on Bluntschli I have plundered in chapter 1 and Dr. Ingo Hueck whose writings on the institutional aspects of the German inter-war scene underlies sections of chapter 3. I am grateful for a number of French friends and colleagues, too, among them in particular Professors Pierre Michel Eisemann and Charles Leben, who directed me to primary and secondary materials without which I could not have made sense of the French story in chapter 4. I also thank Doyen Vedel for correspondence on Louis Le Fur, Dr. Oliver Diggelmann for a discussion and a copy of his unpublished dissertation on Max Huber and Georges Scelle as well as Professor Geneviève Burdeau and Mr. Pierre Bodeau for providing relevant materials or references. Chapter 6 on Carl Schmitt and Hans Morgenthau and the "fall" of international law collects several strands of conversation over the years. Some of it draws on papers and discussions at a conference organized by Dr. Michael Byers in Oxford in 1998, and a continuous debate I have had with Professor Anne-Marie Slaughter about the meaning and direction of her "dual agenda." David Kennedy's work underlies much of the description of the American scene. People with whom I have discussed various aspects of the following essays but whose influence cannot be clearly allocated to particular sections include Philip Allott, David Bederman, Thomas M. Franck, Gunther Frankenberg, Benedict Kingsbury, Karen Knop, Jan Klabbers, Mattias Kumm, Susan Marks, Reut Paz, Jarna Petman, and Joseph Weiler. The librarians at the Library of Parliament (Helsinki) were again as helpful as ever. Colleagues at the Erik Castrén Institute of International Law and Human Rights (Helsinki) bore without complaint the additional burden of my absent-mindedness about current matters that needed attention. At home, Aino and Lauri took their father's excessive book-wormishness with a fine sense of irony. So did my mother, Anna-Maija Koskenniemi. I thank them all.

I could not have written this book without one year's leave of absence from the University of Helsinki, made possible by a grant received from the Finnish Academy (Suomen Akatemia).

Parts of this book draw on materials that I have published earlier. Chapter 5 on Lauterpacht is essentially the same essay that was published in (1997) 8 *European Journal of International Law* (pp. 215–263). Chapter 2 contains passages included in 'International Lawyers and Imperialism' in *Josephine Onoh Memorial Lecture 1999* (University of Hull,

Preface

2000). Chapter 5 is a development of my 'Carl Schmitt, Hans Morgenthau and the Image of Law in International Relations', in Michael Byers (ed.), *The Role of Law in International Politics* (Oxford University Press, 1999) pp. 17–34.

The cases where I have used existing translations of French or German materials can be seen from the notes and the bibliography. The rest of the translations are my own.

Martti Koskenniemi,
Helsinki, January 17, 2001

Abbreviations

AFDI	*Annuaire français de droit international*
AJIL	*American Journal of International Law*
Annuaire IDI	*Annuaire de l'Institut de droit international*
ARWP	*Archiv für Rechts und Wirtschaftsphilosophie*
ASIL	*American Society of International Law*
BYIL	*British Year Book of International Law*
EJIL	*European Journal of International Law*
ICJ	International Court of Justice
IDI	Institut de droit international
ILA	International Law Association
PCIJ	Permanent Court of International Justice
RdC	*Recueil des cours de l'Académie de droit international*
RDI (Paris)	*Revue de droit international*
RDI	*Revue de droit international et de législation comparée*
Reports	Reports of Judgments, Advisory Opinions and Orders of the International Court of Justice
RGDIP	*Revue générale de droit international public*
ZaöRV	*Zeitschrift für ausländisches öffentliches Recht und Völkerrecht*

Introduction

I

This book grew out of the Sir Hersch Lauterpacht Memorial Lectures that I gave at the University of Cambridge in the fall of 1998. It is, admittedly, quite a bit longer than those original lectures were, but it is still informed by the same interest. This was to expand upon an article I had written a year earlier on Hersch Lauterpacht himself for the *European Journal of International Law* and in which I had attempted to cover the same ground I had done in a book ten years earlier, but from an altogether different perspective. In that book I had described international law as a structure of argumentative moves and positions, seeking to provide a complete – even "totalising" – explanation for how international law in its various practical and theoretical modes could simultaneously possess a high degree of formal coherence as well as be substantively indeterminate.[1] The result was a formal–structural analysis of the "conditions of possibility" of international law as an argumentative practice – of the transformational rules that underlay international law as a discourse – that relied much on binary oppositions between arguments and positions and relationships between them. But as perceptive critics pointed out, whatever merits that analysis had, its image of the law remained rather static. Even if it laid the groundwork for describing the production of arguments in a professionally competent international law practice, it fell short of explaining why individual lawyers had come to endorse particular positions or arguments in distinct periods or places. Even if it claimed that all legal practice was a

[1] Martti Koskenniemi, *From Apology to Utopia: The Structure of International Legal Argument* (Helsinki, Lakimiesliiton kustannus, 1989).

"politics of law," it did not tell what the "politics" of international lawyers had been. Like any structural explanation, it did not situate the lawyers whose work it described within social and political contexts, to give a sense that they were advancing or opposing particular political projects from their position at universities, foreign ministries, or other contexts of professional activity.

The Lauterpacht essay – the only one of the chapters below that has been previously published as such – chose another approach. It tried to put in a historical frame the development of the ideas and arguments of one of the twentieth century's most influential international lawyers. The 1998 lectures were an extension of that essay, an exploration of why Lauterpacht came to hold the positions he did and what happened to the heritage he left. This book can (but need not necessarily) be read as a continuation of that effort. It constitutes an experiment in departing from the constraints of the structural method in order to infuse the study of international law with a sense of historical motion and political, even personal, struggle. To the extent that what emerges is a description of a particular sensibility, or set of attitudes and preconceptions about matters international, it might also be described as a series of essays in the history of ideas. But in such case, no assumption about history as a monolithic or linear progress narrative is involved, nor any particular theory about causal determination of ideas or by ideas of something else. If instead of "ideas," the essays choose to speak of "sensibility," this is because the fluidity of the latter enables connoting closure and openness at the same time, as does the more familiar but slightly overburdened notion of "culture." The international law that "rises" and "falls" in this book is, then, not a set of ideas – for many such ideas are astonishingly alive today – nor of practices, but a sensibility that connotes both ideas and practices but also involves broader aspects of the political faith, image of self and society, as well as the structural constraints within which international law professionals live and work.

Like my earlier work, this book examines the rather surprising hold that a small number of intellectual assumptions and emotional dispositions have had on international law during its professional period. This time, I have attempted to bring these assumptions and dispositions together in the form of a series of narratives that traces the emergence of a sensibility about matters international in the late nineteenth century as an inextricable part of the liberal and cosmopolitan movements of the day, and that dissolved together with them some time during the second decade after the Second World War. Like the liberal reformism which

Introduction

created it, modern international law was defeated as much by its spectacular successes as its equally striking failures. Many of the political objectives of the first modern international lawyers – the men who set up the *Institut de droit international* in 1873 – were sooner or later realized in their domestic societies: general suffrage, social welfare legislation, rule of law. Support for international institutions and advancing the international rule of law became defining attributes to a new multilateral diplomacy, however much "idealist" and "realist" accounts might have disagreed about their centrality to the conduct of foreign policy. But many large objectives proved to be unrealizable – global federalism, peace, universal human rights – while some turned out to have consequences that were the exact opposite of the lawyers' expectations: the projection of Western sovereignty in the colonies is the most conspicuous example. What was distinctive about the internationalist sensibility was not only its reformist political bent but its conviction that international reform could be derived from deep insights about society, history, human nature or developmental laws of an international and institutional modernity. While the first generation of internationalists imagined that those insights were embedded in their shared Victorian *conscience*, later generations sometimes departed from this assumption in one or another direction, only to return to it in a secondary, or default mode some time in the immediate post-war era. The attempt to imagine international law either as a *philosophy* or a *science of the development of societies* that was pursued with energy in Germany and France during the first half of the twentieth century failed to produce or even support viable policies and collapsed with the inter-war world in 1939. The profession never really recovered from the war. It was, instead, both depoliticized and marginalized, as graphically illustrated by its absence from the arenas of today's globalization struggles, or turned into a technical instrument for the advancement of the agendas of powerful interests or actors in the world scene. As a sensibility, it was compelled to fight nostalgia, or cynicism, or both.

II

This book is informed by two intuitions I have had about the history of international law in the period from 1870 to 1960. One was the sense that earlier accounts of the profession's pedigree failed to give an adequate sense of the radical character of the break that took place in the field between the first half of the nineteenth century and the emergence of a new professional self-awareness and enthusiasm between 1869 and 1885. A central thesis of chapters 1 and 2 is that modern international law did not "begin" at Westphalia or Vienna, and that the writings by Grotius, Vattel, G. F. von Martens or even Wheaton were animated by a professional sensibility that seems distinctly different from what began as part of the European liberal retrenchment at the meetings of the *Institut de droit international* and the pages of the *Revue de droit international et de législation comparée* from 1869 onwards. My second intuition was that whatever began at that time came to an effective (if not formal) end sometime around 1960. About that time it became clear that the late-Victorian reformist sensibility written into international law could no longer enlist political enthusiasm or find a theoretically plausible articulation. Chapters 5 and 6 (the essays on Lauterpacht and Morgenthau) contain the argument about precisely in what that "end" consisted – the emergence of a depoliticized legal pragmatism on the one hand, and in the colonization of the profession by imperial policy agendas on the other.

In addition to telling the story of the "rise" and "fall" of international law I wanted also to highlight the profession's academic and political enthusiasms and divisions during the approximately ninety years of its prime, and to do this by focusing on the links between what are too often portrayed as arid intellectual quarrels with the burning social and political questions of the day. Much was at issue in those debates for the participants, and we recognize that in the passionate tone their arguments often took. I did not, of course, want to resuscitate old debates out of antiquarianism, but to examine an additional intuition I had that the profession in its best days could not have been as "idealistic" or "formalistic" as standard histories have suggested. In fact, as chapters 3 and 4 on Germany and France hope to make clear, the received image not only fails to articulate the variety of approaches and positions that lawyers took in their writings and practices, but is sometimes completely mistaken. One of my desires is that the ensuing account will finally do away with the image of late nineteenth- and early twentieth-century lawyers as "positivists" who were enthusiastic about "sovereignty." If any generalization can be made in this regard, it is rather that these men were centrists who tried to balance their moderate nationalism with their liberal internationalism. In Europe, they saw themselves as arguing against the egoistic policies of States and in favor of integration, free trade, and the international regulation of many aspects of domestic society, including human rights. Their *credo* was less sovereignty than a *critique of sovereignty*.

Introduction

The most important exception to this was their support of official imperialism, as discussed in chapter 2 below. Until 1914, they did advocate the extension of Western sovereignty beyond Europe as the only organized way to bring civilization to their "Orient." After the First World War, however, they started increasingly looking for internationalized solutions to colonial problems.

Finally, the recounting of the story about the "rise" and "fall" of international law seemed to me necessary not only because of what it might tell us of the profession as it was then but what it could say of it as it is now. I hope that these essays provide a historical contrast to the state of the discipline today by highlighting the ways in which international lawyers in the past forty years have failed to use the imaginative opportunities that were available to them, and open horizons beyond academic and political instrumentalization, in favor of worn-out internationalist causes that form the mainstay of today's commitment to international law.[2] This is not to say that I should like to propose a return to the themes of academic or political controversy in which the protagonists of this book were once engaged. Return to "gentle civilizing" as a professional self-definition is certainly no longer plausible. But this is not to say that international lawyers could not learn from their fathers and grandfathers in the profession. Understanding the way they argued in particular situations, often in great crises and sometimes heavily involved as participants or even victims, provides a sense of the possibilities that could exist today. The limits of our imagination are a product of a history that *might have gone another way*. There is nothing permanently fixed in those limits. They are produced by a particular configuration of commitments and projects by individual, well-situated lawyers.

So although this book covers quite a bit of the same ground as the one I published ten years ago, the move from structure to history makes this a completely different work. Or almost does. For the play of apology and utopia is of course effective in the writings of the lawyers I discuss below and continues to account for the fact that they became highly regarded representatives of the profession. But I have consciously tried to downplay that aspect of their work, and to focus instead on the political and in some cases biographical context in which they worked and on the professional and political projects that they tried to advance through their

[2] Cf. also Martti Koskenniemi, "Between Commitment and Cynicism; Outline of a Theory of International Law as Practice," in *Collection of Essays by Legal Advisors of States, Legal Advisors of International Organizations and Practitioners in the Field of International Law* (New York, United Nations, 1999), pp. 495–523.

practice, on the struggles for power and position in which they were engaged, and on their defeats and victories.

III

The move from structure to history in the analysis of international law is thus the first ambition of this book. But to refer to "history" probably begs more questions than it answers. Lawyers – especially those with an interdisciplinary interest – should bear in mind that the grass is not necessarily any greener in the adjoining fields. Historiography, like sociology or philosophy, is at least as much riddled with methodological controversy, and uncertainty about premises, as law is. What *kind* of history, then, do the following chapters offer to the reader? Two alternatives had to be discounted at the outset. One was the grand history that would paint a canvas of "epochs" following each other under some metahistorical law about the workings of "culture" or "power" on the destinies of peoples or civilizations, patterns of creation, flourishing, and decline. There already were such histories and little could be added to them that would be new or interesting.[3] Perhaps more importantly, they implied philosophical, methodological, and political assumptions that seemed hard to sustain. Already the identification of the relevant "epochs," not to say anything about the ways in which they reduced a complex world into hierarchical blocs, following each other in a more or less monotonous parade headed by laws of interdependence, Great Power policies, or perhaps "progress," seemed burdened with contestable assumptions about what was central and what peripheral, what valuable and what harmful in the past, and failed to address the question

---

[3] The standard English-language introduction remains Arthur Nussbaum, *A Concise History of the Law of Nations* (Revised edn., New York, Macmillan, 1954). Like that work, most of the writing in the field has been undertaken by Germans. See particularly Wilhelm Grewe, *Epochen des Völkerrechtsgeschichte* (Baden-Baden, Nomos, 1984) recently published as *The Epochs of International Law* (trans. and rev. by Michael Byers, Berlin and New York, de Gruyter, 2000). Ernst Reibstein, *Völkerrecht. Eine Geschichte seiner Ideen in Lehre und Praxis* (2 vols., Freiburg and Munich, Alber, 1958 and 1963), is a collection of citations, chronologically arranged to support the author's sometimes idiosyncratic theses. Shorter recent introductory overviews are Karl-Heinz Ziegler, *Völkerrechtsgeschichte. Ein Studienbuch* (Munich, Beck, 1994) and Antonio Truyol y Serra, *Histoire du droit international public* (Paris, Economica, 1995). Still impressive is Robert Redslob, *Histoire des grands principes du droit des gens depuis l'antiquité jusqu'à la veille de la grande guerre* (Paris, Rousseau, 1923). An extensive (though not exhaustive) bibliography is Peter Macalister-Smith and Joachim Schwietzke, "Literature and Documentary Sources relating to the History of Public International Law: An Annotated Bibliographical Survey" (1999), 1 *Journal of the History of International Law*, pp. 136–212.

Introduction

of narrative perspective. Moreover, having to pay attention to enormously difficult questions about the miracle of historical progression, or the nature of the "law" employed in such narratives, would have undermined my wish to focus on something much less ambitious and more immediately relevant – namely, how the profession ended up being what it is today. Such histories are reductionist in the sense that they, like the structuralism of my earlier book, flatten the work of individual lawyers into superficial decorations on the surface of the silent flow of periods into one another, the emergence and transformation of great ideas or legal principles.

I wanted to bring international law down from the epochal and conceptual abstractions. I wanted to examine the way it has developed as a career choice for internationally minded lawyers in the course of a relatively brief period, the experiences of which would still resonate in the lives of today's international lawyers. It may be too much to say that international law is *only* what international lawyers do or think. But at least it is that, and examining it from the perspective of its past practitioners might enhance the self-understanding of today's international lawyers in a manner that would not necessarily leave things as they are. Quite apart from such a practical concern, I also wanted to look beyond the commonplace view that there are single, homogeneous periods when "international law" has been either this or that. Like any social phenomenon, international law is a complex set of practices and ideas, as well as interpretations of those practices and ideas, and the way we engage in them or interpret them cannot be dissociated from the larger professional, academic or political projects we have. I wanted to articulate some of those projects, and thus to describe the lawyers as actors in particular social dramas. International law is also a terrain of fear and ambition, fantasy and desire, conflict and utopia, and a host of other aspects of the phenomenological lives of its practitioners. I also wanted to take a step in the direction of describing it in terms of their occasionally brilliant insights and (perhaps more frequently) astonishing blindness, the paradoxes of their thought, their intellectual and emotional courage, betrayals and self-betrayals.

For the fact is that although international lawyers were of course interested in the same phenomena in particular periods, they treated those phenomena from a variety of standpoints that reflected national backgrounds, political preferences, and personal idiosyncrasies. Although all inter-war lawyers were writing about the League of Nations, it would be completely wrong to assume that they wrote from a similar perspective – indeed, that there would have been an orthodox position about the League in the profession in the first place. Although the alternative positions were perhaps not so many – one could be either broadly "enthusiastic" about or "disappointed" with the League, or take a principled or a strategic attitude towards it – merely to describe those positions seemed still too "flat." One needed to describe those positions in the context in which they were taken. For example, one could be "for" the League because one was a pacifist, because that suited the foreign policy of one's *patria*, or in order to forestall attempts towards a more intrusive federalism in Europe, or any mixture of such reasons. In order to attain a credible description that accounted for unity as well as variety one needed to understand each position by reference to some sort of a contextual background from which it arose.

The opposite alternative would have been to abstract the larger context altogether and to write biographies of individual lawyers. This, too, is an old tradition of writing history in the profession, though it had fallen out of fashion in recent decades.[4] The "realist" spirit was incompatible with the assumption that individual lives could have a significant effect on the grand course of international politics. However, the discredit into which "grand history" has more recently fallen as well as the changing political circumstances may be giving biographical history a new relevance. The recapitulation of the Western Canon in the field, as begun in the pages of the *European Journal of International Law*, follows naturally from the political changes since 1989. It may now (again) seem possible to describe the history of the field in terms of the progress of Western humanitarian liberalism from Vitoria to Gentili, Grotius to Vattel, Oppenheim to Lauterpacht.[5] But whatever the value of such a biographical orientation, as method it seems no more credible than epochal history. It, too, reduces the field – this time to a projection of a few great minds – and fails to account for the external pressures to which the doctrines of those men sought to provide responses. Much of recent historiography emphasizes history as narratives. This seemed a much more useful perspective and a challenging one as well.

---

[4] Cf. Albert Geouffre de Lapradelle, *Maîtres et doctrines du droit des gens* (2nd edn., Paris, Editions internationales, 1950); *Les fondateurs du droit international* (Intr. Antoine Pillet, Paris, Giard, 1904). Truyol y Serra, *Histoire*, also belongs largely to this group.

[5] Cf. the Symposia in the *European Journal of International Law* on Georges Scelle (1990), 1 *European Journal of International Law* (*EJIL*), pp. 193–249; Dionisio Anzilotti (1992), 3 *EJIL*, pp. 92–169; Alfred Verdross (1995), 6 *EJIL*, pp. 32–115; Hersch Lauterpacht (1997), 8 *EJIL*, pp. 215–320; Hans Kelsen (1998), 9 *EJIL*, pp. 287–400.

Introduction

No doubt, interest in the historical aspects of the profession is increasing, even dramatically, as evidenced for instance in the launching of the *Journal of the History of International Law / Revue d'histoire du droit international* in 1999. The best new writing in the field emerges from a theoretical awareness of the difficulties in continuing doctrinal work as in the past without taking stock of the narratives with which the field has justified them and re-telling those stories so as to make methodological or political points. As elsewhere in the social sciences, Michel Foucault's work has been very influential in proposing a study of international law's past that would focus on discontinuities rather than continuities, the relationship between narratives and power as well as delineations of disciplinary autonomy so as to effect subtle maneuvers of exclusion and inclusion. One of the most remarkable feats in the discipline's self-construction has been its overwhelming Eurocentrism: so it is no wonder that much of that new work has concentrated in describing international law as part of the colonialist project.[6] Chapter 2 makes a small contribution to those studies. But there are other exclusions and inclusions as well, some of which have to do with disciplinary struggles within the legal profession (international law's relations to private international law, or constitutional law, or public law generally), some between law and other areas of study, such as sociology or philosophy, some between professional activities (law – politics – diplomacy), others with the production or reproduction of more general cultural hierarchies. If all the protagonists in this book are white men, for instance, that reflects my concern to re-tell the narrative of the mainstream as a story about its cosmopolitan sensibilities and political projects: indeed to articulate precisely in what the limits of its horizon consisted. This should not, however, be read so as to exclude the possibility – indeed, the likelihood – that in the margins, for instance as objects of the administrative regimes developed by or with the assistance of international lawyers, there have been women and non-Europeans whose stories would desperately require telling so as to provide a more complete image of the profession's political heritage.

Thus the following essays are neither epochal nor biographical in the various forms in which such histories are usually written. They form a kind of experimentation in the writing about the disciplinary past in

---

[6] Here I think especially of the new work by Antony Anghie, David Bederman, Nathaniel Berman, Anthony Carty, David Kennedy, Karen Knop, Outi Korhonen, Carl Landauer, and Annelise Riles.

which the constraints of any rigorous "method" have been set aside in an effort to create intuitively plausible and politically engaged narratives about the emergence and gradual transformation of a profession that plays with the reader's empathy. The essays do not seek a neutral description of the past "as it actually was" – that sort of knowledge is not open to us – but a description that hopes to make our present situation clearer to us and to sharpen our own ability to act in the professional contexts that are open to us as we engage in our practices and projects. In this sense, it is also a political act. I hope that it does not treat its protagonists unjustly. But if it seems that it does, then I have Goethe's ironic response to fall back on, namely, that it is the one who acts that is always unjust, and the one that merely observes, that is just.

1

"The legal conscience of the civilized world"

> Man in his conscience is no longer bound by the ends of particularity. This is the higher standpoint, the standpoint of the modern world. We have now arrived at the stage of consciousness, which involves a recoil upon itself. Earlier ages were more sensuous, and had before them something external and given, whether it was religion or law. But conscience is aware of itself as thought, and knows that my thought is for me the only thing that is binding.
> G. W. F. Hegel, *Philosophy of Right*, § 136. *Addition.*

An observer of international politics in the 1860s with liberal sympathies could not fail to be disturbed about the apparent coincidence of two facts. The preceding half-century had constituted one of the longest periods of peace in European history, punctured only by occasional and limited military conflict in the margins. The long calm had created conditions for an unprecedented economic growth whose fruit may have been unevenly distributed but seemed tangible enough as proof that European civilization had been launched on an irreversible march towards economic and spiritual progress.

On the other hand, peace had been created and enforced through a pact among five Great Powers, three of which (Austria, Prussia, and Russia) were governed by absolutist monarchs whose main motive for co-operation seemed to be their shared wish to curb any proposal for representative government or increased franchise. If there was indeed economic progress, its geographic scope was limited to the West while much the largest part of Europe was untouched by the benefits of industrialization or free trade. Progress, while undeniable, had grown out of a peace that seemed both precarious – as had been shown by the Crimean

War – and a positive obstacle to the spread of liberal ideas.[1] Men who extolled the spirit of liberalism in the mid-Victorian age were compelled to conclude that the prevailing economic and political conditions by no means guaranteed further progress and were positively responsible for the presence of that other redoubtable nemesis, revolution.

A manifesto

Under such conditions, many felt that action needed to be taken in order to ensure the spread of liberal ideas. This was one of the purposes of the *Association internationale pour le progrès des sciences sociales* that was set up in Brussels in September 1862 following the example of a British association that had been established five years earlier with the same name.[2] Among the participants to the Brussels Conference were three young lawyers, Gustave Rolin-Jaequemyns (1835–1902), an *avocat* from Ghent, Tobias Asser (1838–1913), 24-year-old lawyer from Amsterdam who had just been appointed Professor of Contemporary Law at what today is the University of Amsterdam, as well as John Westlake (1828–1913), barrister of Lincoln's Inn, author of a well-received 1858 treatise on private international law and Secretary to the British association.[3] The three men met at and outside the formal sessions of the conference and became friends. The following year Rolin invited Asser and Westlake to stay with him in Ghent during the Association's second conference, of which he was the principal organizer.

The *Association internationale* advocated liberal ideas, religious tolerance, freedom of opinion and free trade, as well as the development of contacts between peoples.[4] It sought to provide a secular and scientific

---

[1] Cf. e.g. Charles Vergé, "Le droit des gens avant et depuis 1789," in G. F. de Martens, *Précis de droit des gens moderne de l'Europe, précédé d'une Introduction et complété par l'exposition des doctrines des publicistes contemporains et suivi d'une Bibliographie raisonnée du droit des gens par M. Ch. Vergé* (2 vols., 2nd French edn., Paris, Guillaumin, 1864), pp. xlv–xlvi.

[2] The National Association for the Promotion of Social Science (NAPSS) had been set up in Britain in 1857 to deal with social reform and improvement of legislation. It was divided into five "departments" (legal reform, penal policy, education, public health, and social economy), functioning as a kind of unofficial Parliament that was regularly addressed by leading liberal politicians and intellectuals such as Gladstone or John Stuart Mill. Stefan Collini, *Public Moralists. Political Thought and Intellectual Life in Britain 1850–1930* (Oxford, Clarendon, 1991), pp. 210–211.

[3] *A Treatise on Private International Law, or the Conflict of Laws, with Principal Reference to its Practice in the English and Other Cognate Systems of Jurisprudence* (London, Maxwell, 1858). Another participant at the meeting was Rolin's friend the Swiss Alphonse Rivier, later Professor at the University of Brussels and Secretary-General to the *Institut de droit international*.

[4] Cf. Ernest Nys, "Notice sur Rolin-Jaequemyns" (1910), *Annuaire de l'Académie royale des sciences, des lettres et des beaux-arts de Belgique*, pp. 57–58; T. M. C. Asser, "Le droit

basis for liberal politics, no longer associated with early Enlightenment rationalism or deductive utilitarianism.[5] Some French members, however, wished to use the Association for radical or revolutionary purposes and after four conferences it broke up leaving in the minds of the three men their fruitful co-operation in the section on comparative law, and their friendship.

In the course of a business visit to Amsterdam in July 1867, Rolin again met with Asser and, during a walk in the forest of Haarlem, the idea to set up a scientific legal journal on an international basis arose.[6] Such a journal could propagate liberal views and experiences with legislative reform all over Europe. Later that same summer Rolin visited London, carrying the proposal to Westlake, who agreed that the idea was excellent but declined to assume a principal role in the project. Rolin and Asser then prepared a first plan for a publication that would treat questions of private international law and comparative law on an international and reformist basis. In a prospectus, they observed two important features of the age: The national spirit was waking up and being strengthened all over Europe; simultaneously, it was being tempered by *l'esprit d'internationalité*, a new spirit that taught nations and races to follow certain common principles not only in their mutual relations but also in their domestic legislation. Without renouncing their autonomy, States had come to co-operate and to recognize "the superior unity of the great human society."[7] Thanks to this new spirit, exact sciences, industry, and economics had recently made great progress. Now it was law's turn.

---

international privé et droit uniforme" (1880), XII *Revue de droit international et de législation comparée* (*RDI*), pp. 7–9. On the strength of an appeal signed, among others, by Rolin, Asser, and Westlake, the association was re-established in 1889 under the name *Société d'études politiques et sociales*. Cf. Gustave Rolin-Jaequemyns, "Fondation, à Bruxelles, d'une société politique et sociale" (1889), XXI *RDI*, pp. 501–505.

[5] The Association sought to back its reform proposals with sociological studies of European and "primitive" societies, responding thus to the need for a historical and functionally oriented method that had seized liberal imagination in the second third of the century. Cf. generally J. W. Burrow, *Evolution and Society. A Study of Victorian Social Theory* (Cambridge University Press, 1966).

[6] T. M. C. Asser, "Fondation de la revue" (1902), 2/IV *RDI*, p.111. Cf. also Ernest Nys, "La science de droit des gens," in *Memories of John Westlake* (London, Smith & Elder, 1914), pp. 48–52.

[7] "L'unité supérieure de la grande société humaine," "Prospectus" (avant-projet, 1867) (1902), 2/IV *RDI*, pp. 116–117. The concept of "internationalité" went further than "internationalism," that connoted the interdependence-driven process of increasing co-operation and development of common interests between States. The former notion also connoted the humanization of national policies and the development of a liberal spirit. Cf. Betsy Roeben, "Johann Caspar Bluntschli, Francis Lieber und das moderne Völkerrecht," PhD thesis, University of Frankfurt, on file with author (2000), pp. 153–156.

Legislators and jurists needed to learn about the laws and legislative projects of different countries so as to better appreciate the effects of proposed domestic reforms and to reduce conflicts that might be caused by differing laws. Today, the prospectus declared, nobody who wanted to ameliorate social conditions could afford to neglect the study of comparative law.[8]

Westlake agreed to the scope and spirit of the prospectus although he wondered whether the national spirit always worked in the direction of peace and objected to the appeal to vague notions such as the "conscience of the age." The text was therefore amended so as to replace the *esprit d'internationalité* by a less controversial reference to how nations ("ces grandes individualités collectives") had recently ceased regarding each other as enemies and started to co-operate for the furtherance of common aims.[9] Rolin and Asser then communicated the prospectus to Pasquale Mancini (1817–1888) of Turin, Professor of Public, Foreign, and International Law[10] and member of Sardinia's Parliament from the constituency of the Democratic Left, already a famous advocate of the nationalities principle, whose prestige and experience they wished to enlist. Mancini gave enthusiastic support to the project, proposing that the journal should also treat questions of international law proper.[11] The text was revised accordingly and the first issue of the *Revue de droit international et de législation comparée* – the first international law journal – was published at the end of 1868.

In the manifesto that headed the first issue, Rolin inaugurated the *Revue* as a professional forum for liberal legislative reform in Europe. Comparative study of legislation was instrumental in this, he noted, with specific reference to Bentham and Montesquieu, and then listed his agenda:

In the matter of personal status, the abolition not only of slavery but of servitude; in civil matters the freedom of establishment; in penal matters, the creation of a more just relationship between the crime and the punishment and the application of the punishment in the interests of the criminal as well as that of society; the suppression of the criminalisation of usury, and of privileged corporations, the liberation of the value of gold and silver, and the freedom of association.[12]

---

[8] Roeben, "Bluntschli," pp. 117–118.   [9] Asser, "Fondation de la revue," p. 112.
[10] A Chair instituted for him in 1850. Cf. Rodolfo di Nova, "Pasquale Stanislao Mancini," in *Institut de droit international, Livre de centenaire: évolution et perspectives du droit international* (Basle, Karger, 1973), p. 5.   [11] Asser, "Fondation de la revue," p. 113.
[12] Gustave Rolin-Jaequemyns, "De l'étude de la législation comparée et de droit international" (1869), I *RDI*, p. 11.

"The legal conscience of the civilized world"

And so on. It was a veritable shopping-list of liberal reform that was to be promoted by the new journal. But the manifesto also dealt with questions of international law proper. Rolin pointed to the increasing influence of humanitarian ideas in the limitation of warfare and in the conduct of hostilities. The 1864 Geneva Convention had established provisions for the treatment of wounded and sick soldiers and, while Rolin was writing, a conference was sitting in Brussels, aiming to agree on additional principles for the humanization of warfare. The journal could discuss such projects so as to spread awareness about them. For, Rolin wrote, although it had become common to treat unilateral acts by and treaties between States as the sources of international law, their force was not due to their form – after all, "on les viole aussi souvent qu'on les invoque."[13] Their force arose from public opinion. Even in breaching their compacts, States made excuses in a way that showed that they sought justification before such opinion.

Diplomacy was not trustworthy. In 1815, the Great Powers had arrogated to themselves the role of guarantors of peace. But had they abided by their proclaimed principles? Had they defended the weak against the strong? The questions were purely rhetorical. The Holy Alliance and the Congress, Rolin wrote, "had turned Kantian ideas in favor of absolutism and dressed them in the garb of mysticism." The reaction had been inevitable: revolutionary ideas spread everywhere and Europe was divided into two hostile camps: "the alliance of peoples challenged that of the Princes."[14] In this situation, public opinion took on a mediating role:

In international law this opinion is really and rightly the queen and legislator of the world. It is the voice of reason itself . . . And it is finally also the progressive expression of that natural law which Grotius had defined so well and so profoundly.[15]

But public opinion was not whatever uncultivated whim pleased the masses. On the contrary:

We mean a public opinion that is serious and calm, that is based on the application of certain principles of universal justice, with constant elements, an

---

[13] Rolin-Jaequemyns, "De l'étude de la législation comparée et de droit international," p. 235.
[14] Rolin-Jaequemyns, "De l'étude de la législation comparée et de droit international," p. 256.
[15] Rolin-Jaequemyns, "De l'étude de la législation comparée et de droit international," pp. 225–226.

opinion that is gradually confirmed and generalized into the judgment of history.[16]

Formal State acts may be just or unjust, right or wrong. They could therefore not be the fundamental source of the law of nations. Whether they should be obeyed depends on whether they were accepted by the civilized conscience of peoples:

> Thus the documents usually referred to as the sources of international law receive their binding force from a common source, human conscience, manifested in the collective opinion of enlightened men. But this conscience is not stationary; it is eminently progressive.[17]

But public opinion was ephemeral and without a formal channel of expression. There was no international legislation. Therefore, a particular burden for the development of international law fell upon science: "In external law it is science, or rather the conscience of humanity that is the source, the tribunal and the sanction of positive law."[18] In this way, Rolin's imagination amalgamated the two great nineteenth-century ideas, science and conscience. The man of legal science became the representative – the organ – of humanity's conscience. Public opinion crystallized in a legal scholarship that proceeded by way of introspection.

At the time of writing his manifesto, Rolin was a member of the Belgian liberal party's moderate – "doctrinaire" – wing and an activist of social causes.[19] Two years earlier he had set up the *Gentsche Volksbank* on the basis of German co-operative ideals that he admired. He had no background in international law. He was no naturalist or philosopher. On the contrary, he was a man of action, a parliamentarian and future minister in Frère-Orban's liberal government in 1878–1884 and a legal adviser to the King of Siam in 1892–1901. The reflexions in the first issue of the *Revue* were not drawn from philosophical contemplation but expressed Rolin's confidence in the ability of his liberal sensibility to capture reason and progress in their authenticity.

After the manifesto, Rolin seldom ventured into legal or political

---

[16] Rolin-Jaequemyns, "De l'étude de la législation comparée et de droit international," p. 225. For the role of public opinion, cf. also Francis Lieber, *On Civil Liberty and Self-Government* (Philadelphia, Lippincott, 1859), pp. 405–416.

[17] Rolin-Jaequemyns, "De l'étude de la législation comparée et de droit international," p. 228.

[18] Rolin-Jaequemyns, "De l'étude de la législation comparée et de droit international," p. 225.

[19] For biographical details, cf. the obituaries in (1902), 2/IV *RDI*, pp. 88–122 and Nys, "Notice sur Rolin-Jaequemyns," pp. 53–87.

"The legal conscience of the civilized world"

theory. In his prolific writings in the *Revue* he often reported on the activities of professional organizations and inaugurated a new genre of legal writing – the *chronique de droit international* – that allowed him to review and comment upon the international events of the day. This created a practical means for him to apply the view of the jurist as the organ of liberal public opinion that often felt strongly about international matters such as the Balkan War of 1887–1888, the Russian advances in the Caucasus, or the Turkish treatment of Christians, on which he focused his detailed commentary.

In fact, none of the men behind the *Revue* came from the tradition of Grotius, or the school of "European Public Law" that had dominated international legal writing from Vattel well into the mid-nineteenth century. None was a lawyer–philosopher in the vein of Suarez or a diplomat like Wheaton. Like Rolin, Asser was and continued as a practicing lawyer in addition to holding a university chair. In later years, he was instrumental in setting up the Hague Conference on Private International Law and undertook a number of activities in the field of unification of private law. He failed to get elected to the Dutch Parliament but did secure the Nobel Peace Prize in 1911. Westlake had practiced as a barrister since 1854 and, aside from being a "thoroughly trained and competent equity lawyer"[20] was also a "convinced and unflinching liberal."[21] After a brief period in the House of Commons he was elected Whewell Professor of International Law in Cambridge in 1887 but continued taking part in various foreign policy activities including the British Government's Balkan Committee and the manifesto in favor of Finland.

Establishing professional journals was one means whereby the mid-Victorian generation institutionalized the various scientific disciplines – including economics and social sciences.[22] Rolin's objective, too, was to organize reformist lawyers interested in contacts with other countries and in international affairs around a tangible focal point that his journal was to provide. Up until then, international law had been an affair of professors and philosophers, diplomats with an inclination to reflect on the history and procedure of their craft. Now it was to be discussed in the pages of the *Revue* like any legal problem from the status of women

---

[20] A. V. Dicey, "His Book and His Character," in *Memories of Westlake*, p. 24.
[21] Lord Courtney of Penwith, "Public Affairs," in *Memories of Westlake*, p. 61.
[22] Cf. Peter Gay, *The Cultivation of Hatred. The Bourgeois Experience: From Victoria to Freud* (5 vols., New York, Norton, 1993–2000), III, pp. 484–485; Collini, *Public Moralists*, p. 213.

to the reform of labor legislation, with focus on recent events and reforms and contributions from all over Europe.

The *Revue* reflected the agenda of its founders in a variety of ways.[23] The initial volumes focused on the reform of penal law – particularly the abolition of capital punishment – as well as on new social legislation, including laws on child labour, education, and public assistance. Private international law figured prominently in the form of articles on nationality, extradition, and enforcement of sentences. These were standard reformist themes. During its first twenty years, the *Revue* reported extensively on proposals for increasing arbitration and on the meetings of peace movements, on the *Institut de droit international* and on the Committee for reform and codification of international law (in 1895 renamed the International Law Association). Gradually, however, public international law came to occupy increasing space, mainly at the expense of comparative law and commentary on domestic legal reform, marking the deepening specialization of these fields and the gradual replacement of Rolin's culturally oriented *esprit d'internationalité* by a more professional focus on intergovernmental co-operation and conflict.

The *Revue* was born out of a sensibility that looked for social progress, emphasized responsibility, and sought a *via media* between individualism and collectivism, abstract speculation and political action. It was democratic but fearful of the masses, reformist but bourgeois. In psychoanalytic language it might be characterized in terms of the repression of extremism and a sublimation of aggression into a more or less successful toleration of variety, of different shades of grey.[24] Its spirit was both nationalist and internationalist – though opposed to "extreme" variants of both. It was politically "progressive" inasmuch as it rejected monarchic absolutism and "conservative" to the extent that it saw revolution

---

[23] Aside from Rolin's programmatic articles on private and public international law, and the first of his series of *chroniques*, the first issue contained an article on the abolition of corporal punishment in France in 1867 together with a comparative review of corporal punishment in various European States. Franz von Holtzendorff (1829–1889) from Berlin reviewed recent publications on the prison system, arguing against absurdly long sentences and in favor of prison leave. Pradier-Fodéré (1827–1904), consultant to South American governments, criticized the Western misuse of capitulations in Turkey and argued in favor of their abolition. The French essayist, poet, and historian Edouard Laboulaye (1811–1883), Professor of Comparative Legislation at the Collège de France and later a member of the French National Assembly, wrote a short piece on the lack of historical perspective in Montesquieu's *Esprit des lois* while the Argentinian lawyer–diplomat Carlos Calvo (1824–1906), reiterated the Calvo doctrine – that governments should not be held responsible for damage caused by acts of domestic insurgents.   [24] Gay, *The Cultivation of Hatred*, p. 526.

"The legal conscience of the civilized world"

in every shade of socialist agitation. Unlike the peace movement, it was not averse to governmental activities – after all, liberals were increasingly involved in European governments – and hoped to channel its reforms through diplomacy. Its active base was narrow, however. The number of contributors remained low even after the journal became an organ of the *Institut de droit international* in 1875 and decreased by the establishment of the *Revue générale de droit international public* in Paris in 1894, after which time it started to become identified as a distinctly "Belgian" publication (an assessment hardly counteracted by the fact that as Rolin left his editorship it was continued by his brother Albéric and his son Edouard).

An old-fashioned tradition

In his manifesto, Rolin made no reference to earlier continental writing on international law – although he did dwell briefly on humanitarian ideas and federalist proposals by Rousseau, Kant, and others. He completely passed over the treatises that had come out earlier in the century, particularly in Germany, written by experts in public law, with an interest in international affairs often triggered by consultant work to a sovereign. The founders of the *Revue* sought a complete break from that tradition: its focus had been too narrow, its ambition too limited. Indeed, it must have seemed more part of the problem than an instrument for its resolution.

Perhaps the most famous representative of that tradition had been Georg Friedrich von Martens (1756–1822), Professor at the University of Göttingen until 1808 and counsellor to the Courts of Westphalia and Hanover.[25] A close observer of diplomatic events and publisher, since 1790, of the extensive *Recueil de traités*, von Martens had prepared in 1821 a completely revised third edition (in French) of his 1796 introduction to European international law.[26] The concept of law employed in that book had been that of the fully rational social compact.[27] Like individuals in the natural state, European States had contracted positive rules so as to complement and mitigate natural law and to guarantee its realization – to determine uncertain points, to modify its rigors, sometimes to set aside the reciprocity of rights that it initially provided.[28] But

---

[25] For biographical detail, cf. Arthur Nussbaum, *A Concise History of International Law* (2nd rev. edn., New York, Macmillan, 1954), pp. 179–185.
[26] I have here used the 1864 edn. prepared by Vergé of the *Précis du droit des gens moderne de l'Europe*.   [27] Martens, *Précis*, I, pp. 37 § 2, 40–41 § 4.
[28] Martens, *Précis*, I, p. 46 § 6.

no general code had emerged to link Europe into a federation. It was up to legal science to abstract general rules from the relations between European States in order better to serve as the handmaid of cultivated European diplomacy.[29]

What von Martens understood by this was reflected in how he guided his reader by the hand through the political relations of European States after the Congress of Vienna, proceeding by an almost endless series of definitions and classifications – distinctions between fully sovereign and half-sovereign States, maritime and continental powers, powers in different geographic locations and of different rank, States classified by reference to constitutional type (democracy – aristocracy – monarchy), again divided and subdivided into several variants.[30] The discussion of the law's substance – treaties, commerce, war – was constituted of typologies of procedural relationship.[31] The natural starting-point was always the existence of States, treated by analogy as individuals, self-sufficient, independent, and free.[32] Political society emerged from the formal reason that created constraint out of pure self-regard. That is why every State was entitled to take action – even military action – if a disruption of the balance of power might threaten its independence.[33]

Such purely rational law was completely static. There was no progress or improvement – apart from the narrow sense of universal reason being sometimes less, sometimes better observed. Its history was Enlightenment history: *jus gentium* had been known to Greek and Roman antiquity but fallen with Rome. Now it was time for reason to reassert itself against the superstitions of the intervening ages. After the Napoleonic intermission, the law would now return to its rational basis, agreed at Westphalia and Utrecht, fortified by the lessons of the Enlightenment.[34] This was also a completely procedural law, dealing with how treaties were made, how territory was acquired, how war was waged. It contained no conception of society or culture beyond diplomatic form and protocol. It was not a conservative, even less a legitimist law that von Martens described. It could even be seen as an extrapolation of the principles of the liberal *Rechtsstaat*. But it was a narrow and a distant law that looked like the complex rules of some exotic variation of the game of chess. As such it was completely alien to the *esprit d'internationalité* that animated the circle of Rolin and his friends.

---

[29] Martens, *Précis*, I, p. 56 § 8. [30] Martens, *Précis*, I, pp. 91–117 § 18–29.
[31] Cf. e.g. Martens, *Précis*, II, pp. 201–273 § 263–289.
[32] Cf. e.g the analogy between possession of territory and ownership, in Martens, *Précis*, I, p. 151 § 44. [33] Martens, *Précis*, I, pp. 322–336 § 120–124.
[34] Martens, *Précis*, I, p. 60 § 10, p. 83–88 § 17.

"The legal conscience of the civilized world"

It was no different with the teachings of Johann Ludwig Klüber (1762–1837), perhaps the most important representative of the *Vormärz* period in German public law in 1815–1848. Klüber had published his *Droit des gens moderne de l'Europe* in 1819 as Professor of Public Law at the University of Heidelberg and counsellor to the Grand Duke of Baden.[35] His good contacts with the Prussian Chancellor Hardenberg – a "liberal bureaucrat out of the eighteenth-century school of enlightened despotism"[36] – had provided him entry into the Vienna negotiations in 1814–1815 of which he published a nine-volume overview.[37] In his work on the public law of the German Confederation he had advocated a "dogmatic–historical" method[38] with a stress on exact documentation and literary referencing – tasks which he combined with a talent for precise albeit somewhat dry synthesis.

Klüber had written self-consciously for the education of diplomats and men of public affairs, becoming – wrote Jellinek later – the most appreciated academic teacher in the courts of Europe at the time. No doubt his audience was pleased to learn that the sovereignty of their States, understood "in a strictly legal sense," was to be seen as independence from the will of all other States[39] while the substance of the law that bound them was to be seen in terms of their "absolute" rights – the rights to self-preservation, independence, and equality and the "relative" rights they contracted with each other.[40]

Von Martens and Klüber each interpreted the diplomacy of the restoration as if it had to do with the realization of contractarian principles between a determined number of independent and legally equal European States-as-persons. From ideas that came from Enlightenment rationalism (and closely resemble those of Vattel) they constructed "Europe" as a political organization of independent States, seeking each

---

[35] Johann Ludwig Klüber, *Europäisches Völkerrecht* (2nd edn., by Carl Morstadt, Schotthausen, Hurter, 1851). The text essentially follows the 1st edn. For biography and comment, cf. A. de La Pradelle, *Maîtres et doctrines du droit des gens* (2nd edn., Paris, Editions internationales, 1950), pp. 183–193.
[36] Leonard Krieger, *The German Idea of Freedom. History of a Political Tradition* (Boston, Beacon, 1957), p. 156.
[37] In a period of reaction and secrecy, this was understood as part of liberal resistance. Michael Stolleis, *Geschichte des öffentlichen Recht in Deutschland* (3 vols., Munich, Beck, 1992–1998), 2: 1800–1914, pp. 71–72, 83–85.
[38] Cf. also Klüber, *Europäisches Völkerrecht*, pp. 10–11 § 9.
[39] Klüber, *Europäisches Völkerrecht*, pp. 23 § 21, 54 § 45.
[40] The three absolute rights are quite analogous to the rights of citizens under the American Declaration of Independence, namely the rights of life, liberty and the pursuit of happiness.

its own perfection[41] – with the assumption that natural development would lead to the greatest happiness of all.[42] Although Klüber recognized the existence of a European moral community (*Europäische Völkersitte*), based on historical and religious affinities, he insisted on a sharp distinction between it and the legal relations between individual States.[43] Law was to be strictly distinguished from politics, morals, and courtesy, Roman and Canon law and theology as well as from "dialectical" or "metaphysical" speculations.[44] Diplomacy was to pay no attention to internal constitutions or forms of government; no intervention on an ideological basis was allowed.[45] This did not mean that lawyers could not have recourse to analogy or natural law. (Was not the argument from "absolute rights" a naturalist point *par excellence*?) But they did little else than refer back to the State's initial independence.[46] In this way, the society of European States with which von Martens and Klüber worked grew out from a rationalistic political theory. It "flattened" the history of European societies into universal reason's struggle to realize itself and did not bother with the cultural, political, or economic developments that were transforming these societies out of all recognition.

For the liberals of the 1860s, such treatises legitimized a politically suspect settlement and the monarchic absolutism they fought against. It was impossible to use von Martens or Klüber to argue about the needs of economic or humanitarian progress, national self-determination, or the primacy of an international public opinion.[47] Their European society was a society of Kings and diplomats, their history a history of

---

[41] "Die Staat ist eine Gesellschaft; – eine freie Gesellschaft." It is composed of individuals and families that have joined together for this very purpose, Klüber, *Europäisches Völkerrecht*, p. 47 § 37.

[42] Hence, for instance, the principle of equilibrium, unless agreed in the form of a treaty, has no legal meaning and acts purportedly seeking to maintain or redress the balance are conducive only to endless power struggle and encouraging suspicion and conflict. By contrast, each State is entitled to struggle against *illegal* pursuit of hegemony, Klüber, *Europäisches Völkerrecht*, pp. 51–52 § 42.

[43] Klüber, *Europäisches Völkerrecht*, pp. 43–45 § 34–35.

[44] Klüber, *Europäisches Völkerrecht*, pp. 10 § 9, 60–61 § 51.

[45] Klüber, *Europäisches Völkerrecht*, pp. 24–25 § 22.

[46] Klüber, *Europäisches Völkerrecht*, Introduction, p. xi and pp. 4–7 § 3–5. Rational law's principal sphere of application is – as in Montesquieu – relations between Europe and the outside world. About these, however, Klüber has very little to say.

[47] Indeed, Martens had reprinted in successive editions his 1796 critique of the revolutionary *Projet de 21 articles sur le droit des gens* that had been proposed to the French National Assembly. A declaration of general principles on the rights and duties of nations, on peace and self-determination, he held, was not only unrealistic but useless as there would be no agreement on their application – and only agreement between States would count, cf. Martens, *Précis*, I, pp. 9–21.

dynasties and wars and their politics the conservative principle of the balance of power. They provided no foothold for activism outside governmental diplomacy, indeed any activism seemed *a priori* suspect inasmuch as it tended to disturb the balance of power that both associated (sometimes seemed to think identical) with the maintenance of the States.[48]

But the two books also seemed untenable from a scientific perspective. As an explanation of society, rationalism was on the way out. In Germany, Fichte and Hegel had focused on society in terms of the spirit that occupied it, in the case of the latter, a spirit that was, though universally inclined, embedded in the nation's specific history and culture. Savigny's historical school of law made much the same argument – coming to the paradoxical conclusion that identified the German legal *Bewusstsein* with the maxims of Roman law. In France, Comte had taught that in a study of society rationalist imagination should be replaced by observation. Society, like nature, was not only to be examined by expert savants but also developed in accordance with the causal–instrumental insights they had produced. In Britain, Benthamite abstractions were being overridden by the writings of John Stuart Mill – whose *On Liberty* was published in 1859 – that were not only compatible with but drew express inspiration from Comtean sociology. However rationalistic a basis utilitarianism had as theory, its practice encouraged legislators to fieldwork rather than armchair imagination. As James Reddie (1773–1852) observed in 1842, through a tortuous prose perhaps inevitable in a transitional work, it was time:

> [t]o give up the idea of transferring the rules applicable to men viewed abstractly, apart from any condition, in which they have ever been found to exist, to nations or communities, formed by union of men in civil society; and to investigate the principles of the human constitution, as ascertained by observation, experience, and the records of history.[49]

By the 1860s, the international law taught by von Martens and Klüber had become old-fashioned. It had compressed European reality into an *a priori* system of political ideas with little attention to the special nature and history of the relations between European sovereigns and even less to the political consciousness of European societies. It possessed no

---

[48] Martens, *Précis*, I, pp. 323–336 § 121–124. Klüber did not think the balance a legal principle. Disturbing it was not a legal ground for war – although it was, he said, self-evident that all States were entitled to oppose any *illegitimate* attempt at supremacy, Klüber, *Europäisches Völkerrecht*, pp. 50–52 § 42.

[49] James Reddie, *Inquiries in International Law* (Edinburgh, Blackwood, 1842), p. 114.

A transitional critic: Kaltenborn von Stachau

Many of such criticisms had been voiced by Carl Baron Kaltenborn von Stachau (1817–1866), *Privatdozent* from Halle and later Professor of German Public Law in Königsberg and member of the Kur-Hessian Foreign Ministry in Kassel.[50] In his *Kritik des Völkerrechts* of 1847, Kaltenborn had noted the *Grabesstille* in the field between 1820 and 1840 and had aimed to introduce a scientific study of international law that would collect the facts of international life into a system of principles ("ein organisches System von Grundsätzen").[51] He wanted to connect the reality of the Vienna settlement – in particular the central role of sovereignty – with a standpoint *outside* sovereignty by the systematic ordering of the law's leading principles.

Kaltenborn's scientific ambition expressed itself in his stress on international law as a *historical* subject (as well as a distinctly Protestant discipline).[52] He attacked the abstract rationalism of earlier writers as well as their frequent failure to discern any principle beyond the positive facts of diplomacy.[53] He shared the mid-century view that science was constituted of "the rational organisation of ideas"[54] and the peculiarly German understanding that this meant that legal science was to group its facts into a system of concepts.[55] Previous scholarship had worked with arbitrarily chosen concepts, confusing Roman law and natural law with international law, positive law with philosophical law.[56] By abstracting principles from the normative relationships between individuals von

---

[50] Stolleis regards him a "conservative" – assessed by reference to his *Einleitung in das constitutionelle Verfassungsrecht* (1863) that sided with Bismarck. His critique, and especially the objective/subjective distinction at the heart of it, came from the legal philosophy of the monarchist–conservative professor Friedrich Julius Stahl. Cf. Erich Kaufmann, *Das Wesen des Völkerrechts und die Clausula rebus sic stantibus* (Tübingen, Mohr, 1911), pp. 185–186.

[51] Carl Kaltenborn von Stachau, *Kritik des Völkerrechts* (Leipzig, Mayer, 1847), pp. 92, 111.

[52] Kaltenborn, *Kritik*, pp. 24–25. Only Protestantism could make room for freedom, and for a modern concept of sovereignty as representative of such freedom.

[53] Natural law theory being an arbitrary product of the author's mind, Kaltenborn, *Kritik*, pp. 28, 52.

[54] Roger Cotterell, *The Politics of Jurisprudence: A Critical Introduction to Legal Philosophy* (London, Butterworth, 1989), p. 47.   [55] Cf. Kaltenborn, *Kritik*, pp. 243–246.

[56] Cf. especially Kaltenborn, *Kritik*, pp. 103–127.

"The legal conscience of the civilized world"

Martens and Klüber had failed to arrive at any autonomous understanding of international relations.[57] This was to be corrected by a historically based and system oriented legal study.

Kaltenborn wished to transcend the old opposition between positive and philosophical law.[58] He generously granted that this might not have been possible in the political atmosphere of earlier times. The conditions for an "objective" science of international law had emerged only after the re-establishment of the European system in the first decades of the nineteenth century.[59] Only now it had become possible to see how human consciousness was reflected in legal sources, custom, and treaties, and received its highest expression in legal science.[60] Kaltenborn gave science a much more active role than it had had for von Martens or Klüber.[61] Legal sources were interpreted and new sources were constantly created through the work of legal science. From innumerable customary and treaty rules science created more basic, interrelated principles whose positivity would be proved by their future application.[62]

Like von Martens and Klüber, Kaltenborn accepted that Europe was naturally divided into sovereign States.[63] Unlike them, however, he saw these States also joined in a historical and cultural community to which his new science would give reality. It would describe legal *subjects* (States) in their relation to certain *objects* (territory, commerce) and the legal *forms* (treaties, diplomacy) whereby these were linked together. Such a relational systematic was derived from sovereignty (the older doctrine of absolute rights) but gave reality to the principle of international legal community (the old doctrine's relative rights) as well.[64] This enabled Kaltenborn to respond to the "deniers" who had doubted whether international law was law in the absence of legislation, adjudication, and enforcement through an argument that was to become the profession's

---

[57] Kaltenborn, *Kritik*, pp. 112–113, 175–185.   [58] Kaltenborn, *Kritik*, p. 97.

[59] Kaltenborn, *Kritik*, pp. 91, 130–132, 170–171. Kaltenborn did appreciate the recent work by Heffter and Oppenheim and saw his own writing as an attempt to bring to fruition the construction attempted by Ch. E. Gagern in his *Kritik des Völkerrechts. Mit practischer Anwendung auf unsere Zeit* (Leipzig, Brockhaus, 1840).

[60] Kaltenborn, *Kritik*, pp. 231–234.

[61] Kaltenborn distinguished between the historical, dogmatic, philosophical, and legal policy tasks of legal science. Kaltenborn, *Kritik*, pp. 240–255.

[62] In relation to custom, for instance: "Die Rechtswissenschaft hat die Aufgabe, die Rechtgewohnheit aufzufassen und aus ihrer Unbestimmtheit und Unmittelbarkeit zur Klarheit und Bestimmtheit eines Theoretischen Rechtssatzes zu erheben," Kaltenborn, *Kritik*, p. 235.   [63] Kaltenborn, *Kritik*, pp. 256–272.

[64] Kaltenborn, *Kritik*, pp. 295–300.

standard way of reconciling sovereignty and community.[65] In reality, he claimed, States themselves were legislators and judges and war international law's ultimate enforcement. This procedural fact reflected the special character of the States-society. Failure to understand it was the source not only of the deniers' skepticism but also of the gap between the science of the previous period and international reality. Though international law was occasionally breached, it was more often spontaneously complied with, sometimes through pressure of public opinion, sometimes through coalitions and alliances.[66] It was true that sometimes such alliances also violated the law. Nothing guaranteed that war would always be won by the originally aggrieved party. But then, law was a subsidiary element in history and war one of its primary movers, a means of renewal when the existing order no longer corresponded to "reality."[67]

Kaltenborn hoped to articulate the reality of a European political system that sought legitimation from national sovereignty but acknowledged the existence of a larger cultural community. The depiction of that community in the language of general principles would now become one of the tasks of legal science. But like a true realist, Kaltenborn was conservative. He accepted that law's role in international relations was limited. The notable political facts of the day were the demise of pretensions to universal monarchy as well as the "chimerical" constructions of those who wished to introduce the democratic principle into European societies – "May God still spare us from that for a long time!"[68] He was satisfied with the way governmental policies increasingly reflected national consciousness and depicted constitutional monarchy in an organic relationship with it.[69]

Though Kaltenborn's views of the role of international lawyers went much further than those of von Martens or Klüber, they provided no agenda for legal reform. They failed to explain, let alone to assist in, the social and cultural progress that the liberals of the 1860s saw around themselves. Whatever their scientific merits, rationalism and humanitarianism had at least been a comfortable part of the outlook of the European educated elites. Kaltenborn's pedantic insistence on system,

---

[65] "Zur Revision der Lehre von internationalen Rechtsmitteln," (1861), 17 *Zeitschrift für Staatswissenschaft*, pp. 69–124.   [66] Kaltenborn, "Zur Revision," pp. 89–94.
[67] Kaltenborn, "Zur Revision," pp. 122–123.
[68] "Davor möge uns freilich Gott noch recht lange bewahren!," Kaltenborn, *Kritik*, p. 13.   [69] Kaltenborn, *Kritik*, pp. 13–14.

the paradoxical absence of a theory of legislative change from his writing and his "heroic" submission to war as vehicle of world history could not resonate with an *esprit d'internationalité* that introduced liberal–humanist principles into the law proper and not merely into its philosophical background. For all its stress on scientific objectivity and facts, Kaltenborn's writing was remarkably distant from *life*.[70]

By contrast, the new reformist spirit from which Rolin's *Revue* emerged was strikingly present in Charles Vergé's (1810–1890) more than fifty-page introductory essay to the second French edition of von Martens' *Précis* of 1864.[71] The essay enthusiastically described the developments that had in the past half-century brought European peoples closer to each other. Economic relations had come to be based on division of labor, making States increasingly interdependent. Liberation of trade had been carried out through new agreements, abolishing customs and other duties, and providing for freedom of navigation in international waterways. New technology – railways, telegraph, postal connections – disseminated new ideas with unprecedented efficiency. International associations were set up and conferences held in order to speed up international co-operation in a variety of professional fields. Humanitarian and charitable societies were active everywhere. Even the new financial system brought States closer through rapid movements of capital over boundaries – "L'argent n'avait jamais eu de patrie."[72]

For Vergé, the natural development of humanity was from independence to solidarity, patriotism to community.[73] The developments were "signs of a new period, symbols of a universal law."[74] True enough, there were obstacles on the way, such as the principles of legitimacy and *fait accompli*, both valuing the past over the future. Citing Constant against de Maistre, Vergé opined that the divine right of Kings had become an empty form over arbitrary privileges.[75] The Vienna system

---

[70] This applies also to the systematization a decade later by Professor August Bulmerincq, who sought an even fuller purification of positive law from "extraneous" philosophical or political elements. Cf his *Die Systematik des Völkerrechts von Hugo Grotius bis auf die Gegenwart* (Dorpat, Karow, 1858).

[71] Vergé, "Le droit des gens avant et depuis 1789," pp. i–lv.

[72] Vergé, "Le droit des gens avant et depuis 1789," p. xxxi.

[73] This was in line with the Victorian anxiety to overcome selfishness and egoism – seen as primitive desires – and to develop a more sophisticated altruistic outlook on society. Cf. Collini, *Public Moralists*, pp. 60–90.

[74] Vergé, "Le droit des gens avant et depuis 1789," p. xxxvii.

[75] Vergé, "Le droit des gens avant et depuis 1789," pp. xxii–xxiii.

of 1815–1830 might have been able to preserve a relative peace – but it had been "a work of diplomacy and authority, not a work of justice and franchise."[76] But there was no reason to run behind chimeras of eternal peace. The transformations of the age would remove those obstacles – particularly through that most potent of forces, public opinion, "this queen of the world that expresses only what is the most elevated duty and interest of everyone."[77] That change was already on the way could be seen in the difference between the Vienna settlement and the Peace of Paris of 1856, the former having taken place in secrecy, the latter in an unprecedented light of publicity. Where Vienna had been a great power *diktat*, Paris had declared progressive rules and accepted Turkey in the European system.

Finally, Vergé cited the Whig potentate Lord Brougham's prophecy on how progress and the interdependence of European States were to produce a peaceful international system:

> The formation of the European system which is expressed by Lord Brougham with his most elevated liberalism, the solidarity between different States that provides for the protection of the weak and the hindrance of the strong, is produced by international law and fortified by public opinion. By this means all the improvements and reforms, whether in the internal affairs of States or in their international relations, have been predetermined.[78]

An amateur science

At the time when Vergé wrote his introduction to von Martens' old treatise, and Rolin began his *Revue*, there was very little consciousness of international law as a discipline of its own, separate from philosophy, diplomacy, or public and civil law.[79] In France, the writings of the *philosophes* continued to dominate the way in which the subject was conceived well into and beyond the Napoleonic era.[80] Works such as that by Gérard de Rayneval (1736–1812) on *Institutions du droit de la nature et des gens* (1803) derived international law from a discussion of the origin of human society in the natural state and restated the principles of

---

[76] Vergé, "Le droit des gens avant et depuis 1789," p. xlvi.
[77] Vergé, "Le droit des gens avant et depuis 1789," p. lii.
[78] Vergé, "Le droit des gens avant et depuis 1789," p. liv.
[79] For reviews of the study of international law teaching in Europe in the 1870s, cf. (1878), 2 *Annuaire de l'Institut de droit international (Annuaire IDI)*, p. 344; (1879–1880), 3–4 *Annuaire IDI*, pp. 324–347.
[80] Cf. e.g. Paul Challine, *Le droit international public dans la jurisprudence française de 1789 à 1848* (Paris, Loviton, 1934), pp. 10–14.

"The legal conscience of the civilized world"

natural independence, equality, and the balance of power under a utilitarian rhetoric adopted from Montesquieu[81] and Vattel.[82] The obligation to keep treaties was derived from "the honor and dignity of the sovereign, the health and real interest of the State."[83] Rayneval and others were, perhaps, balancing their fear of the *ancien régime* with their dread of the return of Jacobin terror.

Neither restoration nor the revolutionary turmoils of 1830 and 1848 provided a foothold for juristic points about a stable European legal system. On the other hand, the Napoleonic disaster in Russia had made the argument sound compelling that the time of conquest was over and that economic liberalism was making war an anachronism.[84] Saint-Simonian optimism assumed that the development of industry and positive science would completely transform the public space of European societies. Auguste Comte (1798–1857) described societies as functional "systems" developing in accordance with their intrinsic laws: from theological to positive, military to industrial. The diplomacy of States was an outdated growth of earlier, pre-positive eras – and so were the diplomatic laws that regulated it. The future was for industrial chiefs, the proletariat and the unification of Europe under the spiritual leadership of public opinion enlightened by positive science.[85] Saint-Simon dismissed lawyers altogether as a "bastard class"[86] while Comte still allowed them (together with the "littérateurs") subsidiary functions in the coming industrial utopia.[87]

---

[81] "The law of nations is naturally founded on this principle, that different nations ought in time of peace to do one another all the good they can, and in the time of war as little injury as possible, without prejudicing their real interests." *The Spirit of the Laws* (trans. Thomas Nugent, New York, Hafner, 1949), p. 5.

[82] Gérard de Rayneval, *Institutions du droit de la nature et des gens* (Paris, Leblanc, 1803), p. 129 *et seq*; 203–206, 333.

[83] "L'honneur du souverain, sa dignité, le salut, l'intérêt véritable de l'Etat," Rayneval, *Institutions*, pp. 145, 147.

[84] Benjamin Constant, *The Spirit of Conquest and Usurpation and their Relation to European Civilization*, in Biancamaria Fontane (ed.), *Benjamin Constant. Political Writings* (Cambridge University Press, 1988), pp. 51–83.

[85] Cf. Auguste Comte, *La sociologie*, résumé par Emile Rigolage (Paris, Alcan, 1897), esp. pp. 373–407. Comte advocated a complete reorganization of society under the spiritual leadership of "chefs d'industrie." In contrast to "government" and "coordination," he had very little to say about the role of law. He was a federalist, advocating European unification and the civilization of non-European peoples under a *Comité positif occidental*, led by the five European great powers, Comte, *La Sociologie*, pp. 405–407. Cf. also Marcel Merle, *Pacifisme et internationalisme* (Paris, Colin, 1966), pp. 217–234.

[86] Geoffrey Hawthorn, *Enlightenment and Despair. A History of Social Theory* (2nd edn., Cambridge University Press, 1987), p. 76.   [87] Comte, *La sociologie*, pp. 403–404.

Hence, until late in the second half of the century, international law received no general academic treatment in France that would have been separate from a discussion of natural law.[88] In the 1868 edition of his great treatise on the rights and duties of neutrals in maritime war Hautefeuille (1805–1875) had still this to say about the basis and proper method of his science:

> International law finds its basis in divine and primitive law; it is completely derived from this source. With the help of only this law, I firmly believe that it is not only possible but even easy to regulate all relations that exist or might exist between all the peoples of the universe.[89]

Only a few specialized treatments of maritime law, arbitration or diplomatic and consular law appeared in France before the 1870s. French diplomats and courts were satisfied by general treatises written by foreigners – particularly those by von Martens and Klüber and the American diplomat Henry Wheaton (1785–1848) – either directly in French or translated for the French audience.[90]

Nor had international law enjoyed a separate existence in the *facultés de droit*. Indeed, international law fitted uneasily into the juristic atmosphere of the French mid-century, dominated by the exegetic school that recognized no positive source beyond the *Code Civil*. In the *Collège de*

---

[88] Rayneval's 1803 book (with a 2nd edn. in 1832) on international and natural law remained the only French general treatment of the topic. Cf. Paul Fauchille, "Louis Renault (1843–1918)" (1918), XXV *Revue générale de droit international public* (*RGDIP*), pp. 20–21. Cf. also Marc Barreau, *Précis du droit de la nature et des gens* (Paris, Ladvocat, 1831); L. B. Cotelle, *Abrégé d'un cours élémentaire du droit de nature et des gens* (Paris, Gobelet, 1820); François André Isambert, *Tableau historique des progrès du droit public et du droit des gens, jusqu'au XIX siècle* (Paris, Paulin, 1833).

[89] L. B. Hautefeuille, *Des droits et devoirs des nations neutres en temps de guerre maritime* (3rd edn., Paris, Guillaumin, 1868), p. x. Hautefeuille practiced what he preached. Holding that human beings had access to divine and natural law in the form of innate ideas, and that historical facts should have no influence whatsoever on legal study, he inferred freedom of the seas, for instance, from the natural law of property that excluded inappropriable objects of sufficient abundance for everyone to use, pp. ix–xi, xvii, 71–87.

[90] This is the reason given in Henry Bonfils, *Manuel de droit international public* (2nd edn. by Paul Fauchille, Paris, Rousseau, 1898), p. 61, for the absence of an overview of the field in France until the publication of Pradier-Fodéré's 8-volume *Traité de Droit international public européen et américain* (Paris, Pedone-Lauriel, 1885–1906) – although, in fact Louis Renault had already published his *L'introduction à l'étude de droit international* (Paris, Larose, 1879, also published in *L'Oeuvre internationale de Louis Renault*, Paris, Editions internationales, 1932, pp. 1–68) and Funck-Brentano and Sorel had written their policy oriented *Précis de droit des gens* (Paris, Plon, 1877). On these cf. Chapter 4 below. A short overview of French works is in A. Truyol y Serra, *Histoire du droit international public* (Paris, Economica, 1995), pp. 119–120. A much better review appears in Challine, *Le droit international public*, pp. 14–23.

"The legal conscience of the civilized world"

France in 1880, for example, the relevant position was Chair of *Droit de la nature et des gens*.[91] After the Chair of International Law in Strasbourg was abolished in 1867 the only international law professorship remained in Paris. This had been established in 1829 but the courses given by its holders – Royer-Collard (1830–1864) and Charles Giraud (1864–1874) – had been more about diplomatic history than positive law. Only in 1889 was international law introduced at French universities as a compulsory subject with an examination.[92] The situation was not very different in other continental States. When in Holland a law of 1876 prescribed the teaching of international law in State universities there was still no chair for public international law in the country. And in 1884 the University of Brussels decided to allocate the teaching of international law to a Professor of Roman Law, Rolin's close friend and collaborator, Alphonse Rivier (1835–1898).[93]

In France as in Germany the old theory of the *ius publicum universale* continued to form the mainstay of public law teaching well into the nineteenth century. This is easy to understand. It did not need to rely on a weak and politically suspect domestic sovereignty and its rationalism was available both to counter *de facto* political fragmentation (as in Germany) in terms of the unity of a legal system and to criticize reactionary governments (as in France) by reference to principles of liberal, perhaps even democratic, constitutionalism. But although rationalism, through its roots in Roman law, did make a distinction between private and public law, it did not found a technical discipline that would have focused on the external affairs of the government in contrast to its internal activities – this had been precisely the gist of Kaltenborn's critique. In France as in Germany, the *Droit public de l'Europe* was simply one part of public law, von Martens' *äusseres Staatenrecht*, external public law.[94]

German public lawyers writing during the period of Napoleon's *Rheinbund* (1806–1815) and the early years of the Confederation normally carried over their *Aufklärungsideale* from the eighteenth to the nineteenth century.[95] We have seen how this was done by von Martens and Klüber. Many of their followers sought to balance popular sovereignty with the monarchic principle by "organic" language that fused the elements of the

---

[91] Cf. (1878–1879), 3–4 *Annuaire IDI*, II, p. 329.
[92] Fauchille, "Louis Renault," pp. 31–32.
[93] By that time, Rivier had already established a name as internationalist by frequent contributions in Rolin's *Revue* and through activities within the *Institut de droit international*. Cf. "Nécrologie" (1898), XXX *RDI*, pp. 382–393 and Ernest Nys, "Alphonse Rivier, sa vie et ses oeuvres" (1899), XXXI *RDI*, pp. 415–431.
[94] Martens, *Précis*, p. 45.   [95] Stolleis, *Geschichte* II, pp. 62–75.

public realm together in more or less conservative or liberal positions. The predominant concern to construct a distinctly German realm of public law buttressed by arguments about the workings of the *Volksgeist* led some to deny the very possibility of an international law proper – seen as a survival from earlier rationalist moorings. Neither Hegel nor Savigny were simple "deniers," however, but held international law to be a qualitatively different type whose existence and reality depended on the degree of cultural integration of European nations.[96]

However, the liberal disappointment of 1848 turned the attention of German constitutional lawyers to international reform. After all, it was through international action – the Russian intervention in Hungary – that reaction had combated progress. Thus, a leading liberal Professor of State and Administrative Law from Tübingen (later Heidelberg), Robert von Mohl (1799–1875), suggested in the 1850s – by express reference to Kaltenborn – a reconceptualization of international law on a scientific basis, that is to say, on a theory of the international community (*die Lehre von der internationalen Gemeinschaft*).[97] Previous theory had started from the axiomatic existence of sovereign States and had sought to derogate from independence as little as possible. By contrast, a scientific theory would understand all forms of social organization as instruments for human purposes (*Lebenszwecke*) and would grant the need for different kinds and levels of such organization. International law, too, should seek to contribute to the ability of the international community to fulfill effectively those human purposes that were best suited for international realization.[98] This required, however, accepting that alongside a community of States there were also a community of individuals and communities of societies that interacted with each other in a myriad ways. In accordance with a liberal view of representation – that grounds his theory of the *Rechtsstaat*[99] – von Mohl saw States in their international relations as representatives of individuals, societies, and of the international community whose interests and aims they were called upon to realize.[100]

Not all German public lawyers shared von Mohl's theory of the representative State or, even if they did, drew as far-reaching conclusions from it. For Adolf Lasson (1837–1917), for instance, the Hegelian legal

---

[96] Cf. G. W. F. Hegel, *Philosophy of Right*, trans. by S. W. Doyle (London, Prometheus, 1996 [1896]), pp. 340–341.
[97] Robert von Mohl, *Staatsrecht, Völkerrecht, und Politik, I: Staatsrecht und Völkerrecht* (3 vols., Tübingen, Laupp, 1860), p. 580.   [98] von Mohl, *Staatsrecht*, p. 585.
[99] von Mohl, *Staatsrecht*, pp. 8 *et seq.*   [100] von Mohl, *Staatsrecht*, pp. 599–636.

philosopher from Berlin, arguing perhaps significantly in the year 1871, international law was possible only as an expression of the sometimes parallel interests of States, a means of co-ordinating their action for a more effective attainment of the objects they desired. The world was irreducibly divided into separate nations between which reigned a constant *bellum omnium*, or at least a threat thereof. An international community – or indeed a law above States – was a conceptual, historical and psychological absurdity.[101]

If in France international law existed as a somewhat exotic branch of natural law and in Germany as an outgrowth of public law and diplomacy, in England there was virtually no university teaching in the subject at all in the first half of the century. In 1842 James Reddie pointed out that aside from translations of Grotius, Bynkershoek, and Vattel, a systematic treatment of the topic "appeared to be still a desideratum in the legal or juridical literature of Great Britain."[102] Even general legal education had until then been carried out through apprenticeship so that a Parliamentary Select Committee had been compelled to conclude in 1846 that "[n]o Legal Education worthy of the name, of a public nature, is at this moment to be had in either England or Ireland."[103] After the reform of legal education in the mid-century, the first chairs of international law proper were set up quite rapidly in Oxford in 1859 (the Chichele Chair with Montague Bernard [1820–1880] as its first occupant) and in Cambridge in 1866 (the Whewell Chair with William Harcourt [1827–1904]).[104] The position held by the eccentric Scotsman James Lorimer (1818–1890) in Edinburgh after 1862 continued to be a chair in the Law of Nature and of Nations, a combination well reflected in Lorimer's teaching.[105] Sir Travers Twiss (1809–1897) who was much used as Foreign Office consultant, taught at King's College London in 1852–1855, but moved from there to hold the *Regius* chair of civil law in Oxford until 1870. In addition, private grants enabled the teaching of international law at other universities as well.

---

[101] Adolf Lasson, *Princip und Zukunft des Völkerrechts* (Berlin, Hertz, 1871).
[102] Reddie, *Inquiries in International Law*, pp. 1–2.
[103] Quoted in Collini, *Public Moralists*, p. 266. For the (largely unsuccessful) initiation of the study of "Law and Modern History" in Oxford 1850–1865 and the consequent setting up of an independent law school, cf. F. H. Lawson, *The Oxford Law School 1850–1965* (Oxford, Clarendon, 1968), pp. 1–33.
[104] The syllabus for international law at Oxford in 1877–1884 contained two American textbooks (Wheaton and Woolsey), one German (Heffter) and one French (Ortolan) textbook but no English works, Lawson, *Oxford*, pp. 39–41.
[105] The Chair had been established as early as 1707.

The Gentle Civilizer of Nations

In Britain, a self-confident legal positivism sought the basis of law from well-entrenched secular sovereignty. The 1832 lectures of John Austin (1788–1859) famously disqualified international law as law through an argument that conceived legal rules in terms of the commands of a sovereign enjoying habitual obedience. Well-suited for a domestic system whose legitimacy was taken as self-evident, it found no room for a law beyond sovereignty. If Benthamite utilitarians agreed that the principles of the greatest pleasure of the greatest number were as applicable in the international as in the domestic field ("common and equal utility of nations"), and conceded to public opinion the role of an informal enforcement agency,[106] there was little in such construction that would have provided a tangible foothold for an independent profession. More than their continental colleagues, British lawyers such as Lorimer or Sir Robert Phillimore (1810–1890) argued on the basis of God's will and natural reason[107] – which is perhaps why Prime Minister Salisbury could report to the Parliament in 1887 that "international law has not any existence in the sense in which the term 'law' is usually understood. It depends generally upon the prejudices of writers of text-books. It can be enforced by no tribunal, and therefore to apply to it the phrase 'law' is to some extent misleading."[108]

Such an attitude may not have been only a reflection of disinterested speculation. As the only industrial economy and naval power since 1815, Britain could confidently believe that the benefits that law claimed to offer could better ensue from the continued expansion of British economy and territory. An Empire is never an advocate of an international law that can seem only an obstacle to its ambitions. The persistent British refusal to underwrite a legal system of collective intervention in the legitimist cause may have been justified by a genuine aversion against absolutism – but the absence of common rules or agreed procedures also automatically played into its hands.[109]

---

[106] Cf. Jeremy Bentham, *Principles of International Law*, in *The Works. Published under the superintendence of John Bowring* (9 vols., Edinburgh, 1843), II, pp. 537–560.

[107] Cf. Wilhelm Grewe, *Epochen des Völkerrechts* (Baden-Baden, Nomos, 1983), pp. 597–601.

[108] Quoted in T. E. Walker, *The Science of International Law* (London, Clay, 1893), p. 1.

[109] "Never in the entire history of the world has a single power exercised a world hegemony like that of the British in the middle of the nineteenth century . . . Never since then has any single power succeeded in re-establishing a comparable hegemony . . . for no power has since been able to claim the the exclusive status of 'workshop of the world,'" Eric Hobsbawm, *The Age of Revolution* (London, Abacus, 1997 [1962]), p. 365.

"The legal conscience of the civilized world"

It is not difficult to see why a professional international law would not have come into existence during the first half of the century. The ascendant liberalism of 1815–1848 was radically activist and internationally organized within peace societies and federalist and pacifist movements.[110] These movements found their strongest base within the Anglo-American world and a natural ally in the groups of exiles from the revolutionary movements of 1830 and 1848.[111] They did not need lawyers to argue what was seen as a political, even a radical task of transformation. The distrust of governments by liberal radicals, and, *a fortiori*, socialists, was incompatible with an attempt to conceptualize the post-Napoleonic system in terms of legal rules: an international law of the governments rallied around a Holy Alliance was simply anathema. Peace would follow from the uniting of nations (and their working classes) brought about by the natural development of free trade and increasing popular enlightenment – or, as some assumed, of impending revolution.[112]

Writing in lonely exile in Brussels in 1861 the French socialist and political thinker Pierre Joseph Proudhon (1809–1865) agonized over the difficulty of fitting the French military campaign in Northern Italy into the commonplace theory about the growth of civilization and the needs of an interdependent economy doing away with war. No prevailing system of concepts could realistically grasp war. This was particularly the case with lawyers' concepts: "This so-called science of the law of nations of theirs, what should be said about it? The whole body of law they have conceived and articulated is a scaffolding of fictions which they themselves fail to think credible."[113]

A time of danger

The Crimean War could still be interpreted by contemporaries as not really a threat to the European peace system – for it had to do with the perennial "Eastern Question" and the ambitions of that only marginally European country, Russia. But faith in the intrinsic peacefulness of European societies facing unprecedented economic growth and the

---

[110] Cf. F. H. Hinsley, *Power and the Pursuit of Peace. Theory and Practice in the History of Relations between States* (Cambridge University Press, 1963), pp. 92–113.
[111] Hobsbawm, *The Age of Revolution*, pp. 160–162.
[112] Hinsley, *Power and the Pursuit of Peace*, pp. 111–113.
[113] P.-J. Proudhon, *La guerre et la paix. Recherches sur la constitution du droit des gens* (Oeuvres complètes, nouvelle édition, Paris, Rivière, 1927), p. 9.

spread of liberal and democratic ideas was crushed by the Franco-Prussian war of 1870–1871 which Maine described a few years later as "one of the greatest of modern wars, which probably never had a rival in the violence and the passion which it excited."[114] The war and the establishment of the German Empire inaugurated a new era in foreign policy. There was a change of feeling, a turn "from an international moral order to a *Realpolitik*."[115] Militarism was on the rise.[116] The creation of Germany and Italy seemed to confirm that war was sometimes not only inevitable but necessary. Germany's *Weltpolitik* created successive war scares in Britain which did nothing to curb the increasing levels of armaments. Moreover, French desire for *revanche* after Sedan went through all factions of society.

Contemporaries, too, saw the period as one of grave danger. In a book that came out in 1873, the Christian-socialist economist Emile de Laveleye (1822–1892), one of the founding members of the *Institut de droit international*, the subject of the following section, concluded that popular sentiment was not necessarily oriented towards peace. On the contrary: "Today, unfortunately, Europe's horizon is more threatening than ever; not only some black spots appear but dark, blood-colored clouds cover it."[117]

Mid-Victorian faith in the ability of science and industrialism to bring about peace and harmony was eroding. Taking up a professorship in Göttingen in 1872, Rudolf Jhering (1818–1892) published his famous pamphlet on Struggle for Law (*Der Kampf ums Recht*), in which he argued that, as individuals were called upon to struggle over their rights, and in this struggle to vindicate the authority of the legal order, nations were not entitled to let injustice pass without opposition; a nation that would do so would compromise its own honor and dignity and undermine international legality. Contrary to Savigny and the historicists Jhering claimed – probably only dimly aware of the Darwinian tone of his argument – that struggle and not slow development and harmony was the core of law. Through struggle the nation creates self-awareness and

---

[114] Henry Sumner Maine, *International Law. The Whewell Lectures* (London, Murray, 1887), pp. 128–129.
[115] Owen Chadwick, *The Secularization of the European Mind in the 19th Century* (Cambridge University Press 1995 [1975]), pp. 134, 132–137.
[116] Cf. Brian Bond, *War and Society in Europe 1870–1970* (London, Fontana, 1983), pp. 26–28.
[117] Emile de Laveleye, *Des causes actuelles de guerre en Europe et de l'arbitrage* (Brussels and Paris, Muquerdt and Guillaumin, 1873), p. 11.

"The legal conscience of the civilized world"

becomes attached to its rights and the law.[118] This was part of a new literature that turned away from materialism and rationalism and sought to invoke struggle and the depths of feeling. It now seemed that the "positivist system of morality failed to satisfy at some ultimate point of truth about the human predicament."[119]

Such sentiments were expressed in Adolf Lasson's 1871 book on the principles and future of international law which attacked the popular Kantian mistake about international development being necessarily towards a more peaceful, cosmopolitan world. The world was naturally divided into several nations between which reigned an irreducible antagonism:

> with peoples of lower and higher culture – everywhere, and to the highest degree with peoples of the most noble pedigree, between people and people, between State and State, all over we find the deepest oppositions and as a consequence an interminable struggle.[120]

States were always full of fear of each other, and hungry for more wealth, honor, *Herrschaft*. No rational explanation could change this aspect of their nature – to fantasize to the contrary would leave only bitter disappointment.[121] States had no purposes outside themselves: indeed could not have because their very definition lay in the aim of advancing the nations that inhabited them. They could not accept a law above themselves without self-mutilation. There was no analogy with individuals in the natural state:[122]

> this dream of a legal order over and between States is a confused and mindless dream that is born of weakness and false sentimentality and has received the appearance of realisability and reasonableness only through the misuse of words and unclear ideas.[123]

But if the Catholics were wrong, so were the Machiavellians. States did develop a kind of Ersatz-law so as to facilitate the fulfillment of their desires (to exchange goods, for example).[124] The higher the cultural level

---

[118] Rudolf Jhering, *Der Kampf ums Recht* (Berlin, Philo, 1925), pp. 58–62. Cf. also Frantz Wieacker, *A History of Private Law in Europe. With Particular Reference to Germany*, trans. Tony Weir (Oxford, Clarendon, 1995), p. 357.
[119] Chadwick, *Secularization*, p. 248. [120] Lasson, *Princip und Zukunft*, p. 6.
[121] Lasson, *Princip und Zukunft*, pp. 31–32. Cf. also pp. 7–9.
[122] Lasson, *Princip und Zukunft*, p. 22. [123] Lasson, *Princip und Zukunft*, p. 26.
[124] The rules of international law are rules of prudence rather than law while obedience to them is dictated only by clever egoism, Lasson, *Princip und Zukunft*, pp. 42–55.

of States, the more their desires diversified, and the more co-ordination was needed. States were even compelled to honesty by this law: all co-ordination was premised upon some firmness of commitment. However, in matters of vital interest, nothing may constrain the State, and obligations rested valid only so long as they were useful.[125]

Lasson wrote as a German patriot in the immediate aftermath of the establishment of the German Reich. It would have been odd had he not assumed that war sometimes was a necessity and that if treaties and real conditions conflicted, all the worse for treaties.[126] But though international lawyers have regarded Lasson's arguments as nothing less than scandalous, in fact his preference was for peace and he argued that if States understood their self-interest correctly, so was theirs.[127] His nine-point program for an international law that would aim at further understanding between States and prevent unnecessary war captured much of the liberal sensibility.[128] That he was a realist who stressed the degree to which States were motivated by self-interest and used law – or their interpretations of it – to further their objectives hardly differentiated him from how contemporaries viewed the matter. What made Lasson seem the paradigmatic "denier" was perhaps the bluntness with which he concluded that the primary mover of inter-State relations was power, that democratic institutions or a well-developed cultural life did nothing to prove the political wisdom of a people (here he had France in mind) and that if war was necessary, then a well-informed popular opinion strengthened the belligerent spirit rather than mitigated it.

If Lasson's argument that modernity and culture did not automatically engender peacefulness was right, then the time of political *laissez-faire* was over. Nationalist ambition and ideas that Spencerian acolytes had popularized in France under the neologism of "survivaldefitisme" needed to be positively counteracted in order to support the internationalist spirit.

---

[125] Lasson, *Princip und Zukunft*, p. 54.
[126] "Den neuen Zuständen sollen neue Verträge entsprechen," Lasson, *Princip und Zukunft*, p. 69.
[127] Lasson shared the Clausewitzian view of war as an instrument of politics. It was a "method of negotiation" whereby States hoped to attain an agreement in the peace treaty, Lasson, *Princip und Zukunft*, pp. 66–75.
[128] These points included basing law on the "real nature" of international relations, codifying it in the form of laws, providing for a maximal openness of international negotiations, increasing the use of permanent congresses and arbitration and so on, Lasson, *Princip und Zukunft*, pp. 84–116.

"The legal conscience of the civilized world"

A meeting in Ghent, 1873

The failure of both sides in the Franco-Prussian war to honor the 1864 Geneva Convention, including widespread misuse of Red Cross insignia, deeply disturbed the humanitarian activists. In his memoirs Gustave Moynier (1826–1910), Professor of Law at the University of Geneva who had presided over the 1864 Conference, writes that having followed the conduct of the 1870 war, he

> had often been painfully struck by the uncertainty surrounding legal regulation governing the conduct of hostilities . . . This state of affairs seemed to me to have done much to intensify already inflamed passions and to give the fighting a savagery unworthy of civilized nations.[129]

Action needed to be taken. Not being able to proceed alone, Moynier felt that "only one man had the qualities required" for initiating a collective effort. This man was Rolin-Jaequemyns whom Moynier had met at an international charity conference in London in 1862 and who had since then received a reputation as someone who was able to achieve things. Consequently Moynier wrote to Rolin suggesting that action be taken in order to set up a congress composed of the principal international jurists, "une espèce de concile juridique-oecuménique, sans pape et sans infallibilité."[130] Through a common friend, Alphonse Rivier from Brussels, Moynier then arranged a meeting with Rolin in Ghent in November 1872 where he learned that a number of lawyers from Europe and elsewhere had already made a similar proposal. Among them had been Francis Lieber (1800–1872) from the United States, the drafter of the famous "Lieber Code" for the use of the Union army in the American Civil War,[131] a liberal adventurer and a political essayist

---

[129] Quoted in André Durand, "The Role of Gustave Moynier in the Founding of the Institute of International Law (1873)" (1994), 34 *ICRC Review*, p. 544.

[130] Alphonse Rivier, "Notice historique sur l'Institut de droit international. Sa fondation et sa première session. Gand 1873" (1877), 1 *Annuaire IDI*, p. 12; Durand, "The Role of Gustave Moynier," pp. 543–563.

[131] *Instruction for the Government of Armies of the United States in the Field* (also known as General Orders No. 100), approved by President Lincoln in 1863. For the text and background of the Lieber code, cf. Richard Shelly Hartigan, *Lieber's Code and the Law of War* (Chicago, Precedent, 1983). After a tumultuous career as a liberal adventurer in Europe, Lieber had settled in the United States in 1827 and in 1857 become Professor of History and Political Economy at Columbia University in New York. He was a moderate liberal in whom the adjective "moderate" became increasingly appropriate with the advancement of age. He hated monarchy and absolutism – but he also detested the way the Communards of Paris in 1871 had adopted his motto "No right without its duties, no duty without its rights" as theirs. For biographical

who a few years earlier had given the "Anglican Race": "the obvious task ... among other proud and sacred tasks, to rear and spread civil liberty over vast regions in every part of the earth, on continent and isle."[132]

On the basis of such suggestions Rolin contacted several other eminent lawyers, including Johann Caspar Bluntschli (1808–1881) from Heidelberg, Baron Franz von Holtzendorff (1829–1889) from Berlin, Carlos Calvo (1824–1906), the Argentine lawyer and diplomat living in Paris, the French lawyers and politicians Edmond Drouyn de Lhuys (1805–1881), and F. Esquirou de Parieu (1815–1893) as well as the Russian D. I. Katchenowski (1827–1872).[133] From his initial soundings, Rolin drew the conclusion that instead of a conference there was support for a permanent institution or an academy of international law.

The successful conclusion of the *Alabama* affair by the rendering of the first significant arbitration award in Geneva on September 14, 1872 provided publicity and political support for such efforts. As Rolin was corresponding with his acquaintances in Europe, the American pacifists Elihu Burritt (1810–1879) and James B. Miles (1823–1875) took up the proposal for a conference to draw up a code of international law that their compatriot, the legal reformist David Dudley Field (1805–1894) had already made in 1866 at the British Association for the Promotion of Social Sciences. Miles – who could speak no foreign language – was despatched to Europe in January 1873 and having met with peace activists and lawyers in Britain, France, Italy, Austria, and Germany conferred with Rolin in Ghent in early March 1873. Despite initial enthusiasm for the American proposals, Rolin and the Europeans soon decided that they went much further than the scientific restatement they had had in mind. The Americans were seeking to establish an open organization whose composition, aims, and working methods were directed towards political influence, especially the revival of the peace conferences, and deviated from those of the limited scientific organization that had been contemplated in Europe.[134] They were part of an

---

Footnote 131 *(cont.)*
    detail, apart from the above book by Hartigan, cf. Frank Freidel, *Francis Lieber. Nineteenth-Century Liberal* (Baton Rouge, Louisiana State University Press, 1940), and Roeben, "Bluntschli," pp. 17–44.

[132] Lieber, *On Civil Liberty and Self-Government* (Philadelphia, Lippincott, 1859), p. 21.

[133] Albéric de Rolin, *Les origines de l'Institut de droit international, 1873–1923. Souvenirs d'un témoin* (Bruxelles, Vromant, 1923), p. 11. Cf. also August Schou, *Histoire de l'internationalisme* (3 vols., Publications de l'Institut Nobel Norwégien, Oslo, Aschenhoug, 1963), 3, p. 311. Cf. also Rolin-Jaequemyns, "De la nécessité," p. 481.

[131] Cf. Rolin-Jaequemyns, "De la nécessité," pp. 475–477, 482; Irwin Abrams, "The Emergence of the International Law Societies" (1957), 19 *Review of Politics*, pp. 361–380; Fritz Münch, "L'Institut de droit international: Ses debuts comme organe

"The legal conscience of the civilized world"

eminently political effort and improper for a scientific body as well as impractical, as there seemed to be no realistic prospect that governments would approve of a code drafted without their involvement.[135]

Rolin counted that there were about twenty–thirty men in Europe who had been actively engaged in the development of international law and about twenty with significant contributions in the field of politics and diplomacy.[136] In March 1873, he sent a confidential note to a limited number of these men, proposing the establishment of a permanent institute or academy for the organization of collective scientific activity in international law. He pointed out that in most fields of intellectual cultivation, there was a tendency to organize internationally – a tendency made so much easier by the development of new means of communication – after all, this was the year of the publication of Jules Verne's *Around the World in 80 Days*. It was, he wrote, "une idée *essentiellement moderne*."[137]

The first Meeting of the *Institut de droit international* was held in Ghent on September 8–11, 1873 under the presidency of Italy's Mancini. Out of the thirty-three invitees, eleven arrived in Ghent and the rest soon joined as permanent or associate members. Among other decisions, the Ghent meeting adopted a Statute for the institute Article 1 of which laid down as the purpose of the institute: "De favoriser le progrès du droit international, en s'efforçant de devenir l'organe de la conscience juridique du monde civilisé." The "legal conscience [or perhaps consciousness, there is an important ambivalence in the original French language] of the civilized world" – language that to our ears seems old-fashioned and difficult to take in full seriousness. To be an organ of the conscience – or consciousness – of the civilized world; what might *that* feel like?[138]

---

collectif de la doctrine," in *Estudios de derecho internacional. Homenaje a.g. Antonio de Luna* (Madrid, C.S.I.C., 1968), p. 386.

[135] The American proposal led to the convening of the Conference on Reform and Codification of International Law in Brussels on October 13, 1873 – only five weeks after the Conference that set up the *Institut de droit international*. Present in Brussels were thirty lawyers, philanthropists, diplomats, and representatives of peace societies as well as three representatives of the newly established *Institut*. The conference failed to establish the planned code of international law and the sweeping proposals in support of arbitration were gradually set aside as attention was directed at technical questions of private international law and maritime law. To this extent, the peace activists had failed. Cf. Abrams, "The Emergence of the International Law Societies," pp. 376–379; Schou, *Histoire de l'internationalisme*, pp. 321–325.

[136] Nys, "Notice sur Rolin-Jaequemyns," p. 63.   [137] (1877), 1 *Annuaire IDI*, p. 13.

[138] In the course of the discussion in Ghent it had been argued that the provision was quite ambitious. Nonetheless, it was maintained because: "on a pensé qu'il était essentiel d'affirmer, pour ainsi dire en tête des statuts, le lien intime qui doit exister entre le science véritable du droit international et les inspirations de la conscience public du monde civilisé" (1873), V *RDI*, p. 683.

A romantic profession: Bluntschli

The language came from the pen of the Swiss lawyer, Johann Caspar Bluntschli, then Professor of Political Science at the University of Heidelberg, an accomplished publicist in civil and public law, a moderate-liberal politician and a Protestant activist. Already in November 1872 Bluntschli had been in contact with Rolin about this suggestion. Having received Rolin's note, Bluntschli seized the opportunity and in his response of March 22 (the Emperor's birthday, as Bluntschli points out in his memoirs) annexed drafts for the Statutes of an *Akademie des Völkerrechts* as well as an International Society for International Law. The following May, Rolin and Westlake met with Bluntschli in Heidelberg to discuss the drafts. Article 1 of the Statute for the Institute as it was prepared then read: "The *Institut de droit international* shall act as the scientific organ of the common legal consciousness [*dem gemeinsamen Rechtsbewusstsein*] of the civilized world."[139]

This had not been the first time Bluntschli had had recourse to the idea of a *Rechtsbewusstsein der civilisierten Welt*. In 1867 he had had published his *Das moderne Völkerrecht der civilisierten Staaten als Rechtsbuch dargestellt*. This book – like the idea of the Institute – was also credited to Lieber and followed Lieber's example in taking the form of a prepared codification.[140] Bluntschli explained that he had chosen this form as he had not wished to report merely the contents of existing treaties or customs – this would have been unnecessary (as many books already did this) but also counter-productive as it would have frozen the law's development:

> I was rather seduced by the contemporary idea to formulate international law in terms that were clear and correct and to articulate the legal norms that were held necessary or useful by the consciousness of the civilized world. In this way I hope to contribute as much as possible to the development of international law.[141]

For Bluntschli, the essence of the legal craft was neither the reporting of treaties, negotiated by diplomats with an eye for immediate benefit, nor

---

[139] "Das internationale institut für Völkerrecht (Institut de droit international) soll dem gemeinsamen Rechtsbewusstsein der civilisierten Welt zum wissenschaftlichen Organe dienen." J. C. Bluntschli, *Denkwürdiges aus meinem Leben*, auf veranlassung der Familie durchgesehen und veröffentlicht von Dr. Rudolf Seyerlen (3 vols., Nördlingen, Beck, 1884), III, p. 331.

[140] In fact, Lieber had opposed governmental codification and preferred a scientific restatement, independent of official scrutiny. Cf. Ernest Nys, "François Lieber," (1902), 2/V *RDI*, p. 687. For the correspondence, cf. Roeben, "Bluntschli," *passim*.

[141] Bluntschli, *Denkwürdiges*, III, p. 171.

"The legal conscience of the civilized world"

the elucidation of customs, always developed for local situations and for particular needs. Law was, in accordance with the catch-word of the times, dynamic, and it was the task of legal science to capture and describe it in its dynamism. Old scholarship had portrayed a static image of law, one that neglected its constant becoming, its being a part of the living, evolving order of humanity.[142] Moynier would not have disagreed. Reflecting upon his own initiative to Rolin he tells that what had been in his mind was:

> to bring together those most experienced in international law so that they would proclaim, with a single voice if possible, the rules of moderation which the legal conscience of the time found indispensable.[143]

Through Bluntschli, the proposal for a scientific institute to act as an "organ" of legal conscience-consciousness of the civilized world can be traced to the teachings of the German historical school of law, associated particularly with Friedrich Carl von Savigny (1779–1861). As is well known, the historical school emerged as a reaction against the abstract rationalism of Enlightenment thought and appeared in the critique against the legislating of comprehensive codes – such as Napoleon's *Code Civil* – that were felt by Savigny to neglect the organic development of law by popular conviction and to freeze it into inflexible and abstract maxims.[144] By contrast, Savigny stressed the *völkisch* character of law: "Positive law lives in the common consciousness of the people."[145] The word "positive" here had nothing to do with recognition by each and every member of the *Volk*, nor with majority decision. It denoted a real, supra-individual historical process. For Savigny, law emerged and was connected to the *Volksgeist* like language, not as abstract rules but as living institutions.[146]

That all (positive) law was *Volksrecht* did not contradict the possibility of a general human law: "What lives in a single people is only the general human nature that expresses itself in an individual way."[147] For example, Savigny constructed private international law in a way diametrically

---

[142] Johann Caspar Bluntschli, *Das moderne Völkerrecht der civilisierten Staaten als Rechtsbuch dargestellt* (2nd edn., Nördlingen, Beck, 1872), p. vi.

[143] Durand, "The Role of Gustave Moynier," p. 544.

[144] Cf. Friedrich Carl von Savigny, *Vom Beruf unserer Zeit für Gesetzgebung und Rechtswissenschaft* (Reprint of the 3rd edn. [1840], Freiburg, Mohr, 1892).

[145] "In dem gemeinsamen Bewusstsein des Volkes lebt das positive Recht . . .," Friedrich Carl von Savigny, *System des heutigen römischen Rechts* (8 vols., Berlin, Veit, 1840), I, p. 14.

[146] Savigny, *System des heutigen römischen Rechts*, I, pp. 14–16.

[147] Savigny, *System des heutigen römischen Rechts*, I, p. 21.

opposed to the old rationalist theory of statutes, emphasizing that types of legal relationship were rooted in particular historical contexts and that it was this organic link and not the nationality of some aspect thereof that should determine applicable law. Private international law was a supranational expression of legal relationships, not a part of the national law of this or that State.[148] This was precisely the ethos of Westlake and Mancini, too, who had both attacked the standard view that the use of anything else than the *lex fori* was always merely a matter of *comitas gentium*.[149]

But if law was an expression of community spirit and there was no universal community, what then became of international law? In Savigny's mind, advanced nations such as the Romans and later the "Christian–European world" had developed legal rules to govern their behavior not only *inter se* but sometimes towards other nations as well – although there were neither tribunals nor a legal profession to administer them.[150] But this was not all. The organic theory was directed more towards a renewal of legal scholarship than inaugurating a radically populist legal ontology. The "*Volk*" was in Savigny's conservative mind a cultural concept, an intellectual tradition and not an actual people. A community was neither a raw nation nor a bundle of free-floating individuals but an institution and a history. Inherited traditions made people what they were. Savigny was a cosmopolitan humanist who felt alien towards emerging German nationalism, and led the "Romanist" wing of the historical school against those who sought to replace the study of classical Roman law by enquiries into the Germanistic *ius commune*.[151]

The argument highlighted the position of the academic jurist. It was the jurist's task to bring, through a combination of historical and "philosophical" study, the *völkisch* law into consciousness.

In the specific consciousness of this estate law is only a continuation and special development of the popular law [*Volksrecht*]. It now comes to lead a double life: as the consciousness of the people whose more detailed development and use in individual situations is the special calling of the juridical estate.[152]

---

[148] Savigny, *System des heutigen römischen Rechts*, VIII.
[149] Cf. Stanislao Mancini, "De l'utilité de rendre obligatoire, sous la forme d'un ou de plusieurs traités internationales, un certain nombre de règles générales du droit international privé pour assumer la décision uniforme des conflits entre les différentes législations civiles et criminelles" (1874), 5 *Journal de droit international privé*, p. 229.
[150] Savigny, *System des heutigen römischen Rechts*, I, pp. 33–34.
[151] Cf. Wieacker, *A History of Private Law*, pp. 303–316.
[152] Savigny, *System des heutigen römischen Rechts*, I, p. 45.

"The legal conscience of the civilized world"

The jurists stand in a reflexive relationship to the *Volk*; taking the law as they find it in a nation's history and customs and exposing it in the codes they prepare for the nation.[153] For Savigny, Wieacker notes:

> the jurist is the exclusive representative of law in the people. Although law had originally evolved in the people as a whole, possibly through the medium of priests and judges, a class of learned jurists then arose, and it is they who now have the sole control on the development of the law.[154]

The view of the jurist as a representative of popular sentiment was taken further by Pandectist jurisprudence for which it was the principal task of legal science to articulate the consciousness of the people into a logically organized conceptual system. Now the jurist became – in the words of the leading Pandectist, Georg Friedrich Puchta (1798–1846), as in Article 1 of the Statute of the Institute – an "organ" of the people that possesses a monopoly on the theory and practice of the law.[155] In practice, this supported the writing of scholarly tracts in the form of codes; the concepts of the law derived not from some momentary (and arbitrary) legislative will but from the jurists' historical and conceptual studies. In the same way, international law could have reality as the juridical articulation of common European institutions.

Bluntschli had studied under Savigny in Berlin in 1827–1828 and admired him greatly. By the 1860s, however, the battle between historicism and rationalism in Germany was largely over and, with many others, Bluntschli now stressed the need to transcend their opposition or to find balance between the two.[156] Nevertheless, he felt that public law was still studied by predominantly rationalist techniques.[157] It was necessary to reform it by relating it to the development of the people and the State within the larger context of world history:

> It now is necessary to examine the State not as a dead machine that functions under the laws of mechanic movement but as a living entity, an organism inhabited by a spirit. This must, however, take place by situating the State's development in world history and in light of ideas that determine the development of world history.[158]

Bluntschli spoke the language of Savigny's supranational historicism. This language was familiar to Westlake, too, whose 1858 treatise on

---

[153] Savigny, *System des heutigen römischen Rechts*, I, pp. 46–47.
[154] Wieacker, *A History of Private Law*, p. 311. Cf. also Carl Joachim Friedrich, *The Philosophy of Law in Historical Perspective* (2nd edn., Chicago University Press, 1963), p. 140.
[155] Cf. Wieacker, *A History of Private Law*, p. 316.
[156] Roeben, "Bluntschli," pp. 106–109.   [157] Bluntschli, *Denkwürdiges*, III, pp. 196–201.
[158] Bluntschli, *Denkwürdiges*, III, p. 199.

private international law had been systematically written to familiarize English jurists with continental scholarship, and Savigny in particular.[159] There was, in this respect at least, no fundamental divide between the continental and the British jurists behind the Institute. Both held that law was rooted in the actual histories of peoples and nations. But its essence was universal; national laws were but aspects or stages of the universal development of human society.

Such ideas were expressly related to international law by the leading British legal historian Sir Henry Sumner Maine (1822–1888) who also occupied the Whewell Chair in Cambridge for a brief period before his death. Maine regarded international law as essentially a product of Roman law – often under the pseudonym of Natural Law, as interpreted and expanded by the great writers, Grotius and de Vattel in particular. These were Maine's "race of law-making jurists":

> the process by which International Law obtained authority in a great part of Europe was a late stage of the process by which Roman Law had also obtained authority over very much the same part of the world . . . this process had little or no analogy to what is now understood by legislation, but consisted in the reception of a body of doctrine in a mass by specially constituted or trained minds.[160]

In Germany, Bluntschli's "organic" view was soon to be overshadowed by the Gerber–Laband school of voluntarist positivism.[161] But by importing this older view to international law Bluntschli was able to avoid the consequence that was inevitable in later public law that the question of international law's binding force would become the central dilemma in the way that Austin had argued in Britain in the 1830s. If law did not emerge from the will of the (formal) sovereign but was part of the society's (organic) development, the problem of how it could bind the sovereign would simply not arise.

All this was commonplace to Bluntschli as he turned to international law in the 1860s at an advanced age and as an already recognized authority in politics and law.[162] He had published works on Swiss (especially Zürich's) and German civil and public law as well as tracts in theology,

---

[159] A. V. Dicey, "His Book and His Character," in *Memoirs of John Westlake*, pp. 26–27.
[160] Maine, *International Law*, p. 26.
[161] Cf. e.g. Peter von Oertzen, *Die soziale Funktion des staatsrechtlichen Positivismus* (Frankfurt, Suhrkamp, 1974), pp. 60–71, 118–123, 154 *et seq*. Cf. also pp. 184–185 below.
[162] His first publication in the field was *Das moderne Kriegsrecht der civilisierten Staaten* (Nördlingen, Beck, 1866), a section of the 1867 work brought out in advance due to the Austro-Prussian war.

psychology and politics. Most significantly, he had followed the historicist school and adopted the Pandectist technique, drafing a Code for Private Law for Zürich in 1853–1856 that had been used later in the preparation of the Swiss Civil Code and is still held to be "outstanding."[163] He followed this technique in his 1867 code of modern international law of civilized States. He explains: "I was convinced that international law existed in a relationship of reciprocal influence with the growing civilization and that every large human progress meant also progress for international law."[164] Bluntschli interpreted his international code-writing in the same light as his earlier assignment to write a civil code for Zürich: it was not for Parliaments or sovereigns to enact written laws but for the publicists to write down the living law of the people's *Bewusstsein*. This was also to be the vocation of the *Institut de droit international*.

A social conception of law

The "conscience juridique du monde civilisé" in Article 1 of the Institute's 1873 Statute refers to a historico-philosophical concept of law and highlights legal scholarship's role in expressing it. The double meaning of *conscience* is exploited to merge a romantic sensibility with Enlightenment rationalism.[165] On the one hand, as "conscience," it looks beyond the vicissitudes of diplomacy towards the moral sentiments of European societies, a normative–psychological dictum about the deepest feelings about right and wrong in (civilized) contemporaries. On the other hand, as "consciousness," it separates the true from the false, knowledge from superstition, employing a multilayered image of the human psyche at the top of which "consciousness" merges individual (subjective) understanding with that which is (objectively) true for everybody.

To articulate and to represent this *conscience* became the task of the international law profession. The second paragraph of Article 1 of the Institute's Statute links this general purpose to the functions of the Institute: "De formuler les principes généraux de la science, ainsi que les

---

[163] Wieacker, *A History of Private Law*, p. 388. Marcel Senn observes that Bluntschli was "einer der bedeutendsten Staatsrechtstheoretiker deutscher Sprache des 19. Jahrhunderts," "Rassistische und antisemitische Elemente im Rechtsdenken von Johann Caspar Bluntschli" (1993), 110 *Z. der Savigny-Stiftung für Rechtsgeschichte*, p. 376.
[164] Bluntschli, *Denkwürdiges*, III, p. 170.
[165] For the combination of rationalist and romantic elements in the historical school, cf. Wieacker, *A History of Private Law*, pp. 286–299.

règles qui en dérivent, et d'en répendre la connaissance." Again, our modern sensibility may find this way of speaking of international law as "science" a rather contrived way to characterize an essentially technical profession. But for Rolin, Westlake, and Bluntschli, the "scientification" of law seemed important precisely to enable the articulation of the organic relationship between the popular conscience and the law.

The image of nineteenth-century international law today is focused on a deviation, and thus fails to grasp the project of the men of 1873. The deviation consists of what is usually called the Austinian challenge[166] – though similar ideas had surfaced in German *Staatslehre* and French jurisprudence as well. This challenge has to do with the command theory of law, espoused by John Austin in the *Province of Jurisprudence Determined* (1832) but receiving wider appreciation only after the posthumous publication of his *Lectures on Jurisprudence* in 1863.[167] By reference to *a priori* definition Austin disqualified international law as "law" in the absence of a common sovereign whose commands would be habitually obeyed by members of the international society. But the men of 1873 did not share a command theory of law. They represented a historical and organic jurisprudence that linked law to popular consciousness as represented by the legal profession.

Richard Wildman's 1849 treatise, for instance, made no mention of Austin, derived international law from custom and excluded sovereign compacts from general law altogether: they created obligations, not law, and were of doubtful significance as evidence of a general consent of nations.[168] But even after Austin's fame had grown, his reasoning was opposed by English historical jurisprudence. Maitland saw little value in it and Maine held it "very interesting and quite innocuous."[169] For Maine – as for the men of 1873 – international law did not emerge from legislation by sovereigns. Its essence did not lie in the presence of effective sanctions but in the "law-abiding sentiment" that lay behind it, that

---

[166] Cf. also Martti Koskenniemi, *From Apology to Utopia. The Structure of International Legal Argument* (Helsinki, Lakimiesliiton kustannus, 1989), pp. 101–102.

[167] For instance, the most recent edition of Oppenheim mentions Austin and "his followers" as the only reference to nineteenth-century jurisprudence in connection with a discussion of international law's legal force. Robert Jennings and Arthur Watts, *Oppenheim's International Law* (1 vol, parts 1–4, 9th edn., Harlow, Longman, 1992), p. 9. In his illuminating study of nineteenth-century international law, Anghie, too, sees Austin's theory as central to nineteenth-century international law. Cf. Antony Anghie, "Finding the Peripheries: Sovereignty and Colonialism in Nineteenth-Century International Law" (1999), 40 *Harvard International Law Journal*, pp. 13 *et seq.*

[168] Richard Wildman, *Institutes of International Law* (2 vols., London, Browning, 1849), *I: International Rights in Time of Peace*, pp. 1–14.

[169] Maine, *International Law*, p. 49. Cf. also Collini, *Public Moralists*, p. 303.

"The legal conscience of the civilized world"

is to say, in the civilized conscience-consciousness of which the body of liberal jurists was a collective representative.[170]

True enough, Rolin, Bluntschli, and Westlake each recognized that international law was a special kind of law with special problems relating to the absence of a common sovereign, legislative or executive power.[171] If law was not a creation of sovereign will, but an organic growth of popular *conscience*, then this was merely an incidental problem which, however important in diplomatic practice, had no conceptual repercussions whatsoever on treating international law as proper "law."[172] Westlake was express about this. Not a sovereign but a society was the precondition of law: "When we assert that there is such a thing as international law, we assert that there is a society of states: when we recognize that there is a society of states, we recognize that there is international law."[173] This society was the Europe that – as Westlake's 1894 book canvassed it – was born with classical Greece and Rome, was consolidated at Westphalia, and now extended to native territories, colonial government, and war. It consisted of European and American States plus a few Christian nations elsewhere, such as "the Hawaiian Islands, Liberia and the Orange Free State."[174] This was not just some privileged political conglomerate but, in the words of Francis Lieber "one family of advanced nations"[175] whose "habits, occupations and ideas . . . [f]amily life and social life"[176] – were the basis of international law:

> The society of states, having European civilization, or the international society, is the most comprehensive form of society among men . . . The consent of the international society to the rules prevailing in it is the consent of the men who are the ultimate members of that society.

Bluntschli's law was neither fixed on sovereign will nor drawn from Roman law or moral theory but emerged spontaneously through the lives of (European) peoples. Because spontaneous, this was a fragile law

---

[170] Maine, *International Law*, p. 51. Maine even held "that the Law of Nations is essentially a moral and, to some extent, a religious system," p. 47.
[171] Cf. Bluntschli, *Das moderne Völkerrecht*, pp. 2–12.
[172] Wheaton had already tackled the issue. Law of nations did not have "laws" – for laws emanate from a political superior. If laws are a necessary element of law, then international law is law only in a metaphorical sense. But this had no effect on the tangible reality of sovereigns everywhere aligning their behavior with certain rules of conduct to which they had expressly or tacitly agreed. Cf. Henry Wheaton, *Histoire de progrès du droit des gens en Europe depuis la paix de Westphalie jusqu'à nos jours* (2 vols., 3rd edn., Leipzig, Brockhaus, 1853), II, p. 370.
[173] John Westlake, *Chapters in the Principles of International Law* (Cambridge University Press, 1894), p. 3.   [174] Westlake, *Chapters*, p. 81.
[175] Lieber, *On Civil Liberty*, p. vii.   [176] Westlake, *Chapters*, p. 101.

that did sometimes – as in war – break down. In such cases, it became the jurist's task to articulate it anew: in its coming into being, its past as well as its future. If, says Bluntschli, scholars such as Wheaton and Phillimore, Kent and Wildman, Heffter and Oppenheim agreed on a proposition of law, then it was part of the law even if there existed no treaty or clear practice on the matter.[177] Bluntschli, Rolin, and Westlake each worried that international law's special nature had not been properly understood. But none of them held that for it to qualify as law it had to parade in the form of sovereign commands: "It is not up to the arbitrary will of the State to follow or reject international law."[178]

The organic position was a liberal position, not too far removed from Rousseau's views about national self-determination and radically opposed to the conservative-monarchist tradition of early nineteenth-century public law.[179] As we have seen, already von Mohl, Bluntschli's predecessor in Heidelberg, had in 1860 constructed public law on the basis of a theory of representative government, advocating a three-level analysis of international law as relations between States, communities (or civil societies, *Gesellschaften*), and individuals. This had led him to focus on extradition law which emphasized the juxtaposition of statehood and individual rights and allowed a terrain for a liberal politics in favor of non-extradition for political offences.[180] Bluntschli simply followed up by arguing that sovereignty was always limited by the obligation to guarantee the human rights of citizens and non-citizens alike.[181] However weak and undeveloped the international guarantees for such rights were, he wrote, it had become a fact of cosmopolitan modernity that the German Everyman could now travel as secure in Paris, New York, and Calcutta as he lived in Berlin. In the civilized world, a Kantian *Weltbürgerrecht* had become a partial reality.[182] The definition of legal subjecthood in organic terms also allowed a flexible means of conceiving international law as having a sphere of application wider than that of European States.[183] Although nomadic tribes, for instance, did not qualify as formal States, if they were able to formulate a common public

---

[177] Bluntschli, *Das moderne Völkerrecht*, p. 65.
[178] "Es hängt nicht von der Willkür eines Staates ab, das Völkerrecht zu achten oder zu verwerfen," Bluntschli, *Das moderne Völkerrecht*, p. 58. On Rolin's anti-voluntarism, cf. Nys, "Notice sur Rolin-Jaequemyns," p. 67.
[179] Cf. von Oertzen, *Die soziale Funktion*, pp. 114–117.
[180] Von Mohl, *Staatsrecht*, pp. 637–764.
[181] Bluntschli, *Das moderne Völkerrecht*, p. 20.
[182] Bluntschli, *Das moderne Völkerrecht*, pp. 26–27.
[183] "Das Völkerrecht ist nicht auf die europäische Völkerfamilie beschränkt. Das Gebiet seiner Herrschaft ist die Ganze Erdoberfläche, so weit auf ihr sich Menschen berühren." Bluntschli, *Das moderne Völkerrecht*, p. 60.

"The legal conscience of the civilized world"

will, they should nevertheless be treated analogously and conclude treaties with binding force towards European parties.[184]

In summary, the founding conception of late nineteenth-century international law was not sovereignty but a collective (European) *conscience* – understood always as ambivalently either consciousness or conscience, that is, in alternatively rationalistic or ethical ways. This view emerged less as a reaction to Austin than an independent stream of historical jurisprudence, linked with liberal–humanitarian ideals and theories of the natural evolution of European societies. Even in the absence of a common sovereign, Europe was a political society and international law an inextricable part of its organization.[185] This was the metaphoric sense of Westphalia that: "group[ed] for the first time together the States of Central Europe after the fashion of a family, the members of which were acknowledged to be independent, and, although of unequal power, were recognized as possessing an equality of Right."[186] In the last years of the century, international lawyers routinely responded to the Austinian criticism by noting that law does not only come down by sovereign enactment but equally from the spontaneous functioning of society. Customary law had always emerged in that way; and much of European law was customary in the sense of having spontaneously come to regulate inter-European relations. If law was the effect of a common consciousness, and the existence of a common European consciousness seemed an undeniable fact, then international law's reality was firmly grounded in a social and cultural fact.

Method: enlightened inwardness

The men of 1873 thought that to find out the law it did not suffice to record what States had done or said. It was necessary to delve deeper into the spirit and history of the community. But how does the scholar do this? Where does one find international law, asks Rolin, and responds:

> Not in express enactments which do not exist, nor in precedents that may themselves be just or unjust, but in the testimony of his conscience, illuminated and fortified by what the wisest of men have decided in analogous cases. Thus the principles posed by publicists in external law find their juridical and legislative authority in their presumed conformity with human conscience.[187]

---

[184] Bluntschli, *Das moderne Völkerrecht*, p. 67.
[185] I am indebted for this argument to Antony Anghie.
[186] Travers Twiss, *The Law of Nations Considered as Independent Communities* (2nd edn., 2 vols., Oxford, Clarendon, 1884), I, p. xvii.
[187] Rolin-Jaequemyns, "De l'étude de la législation comparée et de droit international," p. 226.

The law could be found only by looking inwards, into one's own normative intuitions whose authority lay in their being those of a person educated in the canon of Western civilization. This was an anti-formalist view: "International law increases in substance and binding force in relation to the degree that the common conscience of humanity increases in clarity and energy."[188] Bluntschli's 1867 code, for instance, contained no separate treatment of formal legal sources at all. Treaties appear only in paragraph 402 while the law in the preceding 401 paragraphs emanated from a formless *Anerkennung* or a consensus, extracted and justifiable partly through history – that is to say custom – and partly through philosophy – that is, the dictates of reason and ethics, including "Grundsätzen des natürlichen Menschenrechts." They were not reducible to formal expressions of State will.[189]

Though Westlake did present a theory of legal sources, it looked behind formal acts of State diplomacy. His sources were custom, reason and Roman law[190] – a nice recapitulation of late historical jurisprudence: law was a function of history and reason – while Roman law could be presumed to reflect both. Treaties created no law but only obligations between the parties. They were equivalent to private law contracts. Nor was custom mere habit but "that line of conduct which the society has consented to regard as obligatory."[191] What one needed to show when showing custom was "that the general consensus of opinion within the limits of European civilisation is in favor of the rule." And there was the liberal assumption: "The consent of the international society . . . is the consent of the men who are the ultimate members of that society."[192] In practice, such consent could be found in the writings of jurists "especially when the writer's reputation proves that he represents many persons besides himself."[193] The idea of the representativity of the writer may seem odd – but only if one fails to take seriously the theory of the writer as an "organ" of a juridical *conscience*.

By the 1890s a new generation of textbooks expressed the ethos of the men of 1873 in a more or less systematic form, bringing to light its strengths and weaknesses. Central to these books was the conception of international law as part of European history and *conscience*. Alphonse Rivier, for instance, who took over as Secretary-General of the Institute

---

[188] Bluntschli, *Das moderne Völkerrecht*, p. 59.
[189] Bluntschli, *Das moderne Völkerrecht*, pp. 61–64.
[190] John Westlake, *International Law* (2 vols., 2nd edn., Cambridge University Press, 1910), I, p. 14.   [191] Westlake, *International Law*, I, p. 14.
[192] Westlake, *International Law*, I, p. 16.   [193] Westlake, *International Law*, I, p. 17.

"The legal conscience of the civilized world"

while Rolin was in government during 1878–1885, started his 1889 textbook with the dictum that international law was developed among States that shared a "gemeinsames Rechtsbewusstsein." The extent of that consciousness marked the sphere of international law's validity; it extended to the family of nations that shared the Christian faith, together with the Ottoman Empire that had been expressly admitted to the family in 1856. The family was not closed but open: through express recognition other nations could and would be admitted to it.[194] It was this family's legal consciousness that was international law's "source of sources": the validity of treaties and custom was constantly checked by what common consciousness held to confirm with "*necessitas und ratio.*"[195]

Such a flexible concept of law allowed lawyers to read their humanitarian sentiments as parts of the law proper while still complying with the dictates of an emerging evolutionary sociology. The combination of the two constituted a restatement of their political project: the law that was derived from European liberal consciousness–conscience was an agnostic law, freed, as Bluntschli wrote, from religious imprisonment and oriented towards expansion: "its objective is a human world order."[196] In this cosmopolitan order no essential distinction existed between matters internal and international; a humanitarian order that focused on communities and individuals alike.

In their legal theory, the men of 1873 turned inwards to look for a law that they believed existed in their moral conscience, cultivated by a humanitarian sensibility whose outward expression was their alignment with the political liberalism of the day. The theory of the text-writer as an organ of popular conscience–consciousness legitimized the projection of that morality as an expression of what was best in the cultural heritage of nineteenth-century Europe. The microcosm of individual sensibilities and the macrocosm of public law were experienced as aspects of one and the same reality. Emphasis was less on the construction of rational systems – this was an old-fashioned idea – than on the development and cultivation of appropriate personal attitudes – on becoming "civilized," in a word. It is not by chance that most of the

---

[194] Whether and to what extent its precepts already applied outside its formal sphere of validity was a problem that could be solved neither in a fully egoistic way nor through some "pseudo-philanthropic Utopia." Alphonse Rivier, *Lehrbuch des Völkerrechts* (Stuttgart, Enke, 1889), pp. 3–5.   [195] Rivier, *Lehrbuch*, pp. 9–11.
[196] "sein Ziel ist die menschliche Weltordnung," Bluntschli, *Das moderne Völkerrecht*, pp. 18–19, 59.

founders of the *Institut* were active Protestants whose activism also constituted a demonstration – to oneself at least as much as to others – that the internal qualities needed for salvation were indeed present.

Towards a culture of human rights: Fiore

One book that captured such a vision admirably was that by Pasquale Fiore (1837–1914), *Le droit international codifié et sa sanction juridique*, a translation of the Italian original that came out in 1890. Fiore had been Professor of Philosophy in Cremona and later of International Law in Pisa and Naples. The book – which Fiore dedicated to his colleagues at the *Institut* – was written in the form of a codification that moved freely between a scientific restatement and a proposal *de lege ferenda*. The fluidity with which it transgressed those categories illustrates the force of the author's humanitarian–liberal intuitions as well as his conviction that they expressed a collective European *conscience* that arose from the highest form of civilization ever known.

The ultimate source of international law, Fiore wrote, was the juridical conscience of European peoples ("convictions juridiques populaires"). Though the interests of political elites and peoples often conflicted, public opinion increasingly compelled governments to take account of the latter.[197] In due course, general suffrage and capitalism would do the work of internationalism:

> It is above all desirable that the industrial bourgoisie, agriculturalists and the other social classes whose activity and international division of labor are the sources of prosperity have a greater influence in the administration of the republic. These classes will then compel the nation's representatives to put the interests of humanity above the sectional and momentary interests that result from the narrow policies of governments.[198]

Again, Fiore's public opinion was not an irrational popular passion. It was enlightened by reason and "follow[ed] the movement of incessant progress and history."[199] Its ambivalent connection to his theory of

---

[197] Pasquale Fiore, *Le droit international codifié et sa sanction juridique* (Paris, Pedone, 1890), p. 9.

[198] "Il est avant tout désirable que la bourgeoisie industrielle, les agriculteurs et les autres classes sociales dont la commerce et la division internationale du travail font la prospérité, aient une action et une influence plus considérables dans l'administration de la République. Ces classes forceront alors les représentants de la nation à mettre les intérêts de l'humanité au-dessus de ces intérêts factices et trompeurs, résultats de la politique étroite des gouvernements," Fiore, *Le droit international codifié*, p. 10.

[199] Fiore, *Le droit international codifié*, p. 7.

historical development reconciled the liberal ethos with the need to look at something more tangible than mere "opinion" – namely the hard facts of history. This enabled Fiore to contrast the law of 1815 with his own time: dynastic legitimacy had been overcome by the idea that all peoples are autonomous and individuals enjoy human rights. Today, he wrote, "certain juridical notions" had crystallized in the conscience of civilized peoples.[200] Three of them were particularly sigificant.

First, individual freedom and human rights had become the fundamental objects of protection by international law. Individuals were entitled to choose their nationality and citizenship freely, having duties to States only in exchange for benefits received.[201] Six of such rights ("autrement dit les *Droits de l'homme*") bound even the national legislator:[202] personal freedom and inviolability, the right of civil liberty and nationality, the rights of emigration, commerce, property, and the freedom of conscience.[203] All individuals enjoyed such rights (with certain restriction as to married women)[204] irrespective of race, nationality, or degree of civilization.[205] They were "under the collective juridical guarantee by all civilized States" so that their violation allowed collective intervention.[206]

Second, law was not an effect of sovereign decision, but a spontaneous outgrowth of society. Fiore's methodological *a priori* was the historical emergence of his own society, the tangible base for "civilized consciousness." Through commerce and increasing contacts with other nations it was expanding so that it was no longer possible to speak of "European international law." The human society was one: "The unity of the human species conduces to the recognition that the empire of legal rules that are applicable to all forms of human activity in the *Magna civitas*, must be universal."[207] But how to give expression to the undeniable and constant experience of cultural difference while preserving the idea of one single law? This was possible by adopting a theory of stages

---

[200] Fiore, *Le droit international codifié*, p. 16.
[201] Fiore, *Le droit international codifié*, p. 92 (a State as "libre agglomération d'individus réunis en communauté en vertu d'un consentement exprès ou tacite").
[202] Fiore, *Le droit international codifié*, p. 15. Fiore's subjects of international law are States, individuals, and churches, pp. 87–90.
[203] Fiore, *Le droit international codifié*, pp. 164–177.
[204] Although the imposition of a nationality violated human rights, Fiore accepted that "social necessities and the need to maintain the unity of the family" required that the wife acquire the husband's nationality, Fiore, *Le droit international codifié*, p. 167.
[205] In particular, civilized nations have the obligation to eradicate (black) slavery and all forms of activity contributing to it, Fiore, *Le droit international codifié*, p. 165.
[206] Fiore, *Le droit international codifié*, p. 177.   [207] Fiore, *Le droit international codifié*, p. 74.

of civilization which in Fiore – as in most other international lawyers – was only implicit, playing upon the prejudices of the European bourgeoisie. Only fully civilized States could be members of the *Magna civitas*, the juridical community. For "[t]his community is already a product of civilization. To the extent that it expands to savage countries, it gives rise to needs and interests that unite the civilized nations with barbaric or other peoples less advanced in the path of progress."[208] Full membership in the legal community required the possession of "un certain niveau de culture." This level was first attained in Europe but through commerce and other contacts it was slowly spreading.[209] Fiore made the commonplace distinction between the somewhat civilized cultures of Asia (such as Turkey and the "great Oriental empires") and the less civilized ("peut-être barbares") of Asia and Africa that did not possess a stable political organization that would make the development of a juridical culture possible.[210]

Third, Fiore emphasized the policy oriented tasks of international jurisprudence. The combination of the rationalist and historical arguments enabled him to interpret his own political intuitions as expressive of popular convictions as well as the determined consequences of historical progress. By focusing more closely on the juridical convictions of different ages and peoples, legal science would "foresee and prepare the progressive amelioration of the laws."[211] From a study of actually existing societies legal science could proceed to formulate concrete proposals "without ever losing sight of the requirements of real life as it manifests itself in the different epochs of humanity's history. It must not be occupied by humanity's hypothetical development but its real and tangible development."[212] This meant, for instance, a rejection of the claims of the papacy and the recognition of the right of peoples to freely govern themselves.[213] Fiore's historiography would not simply record past facts. It would be an "experimental philosophy" through which historical facts would be linked to causes and consequences that enabled drafting utilitarian rules "in order to attain the best and avoid the worst," to decide

---

[208] Fiore, *Le droit international codifié*, pp. 74, 82. New States may enter the community only by recognition by existing ones, pp. 93–94.
[209] Fiore, *Le droit international codifié*, pp. 75, 81–82.
[210] Where nomadic communities may be treated by reference to international law (if they have a political organization and a representative chief), barbarians have a claim only to "humanity" and the protection of human rights, Fiore, *Le droit international codifié*, pp. 92–93. [211] Fiore, *Le droit international codifié*, p. 85.
[212] Fiore, *Le droit international codifié*, p. 48.
[213] Fiore, *Le droit international codifié*, pp. 50–51.

"The legal conscience of the civilized world"

which facts or which behavior, which treaty or declaration could be elevated "à la hauteur de droit."[214]

In Fiore's 1890s treatise, many aspects of the professional ethic of a new international law were brought together: it responded to the needs of European economic and imperial expansion while remaining sensitive to the problems that accompanied it. It embraced a commercial spirit and had no doubt about the peaceful and enlightened quality of (European) public opinion. As legal theory, it was neither naturalist nor positivist but sought a pragmatic reconciliation of history with reason: development was "progress," associated with the spread of liberal political institutions, protection of individual rights, freedom of trade, interdependence and the civilizing mission.

The weakness of a book such as Fiore's was that it failed to confront the disturbing evidence from Europe and elsewhere that social or economic development was not always necessarily felt as "progress"; that European peoples were not always peaceful, enlightened, or in agreement with the cosmopolitan sentiments of elite lawyers; that non-European peoples had often little reason for gratefulness over the fruit of "civilization"; and that even if there had been agreement on the direction of reform of European societies (which there was not) this might not automatically strengthen the international system. Its most utopian aspect was its implicit federalism, the view of (European) States becoming increasingly bound to act through conferences, treaties and dispute-settlement procedures.[215]

Advancing the liberal project

The legal theory and the *esprit d'internationalité*[216] of the men of 1873 put the jurist in the position of the Roman *praetor* in whom the functions of restatement and reform were inextricably intertwined. For Asser, for instance, the tasks of the *jurisconsulte* in the codification of private international law followed "from the necessity to subordinate interest to justice – in preparation of general rules for the acceptance of governments to be used in their external relations."[217] The jurists should not remain in the scholar's chamber but were to contribute to social

---

[214] Fiore, *Le droit international codifié*, pp. 48, 49–50, 51.
[215] Cf. Fiore, *Le droit international codifié*, pp. 84–85, 275–283. Cf. also J. C. Bluntschli, *Gesammelte kleine Schriften* (2 vols., Nördlingen, Beck, 1879), II, pp. 279–312.
[216] T. M. C. Asser, "Droit international privé et droit uniforme" (1880), XII *RDI*, p. 5.
[217] Asser, "Droit international privé," p. 6.

progress. As we have seen, Rolin had in his manifesto directly associated the project of comparative and international law with progressive legal reform.[218] And Bluntschli, who had been a leading member of Zürich's liberal party until 1848, continued to regard his political activities in Munich and Heidelberg as no less important than his scientific work. From his chair in public law and politics he became a vigorous advocate of German unification under Prussia – through war if necessary – which he interpreted as a struggle between liberal modernity against the autocratic Medievalism of the Habsburgs.[219] Yet the atmosphere of the 1870s demonstrated that one could not count on automatic victory. Economic stagnation and the increasingly visible social problems associated with *laissez-faire* capitalism were hardening nationalist and class antagonisms as well as racism all over Europe.

The great economic slump had started in Europe in the very year the *Institut* was established. Apart from Britain, all European countries returned to protective tariffs. The negative effects of industrialization had become visible: pauperization of large populations was a reality around many industrial centers – yet agriculture was the hardest hit by the depression. As Bluntschli noted, in parts of civilized Europe the condition of workers and peasants was worse than that of the slaves of antiquity.[220] While the tone of the economic debate changed from optimism to pessimism, socialists could interpret the turn to monopoly capitalism as the system's last gasp before final collapse.[221]

International lawyers reacted to this situation with ambivalence. On the one hand, they continued to advocate free trade and to argue against protectionism. They were active supporters of the "open door" policy and proposed regimes of freedom of navigation and free trade in the colonies.[222] They were enthusiastic about new forms of postal, telegraphic, and monetary co-operation and other aspects of what they saw as an increasingly transnational economy. By temperament and position, they

---

[218] Rolin-Jaequemyns, "De l'étude de la législation comparée et de droit international," pp. 1–17.
[219] Cf. especially Bluntschli's position on the Austro-Prussian war in *Denkwürdiges*, III, pp. 137–168. [220] "Eigenthum," in *Gesammelte kleine Schriften*, I, p. 221.
[221] Although some historians have doubted the reality of the depression of 1873–1895, there was no doubt that contemporaries saw it as "an unprecedented disturbance and depression of trade." Eric Hobsbawm, *The Age of Empire 1875–1914* (London, Abacus, 1989), pp. 34–55.
[222] Cf. Emile de Laveleye, "La neutralité du Congo" (1883), XV *RDI*, p. 254; Travers Twiss, "La libre navigation du Congo (1883)," XV *RDI*, pp. 437, 547.

"The legal conscience of the civilized world"

were supporters of private property.[223] Lieber declared that "[o]ne of the staunchest principles of civil liberty is the firmest protection of individual property" and Bluntschli saw the right of inheritance as an essential part of "Aryan" law without which civilization would slide into barbarism.[224] On the other hand, even as liberals, they also advocated increasing and even massive governmental involvement through legislation in correcting the social problems brought about by industrialization – however much they justified such measures by the need to secure private property and to avoid the repetition of 1848.[225] The State's increasing role in social reform and the seemingly inevitable advance towards centralization all over Europe were unmistakable signs that the days of Victorian voluntarism were gone forever.[226]

Westlake, too, a late follower of the Benthamites, a great believer in progress and reason, engaged in considerable activity outside the purely legal realm. Like many other radical–liberals he thought education as central for social progress. In 1854, at the age of twenty-six, he became one of the founders of the Working Men's College "where Christian socialists mingled with the later utilitarians."[227] This was an eccentric move by a young barrister. As A. V. Dicey puts it, it was a company to be joined at the risk of being deemed by older colleagues as "pretty much what we now call a crank."[228] Westlake was a supporter of the rights of minorities and especially of the enfranchisement of women, and an activist in the temperance cause. Aside from acting as Secretary to the British Association for the Promotion of Social Science, Westlake was President of its Jurisprudence (legal reform) Department and even a liberal–radical Member of Parliament in 1885–1887.[229]

---

[223] This was visible, for instance, in Bluntschli's extensive arguments to keep private property away from the right of capture and destruction in maritime war. Cf. Johann Caspar Bluntschli, *Beuterecht im Krieg* (Nördlingen, Beck, 1870). Cf. also the discussion in Roeben, "Bluntschli," pp. 201–219.

[224] Lieber, *On Civil Liberty*, p. 103; Bluntschli, "Arische Völker und arische Rechte," in *Gesammelte kleine Schriften*, I, pp. 77–78.

[225] Cf. Bluntschli, "Eigenthum," in *Gesammelte kleine Schriften*, I, pp. 218–224. Bluntschli discussed at great length the proper limits of State intervention in "Zur Revision der staatlichen Grundbegriffe," in *Gesammelte kleine Schriften*, I, pp. 305–317.

[226] David Newsome, *The Victorian World Picture* (London, Fontana, 1979), p. 231. Cf also Chadwick, *Secularization*, p. 46.

[227] For an account cf. C. P. Lucas, "The Working Men's College," in *Memories of Westlake*, pp. 130–137.

[228] Dicey, "His Book and Character," in *Memories of Westlake*, p. 37. At the College, Westlake taught mathematics.

[229] J. Fischer Williams, "Introduction," in *Memories of Westlake*, pp. 10–11, 13.

Westlake supported proportional representation and the Reform Bill of 1867. He advocated liberty of opinion within the Church, defending his old tutor Colenso, the Bishop of Natal, against the much-publicized efforts to deprive him of his diocese by the Bishop of Capetown owing to a religious disagreement. Despite his many welfare activities, however, he seems to have had "profound distrust" of the extension of the activities of the State and the municipality – a position attributed less to a belief in the benefits of the invisible hand than in the individual's sense of right and wrong.[230] However, though Westlake made it clear that "our sympathy should be on the side of liberty," he stressed that the increasing complexity of modern economy and the resulting interdependence between individuals necessitated "more regulation" in the domestic as well as in the international realm.[231]

One of the eleven founding members of the *Institut* was the Belgian economist and Christian socialist Emile de Laveleye, who not only participated actively in drafting its Statute but was the main author of the Declaration that was intended to serve as the Institute's *profession de foi*.[232] De Laveleye was vice-president of the *Institut* in 1882–1883 and a frequent collaborator in Rolin's *Revue*.[233] Most of his works have to do with political economy, however, and many of them went into several editions and were widely translated.

De Laveleye argued that political democracy did not suffice to maintain social peace. Growing social and economic inequality threatened to destroy the European order as it had once destroyed Greece and Rome. A principal reason for this, he maintained, was unrestricted protection of private property, based on an erroneous rationalism. Historically, forms of collective property had been the rule and private property the exception. As Maine had noted, the original contract was pure fiction. Property regimes were an effect of power. It was now time to recognize the social role of property as a condition of political freedom and economic justice. This could be done, he suggested, by conceiving a part of the land of every municipality as public domain to be divided equitably between families in the way that was customary in certain Swiss Cantons.[234]

---

[230] Fischer Williams, "Introduction," p. 11. [231] Westlake, *Chapters*, p. 50.
[232] Cf. (1877), 1 *Annuaire IDI*, pp. 21–27.
[233] For a short biography, cf. the obituary by Alphonse Rivier in *Institut de droit international, Livre de centenaire 1873–1973: Evolution et perspectives du droit international* (Basle, Karger, 1973), pp. 74–79.
[234] Emile de Laveleye, *De la propriété et de ses formes primitives* (Paris, Baillière, 1874). Bluntschli did not think of property as an effect of legislation but conceived its pro-

"The legal conscience of the civilized world"

As economist, de Laveleye was opposed to the naturalist individualism of Adam Smith and the physiocrats, agreeing with the German *Katheder-socialisten* that national economies were also based on a collective consciousness by reference to which individuals were sometimes ready to sacrifice their private good for that of the fatherland, humanity, or truth.[235] For him, the State was a representative of the national consciousness, "l'organe suprême du droit, l'instrument de justice." It was therefore for the State, and its law, to create the conditions for a just economic system. At the international level, de Laveleye advocated the drafting of a code of international law to be enforced by a general system of international arbitration.[236] This would be the first step towards the increasing integration, through economy, of Europe into a federation of free nations.

Irrespective of their wide-ranging political engagements, however, the members of the *Institut* simultaneously highlighted the scientific neutrality of their common venture. This was already visible in Rolin's attempt to maintain a careful distance from the American initiative that had led to the establishment of the Association for the Reform and Codification of International Law in Brussels only a few weeks after the *Institut* had been set up.[237] Rolin and Mancini both advocated a kind of centrism, staying aloof from "the virtuous utopists that wanted the immediate abolition of war" as well as from those "timid spirits" that regarded the present state of affairs as beyond correction. By not taking a position on diplomatic conflicts – or at least conflicts between European powers – they hoped the Institute would receive enough prestige to be able to

---

tection as one of the State's principal tasks. However, he recognized the dangers in massive inequalities of ownership and agreed that an acceptable way to alleviate them was to provide allotments of common property to poor families: "Sie verdanken dann ihre Kartoffeln und Gemüse vornehmlich der eigenen Arbeit und Sorge, und dieses Gefühl wirkt in moralischer Beziehung ebenso belebend und erfrichend, wie die Arbeit in freien Luft in leiblicher Hinsicht." "Eigenthum," in *Gesammelte kleine Schriften*, I, p. 231.

[235] Emile de Laveleye, *Le socialisme contemporain* (Paris, Baillière, 1881), p. 5.
[236] de Laveleye, *Des causes actuelles*, pp. 161 *et seq.*
[237] Many *Institut* members did participate in the activities of the Association, drawing it closer to governments and channeling its activities to more modest proposals for arbitration, rules of warfare, and the codification of private international law. This disappointed the philanthropists who had originally conceived the Association as a forum for far-reaching legislative change and who now gradually shifted their emphasis away from international law to other forms of cultural or economic cosmopolitanism and work for peace societies. Cf. Hinsley, *Power and the Pursuit of Peace*, pp. 126, 133, 267.

influence the domestic policies of European governments and to contribute to international concord.[238]

To make sure that the *Institut* would not appear to take sides in political controversy, its early work concentrated on a pet theme of Mancini's and Asser's, the drafting of international conventions on private international law – particularly conflict of laws in civil, commercial, and criminal matters. It also dealt with the procedures of international arbitration and sought to codify the Washington Rules that had been written into the Alabama *compromis*. When the *Institut* did take a more activist line – appealing against the use of irregulars and in favor of disseminating humanitarian law in the 1877–1878 Balkan war[239] – it did so in thinly veiled criticism of Turkey. When in 1887 Rolin suggested that the Institute might propose to European governments the conclusion of a convention on the limitation of armaments and military budgets, the majority strongly opposed such a venture into an eminently political domain and no action was taken on it.[240] Nor was there any action to further the schemes for European government that had been proposed in their academic writings by Bluntschli and the Edinburgh scholar James Lorimer. "Politics" was for the *Institut* an affair that concerned European diplomacy, too sensitive or controversial to embark upon. By contrast, if a matter related to colonial affairs – for instance, freedom of navigation in the Congo or the conditions of effective occupation in Africa under the 1885 Act of Berlin – no such procedural obstacle was conceived.

Around this time European nationalism separated from enlightenment rationalism and turned to the right. It became part of the revolt against positivism that characterized the cultural atmosphere of the century's last two decades.[241] At the same time, Napoleon III succeeded in co-opting it for a patriotic cause and in 1861 and 1870–1871 Italy and Germany were united under it. The use of nationalist rhetoric as part of the foreign policy of European powers did nothing to soothe the emotions

---

[238] Rolin-Jaequemyns, "De la nécessité," pp. 478–480, 483, 486–487. The same is also the gist of James Lorimer's speech at the University of Edinburgh on November 4, 1873, as reported in (1874), V *RDI*, pp. 168–172.

[239] Cf. (1878/2), *Annuaire IDI*, pp. 132–137 and (1879–1880/1), 2 *Annuaire IDI*, pp. 13–17. A proposal by Hall to criticize Russian behavior in the war was expressly rejected (1879–1880), 3 *Annuaire IDI*, pp. 38–49.

[240] (1887–1888), 9 *Annuaire IDI*, pp. 344–356.

[241] For the transformation of nationalism from a liberal to a conservative force at this time, cf. E. J. Hobsbawm, *Nations and Nationalism since 1870: Programme, Myth, Reality* (Cambridge University Press, 1990), pp. 101–130.

of the masses. Liberal cosmopolitanism was increasingly limited to the outlook of bourgeois and aristocratic classes.

International lawyers never formally adopted the language of Mancini's "principle of nationalities." However, nationalism was such an important part of the political reality that a legal doctrine in search for a firm cultural basis could hardly ignore it. All the men of 1873 accepted nationhood as a fundamental fact of the international society and were thus called upon to explain how it could be reconciled with their cosmopolitanism. They did this by distinguishing between what Rolin called *l'esprit national* and *le préjuge national*, nationalism in its beneficial and malignant forms and held the former quite compatible with a well-ordered international realm.[242] Baron Franz von Holtzendorff (1829–1889) from Berlin, for example, a frequent commentator in Rolin's *Revue* and a member of the inner circle of the *Institut*, described the dialectic of nationalism and cosmopolitanism as analogous to that between individual autonomy and communal solidarity in domestic society. Its national properties did not exhaust the identity of a State; like an individual it was both independent of and related to the outside world. As currents of air circulated through space irrespectively of political boundaries, so the spirit of humanity animated the lawbooks of different nations.[243]

In such and other metaphors international lawyers integrated their nationalism in a larger, humanist vision of European civilization, sometimes defining nationhood as Fiore had done, in a cosmopolitan way, as an aggregate of, or political compact between, individuals.[244] Westlake, for instance, seemed to have no theory of nationhood at all but thought that the State's duties and rights were "only the duties and rights of the men who compose them."[245] But even continental lawyers who generally did share an organic conception of the nation refrained from drawing the kinds of *legal* conclusions from it that Lasson had done in

---

[242] Rolin-Jaequemyns, "De l'étude de la législation comparée et de droit international," p. 16.
[243] Franz von Holtzendorff, *Handbuch des Völkerrechts. Erster Band. Einleitung in das Völkerrecht* (4 vols., Berlin, Habel [vol.I] and Hamburg, Richer, 1885), I, pp. 38–39. Similarly, cf. James Lorimer, *Institutes of the Law of Nations* (2 vols., Edinburgh and London, Blackwood, 1883), I, pp. 9–11. Holtzendorff also argued that the importance of nationhood lay in the fields of history, culture, and psychology – it was normally sufficient for lawyers to focus on States and to dismiss speculation about principles of nationalism. While nationalism might have a *factual* influence on the law, it remained outside normative analysis. Holtzendorff, *Handbuch*, I, pp. 40–41.
[244] See e.g. Twiss, *The Law of Nations*, I, pp. 1, 7–9.   [245] Westlake, *Chapters*, p. 78.

1871. Bluntschli certainly never imagined that there was any conflict between his nationalism and individual rights: each was defined in terms of the other.[246] The two also came together in his theory of national self-determination: a law denying this, Bluntschli wrote, would simply be an *Unrecht*.[247] For him as for Lieber, the defense of individual liberty went hand in hand with a (moderate) nationalism.[248]

Yet, all international lawyers espoused the cause of their State and felt that its particular nationalism was of the beneficial variant. From his seat in the first chamber of the Baden Parliament Bluntschli became an active supporter of Bismarck's "energetic" unification policy.[249] He even defended the integration of Schleswig-Holstein into the German Confederation in 1863 on the basis of the national idea – and not following the principle of dynastic succession as provided in the London Treaty of 1852. He had no reservation about the legitimacy of war to defend German honor if its just claims were opposed: "We have to invest all, and thus we can accomplish all . . . A nation of Germany's greatness that defends its right and honor will also emerge victorious from a difficult war."[250] Here nationalism prevailed over individual rights; at least in Schleswig-Holstein it sufficed that unification was "necessary," even if the population opposed it.[251] Bluntschli also saw unification (at least under Prussia) as a safeguard against French imperialism. But he was critical both of German pride (*Hochmut*) and French vanity (*Eitelheit*) and ready to admit that French "femininity" counterbalanced German "manliness" to humanity's benefit: "a female property is naturally quite charming and less offensive than . . . manly vice."[252]

Commenting upon the on-going Boer War in 1896, Westlake was careful not to appear to take a "propagandist" pro-British position. The war, he felt, was a war between two ideals, the racial ideal – the Transvaal ideal – and the English ideal of "a fair field for every race and every language, accompanied by a humane treatment of the native races." But it did happen that "the English language and institutions [were] taking possession of a large part of the world, as being those

---

[246] Bluntschli, *Das moderne Völkerrecht*, p. 20.
[247] Bluntschli, "Die Entwickelung des Rechtes und die Recht der Entwickelung," in *Gesammelte kleine Schriften*, I, pp. 44–55.   [248] Cf. Roeben, "Bluntschli," p. 184.
[249] Bluntschli, "Die nationale Statenbildung und die moderne Deutsche Stat," in *Gesammelte kleine Schriften*, I, pp. 99–113.   [250] Bluntschli, *Denkwürdiges*, III, p. 78.
[251] "A part should not obstruct the whole," Bluntschli, *Das moderne Völkerrecht*, pp. 174–175 (with reference to Schleswig-Holstein).
[252] "[J]ene weibliche Eigenschaft ist doch liebenswürdig und weniger verletzend als . . . männliche Fehler." Bluntschli, *Das moderne Völkerrecht*, pp. viii–ix.

"The legal conscience of the civilized world"

which most successfully compete in that fair field; but although that may be the result it is not the object of the English ideal."[253] Westlake's admiration of the "English ideal," indissociable from his admiration of liberalism, turned in this way into a nationalism that provided no understanding for President Kruger's position in the war. Had the English *Uitlanders* been given a right to vote, Transvaal would have ceased being independent. From Westlake's perspective, however, such independence had no real weight. He had no trouble canvassing the eventual British annexation of Transvaal and the Orange Free State.[254]

The nationalism of the founders of the Institute must be seen in the context of their Protestant politics. The contrary to nationalism was universal monarchy – something they associated with Papist (or possibly French) ambition and against everything they thought valuable. Hence they preached freedom of thought and religion as central parts of their politics.[255] If the Pope had refused to reconcile himself with liberalism in the infamous encyclical *Syllabus of Errors* (1864) – which Bluntschli called a "manifesto of war by ecclesiastic Absolutism over the modern world and its culture" – this only strengthened their conviction that the Westphalian peace was a continuously valuable core of Europe's political and legal system.[256] As minister of interior in Belgium in 1878–1884, Rolin struggled against Catholics (Jesuits in particular) during the "school wars" – the establishment of non-confessional primary and secondary schools – and achieved the rupture of diplomatic relations with the Vatican.[257] Bluntschli and von Holtzendorff had both been involved in the establishment of the *Protestanten-Verein* in Germany in 1863 and sided squarely with Bismarck in the *Kulturkampf*. For them, Protestantism, liberalism and nationalism formed an inextricable whole.[258] This did not necessarily mean that international law was inapplicable beyond the Protestant or even the Christian realm: in contrast to all other religions,

---

[253] John Westlake, "The Transvaal War" (1899), in *The Collected Papers of John Westlake on Public International Law* (L.Oppenheim ed., Cambridge University Press, 1914), p. 422. [254] Westlake, "The Transvaal War," pp. 457–459.

[255] Cf. Bluntschli, "Geschichte des Rechtes der religiösen Bekenntnisfreihet," in *Gesammelte kleine Schriften*, I, pp. 100–133. Cf. also Roeben, "Bluntschli," pp. 184–189.

[256] Cf. Bluntschli, "Das römische Papstthum und das Völkerrecht," in *Gesammelte kleine Schriften*, II, p. 243. Bluntschli denied that the relations between States and the Pope could come under international law – although certain analogies – conclusion of concordats and the right of legation – did exist, pp. 248–255. Lorimer agreed. For him, "Roman Catholicism is moribund," *Institutes*, I, p. 117.

[257] Cf. Georges-Henri Dumont, *Léopold II* (Paris, Fayard, 1990), pp. 198–201.

[258] Cf. also generally James J. Sheehan, *German Liberalism in the 19th Century* (Chicago University Press, 1978), pp. 123–180.

Lorimer wrote, Christianity preached universality and full reciprocity between human communities. But it did mean that communities governed by "intolerant religious creeds" (practically the whole non-Christian world) could not enter the community as full-fledged members.[259]

The need to balance between universalism and nationalism required delicate assessments about what kinds of reform to propose. There could be no doubt about Mancini's nationalist credentials. His nationalism was based on a cosmopolitan liberalism that looked and, increasingly after 1861, worked towards European unification. In 1867 Mancini had Italy propose a European convention on conflicts of laws. As this did not succeed (owing to Franco-German hostility) he reformulated his proposal in 1874 in a famous speech at the *Institut* in which he reiterated the old distinction between the rational law that was applicable everywhere and cultural law whose immediate unification – for instance, in the form of a uniform European civil code – was not desirable. The differences between European peoples were still too important. By contrast, a code on the conflict of laws would be a suitable compromise. It would not encroach on national laws – on the contrary, it would make certain that national laws were to be applied as a matter of duty, not merely of comity, irrespectively of which jurisdiction it was that decided the case. By defining the relevant national link such a code would give effect to the national character of the dispute wherever it was to be decided.[260]

A few years later, Asser succeeded in mobilizing the Netherlands in a massive effort for the development of rules of private international law and the unification of law.[261] His approach was entirely pragmatic. He readily admitted that legal unification was not always beneficial but sometimes required compromises on the part of national legislatures that might violate the national sentiment.[262] Care was to be taken so as not to direct international reform against the autonomy of States or the powers of legislative organs. Unification was to commence in the field of conflicts of laws where reform seemed most urgent and least threatening to national authorities.[263]

Such a reconciliation of nationalism with a (European) political order

---

[259] Lorimer, *Institutes*, I, pp. 109–125.   [260] Mancini, "De l'utilité," pp. 221–239.
[261] He shared the Prize in 1911 with the Austrian pacifist August Fried. On the setting up of the Hague Conference on Private International Law in 1894 cf. the report by Asser in (1894–1895), 13 *Annuaire IDI*, pp. 369–374.
[262] T. M. C. Asser, "Droit international privé et droit uniforme," (1880), XII *RDI*, p. 12.
[263] Asser, "Droit international privé," pp. 14, 17.

"The legal conscience of the civilized world" was programmatically argued in Francis Lieber's short essay of 1868 on nationalism and internationalism. The two ideas were not only compatible but interlinked: "The multiplicity of civilized nations, their distinct independence (without which there would be enslaving Universal Monarchy), and their increasing resemblance and agreement are some of the general safeguards of our civilization."[264] There was, on the one hand, "the manly idea of self-government applied to a number of independent nations" and, on the other hand, "the all-pervading law of interdependence." Nationalism and internationalism were brought together by the concept of a community of independent, yet increasingly interdependent civilized nations: "The civilized nations have come to constitute a community, and are daily forming more and more a commonwealth of nations, under the restraint and protection of the law of nations."[265] Towards the external world, Europe was a historical, political, and cultural unity. Internally, its unity consisted in organization into separate, secular States. Projects for European unification drafted by *Institut* members sought to respect this duality: to give expression to what was common to European States without encroaching on their political independence.[266]

Limits of liberalism

In addition to seeking to defend their liberal world-view against increasing economic problems and nationalist agitation the men of 1873 waged a defensive war against the socialists and communists on the left. When the German Emperor convened an international conference in Berlin in 1890 on the protection of workers, Rolin attacked the initiative as a form of international socialism that encroached on the freedom of labor. The good that would result from State intervention in matters of this nature were far outweighed by the disadvantages of increased bureaucracy. This was not to deny the need for better worker protection or social welfare schemes, he wrote, but to insist that how these should be carried out was best left to national legislators.[267] Alphonse Rivier, Rolin's friend from Brussels, wrote that the great dangers of the time were racial hatred

---

[264] Francis Lieber, *Fragments of Political Science on Nationalism and Inter-nationalism* (New York, Scribner, 1868), pp. 20–21.   [265] Lieber, *Fragments of Political Science*, p. 22.
[266] Cf also Bluntschli's proposal for a European Community in *Gesammelte kleine Schriften*, II, p. 279. Likewise, von Holtzendorff, *Handbuch*, I, pp. 38–41.
[267] Gustave Rolin-Jaequemyns, "La conférence de Berlin sur la législation du travail, et le socialisme dans le droit international" (1889), XXII *RDI*, pp. 14–27.

and "certain continental aberrations of Parliamentarism . . . as well as the exaggeration of general franchise that had in certain States supported the raw and unthinking popular opinions through the misuse of freedom by an unthinking and often unpatriotic and speculating press."[268] Lorimer held "communism and nihilism" to be simply prohibited by international law.[269] In that matter, the language of the men of 1873 sometimes took a tone of excitement that appears symptomatic of the repressive impulses their otherwise balanced centrism must have entailed. One controversial item concerned the treatment of foreign political exiles.[270] In 1859, Lieber – himself a refugee from Europe – was able to congratulate the British House of Commons for rejecting a bill that would have made it an offence to foment conspiracy against foreign princes in England and for freeing of Orsini, suspected of a plot against the life of Napoleon III – decisions that were "hailed with joy by every man on the European continent, who wishes well to liberty."[271] Indeed, not only Orsini but Mazzini, Kossuth, Garibaldi, and Herzen together with numerous other refugees of 1848 had all at one point been able to demonstrate publicly in London while enjoying asylum in England much to the dismay of their governments.[272]

Twenty years later, Fedor (Friedrich) Martens (1845–1909), the famous Baltic–Russian professor and diplomat, argued at the *Institut*, in a somewhat circular way, that times had changed. While the number of "real" political refugees had diminished, the number of political "criminals" had increased – members of the Commune, nihilists or socialists who through the use of murder and arson desired anarchy and celebrated the "instincts bestiaux de l'homme."[273] Now Bluntschli, too, demanded extradition for political crimes, denouncing "communist and nihilist conspiracies" which, he maintained, "have an international character and threaten all authorities in all countries."[274] In 1879 the Institute voted (19–7) to adopt a provision that enabled States to exercise extraterritorial criminal jurisdiction for acts committed anywhere and by anyone, if such acts constituted attacks "on the social existence

---

[268] Rivier, *Lehrbuch des Völkerrechts*, p. 28.
[269] James Lorimer, "La doctrine de reconnaissance. Le fondement de droit international" (1884), XVI *RDI*, p. 351.
[270] For a general treatment of the right of asylum in mid-century Europe cf. Robert von Mohl, *Staatsrecht, Völkerrecht und Politik*, pp. 637–764. Cf also "Rapport de M. Charles Brocher sur l'extradition" (1879–1880), 3–4 *Annuaire IDI*, pp. 213–220.
[271] Lieber, *On Civil Liberty*, p. 59.
[272] Cf. the colorful account in E. H. Carr, *The Romantic Exiles* (London, Serif, 1998 [1933]), pp. 122–123.   [273] (1879–1880), 3–4 *Annuaire IDI*, pp. 268–269.
[274] Cited in Nys, *Le droit international*, II, p. 303. Cf. (1881–82), 5 *Annuaire IDI*, pp. 102, 103.

"The legal conscience of the civilized world"

of the State" or endangered its security.[275] The following year, the Institute adopted a series of articles that did provide for non-extradition for political crimes – but limited this strictly to activities that would not compass normal crimes as well.[276]

In a lengthy article on anarchism in the 1890s Rolin's brother, the President of the University of Ghent and Vice-President of the *Institut*, Albéric Rolin (1843–1937, later Baron Rolin) denounced universal suffrage as it led the uneducated to socialism, collectivism, and anarchism. There was only a theoretical difference between socialism and anarchism: the one led automatically to the other: "If modern society carries socialism within itself, it has contracted a sickness, it is a cancer that has to be removed, if possible, from which it must heal itself, for the malady is serious."[277] Albéric Rolin agreed with Lorimer, Bluntschli, and Martens: anarchism and communism were crimes against all States, to be combated by all available means.[278] In this respect, many legislations – particularly those of France and Belgium – still contained gaps. But his point was more general. The threat came not only from anarchist acts but from the very spread of socialism: "Socialist, collectivist and anarchist theories address themselves to man's basest instincts, they flatter and seduce his vilest appetite: they have assured clients among the outcast and especially among criminals."[279]

Within the Institute, such views were not too extreme[280] – even Lieber associated socialism with despotism, "those fatal negations of freedom," demonstrating how easily the men of 1873 could fall back on repression in order to defend their aristocratic liberalism. At Albéric Rolin's initiative, the Institute tightened the conditions for non-extradition for political crimes in 1892, exempting acts that could be described as being "dirigés contre les bases de toute organisation sociale."[281] The Institute's *esprit d'internationalité* was tolerant but paternalistic and repressive. Not

---

[275] (1879–1880), 3–4 *Annuaire IDI*, pp. 276–281. Westlake voted against this provision, arguing that such acts could better be dealt with by diplomacy than criminal law. Westlake, *Chapters*, pp. 127–128.

[276] Déclaration internationale relative au droit d'expulsion des étrangers (8–9 septembre 1880), Arts. 13–14 (1881–1882), 5 *Annuaire IDI*, pp. 127–130.

[277] Albéric Rolin, "La repression des attentats anarchistes" (1894), XXVI *RDI*, p. 126.

[278] At its session of Geneva in 1892 the Institut did modify the resolution of 1882 to the effect of exempting from non-extradition crimes that were "directed against the basis of all social organization, and not only against a determined State or a particular form of government" (Art. 4). Règles internationales sur l'admission et l'expulsion des étrangers, 9 September 1892 (1892–1894) 12 *Annuaire IDI*, p. 183.

[279] Rolin, "La repression," p. 128.

[280] Cf. also the remarks by Martens and Saripolos (1879–1880), 3–4 *Annuaire IDI*, pp. 265–276.   [281] (1892–1894), 12 *Annuaire IDI*, pp. 182–183.

without reason, Rolin-Jaequemyns sometimes defined it as "un esprit à la fois libéral et sagement conservateur."[282] And Westlake confessed that although as a young man in 1867 he had been in favor of proportional representation and abolishing the House of Lords, he had later seen the virtues of control on the whims of public opinion.

Cultural consciousness

If international lawyers espoused an ambivalent centrism in their attitudes towards European nationalism, and manly determination to repress the spread of socialist ideas, they were anything but averse to giving legal recognition to cultural difference between Europe and the rest of the world. Darwin's *Origin of Species* was published in 1859 and within thirty years, social Darwinism had become the principal competitor of liberalism among educated classes in Britain.[283] Herbert Spencer's popular works suggested that social evolution took place through a move from homogeneity to heterogeneity, increasing differentiation and specialization, and thus worked against egalitarian ideas.[284] With disappointments in the colonies, and the horror stories that explorers and frustrated missionaries brought back from Africa, humanitarianism often transformed into racism.[285]

With express reference to these new doctrines, James Lorimer, the *Institut* member who did the most to attempt a theoretical articulation of a new international law, forecast in 1884 that no other modern science would have as much effect on international law as ethnology, or the science of races, as he called it. Speculating about the connection of racial background and political organization he canvassed two possibilities for the future of British rule in India. Either British domination would continue – or else something would happen "that had never happened before," namely the birth of a proper Oriental political organization. Because political organization was a European concept, only

---

[282] Gustave Rolin-Jaequemyns, "Le droit international et la phase actuelle de la question de l'Orient" (1876), VIII *RDI*, p. 380. Bluntschli, too, characterized his own political ideas with the epithet "liberal–conservatism."

[283] G. N. Sanderson, "The European Partition of Africa: Coincidence or Conjecture?," in E. F. Penrose (ed.), *European Imperialism and the Partition of Africa* (London, Cass, 1975), p. 43. On Darwin's (or rather Darwinism's) influence in various European countries at the time, cf. Chadwick, *Secularization*, pp. 241, 175–188; Gay, *The Cultivation of Hatred*, pp. 45–68.

[284] Cf. Hawthorn, *Enlightenment and Despair*, pp. 90–100.

[285] Cf. Hobsbawm, *Age of Empire*, pp. 31–32.

"The legal conscience of the civilized world"

European States merited full recognition as States while "barbaric" and "savage" communities merited only a partial or "human" recognition.[286] On the other hand, in 1885, de Laveleye did accuse Spencer of being "anxious to see the law of the survival of the fittest and of natural selection adopted in human society."[287] Even as international lawyers had no doubt about the superiority of European civilization over "Orientals," they did stress that the civilizing mission needed to be carried out in an orderly fashion, by providing good examples, and not through an unregulated scramble.

This was a novel doctrine. Early nineteenth-century lawyers such as von Martens and Klüber had professed that a universal law could be derived from a universal human nature. Though they had understood international law as a European heritage they had seen that heritage in a universal light. Rational law was first realized in Europe but its validity was not limited to Europe.[288] It is important not to overstate the extent of their universalism, however. For James Reddie, writing in mid-century, it was clear that "a body of practical international law has grown up, and been formed, in the course of the last three centuries, among the Christian nations; namely what the German jurists call the practical science of the *Droit des Gens Moderne de l'Europe*."[289] After all, it was precisely that "practical law" that filled the textbooks of von Martens and Klüber. But the European culture they wrote about, or pretended any knowledge of, was diplomatic culture: the culture of sovereign protocol, great congresses, alliances, and war. If that was a European heritage, it was narrow and technical, unconnected to the spiritual awakening of European nations. Even as they wrote of the history of international law as part of the development of civilization, they meant "civilization" in the Kantian sense as a state of cultivation of the human faculties, manifested in diplomacy's complicated forms, and not in the sense of the idiosyncratic *Kultur* of any particular nation.[290]

The liberal jurists of 1873 could not fail to see the limitedness of such concept of culture. Its mastery was hardly an adequate basis for imagining oneself as the "organ" of a popular conscience–consciousness. The old German textbooks gave much too much weight to formal treaties

---

[286] Lorimer, "La doctrine de reconnaissance," p. 335.
[287] Quoted in Gay, *The Cultivation of Hatred*, p. 45.   [288] Cf. chapter 2 below.
[289] Reddie, *Inquiries in International Law*, p. 146.
[290] For the distinction, cf. e.g. Raymond Geuss, *Morality, Culture, and History. Essays on German Philosophy* (Cambridge University Press, 1999), pp. 33–44 and Terry Eagleton, *The Idea of Culture* (Oxford, Blackwell, 2000), pp. 10–14.

which, after all, and despite elaborate explanations to the contrary, failed to bind anyone but parties. The real law was to be founded on something more inclusive. Reddie had imbibed the message of the historical school and argued that positive law "has chiefly arisen or grown up gradually, from customs and usages, adapted from time to time in the course of ages." It was not sufficient for legal study to search and organize formal acts of diplomacy. One must, rather "search therein, for the notions, which serve as guides, to unfold these rules as derived from the fundamental principle of right or wrong."[291] Reddie mixed diplomatic form and national substance, rational and positive law, custom and justice in a fashion that was only a step away from Rolin's arguments about the jurist as public opinion's enlightened mouthpiece. As soon as skepticism about a general, abstract right stepped in, Reddie's methodological dictum could be rewritten so as to imply that what must be fundamental is the jurist's moral sensibility.

From mid-century onwards, a sociological consciousness was increasingly propagated by bodies such as the British Association for the Advancement of Social Sciences at which Rolin and his friends had met. Legislative reforms had to be based on the actual conditions of societies. Hence the early stress on comparative law and conflict of laws in the *Revue* and the *Institut*.[292] This created a practical problem, however. It could hardly be expected that international lawyers undertake ethnographic or sociological studies as a condition for being able to say anything general about international law. Though Bluntschli, for instance, argued that nations had different character and that successful reform must be compatible with such character,[293] his 1867 code-book contained no character studies of European nations. For the purposes of international law, he and his colleagues assumed that whatever differences there existed between European nations, they were sufficiently similar for there to be an international law among them, and sufficiently different from non-European peoples so as to preclude the extension of such law to the latter.

The explanation of international law as an effect of European culture, instead of habits of diplomacy, was elaborated in the great textbooks of the last two decades of the century. Franz von Holtzendorff's

---

[291] Reddie, *Inquiries in International Law*, p. 153.
[292] Bluntschli engaged in lengthy discussions of Jewish and Mohammedan law, Chinese and Buddhist law, etc., cf. "Der Rechtsbegriff," in *Gesammelte kleine Schriften*, I, pp. 7–20.
[293] Bluntschli, "Der Stat ist der Mann," in *Gesammelte kleine Schriften* I, pp. 269–271.

many-volume *Handbuch des Völkerrechts* (1885–1889), for instance, discussed the "ethnographic basis of international law" and concluded that international law governed the relations between States "whose external relations could be regulated by a uniform set of norms on the basis of a shared legal consciousness of peoples."[294] National law developed in relation to the cultural process of the nation. In the same way, international law was based on the cultural process of Europe, a process of "civilization" – in contrast to which the cultural process of other nations could be understood as half-civilized or savage.[295] Because international law was a fruit of European civilization it could not be automatically applied outside its realm.[296]

In their textbook, much-used after 1898, Henri Bonfils (1835–1897) and Paul Fauchille (1858–1926) explained that international law emerged through increasing contacts between nations with a common civilization: "The foundation of international law resides thus in the undeniable and necessary fact of the existence of a durable and legally recognized community among States that have attained or exceeded a certain level of civilization."[297] There was a natural international law ("principles of justice and humanity") that applied to all peoples irrespective of cultural difference – and it had not always been honored by Europeans. But the bulk of the law concerned only European States: "They form a community of nations that is united by religion, customs, morality, humanity, science as well as as the advantages of commercial relations, together with the habit of forming alliances and concluding treaties with each other."[298] To participate in international law required a certain resemblance of habits, customs, and procedures. Citing John Stuart Mill against Pufendorff and Montesquieu, Bonfils and Fauchille observed that to apply European international law in regard to barbarian nations was to misunderstand the reciprocity underlying it. If some parts of the law had sometimes been applied to States such as Turkey or the great Asiatic empires, this had taken place only on an "exceptional and limited fashion" and for a particular purpose. Their full application

---

[294] Holtzendorff, *Handbuch*, I, p. 11.
[295] This classification comes from Lorimer, *Institutes*, I, pp. 101 and *passim*.
[296] Holtzendorff observes that the concepts of "culture" and "civilization" are not unambiguous and that their definition is not the task of lawyers but of historians and ethnographers. For the jurist, it suffices to observe the peaceful interaction between European States and the recognition by those States of certain binding rules as "entscheidendes Merkmal der politischen Cultur in Völkerrechtlichen Sinne," *Handbuch*, I, p. 13.   [297] Bonfils–Fauchille, *Manuel*, p. 5
[298] Bonfils–Fauchille, *Manuel*, pp. 17–18.

was impossible in the absence of "this community of historical tradition, this mutual understanding that even in Europe needed thousands of years."[299]

A cultural approach was closely linked with an evolutionary one. In the 1860s and 1870s colonization produced new data on primitive societies that needed to be integrated into the Victorian world-view. The eighteenth-century notion of the Noble Savage, an uncorrupted specimen of the universal man, could no longer be sustained.[300] First, it was at odds with much of the colonizers' experience, indeed failed to account for the European fascination with Oriental "vice." Second, to the extent that it did seem correct, it posed embarrassing questions about the virtues of European civilization both in regard to the manner the civilizing process was being conducted and with respect to the astonishing tolerance by civilization of pockets of massive injustice within itself. Faced with this dilemma, humanitarian liberals needed reassurance. Such reassurance was, as the British philosopher Henry Sidgwick noted in 1902, received from a theory of progress in which the otherness of the non-Europeans could be seen as backwardness, a lagging behind in the great chain of evolution:[301]

The attraction of evolutionary social theories was that they offered a way of reformulating the essential unity of mankind, while avoiding current objections to the older theories of a human nature everywhere the same, but because the differences represented different stages in the same process. And by agreement to call the process progress one could convert the social theory into a moral and political one.[302]

If international lawyers were truly for progress, then they could not avoid also being preachers of the conversion of non-Europeans into "civilized" behavior. Although international law had been created by Christian nations, Bluntschli wrote at the end of the 1860s, it aimed at true universality.[303] Or, in Lieber's words, it was modernity's great task to teach nations to co-exist through *one* international law, *one* religion, and *one* education (*Bildung*) – but nevertheless persist as *nations*.[304]

---

[299] Bonfils–Fauchille, *Manuel*, p. 19.
[300] Cf. Bluntschli, "Der Stat ist der Mann," in *Gesammelte kleine Schriften*, I, pp. 278–283.
[301] Cf. Henry Sidgwick, *Philosophy. Its Scope and Relations. An Introductory Course of Lectures* (London, Macmillan, reprinted by Thoemmes, 1998 [1902]), pp. 174–211.
[302] Burrow, *Evolution and Society*, pp. 98–99.
[303] Bluntschli, *Das moderne Völkerrecht*, p. 59.
[304] Lieber in a letter to Professor Karl Joseph Anton Mittermeier (1787–1867) on August 26, 1867, emphasis in original, quoted in Roeben, "Bluntschli," p. 183.

"The legal conscience of the civilized world"

The evolutionary framework suggested that non-European communities were not only different but inferior in the sense of being more primitive. None of the lawyers, however, developed a detailed theory about that difference or how the evolutionary process would work in the future. Most were content with generalizations such as Lorimer's threefold classification (civilized/barbarian/savage) and simply assumed European modernity as the natural end-point of development everywhere. Westlake professed the possession of government as the test of civilization. But this merely pushed the difficulty one step further: what was government? Clearly, for him, as well as for all those lawyers who admitted Japan into the international society only after the end of the Tokugawa period, the notion of "government" meant "government of the European type."

One lawyer to sketch a theory of legal development was the leading British legal historian, Sir Henry Sumner Maine. There is no evidence that Maine's *Ancient Law* that came out only two years after the *Origin of the Species*, was influenced by Darwin or Spencer.[305] Its evolutionary outlook can perhaps better be accredited to the historical school and its enthusiastic reception to a *Zeitgeist* that looked for assurance about evolution being on the side of the West. For this purpose, Maine's distinction between "dynamic" and "stationary" societies fitted nicely. But neither did Maine go much beyond the dictum of "from status to contract" and chronicling a general move from judgments to custom and written law. The historicism of his 1887 Whewell lectures on international law consisted more of a literary style than well-argued propositions. Maine's intuitions about what aspects of his own society were valuable were assumed rather than argued as the highest forms of civilization.[306]

But Maine's influence in the field remained negligible. He did not become a member of the *Institut* where his idiosyncratic views – his defense of the *Dreikeiserbund* as a peace-keeping compact, for instance – would hardly have been appreciated.[307] It was left for his successor in Oxford (after Pollock), Sir Paul Vinogradoff, much later to produce an express theory of international law's evolution through stages.[308] As will be argued in more detail in chapter 2, when European expansion

---

[305] In fact, the materials for Maine's *magnum opus* had already been compiled and lectured on by him in the early 1850s. Cf. Burrow, *Evolution and Society*, pp. 142–143.
[306] Cf. also Collini, *Public Moralists*, p. 273. [307] Maine, *International Law*, p. 226.
[308] Paul Vinogradoff, *Historical Types of International Law*, I (1923), Bibliotheca Visseriana, pp. 3–70.

reached its peak in the 1880s and 1890s, international lawyers made only a superficial use of the theory of the degrees of civilization in their attempt to grasp the legal aspects of the expansion.

Culture as character

The standard opposition of "civilization" to "barbarism" by Rolin and his friends invoked a set of shared intuitions about what was valuable and what was base in social life. If "barbarian" societies were uncivilized, this meant they indulged in vice, lacked restraint and moderation, that they were "fanatical," untrustworthy, and uneducated. Even at best, barbarians were, in the favourite metaphor, like children who allowed their passions to rule their behavior.[309] If, as in Westlake, a more formal criterion such as "absence of government" was invoked, it was done to draw attention to the chaotic state of native life in which a "king or chief" might sign away anything simply because of being "such a drunkard as to be subject to *delirium tremens*."[310] Westlake seems to have "found the key to social problems in the development of individual character."[311] He was a friend of Thomas Hughes, a later Principal of the Working Men's College of which Westlake was one of the founders and the hugely popular theorist of Victorian character in *The Manliness of Christ*.[312] In his inaugural lecture at Cambridge Westlake emphasized activism, charity and the sense of personal responsibility, as central ideas around which international law was constructed, over the narrow and technical definitions of the subject as rules or principles formulated as mere abstractions.[313] Moreover: "No law national or international, will be durable unless it is fairly well adapted to the character and circumstances of the men who are to observe it."[314] Such and analogous statements focused on personal virtue and especially on proper character as cornerstones of a civilized morality, equally applicable in human lives as in the lives of nations. But they were projections of what the men of 1873 valued in each other as persons and colleagues, not derivations from a well-developed sociology of civilization or an articulated moral theory.

This was also Rolin's message in his programmatic article of 1869. If

---

[309] Cf. e.g. Joseph Hornung, "Civilisés et barbares" (1886), XVIII *RDI*, pp. 188–189.
[310] Westlake, *Chapters*, p. 151.   [311] Fischer Williams, "Introduction," pp. 10–11.
[312] *Memories of Westlake*, p. 62.
[313] John Westlake, "Introductory Lecture on International Law," in *Collected Papers*, pp. 411–412.   [314] Westlake, *Chapters*, p. 80.

"The legal conscience of the civilized world"

the law lay in the *conscience* of enlightened jurists, was it not precisely the quality of that conscience–consciousness – virtuous or base – that would be central to law? Did not "method" then equal the exploration of aspects of virtuous character? When Savigny defined the jurist as the mouthpiece of popular consciousness he thereby transferred that jurist as the measure of the legal system: the examination of the law was always also an examination of the lawyer's soul; in his own personal virtue he recognized the justice embedded in law. If the morality of late nineteenth-century liberals was a morality of personal virtue, this was less euphoria than a logical consequence of a view of cultural determination that focused on individuals: "what is bred in the bone, comes out in the flesh."

The rhetoric of honor and virtue was everywhere. Francis Lieber's writings – and he was certainly one of the more politically conscious activists behind the Institute – were permeated by the idea of "manliness," associated with self-government, self-reliance, and self-institution – ideas according to which "government . . . should do nothing but what it necessarily must do."[315] There was an idea of nobility involved here, of knowing one's place and being proud of it, as Lieber put it, "readiness of resigning the use of power which we may possess, quite as often as using it."[316] Some of the values of Victorian character have been canvassed in terms of "self-restraint, perseverance, strenuous effort, courage in the face of adversity."[317] Such adjectives are closely linked with duty, or the fulfillment of duty, or perhaps aggression disciplined and sublimated.[318] A noble character did not exhibit weakness of will and "sentimentalism" – these were precisely what disqualified the peace activists as serious partners in Rolin's eyes. Instead, Bluntschli praised the sense of honor and the will to overcome difficulties in an effort to constantly improve the human condition which he associated with the "Aryan races." This was what made the secular State as a distinctly "European–Aryan" political form seem so much superior to the "dumpfe Religiosität, welche ein alter Erbteil Asiens ist."[319] Lorimer compared Oriental communities without internal freedom to immature or irrational individuals deprived of legal capacity and described the relationship between superior and inferior races in terms of a trust the former had over communities suffering from a "weakness of spirit" that

---

[315] Lieber, *On Civil Liberty*, p. 253.   [316] Lieber, *On Civil Liberty*, p. 256.
[317] Collini, *Public Moralists*, p. 100.   [318] Gay, *The Cultivation of Hatred*, p. 502.
[319] Bluntschli, "Arische Völker," p. 89.

rendered them incapable of full membership in the civilized community.[320]

The idea of moral character as the nucleus of civilized conscience–consciousness was developed in two directions. On the one hand, moral character defined the international jurists themselves and bound them into a transhistorical fraternity of aristocratic heroes. On the other hand it was projected on collectivities and gave the measure whereby their civilization could be measured so as to determine, for example, whether they qualified for entry into the family of nations. In its former role, moral character was emphasized in the discussions of the writings of earlier jurists. Here is how Sir Travers Twiss discussed Vitoria's and Las Casas' defense of the Indians:

> It is difficult for us, in the present age, to measure the degree of courage and noble principle which impelled these excellent monks to vindicate the right of the oppressed against the authority of the Church, the ambitions of the Crown, the avarice and pride of their countrymen, and the prejudices of their own Order.[321]

There is nothing hyperbolic in this writing. It could have come from the pen of any late nineteenth-century international lawyer. In vindicating their profession, they repeatedly drew examples from past lawyers – Vitoria, Suarez and Las Casas were the favorites, perhaps as they opposed Empires that had since collapsed – whose merit had been their resolution against adversity. Grotius, too, was often portrayed in this light and Bluntschli praised Pufendorff's courage in his separation of international law from Christian religion.[322] In a way, international legal history became a story of individual lawyers acting like so many chivalrous knights, defending the oppressed against the oppressors, peace against war, carrying the torch of civilization (from Greece and Rome) through dark ages to the present. It was not kings or diplomats but writers and scientists who finally woke up "das schlummernde Rechtsbewusstsein der civilisierten Welt."[323] Twiss projected this ideal directly to the jurists of his day. The international lawyer was "by his vocation placed sentinel upon the outworks of this system":

> and no nobler end can be proposed to his ambition or sense of duty than to keep vigilant watch, ready to defend the weaker against the aggressions of the

---

[320] Lorimer, "La doctrine de la reconnaissance," p. 351.
[321] Travers Twiss, *Two Introductory Lectures on the Science of International Law* (London, Longman, 1856), p. 8.   [322] Bluntschli, *Das moderne Völkerrecht*, p. 19.
[323] Bluntschli, *Das moderne Völkerrecht*, pp. 17–18.

more powerful, and to control the spirit of war and conquest, when it attempts to overthrow the established doctrines of public law[324]

So much was placed on the international lawyer's shoulders that it is no wonder that discussion turned to the requirements of character that such a person must have. Rolin did not fail to use the opportunity to speculate on this: the international jurist needed to demonstrate a progressive spirit, "progress" being measured as development from vice to virtue, like a collective *Bildungsroman*. In the liberal age, Princes could no longer be instructed to be lions or foxes as Machiavelli would have had them; no more could a regent get away with what Alexander VI was reputed to have said, namely that his sole occupation was to fool people. For "the public judgment that falls upon public acts has become more severe, more enlightened, more honest."[325] When Rolin argued that the conscience of enlightened men was the real legislator, adjudicator, and sanction of international law, he meant a conscience of restraint – "the calm search for truth and justice" – that could be more powerful than diplomacy and even war, if only it maintained control and moderation: "that it renounces the shadows of passion for the light of reflective study."[326]

The focus on character opened a way to avoid the problems involved in the available alternatives: a more or less religiously inclined naturalism or a legal formalism highly developed in the French and German domestic legal contexts. The former avenue was closed by the Protestantism of the majority of *Institut* members, their aversion against the secular pursuits of the Catholic church. Freedom of thought and religion was an article of faith for them. But to establish legal study on secular "values" – to which of course they made constant reference – must have seemed no less difficult. Nietzsche was not alone in the 1890s to feel that human beings did not discover values but created them instead: his moral genealogy assumed a thorough-going relativism in his contemporaries that was only thinly hidden behind a facade of righteousness that he interpreted as part of a culture of *ressentiment*.[327] Those values could not be articulated as axioms of a legal *system* without being immediately revealed as inconsequential generalizations or, if concrete, indissociable

---

[324] Twiss, *Two Introductory Lectures*, p. 60.
[325] Rolin, "De l'étude de la législation comparée," p. 231.
[326] Rolin, "De l'étude de la législation comparée," pp. 231–237, 243.
[327] Cf. Friedrich Nietzsche, *On the Genealogy of Morals: A Polemic*, trans. with introd. and notes by Douglas Smith (Oxford University Press, 1996 [1887]), pp. 22–25, 29–30, 54–57.

from the political program of this or that liberal faction. Recourse to a legal formalism of the French or the German type, again, although not completely alien to the membership of the *Institut*, was expressly repudiated by Rolin, Bluntschli, and Westlake as overly oriented to the past, and in any case problematic in an international context where no formal legislation existed. Their dilemma was later discussed by Max Weber, reflecting on the conditions of politics in modern society: between nihilism and an ethics of ultimate ends, there lay an ethics of responsibility, the pragmatic *via media* that might provide a means of struggling against capitalism and bureaucracy on the one hand, and socialism on the other.[328] This was to reach for the person over the institution, and to focus on the politician's (or administrator's, lawyer's) conscience–consciousness ("responsibility") as the ultimate criterion of the political good.

The role of personal virtue and responsibility did not stop at describing the character traits of men who were to be the juridical conscience–consciousness of the civilized world. States were vested with human qualities first perhaps by way of metaphor. But metaphor soon transformed into a description of reality, however, as inter-State relations received some of those intrinsically humane epithets of "culture" and "civilization." Nations became real, not metaphoric entities, with a spirit, mind, and will of their own. As Bluntschli put it in 1869: The nation was above all a community of spirit and character ("*Geistes- und Charactergemeinschaft*").[329] Human qualities such as femininity and manliness became thus quite central for Bluntschli's discussion of Franco-Prussian relations. The same applied to the relations between the State and the Church: the former was the commanding, active figure, the latter a soft, tempering spirit. In his essay "Der Stat ist der Mann" ("The State is the Man"), Bluntschli argued that humanity was divided into men and women; there was no abstract human person. This applied to States as well. Aristotle had already associated the public realm with men – the woman's natural timidity made her unsuitable for politics. The State must therefore obviously be a man: "Men form and lead the State. It is the image of their spirit."[330]

---

[328] Cf. Max Weber, "Politics as Vocation" (1919), in *From Max Weber: Essays in Sociology*, trans., ed., and with an introd. H. H. Gerth and C. Wright Mills (London, Routledge, 1967), pp. 77–128.

[329] Bluntschli, "Die Einwirkung der nationalität auf die religion und kirchlichen Dinge," in *Gesammelte kleine Schriften*, II, p. 133.

[330] Bluntschli, "Der Staat ist der Mann," in *Gesammelte kleine Schriften* I, p. 284.

"The legal conscience of the civilized world"

In Bluntschli's organic theory States were neither formal–rational structures nor aggregates of individuals or communities. They were "unitary wholes, persons, that is to say, legal bodies in possession of a will, just like individuals."[331] A State lived as a person, experiencing youth, adulthood, old age, and death. In its different ages, the State's character changed – as did its laws.[332] This was standard nationalism. The principle of self-determination was an analogy of personal freedom. The Napoleonic Empire had seemed such a burden precisely as it had suppressed the individual spirituality of the nations it overrode. Yet, precisely in the struggle against external oppression nations – like the best of men – cultivated their character: even the lowest Frenchman had the warmest feelings towards *La Patrie* and acted "wie ein Mann" if such feelings were violated.[333] The recognition of such character in nations as well as in individuals was precisely what made the law think of them as persons in the first place.[334]

For Rolin, the duty to keep the treaties was a matter of honesty and of forthrightness; there was nothing more to it. External sanction, for instance, was not a criterion of whether one was obligated or not.[335] The perspective of the Holmesian "bad man" is completely absent from this image. Inasmuch as it sufficed to say *ibi jus, ubi societas* to prove the existence of international law, the law's basis was set on a morality of sociableness. The system could work if States were – or could be persuaded to become – reasonable and moderate individuals whose main concern would be with the protection of their freedoms (often seen as "fundamental rights") and the pursuit of material and spiritual progress through co-operation.

The personalization of inter-State relationships did not limit itself to organic conceptions of public law or other tracts of continental theory. William E. Hall (1835–1894), an avowed positivist and a pragmatist, the author of perhaps the most influential English-language textbook of the period, pictured the relations between States as if they were members of

---

[331] Bluntschli, *Das moderne Völkerrecht*, p. 2.
[332] "Die Entwickelung des Rechts und das Recht der Entwickelung," in *Gesammelte kleine Schriften*, I, pp. 53–55.
[333] "Arische Völker," pp. 74–75. A world State was impossible for just this reason: "Denn die Völker und Nationen haben ihre eigenthumliches Dasein. Ihr individuelle Character hat auch sein Recht und seine Bedeutung. Sie sind zwar nur Gestaltungen innerhalb des sie alle umfassenden Wesens der Menschheit, aber in dieser ihrer Existenz unvertilgbar und nothwendig," "Der Stat ist der Mann," p. 281.
[334] Bluntschli, "Person und Persönlichkeit," in *Gesammelte kleine Schriften*, I, pp. 91–93.
[335] Rolin, "De l'étude de la législation comparée," pp. 231–233.

a Victorian social club. Admission to the club was conditional on the possession of a sufficient degree of European culture so that its internal rules "can . . . be supposed to be understood or recognized by countries differently civilised."[336] Having pointed out that States were independent persons possessing inalienable rights, in particular the right of property, he laid down the basic rules of the society between them as follows: "It is also considered that their moral nature imposes upon them the duties of good faith, of concession of redress for wrongs, of regard for the personal dignity of their fellows, and to a certain extent sociability."[337] States were above all right-holders whose rights were limited by those of others as well as a moral code akin to that between honorable gentlemen in bourgeois society: "A state is enabled to determine the kind and amount of intercourse it will maintain with other countries, so long as it respects its social duties."[338] It is this dialectic between the right of independence, of liberty as a "moral person" and the duties towards the other members of the states–society that constitutes such striking analogy to the way liberal society conceived itself. Even as Hall was the paradigmatic late nineteenth-century legal positivist, the basic rules of his law did not emanate from treaty or custom but from "fundamental rights" and a "duty of sociability" that are taken as the self-evident foundations of civilized behavior. The first sentence of the treatise defined international law as rules that civilized States hold binding "with a force comparable in nature and degree to that binding the conscientious person to obey the laws of his country." As club members, States had "feelings of honour and personal dignity" that sometimes call for external recognition.[339] Those aspects of Hall's own society that seem valuable to him were always transposed to his texts: "A large part of international usage gives effect to principles which represent facts of state existence, essential under the conditions of modern civilized state life."[340] As with other jurists of the period, international law was part of "modern civilised state life"; it was not legislated into existence by a sovereign but derived from membership in a de facto society – "a society and the moral principles to which that society feels itself obliged to give legal

---

[336] W. E. Hall, *A Treatise on International Law* (4th edn., Oxford, Clarendon, 1895), p. 42. One mark of the possession of the capacity for membership was the possession of a municipal law "consonant with modern European ideas," p. 55.
[337] Hall, *A Treatise*, p. 45.　[338] Hall, *A Treatise*, p. 50.
[339] Hall, *A Treatise*, pp. 61–62. Bonfils–Fauchille conceived this a matter of law, *Manuel*, p. 138.　[340] Hall, *A Treatise*, p. 6.

effect."[341] As members of this society, this social club, States had the duty of sociability, including the duty to preserve good faith – to hold compacts – with the risk that their membership will be canceled, they become "outlaws."[342]

The projection of States as members of a social club plays on a domestic analogy that transposes the morality of conscience that the men of 1873 experienced as the foundation of their professional competence onto the level of States. States become individual right-holders in an exclusive society, entry to which is governed by a flexible standard of civilization. The rules of the society pre-exist membership in it and are found not in any agreement or rule-book but in the implicit cultural conventions of the day whereby the members of the club recognize their respective moral worth, honor and dignity.

For the liberal jurists, war – the "war phenomenon" – was an enigma, as it has remained for liberals and humanitarians ever since. On the one hand, most of them were opposed to war, regarding it as a manifestation of the primitive and destructive instincts that it was the point of law to eradicate from civilized life. They shared the critique, commonplace since Cobden in Britain and Constant in France, that there were no good political or economic arguments in favor of war, that war was an irrational departure from Victorian normality.[343] On the other hand, they were equally averse against the utopians who failed to see that war was occasionally needed to change an obsolete situation[344] or as enforcement against the law-breaker.[345] None of them joined Clausewitz or von Moltke to argue that war usefully supported such valuable character traits as courage, unselfishness, honor, sacrifice – though at least Bluntschli admitted that it sometimes did have that consequence. For better and for worse, it was a part of an imperfect human society.[346]

War was to be controlled, exorcized from the social normality of

---

[341] Hall, *A Treatise*, p. 6. [342] Hall, *A Treatise*, p. 58.
[343] Cf. De Laveleye, *Des causes actuelles*.
[344] Cf. Bluntschli, *Das moderne Völkerrecht*, pp. 10–11 (dissociating himself from von Moltke's glorification of war but holding it still sometimes a necessary instrument for the breaking of the "abgestorbenen Formen des veralteten Rechts").
[345] The general view was that war was a last resort for a State for the vindication of its rights. Cf. e.g. Bonfils–Fauchille, *Manuel*, pp. 522–523. But note also Fiore, *Le droit international codifié*, advocating collective war against the law-breaker, pp. 60–63.
[346] "La guerre est donc un mal; mais, un mal inhérent à l'humanité et indéracinable." Bonfils–Fauchille, *Manuel*, p. 517.

nations, made an "état exceptionnel, transitoire, passager."[347] But its abolition could take place only through the growth of human nature itself. The ambivalence of these attitudes was summarized by a Japanese diplomat in about 1898–1899, observing that: "We show ourselves at least your equals in scientific butchery, and at once we are admitted to your council tables as civilized men."[348] The trauma of the Franco-Prussian war was that it demonstrated that humanitarian laws did not become applicable merely by the good will of the belligerents, even when they were undoubtedly civilized European nations. Clearly, technical improvements were needed, but even they did not do away with the difficulty that there was no one to sanction belligerent behavior. What were international lawyers to think of this?

In December 1880, the Chief of the German General Staff, Count von Moltke (1800–1891) – the hero of the Franco-Prussian war – wrote a letter to Bluntschli. Moltke thanked Bluntschli for having sent him the *Manuel des Droits de la guerre* ("Oxford Manual") that had been adopted by the *Institut* early that same year and expressed agreement with its humanitarian sentiments. But he raised a number of problems with its legalistic attitude to warfare arguing, among other things, that decent conduct in war would not be attained by legal rules – moreover rules that did not have an effective sanction. The best humanitarianism, he wrote, was to carry the war efficiently to a conclusion.

In his response, Bluntschli did not deny the weaknesses of humanitarian law. Like von Moltke he testified to an increasing humanity in recent warfare, brought about by general conscription that had also brought gentlemen to the battlefield, and not merely rogues. But he argued that this was also a result of the development of the legal conscience of European *Kulturvölker*. War created an abnormal situation in which the dictates of conscience were sometimes lost. This is why it was imperative that the jurists took it upon themselves to articulate ("in klarem Ausdrucke vorzulegen") these dictates in the form of legal rules. As such they could be effectively integrated in the consciences of the belligerent masses.[349] The soldier and the jurist congratulated each other on what in 1880 seemed undoubted progress in comparison to 1648. The soldier – who of course was a nobleman – and the jurist – who felt himself no

---

[347] "La guerre est un état de fait, contraire à l'état normal de la communauté internationale qui est la paix," Bonfils-Fauchille, *Manuel*, p. 521.

[348] Quoted in Geoffrey Best, *Humanity in Warfare* (London, Weidenfeld & Nicolson, 1980), p. 141.

[349] For the correspondence, cf. Bluntschli, *Denkwürdiges*, III, pp. 470–476.

less – could at least agree on how wonderfully civilized their period was and look confidently to the future, whatever their differences.

In their correspondence, von Moltke and Bluntschli agreed that humanitarian behavior in war was a matter of civilization. Bluntschli's defense of humanitarian law rested on the way it would educate the fighting men's sensibilities so as to bring about those traits of character that were associated with civilized behavior. Unlike von Moltke, he did not assume that the significance of humanitarian rules was dependent on enforcement. Such rules were rather a form of *Bildung*, of educating European men to develop their sentiments towards peacefulness and moderation. Coming to know the rules would thus already work towards humanitarian objectives. Such ideas permeated all writing about war.

Westlake, for instance, talks about war as if it were a duel between honorable gentlemen – a "prosecution of a public quarrel"[350] – and thus associates it with his society's popular psychological imagery. Law cannot determine the outcome of struggle but must (like the seconder in a duel) "stand aside while they fight the quarrel out." War is a natural procedure of the human species mitigated not by law but by "the better qualities of our mixed humanity." The idea of *Bildung* emerges. The laws of war are needed in order to spell out "acts which would degrade the doer" and acts that would "exceed the object and be inhuman."[351] Personal honesty is the guiding thread: "benevolent neutrality," for instance, or the sudden commencement of war without adequate notice, would break the rule of "frank sincerity," based on the need of "good order that states should know how they stand with regard to one another."[352] For Maine as well, the laws of war (that is to say, the British Manual of 1887 on which his lectures were based) were less law in a technical sense than in a moral, psychological sense. They spelled out what a "humane commander" (such as the Duke of Wellington!) would or would not do – basically to try to avoid causing more harm than dictated by military necessity.[353] That spying was punishable by death

---

[350] Westlake, *International Law*, II, p. 81.
[351] Westlake, *International Law*, II, pp. 56, 57, 58.
[352] Westlake, *International Law*, II, pp. 191, 192. Likewise, Fiore, *Le droit international codifié* ("Sera considérée comme déloyale et contraire au droit moderne la conduite de l'Etat qui commencerait les hostilités sans déclaration de guerre préalable"), p. 306. A majority of writers held the view, however, that no declaration of war was necessary. They did not dispute the need for loyalty, however, but pointed out that "no forms give security against disloyal conduct," Hall, *A Treatise*, p. 399.
[353] Maine, *International Law*, pp. 126, 127, 138, 149.

reflected for both Westlake and Maine the way in which it violated the honorable conventions of the duel.[354]

The rules of such dueling, it goes almost without saying, apply only in combat between the civilized. In colonial wars Westlake did not find it difficult to imagine that a colonizer might need to take "punitive expeditions" in cases of "inroads or other outrages committed by savages of half civilised tribes." In such cases "the whole population must suffer for want of a government sufficiently marked off from it." Constraints in colonial war were, again, internal to the belligerents' virtue: "no humane officer will burn a village if he has any means of striking a sufficient blow that will be felt only by the fighting men."[355]

Civilized war was imagined in strictly utilitarian terms. It was not allowed for reasons of abstract justice or religion, only for the vindication of rights, conceived broadly as what was deemed necessary for self-protection. A lawful war was waged neither out of passion nor as ritual. Its object was always the seizure of territory or the attainment of some other rational objective. The means of war were to be fitted to its ends – hence the interminable discussions about what actually was allowed by "military necessity." Because passion and ritual were excluded, shaming the adversary, or symbolic destruction of life or property, were prohibited as uncivilized savagery.[356] Excluded were acts that the lawyers perceived as having the character of "cruauté, déloyalté, perfidie ou barbarie."[357] The main thing was to eradicate passion; war was to be seen as Rousseau had written, not as a relationship between men but between States – no personal animosity was therefore to be felt. The fighting men were to be killing machines: kind, considerate, and effective.

Even in war, the social life of the members of the family of nations was supposed to continue. No one was to be cast outside: the complex norms regarding maritime neutrality (of the right of visit and seizure, blockade, lists of contraband goods), for instance, were disputed in detail between the British and the French – though Harcourt's criticism of Hautefeuille ironically shows just to what extent national passions were involved.[358] And when Bluntschli advocated the almost complete leaving of private relations, including commercial relations between the citizens

---

[354] Maine, *International Law*, pp. 148, 149. Cf. also Art. 88 on spies and 101 on deception in war of the Lieber Code, Hartigan, *Lieber's Code*, pp. 61, 63.
[355] Westlake, *International Law*, II, p. 59. Cf. also p. 87 on the bombardment of non-civilized towns and villages.
[356] Cf. e.g. Art. 14–16 of the Lieber Code, Hartigan, *Lieber's Code*, p. 48.
[357] Fiore, *Le droit international codifié*, p. 315.
[358] Cf. e.g. "The Territoriality of a Merchant Vessel," in *Letters by Historicus on Some Questions of International Law* (London, Macmillan, 1863), pp. 199–212.

"The legal conscience of the civilized world"

of the belligerents, beyond the compass of war, this was quite logical from the perspective of the effort to draw a rational limit between the public and private realms – however much it went against earlier teaching on the matter.[359] But the very concept of such rules, and their having a sensible objective, was never seriously questioned. Indeed, the laws of war have perhaps never before nor since the period between 1870 and 1914 been studied with as much enthusiasm. Optimism in reason and the perfectibility of human nature laid the groundwork for the view that men could be educated to wage war in a civilized way. The "later Enlightenment consensus" (an implicit agreement about the general rules: sparing civilians, minimizing unnecessary harm, directing one's acts at formal enemies) mapped the mental terrain of civilized warfare.[360]

Where did this consensus come from? Until the Hague Conferences, there were no general treaties on the laws of war.[361] Grotius had drawn from stories of chivalry, courage, and pity shown by fighting men through history that reflected ideas of honor that were partly constitutive of what he thought of as European civilization. That such acts were cited in demonstration of natural law conceptualized them within a framework of explanation with which cultured Europe was familiar. The code proposed by Lieber and adopted by Lincoln in 1863 to govern the conduct of the armies of the Union was largely a compilation of humanitarian principles taken from publicists from Grotius onwards; it was animated by the need to define clearly the distinction between public and private property; and it followed the idea that war was a rational, public pursuit of limited objectives. "Humanity" and "honor" were its guiding principles.[362] The *Martens clause* that became part of the 1899 conventions plays on the continuing intuition that restraint in warfare is an intrinsic part of European conscience. Under the clause, namely, so long as positive law had not been adopted on some issue:

populations and belligerents remain under the protection and empire of the principles of international law, as they result from the usages established between civilized nations, from the laws of humanity, and the requirements of public conscience.[363]

---

[359] Bluntschli, *Das moderne Völkerrecht*, pp. 296–297 and Roeben, "Bluntschli," p. 195.
[360] Best, *Humanity in Warfare*, pp. 31–74.
[361] The Brussels Declaration Concerning the Laws and Customs of War of 1874 that complemented the 1864 Geneva Convention was a partly abortive document. In particular, nothing came of the attempt to set up an international enforcement of the earlier instrument.   [362] Cf. Roeben, "Bluntschli," pp. 192, 228.
[363] James Brown Scott, *The Reports to the Hague Conferences of 1899 and 1907* (Oxford, Clarendon, 1917), pp. 547–548.

As late Victorian lawyers elaborated on such requirements, it became evident that they had to do with the control of the passions that war was seen to launch. Even before 1899, the general view was that in the course of hostilities, "the measure of permissible violence is furnished by the reasonable necessities of war."[364] The significance of "reasonable necessity" was less to provide a criterion for measuring the permissibility of an act than to direct the combatants – in practice, superior officers – to examine their conscience even in the midst of fighting and to suppress their desire to engage in "irrational" violence – just as the lawyers of the late Victorian era were to accept the conventions of normality (and the accompanying *ressentiment*) as the price to pay for a life of security. Already to speak in terms of "necessity" was to refer to rationally defensible objectives and to oppose the Clausewitzian view that war tends to generate its own aims – revenge, dishonoring the enemy – under which a wholly different scale of passions becomes functional.

Qualities of personal character, cultivated by tradition and learning constituted the framework through which the men of 1873 identified the legal *conscience* of which they felt they were the organ. Matthew Arnold, a perceptive commentator on Victorian society had some years earlier described this in terms of an aristocratic sensibility, a striving for inner perfection of "sweetness and light" (or beauty and knowledge). Culture, he had written, in a way reminiscent of Rolin's definition of law, was to be found "in an inward condition of the mind and spirit, not in an outward set of circumstances."[365] All this was a matter of feeling, and of intuition, that was impossible to articulate in terms of rules or criteria. This is why the men of 1873 did not possess a "theory of European civilization" even as they stressed the need to find a historical and cultural basis for law. *Ubi societas ibi jus* may have been a necessary argument for a profession looking beyond naturalism and formalism, but it did not ground a sociological program for the lawyers – as it did for Marx, Durkheim, or Weber. But of course, none of these men felt able to bank their reformism on the individual moralities of a class of lawyers.

The elusive sensibility

The stories of the *Revue* and of the *Institut* are undoubtedly narratives of (relative) failure. From its early association with broad liberal–reformist

---

[364] Hall, *A Treatise*, p. 411.
[365] Matthew Arnold, "Culture and Anarchy," in *Culture and Anarchy and Other Writings*, Stefan Collini ed. (Cambridge University Press, 1993[1859]), p. 62.

"The legal conscience of the civilized world"

themes, the *Revue* transformed gradually into a rather standard public international law periodical without a conscious political or professional program. The activities of the Institute continued to focus on technical topics but very little came to be seen by way of governmental implementation of its proliferating resolutions. In a melancholy passage in the Secretary-General's 1888 report Rolin-Jaequemyns admitted that the proposals of the Institute had not been transformed into national laws or treaty texts and perhaps never would be. He could cite only one official reference to the works of the Institute – a passage from a settlement of a dispute between Mexico and the United States where the latter had referred to an 1878 resolution on criminal jurisdiction. Despite his *ex officio* assurance that the Institute was not *vox clamans in deserto*, it was precisely that impression his text conveyed.[366] As the Institute in the 1890s twice instructed Rolin's successor to seek the implementation of its decisions with governments, the Secretary-General was in both cases compelled to admit that no implementation was forthcoming.[367]

One set of reasons for such relative failure must be sought from the general atmosphere of the period towards the turn of the century which witnessed the general decline of European liberalism. The 1890s were a time of intellectual revolution in which the scientific and political certainties of mid-century and of the 1880s – that "stuffy decade" – were gradually brushed aside.[368] Writing a farewell address to his colleagues at the Institute on board a ship that took him and his family to the Far East in September 1892, Rolin expressed the wish that the Institute would not succumb to a time of "the most extreme opinions" and his conviction that moderation would prevail, "persuadé que la verité, comme la vertu, se trouve au milieu."[369] Yet, such optimistic centrism was increasingly viewed as shallow theory and unworkable practice. It had failed to engage accumulating evidence that passion and desire – "extreme opinions" – could not be eradicated from civilized society –

[366] "Rapport du Secrétaire-Général," (1888–1889), 10 *Annuaire IDI*, pp. 48–49. At the next session, held only after a three-year interval in 1891, he suggested that the Institute adopted perhaps too many resolutions and that one should have no illusions about their direct effect with governments. Nonetheless, he hoped that their moral authority would have an indirect influence through public opinion. "Rapport du Secrétaire-Général" (1889–1891), 11 *Annuaire IDI*, pp. 45–46.

[367] These were the proposals for the setting up of an International Union on the Publication of Treaties and for a conference on penal sanctions to ensure the implementation of the Geneva (Red Cross) Convention of 1864. Cf. "Rapport du Secrétaire-Général" (1896), 15 *Annuaire IDI*, pp. 174–181.

[368] See in particular, H. Stuart Hughes, *Consciousness and Society. The Reorientation of European Social Thought 1890–1930* (New York, Knopf, 1958), pp. 33–66.

[369] (1892–1894), 12 *Annuaire IDI*, p. 68.

that, on the contrary, they also constituted a necessary aspect of and sometimes a much-admired motivation for economic and political action.

Rolin himself felt the transformation very close to home. Having struggled six years from a position in Belgium's liberal government against Catholic ultramontanes on the right and liberal radicals on the left, Rolin finally lost his parliamentary seat in the elections of 1886 that brought Catholics back to power. He returned as Editor-in-Chief of the *Revue* and Secretary-General of the Institute, but having spent most of his appreciable fortune for political and humanitarian causes, as well as helping out a relative in financial distress, he was compelled to exercise his reformism at the service of the King of Siam in 1892 for the last ten years of his professional life. As he returned to Ghent in 1902 he had been already broken by the disease that was to lead him to the grave a few months therafter.

Westlake was elected to Parliament as a liberal radical in 1885. He was known for his strong opinions and in 1886 broke with Gladstone in joining the liberal Unionists against Home Rule for Ireland. He lost his seat the following year and failed to get re-elected in 1892.[370] As a politician, he was not a success. His speeches tended to turn into lectures and were apt to weary the audience.[371] Having lost his parliamentary seat he began a career as Professor of International Law. This offered him a platform not only for academic writing – he continued contributing commentaries on current events and recent disputes to Rolin's *Revue* and to British journals – but also for political action. He took a leading role in the international jurists' campaign in support of Finland against the Russification measures of 1899–1907, presided over the British Government's Balkan Committee in 1905–1913, and remained an active member of the Political Economy Club up to 1913.[372]

Bluntschli's fate was different.[373] He had begun a successful career as a liberal–conservative politician in his native Zürich in the 1830s with the Radicals as his main opponents, only narrowly losing a competition for the position of Mayor at a time when this would also have meant

---

[370] Courtney of Penwith, "Public Affairs," in *Memories of Westlake*, pp. 64–67.
[371] *Memories of Westlake*, p. 99.
[372] Cf. the obituaries of Westlake by Edouard Rolin (1913), XLV *RDI*, pp. 265–270; T. E. Holland (1913), 26 *Annuaire IDI*, pp. 698–700; Albéric Rolin (1913), 26 *Annuaire IDI*, pp. 701–712. Cf. also Fischer Williams, "Introduction," pp. 10–11, 13 as well as the essays on Westlake's life in *Memories of Westlake* generally.
[373] For biographies, cf. Roeben, "Bluntschli," pp. 45–67.

"The legal conscience of the civilized world"

leadership of the Swiss federation. Radical victory in the civil war compelled him to leave for Munich in 1847 from where he moved on to Heidelberg in 1861, continuing an active political career (often advocating the liberal views he had opposed when still in Zürich) as member of the Parliament of Baden and elected representative in the *Zollverein*. He became one of the founders of the Protestant Union (*Protestanten-Verein*) as well as of the German jurists' meetings (*Juristentag*), using both as a basis from which to argue for German unification under Bismarck and against a *Grossdeutsch* solution headed by the Habsburgs. During the 1870s Bluntschli regarded his political activities as at least as significant as his teaching. Much of his activism was targeted against Catholic influence (especially the Jesuits). His political writings combined liberal–humanitarian themes and a stress on individual rights with occasional lapses into anti-semitism and adherence to the obscure Christian dogmas of his admired Fredric Rohmer.[374] When Bluntschli died in 1881 his branch of conservative–liberalism was still successfully engaged in the alliance with Bismarck that would towards the end of the century tie liberals to compromises that perpetuated the split in the party and slowly undermined its ability to fight the onslaughts from left and right.[375]

But the failure of international law to become the avant-garde of a new internationalism was also a consequence of factors internal to the way the men of 1873 argued about it. Key problems were their ambivalent notion of civilized conscience–consciousness, accompanied by superficial organic metaphors about the State or the condition of international politics, the projection of personal morality onto international problems, as aspects of what was perceived from the outside as a technical profession. Neither contemporary internationalists, nor future generations of lawyers, could sustain that kind of political jurisprudence. Its politics was too closely associated with the reform agendas (and fate) of domestic liberalism. And it was too arrogant to suggest that the intuitions of a group of lawyers with a cosmopolitan orientation might provide a credible foundation for thinking about international relations or conducting foreign policy. Even as the theory of the "organ of the juridical conscience–consciousness of the civilized world" offered a basis on which to avoid critiques directed against rationalism, naturalism, and positivism, and to carry on with doctrinal work without too

---

[374] Roeben, "Bluntschli," pp. 67–74.
[375] Cf. Sheehan, *German Liberalism*, pp. 258–271.

much constraint, as constructive theory it was hopelessly *manqué*: an eclectic, fragile facade over what must often have seemed as the banal prejudices of a cultured but declining bourgeoisie.

Rolin, Westlake, Asser, and most of the other members of the Institute had little ambition as theorists. Lorimer's idiosyncratic naturalism received no following. Even Bluntschli's organic generalizations were dismissed by the following generation as "Diletanttismus und politisches Räsonnement."[376] The men of 1873 were not interested in philosophy but in extending the mores of an *esprit d'internationalité* within and beyond Europe. To get on with their politics, however, they needed distance from the available legal–dogmatic positions – from the rationalism of von Martens or Klüber and the statist positivism of Austin or Lasson. But their reluctance to occupy confidently any one of the three major positions of the period's legal theory (rationalism, naturalism, positivism) was accompanied by their constant borrowing of aspects of each.[377] This explains the difficulty of classifying late nineteenth-century international lawyers and makes it such a profound mistake to follow Lassa Oppenheim (1858–1919) and to label them simply as "naturalist" "Grotians" or "positivists."[378] In order to appreciate their pragmatic and eclectic spirit, and to understand why the next generation could dismiss them so easily, yet building upon the foundations they had erected, I would like to conclude by a brief interpretation of their significance as "founders" of the modern international law profession.

The men of 1873 were not satisfied with the rationalism of the successive editions and translations of von Martens and Klüber, nor the passion for "system" in Kaltenborn's 1847 treatise. These were too abstract and cold for the tastes of men educated in the teachings of the historical school and active politicians in the liberal cause. The contribution of Grotius or Pufendorff had been valuable in its time but incompatible with modern legal science, unable to see law as a historically and

---

[376] Oertzen, *Die gesellschaftliche Funktion*, p. 119. Similarly, Georg Jellinek, "Johann Caspar Bluntschli," in *Ausgewählte Schrifte und Reden* (2 vols., Berlin, Häring, 1911), II, pp. 289–291.

[377] Bluntschli adopted his eclecticism quite consciously, hoping to overcome the old controversy between rationalism and historicism by the creation of a third way that would not fall into a shallow and technical positivism, either. Cf comments in Roeben, "Bluntschli," pp. 232–233.

[378] For Oppenheim's discussion of nineteenth-century international lawyers as an account of positivism's victory, cf. *International Law. Volume I: Peace* (2 vols., 3rd edn., 1920), pp. 114–118.

"The legal conscience of the civilized world"

a geographically bounded construction. For the men of 1873, international law was to be social and cultural in a deep sense: not as a mere succession of treaties or wars but as part of the political progress of European societies. They each read individual freedoms and the distinction between the private and the public into constructive parts of their law. If they welcomed the increasing interdependence of civilized nations, this was not only to make a point about the basis of the law's binding force but to see international law as part of the progress of modernity that was leading societies into increasingly rational and humanitarian avenues.[379]

Yet they could not fully reject rationalism, either, for it was an aspect of the culture they so appreciated. They needed it to oppose the *fin-de-siècle* dangers of anarchism, nationalism, and war as well as to create distance between their societies and what colonial administrators encountered as they penetrated deeper into "uncivilized" territory. So they theorized rationalism and natural law into a default position, a last reservoir from which to grasp arguments when other sources ran dry. Bluntschli, for example, postulated a universal human nature as a guiding idea (*Rechtsidee*) behind all law, but also that this idea was not in itself law but an inspiration to it.[380] Nevertheless, he constantly referred to human nature as an additional point to strengthen whatever conclusion he wished to defend. Like Maine, Westlake held that recourse to natural law when positive principles of private international law ran out either camouflaged a reference to Roman Law or then amounted "in practice to little else than the judge's private opinion of what is equitable."[381] Yet he, too, made constant references to rational arguments and

---

[379] Nobody made these points more forcefully than Lorimer, for whom "empiricism, utilitarianism, and the like, degenerate into mere objectless groping among lifeless facts and life-destroying fictions." His argument for an international law that was a *necessary* aspect of international relations, only *declared* by positive sources (but never created by them), has been too easily dismissed as a revival of old natural law. In fact, Lorimer's "necessity" was a socially and ethnically based, teleologically oriented concept that grounded international law as science. Like the others, he accepted inductive and historical studies as part of legal science, but stressed the need to collect the facts they produced under a general theory about social specificity and development. He had a clear view about why this had not traditionally been so: "there has been all along a sad lack of consistent application to the subject of men of first-rate ability." This was now being corrected, however, with "the writings of Bluntschli, or Mancini, or Rolin Jaequemyns." Lorimer, *Institutes*, I, p. 83.

[380] Cf. Roeben, "Bluntschli," p. 233.

[381] John Westlake, "Relations between Public and Private International Law" (1865), in *Collected Papers*, p. 287.

the virtues and honorable conventions of his society when arguing about particular international institutions.[382] It is easy to see why the men of 1873 could not adopt a completely cultural view of the law, either. For that would have left them no platform from which to argue for their preferred reforms.

For example, in 1849, the English barrister Richard Wildman (1802–1881) had vehemently criticized the famous 1822 American case of *La Jeune Eugénie*, in which Justice Joseph Story had held the slave trade as "a violation of the law of nature, and therefore contrary to the law of nations." Instead he accepted Chief Justice Marshall's ruling in the *Antelope* to the effect that as the slave trade had not been decreed to be illegal by positive treaty, it could only be deemed lawful.[383] Most nations of the world, including in Africa, had, until recently, continued to pursue it and if the standards of international law were (as Wildman thought they should be) "usages, national acts and general assent," then there was no basis on which to decide otherwise than in favor of the master suing for his property and return a slave to him "with costs and damages."[384] The slave trade might be contrary to the law of nature, but that did not mean it was contrary to the law of nations. If law was indeed cultural, then there was no basis for applying the moral intuitions of European elites against practices in which European States had undoubtedly been long involved.

The lawyers of the *Institut* could not have accepted such a conclusion. For them, the legal status of slavery or the slave trade could not be inferred from cultural habits but directly from human nature: that the slave trade had been agreed as illegal by treaty was a measure of the moral conscience of European nations. But illegality could not be dependent on such agreement – even if there might not always exist positive guarantees to enforce it.[385] The new generation would not allow cultural arguments to encroach upon its liberal conscience. That conscience might sometimes express itself through a formal natural law argument, but more often it was simply taken for granted that the equal freedom of human beings was applicable everywhere and transgressed the limits of relativism justifying, for instance, Christian intervention (as

---

[382] For an early example, cf. John Westlake, "Commercial Blockade (1862)," in *Collected Papers*, pp. 312–361.

[383] For a recent discussion of these cases, cf. Alfred B. Rubin, *Ethics and Authority in International Law* (Cambridge University Press, 1997), pp. 101–108.

[384] Richard Wildman, *Institutes of International Law* (2 vols., London, Benning, 1849), I, pp. 9–14.   [385] Bluntschli, *Das moderne Völkerrecht*, pp. 21–23.

"The legal conscience of the civilized world"

in Greece in 1826–1828 or in the Principalities in 1877–1878) when the interests of humanity were being infringed by the excesses of a barbarous or despotic government.[386]

The successive rejection of rationalist, naturalist, and positivist positions, yet the partial retention of arguments from each, offered a *mélange* of tropes and styles, doctrines and understandings, that came together only through the fact that the Rolin *Kreis* used them as parts of its worldview and interpretative framework. The acceptability of this was received from the additional argument that their intuitions were an intrinsic part of a profession that saw itself as the "organ of the juridical *conscience* of the civilized world." To speak from such a position provided a remarkably flexible basis for legal argument. The evolutionary view justified differing treatment of de facto different situations. It allowed rationalist and utilitarian arguments when passion and excess seemed to be the enemy. Its rationalism was, however, an instrumentality of the liberal heart, and not an autonomous theoretical dogma. It was not the rationalism of Kaltenborn in the 1840s that aimed towards scientific "systems" but one that looked for political effect. It was the rationalism of uniquely "rational" liberal values.

The men of 1873 were, of course, a heterogeneous group. Their scientific positions differed, as sometimes did their political preferences. But they were united in their wish to be seen as neither rationalists nor moralists, nor mere describers of valid (positive) law. Centrists in this respect, too, I want to think of them as amateur sociologists, who thought that law emerged from human society in some spontaneous, even mystical way, and that it was the point of international law as science (instead of a taxonomy of rules or a diplomatic technique) to

---

[386] For Rolin, intervention in the Danubian principalities against Turkey was "un droit et un devoir imposé par l'humanité et par des exigences supérieures aux convenances individuelles de chaque Etat," "Chronique du droit international" (1878), X *RDI*, p. 19. Though Westlake allowed intervention formally only in the cases where general peace was threatened, he accepted that it would be idle to argue that in cases of religious or ethnic oppression neighboring States should look on quietly: "Laws . . . must not create or tolerate . . . situations which are beyond endurance . . . of the best human nature." This was the principle by which interventions in Turkey were to be tried, *International Law*, I, p. 320. Bluntschli justified forcible intervention against those committing particularly serious ("gemeingefährlich") violations of international law, including slavery, religious oppression, the suppression of independent peoples, and in case of break-up of constitutional order, *Das moderne Völkerrecht*, pp. 264–265, 269. For a general argument in favor of Christian intervention everywhere against despotism and barbarism, and for disinterested Christian trusteeship over "barbarians" cf. Hornung, "Civilisés et barbares," pp. 201–206 and 281–298.

canvass how this came about. Choosing a sociological language allowed them to avoid the standard criticisms that were voiced against abstract rationalists or utopian moralists on the one hand, or codifiers of diplomatic practices on the other. Simultaneously, it pushed the profession of international law into the forefront of progress as the "organ" of the popular consciousness in which it saw the law's ultimate foundation.

Yet, as sociologists, they were *amateurs*. They had no sociological theory beyond Bluntschli's crude and sometimes outright racist ponderings about an organic link between statehood and the human community. Lorimer fared no better with his "de facto principle," the division of humankind into civilized, barbarian, and savage communities and his awkward naturalism that divested the human will altogether from law-creating effects. What little generalization others employed was usually constituted by short discussions of the increasing interdependence – a word that Lieber claimed to have invented – that European modernity seemed to bring along. Whatever sociology was employed in actual situations or problem areas was received from introspection of their own cultural or moral sensibilities. Such introspective sociology was – within limits – an effective form of argument as it was accompanied by bits of evolutionary science. Unpleasant things could be opposed as being outdated, or barbarian, without resort to what otherwise might have appeared openly political positions. If evolution was indeed scientific truth then the fact that you were a half-civilized Oriental in a way that justified the continued maintenance of Western consular jurisdiction in your territory was merely stating a fact. Such argument appeared both normative and rational because scientific. Its truth seemed based on sociological evidence that was easily verifiable: the Oriental did, in fact, look different.

Such shifting between fact and evaluation was a constant feature in their writings, present already in the ambivalence concerning the translation of the expression *"conscience juridique"* in the Institute's Statute. While the German original of *Bewusstsein* had to do with cognition of facts, the French term was closer to the English "conscience," connoting a world of partly unselfconscious, emotional sensibility. It is precisely such shifting that makes it pointless to try to class these writers – any one of them – as "positivists" or "naturalists." They were always both at the same time – their arguments about valid positive law implying loaded assumptions about political worth, and their humanitarian sentiments always receiving expression in the practices of their own States or in some sociological understanding of the fact of European civilization.

"The legal conscience of the civilized world"

Society – *conscience* – organ – law; with all its flexibility, the inference proved shallow. The concept of *conscience* and the organ theory opened up the way to present aspects of the lawyers' private morality as public law but hardly served as serious sociology. It proved a useful ground of attack but quite useless as a quarter of defense. What after all was this *conscience* but a set of unanalyzed prejudices about good manners? What was its relationship to (political) will – and if it was "will," did it not take away the distinction between science and legislation? If, on the other hand, it referred to some non-will-related fact (whether natural or structual), then an explanation was owed of the striking coincidence that the superiority of Western culture was revealed precisely to that Western elite whose privileges it justified.

2

Sovereignty: a gift of civilization – international lawyers and imperialism, 1870–1914

Surveying the state of international law at the turn of the century, Enrico Catellani (1856–1945), Professor at the University of Padua and member of the *Institut de droit international* gave a gloomy view of the situation. If there was one tendency, he wrote, that was evident from the first moments of the new century, it was the increasing use of force in the determination of the fate of peoples.[1] The law was moving away from the mid-nineteenth-century ideals of justice and equality. No doubt, there had been many developments in a positive direction: the increase and technical improvement of treaty law and private international law, progress in arbitration and the emergence of functional international co-operation.[2] These developments were, however, overweighed by negative ones. No real international society had come to existence beyond Europe and the fundamental rights of peoples or States were no better protected than a century before. Europeans still acted from a position of superiority towards others: capitulation regimes, consular jurisdiction, and brutal colonial wars had become banal aspects of the international everyday. Advancing civilization oppressed and impoverished indigenous populations to the point of extinction – a fact accepted by imperial powers as an inevitable consequence of modernity. Even in Europe, powerful States had set up a permanent reign of control over the continent so that smaller powers enjoyed less autonomy than ever.[3] All in all, Catellani exclaimed, the nineteenth century had closed with imperial domination, methodological enslavement of populations, and war.

The particularly worrisome feature of this was, he then pointed out,

---

[1] Enrico Catellani, "Le droit international au commencement du XXe siècle" (1901), VIII *RGDIP*, p. 585.   [2] Catellani, "Le droit international," pp. 386–400.
[3] Catellani, "Le droit international," pp. 400–408.

Sovereignty: a gift of civilization

that instead of being hidden behind hypocritical justifications such practices were openly advocated as consistent with new philosophical and scientific doctrines, especially sociology and evolutionism. Collectivist theories – such as the doctrine of the survival of the fittest – had become acceptable defenses to override individual rights. The historical school in Germany and Comtist sociology in France had taught that individuals were determined by their collectivities and that there were no universal principles, that laws and moralities were relative to particular periods and locations.[4] All of this was invoked by great powers to give war a new justification. Catellani ended his melancholy overview as follows: "if the international society must in the immediate future live and develop in accordance with the law of the struggle for life and the survival of the fittest, I myself wish that my country will not remain on the side of the weak and the incapable, destined for submission and disappearance."[5]

Ambivalent attitudes

International lawyers were confronted by imperialism at a time when the optimistic faith in the universal spread of civilized principles had entered a crisis.[6] But if Catellani and others were disappointed by European

---

[4] Catellani, "Le droit international," pp. 408–413.
[5] Catellani, "Le droit international," p. 586.
[6] Very little has been written on imperialism and international law. Not only does there seem to exist no full-length study of the matter, there is an almost complete silence on it. There is, for instance, no entry for "imperialism" in the *Max Planck Encyclopaedia of International Law*. Nor is the word "imperialism" carried in the indexes of major international law textbooks. With few exceptions, international lawyers have treated the subject as part of the history of territorial acquisition. The most comprehensive treatment is Jörg Fisch, *Die europäische Expansion und das Völkerrecht* (Stuttgart, Steiner, 1984). Perhaps there is a sense that "imperialism" is too much a politically loaded word, "no word for scholars." The equation works both ways: in the voluminous amount of historical publication on European imperialism, international law is practically absent – with the exception of references to effective occupation as the basis for title in non-European territory (with particular reference to the Act of Berlin of 1885). "Imperialism" always appears as a political, economic, military, social, or cultural "fact," a series of incidents or relationships instead of a normative category. It was first used in the 1850s and 1860s as a (British) characterization of French policies conducted under Napoleon III. Thereafter, it has been linked to the expansive foreign policies of individual countries more generally, usually with a tint of criticism, perhaps by reference to Lenin's famous thesis about the highest stage of capitalism. One general definition of imperialism reads: "the process by which either formal empires or significant influence and control short of direct rule – 'informal' empires – came into being and then grew." Andrew Porter, *European Imperialism 1860–1914* (Basingstoke,

behavior in the colonies, the ground from which they argued for humane treatment of the natives was an outdated concept of natural law that had little intellectual credibility even in their own professional milieu. Most of them agreed with Theodor Woolsey (1801–1889), President of Yale and the author of a leading American textbook of the period, that lawyers making use of natural principles were in fact spinning the web of a system out of their own brains as if they were legislators of the world.[7] In their nostalgic references to a universal natural law they were ignoring the extent to which even the *philosophes* had wondered about the appropriateness of applying identical precepts for the administration of all societies. The ambivalence about the powers of natural reason was plainly evident in Montesquieu whose *Esprit des lois* distinguished between "laws in general" that were based on human reason and thus applicable to all nations and laws in particular: "that should be in relation to the nature and principle of each government . . . to the climate of each country, to the quality of its soil, to its situation and extent . . . to the religion of the inhabitants, to their inclinations, riches, numbers, commerce, manners and customs."[8] The view of law as reflection of society and culture and not as derivation from universal principles could not simply be unlearned. Even if most late nineteenth-century lawyers agreed that a world without some conception of universal, rational law would be unthinkable, they emphasized law's social and historical basis and struggled over complex formulas to fix the relationship between the two. Yet it was hard to accept that one's own position shared in such contextuality: where Savigny's historical explorations revealed that the German *Geist* resided in the rational formulas of Roman law, Maine contextualized the use of rational law by English and international jurists as a culturally specific adoption of analogies from the Romans. But though variations between European cultures might be satisfactorily accounted

---

Footnote 6 (*cont.*).

Macmillan, 1994), p. 2. Another definition draws a line between imperialism and colonialism: "Imperialism presupposes the will and the ability of an imperial center to *define* as imperial its own national interests and enforce them worldwide in the anarchy of the international system. Imperialism implies not only *colonial* politics but *international* politics for which colonies are not just ends in themselves, but also pawns in global power games." Jürgen Osterhammel, *Colonialism. A Theoretical Overview* (trans. from German S. L. Frisch, Princeton, Wiener, 1997), p. 21. In this chapter, imperialism appears as an insistence on the extension of formal European sovereignty in the colonies.

[7] T. D. Woolsey, *Introduction to the Study of International Law* (5th edn., London, Sampson, 1879), p. 13.

[8] Baron de Montesquieu, *The Spirit of the Laws*, trans. T. Nugent, introduction F. Neumann (New York and London, Hafner & Collier, 1949 [1748]), p. 6.

for by reference to history and context, it seemed nonetheless impossible not to believe that what was common to Europeans encapsulated some kind of a non-contextual, objective form of experience, civilization *tout court*.

Penetrating deeper into the colonies – Africa in particular – Europeans came into contact with societies and cultural forms that seemed to share little of what they felt was the common core of their civilized identity. How were they to think of such societies and Europe's relationship to them? In the eighteenth century, Europeans had often either dismissed primitive societies on account of their not partaking of the same kind of humanity as that enjoyed by the Europeans, or idealized them into Noble Savages, representatives of a Golden Age lost to Europe.[9] Neither attitude had much by way of reasoned background and they often emerged in connection with stories intended to make a political point about present Europe rather than to provide a basis for thinking about foreign cultures. In the course of the first half of the nineteenth century, such attitudes gave way to more historicized explanations such as the Comparative Method that viewed primitive peoples as earlier stages of human development in an overall law-like frame of progressive history.[10] By the 1870s the assumption of human development proceeding by stages from the primitive to the civilized had come to form the bedrock of social anthropology and evolutionary sociology that provided much of the conceptual background for cultivated European reflection about what Europeans often sweepingly termed the Orient.[11]

---

[9] Cf. e.g. Jean-Jacques Rousseau, *A Discourse on Inequality*, trans. with introduction by M. Cranston (London, Penguin, 1984 [1755]), citing travellers' stories about "the strength and vigour of men in barbarous and savage nations," pp. 143–145 and *passim*. For comment, cf. J. W. Burrow, *Evolution and Society. A Study in Victorian Social Theory* (Cambridge University Press, 1966), pp. 4–6, 75–76. On the two modes of thinking about the primitive and of the Noble Savage idea as a strategy to undermine the idea of nobility itself, cf. also Hayden White, *Tropics of Discourse. Essays in Cultural Criticism* (Baltimore and London, Johns Hopkins University Press, 1985 [1978]), pp. 183–196. [10] Burrow, *Evolution and Society*, pp. 11–14, 78–82.

[11] Of particular importance were E. B. Tylor, *Primitive Culture: Researches into the Mythology, Philosophy, Religion, Language, Custom, and Art* (7th edn., New York, Brentano, 1924 [1871]) and *Primitive Culture* (2 vols., New York, Harper, 1958). The idea of a universal history as "the realization of a hidden plan of nature to bring about an internally – and for this purpose also externally – perfect political constitution" is most influentially presented in Immanuel Kant, "Idea for a Universal History with a Cosmopolitan Purpose," in *Political Writings*, Hans Reiss, trans. H. B. Nisbet (Cambridge University Press, 1991), pp. 41–53. The quote is from Kant's *Eighth Proposition*, p. 50.

Like much nineteenth-century social reflection, international law imagined itself in terms of progressive, or pedigree history. It posited an early origin – usually somewhere in Western Antiquity, perhaps the universalism of Stoic thought – and then described itself in terms of how the promise of that origin had been preserved or enhanced by later developments, and how the present could be seen as its highest (though always incomplete) stage of flourishing.[12] A random example of how pedigree history worked can be gleaned in the popular German textbook by Franz von Liszt (1851–1919), for whom international law was a historical–contextual aspect of European culture and not a set of immutable, God-given principles. Although legal relations between communities had existed since Greek and Roman Antiquity, the origin of a systemic law lay in the Westphalian treaties. It was a necessary precondition of international law, he wrote, that there exist independent States of approximately equal power that owing to common culture and interests engage in frequent contacts on a secular basis. From that point he traced international legal history through five subsequent periods in which the original idea of a universal law between formally equal communities was gradually strengthened through increasingly complicated legal arrangements – with the last (and highest) period coinciding with the Hague Conferences and forceful European penetration in Africa, Asia and the Far East.[13]

This type of history aimed at more than a neutral description of the flow of past events into the present.[14] Its point was to justify present European expansion by making it appear as the fulfillment of the universalist promise in the origin.[15] In the case of Liszt and others, the positive substance of this development was captured in the concept of "civilization" that now took the place of natural law as the universal standard of evaluation and with the force of apparent natural necessity called for European expansion. Law, wrote Bluntschli's successor in Heidelberg, August von Bulmerincq (1822–1890), was the guardian of

---

[12] For a good description of "pedigree history," cf. Raymond Geuss, *Morality, Culture and History. Essays on German Philosophy* (Cambridge University Press, 1999), pp. 1–3.

[13] Franz von Liszt, *Das Völkerrecht. Systematisch dargestellt* (5th edn., Berlin, Häring, 1907), pp. 15–38. A brief standard history that specifically identifies the Stoics as the initiators of a general human law is Frantz Despagnet, *Cours de droit international public* (2nd edn., Paris, Larose, 1889), pp. 5–26.

[14] Cf. also Burrow, *Evolution and Society*, pp. 93–100.

[15] This view is expressly argued in Joseph Hornung, "Quelques vues sur la preuve en histoire, comparée avec la preuve judiciaire, sur les documents de l'histoire contemporain et sur l'importance historique de l'actualité" (1884), XVI *RDI*, pp. 71–83.

civilization. As shadows escape the light, law and civilization constantly reduced the space left for their antitheses: politics and barbarism.[16] As we have seen in chapter 1, much of what the lawyers behind the *Institut de droit international* had to say about the conditions of international society related to the degrees of civilization possessed by its members. That "civilization" was not defined beyond impressionistic characterizations was an important aspect of its value. It was not part of some rigid classification but a shorthand for the qualities that international lawyers valued in their own societies, playing upon its opposites: the uncivilized, barbarian, and the savage. This provided a language for attitudes about social difference and for constructing one's own identity through what the historian Hayden White has called "ostensive self-definition by negation" – a reflex action pointing towards the practices of others and affirming that whatever we as Europeans are, at least we are not *like that*.[17]

Although there is no *necessary* relationship between the Comparative Method, pedigree history, and racism, on the one hand, and expansion, on the other, for men of liberal conscience such equation seems practically inevitable. In Bluntschli, the narrative about progress as civilization came together with racial speculation in a striking way. In an article written in 1857 to the German *Staatswörterbuch*, he observed that of all the races the highest were the Aryan and the Semitic, the former a race of rationalism and philosophy, the latter a race of emotion and religion. In particular, he opined, "All higher science is of Aryan origin."[18] The superiority of the Aryan races lay in the way they emphasized the dignity and honor of the human being. The Negro, for example, allowed his master to enslave him, even threw himself on the ground before his master, and "lifted the master's foot himself on his head." The Aryan would never suffer such. The Aryan would also stress the honor of women – expressed in monogamy – and the honor of the family – expressed in the fact that although the man was the head of the household, his power over family members was not unlimited. The right of property and especially of the ownership of land were distinctly Aryan institutions, designed to give human beings "eine feste Heimat."[19]

Above all, the Aryans were State people, Bluntschli wrote, having

---

[16] A. Bulmerincq, "La politique et le droit dans la vie des états" (1877), IX *RDI*, p. 364.
[17] White, *Tropics of Discourse*, pp. 151–152.
[18] J. C. Bluntschli, "Arische Völker und arische Rechte," in *Gesammelte kleine Schiften* (2 vols., Nördlingen, Beck, 1879), I, p. 66.
[19] Bluntschli, "Arische Völker," pp. 74–77, 78.

already organized in political societies in ancient India. This progressive idea had been realized in Europe and was apparent in Europe's world-dominance. Even if lower races sometimes succeeded in organizing themselves into States, these were theocracies lacking a balanced relationship between State and religion.[20] Only Aryan States had realized human rights while in most non-Aryan communities the masses were treated as slaves or lived in wild independence. Only Aryan states had developed into rule-of-law States in which the King "liebt das Licht und ist ein Rechtskönig."[21] The Aryans had a natural drive for progress (*Vervollkommnung*): from the earliest days they had organized their political lives for the attainment of common purposes instead of waiting for divine intervention. No race could compete with them in the theory of the State which among Aryans had come to the greatest "elevation and clarity of ideas" in the Germanic people.[22] And there was a *Missionsbewusstsein*: the Aryans were to educate other races in political theory and statehood so as to fulfill their great historical assignment: "to develop and complete the domination of the world which already lies in the hands of the Aryan peoples in a consciously humanistic and noble way so as to teach civilization for the whole mankind."[23]

Bluntschli's ideas may have been expressed in a language that many of his colleagues might have found distasteful – and he himself later avoided it. Though Lorimer went even further in his antisemitism, and in his indictment of "Mohammedism," his arguments were dressed in a more conventionally Darwinistic garb.[24] Yet there is no reason to assume that the properties which they valued in "Aryan races" would not have been valued by *Institut* members generally. Generalizations about the lack of a proper concept of the State in the Orient, about the fatalism or stagnation of non-European societies – such as Maine's casual division of societies into progressive and stationary ones – were a part of the educated common sense of the period that portrayed the East as voiceless, feminine, irrational, despotic, and backward and the West as rational, male, democratic, and forward-looking.[25] Despite all the talk about Turkey's

---

[20] This fact was cited against Turkey in Bluntschli, "Le Congrès de Berlin et sa portée au point de vue de droit international" (1879), XI *RDI*, pp. 420–430.

[21] Bluntschli, "Arische Völker," pp. 82, 86.   [22] Bluntschli, "Arische Völker," p. 89.

[23] Bluntschli, "Arische Völker," p. 90.

[24] James Lorimer, "La doctrine de la reconnaissance. Fondement du droit international" (1884), XVI *RDI*, pp. 333–359.

[25] Cf. Edward Saïd, *Orientalism. Western Conceptions of the Orient* (Harmondsworth, Penguin, 1995 [1978]), pp. 57–73 and comment in Bart Moore-Gilbert, *Postcolonial Theory. Context, Practices, Politics* (London, Verso, 1997), pp. 35–40.

Sovereignty: a gift of civilization

admission into the European community of nations in 1856, little had changed in terms of attitudes. Lorimer had nothing but scorn for those who forecast Turkey's rapid integration into the community of civilized nations: the Turks probably did not even belong to the progressive races![26] Even the Swiss critic of Western imperialism and member of the *Institut*, Joseph Hornung (1822–1884), held the Orient to be profoundly decadent and worth study only insofar as it had participated in the origin of civilization, a kind of living souvenir of the West's pre-history.[27]

This is not to say that international lawyers would have developed a fully homogeneous colonial discourse. There were significant variations of tone and emphasis in the way they treated European expansion, some of which reflected national backgrounds, some political leanings or personal idiosyncrasies. Many had preserved Rousseau's ambivalence about the ethical value of this development and spoke about colonization, at least of colonization by others, through a complicated language of humanitarian regret and historical inevitability. The ambivalence was particularly evident in the French lawyers, perhaps in part as a reflection of the persistence of the discourse of the *philosophes* in French culture generally and a strong sense of a *mission civilisatrice* based on republican ideals.[28] Louis Renault (1843–1918), for example, the future doyen of the French international law community, writing in 1879, repeated Montesquieu's distinction between a natural law (that was largely negative, prohibiting the causing of harm to others) and a cultural law, based on the progress of civilization, the marvelous discoveries of modern science, and common traditions. Yet it was the former that controlled what could be achieved by the latter: too often, he wrote, the Europeans had misused their power against the "so-called barbarians" and waged unjust wars against them, violating the most elementary rules of international law.[29] Such a general criticism in a textbook hardly counted as

---

[26] Lorimer, "La doctrine de la reconnaissance," pp. 342–343.

[27] Joseph Hornung, "Civilisés et barbares," (1884), XVI *RDI*, p. 79.

[28] Alice Conklin defines the French civilizing ideal in terms of "mastery" – not only of others but of oneself, nature and society: "the French believed that they had triumphed over geography, climate and disease to create new internal and external markets, and because they before all other nations had overcome oppression and superstition to form a democratic and rational government." The non-European world lacked precisely these qualities: "the crucial ability to master – that they were just as obviously barbarians, in need of civilizing." Alice L. Conklin, *A Mission to Civilize. The Republican Idea of Empire in France and West Africa 1895–1930* (Stanford University Press, 1997), p. 6.

[29] Louis Renault, *Introduction à l'étude de droit international*, in *L'oeuvre internationale de Louis Renault* (Paris, Editions internationales, 1932 [1879]), pp. 11–12, 17.

serious resistance to colonization, however. Renault had nothing but sympathy for French consular jurisdiction in Turkey and China.[30]

A more critical full-length survey of European colonization was published in Paris a decade later by Charles Salomon (1862–1936) who was genuinely ironical about the civilizing mission: "No word is more vague and has permitted the commission of more crimes than that of civilization."[31] With the exception of Vitoria and Las Casas, no attention had been paid to indigenous rights. Salomon condemned "the deplorable excesses that tarnished the history of Spanish colonisation."[32] Although Salomon admired the tolerant spirit in France in the seventeenth century and noted a marked improvement in the way the natives now were treated by the English – especially by the Quakers – he still held colonization as violent and unjust for the natives: "the history of all colonies begins with violence, injustice and shedding of blood: the result is everywhere the same; the disappearance of the native races (des races sauvages) coming into contact with civilized races."[33] Although the requirement of effective occupation did mean an improvement in the law, the result of the 1884–1885 Berlin Conference had made little practical difference. "It cannot be said that the history of colonization during the past five years would present a morally more adequate image than that of the past century." "[34] Salomon read the contemporary language of civilization as pure hypocrisy that sought only the advancement of commerce.[35] To be civilized, he thought, gave no basis for more extensive rights but in fact imposed duties: lack of civilization was a problem, not a vice. But though he made detailed references to past and contemporary European excesses, and spoke in favor of treating indigenous communities in a humane way, and sometimes from a basis of equality, Salomon's book hardly constituted an attack on colonialism itself. Its problems were attributed to external causes: egoism, greed, and vanity. Gaston Jèze (1869–1953), too, who achieved moderate fame in the 1930s as the legal adviser of the Ethiopian Negus and as target of right-wing protests in Paris, in 1896 wrote critically about the way colonization had been left for adventurers and profit-seeking private companies.[36] He joined Salomon in condemning the destruction of

---

[30] Renault, *Introduction*, p. 16n.1.
[31] Ch. Salomon, *L'occupation des territoires sans maître. Etude de droit international* (Paris, Giard, 1889), p. 195.   [32] Salomon, *L'occupation*, p. 64. Cf. also p. 193.
[33] Salomon, *L'occupation*, p. 68.   [34] Salomon, *L'occupation*, pp. 83–84.
[35] Salomon, *L'occupation*, p. 197.
[36] Gaston Jèze, *Etude théorique et pratique sur l'occupation comme mode d'acquérir les territoires en droit international* (Paris, Giard & Brière, 1896).

native communities during the early history of European expansion.[37] Likewise, Edouard Engelhardt (1828–1916), Jules Ferry's assistant and one of the French delegates at the Berlin Conference,[38] published a series of articles on the proper notion of the protectorate, waging a brief battle within the *Institut* in order to insist that territorial acquisition be connected with administrative duties.[39] Salomon, Jèze, and Engelhardt each advocated the formal extension of European sovereignty into colonial territory as the only means to check the excesses of purely commercial colonization. This was not a radical point by Frenchmen, however, as French colonization had always been conducted as official State policy, often through military conquest. French lawyers were as enthusiastic about the colonial venture as any, and never failed to mention how the native treaties concluded by the French–Italian adventurer Pierre Savorgnan de Brazza (1852–1905) in the French Congo in 1880 had been negotiated in an atmosphere of friendly brotherhood with local chiefs in contrast to the aggressive manipulations of the British–American H. M. Stanley (1841–1904) at the service of the King of the Belgians or the German Carl Peters (1856–1918) acting on his own in East Africa.[40]

Humanitarian sentiments and regret about European brutality were of course not simply a preserve of the French. A representative mixture of historical and racial generalization, ambivalence about progress and popular humanitarianism can be gleaned from a speech by Lord Russell (1832–1900), speaking as an Englishman to the American Bar Association in 1896. Affirming the progressive nature of human history, he added "progressive, let us hope, to a higher, a purer, a more unselfish ethical standard."[41] He had no doubt that as with religion, countless crimes had been committed in the name of civilization in the course of European expansion. "Probably it was inevitable that the weaker races should, in the end, succumb, but have we always treated them with consideration and with justice?" Having rhetorically asked his audience "What indeed is true civilization?," he let himself define it by an unambiguously Victorian set of virtues:

---

[37] Salomon, *L'occupation*, pp. 29–81; Jèze, *Etude théorique*, pp. 90–103.
[38] Jules Ferry (1832–1893) was a liberal politician, minister of foreign affairs and an advocate of French colonialism in Africa and the Far East.
[39] Many of these articles are collected in Edouard Engelhardt, *Les protectorats. Anciens et modernes. Etude historique et juridique* (Paris, Pedone, 1896).
[40] Cf. e.g. Jèze, *Etude théorique*, pp. 152–160.
[41] Lord Russell of Killowen, "International Law" (1896), XLVIII *Law Quarterly Review*, pp. 315, 317.

Civilization is not a veneer; it must penetrate the very heart and core of societies of men. Its true signs are thought for the poor and suffering, chivalrous regard and respect for woman, the frank recognition of human brotherhood irrespective of race or colour or nation or religion, the narrowing of the domain of mere force as a governing factor in the world, the love of ordered freedom, abhorrence of what is mean and cruel and vile, ceaseless devotion to the claims of justice.[42]

It is a measure of the complex *innerlichkeit* of a Victorian lawyer and nobleman that he could dwell on such attributes after having in the early part of his lecture decisively dismissed natural law and morality as stable bases for international law. His "civilization" consisted of a set of psychological dispositions that appeared as simple "facts" imbedded in a reassuringly progressive historical frame. Although progress required some tragic sacrifices, it was still possible to perceive its benefits in the opposition between Western humanitarian sensitivity and Oriental barbarism: did not recent reports tell that Menelik, the victorious Emperor of Abyssinia, had ordered the cutting off of the right hands and feet of 500 Italian prisoners? Here finally there was an unambiguous measure of progress. Though similar acts had been quite common in Europe some time ago, today the civilized world had learned to react to them with horror.[43]

In general, however, British lawyers such as Twiss, Westlake, and Hall had a much more matter-of-fact view of colonization than their French colleagues. Sir Travers Twiss, for instance, who acted as legal counsel to King Léopold in the early 1880s, argued against the majority view that private associations could not receive right of dominion in the colonies. On the contrary, citing the cases of Maryland and Liberia – and anticipating what the Congo might in his view become – he described their activities in predominantly philanthropic terms. Quoting Vattel and Chief Justice Marshall approvingly, he also limited indigenous territorial rights by reference to the extent they had come to be effectively used.[44] Westlake and Hall absented public law completely from the relations of protecting and protected communities: the only international law duties owed by the colonizer were towards other colonizers. Nor did colonization bring any determinate administrative duties. The situation in different protected territories differed so radically that the colonizing State "must be left to judge how far it can go at a given time, and through what form of organisation it is best to work."[45]

---

[42] Russell, "International Law," p. 335. [43] Russell, "International Law," pp. 325–326.
[44] Travers Twiss, *The Law of Nations Considered as Independent Political Communities* (2 vols., 2nd edn., Oxford, Clarendon, 1884), I, pp. x–xvi and 217–224.
[45] W. E. Hall, *A Treatise on International Law* (4th edn., Oxford, Clarendon, 1895), pp. 132, 133.

Sovereignty: a gift of civilization

While German lawyers started to write about colonialism only after Bismarck's famous *volte-face* in 1884, their treatment of it drew more upon the tradition of national public law than upon international law: the focus of German interest lay in how the German *Schützgebiete* should be seen from the perspective of the imperial constitution.[46] Early commentators such as Paul Heilborn (1861–1932), Karl Heimburger (1859–1912), or Friedrich Geffcken (1830–1896) showed little awareness of the moral ambivalence of the civilizing mission and concentrated their energy on clarifying the meaning and limits of concepts such as "protectorate" or "territorial sovereignty" (*Gebietshoheit*) or defending Germany's right as a latecomer to the imperial game that would correspond to its role as a Great Power.[47] They understood colonization as a perfectly natural drive; just as ownership was a projection of the owner's person in the material world, colonial possession was an aspect of the healthy State's identity and self-respect. One early German study maintained that international law held the State's quest for territory a justified expression of its life-energy ("eine berechtigte Äusserung seine Lebensenergie"), and protected this as long as it did not conflict with the legal spheres of other (European) States.[48]

But despite occasional disagreement about particular geographical disputes or doctrinal matters such as the conditions of effective occupation, the effect of native treaties or the legal position of colonial companies, international lawyers shared a sense of the inevitability of the modernizing process. Even Hornung dressed his criticism of European behavior in the colonies in the form of an appeal to charity and concern for the weak and the uneducated.[49] International lawyers were not insensitive to the humanitarian problems that accompanied colonialism. They all admired the Spanish scholastics of the sixteenth century.[50] They saw it as their role to minimize such problems through the export of rational, public law-based administrative structures to manage the colonial encounter, to include sovereignty among the benefits civilization would

---

[46] Cf. Carl Von Stengel, "La constitution et l'administration des colonies allemandes" (1895), III *Revue de droit public et de la science politique en France et à l'étranger*, pp. 275–292.
[47] Paul Heilborn, *Das völkerrechtliche Protektorat* (Berlin, Springer, 1891); Karl Heimburger, *Der Erwerb der Gebietshoheit* (Karlsruhe, Braun, 1888).
[48] Heimburger, *Erwerb*, p. 45. Likewise, F. H. Geffcken, "L'allemagne et la question coloniale" (1885), XVII *RDI*, p. 114.
[49] Hornung, "Civilisés et barbares" (1886), XVIII *RDI*, p. 188.
[50] This was hardly a radical position, as even the Spanish government had officially adopted the view of Las Casas against that of Sepulvéda. V. G. Kiernan, *Imperialism and Its Contradictions*, ed. and introduction by Harvey J. Kaye (New York and London, Routledge, 1995), p. 102.

bring. If they also thereby legitimized some of the worst injustices in the history of modernity, they did this unwittingly, and it is a moot question whether their absence from the scene – marginal as they always were – would have provided the Age of Empire with any better credentials.

Informal empire 1815–1870: *hic sunt leones*

After the Napoleonic wars, European expansion took place with little sense of a conscious process. Europeans had expressed some systematic interest in the exploration of non-European spaces in the eighteenth century but the upheavals of century's end made the society turn inwards. Great Power diplomacy sought to reconstruct the European equilibrium and with the exception of the Eastern Question, the European Concert focused until 1884 exclusively on European affairs.

In some ways, official Europe was losing ground. The independence of Spanish America (1822) and the secession of Brazil from Portugal brought the decay of two empires to a conclusion. French energies were absorbed by three revolutions. The seizure of Algeria in 1830 as part of the restaurationist policy of Charles X had led France into an endless and unpopular guerrilla war. The French Parliament had no enthusiasm for colonial ventures and when the Empire fell in 1870, many felt that imperial ambition was partly to blame.[51] Likewise, the "great mass of German bourgeoisie wanted no part in colonial adventure."[52] German attention was focused on the continent, on unification as well as on constitutional and social conflict at home. In the 1870s Bismarck still rejected proposals by the German *Kolonialverein* to set up colonies. He thought them expensive and was against the idea of having to request funds from the *Reichstag* in a way that might have strengthened the latter's hand against the Chancellor.[53] Italy, too, was busy getting united. Russia moved back and forth in the east and Austria was preoccupied in the Balkans.

European populations had little interest in colonies. Attention was directed at social upheaval at home and at the advantages and problems of industrialization. Questions relating to non-European regions were

---

[51] James J. Cooke, *New French Imperialism 1880–1910: The Third Republic and Colonial Expansion* (Newton Abbot, Archon, 1973), pp. 13–14.
[52] L. H. Gann, and Peter Duignan, *The Burden of Empire. An Appraisal of Western Colonialism in Africa South of the Sahara* (Stanford University Press, 1971), p. 187.
[53] Cf. e.g. Henri Wesseling, *Le partage de l'Afrique 1880–1914*, traduit du néerlandais par Patrick Grilli (Paris, Denoël, 1996), pp. 152–154.

Sovereignty: a gift of civilization

the preserve of humanitarians and Christian missionaries. The State limited itself to the adoption of legal provisions under which private trade and economic development, education and technological regeneration might be undertaken through commercial or humanitarian societies.[54] The establishment of Sierra Leone (1791) and Liberia (1822 and 1847) were understood as mainly private, humanitarian ventures, only slightly colored by economic motives.[55] The main interest in Africa was not colonization but the prevention of the slave trade, organized on the basis of a Declaration from Vienna in 1815 and through bilateral treaties that granted Britain the privilege of patrolling the African coasts in search of vessels suspected of slaving.

The years 1815–1870 constituted the heyday of British predominance overseas. But in Britain, too, successive Prime Ministers from Castlereagh onwards opposed the formalization of British rule. As Macaulay pointed out in 1833: "To trade with civilized men is infinitely more profitable than to govern savages."[56] Britain's was an "empire of free trade," maintained by unchallenged naval supremacy and the absence of serious industrial or diplomatic competition from potential European rivals.[57] Britain's advocacy of free trade was firmly grounded in self-interest. Not without justification, colonization was understood to be contrary to free trade and colonies were regarded as an economic burden.[58] In 1846, British colonial defense cost the value of half of the total colonial trade.[59]

[54] Ronald Hyam, *Britain's Imperial Century 1815–1914. A Study of Empire and Expansion* (London, Macmillan, 1976), pp. 108–116.
[55] Winfried Baumgart, *Imperialism; The Idea and Reality of British and French Colonial Expansion 1880–1914* (Oxford University Press, 1982), pp. 11–13; Hyam, *Britain's Imperial Century*, pp. 91–97.
[56] Quoted in Hyam, *Britain's Imperial Century*, pp. 106, 105–108.
[57] Cf. generally Ronald Robinson and John Gallagher, with Alice Denny, *Africa and the Victorians. The Official Mind of Imperialism* (2nd edn., London, Macmillan, 1981). This did not mean that there would have been no advances in official empire at the time. Between 1839 and 1851, for instance, Britain obtained as formal colonies New Zealand, the Gold Coast, Natal, Punjab, Sindh, and Hong Kong. Cf. Hyam, *Britain's Imperial Century*, pp. 8–15, 86–90, 120–121.
[58] Cf. e.g. Gann and Duignan, *The Burden of Empire*, pp. 12–14, 18–19. As late as 1876, the capitalist and humanitarian William Mackinnon aimed to conclude a treaty with the Sultan of Zanzibar that would have given Mackinnon's company sovereign rights over the area between the East African coast and the Great Lakes. Salisbury intervened out of fear of formal engagements that this might have entailed. Five years later still, Gladstone politely refused the Sultan's request for the establishment of a British Protectorate over this strategically placed island. Cf. Wesseling, *Le partage de l'Afrique*, pp. 189–190.
[59] David Newsome, *The Victorian World Picture* (London, Fontana, 1997), p. 131.

Instead, recourse was had to strategies of informal influence. The largest piece of the Empire, India, had been ruled by the British East India Company since 1600 and its charter was not taken under direct administration until after the Indian mutiny of 1857.[60] Predominance in China was based on treaties (of Nanking, 1842 and Tientsin, 1858) that guaranteed the entry of goods through and extraterritorial rights in determined treaty ports, limiting the need for imperial intervention to "gingering up" operations through gunboat diplomacy.[61] In West Africa and elsewhere, the occasional show of limited military or naval strength was normally sufficient to protect British trade and missionaries.[62] White settlement colonies (Australia, Canada, New Zealand, Cape Colony) were granted responsible government in an effort to minimize the British taxpayers' burden. During 1815–1870 the slogan "trade, not rule" formed the core of British overseas policy.[63]

The lawyers 1815–1870

At this time, as we have seen in chapter 1, no profession of international law existed. Von Martens and Klüber had written for the education of diplomats and men of public affairs. Their outlook reflected the preoccupations of the powers engaged in the reconstruction of European States–society and they had little to say about colonial expansion. Their *Droit public de l'Europe* was, however, intended less as an instrument of exclusion than of integration – however much the idea of a specifically European political or cultural realm was premised upon a projected non-European otherness. They were of course not the only lawyers with

---

[60] Cf. generally, John Keay, *The Honourable Company. A History of the English East India Company* (London, Harper-Collins, 1991).
[61] Cf. Hyam, *Britain's Imperial Century*, pp. 123–133, Kiernan, *Imperialism and Its Contradictions*, pp. 152–187; Gerrit W. Gong, *The Standard of "Civilization" in International Society* (Oxford, Clarendon, 1984), pp. 130–153; and generally Frances Wood, *No Dogs and Not Many Chinese. Treaty Port Life in China 1843–1943* (London, Murray, 1998).
[62] In 1860–1870 British traders sought to open the Niger especially for palm oil trade: for this purpose, they received protection by the navy and there was occasional stiff fighting to protect trade, Gann and Duignan, *The Burden of Empire*, p. 173. On British gunboat diplomacy in 1815–1870, cf. Hyam, *Britain's Imperial Century*, pp. 15–21.
[63] Conventional histories of the British Empire depict a clear break between an essentially anti-imperial mid-Victorian era and the "new imperialism" of the last two decades of the century. This break has been questioned by the Robinson–Gallagher thesis (Robinson and Gallagher, 1981) about the "imperialism of free trade" of the early period: instead of "trade, not rule," it was "trade if possible, otherwise rule." In any case, the British possessions did grow steadily, even during the early period of informal empire in 1815–1870.

Sovereignty: a gift of civilization

a program of cultural integration. Friedrich Saalfeld (1785–1834), for instance, writing in 1833, pointed out that the uniform culture of and reciprocal relations between Christian nations had created a consensus over central international law principles.[64] When Saalfeld wrote that international law was part of public law, he thereby based it firmly on Western jurisprudential categories: to know international law was to know it as "part of" public law and European diplomacy.[65] Both von Martens and Klüber opened their discussion of the law by a classification or even an enumeration of European States. The law's substance then followed in terms of the absolute and relative rights of those States and the sum total of their (peaceful and hostile) relationships. Their texts became portraits of European political society as it stood in 1815.

On the other hand, however, von Martens and Klüber both felt they needed to say something of the world beyond Europe. Both were educated in the *Aufklärungsideale* of the eighteenth century and like Montesquieu, Kant, or Rayneval held that natural law provided for the equal worth of individuals, irrespective of race or religion. They thus espoused quite a liberal conception of the right of native ownership. Klüber, for instance, pointed out that: "no nation is authorized, whatever its qualities, including a higher level of culture, to divest another nation of its property, not even savages or nomads."[66] And von Martens agreed:

> The law of property being the same for everybody, independently of their religion or habits, natural law does not authorise Christian peoples to appropriate areas that are already occupied by savages against their wishes, even if practice offers only too many examples of such usurpations.[67]

Such a well-entrenched right of property did not, of course, position native communities as equal to European States. As later lawyers

---

[64] This is visible not only in regard to the treaties and customs of European nations – that was evident – but also in how secondary sources (the nature of the thing, tacit agreement and analogy) presuppose a cultural knowledge of the sphere in which it is to be applied. Friedrich Saalfeld, *Handbuch des positiven Völkerrechts* (Tübingen, Ostander, 1833), pp. 4–5.   [65] Saalfeld, *Handbuch*, p. 5.
[66] J. L. Klüber, *Droit des gens moderne de l'Europe* (Stuttgart, J. G. Cotta, 1819), p. 194.
[67] G. F. de Martens, *Précis du droit des gens moderne de l'Europe, précédé d'une Introduction et complété par l'exposition des doctrines des publicistes contemporains et suivi d'une Bibliographie raisonnée du droit des gens par M. Ch. Vergé* (2 vols., 2nd French edn., Paris, Guillaumin, 1864), 1, pp. 128–129 § 36 (footnotes omitted). However, in an appendix to the first edition as well as in his *Recueil des traités*, von Martens included treaties with North American Indians "as well as treaties with rulers of the Barbary States, the Philippines . . . Persia, China and Ceylon," Dorothy V. Jones, *License for Empire; Colonialism by Treaty in Early America* (University of Chicago Press, 1982), p. 6 and generally on treaty relations with non-Europeans, pp. 5–18.

routinely remarked, the property rights of indigenous populations that were taken from the Roman concept of occupation fell short of public law *imperium*, or of sovereignty, and to invoke them against European sovereigns was to confuse categories that were to be held distinct.[68] Klüber and von Martens would probably have agreed. At any rate, they took no exception to the famous construction of British title to American territory by the argument crystallized in Chief Justice Marshall's 1823 decision that allowed the Indians a right of occupancy but gave the Federal Government as possessor of sovereignty the power to extinguish it.[69] On the other hand, they were not dealing with European public law claims over vast stretches of territory. When they wrote, the Orient was still principally an object of commerce, travel, and proselytizing. The colonial encounter took place between individual natives or native tribes on the one side and private individuals, missionaries, humanitarian associations, and trade companies on the other. Beyond appealing to humane behavior on both sides, there was no need to envisage norms governing the formal relations between European and non-European communities, even less of jurisdictional boundaries between European States.

At the same time, lawyers were digesting the lesson of the historical school, and emphasized the cultural limits of European diplomatic law. Here is the definition of international law given by Henry Wheaton (1785–1848), an attorney with the United States Supreme Court and a diplomat posted in Europe, whose *Elements of International Law* became one of the most widely used treatises by the middle of the century: "The ordinary *jus gentium* is only a particular law, applicable to a distinct set or family of nations, varying at different times with the change of religion, manner, government, and other institutions, among every class of nations."[70] For Wheaton – who knew his Savigny well – European positive law was a compilation of the "customs, usages, and conventions

---

[68] Cf. e.g. John Westlake, *Chapters on the Principles of International Law* (Cambridge University Press, 1894), pp. 129–133, also published in *The Collected Papers of John Westlake on Public International Law* (ed. L. Oppenheim, Cambridge University Press, 1914), pp. 131–135. For the development of the public law concept of territorial right in terms of *imperium* in the nineteenth century, cf. e.g. Anthony Carty, *The Decay of International Law? The Limits of Legal Imagination in International Affairs* (Manchester University Press, 1986), pp. 50–64.

[69] The decision recognized that British right had been received by discovery. It gave right to the Federal Government (against the States) to extinguish title of occupancy – but only "either by purchase or by conquest." *Johnson v. McIntosh*, 21 US (1822), p. 579. Cf. also *Cherokee Nation v. Georgia*, 30 US (1831), p. 1.

[70] Henry Wheaton, *Elements of International Law. With a Sketch of the History of the Science* (2 vols., London, Fellowes, 1836), I, pp. 50–51.

Sovereignty: a gift of civilization

observed by that portion of the human race in their mutual intercourse." From this it followed that: "the international law of the civilized, Christian nations of Europe and America, is one thing; and that which governs the intercourse of the Mohammedan nations of the East with each other, and with Christian, is another and a very different thing."[71] Klüber and von Martens did not call their international law the *Droit public de l'Europe* for nothing. For Wheaton, as for later professional lawyers, Western consular jurisdiction as it existed in 1836 in Turkey, the Barbary States, and other Islamic countries was but a logical offshoot of the law's cultural peculiarity: Europeans were to be governed by European law; anything else would be arbitrariness.

For early nineteenth-century lawyers, native communities remained outside international law in the technical sense that the *Droit public de l'Europe* did not regulate their relations with the Europeans. It sufficed that the individuals – Europeans and natives – would receive the protection of a natural law that would treat them as equal traders or travelers, equally obliged to show courtesy to and remain from violence against each other. For the situation in the colonies, this was for a long time quite sufficient. The extension of natural law – in particular that concerning property – explained why the natives were bound to honor the lives and possessions of Europeans moving beyond the reach of European legal principles and on what basis the commercial relations between Europeans and natives would be conducted. Private interest in land was protected by the natural law argument which linked territorial rights to the cultivation of land, and implied the distinction between nomadic and sedentary populations that opened much the largest part of non-European territory for European settlement.[72]

Such a personalized natural law was embedded in the cosmopolitanism of the eighteenth century, its admiration of the unspoiled ways of life in savage communities.[73] Voltaire, Rousseau, and Diderot had professed sympathy towards the natives as an instrument of their critique of the religious and political establishment in Europe. Their knowledge of non-European cultures remained, however, anecdotal and their admiration reflected at least in part the scarcity of actual contacts with them. The same is true of the discussions of non-European cultures by early

---

[71] Wheaton, *Elements of International Law*, I, p. 51.
[72] Salomon, *L'occupation*, pp. 202–204; Jèze, *Etude théorique*, pp. 103–112 and Johann Caspar Bluntschli, *Das moderne Völkerrecht der civilisierten Staaten als Rechtbuch dargestellt* (2nd edn., Nördlingen, Beck, 1872), pp. 168–169.
[73] Burrow, *Evolution and Society*, p. 52.

nineteenth-century lawyers. No in-depth studies were available of the political or legal systems of non-European societies that could have provided a basis for inferences about a distinct legal sphere beyond Europe. Europe's natural law continued to hold an image of the native as the "savage" that was more a reflection of Europe's own fears and desires than experience of native ways of life.[74]

But natural law is – as Rousseau famously pointed out against Grotius – a weak system of legitimation and always amenable for the justification of the policies of the day. There was nothing in Klüber, von Martens, or Wheaton that would have been critical or even suspicious of official colonialism. Each held, as a matter of course, that European nations had – by all lawful means – the right to extend their settlement and authority by discovery and effective occupation in new countries.[75] As Robinson and Gallagher observe in their important study of British expansion in Africa after 1879: "Because those who finally decided the issue of African empire were partly insulated from pressures at Home, and remote from reality in Africa, their historical notions, their ideas of international legality and the codes of honour shared by the aristocratic castes of Europe had unusually wide scope in their decisions."[76]

If politicians, ministers, and colonial officials had a relatively free hand in deciding on what action to take, it is not insignificant to what extent abstract notions of natural law buttressed their confidence that expansion was not simply an economic or strategic problem but also – and perhaps even largely – "a moral duty to the rest of humanity."[77]

The demise of informal empire in Africa

The reasons for the sudden acceleration of the pace of European expansion has been subject to much controversy. Explanations referring to developments in Europe ("metropolitan theories") have been contrasted with changes outside Europe ("peripheral theories").[78] Economic, social,

[74] For a discussion of this aspect of European writing about what lies outside, cf. Tzvetan Todorov, *The Morals of History* (trans. Alyson Waters, Minneapolis and London, University of Minnesota Press, 1995).
[75] Cf. Wheaton, *Elements of International Law*, I, pp. 109–110.
[76] Robinson and Gallagher, with Denny, *Africa and the Victorians*, p. 21.
[77] Robinson and Gallagher, with Denny, *Africa and the Victorians*, p. 2.
[78] For a general overview of different explanations, cf. Porter, *European Imperialism*; Michael Doyle, *Empires* (Ithaca, NY, Cornell University Press, 1986) and with special reference to Africa, G. N. Sanderson, "The European Partition of Africa: Coincidence or Conjecture?," in E. F. Penrose (ed.), *European Imperialism and the Partition of Africa* (London, Cass, 1975), pp. 1–54.

and ideological causes have been set against more traditional diplomatic and political explanations. To what extent the "new imperialism" that led to the partition of Africa soon after the Berlin Conference of 1884–1885 and the intensification of European penetration in the Pacific and South-East Asia was a qualitatively "new" phenomenon or merely the logical extension of old European policy has likewise seemed uncertain. The facts can hardly be contested, however: Despite initial and sometimes quite open resistance by leading politicians and populations at large, from 1879–1882 onwards European powers suddenly took active steps for the creation of formal empires.

By 1870, British overseas predominance had eroded. Other powers assumed an increasingly active imperial policy. The first steps were taken by France whose influential *Ministère de marine et des colonies* had since 1865 pursued large-scale military operations from Senegal deep into Western Sudan, against the Tukolori and other native kingdoms. In 1876 and 1881 France set up formal protectorates in Annam and Tunisia.[79] Britain reacted by intensifying informal influence. One of these ways was a revival of chartered companies that had come under much criticism earlier in the century. Expansion in Africa had always been conducted by mercantile associations (Royal African Company, African Company of Merchants) led by ambitious capitalists such as George Goldie, William Mackinnon, and Cecil Rhodes.[80] With the chartering of the British North Borneo Company in 1881[81] a new precedent was created for the exercise of informal rule without having to request funds from Parliament or the Treasury – which in all probability would not have been granted. By the time the scramble was over, more than 75 percent of British acquisitions south of the Sahara were acquired by chartered companies.

---

[79] Cf. Wesseling, *Le partage de l'Afrique*, pp. 238–252; David Levering Lewis, *The Race to Fashoda. Colonialism and African Resistance* (New York, Weidenfeld & Nicolson, 1987), pp. 75–83.

[80] For example, in 1870 British possessions in West Africa were restricted to isolated coastal spots while occasional military excursions (e.g. against the Ashanti in 1874) were without lasting territorial effect. A Parliamentary Select Committee in 1865 even advocated partial withdrawal – no such withdrawal took place. Cf. Gann and Duignan, *The Burden of Empire*, pp. 171–172; Baumgart, *Imperialism*, pp. 14–15.

[81] The company's powers included "life and death over the inhabitants, with all the absolute rights of property vested in the Sultan over the soil of the country," cf. M. F. Lindley, *The Acquisition and Government of Backward Territory in International Law* (London, Longmans, 1926), pp. 100–101. For the early activities of the chartered companies in Africa and elsewhere, cf. J. Flint, "Chartered Companies and the Transition from Informal Sway to Colonial Rule in Africa," in Stig Förster, Wolfgang J. Mommsen, and Ronald Robinson (eds.), *Bismarck, Europe and Africa. The Berlin Africa Conference 1884–1885 and the Onset of Partition* (Oxford University Press, 1988), pp. 69–71.

German colonization followed similar lines. In his famous imperial manifestos of 1884 and 1885 Bismarck repeated his staunch opposition to the "French system" that involved expansion by formal armies followed by resident colonial officials.[82] What eventually became German South West Africa was acquired in 1882 by a tobacco merchant from Bremen, Adolf Lüderitz who had set up shop in Angra Pequeña north from the British Cape Colony and to whom Bismarck, greatly irritated by British reluctance to acknowledge him freedom of action in the area, wrote a *Schutzbrief* in April 1884. In the following June he told the *Reichstag* that his negative attitude towards annexation had not changed and that material responsibility for the colony should always be left to the company.[83]

This technique provided only temporary relief for European governments, however. Eventually the companies resorted to protectionist practices (in breach of their charters), proved unable to administer territories granted to them, or failed to forestall expansion by other powers. Governmental interference was required to protect traders and settlers or to prevent anarchy and, eventually, to set up formal rule.[84] A typical development took place in Western Africa where Sir George Goldie's (1846–1925) United (National) African Company had started out in the Niger region in 1879 in which both France and Germany were seeking possessions. In 1883, Sir Percy Anderson, the head of the Foreign Office's African bureau wrote: "Action seems to be forced on us . . . Protectorates are unwelcome burdens, but in this case it is . . . a question between British protectorates, which would be unwelcome, and French protectorates, which would be fatal."[85] The British received a free hand in the area from the powers united at Berlin in December 1884. The Berlin Act, however, required that acquisition be accompanied by effective occupation. As the colonial office was not ready to set up an administration in the area – nor the Treasury to pay for a formal protectorate – Goldie's company was chartered in June 1886 to "enforce treaty rights, to collect customs duties and to spend the receipts solely on the expenses of rule."[86] But Goldie never had any intention to implement the trade

---

[82] Cf. Salomon, *L'occupation*, pp. 117–118.
[83] Quoted in K. J. Bade, "Imperial Germany and West Africa: Colonial Movement, Business Interests, and Bismarck's 'Colonial Policies,'" in Förster, Mommsen, and Robinson, *Bismarck, Europe, and Africa*, p. 137.
[84] Earlier – as in Fiji in 1874 – there had already been genuine fears of abuses against the indigenous population by unscrupulous traders, triggering governmental intervention. Cf. Hyam, *Britain's Imperial Century*, pp. 208–209.
[85] Quoted in Sanderson, "The European Partition of Africa," p. 11.
[86] Robinson and Gallagher, with Denny, *Africa and the Victorians*, p. 182.

Sovereignty: a gift of civilization

or humanitarian provisions of the Act.[87] He immediately excluded all competition in the river (including competition by Africans). In 1891 Britain was forced to increase its direct administration in the region and two years later to set up the Niger Coast protectorate.[88]

In East Africa as well, formal rule fell upon Europeans as a result of private pre-emption. With a *Schutzbrief* of March 3, 1885 Bismarck brought the Zanzibar inland regions that had been the object of frantic treaty-making between the eccentric adventurer Carl Peters and native chiefs under a German protectorate whose administration was granted to the German East Africa Company (*Deutsch-Ostafrikanische Gesellschaft*, DOAG).[89] On the British side, William Mackinnon (1823–1891), the founder of the British and India Steam Navigation Company, insisted that the British make a similar move. In October 1886 Britain and Germany divided the area formerly claimed by the Sultan of Zanzibar between themselves. Mackinnon's Imperial British East Africa Company (IBEAC) was chartered on September 3, 1888.[90]

Neither company lived up to imperial expectations. Mackinnon remained on the brink of bankruptcy and projects to subsidize his company fell to naught. The company's agents were withdrawn from Uganda in 1891. After a period of indecision and political conflict, the charter of the IBEAC was withdrawn and formal protectorate was established over Uganda on August 27, 1894 and over all territory between Buganda and the coast on July 1, 1895.[91] The DOAG mismanaged its territory by excessive taxation with the result that a rebellion ensued. As the company proved unable to put up a meaningful resistance, German officers and a force of African mercenaries were sent in to crush the rebellion – a task that was carried to a conclusion by 1889.

---

[87] J. Flint, "Chartered Companies and the Transition from Informal Sway to Colonial Rule in Africa," in Förster, Mommsen and Robinson, *Bismarck, Europe, and Africa*, pp. 78–79. Cf also the detailed criticism of Goldie's blocking of the Niger by A. de Lapradelle, "Chronique internationale" (1899), XI *Revue du droit public et de la science politique en France et à l'étranger*, pp. 279–289.

[88] Cf. Robinson and Gallagher, with Denny, *Africa and the Victorians*, pp. 180–189; Wesseling, *Le partage de l'Afrique*, pp. 253–264. Goldie's charter was withdrawn in 1900.

[89] The Charter of Protection was granted to the German *Kolonialverein* (Colonization Society) on February 27, 1885. The Charter went as follows: "We grant unto the said Society, on the condition that it remains German . . . the authority to exercise all rights arising from the Treaties submitted to us, including that of jurisdiction over both the natives and the subjects of Germany and of other nations established in those territories . . . under the superintendence of our Government," Edward Hertslet, *The Map of Africa by Treaty* (3rd edn., 3 vols. London, HMSO, 1909), II (no. 209), pp. 681–682.

[90] Cf. Robinson and Gallagher, with Denny, *Africa and the Victorians*, pp. 193–202.

[91] Cf. Robinson and Gallagher, with Denny, *Africa and the Victorians*, pp. 290–294, 307–330; Wesseling, *Le partage de l'Afrique*, pp. 253–264.

Two years later, Germany took over German East Africa as a formal protectorate.[92] By 1895 all German colonies in Africa (South West Africa, Togo, Cameroons, German East Africa) had come under direct imperial *Schutzgewalt*, as much parts of the Empire under international law as departments or provinces.[93] With the brutal crushing of the Herero uprising in South West Africa in 1905 and the "Maji-Maji" rebellion in German East Africa the following year, German rule in Africa was irreversibly turned into military conquest and direct imperial administration.[94]

The most ambitious scheme to exercise empire in Africa without the burden of formal sovereignty was the granting of a charter to Cecil Rhodes' (1853–1902) British South Africa Company (BSAC), on November 29, 1889.[95] In exchange for requiring no subsidy from government, and against the opinion of humanitarian societies, Rhodes received a practically free hand to administer the area (Matabeleland, Barotseland, Zambesia, and other territories north of the British Bechuanaland).[96] But his irresponsible policy and particularly his association with the privately organized Jameson raid on the Transvaal government at the end of 1895 led "almost inevitably" to the most devastating colonial war ever, the Boer War.[97]

None of the attempts at keeping formal sovereignty – with all the attendant burdens – at arm's length were successful. The strategy of the "cat's paw," i.e. the use of local rulers such as the Sultan of Zanzibar or Ismaïl Pasha in Egypt and the enlisting of local assistance in administration to carry out imperial purposes, fell because it was intrinsically contradictory. It was impossible not to rule and yet insist on internal reform and abolition of the slave trade.[98] Even Gladstone's liberal government that had in 1880 come to power on a vocally anti-imperialist platform two years

---

[92] Cf. Wesseling, *Le partage de l'Afrique*, pp. 200–203, 221–222; Thomas Pakenham, *The Scramble for Africa 1876–1912* (New York, Random House, 1991), pp. 346–349.
[93] von Stengel, "La constitution et l'administration," pp. 275–292.
[94] For the two wars, cf. e.g. Pakenham, *Scramble for Africa*, pp. 602–628.
[95] In this case, the British Government might have extended direct rule had it wished to do so. But "[t]he British public opinion, Parliament, the Treasury, and the Cabinet were no more eager in 1889 to undertake new costs in Africa than they had been in 1884. In fact, it was British government intervention and prodding, as much as Rhodes' ambition, which secured the granting of the charter in 1889," Flint, "Chartered Companies," pp. 81–82.
[96] As Robinson and Gallagher, with Denny put it, "the company in operation was a colonial enterprise effectively under colonial, not imperial, control," *Africa and the Victorians*, p. 243.   [97] Flint, "Chartered Companies," p. 72.
[98] Cf. e.g. Hyam, *Britain's Imperial Century*, pp. 117–118; Sanderson, "The European Partition of Africa," pp. 15–16; Gann and Duignan, *The Burden of Empire*, p. 185.

Sovereignty: a gift of civilization

later blundered into military occupation of Egypt as a response to the worsening financial crisis and a nationalistic revolt in the country, leading first to an international financial administration and finally in 1914 to the declaration of a formal British protectorate.[99] As the Marxist historian V. G. Kiernan has observed, "There was always an ambiguity between preserving native institutions and culture and controlling the many through the few. It would mean at least a dilution of the civilising mission, at worst its abandonment."[100]

The end of informal empire meant that European public institutions – in particular, European sovereignty – needed to be projected into colonial territory – something that only the assimilationist French had advocated earlier in the century. Arguments about sovereignty and international law then appeared with particular intensity in two contexts: to deal with conflicts of jurisdiction between European powers and to determine the rules applicable in the relations between the colonizing power and the indigenous population. To agree on such principles was the ostensible purpose of the Berlin Conference of 1884–1885. Here law became part of the moral and political controversy about the justice of colonialism.

The Berlin Conference 1884–1885

At the meeting of the *Institut de droit international* in Paris in September 1878, Gustave Moynier drew the attention of his colleagues to the increasing interest that the exploration of the Congo river had had after Stanley's spectacular resurgence at the mouth of the river on August 5, 1877. It was necessary to check the impending scramble and to see to the orderly progress of the civilizing mission in this enormous region of central Africa. This could be done, he suggested, by setting up a regime of free navigation in the Congo river, administered by an international commission after the example of the Danube. The proposal was not felt as urgent, however, and no action was taken on it.[101]

Five years later, the Belgian de Laveleye proposed in Rolin's *Revue* an international regime of neutralization for the region in an attempt to avoid its division between the colonial powers.[102] He confessed that full neutralization might be utopian, however, and suggested as an alternative (which may in fact have been his principal intention) that the *Association internationale Africaine* that had been set up in 1876 through the

---

[99] Cf. e.g. Robinson and Gallagher, with Denny, *Africa and the Victorians*, pp. 122–159.
[100] Kiernan, *Imperialism and its Contradictions*, p. 130.
[101] (1879–80), 3–4 *Annuaire IDI*, p. 155.
[102] Emile de Laveleye, "La neutralité du Congo" (1883), XV *RDI*, p. 254.

initiative of Léopold II, King of the Belgians, be recognized as a "neutral and independent" administrator of the territory. To those who doubted whether a private organization might be granted such status, he responded in advance by referring to the position of the Red Cross as well as the recent chartering by Britain of the North Borneo company.[103] Though members largely agreed, many of them – particularly Twiss – protested against the word (and possibly the concept of) "neutralisation." In fact, military forces and vessels were needed in the river to protect traders and natives against each other and against pirates and slave traders. Instead, an agreement on the internationalization and freedom of navigation in the river might be concluded and a declaration of disinterest made by the powers. The *Association* could, he suggested, be vested with the mission to proselytize and exercise sovereign rights over the territory in the image of medieval orders such as the Teutonic knights, the colonization societies that set up Liberia and Maryland, or indeed the British North Borneo Company.[104] In September 1883 Moynier repeated his suggestion, observing that with Stanley's more recent discoveries, an uncontrolled scramble was beginning and action needed to be taken soon.[105] In response, the *Institut* adopted a *voeu*, prepared by its Secretary-General, the Belgian Professor Egide Arntz (1812–1884), appealing to the powers for the realization of freedom of navigation in the Congo in the interests of Europeans as well as the natives.[106] Later, the expert statements of Twiss and Arntz appeared in

[103] de Laveleye, "La neutralité du Congo," pp. 256–258.
[104] Sir Travers Twiss, "La libre navigation du Congo" (1883), XV *RDI*, pp. 436–442, 547–563, and (1884), XVI *RDI*, pp. 237–246. Twiss made a distinction between the lower and the upper Congo and suggested for the former an international protectorate under Portugal's presidency and for the latter a system of "free towns" consisting of the stations of the *Association internationale* or the *Comité des Etudes* with which Stanley was formally employed.
[105] Cf. Gustave Moynier, "Mémoire à l'Institut de droit international, à Munich, le 4 septembre 1883," in *La question du Congo devant l'Institut de droit international* (Geneva, Schuchardt, 1883), p. 7.
[106] "Navigation sur le fleuve Congo," Résolution du 17 septembre 1883 (1883–85), *Annuaire IDI*, p. 278. Moynier's proposal was also opposed in view of its "unrealistic" nature, *ibid.*, pp. 275–278. Originally, the Portuguese Government protested against the declaration which it saw as contrary to its territorial claims in the region. For his part, Arntz responded by pointing out that unlike the Portuguese had assumed, the declaration did not suggest a neutralization of the area but only agreement on freedom of navigation and free trade – something, he argued, to which the Portuguese could and did seem to have no objection. Egide Arntz, "Le Gouvernement portugais et l'Institut de droit international" (1883), XV *RDI*, pp. 537–546.

Sovereignty: a gift of civilization

the debates within the US Senate in support for the decision to recognize King Léopold's *Association* as a sovereign State.[107]

The Berlin West African Conference was opened on November 15, 1884 and the General Act was signed on February 26, 1885. The Conference had three official aims: the organization of freedom of navigation in the Congo and Niger rivers, the guarantee of freedom of trade in the Congo basin and mouth, and agreeing over the rules concerning the acquisition of new territory.[108] It was a multilateral attempt to channel the scramble in Africa into pacific channels. From the perspective of its initiators (Germany and France) it also constituted an attempt to limit the exorbitant claims that they saw Britain making on vast stretches of practically unexplored African territory. International lawyers have invariably focused on the territorial aspects of the Conference and have therefore, unsurprisingly, been disappointed by the result.[109] Only two articles of the Final Act dealt with territorial acquisition, and even they through general formulations whose applicability was limited to an almost meaningless minimum. Article 34 required powers to inform each other of new acquisitions. Article 35 read: "The Signatory Powers of the present Act recognize the obligation to insure the establishment of authority in the regions occupied by them on the coasts of the African Continent sufficient to protect existing rights and, as the case may be, freedom of trade and of transit under the conditions agreed upon." The Conference rapidly agreed on the principle of effective occupation, although it had originally been directed against the British whom Bismarck had accused of espousing a kind of a Monroe doctrine for Africa. The British, however, had no difficulty in agreeing to the result as no criteria for what would constitute "effectiveness" were

---

[107] Cf. US Congress, Senate Committee on Foreign Relations, Session of March 26, 1884, Report (Occupation of the Congo Country in Africa), no. 393, pp. 16–37.

[108] In his opening words, Bismarck emphasized the humanitarian objectives of the Conference that aimed to: "d'associer les indigènes d'Afrique à la civilization en ouvrant l'intérieur de ce continent au commerce, en fournissant à ses habitants les moyens de s'instruire, en encourageant les missions et entreprises de nature à propager les connaissances utiles et en préparant la suppression de l'esclavage, surtout de la traite des Noirs." Protocoles de la Conférence de l'Afrique occidentale réunie à Berlin, du 15 novembre 1884 au 26 février 1885, De Martens (1885–1886), X *Nouveau recueil général*, 2nd series, p. 201. For a general history of the Conference, cf. S. E. Crowe, *The Berlin West African Conference 1884–1885* (London, Longmans, 1942).

[109] Cf. e.g. Salomon, *L'occupation*, p. 96; Jèze, *Etude théorique*, pp. 32–36 and Jörg Fisch, "Africa as *terra nullius*. The Berlin Conference and International Law," in Förster, Mommsen, and Robinson, *Bismarck, Europe, and Africa*, p. 348.

laid down.[110] Chartering a company would continue to suffice. In fact, Bismarck's letter of protection to the German East Africa Company was dated only one day after the Conference.

The rule was also limited in time and space: it was to apply only to *new* acquisitions and only to acquisitions on the coasts – at a time when there was practically no coast left to occupy. Significantly, the Conference refused to apply it to the African interior because this would have required an exact determination of the formal claims of the powers and would have resulted "en fait à une partage de l'Afrique" – something the Conference was desperate to avoid.[111]

Finally, at a British proposal, protectorates were excluded from the ambit of Article 35 – although they had become the main form of European influence in Africa and often indistinguishable from annexation – despite criticism about such an unscrupulous blurring of jurisprudential distinctions.[112] In contrast to the traditional concept of a protectorate as a taking over of the foreign affairs of a State that otherwise remained sovereign (or "semi-sovereign"), the African protectorates were established by treaties with native chiefs or unilateral letters from European capitals with the most varied content and certainly without implying that any kind of sovereignty resided in the native community. They constituted a flexible means for staking a claim of precedence and maintaining a free hand against such communities without the establishment of formal administration.[113] They allowed the British, for instance, to uphold their unlimited commercial empire while at the same time avoiding the financial and administrative burdens (e.g. keeping the peace and abolishing the slave trade) that would have resulted from formal occupation.[114] The British

---

[110] Cf. e.g. Fisch, "Africa as *terra nullius*," pp. 349–350. For the anti-British aims of the conference, cf. also Salomon, *L'occupation*, pp. 86–90.

[111] Conférence de Berlin, De Martens, *Nouveau recueil*, X, p. 343.

[112] Cf. e.g. Salomon, *L'occupation*, pp. 226–242; Heilborn, *Das völkerrechtliche Protektorat*, pp. 5–7, and Fisch, "Africa as *terra nullius*," pp. 358–360, 363–366. For a positive assessment, cf. Sir Travers Twiss, "Le congrès de Vienne et la conférence de Berlin" (1885), XVII *RDI*, p. 215.

[113] For contemporary commentary, cf. e.g. S. McCalmont Hill, "The Growth of International Law in Africa" (1900), LXIII *Law Quarterly Review*, pp. 250–255; A. Mérignhac, *Traité de droit public international* (3 vols., Paris, LGDJ, 1905–1912), II, pp. 180–225; Ernest Nys, *Le droit international: Les principes, les théories, les faits* (3 vols., new edn., Brussels, Weissenbruch, 1912), II, pp. 98–105. As John Hargreaves notes, "Europeans reinterpreted their doctrine of protectorates to justify arbitrary exercises of power," "The Berlin Conference, West African Boundaries, and the Eventual Partition," in Förster, Mommsen, and Robinson, *Bismarck, Europe, and Africa*, p. 319.

[114] As Lindley points out, a treaty of protectorate secures exclusive control over the area concerned "with the ultimate right of annexing it." *Acquisition and Government*, p. 186.

Sovereignty: a gift of civilization

Bechuanaland protectorate of 1884, for example, was "an interesting example of a protectorate in which the internal as well as the external sovereignty has passed to the protecting Power, but the territory has not been formally annexed, so that, in the eyes of British law, it is not British territory."[115] Not being British territory, British law, including that against slavery, for instance, did not apply in Bechuanaland.

Imperial powers opposed formal sovereignty as it constituted a burden to the one who had it and limited everyone else's freedom of action. To have enacted a clear rule on the conditions of colonial sovereignty would too easily have encompassed the wrong situations. Its consequences would have been impossible to calculate – though the British were certain that it would have gone against their claims all over the world.[116] Instead of agreeing on a rule, it was better to leave conflicts to be settled by ad hoc agreements between the powers, free to take into account whatever conditions they might think relevant. Much the larger part of the Conference was used in bilateral behind-the-scenes talks.[117] Hence the two important treaties of 1890, the Anglo-French Treaty on the spheres of interest in Western Sudan and the corresponding Anglo-German treaty on East Africa had nothing whatsoever to do with an application of formal rules. The exchange of Zanzibar for Helgoland by Germany in the latter treaty – the absolute *sine qua non* of the agreement – would never have been attained by the application of fixed rules about territorial entitlement. The agreements effectively determined the rights of precedent that the three principal powers accorded to each other – without requiring them to take formal action. Inevitably, lawyers came to see such agreements as a return to fictive sovereignty – deliberate attempts to undermine what few administrative duties had been imposed on the colonizing powers by the Berlin Act.[118]

Today, historians dismiss the Berlin Act as in practice irrelevant for the scramble.[119] However, this is not wholly adequate.[120] Although the words

---

[115] Lindley, *Acquisition and Government*, p. 187.
[116] Which is why the Franco-German invitation to the Conference "sent Granville and his officials scurrying to consult legal experts and compile the precedents and places likely to be affected," Robinson, "The Conference in Berlin and the Future in Africa, 1884–1885," in Förster, Mommsen, and Robinson, *Bismarck, Europe, and Africa*, p. 9.
[117] For a rapid overview of the bilateral agenda of the Conference, cf. Robinson "The Conference in Berlin and the Future in Africa, 1884–1885," pp. 11–15.
[118] For an early criticism, cf. Salomon, *L'occupation*, pp. 254–256.
[119] "none of the thirty-eight clauses of the General Act had any teeth. It had set no rules for dividing, let alone eating, the cake." Pakenham, *Scramble for Africa*, p. 254.
[120] Cf. also G. N. Uzoigwe, "The Results of the Berlin West Africa Conference: An Assessment," in Förster, Mommsen, and Robinson, *Bismarck, Europe, and Africa*, pp. 542–544.

of the General Act did not determine anything about the behavior of European States, they both divested European expansion from some of its potential burdens (by limiting "effectiveness" undefined) and allowed private interest to parade as public interest – as well as irreversibly excluding any pretensions to sovereignty that indigenous communities might have entertained. Articles 34 and 35 treated "sovereignty" as a quality that could attach only to a European possession.[121] Moreover, sovereignty was treated first and foremost as an exclusivity, unaccompanied by clearly defined obligations. Much of the drafting process was constituted of the watering down of the duties of the colonizing power. The word "jurisdiction" in the original Franco-German draft was replaced by the less formal expression "authority" in the final text of Article 35. The duty "to establish and maintain sufficient authority" was amended to read "to ensure sufficient authority" so as to allow the maintenance of indigenous administration where feasible. The requirement to "keeping the peace" in the original draft was deleted as too broad and the occupying power's main duty was defined in terms of safeguarding "acquired rights." Finally, the exclusion of protectorates from the ambit of the rule – a condition without which the British might not have assented to anything – went a long way towards undermining whatever guarantees had been attained for the establishment of a stable system of colonial sovereignty.[122] How all this was to be applied in practice was left for the powers to agree on a case-by-case basis. As Ronald Robinson concludes: "The leading powers who decided the issue were clearly intent on avoiding colonial liabilities, on averting a scramble for the interior, and frustrating the supposed colonial ambitions of their rivals."[123] By contrast, the articles on freedom of navigation and free trade did constitute a "genuine attempt to internationalise future trade in Central Africa."[124] In this, however, they failed miserably. No effective internationalization took place. The provisions that ostensibly dealt with free trade in practice consolidated Goldie's monopoly in the lower Niger.

---

[121] The proposal was made by the United States delegate Mr. Kasson that the conference might also discuss the rights of indigenous tribes, pointing out that international law: "suit fermement une voie qui mène à la reconnaissance de droit des races indigènes de disposer librement d'elles-mêmes et de leur sols héréditaires," and suggesting that his government would be prepared to require that acquisition be based on free consent. To this, the Chairman Mr. Busch observed that "M. Kasson touche à des questions délicates sur lesquelles la Conférence ne saurait pas éxprimer d'opinion," "Le Conférence de Berlin," de Martens, *Nouveau recueil*, X, pp. 335–336.

[122] Cf. the criticism in e.g. Jèze, *Etude théorique*, pp. 265–267.

[123] Robinson, "The Conference in Berlin and the Future in Africa, 1884–1885," p. 25.

[124] Robinson, "The Conference in Berlin and the Future in Africa, 1884–1885," p. 16.

Sovereignty: a gift of civilization

The international commission planned for the Congo was never set up and Léopold established a fully exclusionary system in the river. As Sheryl Crowe has written in her authoritative history of the Conference: "Free trade was established in the basin and mouths of the Congo and the Niger. Actually highly monopolistic systems of trade were set up in both these regions. The centre of Africa was to be internationalized. It became Belgian."[125]

The myth of civilization: a logic of exclusion–inclusion

As European States were struggling in Africa and elsewhere to minimize their colonial liabilities, yet to maximize their influence, the international law profession organized itself through the establishment of Rolin's *Revue* and the setting up of the *Institut de droit international*. As we have seen, the new generation of lawyers – Rolin, Bluntschli, Westlake – reaffirmed international law's European pedigree, holding international law to be a product of European history and culture, and used the distinction between civilized and non-civilized communities to deal with the process of European expansion. Although they discussed colonial problems from a variety of perspectives, some more, some less critical, their discourse provides a uniform logic of exclusion–inclusion in which cultural arguments intersect with humanitarian ones so as to allow a variety of positions while at every point guaranteeing the controlling superiority of "Europe." The most frequent commentator on the colonial process among members of the *Institut* was Westlake who in 1894 – the year when Britain finally turned to official empire in Africa by the annexation of Uganda – wrote: "International law has to treat natives as uncivilised. It regulates, for the mutual benefit of the civilised states, the claims which they make to sovereignty over the region and leaves the treatment of the natives to the conscience of the state to which sovereignty is awarded."[126] For Westlake, it was absurd to think of native possession in terms of sovereignty, or colonial expansion, as conditional upon treaties with native chiefs. "Sovereignty" was a purely European notion. Just as a person cannot transfer what he does not have, the chief cannot transfer a sovereignty of which he has no concept.[127] Westlake followed a long tradition of lawyers by granting that the natives did possess the concept of occupancy, or of private ownership, and were thus perfectly capable of holding or disposing of property. But in European eyes this could be only

---

[125] Crowe, *The Berlin West African Conference*, p. 3. [126] Westlake, *Chapters*, p. 143.
[127] John Westlake, "Le conflit Anglo-Portugais" (1891), XVIII *RDI*, pp. 247–248.

a private law matter. Native treaties dealing with large territories could create acquired rights under Article 35 of the Berlin Act, but they could not transfer sovereignty.[128] Colonial title was always original and never derivative; it followed from European law's qualification of the acts of European powers, not from native cession.

But though Westlake had few scruples about colonization, even he did not suggest that the colonial encounter took place in a legal vacuum. After all, even he held that the treatment of the natives was a matter of Western conscience – a notion not bereft of legal implications, as we saw in chapter 1. In a polemic of 1910 concerning the character of the relationship between the British Government and the native States of India (that is to say, the "territories outside British India [ruled by] Native Princes and Chiefs under the suzerainty of the Crown"), Westlake emphatically rejected the idea that such relations could ever come under international law. They were relations of British constitutional law – yet this meant also that "the same principles of natural justice which underlie international law must be applied to their relations."[129]

Late nineteenth-century textbooks normally affirmed international law's non-applicability in non-civilized territory – but not without provision made for the universal validity of humanitarian and natural law principles or human rights.[130] Bluntschli and Fiore, for instance, both argued that international law provided a number of human and private rights to all individuals regardless of their citizenship or the degree of civilization of their communities.[131] In 1909 Fiore regarded it an urgent task to define more clearly the rules that would govern the European–savage relationship.[132] Even Robert Adam's detailed early study of German colonization law which completely rejected the idea of native sovereignty held it self-evident that the natives enjoyed rights "provided by reason and nature" that included the rights of private ownership and contract over lands actually taken to use.[133]

---

[128] Westlake, "Le conflit Anglo-Portugais," pp. 247, 249. Likewise, Salomon, *L'occupation*, pp. 233–235.

[129] John Westlake, "The Native States of India," in *Collected Papers*, p. 624.

[130] For a useful early review, cf. Mérignhac, *Traité de droit public international*, II, pp. 430–435.   [131] Bluntschli, *Das moderne Völkerrecht*, pp. 19–20, 60–61.

[132] Pasquale Fiore, "La science de droit international. Horizons nouveaux" (1909), XVI *RGDIP*, pp. 478–479.

[133] Robert Adam, "Völkerrechtliche Okkupation und deutsches Kolonialrecht" (1891), VI, *Archiv des öffentlichen Rechts*, pp. 234–240. Cf. also E. von Ullmann, *Völkerrecht* (Freiburg, Mohl, 1898), p. 195; P. Schoen, "Zur Lehre von dem Grundlagen des Völkerrechts" (1914–1915), VIII *Archiv für Rechts und Wirtschaftsphilosophie* (*ARWP*), pp. 314–315.

Sovereignty: a gift of civilization

But if all lawyers accepted that individual non-Europeans enjoyed natural rights, only a few extended such rights to non-European communities. However, both major French studies of the period concluded that if only savages lived in a more or less organized community, their land would escape being labeled as *terra nullius* and colonial title could be created only by cession.[134] This was not to say they thought that native communities enjoyed equality with European States, only that they were not automatically open for European occupation or conquest. In this respect, international lawyers routinely distinguished between non-European communities of different degrees of civilization. For example, in a 1891 study of the concept of the protectorate, the German public law expert Paul Heilborn used Lorimer's scheme to distinguish between the relations Europeans had with civilized non-European States (such as Japan, China, Persia) and with non-civilized communities (*Stämmen*). While international law as a legal system was inapplicable to both, a number of its rules could be applied in the relations Europeans maintained with the former group: the rights of independence and non-intervention were applicable to such communities, as were all the rights contracted with Europeans. The relations between European States and *Stämmen*, on the other hand, never possessed an international law character.[135]

At the other end of the spectrum were the critical articles and interventions within the *Institut* by the Swiss lawyer Joseph Hornung. He attacked not only Western brutality in the colonies but also its double standards: if intervention in favor of oppressed Christians in Turkey had been lawful throughout the century, it should also have been possible to intervene in favor of Africans and Asians living under tyrannical rule. But we Europeans, he insisted, have treated the Orient in terms of *our* commerce, the protection of *our* nationals. Colonialism was justified, Hornung claimed, but only in the interests of the colonized. Colonization should become a part of the moral mission towards world federation.[136] None of this implied that European and non-European communities were equal. Hornung had no appreciation for Oriental cultures and lived securely in the prison-house of paternalism. The barbarian is not such because he is bad: "Those who know them well are able to say that with good treatment, much will be received from

[134] Cf. Salomon, *L'occupation*, pp. 201–242; Jèze, *Etude théorique*, pp. 112–121.
[135] Paul Heilborn, *Das völkerrechtliche Protektorat*, pp. 7–28.
[136] Joseph Hornung, "Civilisés et barbares" (1885), XVII *RDI*, pp. 1–18, 447–470, 539–560 and (1886), XVIII *RDI*, pp. 188–206 and 281–298. Cf also Hornung (1879–80), 3–4 *Annuaire IDI*, pp. 305–307.

them."[137] Moreover: "They are children, of course, but then, let us treat them as one treats children, through gentleness and persuasion . . . We accept the hegemony and trusteeship of the strong but only in the interests of the weak and in view of their full future emancipation."[138] Even if Hornung was considered somewhat of a humanitarian radical, not many members of the *Institut* disagreed with him – though they may not have shared his pathos.[139] They had by now learned to integrate cultural distinctions into a hierarchical ordering of developmental levels. Again, this is not to say that they wrote or thought in identical ways. Some such as Adam or Westlake stressed the law's cultural background and thus excluded the native from the ambit of European law – while immediately qualifying this through a secondary position that re-integrated the native in a European conceptual system as a beneficiary of human rights or the dictates of civilized conscience. Others such as Salomon or Hornung appealed in favor of humanitarian attitudes – while as a secondary position always excluded native communities from equality with European sovereigns. The colonial discourse of late nineteenth-century international law was able to accommodate positions as apparently wide apart as Westlake's and Hornung's to create a solid defense of the extension of European influence. It was a discourse of exclusion–inclusion; exclusion in terms of a cultural argument about the otherness of the non-European that made it impossible to extend European rights to the native, inclusion in terms of the native's similarity with the European, the native's otherness having been erased by a universal humanitarianism under which international lawyers sought to replace native institutions by European sovereignty.[140]

It is sometimes suggested that a universalist conception of international law represented by Enlightenment jurists fell due to the rise of

---

[137] Hornung, "Civilisés et barbares" (Part 3, 1885), XVII *RDI*, p. 559.
[138] Hornung, "Civilisés et barbares" (Part 4, 1886), XVIII *RDI*, pp. 188, 189.
[139] Robert Adam, for instance, held his federalism as a complete utopia but agreed in the characterization of the civilized–uncivilized relationship as that between the mature and the immature, or parent and child, "Völkerrechtliche Okkupation," p. 245.
[140] The two attitudes – full differentiation and full identification – structured European attitudes towards the natives from the outset. A classic discussion of the way that the logic of identification in a Spanish "defender of the Indians" such as Bartolomé de Las Casas and the logic of difference in the *conquistador* Hernando Cortés betrayed "agreement on one essential point: the subjugation of America to Spain" is in Tzvetan Todorov, *The Conquest of America. The Question of the Other* (trans. by Richard Howard, New York, Harper, 1982), pp. 177, 168–182 (and also pp. 151–167 on the isomorphic contrast between Las Casas and Sepúlveda).

Sovereignty: a gift of civilization

"positivism" in the late nineteenth century.[141] This is not an adequate image of the structure of colonial law. In the first place, as was argued in chapter 1, the leading international jurists were not "positivists" in any clear sense but made constant use of arguments about morality or natural law – as even Westlake did in his contemplation of the British–Indian relations. A right or a duty to intervene outside Europe was routinely asserted, as the French lawyer–diplomat Engelhardt put it, in order to ensure respect for "une loi générale et absolue établie par le consensus gentium."[142] If the lawyers sometimes disagreed on the opportunity or manner of conducting intervention, they never doubted its principle.

In the second place, this gives too much credit to the "universalism" of earlier jurists such as Grotius or Vattel, or indeed Klüber and von Martens. They used natural law because in the absence of large numbers of treaties, arbitrations, or a profession of commentators there was little else on which they could rely. More importantly, their "universalism" was a projection of their Western humanism, a secular variant of the Christian view of a single God. This may or may not have been politically admirable (the *Conquistadores*, after all, were also universalists). But in terms of dealing with otherness, the historical school had at least recognized the hypocrisy that was the flip side of universalism – the technique of including the non-European into a universe of European concepts by doing away with native identity (for instance, by excluding native ownership of land through the imposition of a thoroughly European standard of "cultivation of the soil" as condition of ownership).[143]

But if the distinction between the civilized and the uncivilized did structure colonial international law at the end of the nineteenth century, it did so accompanied by considerable doubt about its adequacy. Even Lorimer's threefold division between civilized, barbarian (or half-civilized), and savage (uncivilized) nations seemed too crude for application in special studies that increasingly drew upon anthropological and sociological accounts such as Tylor's 1871 study of primitive culture.[144]

---

[141] This has been the influential thesis in Charles Henry Alexandrowicz, *The European–African Confrontation. A Study in Treaty-Making* (Leyden, Sijthoff, 1973).

[142] Edouard Engelhardt, "Le droit d'intervention et la Turquie" (1880), XII *RDI*, p. 365.

[143] Cf. Richard Tuck, *The Rights of War and Peace. Political Thought and the International Order from Grotius to Kant* (Oxford University Press, 1999), pp. 106–108 and 195–196.

[144] James Lorimer, *Institutes of International Law. A Treatise of the Jural Relations of Separate Political Communities* (2 vols., Edinburgh and London, Blackwood, 1883), I, pp. 93 *et seq.*

Charles Salomon, for instance, concluded that there were an infinite number of degrees of civilization and forms of statehood. Had not "stories of travelers" suggested that "there existed in the heart of Africa Negro communities that offered practically all the characteristics of a State"?[145] Franz von Holtzendorff held that it was not at all the lawyer's task to define notions such as "culture" or "civilization": it should suffice to record the existence of peaceful relations between independent States that allowed common rules to govern their behavior.[146] For Jèze, all such distinctions were arbitrary and subject to misuse: "there is no reason to distinguish between different States on the basis of religion, color, race, or the civilization of their inhabitants."[147]

Looking for a standard

In 1875, the *Institut* sought to provide clarity for this issue by commencing a study under the chairmanship of Sir Travers Twiss on the possibility of applying customary (European) international law "in the Orient." A questionnaire was sent out to experts in Oriental law with the purpose of finding out whether the beliefs and legal institutions of Oriental and Christian States were sufficiently similar to admit the former "into the general community of international law."[148] Out of eight questions the first two were formulated in a general manner: Were the beliefs of the West and the Orient in regard to obligations towards foreigners sufficiently similar? Did Oriental peoples share the same view of the binding force of treaties as Christians? Two questions focused on missionaries: Was there need for special protection of proselytizing activities? Had the behavior of missionaries given occasion to hostility? Two questions dealt with the need to maintain or reform consular jurisdiction and one was formulated as follows: Did experience admit the possibility of common rules on the status and capacity of persons in mixed Christian–Oriental communities?[149]

As responses started coming in it turned out that the questions could

---

[145] Salomon, *L'occupation*, p. 208.
[146] Franz von Holtzendorff, *Handbuch des Völkerrechts, auf Grundlage europäisches Staatenpraxis* (4 vols., Berlin, Habel, 1885), I, p. 13. In practice, the position that the degree of civilization was a factual question left its determination to a case-by-case decision by the European powers. Cf. Adam, "Völkerrechtliche Okkupation," p. 246.
[147] Jèze, *Etude théorique*, p. 210. Likewise, A. Mérignhac, *Traité de droit public international*, II, pp. 430–431.   [148] Text in (1877), 1 *Annuaire IDI*, p. 141.
[149] A final question dealt with the possible need to adopt measures to regulate the maritime transport of Chinese "coolies." Cf. (1877), 1 *Annuaire IDI*, pp. 51, 141–142.

Sovereignty: a gift of civilization

not be answered in general terms. More subtle distinctions were needed. While some Orientals were, Twiss summarized in his report, "pirates and even cannibals," others such as Turkey, Siam, China, and Japan had had long and stable relations with the West.[150] In regard to the former, Europe's superiority would remain a necessity for a long time to come. As to the latter, Twiss had become convinced that there was no such difference between the ideas and faith of Christian and Oriental nations or in their attitudes towards the *pacta sunt servanda*, that the latter could not be admitted in the community of nations. The difficulties lay not in theory but in practice, in enforcement. Many of China's and Turkey's treaties, for instance, had been made after defeat in war. Attitudes to implementation therefore remained hostile. Were China, for instance, free to do so, it would immediately repudiate the treaties of Tientsin and Peking (1858 and 1860) and return to isolation.[151] Religious views were generally tolerant – although a special difficulty concerned Islamic attitudes towards Christians. The experts agreed that the time for lifting the protective veil of consular jurisdiction had not yet arrived, although it should be better organized so as to avoid the injustices that often accompanied it.[152]

Because the problem about the degrees of Oriental civilization turned out too difficult for the Institute to resolve, the project was reformulated so as to focus on technical questions such as what reforms were needed in the judicial institutions of the more developed Oriental nations in view of abolishing consular jurisdiction. It was continued by special studies on individual nations[153] – with not a few lawyers arguing in favor of giving up or reforming consular jurisdiction in Japan and elsewhere.[154] A number of States concluded bilateral treaties with Japan to this effect in 1894 and negotiations were conducted with other Oriental countries until the topic was dropped from the *Institut* agenda in 1895. The matter, noted Rolin, had become "delicate" and its treatment might offend the sensibility of certain nations.[155] Attention was directed away from the abstract standard to a case-by-case negotiation

---

[150] Sir Travers Twiss, "Rapport" (1879–1880), 3–4, *Annuaire IDI*, p. 301.
[151] A. Krauel, "Applicabilité du droit des gens à la Chine" (1877), IX *RDI*, pp. 387–401.
[152] Twiss, "Rapport," pp. 301–304.
[153] Twiss, "Rapport," p. 311; Cf. also the Report by Professor Bulmerincq in (1888–1889), 10 *Annuaire IDI*, pp. 259–263.
[154] Cf. e.g. Paternostro, "La revision des traités avec le Japon au point de vue du droit international" (1891), XVIII *RDI*, pp. 10, 177–182 and the report by de Martens in (1882), XIV *RDI*, pp. 324–328.
[155] Gustave Rolin-Jaequemyns (1895–96), 14 *Annuaire IDI*, p. 201.

of the conditions of integration of particular States into the European system. For a long time, however, private law relations continued to be administered within consular jurisdiction, in some cases by mixed tribunals (with or without appeal to a Western court) while full diplomatic recognition and entry into the public law community had to wait until the 1960s.

No stable standard of civilization emerged to govern entry into the "community of international law." This was implicitly accepted by the Institute as well in connection with a project on the law of colonial occupation after the Berlin conference. The *rapporteur*, Ferdinand von Martitz (1839–1922) from Freiburg, had proposed to classify as *terra nullius* all territory "that is not under the sovereignty or protection of States that form the international legal community, whether or not inhabited." It turned out impossible to define which were such States – and the matter was again left for treatment on a case-by-case basis – with lawyers trying to infer some criterion from the de facto treatment of Turkey, Japan, China, Siam, and Persia.[156] But European behavior never followed a criterion; however much Japan insisted that by any reasonable measure it was at least as civilized as any European State, the way it was treated was a function of what European diplomacy saw as useful.[157] Of course, international lawyers were not ignorant of the existence of civilization outside Europe. But the concept never worked, and was never intended to work, as an all-or-nothing litmus test.[158] Although Westlake admitted that States such as China, Siam, and Persia had attended the Hague Conferences of 1899 and 1907, and had thus been accepted into the "system," that system still fell "short of recognizing their voices as of equal importance with those of the European and American powers."[159] The Ottoman Empire's celebrated entry into the realm of European Public law in 1856 had little consequence for the dismissive treatment that European powers gave to the protests of the Sublime Porte as they encroached gradually deeper into its decaying imperial realm.[160] The

---

[156] For a review of the discussion, cf. Salomon, *L'occupation*, pp. 209–210.
[157] The best study of the matter is Gong, *Standard of Civilization*.
[158] Cf. also Fisch, *Die europäische Expansion*, pp. 284–287.
[159] Westlake, "The Native States of India," p. 623.
[160] The powers, Salisbury pointed out in 1877, had granted Turkey's territorial integrity only on condition that it would not mistreat its subjects. If it did so, in the eyes of the European powers, then that grant was withdrawn. Gustave Rolin-Jaequemyns, "Chronique de droit international: L'année 1877 et les debuts du 1878 au point de vue de droit international" (1878), X *RDI*, pp. 8, 17–18, 20. Turkey's refusal to discuss the matter in early 1877 meant, Rolin opined, that it was henceforth alone

Sovereignty: a gift of civilization

existence of a "standard" was a myth in the sense that there was never anything to gain. Every concession was a matter of negotiation, every status dependent on agreement, *quid pro quo*. But the existence of a *language of a standard* still gave the appearance of fair treatment and regular administration to what was simply a conjectural policy.

Despite their doubts about the possibility or the need to define "civilization," international lawyers were still deeply embedded in the language of the standard. Without such language, it would have been impossible to rationally explain, let alone to justify, why non-European communities could be subjected to massive colonization. Because the European States and their modes of communication were by definition civilized, the whole issue was reduced in practice to the question as to when outside communities would have started to resemble the Europeans to the extent that they could be smoothly integrated into the European system. "Our community of nations is not a closed one," wrote Alphonse Rivier in 1889. "Just as it opened itself for Turkey, it will open itself for other States as soon as these have reached a level of spirituality comparable to ours".[161] Historical optimism and imperial ambition shook hands: progress would gradually bring civilization to non-European communities. And becoming civilized meant becoming like the Europeans' image of themselves: "Everything is reduced to an appreciation, from the point of view of international law, whether a State, by virtue of its organisation, laws, habits, fulfils the necessary conditions to be admitted on the basis of equality to the general community of international law."[162] But the non-European community could never really become European, no matter how much it tried, as Turkey had always known and Japan was to find out to its bitter disappointment. Here was the paradox: if there was no external standard for civilization, then everything depended on what Europeans approved. What Europeans approved, again, depended on the degree to which aspirant communities were ready to play by European rules. But the more eagerly the non-Europeans wished to prove that they played by European rules, the more suspect they became: had not Bluntschli

---

responsible for its fate. After the Berlin Congress Salisbury bluntly noted that the Porte had henceforth only a "relative independence." Edouard Engelhardt, "Considérations historiques et juridiques sur les protectorats." (1892), XXIV *RDI*, pp. 349–383.

[161] Alphonse Rivier, *Lehrbuch des Völkerrechts* (Stuttgart, Enke, 1889), p. 5.

[162] Paternostro, "La revision des traités," p. 7. For an assessment of China in this regard, cf. Joseph Hornung, "Note additionelle" (1882), XIV *RDI*, p. 243.

The Gentle Civilizer of Nations

argued that only "non-Aryans" bowed down in front of their masters? In order to attain equality, the non-European community must accept Europe as its master – but to accept a master was proof that one was not equal.

Between universality and relativism: colonial treaties

In 1878 King Léopold enlisted Stanley's services for a *Comité des Etudes du Haut-Congo*, financed mainly by Belgian interests, ostensibly for the purposes of research of the Congo river and basin but in fact to map out this part of the "magnifique gâteau africain" and to conclude as many treaties as possible with the native chiefs of the region.[163] In these treaties, the chiefs would transfer their lands to the *Comité* which Léopold silently transformed in 1882 into another organization – the *Association Internationale du Congo*, that was to form the nucleus of his future "Independent State of the Congo."[164] These treaties, Léopold's instructions to Stanley read, must "grant us everything." For example, in the treaties concluded on April 1, 1884 the chiefs of Ngombi and Mafela agreed in exchange for "one piece of cloth per month . . . besides present of cloth in hand" to:

> freely of their own accord, for themselves and their heirs and successors for ever . . . give up to the said Association the sovereignty and all sovereign and governing rights to all their territories . . . and to assist by labor and other works, improvements or expeditions which the said Association shall cause at any time to be carried out . . . All roads and waterways running through this country, the right of collecting tolls on the same, and all game, fishing, mining and forest rights, are to be the absolute property of the said Association.[165]

As Stanley was still making provisions for the voyage, de Brazza was advancing on the north bank of the river, formally as an agent of the French national committee of the *Association Internationale Africaine* that

---

[163] The *Comité* was organized as a private company with an initial budget of 1 million Belgian francs, provided by an international group of financers, Pakenham, *Scramble for Africa*, p. 146. Léopold wrote to Stanley at the end of 1881:"La Belgique ne désire aucun territoire en Afrique, mais il est indispensable que vous achetiez pour le Comité des études autant de terrain qu'il vous est possible de obtenir, et que vous placiez successivement sous la souveraineté de Comité, dès que possible et sans perdre une minute, tous les chefs, depuis l'embouchure du Congo jusqu'aux chutes Stanley." Letter reproduced in Georges Henri Dumont, *Léopold II* (Paris, Fayard, 1990), p. 172.   [164] Pakenham, *Scramble for Africa*, p. 161.
[165] Quoted in Adam Hochschild, *King Leopold's Ghost. A Story of Greed, Terror, and Heroism in Colonial Africa* (Boston, Houghton Mifflin, 1998), p.72.

Sovereignty: a gift of civilization

had been set up in Brussels in 1876 but in fact concluding treaties of cession for his beloved but somewhat apprehensive France.[166]

To cite native treaties in the manner of Stanley and de Brazza as irrefutable proof of their employers' sovereignty was controversial from the outset. The French Government, for instance, together with the radical *député* Georges Clemenceau, were initially quite reluctant to accept de Brazza's famous Makoko Treaties from 1880 that granted French sovereignty to vast areas north of the Stanley Pool in the Congo river.[167] The treaties were, however, "forced upon the [French] government under a press campaign whipped up by de Brazza" and duly ratified in November 1882.[168] From 1883 onwards de Brazza was officially instructed by the government to conclude more of such formal acts of cession. The following year Bismarck despatched the German explorer Gustav Nachtigal (1834–1885) to sign treaties of cession with West African chiefs. In a famous race between Nachtigal and the British Consul, Nachtigal came out victorious owing to a delay in the latter's receiving blank treaty forms from London. By July 1884 German colonial protectorates had been set up in Togo and the Cameroons.[169] During his time in King Léopold's service Stanley alone was said to have concluded at least as many as 257 such treaties.[170] As Salomon wrote, "there was scarcely a modern traveller who would not have found himself in the role of a diplomatic agent and would not have attached to his collection of souvenirs some treaty of territorial cession."[171]

It is not difficult to see why imperial expansion took the form of seeking native consent in written form. Both conquest and symbolic annexation were associated with early Spanish and Portuguese colonialisms that contemporaries had learned to reject on moral grounds. Besides, conquest would involve excessive costs. But as Gaston Jèze

---

[166] On the famous race between Stanley and de Brazza, cf. e.g. Robert Stanley Thomson, *Fondation de l'Etat indépendant du Congo* (Brussels, Office de publicité, 1933), pp. 76–100.   [167] Cf. de Martens, *Nouveau Recueil*, X, p. 215.
[168] Baumgart, *Imperialism*, p. 19; Lewis, *Fashoda*, p. 39.
[169] Cf. Wesseling, *Le partage de l'Afrique*, pp. 258–259; Robinson and Gallagher, with Denny, *Africa and the Victorians*, pp. 171–175 and Pakenham, *Scramble for Africa*, pp. 197–199, 207–208.
[170] Marc Ferro, *Colonialism. A Global History* (London and New York, Routledge, 1997), p. 76. Stanley himself boasted of having concluded over 400 treaties during five years in the Congo, Jèze, *Etude théorique*, p. 142. But when the treaties that he had made with the Chiefs of Uganda were examined, it turned out that they were in reality blood brotherhood or non-aggression pacts, Frank McLynn, *Hearts of Darkness. The European Exploration of Africa* (London, Pimlico, 1993), pp. 315–316.
[171] Salomon, *L'occupation*, p. 218.

pointed out: "it must also be asked whether the acquisition conforms to ideas of justice, whether the acquisition of certain territories does not constitute, from a purely moral point of view, a reprehensible act, in a word, whether the occupation, as manifestation of acquisition, is legitimate."[172] Native consent given in a treaty of cession seemed to constitute an irreproachable moral–legal basis for European title and did away with the suspicion that Europeans were merely following in the footsteps of the fifteenth- and sixteenth-century empires. Clearly, it was a problematic practice. Despite the (somewhat ambiguously formulated) proposal by the American delegate at the Berlin Conference, Mr. Kasson, however, no requirement of native consent was included in the Berlin Act – although the conference did recommend that such consent be normally secured. The problem was both conceptual and practical. First, as the Martitz Report pointed out: "[a] treaty of cession cannot be concluded by entities other than States that recognize international law."[173] If native communities lacked international standing – formal sovereignty – treaties with them could hardly enjoy validity under international law. Secondly, many of the treaties had been concluded under circumstances where it was doubtful whether one could speak of the free or informed consent of the native who drew his "x" on it.[174] Stories about the practices of treaty-making followed by Stanley in the Congo or Peters in East Africa did nothing to enhance their credibility.[175]

The lawyers responded to such problems with broadly three types of argument.[176] For one group that included Rolin and Westlake, representatives of two active colonial powers, such transactions were irrelevant from the point of view of international law. Treaties with "ignorant Chiefs" could neither create not transfer sovereignty.[177] They might have a factual effect in consolidating European occupation or creating an environment of confidentiality, and they might create private rights that the sovereign must honor. That is to say, they might be needed for *political* reasons.[178] But they could not be taken account of in international law as basis for European title. Because the native does not possess the

---

[172] Jèze, *Etude théorique*, p. 52.   [173] (1887–88), 9 *Annuaire IDI*, p. 247.
[174] Salomon, *L'occupation*, pp. 218–220; Jèze, *Etude théorique*, pp. 148–153. Cf. also E.-L. Catellani, "Les droits de la France sur Madagascar et le dernier traité de paix" (1886), XVIII *RDI*, p. 153.
[175] The treaties that Peters claimed as the basis of his annexations in East Africa had been made in the German language.
[176] Cf. also Lindley, *Acquisition of Territory*, pp. 10–23, 169–177.
[177] Cf. also Rivier, *Lehrbuch*, p. 136; Nys, *Le droit international*, II, pp. 111–116.
[178] Adam, "Völkerrechtliche Okkupation," pp. 259–261.

Sovereignty: a gift of civilization

concept of sovereignty, he cannot transfer it: a stream cannot rise higher than its source.[179] Seldom has the adage about the connections between knowledge and power been more graphically illustrated: possession of land was the function of possessing a concept.

On the other hand, it was obviously true that the non-European party did not necessarily understand the treaty's meaning to the Europeans. To refuse to recognize the validity of such treaties may have seemed the only way to preclude manipulation of the unequal negotiation situation by the European power.[180] But how then could Western title at all be validated? To rely on de facto presence would have failed to distinguish between peaceful colonization and total war against the inhabitants. Also, it left the European governments in an awkward position as they had regularly referred to native treaties as at least a part of the justification of their title. As the German lawyers, well aware of the ambition of the Kaiser, pointed out, it would have been an inconceivable affront to the honor of His Majesty to insinuate that the treaties he had made with native chiefs were concluded under dubious circumstances and were best treated as scraps of paper.[181] Moreover, if one rationale for colonization was to award the peaceful enjoyment of possession, then *some* proof of peacefulness was required and it was hard to think what else could count as such than some expression of native consent.

For such reasons, a second group insisted that native treaties were indispensable ingredients or even the only legally valid basis of European title.[182] Though the Berlin Conference had not accepted the American proposal to this effect, it had expressly recommended it. And the practice was treated as serious by the powers themselves. By the 1920s, attitudes had changed to the extent that a leading authority on the issue held it to be a majority view that the natives could dispose over their lands and that European sovereignty should normally be based on

---

[179] Cf. John Westlake, *International Law* (2 vols., 2nd edn., Cambridge University Press, 1910), I, pp. 123–124; *Chapters*, pp. 144–155; Pasquale Fiore, "Du protectorat colonial et de la sphère d'influence (hinterland)" (1907), XIV *RGDIP*, pp. 150–151.

[180] Later lawyers have sometimes associated this position with the theory of legal positivism. This, however, is wrong as we have seen, for neither Rolin nor Westlake was a positivist in any clear sense.   [181] Cf. Fisch, *Die europäische Expansion*, p. 336.

[182] This position is in a very absolute form in Henri Bonfils and Paul Fauchille, *Manuel de droit international public* (2nd edn., Paris, Rousseau 1898), pp. 280–281. From the fact that the texts of the treaties often referred to the local chief as sovereign entitled to dispose of land rights, Alexandrowicz draws the doubtful conclusion that they were actually so regarded. Alexandrowicz, *The European–African Confrontation*, pp. 30–40, 118–122, 127–128.

treaties.[183] Already in the 1880s, however, the French lawyers Jèze and Salomon had held that inhabited countries could not be regarded as *terra nullius*. They did not precisely hold that every native community held sovereignty over its land. Sovereignty might be lacking because of the tribe's unorganized or nomadic ways of life, for example. Both held the civilizing mission a perfectly legitimate European pursuit. But even in such cases, native communities enjoyed at least something like a right of self-determination that seemed to call for the necessity of native consent: "it is not permitted to force happiness on people – in this matter, everyone is his own best judge."[184] Jèze even argued that not only was native consent necessary but that consent should be free, intelligent, and given in accordance with local usages.[185]

But this position made little difference as practically all expansion was accompanied by native treaties. A reliable scrutiny of the reality of native consent would have been impossible to carry out and seemed anyway to require the application of European standards. The embarrassing possibility that some part – perhaps a very large part – of European acquisitions was based on formal acts of dubious seriousness could not be easily done away with. Could it be just an accident that Alexandre Mérignhac (1857–1927), Professor at Toulouse and *associé* of the *Institut* came to the conclusion that while Stanley's or Nachtigal's treaties arose from cynical manipulation, French protectorate treaties were concluded in an impeccable fashion?[186] Accepting the validity of the treaties seemed to imply that as legal subjects native communities were equal with European States. For all the lawyers, this would have been an absurdity. Even Jèze expressed the opinion that the need to conclude treaties did not arise from equality between the parties but from the prudential need to carry out the civilizing mission as efficiently as possible. He never even considered the possibility that transfer of territory would not take place.[187]

Most lawyers came to hold an intermediate view. Although colonial title was normally original (and not derivative), native treaties were still relevant – perhaps even necessary – as evidence of the peacefulness of

---

[183] Lindley, *Acquisition and Government*, pp. 20–23, 169–177. It is not clear, however, that Lindley interpreted the views of all the authors he cites in a way they would have accepted.

[184] Salomon, *L'occupation*, p. 207 and the discussion in Fisch, *Die europäische Expansion*, pp. 321–325.   [185] Jèze, *Etude théorique*, pp. 116–117.

[186] Mérignhac, *Traité de droit public international*, II, pp. 435–437.

[187] Jèze, *Etude théorique*, p. 128.

Sovereignty: a gift of civilization

the possession claimed by the colonizer, as "proof of the expansion of the State's influence commercially and politically amongst the tribes."[188] Engelhardt, for instance, held that the parties in Berlin had solved this question by recommending that treaties (either of cession or of protectorate) be always concluded with the non-European community. Although European title would still be original, native consent could be interpreted as an indispensable part of it.[189] The German Heimburger explained this as follows. Because the natives enjoyed no sovereignty (not having that concept), they could not transfer it. The content of what ostensibly were treaties of cession was simply not to oppose the occupation by the colonial power and to agree to European rule. No embarrassing implication of equality was entailed: the relationship was not legal but quasi-legal and the duty to execute the treaty followed from "the natural reasonableness and bona fides of civilized States."[190] The ambivalence of the situation was reflected in the official collections of treaties. Martens' great *Recueil* listed native treaties until around 1880. By 1890, they had disappeared. But both the official British Foreign and State Papers as well as the French de Clerq *Recueil* continued to publish them.[191]

The question of the legal validity of native treaties presents an identical structure to the exclusion–inclusion logic surveyed above. Whichever legal position one took was in the main compatible with colonial interest, yet had its difficulties, too. European predominance could be secured by granting the validity of colonial treaties as well as dismissing them. When colonial enthusiasts such as the Belgian professor and later Secretary-General of the *Institut* Baron Descamps (1847–1933) insisted that indigenous chiefs were perfectly capable of transferring sovereignty, they seemed to imply a normative universe in which the Europeans and the Africans acted as formal equals.[192] Such universalism, however, had nothing to foreclose the possibility or even likelihood of manipulation. To deal with this problem, lawyers automatically retreated to paternalism: the native was unable to understand his interests. To be a universalist and yet to acknowledge cultural difference was

---

[188] Frantz Despagnet, *Essai sur les protectorats* (Paris, Larose, 1896), pp. 246–251; S. McCalmont Hill, "The Growth of International Law in Africa," pp. 254–255. Likewise, Martitz (1887–1888), 9 *Annuaire IDI*, p. 247; Rivier, *Lehrbuch*, pp. 136–137; Ullmann, *Völkerrecht*, pp. 187–188 and e.g. T. J. Lawrence, *A Handbook of Public International Law* (8th edn., London, Macmillan, 1913), p. 52. On Laband's position, cf. Fisch, *Die europäische Expansion*, p. 326.   [189] (1888–89), 10 *Annuaire IDI*, p. 177.
[190] "Der naturliche Billigkeit und der bona fides der zivilisierten Staaten," Heimburger, *Erwerb*, p. 114.   [191] Fisch, *Die europäische Expansion*, p. 337.
[192] E. Descamps, *L'Afrique nouvelle* (Paris, Hachette, 1903), pp. 39–40.

possible – and common – through an argument that arranged such difference in a single hierarchical, evolutionary frame.

A universalism that accepted native treaties not only signified respect for the native but also erased the native's particularity and overlooked the historical nature of the colonial confrontation. In the sixteenth century Vitoria and Las Casas had argued that the American Indians came under a universal natural law in a way that provided ground for their humane treatment. But it also made it possible to discipline Indians as in constant breach of the law which required them to accept European trade and proselytizing.[193] Yet, as the French learned after their originally assimilationist policy in Algeria had failed, the universalism on which it was based had constituted a "philosophic excess bequeathed from the Revolution of 1789 ... a preposterously demanding commitment" – and a receipt for disillusionment and cynicism.[194] By the time of the establishment of the Tunisian protectorate in 1881, French colonialists started to change over to the British technique that sought to leave native institutions in place wherever possible.[195] Late nineteenth-century lawyers usually rejected the indiscriminating universalism of Enlightenment thought and emphasized the cultural difference of the Orient. But this led them to denying the benefits of European law to the non-Europeans. In the former case, imperialism was grounded in an absolute logic of identity, in the latter on the absolute affirmation of difference. Neither position had any determinate consequences: both were equally amenable for a defense as well as criticism of colonialism.[196] Therefore, the question of the legal basis of the colonial encounter could not be treated through a theory of native treaties. Turning away from such theory, lawyers hoped to deal with it in terms of the classical law of occupation – integrating native treaties as a subsidiary category within it. In this way, it could be hoped that European expansion would receive a stable legal base in firmly European thought about the justice of territorial sovereignty – while a

---

[193] The classic is Todorov, *The Conquest of America*, discussing Columbus' turn from initial assimilationism to enslavement and Las Casas' erasure of native particularity through schematic descriptions of the natives' Christian "humility" and "goodness," pp. 42–50 and 160–167. Cf. also Antony Anghie, "Francisco de Vitoria and the Colonial Origin of International Law" (1996), 5 *Social and Legal Studies*, p. 321.

[194] Lewis, *Fashoda*, p. 80.

[195] Nonetheless, in many places – West Africa, for instance – the turn from "assimilationism" to a (democratic) "associationism" was completed only in the aftermath of the First World War. Cf. Conklin, *A Mission to Civilize*, pp. 174–211.

[196] This remains invisible for such critics such as Alexandrowicz and Gong who associate colonialism with positivism.

Sovereignty: a gift of civilization

guarantee might be attained against the manipulation of the colonial relationship for private interests.

The myth of sovereignty: a beneficent empire

While Stanley concluded treaties of cession in the Congo, many wondered about whether a private association such as the *Comité des études* or Léopold's *Association internationale du Congo* was in a position to enjoy sovereign rights. French lawyers in particular, perhaps unsurprisingly bearing in mind de Brazza's simultaneous exploits in the region, vehemently denied this.[197] As the recognition of the Association as the sovereign in the Congo came up in the United States Senate in 1884 Léopold hired Twiss and Arntz, two members of the *Institut*, to make a legal defense on behalf of his Association – although "he had no illusion about the power of juridical arguments."[198] Twiss included his arguments in a series of articles on the Congo in Rolin's *Revue* as well as in the preface of the second edition of his *Law of Nations*, pointing out that in fact colonization by private entities had been the predominant form of Western expansion since the sixteenth century and that for this purpose chartered companies and philanthropic associations had often been vested with sovereign rights. In his view, the analogy between the Congo association and the American Colonization Society that declared itself the Commonwealth of Liberia in 1847 was "striking."[199] Arntz wrote a legal brief that was handed out to the Foreign Relations Committee of the Senate endorsing the arguments by Twiss and providing further examples from Antiquity onwards of cases where States had been founded by private individuals.[200]

However, most international lawyers insisted that the work of civilization required direct rule and effective sovereignty for the European colonizer:

Becoming subjects of the power which possesses the international title to the country in which they live, natives have on their governors more than the common claim of the governed, they have the claim of the ignorant and helpless on the enlightened and strong; and that claim is the more likely to receive justice, the freer is the position of the governors from insecurity and vexation.[201]

[197] Thomson, *La Fondation*, pp. 101–103.
[198] Dumont, *Léopold II*, p. 175. Cf. also Thomson, *La Fondation*, pp. 147–162.
[199] Twiss, *The Law of Nations*, I, p. xiii.
[200] Argument of Professor Arntz, US Senate, Committee on Foreign Relations, 26 March, 1884 (Occupation of the Congo country in Africa), Report no. 393, pp. 33–35.
[201] Westlake, *Chapters*, p. 140.

Laissez-faire had shown its negative effects during domestic industrialization and through disappointments in the colonies. The Indian mutiny of 1857 had already led to the transfer of the administration of the territory from the East India Company directly to the Crown. Jèze pointed out that at least the French nation was constitutionally prevented from delegating sovereignty to private entities: the French people were sovereign and could decide to delegate only the exercise of certain rights of sovereignty, and even this only under extensive and continuous State control.[202] For Salomon, too, a company could never enjoy sovereignty; it was at best an instrument, a *negotiorum gestio* – for the State-sovereign. The British and German technique of informal empire was unacceptable. It was in a way: "to colonize anonymously, without costs and without responsibility, to exclude large territories from the civilising activities of other powers in order to hand them over to private companies that pursue no other objective than immediate personal enrichment."[203] It was the duty of legal doctrine, he added, to work against such practices and to insist that there could be no right without correlative obligations. The German Heimburger agreed with his French colleagues. It was impossible to accept that commercial entities could possess public law sovereignty, with all the rights and duties attached thereto. They could act as agents of States but not as subjects of international law in their own name.[204] In 1889, Rolin argued that colonization by chartering companies to deal with territorial administration failed to distinguish between ownership and *imperium* and to effect the humanitarian treatment of the populations – of this, the Abushiri rebellion in German East Africa should have taught a lesson: direct rule was infinitely better. If early colonization had indeed been undertaken through private companies, the juridical concept of colonization had now been transformed: a company could not carry out the required humanitarian and civilizing tasks.[205] The same critique underlay Salomon's critique of company sovereignty: if a State colonizes through a company, this would then take place only for the company's own enrichment: "It would be naïve to require a limited liability company to

---

[202] Jèze, *Etude théorique*, pp. 344–358.   [203] Salomon, *L'occupation*, p. 186.
[204] Heimburger, *Erwerb*, pp. 48–77. However, Robert Adam argued that although Heimburger was in principle right, international practice had accepted company sovereignty, "Völkerrechtliche Okkupation," pp. 220–225.
[205] Nonetheless, he presumes that "si mauvaise que puisse être l'administration d'une compagnie de marchands européens, elle est toujours meilleure que celle d'un sultan." Gustave Rolin-Jaequemyns, "L'année 1888 au point de vue de la paix et du droit international" (1889), XXI *RDI*, p. 192.

Sovereignty: a gift of civilization

make sacrifices in order to improve the condition of the natives at the risk of diminishing its dividends."[206] Most of the lawyers of the new generation argued that colonization should not be delegated to private entities or hidden behind ambiguous formulas that allowed the colonizer to pick the fruit without paying the price. They insisted on the need to establish effective Western sovereignty in colonized territories not only in order to deal with territorial conflict between the European powers (although that was the reason why the problem had arisen) but to protect European settlers and traders and to see to the civilization of the inhabitants. By the end of the century, the question of principle had largely lost its actuality: private companies had been useful as a means of occupying new territory. In order to exploit and administer the colonies, official State intervention had become a practical necessity.[207]

The legal analysis of colonization was not independent of the purposes that lawyers envisaged for the imperial venture.[208] The economic purpose – securing vital imports and new markets for expanding domestic production – did not necessarily call for formal empire. But already in 1884 when Germany started looking towards Africa the large trade companies of Hamburg refused to take on the administration of the recent annexations in Togo and the Cameroons. In their view, it was the task of the State to set up administration and police in these territories to create and maintain orderly conditions for trade and settlement. This seemed effectively confirmed by the financial and administrative difficulties that led to the withdrawals of the charters of the British and German companies in the 1880s and early 1890s.

The political objective – securing influence or prestige – was also easier to attain by formal than informal means. When de Brazza left for the Congo in 1879 the French insisted that he plant the tricolor and not the flag of the French Committee of the *Association International Africaine* precisely as they held that this enjoyed no protection by international law.[209] In the creation of settlement colonies, too, formalization seemed rational and its justification was received from the Enlightenment idea that territorial rights were based on effective land use. For example, as

---

[206] Salomon, *L'occupation*, p. 197. Likewise, Frantz Despagnet, *Cours de droit international public* (2nd edn., Paris, Sirey, 1899), pp. 430–431.

[207] Arthur Girault, "Chronique coloniale" (1897), VIII *Revue de droit public et de la science politique en France et à l'étranger*, pp. 120–121.

[208] Colonies have been classed as exploitation colonies for principally economic purposes, maritime enclaves as points of commercial penetration into the hinterlands or settlement colonies for European and native settlement. Cf. Osterhammel, *Colonialism*, pp. 10–12. [209] Thomson, *La Fondation*, pp. 80–81.

the first German settlers arrived in Samoa in 1878 – in Germany, colonization was predominantly thought of in terms of finding new territory for a rapidly growing population[210] – Bluntschli expressed his skepticism about whether Bismarck could refrain from taking protective action. Private treaties with the chiefs were, he opined, hardly sufficient to protect the settlers and their trade interests. And when he turned his gaze towards Africa and the first efforts of German colonization there, he saw them bluntly in terms of "the great civilizing mission of the German Reich."[211] Immediately after Bismarck's declaration of a colonial policy in 1884 Geffcken, the editor of Klüber's textbook and a member of the *Institut*, wrote a long article about German colonial policy enthusiastically speculating about the economic and demographic advantages that colonization would bring to Germany, ending his review in the French colonialist Paul Leroy-Beaulieu's famous adage: "la nation qui colonise le plus est la première, et . . . si elle ne l'est pas aujourd'hui, elle le sera demain." Like Bluntschli, Geffcken was from the outset of the opinion that colonization could not continue through the activities of private companies – that stage had been passed – "a colony cannot be governed by private actors, it needs a government, a jurisdiction."[212]

Another argument for formal colonization was received from the increasing disillusionment of the humanitarians as experience of expansion increased. When Livingstone propagated the introduction of his "three Cs" – Civilization, Commerce and Christianity – in Africa in the 1830s, there was no doubt in his mind that Africa needed to be regenerated spiritually as well as materially. He never dreamed, however, that this would take place by annexation. But by the 1870s philanthropic humanitarianism was on the decline. The Indian mutiny of 1857 had come as a shock to the European communities. A great number of Europeans had been killed and the British had reacted by "retributive savagery which is one of the most shameful episodes in British history."[213] Other disappointments followed in Ceylon and Bengal. A war was fought by the British in China and Persia and native disturbances in Africa and elsewhere were met with increasing toughness. The

---

[210] Cf. Geffcken, "L'Allemagne et la question coloniale," pp. 105–114.
[211] Bluntschli, "Eigenthum," in *Gesammelte kleine Schriften*, I, pp. 229–230.
[212] Geffcken, "L'Allemagne et la question coloniale," pp. 105–131, 128. He repeated this view five years later. Cf. Geffcken, "Le traité Anglo-Allemand de 1ᵉʳ juillet 1890" (1890), XXII *RDI*, pp. 599–602. By 1895 all German colonies had become formal parts of the Empire while only in New Guinea did there remain a company to carry out some administrative tasks. Cf. Von Stengel, "La constitution et l'administration des colonies allemandes" (1895), III *Revue de droit public et de la science politique en France et à l'étranger*, pp. 275–292.   [213] Hyam, *Britain's Imperial Century*, p. 137.

Sovereignty: a gift of civilization

Xhosa rebellion in South Africa left over 35,000 natives dead. The 1865 Morant Bay rebellion in Jamaica arose from an insignificant quarrel over land rights: in the resulting skirmishes eighteen people were killed. Governor Eyre reacted by having 439 persons hanged, at least 600 flogged and thousands of homes burned to the ground.[214]

Such events were a shock to those who had hoped that Western civilization would be adopted by indigenous populations almost automatically. Demands were made for a "strong hand" in guiding the natives to the path of civilization. Liberia and Haiti were held by the 1870s as "object lessons concerning the black man's assumed incapacity to take care of his own affairs."[215] By the same time efforts to convert Africans to Christianity in a massive way had almost come to a standstill. Many missionaries who had worked in Africa for decades reacted with bitterness and brought back home stories of the natives' depravity. As servants of explorers they were untrustworthy, as cultivators or agriculturalists, ineffective. Such stereotyping was encouraged in the writings by racist explorers such as Stanley, Burton, and Speke. Tales of atrocity, horror, and of African racism were spread by the papers all over Europe.[216] The attitude was summarized in terms of amateur political theory by the commercial artist Charles Castellani, reflecting on his experience on the Marchand mission from French Congo to the Nile in 1897: "It is the triumph of anarchy, it is the state of nature that I had to learn about first hand."[217]

Most international lawyers of course continued to admire Vitoria and Las Casas and to write critically of the egoism, greed, and inhumanity that accompanied early European expansion. But they could have no illusions about the spontaneity with which the natives were willing to live by European rules. An effective and responsible administration of those rules was needed. Geffcken speculated about teaching the natives European methods of agriculture so that they would leave idleness and barbarism and "would be rendered useful for the world."[218] Rolin interpreted the crushing of the Abushiri rebellion and the full-scale blockade of the East African coast as part of the struggle against slave-trading Arabs.[219] To achieve pacification, international lawyers

---

[214] Hyam, *Britain's Imperial Century*, pp. 150–154.
[215] Gann and Duignan, *The Burden of Empire*, p. 170.
[216] Gann and Duignan, *The Burden of Empire*, pp. 128–129; Hyam, *Britain's Imperial Century*, pp. 159–161. [217] Quoted in Lewis, *Fashoda*, p. 172.
[218] Geffcken, "L'Allemagne et la question coloniale," pp. 119–122.
[219] Gustave Rolin-Jaequemyns, "L'année 1888 au point de vue de la paix et du droit international" (1889), XXI *RDI*, pp. 199–208.

insisted on the importation of European legal and political institutions, that is, European sovereignty – the idea that Bluntschli had envisaged as the most significant heritage of "Aryan" political thought – into the colonies.

Finally, formal sovereignty seemed needed also to deal with the potential of conflicts between rival colonial powers. As soon as Stanley had descended the Congo River in 1877, international lawyers had expressed concern over the eventual disputes between European powers that might ensue and that would give "a sad image of our antagonisms to the Negroes whom we seek to civilize."[220] The need to foreclose such conflicts worked as a powerful argument in favor of the formal extension of public law sovereignty, and the formal delimitation of such sovereignty, in Africa and elsewhere.

For such reasons, from the first clashes of colonial powers outside Europe – in the Far East, in Africa, and in the Pacific Ocean in the 1870s – a public international law doctrine developed that was concerned with the criteria for the establishment and delimitation of European sovereignty in the Orient. This was received from analogies from the Roman law of occupation which performed the double feat of avoiding the embarrassment of having to explain European title as derived from cession by native chiefs and pointing towards the need to set up an effective administration of the territory on which sovereignty was claimed. By this shift of attention from native treaties to the occupation of *terra nullius*, non-European communities became a passive background to the imperial confrontation.[221] The law that was applied to the natives became a kind of a shadow of the inter-European law that laid down the rules for the confrontation. That was the shadow of a disturbed conscience: even if the acquisition of sovereignty was based on unilateral action, attached was always a rejoinder about the civilizing mission and the need of native co-operation.[222]

The law of occupation was seen as great progress from earlier ages. Textbooks described it within a narrative about the law of territory that commenced with the 1494 Treaty of Tordesillas that delimited the Spanish and Portuguese empires by reference to a Papal dictum. They criticized the exaggerated importance given in the sixteenth and seventeenth centuries to discovery and symbolic annexation and emphasized

---

[220] Gustave Moynier, *La question du Congo*, p. 4.
[221] Cf. Fisch, *Die europäische Expansion*, pp. 300–302, 287.
[222] For a particularly striking example, cf. Adam, "Völkerrechtliche Okkupation," pp. 234–235, 260.

Sovereignty: a gift of civilization

the rational basis of the rule that required effective presence as the condition of territorial right.[223] Only actual occupation could be squared with a political theory that linked the right of possession to actual use of the territory for some beneficial purpose.[224] Only occupation with the requirement of publicity as its inextricable part could create a stable system of European sovereignties, provide protection for acquired and indigenous rights, abolish slavery and the slave trade, and do away with the portrayal of Africa in the explorers' books as a continent of superstition, savagery, cultural inferiority, political instability, and overall backwardness.[225]

The limits of sovereignty: civilization betrayed

For such reasons, the members of the *Institut* greeted the proposal for a conference on African affairs with enthusiasm, crediting the idea to the writings by Moynier and de Laveleye. After the Berlin Conference had ended, however, they were quite puzzled about what to think of its results. They welcomed the free trade and free navigation provisions. Twiss, himself a member of the British delegation, predicted that the free trade regime will "prepare the civilization of populations that occupy an area perhaps larger than the whole of Europe."[226] But they were ambivalent about the territorial provisions. Even as they felt that the requirement of effective occupation constituted an important advance, they also held that it had already been part of valid customary law for some time and that its formulation in the Act had been unduly limited: in fact, it had been left to doctrine and practice to generalize it into being applicable outside African coasts.[227] They thus inscribed in the Institute's work program of 1885 a further study of the matter. When would occupation be possible? What type of government was to be accompanied by it? If the Act was not to apply to colonial protectorates, what administrative duties did they entail? Westlake's assessment that "nothing less than a regular government was contemplated as the contribution to be made by a state to the general interest" went clearly further than most States would have conceded, which is probably why

---

[223] Cf. e.g. H. S. Maine, *International Law. The Whewell Lectures* (London, Murray, 1887), pp. 66–67; Westlake, *International Law*, I, pp. 103–105.
[224] Mérignhac, *Traité de droit public international*, II, pp. 458–461.
[225] Westlake, *International Law*, I, pp. 96–113. For the explorers' stories of Africa as part of the case for Empire, cf. McLynn, *Hearts of Darkness*, pp. 310–315.
[226] Twiss, "Le Congrès de Vienne," p. 216.
[227] For some such ambivalence, cf. Salomon, *L'occupation*, pp. 263–273.

he developed the doctrine of "inchoate title" as a right of preference based on acts of lesser intensity than formal government.[228]

In his study for the *Institut* on the effects of the Berlin Act on the law of colonial occupation, the German professor Martitz proposed that it should always be possible to occupy a territory or set up a protectorate over an area that did not already come under the sovereignty or protectorate of one of the States members of the international legal community ("des Etats qui forment la communauté de droit des gens"). This proposal was rejected, however, as many members held that the treatment of almost all non-European territory as *res nullius* in this way went simply too far. As no other proposal was adopted either, the conditions of occupation (or protectorate) were left obscure.[229] As far as the resulting obligations were concerned, Martitz tried almost to reverse the position attained in Berlin by suggesting that occupation and protectorate ("occupation à titre de protectorat") should *both* entail at least some degree of formal rule.[230] Occupation was to be accompanied by the establishment of a responsible local government with sufficient means to ensure the regular exercise of its authority. The establishment of a protectorate would have required setting up some system to protect acquired rights and to see to the education of the natives. However, no formal occupation by Europeans would have been required.[231] Engelhardt produced a draft that was modeled after the French system and applied the requirement of effectiveness also to protectorates, putting them at the level of occupation with regard to duties concerning the protection of natives. The protecting power should have at least the duty to ensure that a local authority was in control of the protected territory.[232]

Neither position was clearly endorsed in the final Declaration adopted in 1888. No agreement was reached on the kinds of territory that could be considered *terra nullius* and thus subject to occupation. There was

---

[228] Westlake, *International Law*, I, pp. 109–111.
[229] For discussion, cf. Fisch, *Die europäische Expansion*, pp. 330–332 and Despagnet, *Essai*, pp. 231–234.   [230] Rapport de M. Martitz (1887–1888), 9 *Annuaire IDI*, p. 249.
[231] Certainly, the very basis of the distinction confirmed at Berlin was to exempt protectorates from such duties, Twiss, "Le Congrès de Vienne," p. 215.
[232] Cf. (1887–88), 9 *Annuaire IDI*, pp. 251–255; (1888–1889), 10 *Annuaire IDI*, pp. 189–190; Salomon, *L'occupation*, pp. 332–333 and Jèze, *Etude théorique*, pp. 240–241. Engelhardt was prepared to accept protection of acquired rights and the duty of keeping the peace. But he also defended the French view that the occupying power should have a duty to guarantee free movement, free trade or non-discrimination. "Etude de la déclaration de la Conférence de Berlin relative aux occupations" (1885), XVII *RDI*, pp. 435–436.

agreement that this did not require that the territory be uninhabited. But Institute members continued to differ about the type of native community whose presence would preclude occupation.[233] As far as protectorates were concerned, they were unwilling to limit the flexibility that was provided by Article 35.[234] In the end, the Declaration failed to propose a change in the prevailing practice that allowed the colonial powers to gain full political control with practically no administrative or humanitarian duties attached.

International lawyers were unable to safeguard the effective extension of the benefits of Western sovereignty into the Orient. What little administrative duties accompanied occupation could always be avoided by setting up a protectorate instead. Despite criticisms, protectorates continued to mean whatever the protecting power wanted them to mean.[235] It was still possible to make extensive spheres of interest and *Hinterland* claims that had nothing to do with the civilizing mission.[236] And whatever the relationship between the colony and the metropolis, the inhabitants of the former invariably became only subjects, never citizens in the latter. In fact, none of the rights valid in European territory were automatically extended to the colony.[237]

In a particularly critical attack in 1909 Jean Perrinjaquet from Aix-en-Provence observed that greed and the wish for exploitation without administrative and policy costs had led European countries to employ hypocritical techniques of annexation without sovereignty. Colonial protectorates had become a regular feature in the French realm (Cambodia, Annam, Tunisia). Annexation of Bosnia-Herzegovina by the Austro-Hungarian Empire was veiled as a lease. So was the British de facto annexation of Cyprus. It was striking how the European States continued to pay lip service to the inviolability of the Ottoman Empire while constantly occupying and bargaining among themselves over large chunks of it. A dangerous gap between appearance and reality was created; different types of annexation were treated differently and their consequences varied, one of the worst injustices being the fact that the

---

[233] (1888–1889), 10 *Annuaire IDI*, pp. 177–184.
[234] Cf. Salomon, *L'occupation*, pp. 94–96, Fisch, *Die europäische Expansion*, pp. 330–332 and Despagnet, *Essai*, pp. 234–240.
[235] Cf. e.g. Adam "Völkerrechtliche Okkupation," pp. 276–281; Nys, *Le droit international*, II, pp. 111–116.
[236] For a critique, cf. e.g. Enrico Catellani, "Les possessions africaines et le droit colonial de l'Italie" (1895), XXVII *RDI*, pp. 429–430.
[237] For the relations between the *Hauptland* and *Nebenland* in Germany, cf. Heimburger, *Erwerb*, pp. 85–87.

inhabitants of the colony were regularly prevented from being citizens and thus deprived of whatever benefit European sovereignty might otherwise have entailed.[238]

The efforts of international lawyers to export formal sovereignty into the colonies had been frustrated by political reality. Egypt, for instance, remained formally a part of the Ottoman empire until the British protectorate was declared in 1914. Yet it had been informally ruled by the British since 1882. Since that time, there existed no important Khedival administration or ministry that was not led by the English: "Every minister has his English legal counsellor or under-secretary for whom he only lends his name, while the provincial administrators are themselves assisted by English *moustechars* . . . As a result, the Khedive rules and England governs."[239]

Occupation is nothing – Fashoda

The requirement of effective administration over colonial territory had already been limited quite drastically in the Berlin Act. In the years that followed, it was further diluted so that by the turn of the century extensive *Hinterland* claims and spheres of interest had become part of a colonial routine whose validity was confirmed in the Fashoda affair.

After the fall of Khartoum in 1885, the Sudan was vacated by European or Egyptian forces and administered as part of the Mahdiyya, a theocracy in perpetual jihad against the infidel under the leadership of the Mahdi.[240] Egypt had formally abandoned the territory, described by one historian as "the largest, most militant and most organized political entity ruled by Africans."[241] Since 1893, Théophile Delcassé (1852–1923), the ambitious French under-secretary of colonies, had entertained the idea of challenging British hegemony in Egypt (as well as the plan for a unified "Cape to Cairo" British African Empire) by undertaking a French advance from the Congo towards the Nile in order to create a horizontal French belt across Africa from the Atlantic to the Red Sea. The British responded the following year by concluding a

---

[238] J. Perrinjaquet, "Des annexations déguisées de territoires" (1909), XVI *RGDIP*, pp. 316–367. Evidently, the author was unaware of the practice that barred even inhabitants of formally annexed territories from full citizenship.

[239] Ed. Engelhardt, "Considérations historiques et juridiques sur les protectorats" (1892), XXIV *RDI*, p. 377.

[240] The Mahdi, or Sheikh Muhammad Ahmad 'Abd Allah, was the leader of the Mahdist rebellion against the English and the de facto ruler of the Sudan in 1885–1898. [241] Lewis, *Fashoda*, p. 137.

Sovereignty: a gift of civilization

treaty with King Léopold in which the territory immediately west from the Nilotic Sudan was leased to him. The French were furious. Gabriel Hanotaux (1853–1944), the Foreign Minister, held the treaty "zero with zero ramifications." Before ratification, Léopold changed his mind, however, and signed a treaty with the French instead, giving France the territory of Upper Ubangi that led straight from the French Congo to the Nile. Now it was time for the British to be angry and in 1895 Foreign Secretary Edward Grey made a declaration in which he affirmed the continued validity of the Cape to Cairo plan and that any attempt to check this – by foreign advance in the Nile region, for instance – would be considered an "unfriendly act."[242]

Nonetheless, the liberal lawyer Léon Bourgeois (of whom more in chapter 3) who served at the time as the French Prime Minister, approved of the plan to send a French occupation expedition, under the leadership of captain Jean-Baptiste Marchand (1863–1934) through the Sudan to establish French presence in the small island of Fashoda, 469 miles south of Khartoum in the section of the White Nile that traverses the Bahr al-Ghazal province of the Sudan. After an epic journey of over two years, Marchand finally hoisted the French flag in Fashoda on 10 July 1898.

Meanwhile, the British government had decided to avenge the loss of Khartoum and to reoccupy the Sudan together with Egyptian forces. For this purpose, Lord Kitchener had been sent to fight the Mahdist dervishes whom he defeated at Omdurman on September 2, 1898. In the morning of September 19 Kitchener appeared outside Fashoda where his army of 24,000 men met with captain Marchand's handful of Europeans and 150 Senegalese *tirailleurs*. At a polite *rendez-vous* not without theatrical qualities Kitchener offered to facilitate an honorable withdrawal for Marchand who responded that he and his men would rather die for *La Patrie* than retreat. After a frantic series of exchanges between London and Paris, the danger of full-scale war between the two countries was averted by the new Foreign Minister Delcassé's decision to give in: Marchand was conveyed thanks and told to prepare the evacuation: "they have the troops . . . we only have the arguments."[243]

The French had assumed that the rules of the scramble had been laid out in Berlin and based sovereign rights on actual occupation (or at least

---

[242] Lewis, *Fashoda*, pp. 47–59; Pakenham, *Scramble for Africa*, pp. 465–467.
[243] For the end of the Fashoda crisis, cf. e.g. Lewis, *Fashoda*, pp. 206–230 and the graphic description in Pakenham, *Scramble for Africa*, pp. 524–556. The quote is from Pakenham, p. 552.

occupation by Europeans, for there had never been any question of recognizing Mahdist sovereignty). From this perspective, the French claim to Fashoda seemed the stronger one.[244] After Egypt and Britain had evacuated the Sudan in 1885, the territory had become a *terra nullius*, available for effective occupation on a first-come-first-served basis.[245] Yet none of this worked out in Fashoda. The 1895 declaration by Sir Edward Grey of a British sphere of interest in the whole of the Nile valley prevailed over French occupation. In the agreement between Britain and France of March 1899 that settled the affair and later in the treaties forming the *Entente cordiale* of 1904, there was no longer any pretence of effective occupation as the governing rule for colonial title. France and Britain agreed on spheres of interest *inter se:* in exchange for a recognition of British predominance in Egypt and the Sudan, France would receive a free hand in Morocco and Tunisia.

French lawyers who commented on the Fashoda affair shared the disappointment of French public opinion – "Never was an affair conducted in poorer way," wrote Albert de Lapradelle (1871–1955) in 1899, outlining the many weaknesses even in the French legal case:[246] the doubts about whether Marchand's small troop had succeeded in establishing de facto effective occupation, the pathetic argument about French title flowing from an agreement with the indigenous Shilluks of the region, the express recognition by Hanotaux a couple of years earlier of the Ottoman Empire's sovereignty in the region. But after Fashoda, international lawyers could hardly continue to insist that colonial title could follow only from setting up effective administration "to protect acquired rights," as required by the Berlin Act. The turn back from effective occupation to abstractly delimited spheres of interest now became an accepted means to manage imperial rivalry.[247] In one sense, at least, this was the more reasonable position: insisting on effective occupation

---

[244] Cf. e.g. Marcel Moye, *Le droit des gens moderne* (Paris, Sirey, 1929), pp. 70–71.

[245] Arthur Girault, "Chronique coloniale" (1898), X *Revue de droit public et la science politique en France et à l'étranger*, pp. 461–462. There was, however, an embarrassing uncertainty about the title of the Ottoman Empire of which Egypt was – formally at least – simply a province over the Sudan. Presumably it had not been in the Egyptian Khedive's power to renounce possessions of the Porte after the Mahdist rebellion. If the English had no basis for their claims over the Sudan, the French, too, may have been bound by their earlier declarations not to encroach on the Porte's possessions. Cf. Georges Blanchard, "L'affaire Fachoda et le droit international" (1899), VI *RGDIP*, pp. 390–427, esp. pp. 395–396, 418–421.

[246] Cf. A. Geouffre De Lapradelle, "Chronique internationale" (1899), XI *Revue de droit public et science politique en France et à l'étranger*, pp. 295–297.

[247] Cf. e.g. Mérignhac, *Traité de droit public international*, II, pp. 444–447.

Sovereignty: a gift of civilization

would have only exacerbated conflicts as enterprising colonial officials would have clashed on the ground seeking to grasp as much territory as possible. In the Anglo-French and Anglo-German treaties of 1890 the principal powers divided West and East Africa between themselves without the slightest concern over effectiveness of occupation: what was important was not the setting up of administration for civilizing or other purposes but to find a suitable *quid pro quo* on which to guarantee interest in future expansion. The key provision of the Anglo-French treaty of July 1898 on the Niger delimited spheres of interest in territories that had hardly been visited by representatives of the parties.[248]

The return to fictive sovereignty at the turn of the century was surveyed by international lawyers with a sense of regret: even if the new treaties provided a new means to fight the slave trade, they were still seen by T. A. Walker (1862–1935) as an incident of "might makes right" – though he then consoled himself that they nonetheless belonged to "the great Scheme of the World's progress."[249] Many lawyers still continued to write as if effective occupation were a principal legal requirement of colonial title but accepted the fact of colonial protectorates and spheres of interest as part of a reality they had to reckon with.[250] By 1914, occupation was no longer seen as an instrument of civilizing mission. A more matter-of-fact type of commentary took over in which the principal protagonists were the colonial powers, not native populations. There was an implicit sense that the civilizing mission had come to naught; the colonial question was transformed into a balance of power problem in which there was scarcely room for philanthropic or humanitarian ideals. Legal commentary on the Act of Algeciras, for instance, was exclusively devoted to analysis of its effects on the relations between Britain, France, and Germany. The standard metaphoric reading of Joseph Conrad's *Heart of Darkness* was enacted in the lawyers' colonial debates: but the journey down the river took place in Europe and led to the cataclysm of 1914.

Sovereignty as terror – the Congo

Perhaps the most striking effort to create European sovereignty – and the greatest disappointment about the civilizing mission – can be gleaned in

---

[248] Cf. text and comment in Girault, "Chronique coloniale," pp. 454–459 and De Lapradelle, "Chronique internationale," pp. 280–284.
[249] T. A. Walker, *The Science of International Law* (London, Clay, 1893), p. 161.
[250] Fiore, "Du protectorat colonial," pp. 151–153.

the story of the "Independent State of the Congo," created in 1884–1885 in part by the private activity of King Léopold II of the Belgians and in part by the concerted action of European powers. The story is familiar, so only its broad outlines need be recalled here. At Léopold's initiative, a conference of private explorers and scientific experts set up in Brussels in September 1876 an *Association Internationale Africain* (AIA).[251] The initiative was enthusiastically applauded by the *Institut* which understood it as having to do principally with the suppression of slavery and slave trade in the Congo basin.[252] Rolin, for instance, commended the scientific and philanthropic objectives of his King though he also doubted whether the setting up of stations in the region could always take place in a peaceful way.[253] Soon thereafter, as we have seen, Moynier and de Laveleye suggested that an effort should be made for the neutralization or internationalization of the river. Simultaneously, Léopold employed Stanley first for his *Comité des Etudes* and in 1882 for the *Association internationale du Congo* (AIC) that was to be the "diplomatic dress [in which] he would found the Congo Free State."[254] By the deliberate confusion of these various bodies Léopold was able to create the impression that a venture that was essentially his private activity bore an international and humanitarian purpose. The securing of the formal recognition of the United States on April 22, 1884 for the Association as possessor of sovereignty over the as yet undefined territory of the Congo was a crucial breakthrough. By the closing of the Berlin Conference in February 1885 the blue flag of Léopold's Association had become recognized by all European States as the flag of a sovereign State and the "Independent State of the Congo," with King Léopold as its head of State, was invited to adhere to the Berlin Act and thus became formally bound by it.[255]

---

[251] For the background, cf. Thomson, *Fondation*, pp. 41–53; Dumont, *Léopold II*, pp. 150–159; Pakenham, *Scramble for Africa*, pp. 11–29, 239–255; Jan Stengers, "Leopold II and the Association International du Congo," in Förster, Mommsen, and Robinson, *Bismarck, Europe, and Africa*, pp. 229–244 and Hochschild, *King Leopold's Ghost*, pp. 61–87.   [252] Reported in (1877), IX *RDI*, pp. 318–319.
[253] Gustave Rolin-Jaequemyns, "L'oeuvre de l'exploration et de civilization de l'Afrique centrale" (1877), IX *RDI*, pp. 288–291.   [254] Pakenham, *Scramble for Africa*, p. 161.
[255] Already the previous year, Léopold's diplomacy in the United States had borne fruit. In the President's address to the Congress of December 4, 1883, he stated: "The objects of the society are philanthropic. It does not aim at permanent political control, but seeks the neutrality of the valley." Pakenham, *Scramble for Africa*, p. 244. For the story of the recognitions and of King Léopold's deliberate obfuscation of the nature and purposes of the Association cf. also pp. 243–253 and Dumont, *Léopold II*, pp. 179–186, Thomson, *Fondation*, pp. 147–162, and Hochschild, *King Leopold's Ghost*, pp. 75–82.

Sovereignty: a gift of civilization

The Independent State was not a formal creation of the Berlin Conference. But nor was it simply the effect of one man's diplomacy either, as some accounts suggest, but served a general European interest. By agreeing on free navigation and free trade in the area European States sought to secure maximal commercial advantage in the enormous territory in the middle of Africa without administrative burdens for any one of them.[256] It is a well-known paradox that to secure freedom of trade, someone has to be given exclusive rights to enforce it. To deal with the paradox, the powers chose an apparently neutral outsider with philanthropic pretensions.[257] This is why Belgian lawyers (Rolin and de Laveleye) were able to interpret the arrangement as an international protectorate and to enlist the enthusiasm of the *Institut*. After the Conference had ended, the institute expressed its gratitude to King Léopold for having assumed the humanitarian task of administering the Congo.[258] The Baltic-Russian Martens who doubted the colonial venture generally thanked the King in gracious terms: "It is without a doubt that thanks to the generosity and the political genius of King Léopold, the Congo State will have a regime in full conformity with the requirements of European culture."[259]

But as soon as Léopold had received the endorsement of the powers, he started building the unprecedented system of wealth-extraction and servitude that characterized his rule over the territory. In 1885 he passed a decree claiming all "vacant lands" as the property of the State. This meant that all uncultivated areas outside native villages – in practice over 90 percent of the country – became at a stroke the private property of the King. Later decrees set up an administrative system under which private companies (in many of which Léopold himself was a substantial shareowner) were granted concessionary monopolies to extract ivory and minerals, and in the 1890s especially rubber. New decrees from 1891–1892 prohibited the inhabitants from collecting products received from the State's property. Unauthorized trade was severely punished. A labor tax was introduced under which the inhabitants were expected to work in principle forty hours a month in order to collect rubber for the State's purposes. Although such a system was in use in other colonial

---

[256] As Robinson observes, the Congo Free State was an elaborate (although faulty) attempt to provide a neutral, international framework under a King whose "international credentials seemed unimpeachable," "The Conference in Berlin," p. 23.
[257] Cf. Robinson, "The Conference in Berlin," p. 17.
[258] Déclaration, Bruxelles 1885 (1885–1886), 8 *Annuaire IDI*, pp. 17–18.
[259] F. de Martens, "La Conférence du Congo à Berlin et la politique coloniale des états modernes" (1886), XVIII *RDI*, p. 268.

territories as well, in the Congo the number of hours was converted to units of quantity (or rubber especially) that, together with the system whereby administrators and company agents received premiums on amounts of produce they were able to collect, turned much of the population into full-time slave laborers. These and other measures were administered with a ruthlessness that saw no equivalent in the African colonies. No schools or hospitals were set up during the King's reign or other measures undertaken in compliance with the provisions of the Berlin Act.[260] Frequent uprisings were suppressed by Léopold's *Force publique*, whose methods of warfare included massacres of the populations of whole villages, the notorious severing of the hands of killed or sometimes simply recalcitrant natives, and the destruction of native cattle and crops.[261] Though statistics of the period are unreliable, as many as 8–10 million Congolese died as a result of these measures.[262]

Criticism of the King's rule first appeared in the international press in the 1890s but increased towards the end of the century. Journalists and missionaries reported on the reign of terror first sporadically but thanks to the indefatigable energy of the humanitarian activist Edmund Morel (1873–1924), soon methodologically and with increasing effect at the political level. In 1903 the British House of Commons passed a resolution calling for an international examination of the allegations. In the same year an official report was produced by the British consul in the Congo, Roger Casement (1864–1916), that graphically described the practices of the King's administration and was of decisive importance in producing the popular outrage that crystallized in the creation of the Congo Reform Association of which Morel became the head.[263] The Casement Report was followed up by a number of similar documents by British and American consuls, and also a 1905 report by a Commission of Inquiry set up by Léopold himself that detailed additional facts of the system of slave labor in the Congo. Finally the pressure on the King built up to the extent that he was compelled to transfer the territory to Belgium in 1908 – though not without

---

[260] There is a wealth of writing on the system of administration set up in the Congo in and after 1885. Cf. e.g. Roger Anstey, *King Leopold's Legacy: The Congo under Belgian Rule 1908–1960* (Oxford University Press, 1966), pp. 1–10. The facts were revealed to Belgian audiences by Félicien Cattier, *Etude sur la situation de l'Etat indépendant du Congo* (Brussels and Paris, Larcier and Pedone, 1906). A more recent account is Hochschild, *King Leopold's Ghost*, pp. 115–181.

[261] On the Swahili wars, cf. Lewis, *Fashoda*, pp. 61–72.

[262] Lewis, *Fashoda*, p. 92; Hochschild, *King Leopold's Ghost*, p. 233.

[263] Anstey, *King Leopold's Legacy*, p. 12.

Sovereignty: a gift of civilization

a sizeable financial compensation.[264] Belgian behavior in the Congo continued, however, to remain subject to criticism until the Congo Reform Association was dismantled in 1913 and the oncoming war directed popular attention elsewhere.

What attitude did international lawyers take in this process? After 1885, textbooks regularly made a note of the anomalous birth history of the Independent State, of the personal union that existed between Belgium and the Congo, and of the neutralization and freedom of navigation regimes that were applicable on paper in its territory. Until 1908, however, they did not normally include any mention of the humanitarian criticisms of the possible violation by the King of the Berlin Act.[265] In the 1890s French lawyers sometimes commented upon the recurrent negotiations between King Léopold and the Belgian Government concerning the eventual Belgian annexation of the Congo.[266] No in-depth studies of the situation in the country – that is to say, on its compliance with the provisions of the Berlin Act – were undertaken by international lawyers. A significant exception to this general silence, however, is constituted by a few Belgian studies on the laws and practices of the Independent State. A first general overview of the treatment of the native population, clearly directed to foreigners, was written by Félicien Cattier (1869–1946), *privat-docent* and professor of public law at the University of Brussels and later Chairman of the *Union minière du-Haut-Katanga* (1932–1939 and 1944–1946), in Rolin's review in 1895. By reference to legislative texts from the Congo administration, and without an independent examination of how they were applied, Cattier sought to demonstrate the admirable way in which the Independent State had fulfilled its humanitarian obligations.[267] The "general spirit" of the administration was, Cattier wrote, to leave as many native institutions as possible to continue as before – although often the inhabitants themselves sought assistance from European laws or tribunals. A slow but perceptible change was underway in the "native mentality" that induced the inhabitants to cultivate the habit of work in order to receive the benefits of civilization. All native rights were recognized by the legislation in

---

[264] For the Congo reform movement and the annexation of the Congo by Belgium, cf. Dumont, *Leopold II*, pp. 275–317; Hochschild, *King Leopold's Ghost*, pp. 185–305.

[265] Cf. e.g. Bonfils–Fauchille, *Manuel*, pp. 81–82, 178; von Liszt, *Das Völkerrecht*, pp. 40, 43–44 *passim*.

[266] The French had an obvious interest in the annexation inasmuch as Léopold had in 1884 promised France a right of first option if he decided to give up the territory.

[267] F. Cattier, "L'Etat indépendant du Congo et les indigènes" (1895), XXVII *RDI*, pp. 263–281.

force, which also contained severe penalties for misbehavior. All in all, he concluded that "the totality of the measures taken form a full body of legislation whose application protects the indigenous people against all forms of oppression and exploitation."[268]

The article was an altogether clumsy work of propaganda and can only partly be excused by Cattier's later disillusionment with the King's operations and his taking a visible role in advocating the handing over of the country to Belgium – "the Belgian solution." Cattier's 1906 *Etude sur la situation de l'Etat indépendant du Congo* created a shock in Belgian political milieus and contributed significantly to the transformation of attitudes in favor of immediate annexation. The target of the book was, however, less the humanitarian aspects of the King's reign than his having stowed away on personal accounts millions of francs borrowed from the Belgian State ostensibly to pay off Congo's budget deficit. But Cattier also had an audience with the British Foreign Secretary, Lord Grey, arranged through the Congo Reform Association, whom he seems to have impressed with his Belgian solution.[269]

None of the other Belgian lawyers, however, expressed public criticism towards the Congo administration. Both Rolin and his friend Rivier from Brussels had been appointed members of the *Conseil supérieur* of the Independent State, an appeals body that was set up by Léopold to respond to the growing criticisms. Both had already left the scene in 1903 as the international campaign against Léopold became official. At that moment, however, the most visible Belgian international lawyers Ernest Nys (1851–1921) and Baron Edouard Descamps (1847–1933) rallied to the vocal defense of their King.[270] Nys, a distinguished legal historian, Professor of International Law at the University of Brussels, and member of the *Institut*, wrote a series of articles as a response to the British *notes verbales*, completely rejecting accusations on inhuman treatment or breach of the free trade or navigation provisions.[271] He responded to the British with a series of *tu quoque* arguments: every State

---

[268] Cattier, "L'Etat indépendent du Congo," p. 281.
[269] Cattier, *L'Etude sur la situation*, pp. 353–358; Anstey, *King Leopold's Legacy*, pp. 10, 15; Dumont, *Léopold II*, pp. 300–303; Pakenham, *Scramble for Africa*, pp. 644–645, 657.
[270] Cf. Ernest Nys, "L'état indépendant du Congo et le droit international" (1903), 2/V *RDI*, pp. 333–379; le chevalier Descamps, "Le différend anglo-congolais" (1904), 2/VI *RDI*, pp. 233–259.
[271] Ernest Nys, "L'état indépendant du Congo et les dispositions de l'acte générale de Berlin" (1903), 2/V *RDI*, 1903, pp. 315–332 and "L'état indépendant du Congo et le droit international," pp. 333–379.

Sovereignty: a gift of civilization

considered vacant lands as State property; all colonial powers used methods that were in use in the Congo. How the State dealt with vacant lands was in any case not a matter for international law but for the State's own constitutional and private law to resolve. "A State uses the territories that constitute its private domain as it wishes; it sells them, it rents them out, it attaches such conditions to the concessions it grants as it sees warranted . . . in none of this does it owe an explanation to other States."[272] No violation of the free trade provisions of the Berlin Act was involved, Nys claimed. Neither State ownership of vacant lands nor the granting of concessionary rights constituted a monopoly under Article 5 which prohibited the parties only from establishing "any kind of commercial monopoly or privilege" ("monopole et privilège d'aucune sorte en matière commerciale"): this concerned only the right to buy and sell, to import and to export, and had nothing to do with property rights over natural resources.[273] In a lengthy, pedantic survey of the status of the Congo State in light of the events of 1884–1885 Nys joined the other Belgians in arguing that the recognitions did not possess constitutive character and that in any case, neither they nor the obligations of the Berlin Act *conditioned* the statehood of the Congo in any way.[274] He maintained that the Congo had carefully complied with all the provisions of the Berlin Act, including those having to do with the protection of the indigenous people: "The Independent State of the Congo has not neglected any effort, has not spared itself any sacrifice in order to realize the humanitarian wishes of the Conference of Berlin of 1884 and 1885."[275]

In the following year Nys was joined by Descamps, Professor of International Law from Louvain, a Catholic politician, advocate of international arbitration, and a member of the Belgian delegation at the Hague Peace Conference of 1899. Descamps later received fame as the member of the *Comité des juristes* that drafted the Statute of the Permanent Court of International Justice on whose proposal "general principles of law recognized by civilized nations" were inserted in the list

---

[272] Nys, "L'état indépendant du Congo et les dispositions de l'acte générale," p. 328.
[273] Nys, "L'état indépendant du Congo et les dispositions de l'acte générale," pp. 329–332.
[274] Nys, "L'état indépendant du Congo et le droit international," pp. 333–371.
[275] "L'Etat indépendant du Congo n'a négligé aucun effort, ne s'est épargné aucun sacrifice pour réaliser les voeux humanitaires de la conférence de Berlin de 1884 et de 1885," Nys, "L'état indépendant du Congo et le droit international," p. 373. As proof he cited an official June 1903 report from the Congo.

of sources the Court was to apply.[276] Now he published a colonialist tract, *L'Afrique nouvelle*, speculating on the advantages small European countries such as Belgium as well as Africa itself would receive from colonization. The book was an over 600-page attempt to refute the attacks against the administration of the Congo from the outside – oddly out of balance, however, by never identifying the attacks that provided its source of energy. In form, it was a history of the Independent State from the Berlin Act to the country's present administrative structures. Much space was devoted to proving that the Berlin Act had created an economic regime of freedom of *commerce* and not *ownership* against those who "have tried to . . . deny the right of the State."[277] The labor tax was defended as a natural form of collecting revenues in African society – rather like military service. In the hands of civilized government, it also taught the natives the value "of regular employment and thus began the work for their moral and material improvement."[278] Whatever problems might have emerged in its application should not be rashly accredited to the State.[279] The book stressed the King's personal role as the century's greatest philanthropist, fighter against the slave trade, and initiator of an altogether new phase in African colonization. Everything possible had been done for the civilizing purpose; autocracy was necessary – but gradually even the (mature) natives would receive rights of citizenship.[280] Critics had "exaggerated the facts, generalized from isolated cases, or formulated impossible demands."[281] Behind the criticisms had been "certain individuals that are unsatisfied for divers reasons, are in a bad mood and throw their complaints to the winds."[282] For Descamps, colonization of Africa was not only justified but "decreed by the double law of conservation and progress that is a proper law of humanity."[283]

In 1904 he returned to the matter in Rolin's *Revue* with the specific intent of responding to the Casement Report.[284] Like many Belgians,

---

[276] Descamps was an active politician, member of the provincial council of Brabant and of the Belgian Senate after 1892. He was Secretary-General and President of the Inter-Parliamentary Union and Minister of Arts and Sciences in 1907–1910. For biographies, cf. A. De Lapradelle, *Maîtres et doctrines du droit des gens* (2nd edn., Paris, Editions internationales, 1950), pp. 325–335; Arthur Eyffinger, *The 1899 Hague Peace Conference* (The Hague and Boston, Kluwer, 1999), pp. 135–136.
[277] Descamps, *L'Afrique nouvelle*, pp. 132, 201–207.
[278] Descamps, *L'Afrique nouvelle*, pp. 140, 150–153.
[279] Descamps, *L'Afrique nouvelle*, p. 259.
[280] Such rights were already enjoyed by the non-indigenous Congolese, Descamps, *L'Afrique nouvelle*, pp. 278–283, 301–305.   [281] Descamps, *L'Afrique nouvelle*, p. 372.
[282] Descamps, *L'Afrique nouvelle*, p. 615.   [283] Descamps, *L'Afrique nouvelle*, p. 594.
[284] Descamps, "Le différend Anglo-Congolais," pp. 233–259.

Sovereignty: a gift of civilization

Descamps assumed that the attacks were based on ulterior motives: the economic interests of Manchester and Liverpool, a wish to direct attention away from Britain's own colonial problems. His substantive response consisted of three points. First, every State needed to make sure that vacant lands are not left for spoliation (something he assumed an automatic effect of "primitive" Congolese agriculture). Second, the humanitarian complaints were in part correct, in part based on mistaken or exaggerated facts. Even as problems had emerged, there was no evidence that they were caused by the State rather than by individual administrators or traders – and action had been taken to punish them and prevent their re-occurrence. Third, Descamps denied that the Berlin Act established any international supervision. Arbitration, for instance, as proposed by the British *note verbal* was out of the question: the provision on the amelioration of the condition of the natives delegated the State a wide discretion on how this should take place. "As such, this engagement is manifestly not among those to which the parties of the Berlin Act had intended to accord each other perfect rights that would involve the authority to exercise their fulfillment or to control their exercise."[285]

Apart from the apologies by Nys and Descamps, the international law community stayed silent during the peak years of the Congo controversy, 1903–1908. The indifference of international lawyers is perhaps best demonstrated by the absence of any reaction to Cattier in 1895 or to Nys and Descamps in 1903 and 1904, despite the fact that by the latter date extensive information on the red-rubber policies of the Congo was readily available. Bearing in mind the pride *Institut* members took in having initiated international action in the Congo in 1878, and their enthusiasm for Léopold's early efforts, it seems odd that neither they nor the *Institut* took a position in regard to the problems. To be sure, many of the early Congo activists had died by 1903 (in addition to Rolin and Rivier, also De Laveleye in 1892 and Twiss in 1897). But Moynier, for instance, had in 1890 become honorary consul of the Congo in Switzerland and continued to write about African and other affairs until his death in 1910. As his biographer notes, his silence over the treatment of the Congolese "throws a shadow over the memory of the philanthropist."[286] Westlake who often commented on African events and disputes, and who felt no scruple to criticize European behavior in the Balkans,

---

[285] Descamps, "Le différend Anglo-Congolais," p. 245.
[286] Bernard Bouvier, *Gustave Moynier* (Geneva, Imprimerie du Journal du Genève, 1918), p. 33 n1.

never wrote on the practices of the Independent State – apart from commenting on its birth history and neutralization.[287] Even as the anti-Congolese movement became part of British foreign policy and British radicals were indicting King Léopold in the House of Commons, Westlake did not feel a need to examine the matter from an international law perspective.[288]

Although a number of French lawyers discussed the status of the Independent State, and the plans of annexation by Belgium, they held aloof from criticisms voiced by the Congo Reform Association – possibly because many of such accusations might have been directed at the practices in the French Congo that had been administered by private companies since the late 1890s after Léopold's model and whose rubber-rich regions experienced a comparable loss of population – in some areas up to 50 percent.[289] Only after 1908, after the transformation of the Congo into a Belgian colony, did international lawyers feel able to say something about the way the King had exercised his sovereignty. Frantz Despagnet (1857–1906), for example, inserted a passage in his treatise in which he speculated that the Congo State might have violated the Berlin Act and that the situation had been "perhaps illegal and certainly contrary to humanity and morality."[290] The same conclusion was made also by Jesse Reeves (1872–1942) in his survey in the *American Journal of International Law* of the status of the Independent State after its incorporation as a Belgian colony in 1909.[291]

The actuality of the matter in 1908 is explained by the fact that some of the powers – in particular Great Britain – refrained from recognizing the annexation of the Independent State – less perhaps as protest against the treatment of its population than owing to a sense that as the Congo

---

[287] Westlake, *International Law*, I, pp. 30, 46.
[288] Westlake continued publishing until his death in 1913 but none of his (published) writings dealt with the humanitarian problem in the Congo. For bibliography, cf. *Memories of John Westlake* (London, Smith & Elder, 1914), Appendix, pp. 147–154. It is difficult to see why this was so. He regularly commented on the on-going disputes in which Britain was involved. He may have agreed with Nys that the matter was purely an internal or constitutional one or, more charitably, held it unnecessary to add his voice to the anyway quite loud British criticisms against the country of so many of his old friends.
[289] Hochschild, *King Leopold's Ghost*, p. 280. For detailed statistics, cf. Catherine Coquery-Vidrovitch, *Le Congo au temps des grands compagnies concessionaires 1898–1930* (Paris and The Hague, Mouton, 1972), pp. 494–506.
[290] Frantz Despagnet, *Cours de droit international public* (4th edn., Paris, Sirey, 1910), p. 101.
[291] Jesse S. Reeves, "The Origin of the Congo Free State, Considered from the Standpoint of International Law" (1909), 3 *American Journal of International Law* (*AJIL*), pp. 117–118.

Sovereignty: a gift of civilization

had been created through international action, its future fate should also be decided internationally. The debate among international lawyers thus focused on the formal status of the Independent State, on whether it owed its sovereignty to the powers that recognized it and which might now be able to "derecognize" it and to take its fate into their hands – or whether its statehood arose independently of the recognitions and the King's cession to Belgium was fully valid.[292] The proposal of international action, however, soon showed itself unrealistic and most international lawyers probably agreed with the conclusion that "[i]t was the anomalous character in international law of the State which has made the Congo question so difficult of treatment" and that the anomaly could now finally be disposed of as: "the Congo Free State now passes out of existence and becomes in fact what it should have been long ago, a Belgian colony."[293]

This view captures the original understanding of the international lawyers that the work of civilization went hand in hand with public law sovereignty. Though the Congo venture was initiated as an extension of European sovereignty into Africa, it failed, and the task was to explain precisely in what that failure resided. For Reeves as for other international lawyers, the original colonial project remained viable and the Congo State had failed only because it had *deviated* from that project. No real public law sovereignty had ever come into existence in the Congo. As Cattier argued in his indictment of 1906: The Independent State was "not a colonial power; it [was] a financial enterprise . . . administered neither in the interests of the indigenous people nor even in the interests of Belgium [but] for the benefit of the King-Sovereign."[294] The annexation by Belgium brought the Congo within the steady advance of civilization by ensuring that the arbitrary reign of private interest and privilege would no longer prevail:

as a colony it will become subject to government by discussion. In a country where party strife is active, where liberal ideas find such ready expression, responsible parliamentary government must surely be a guaranty that the provisions of the Berlin Act will be observed in spirit as well as in letter[295]

Though probably correct, this explanation reveals a blind spot among international lawyers towards the atrocities that went on at the same time in "normal" or "legitimate" French or German colonies in Africa

---

[292] Cf. in particular, Paul Errera, "Le Congo belge" (1908), 28 *Revue de droit public et de la science politique en France et à l'étranger*, pp. 730–753.
[293] Reeves, "The Origin of the Congo Free State," p. 118.
[294] Cattier, *Etude sur la situation*, p. 341.
[295] Reeves, "The Origin of the Congo Free State," p. 118.

and on which they kept an equal or even fuller silence than on the Congo. These cases were no anomalies.

From sovereignty to internationalization

The first decade of the twentieth century saw not only a regime of terror in King Léopold's realm but also in the French Congo as well as in German South West Africa, where of an estimated Herero population of 80,000 in 1903 fewer than 20,000 were alive after General Lieutenant von Trotha's extermination order (*Vernichtungsbefehl*) had been put into effect in 1906.[296] Neither the *Institut* nor international lawyers individually felt it necessary to draw attention to these events, occurring as they did as parts of mainstream imperialism by European great powers. It was easy for international lawyers such as Rolin or Westlake to appeal against the slaughter of Armenian Christians by Turkey, or in favor of Finland's autonomous status within the Russian empire. In these conflicts, the threat came from the outside, and was directed at apparently European cultural and political values. When the threat came from formal (colonial) States, however, and was directed against communities sharing little of what Europeans held valuable, the matter became difficult. Attention to them would either have destroyed the myth of the inseparability of European public law sovereignty and civilization, or it would have posed questions about the meaning of sovereignty whose implications would no longer have been confined to the margins but would have struck at the heart of the legitimating principle of Europe's own political order.

One obvious paradox should have set alarm bells ringing that all was not right. The argument about the civilizing mission was completely unhelpful as discussion turned to disputes between the colonial powers themselves. Reading through the first three decades of Rolin's *Revue*, one gets no sense that colonization was viewed as a common European venture. Although all lawyers spoke in terms of a homogeneous "Europe" acting upon an equally homogeneous "Orient," in fact everyone's *conscience juridique* supported the controversial colonial policy of his homeland. The British lawyers accepted British colonialism in a matter of fact way, having a much more liberal view of the activities of colonial companies than their continental colleagues. Westlake's writings on the Anglo-Portuguese conflict in Southern Africa or between England and

---

[296] Pakenham, *Scramble for Africa*, pp. 611–615.

Sovereignty: a gift of civilization

the Boers faithfully ratified the British positions.[297] The German international law community saw colonization as a natural part of Germany's development into a leading European power.[298] No questions about the justification of expansion were posed: everybody did it and the only problem was that Germany had made its move late in the day. No critical accounts were published by German international lawyers of the extreme brutality with which the native uprisings were suppressed. In the relevant years 1900–1914, the *Archiv des öffentlichen Rechts* that had earlier devoted a number of studies to colonial questions remained silent.

The criticism of commercial colonization by French lawyers was initially quite compatible with French colonial policy. When the French, too, turned increasingly from the 1890s to colonial companies, the criticisms diminished.[299] In disputes with other powers, French lawyers loyally underwrote French positions. The historian and geographer Henri Castonnet des Fossés (1846–1898) had no doubt that the French annexation of Madagascar in 1884 was based on effective possession and consent – the Hovas having been incited to rebellion by the British.[300] Engelhardt defended the French protectorates in North Africa and the Far East. After the 1904 *entente* with Britain and Germany in North Africa, French lawyers turned their attention away from colonial matters – they were removed from the realm of the international. Their patriotism remained unshaken, however. In 1920 Marcel Moye (1873–1939), Professor of International Law at Montpellier, continued to make a sharp distinction between French and non-French colonialism. He contrasted the "regrettable acts" undertaken in the Congo with French North Africa that had, in his view, become "sans contredit un des

---

[297] Cf. e.g. John Westlake, "L'Angleterre et la République Sud-Africaine" (1896), XXVIII *RDI*, pp. 268–300.

[298] Geffcken, "L'Allemagne et la question coloniale," p. 131. He also defends the way German colonizers put indigenous cultivation under European supervision – this was both morally and commercially defensible.

[299] The main critic being Jèze. Good reviews of the new French attitudes towards colonization through commerce in the 1890s are to be found in Coquery-Vidrovitch, *Le Congo*, pp. 25–30 and Pierre Guillen, *L'expansion* (Politique étrangère de la France 1881–1898, Paris, Imprimerie nationale, 1984), pp. 53–69. Despagnet draws critical attention to this practice in the second edition of his *Cours de droit international public*, pp. 429–432.

[300] H. Castonnet des Fosses, "Les droits de la France sur Madagascar" (1885), XVII *RDI*, 1885, p. 442. The French arguments are challenged in E.-L. Catellani, "Les droits de la France sur Madagascar et le dernier traité de paix" 1886, XVIII *RDI*, pp. 151–158.

plus belles colonies du monde" – passing over in silence the continued popular resistance in Algeria and Morocco.[301]

The Belgians, as we have seen, apart from Cattier (who was not an *international* lawyer) were united in the rejection of the criticisms of King Léopold's rule in the Congo. Fedor Martens – otherwise a skeptic about colonization – engaged in a lengthy polemic with Westlake to defend the Russian penetration into the Caucasus.[302] Manuel Torres Campos (1853–1918) saw Spain as the great civilizing force in the dark continent and foresaw a development of four great linguistic empires (English, Chinese, Russian, and Spanish) in which Spain would be "the great representative of the Latin family."[303] Even Catellani, whom we met at the outset of this chapter complaining about the dominance of force in international relations, defended the Italian annexation of Assab and Massawa on the Red Sea in the 1880s. He hoped that Abyssinia would see in Italy "a sincere friend and a precious ally" and regarded it as perfectly natural for Italy to plan the colonization of Tripolitania in order not to fall into the status of a second-rate power.[304] In particular, Catellani defended the Italian reading of the Treaty of Ucciali (1889) against Abyssinia's Menelik in the controversy about whether the Treaty created an Italian protectorate over the country.[305] Though he did not precisely advocate an Italian attack on Abyssinia, when that attack came, and with it Italian disaster at the battle of Adowa on March 1, 1896, he poured his disappointment into the indictment of the use of force by colonial powers generally in his critical overview of *fin-de-siècle* international law.[306]

That international lawyers moved so easily from arguments about the civilizing mission to supporting the controversial policies of their native country should have signaled to them that no single civilization spoke in their voice. The sovereignty which they offered to the colonies was more

---

[301] Marcel Moye, *Le droit des gens moderne. Précis élémentaire à l'usage des étudiants des facultés de droit* (Paris, Sirey, 1920), p. 81.
[302] Fedor Martens, "Chronique de droit international. La Russie et l'Angleterre dans l'Asie centrale" (1879), XI *RDI*, pp. 227–301. For his rejoinder to Westlake cf. (1880), XII *RDI*, pp. 47–59.
[303] M. Torres Campos, "L'Espagne en Afrique" (1892), XXIV *RDI*, pp. 445, 472–473.
[304] M. E. Catellani, "La politique coloniale de l'Italie" (1885), XVII *RDI*, pp. 227–228, 236–237, 238. But he did prefer that Tripolitania remain a part of the Ottoman Empire.
[305] M. E. Catellani, "Les possessions africaines et le droit colonial de l'Italie" (1895), XXVII *RDI*, pp. 423–425.
[306] At Adowa, Menelik's force of 100,000 completely wiped out the Italian invasion force of 20,000. By the end of the battle, half the Italians were dead, wounded, or missing.

Sovereignty: a gift of civilization

an instrument for inter-European struggle than a program to reorganize non-European society. Aside from failing to forestall conflicts between European powers, sovereignty proved disappointing in two ways. First, it was rarely exported outside the metropolitan territory in an effective way. By 1904 colonial protectorates, spheres of interest and *Hinterland* claims, and forms of indirect rule had become accepted parts of empire. Indigenous Kings and other notables continued to rule "as quasi-employees of the colonial administration."[307] The African colonial entity remained an abstraction: its forty or so colonial territories had been amalgamated out of approximately 10,000 indigenous units. In Nigeria, the ratio of British administrators to native inhabitants was 1:100,000.[308] Political emancipation could hardly be achieved under such conditions. Thus, as the first African elites graduated from European universities, their nationalism remained a work of imagination that, when it strove for African sovereignty, could be initially dismissed as practically irrelevant.

But second, where sovereignty did become a reality – as it did in the Congo – its beneficiality was far from evident. When Descamps and Nys claimed that the Congo administration was an internal affair, they detached sovereignty from its liberal justifications. The Congo situation showed that sovereignty and civilization did not automatically go hand in hand and that they did not because sovereignty *had no determined meaning*. It could be associated with liberality and with tyranny, it could justify a limited State that delegated its power to private actors, or an interventionist State – just as it could carry out a politics of assimilation or association (and more frequently hovered between the two). As abstract status it did not dictate any specific colonial policy – after all, it had not replaced the need for domestic politics in the metropolitan territories either. It merely created a right of exclusivity in its European holder.

It was their failure to spell out the meaning of sovereignty in social and political terms, as applied in non-European territory, that in retrospect made international lawyers seem such hopeless apologists of empire. This failure, again, was related to the ignorance of the lawyers of the conditions in the Orient. When an attempt was made by the *Institut* to conduct a study of those conditions, the result was a perplexing variety of data that seemed to exclude all general conclusions. This lack

---

[307] Alexandrowicz, *The African-European Confrontation*, p. 111.
[308] Cf. e.g. H. S. Wilson, *African Decolonization* (London and New York, Edward Arnold, 1994), pp. 11–26.

of a substantive policy of legal reform made the profession fall back on generalities about the civilizing mission – with the risk that supporting the more or less controversial colonial policies of this or that European power involved them every now and then in the quarrels that were waged in European parliaments. In this situation, international lawyers found little room in which to argue in a distinctly professional way – until the failures of sovereignty gave rise to arguments about the internationalization of the civilizing mission.

In Europe, as we saw in chapter 1, liberal lawyers stressed the need to balance nationalism with an enlightened *esprit d'internationalité*. If sovereignty failed to further the civilizing mission in the colonies, why not extend the internationalist spirit there as well? Such an argument had been made already in Joseph Hornung's five articles in Rolin's journal in 1885–1886. Not only must European intervention be organized in a collective way, he had written, its objective must be a Kantian *Völkerstaat*: "directed in the common interest by the most enlightened and the most liberal States."[309] Other lawyers, too, had defined colonization in international terms. Rolin and de Laveleye had interpreted Léopold's rule in the Congo as an international mandate. Catellani redefined "colonial protectorate" as an international protectorate, emphasizing – like Lord Lugard, the leading British colonial ideologist – the colonial power's "dual mandate" towards the population as well as other powers (particularly in terms of commercial access).[310] When Moynier and de Laveleye anticipated inter-European conflict in the Congo, they proposed the "neutralization" of the area to provide for free trade, freedom of navigation and the duties of civilization.

There were only a few precedents for such proposals: the internationalization applied to European rivers and to a few protectorates since 1815, the administration of treaty ports in China and Japan, perhaps the joint financial administration of Egypt by leading European powers, and consular co-operation between Europeans in key Oriental regions. These arrangements were not conceived as international administration but as forms of practical co-ordination between interested powers. They were often controversial, temporary, and anything but central to the civilizing mission. By 1945, however, the League of Nations would cite them (together with the Berlin Conference) as early precedents for the

[309] Hornung, "Civilisés et barbares" (part 3), pp. 542–544.
[310] Catellani, "Les possessions africaines," p. 421.

Sovereignty: a gift of civilization

mandates system that was set up under Article 22 of the Covenant.[311] By that time, the doctrine of the "sacred trust of civilization" had replaced formal European imperialism as the perspective from which international law conceived Europe's outside. In a few years, it was transformed into the notion of trusteeship under the United Nations Charter that, for its part, became only an interim status leading to political sovereignty for non-European territories.[312]

At the end of the First World War, popular opinion had turned decisively against formal empire. Territorial gains had also been excluded from the Allied war aims. Thus the question arose what to do with the former German colonies and the non-Turkish parts of the Ottoman empire that had been handed over to the *entente* powers.[313] As one among his fourteen points, President Wilson declared to the US Senate in early 1919 that the subject peoples' interests should be at the same level as those of established powers and that the "well-being of peoples not yet able to stand by themselves . . . forms a sacred trust of civilization." As is well known, the result was limited League supervision of three classes of former German and Turkish colonies: the "A" mandates (Syria and Lebanon, Palestine and Transjordan, and Iraq), that received internal self-government and were expected to become independent at a future date, the "B" mandates (the Cameroons, Togoland, Tanganyika, Rwanda-Urundi) for whose administration the mandatory remained responsible, and the "C" mandates (South West Africa and the Pacific Islands) that were to be administered as integral parts of the Mandatory's territory.[314] It was unclear how the system should be legally characterized. The involvement of the Allied Supreme Council, the Mandatory powers, the League and individual States (especially the United States) created a long-standing controversy on where sovereignty over the mandated territories lay, and how wide-ranging were the duties

---

[311] Cf. The League of Nations, *The Mandates System; Origin – Principles – Applications* (League of Nations Publications, Geneva, 1945), pp. 7–13. Cf. also Alexandrowicz, *The European–African Confrontation*, pp. 115–116.

[312] R. N. Chowdhury, *International Mandates and Trusteeship Systems. A Comparative Study* (The Hague, Nijhoff, 1955) contains a well-founded criticism of the anachronism in attempts to "see" the origin of the mandates in the writings of nineteenth-century jurists and the Berlin Conference, pp. 13–24.

[313] The distribution was carried out within the Allied Supreme Council in January 1919.

[314] For the establishment of the mandates system, cf. e.g. Albert Millot, *Les mandats internationaux. Etude sur l'application de l'article 22 du Pacte de la Société des Nations* (Paris, Larose, 1924), pp. 5–86.

of the mandatory power and those of the relevant League organ (the Permanent Mandates Commission, PMC) were.[315]

Whatever position lawyers took in the complex debates about where sovereignty with regard to the mandates lay, it soon became clear that there was something artificial about that question.[316] Sovereignty was not a unitary attribute that either was present or absent so that once it was known where it lay, controversies over the rights of the protagonists would be resolved. On the contrary, the abstract question of sovereignty was distinguished from the rights and duties that were distributed in a complex way between the five parties: the mandated territory and its population, the mandatory power, the Allied Supreme Council, the League of Nations, League members. Lawyers such as Henri Rolin (1874–1946), Professor at the University of Brussels, specialist in colonial law, who argued that formal sovereignty lay with the mandatory immediately added that it was, however, limited in a number of ways *vis-à-vis* the territory and League organs.[317] Those who argued that sovereignty lay with the territory itself needed to make fine distinctions between the way it lay in regard to the three classes of mandates and in relation to the mandatory power on the one hand, and League organs on the other.[318] And there were almost as many intermediate positions as there were interested lawyers. In addition, each mandate was governed by the provisions in its specific mandate agreement so that the resulting diversity could not be described under a unitary concept of sovereignty at all.

Such parceling of sovereignty became quite central to the reconstructive scholarship of the 1920s that threw its whole weight against what James Brierly (1881–1955), the occupant of the Chichele Chair in Oxford, called "the extravagances of an anti-social nationalism."[319] The First World War had destroyed belief in political sovereignty in Europe. European lawyers were arguing that there was no "sovereignty" in abstraction from the competencies States had or from the way they were bound into a network of economic and other relations with others, preparing ground for the profession's "turn to international

---

[315] For one overview of positions cf. L. Oppenheim, *International Law. A Treatise* (2 vols., 4th edn. by Arnold McNair, London, Longmans, 1928), I – Peace, pp. 213–215. Cf. also Chowdhury, *International Mandates*, pp. 220–226.

[316] Francis B. Sayre, "Legal Problems Arising from the United Nations Trusteeship System" (1948), 42 *AJIL*, pp. 271–272.

[317] Cf. Henri Rolin, "Le système des mandats coloniaux" (1920), III/1 *RDI*, pp. 329–363. [318] Millot, *Les mandats*, pp. 91–167.

[319] James Brierly, "The Shortcomings of International Law" (1924), V *British Year Book of International Law* (*BYIL*), p. 15.

institutions."[320] Brierly was still criticizing sovereignty in the interests of Great Powers. Now an increasing number of lawyers connected that critique with federalist proposals. Sir John Fischer Williams (1870–1947) observed at the end of the decade the presence of a "feeling so widespread among the general public that international law is largely a failure." With many others, he suggested that "it is in the Covenant of the League of Nations and its development that a remedy may be looked for." Sovereignty was to be understood as the realm of private freedom that international law left to the State.[321] In 1923 the Permanent Court of International Justice had already stated that sovereignty had no fixed content but was wholly dependent on the development of international relations. In its *Wimbledon* judgment it distinguished between sovereignty and sovereign rights: the fact that a State was sovereign did not mean that it could not have contracted out any number of rights. Its sovereignty was not in conflict with binding law; on the contrary, its ability to bind itself was an attribute of its sovereignty.[322] Equally compatible with the situation of a State living in hermetic isolation as with a State in a tightly woven network of obligations, legal sovereignty now became a "bundle of rights and duties," determined from within an overriding international order.[323]

If sovereignty could fail in Europe, it could equally well fail in the colonies. As critiques of sovereignty became louder, they were accompanied by a new language through which to conduct the civilizing mission as well. The mandates grew to represent a form of colonial administration no longer carried out by single colonial sovereigns but by the "international community." By the 1930s, it had become well established in French colonial law, for instance, that mandates constituted a form of international administration, implemented by the administering power on behalf of the international community as represented by the League.[324] In 1931, the *Institut de droit international*, too, defined the mandatory relationship as coming under international law, the mandatory

---

[320] Cf. generally, David Kennedy, "The Move to Institutions" (1987), 8 *Cardozo Law Review*, pp. 841 *et seq.*
[321] Sir John Fischer Williams, *Chapters on Current International law and the League of Nations* (London, Longmans, 1929), pp. 10–11, 64–65, 69.
[322] Cf. Permanent Court of International Justice, *Case of the S.S. Wimbledon*, Ser. A.1 (1923) and *Nationality Decrees in Tunis and Morocco*, Ser. B.5 (1923).
[323] Cf. Martti Koskenniemi, *From Apology to Utopia. The Structure of International Legal Argument* (Helsinki, Lakimiesliiton kustannus, 1989), pp. 212–220.
[324] Cf. Louis Rolland and Pierre Lampué, *Précis de législation coloniale* (2nd edn., Paris, Dalloz, 1936), pp. 93–109.

territory as a subject of international law, and the powers of the mandatory as having been vested in the exclusive interest of the subject population and under the control of the League and the Permanent Mandates Commission. The mandates were considered to be "evolutive" and the League was held to possess the power to modify them in view of the development of the population.[325]

But if the concept of sovereignty was emptied of meaning by the argument that its meaning was derived from international law, the concept of the sacred trust could be emptied of meaning by becoming whatever the administrator wanted it to mean. European predominance continued. In the first place, the Permanent Mandates Commission had only very limited powers. It worked on the basis of reports produced by the mandatory power. Hearing of petitioners or on-the-spot inspections were normally excluded. The assumption was that the League organs and the mandatory power would work in co-operation and in a non-adversarial way.[326] Hence, for example, "the British ruled their Mandated acquisitions as parts of the Empire, administering them like any other Crown Colonies."[327] In the second place, the "science of colonial administration" developed by the PMC had a long-lasting effect by distinguishing political sovereignty from the widespread net of economic dependencies into which the colonial territory was integrated as a source of raw materials and a market for metropolitan products. As Antony Anghie has pointed out, the Commission conceptualized "development" through a liberal understanding that split political emancipation and economic integration from each other, and supported an ideology of modernization that ensured control by Western interests. Through twenty years of internationalized administration, "the civilizing process [was] reproduced by international institutions using the new international law of pragmatism."[328]

The internationalization of colonialism under the mandates and trusteeship systems was part of the civilizing mission in the precise sense that it reinstated Europe's role as the gatekeeper for the benefits of public

---

[325] "Les mandates internationaux" (1931–II), 36 *Annuaire IDI*, pp. 233–234. The last point was, however, disputed among *Institut* members, cf. *ibid.*, pp. 36–67.

[326] Cf. League of Nations, *The Mandates System*, pp. 46–51 and for the conditions of independence under the mandates system, Annex, pp. 118–120.

[327] Jan Morris, *Farewell the Trumpets; An Imperial Retreat* (Orlando, Harcourt, 1978), p. 208.

[328] Antony Anghie, "Time Present and Time Past: Globalization, International Financial Institutions and the Third World" (2000), 32 *New York University Journal of International Law and Politics*, p. 285 and generally pp. 277–286.

diplomacy for the colonial world. It restated the logic of exclusion–inclusion that played upon a Eurocentric view about the degrees of civilization and legal status. Decolonization effectively universalized the European State as the only form of government that would provide equal status in the organized international community. The first generation of political leaders in the third world in the 1950s and 1960s may have disagreed about whether to aim for independence by devolution or revolution. But it had thoroughly integrated Western ideas about the State form as the only viable shell within which to develop into modernity.

In an ironic twist, the more Western politicians and lawyers decried the vices of sovereignty, the more the representatives of the new States emphasized the sacredness of the boundaries they had inherited from their colonial past. Such emphasis on formal sovereignty, however, failed to strike at the heart of European domination: "the extraction of wealth from an already impoverished Africa was in no way halted by the 'transfer of power.'"[329] In an important sense, "neo-colonialism" is a misnomer, the North–South encounter returning since 1960 to the informal, economically driven domination that has formed the mainstream of Empire since the sixteenth century. The State form also failed to provide room for the development of viable alternatives for indigenous political organization, especially in Africa. It was connected with sacred but awkward boundaries as well as authoritarian government, with colonial administration taken over by oligarchies and sometimes tyrants, enjoying the protection of the blind justice of legal sovereignty.

The demise of official imperialism has modified little of the exclusion–inclusion logic. Inclusion in the world of public diplomacy co-exists peacefully with exclusion from the spheres of spiritual and material well-being whose management lies beyond international public policy. The acceptance of the State form and the diplomatic protocol, like Christianity five centuries ago, may have disciplined the non-European world, but has done little to liberate it. The essence of statehood is equality and independence: judged against that standard, redistribution under a New International Economic Order (NIEO) could even at best appear as a temporary return to ideologically loaded authoritarianism.[330] The

---

[329] Basil Davidson, *The Black Man's Burden. Africa and the Curse of the Nation-State* (New York, Times, 1992), p. 219.

[330] Cf. Martti Koskenniemi and Marja Lehto, "The Privilege of Universality. International Law, Economic Ideology and Seabed Resources" (1996), 65 *Nordic Journal of International Law*, pp. 533–555.

spectacular failure of the State form in Africa may have undermined whatever was left of the universalist reformism of public diplomacy without, however, occasioning a rethinking of the conditions of the colonial encounter.[331] Were not Africa's shocking mistakes and failures final proof that the same standards should not be applied to it as were applied to civilized nations?

The story of international law and formal empire in 1870–1914 may be a story of arrogance, misplaced ambition, and sheer cruelty. But it is indissociable from the wider narrative of a liberal internationalism that thinks of itself as the "legal *conscience* of the civilized world" and whose humanitarian aspirations cannot be dismissed as a set of bad-faith justifications for Western domination. Instead, the problem must be sought from the connection liberals have made between progress and civilization on the one hand, and a particular political form, Western statehood, on the other. The men of 1873 saw the great danger in Africa and elsewhere in terms of a continued anarchy inside "primitive" communities and an unrestricted scramble driven by private economic interests between the European powers. They hoped to deal with these dangers by introducing European public administration into the colonies. When that attempt failed, they moved to support the internationalization of colonial administration, again with the view to replacing indigenous political forms with European ones. That most international lawyers enthusiastically welcomed decolonization was completely conditioned by their interpretation that this meant the final universalization of Western forms of government. When in more recent years those forms of government have nonetheless failed, international lawyers have been left uneasily poised between exhaustion and arrogance in face of the endemic political, social, and economic crises in the third world: either leaving the colonies a playground of "tribal" policies and Western private economic domination, or suggesting ever more streamlined versions of civilized guardianship over "failed States." Both are reaction formations to an unarticulated – yet pervasive – liberal unease about the virtues of Western political institutions.

For those institutions do not carry the good society with themselves. The same types of government create different consequences in different

---

[331] A process of rethinking may be starting, however. Cf. Makau W. Mutua, "Why Redraw the Map of Africa? A Moral and Legal Inquiry" (1995), 16 *Michigan Journal of International Law*, pp. 1113–1143 and Obiora Chinedu Okafor, "After Martyrdom: International Law, Sub-State Groups, and Construction of Legitimate Statehood in Africa" (2000), 41 *Harvard International Law Journal*, pp. 503–528.

contexts; there is nothing predetermined about the State form. It can be used for freedom and for constraint, and history is full of examples of both. Equally, empire comes under many disguises. While we often associate it with formal colonies, in fact the more efficient form of hegemony may be invisible, or indirect; the use of freedom to create constraint. In such case, anti-imperialism consists in a struggle for formalism: the establishment of formal administrative structures, police, and government. However, formal sovereignty can undoubtedly also be imperialist – this is the lesson of the colonial era from 1870 to 1960 which in retrospect seems merely a short interval between structures of informal domination by the West of everyone else. Under such circumstances, even a well-meaning internationalism is the Dr. Jekyll for the Mr. Hyde of imperialism. The Congo Free State, a mandates or a trusteeship arrangement may, just like a global trading system or a Multilateral Agreement on Investment under a World Trade Organization (WTO), be used for freedom and for constraint. Administrative structures – whether those of sovereignty or internationalization – only marginally determine the policies for which they are used. We recognize their character only by reference to substantive ideals about the political good we wish to pursue. Here lies the difficulty. Institutions do not *replace* politics but *enact* them. The men of 1873 felt that the introduction of Western institutions in the Orient would be to do history's work, that it would gradually transform backward societies into the European State form. The historical and the normative assumption coalesced in their image of themselves as the juridical conscience–consciousness of the civilized world. None of this language, or this self-image, is available today.

As we look back at periods of formal and informal colonialism, international administration, and independence, whatever technique of administration has been chosen seems often far less significant than how, in fact, the administration has behaved. There is no particular virtue in being tortured or killed by one's own countrymen instead of foreign invaders. A colonial officer, an international administrator, and an indigenous politician may each be susceptible to corruption – but each may be equally able to organize the building of a school, a hospital, or a department store. This is not to say that it should be a matter of complete indifference as to who should rule us, and which technique of rule is being employed. History may teach us to lean in one direction rather than another. In particular, it may often suggest that it is better to live in a political society whose administrators speak our language, share our rituals and know our ways of life. But there is no magic about such relationships, and communities that are closed to outsiders will rot from the inside. But whatever the choice of institution, it should be a matter of debate and evidence, and not of the application of universal principles about "civilization," "democracy," or "rule of law."

3

International law as philosophy: Germany 1871–1933

"[T]he victorious war is the social ideal: the victorious war is the ultimate means for every highest objective. In war the State demonstrates its real being, it is the fullest proof of the special quality of the State... In the victorious war legal thought sets the ultimate norm which decides which State has Right on its side... Who can, may also."[1] These are certainly among the most frequently quoted sentences from Erich Kaufmann's (1880–1972) 1911 book *Das Wesen des Völkerrechts und die Clausula rebus sic stantibus* which expounded a theory of the total State as Europe's historical and spiritual reality. For Kaufmann, a conservative legal theorist and a practitioner – including being a legal adviser at the foreign ministry of the Federal Republic in the 1950s – and a member of the *Institut de droit international*, the view of international law as superior to the State emerged from an unhistorical moral nihilism. Because the State – and not the shallow and discontinuous realm of the cosmopolitan – was the concrete enfolding of human spirituality, international law could never aspire to a normativity higher than the State. Useful as a mechanism of co-ordination, international law possessed no intrinsic value, represented no world-historical process of enlightenment or transcendence. No social ideal was embedded in it. Therefore, all treaties bore an implicit reservation: they were valid only as far as the conditions that were present at their conclusion did not change so that the

---

[1] Erich Kaufmann, *Das Wesen des Völkerrechts und die Clausula rebus sic stantibus* (Tübingen, Mohr, 1911), pp. 146, 153. The first sentence makes a hidden reference to Rudolf Stammler's Kantian view of a "community of persons of free will" as the social ideal. For critical citations, cf. e.g. Leonard Nelson, *Rechtswissenschaft ohne Recht* (Leipzig, von Veit, 1917), pp. 146, 172; Walther Schücking, *Die völkerrechtliche Lehre des Weltkrieges* (Leipzig, von Veit, 1918), p. 12n.

treaty's provisions would have become incompatible with the self-preservation of the State.[2]

Although Kaufmann's 1911 book has been admired as a real *tour de force*, it has also been indicted as an example of "Hegelian" or "nationalist" theory, a specimen of ideas that led to the 1914 cataclysm. This reputation is only partly deserved.[3] Certainly Kaufmann's arguments drew upon Hegel's philosophy of law and responded to an idiosyncratic "German" way of conceiving the nature of Germany's statehood. On the other hand, the critique came from non-disinterested sources: a liberal orthodoxy that imagined law either as human will or formal legality, ideas targeted not only by the 1911 book but by Kaufmann's writings throughout the Weimar era. For Kaufmann, voluntarism and formalism failed to capture life as other than abstract and unhistorical categories: the unconnected individual enjoying "natural rights" and creating social constraint out of free will. No social ideal was embedded in such individualism and it failed to describe a concrete reality existing anywhere. To understand the world required going beyond rationalism. This could be done, he suggested, by following his admired conservative–monarchist constitutional lawyer Friedrich Julius Stahl – "Germany's last significant public law theorist" – who had in the 1830s put forward a "theistic metaphysics, an ethical and religiously grounded irrationalist positivism."[4]

A quarter of a century later, the "Non-Aryan" Kaufmann had been forced to step down from his chair at the University of Berlin – though he was allowed to hold private seminars at his home until he had to flee to the Netherlands in 1938. Three years before, he had traveled to the Hague to give the *Cours général*, speaking there to foreign students as a Platonist idealist:

> I strongly affirm the objective existence and the reality of the phenomenon of the collective spirit . . . The collective spirit rests on the one hand on the existence of trans-subjective and transcendental values and norms that constitute the moral substance of all community and, on the other hand, on the final affinity of the roots of human spirits.[5]

---

[2] Kaufmann, *Das Wesen des Völkerrechts*, p. 204.

[3] Writing 50 years later, Kaufmann still held that this "youthful" work contained the nucleus of all his later oeuvre. Erich Kaufmann, *Rechtsidee und Recht. Gesammelte Schriften (GS)* (3 vols., Göttingen, Schwartz, 1960), III, p. xx.

[4] Erich Kaufmann, "Über die konservative Partei und ihre Geschichte" (1922), *GS* III, pp. 133–134.

[5] Erich Kaufmann, "Règles générales du droit de la paix" (1935), 54 *Recueil des cours de l'Académie de droit international (RdC)*, pp. 554–555.

Was there a contradiction between Kaufmann's views of 1911 and 1935? There was certainly a stylistic transformation that did not only reflect the context and the change of language from the German to the French. What remained common to both texts was Kaufmann's attempt to find a higher level of normativity than provided by formal legality. The total State of 1911 and the "collective spirit" of 1935 both articulate a transgression, an attempt to overcome the liberal dichotomies of the individual and community, force and law, faith and reason. What may have shifted in the years between was the assumption of where that higher level lay, not the conviction that the tangible worlds of the day's law and politics failed to reflect it.

When Kaufmann wrote his 1911 book, Germany had become the European State that had most reason to feel that formal international relations had been superseded by a new constellation of power. As an industrial economy and a military power it had no rival on the continent. The prevailing distribution of the colonies or Britain's arrogant mastery of the seas could not fail to seem anachronistic obstacles to its expansive spirit. Kaufmann's argument about the absence of an objective legal system above the State and his emphasis on the intrinsic limit to the binding force of treaties put in question the legal value of the status quo while entitling Germany to take the necessary action to change it. In this regard, the situation in 1935 was not significantly different. The Versailles Treaty was condemned by practically all German lawyers, right and left, as a *Diktatfrieden*. The League of Nations had not been able to set up an alternative social ideal. Internationalism stumbled from one frustration to another. In 1935 Kaufmann was careful to point out that justice could not be reached by induction from what empirically existed: "it is rather a spiritual, trans-subjective reality that pre-exists any particular social phenomenon."[6]

The story of international law in Germany between 1871 and 1933 is a narrative about recurrent attempts to square the circle of statehood and an international legal order by lawyers trained in public law, often philosophically inclined, and coming from the widest range of political conviction. Nowhere was the challenge to international law posed more strongly than in Germany. Nowhere did lawyers take more seriously the task of responding to that challenge, or develop more sophisticated theories to that effect. Where the members of the *Institut de droit international*

---

[6] Kaufmann, "Règles générales," p. 459.

represented a self-confident, aristocratic liberalism that took for granted the moral superiority of its world-view, German lawyers struggled with complex philosophical arguments to ground the possibility of a scientifically credible and politically legitimate international law, one that would correspond to "concrete reality" and manifest some kind of "social ideal." If the protagonists' arguments sometimes only repeated platitudes about the opposition of German "depth" and Anglo-French "superficiality," the tables were quickly turned as the Germans themselves often found that the deepest legal reality lay as the thinnest form over social life.

The distance between the *völkisch* idealism of German lawyers in 1871 and Hans Kelsen's formalism half a century later may seem as wide as international law itself. In a historical and political sense they are, however, just a step apart, and sometimes merge into each other. The history of international law in Germany during that period is a narrative about philosophy as the founding discipline for reflecting about statehood and what lies beyond. In this narrative "concrete reality" sometimes appears as State power, sometimes as the power of a cosmopolitan history – and "social ideals" sometimes intensively romantic–national, sometimes liberal–individualist. This debate came to an end by the Second World War.

1871: law as the science of the legal form

In the very year when the German empire was declared, Adolf Lasson published his *Princip und Zukunft des Völkerrechts*, which gave expression to the idea that sovereign States could not be members of a legal community above them and that their natural relations could only be those of envy, struggle, even hate. Treaties between States reflected relations of power and could be maintained only as long as those relations remained stable. Far from being illegal, war remained a "means of negotiation" in which the States sought to find out what the real power relations between them were, and to conclude a peace treaty accordingly.[7]

Like Kaufmann later, Lasson drew inspiration from Hegel's view of statehood as the realm of concrete freedom. A people was unfree as long as the legal order that constrained it failed to reflect its inner nature and consciousness. There was evidence to back up this view: *Princip* was an elaboration of an earlier essay on the spiritual–cultural significance of

---

[7] Adolf Lasson, *Princip und Zukunft des Völkerrechts* (Berlin, Hertz, 1871), pp. 66–75.

war that Lasson had written to celebrate Prussia's victorious campaign of 1866.[8] For Lasson, an early convert from Judaism to Christianity, interest in international law was informed by a philosophical critique of rationalism. That human freedom could be realized only in the State made it impossible to accept the Kantian utopia of an intrinsically individualist, cosmopolitan law. It would prevent the people from developing in accordance with its deep spiritual quality, its inner life-principle ("eigenen inneren Lebensprincip").[9]

As we saw in chapter 1, none of this meant, for Lasson, that there should, or could, be no international law. On the contrary, he wished to develop international law into a more effective instrument for cultural co-operation: there should be more openness and codification – treaties on technical and economic matters – as well as diplomatic congresses and permanent institutions. Lasson's view on the future of international law hardly differed from that of the internationalists of the time. But where his arguments came from an anti-rationalist and anti-formalist perspective on Germany's statehood, mainstream public law developed in the opposite direction.

Since 1815, German public law had participated in the creation of a unified identity to the German people. For Savigny, that identity received concreteness in *Juristenrecht,* a common legal consciousness articulated by the profession into positive law. By contrast, later "organic" theory maintained that the unity of the *Volk* was reflected in the German State, manifested in the juridical concepts through which public lawyers sought to establish the autonomy of their discipline. This development was illustrated in the work of Carl Friedrich von Gerber (1823–1891), who came from the organic school but for whom a properly juridical study of statehood was possible only by setting aside the ethical or historical considerations that had infected it in the past. From a juridical perspective, he wrote in a brief but influential book in 1865, the *Volk* became conscious of itself in the State which thus became "the highest legal personality known to the legal order." State power was the power of a personified, spiritual organism.[10] What the "organic" nature

---

[8] *Das Culturideal und der Krieg* (Berlin, 1868). After *Princip,* Lasson never returned to the topic during his long career as a legal philosopher. Cf. Georg Lasson, "Adolf Lasson" (1918–1919), XII *ARWP*, pp. 1–10.   [9] Lasson, *Princip und Zukunft,* p. 9.
[10] "Die Staatsgewalt ist die Willensmacht eines persönliche gedachten sittlichen Organismus," Carl Friedrich von Gerber, *Grundzüge des deutschen Staatsrechts* (3rd edn., Leipzig, Tauchnitz, 1880), p. 19.

of the State meant *juridically*, Gerber argued, was that it had "like all law" to do with formalized relationships of will.[11] The highest will was the monarch's, in whose hands lay the State's monopoly of power. Authoritarianism arose from the organic view: State power was the spiritual power of a people having become conscious of itself.[12]

Von Gerber did not think that State power knew no limits. On the contrary, it became completely constrained by the objective of advancing the common interest. Though these limits were difficult to set *in abstracto*, von Gerber included a number of individual rights and freedoms, as well as socio-cultural objectives, among them.[13] The problem was, as Otto von Gierke (1841–1921) and other liberals retorted, that the limits were determined from the *inside* of State will, and not from the history or interests of autonomous communities (*Genossenschaften*) or an independent theory of subjective rights.[14] This debate brought to the surface the tension between the authoritarian and individualist strands in the theory of the State. On the one hand, the State appeared as a hierarchical structure, and the citizen its passive object; on the other, the State embodied the nation's pursuit of self-determination without which individual freedom would be nothing.[15] Von Gerber dealt with this tension by allowing the State's organic justification to recede to the background, and by concentrating on the State as a conglomerate of (possible) acts of will, described through formal legal concepts that claimed neutrality in regard to the authoritarian and individualist views.[16]

Paul Laband (1838–1918), whose four-volume commentary on the *Reich* constitution started appearing in 1876 was the most influential of von Gerber's successors and completed the development of public law into independence from its social or historical base. Although Laband did not object to the organic theory, he made no use of it and grounded the unity of the *Reich* in its formal character as a *Bundesstaat* (instead of a mere *Staatenbund*). The *Reich* was a single legal person because it

---

[11] On the meaning of "organic," cf. Gerber, *Grundzüge*, pp. 217–225 and the useful commentary by Olivier Jouanjan, "Carl Friedrich Gerber et la constitution d'une science du droit public allemand," in O. Beaud and P. Wachsmann (eds.), *La science juridique française et la science juridique allemande de 1870 à 1918* (1990), 1 *Annales de la faculté de droit de Strasbourg*, pp. 56–58.

[12] Gerber, *Grundzüge*, pp. 1–3, 19–23. Cf. also commentary in Michael Stolleis, *Geschichte des öffentlichen Rechts in Deutschland* (3 vols., Munich, Beck, 1992–1999), II, pp. 334–337.

[13] Gerber, *Grundzüge*, pp. 31–42. Cf. also Jouanjan, "Carl Friedrich Gerber," pp. 60–61.

[14] For these critiques, cf. Stolleis, *Geschichte*, II, pp. 360–362.

[15] For the development of this tension in early nineteenth-century German political theory, cf. Leonard Krieger, *The German Idea of Freedom. History of a Political Tradition* (Boston, Beacon, 1957), pp. 147–165. [16] Von Gerber, *Grundzüge*, pp. 220–225.

enjoyed sovereign rights, because its own organs enjoyed *Kompetenz-Kompetenz*, and because its legislation overrode that of member States.[17] Laband formalized von Gerber's view of laws as commands (*Befehle*) that were constituted of expressions of legislative will.[18] Unlike von Gerber (who wrote before unification, and needed general principles in his constructive work) Laband drew his materials – legal relationships and legal "institutions" – from the positive law of the *Reich* which he subsumed under general legal concepts.[19] From such concepts – which he assumed to be autonomous, like the rules of logic – he then deduced consequences and analogies which enabled him to fulfill the postulate of the closed nature of the legal system.

Laband was no "denier" of international law. On the contrary, he expressly rejected the view of international law as only (external) domestic public law.[20] Of course, treaties were not identical to domestic laws (*Gesetz*). The latter were commands by State authorities to their subjects whereas treaties were contracts (*Rechtsgeschäfte*) that contained reciprocal promises by States to each other.[21] This did not do away with their legal character. They were "acts of will by States," enforceable by States against each other, and binding among them. This was a matter of international law, however. From the perspective of *Staatsrecht*, treaties became binding through the public law enactments that transposed their provisions into national laws.[22]

The new method created a sharp distinction between the material principles through which the German nation was explained and formal law, and directed the lawyers' attention to the latter. In this way, it created an apparently non-political defense of the liberal–authoritarian compromise that the *Reich* constitution was.[23] In his doctoral dissertation the legal philosopher Carl Bergbohm (1849–1927) applied the same technique to defend international law against the "deniers," arguing that

---

[17] Paul Laband, *Das Staatsrecht des Deutschen Reiches* (5th edn., 4 vols., Tübingen, Mohr, 1901, 1911–1913), II, pp. 64–67, 85–88.
[18] Laband's influential two-part theory of material law (*Gesetz*) distinguished between the statement of the law (*Rechtssatz*) and the act of will or command (*Befehl*) that citizens behave accordingly and that public authorities take the necessary action to implement and sanction it. Laband, *Das Staatsrecht*, II, pp. 1–23.
[19] Laband, *Das Staatsrecht*, I, pp. vi–viii.
[20] Paul Laband, *Deutsches Reichstaatsrecht* (5th edn., Tübingen, Mohr, 1909), pp. 160–161n1.
[21] Laband, *Das Staatsrecht*, II, p. 153; Laband, *Deutsches Reichsstaatsrecht*, p. 158.
[22] Laband, *Deutsches Reichstaatsrecht*, pp. 158, 161–165.
[23] Peter von Oertzen, *Die soziale Funktion der Staatsrechtlichen Positivismus* (Frankfurt, Suhrkamp, 1974), pp. 319–326.

international law, too, emerged from State will but existed as a set of autonomous concepts and institutions, particularly in formal treaties. Bergbohm demonstrated that neither law-giver, adjudication, nor sanctions were a *sine qua non* for a legal system, yet that each was present in some rudimentary form as well. His main point, however, was that international law was "law," not because it reflected moral or humanitarian ideals but because it emanated from self-legislation. States were bound because "[t]hey could doubtless make their own will binding on themselves without violating their independence."[24]

This is what "realists" such as Lasson or "moralists" such as Bluntschli had never understood, Bergbohm claimed. The former had confused the fact of competition and struggle among States with the formal question of the possibility of international law. The latter had infused law with historical materials and ethical ideas in a way that made it easy for deniers to ridicule a law they saw violated every day. A clear distinction between existing and desired law was needed, and this was provided by the theory of self-legislation which set international law on the same level as public and constitutional law.[25] However, Bergbohm's "will" was not an elusive, psychological fact. One consequence of modernity, he explained, was precisely the development from vague feelings to more certain knowledge – to science. In international life, this was manifested in the conclusion of an increasing number of law-making treaties to lay down general rules of behavior.[26] This enabled the establishment of a scientific study of law that would not be dependent on mere *Rechtsgefühl*, but could focus on formal State acts independently of their material background.[27]

Before 1871 the organic theory had seen itself as the juridical representation of the German *Volk*. After unification, that function was given over to *Reich* legislation. The resulting *Gesetzpositivismus* opened up the possibility of explaining international engagements as binding on the

---

[24] Carl Bergbohm, *Staatsverträge und Gesetze als Quellen des Völkerrechts* (Dorpat, Mattiessen, 1876), pp. 19, 60–63. [25] Bergbohm, *Staatsverträge*, pp. 7, 42.
[26] Bergbohm, *Staatsverträge*, pp. 3–5.
[27] One difficulty was that the juristic method focused on law as legal enactments (*Gesetz*) that were not available in the international realm. Bergbohm accepted that this fact did not support codification, but he did not believe it disqualified international law as law. Accepting Laband's distinction between the material and the formal notion of *Gesetz*, Bergbohm noted that a (material) *Gesetz* included two parts: the behavioral norm directed to the legal subjects and the directive to the authorities to enact a reaction if the norm was violated. Because most international law did not contain the latter, it was law as *will* but not as *Gesetz*. The failure to make this distinction had often – wrongly – led to the "denial" of international law.

International law as philosophy: Germany 1871–1933

same basis as domestic law – as formal emanations of State will. At the same time, it required distinguishing between the domestic *Gesetz* that implied a hierarchical relationship and the international *Rechtssatz* that did not. Defining international law as co-ordination, German lawyers accepted that there was no principle of political legitimacy above the people – though they often construed the people's normative demands so as to include the protection of fundamental rights or the fulfillment of social or economic needs. Above all, they were now able to work with an autonomous system of legal concepts that avoided collapsing the law into power or humanitarian morality.

The international political context was, however, anything but fruitful for the development of a serious *Gesetzpositivismus*. It was attempted by Paul Heilborn (1861–1932) from Berlin who, drawing on the earlier work by Kaltenborn and Bulmerincq, proposed a logically coherent system of international law concepts that were to be as independent as possible from diplomacy and morality as well as from private and public law. System, wrote Heilborn, was an instrument of knowledge and a way to truth, consisting in the arrangement of concepts that resulted from the ultimate cause of each science, into a consistent and self-contained whole. What was the "ultimate cause" of international law? This did not lie in its material objectives or leading principles. On these, there was too much disagreement. It lay, instead, in its "internal" definitions, of which the most important was this: "international law is the totality of legal norms recognized by States as governing their relationships."[28] From this single sentence – which presumed no external objective, no material principle – Heilborn inferred the concept of the State as legal subject and of law as the effect of its will. The system followed therefrom as the enumeration of legal subjects and their fundamental rights.[29] Heilborn was aware of criticism directed against the "dry abstractions" of systemic exercises. He responded by the Kantian argument that Laband would have endorsed: it was impossible to understand the material world without first having a clear sense of the concepts through which one looks at it.[30] Heilborn's four-page proposal for the systemic arrangement of international law concepts may have had particular didactic advantages or disadvantages – the division of the norms into a general and a special part, the further division of the former into subjects and objects, and the theory of right, and the latter into individual legal relations and

---

[28] Paul Heilborn, *Das System des Völkerrechts aus den völkerrechtlichen Begriffen* (Berlin, Springer, 1896), p. 370.   [29] Heilborn, *Das System*, pp. 2–4.
[30] Heilborn, *Das System*, pp. 414–417.

self-help.[31] As a way to do international law, however, it was already out of step with the anti-formalistic outlook of the times.

From form to substance: the doctrine of the rational will

By the last decade of the nineteenth century legal formalism had become widely criticized as a *Lebensfremd* abstraction that failed to capture the dynamism of social life. But sweeping references to the "conscience of the civilized world," such as routinely made by Bluntschli and his colleagues at the *Institut*, were no less old-fashioned in view of the criteria that natural and historical sciences suggested should be integrated into the study of societies. As early as 1878 the young Georg Jellinek proposed that ethics should finally be divorced from metaphysical speculations and from its obsession with individual morality and instead be aligned with insights received from the workings of human drives (egoism and altruism in particular) in primitive societies by anthropologists and ethnographers. It should have recourse to moral statistics in order to examine the emergence of norms and the effects of social solidarity and focus on the division of labor in the formation of behavioral patterns of collectives. Ethnological studies ought to be used with a view to outlining the emergence of types of consciousness; and principles of political economy ought to be applied to examine the conditions of material growth. All in all, through collaboration from psychology, natural and social sciences, there was hope that "ethics would finally be established in a scientific way" as a social ethics.[32]

The point of a scientific study of society was to seek and articulate *social laws* that could then be translated into political laws, or from a slightly different angle, "to answer the question of how to ground an ethical argument."[33] Whatever other merit science had, it suggested a way to transcend the controversies about the right principles of government that tore European societies and puzzled colonialists and to which there seemed no politically compelling response. In producing an explanation for what held modern, secular, industrial society together, the turn to science

---

[31] Heilborn, *Das System*, pp. 408–412.
[32] Georg Jellinek, *Die sozialethische Bedeutung von Recht, Unrecht und Strafe* (Hildesheim, Olms, 1967, reprint of the 1878 edn.), pp. 1–41, 41.
[33] Geoffrey Hawthorn, *Enlightenment and Despair. A History of Social Theory* (2nd edn., Cambridge University Press, 1987), p. 256. Likewise, Hans Kelsen, *Der soziologische und der juristische Staatsbegriff* (2nd edn., Tübingen, Mohr, 1927), pp. 46–74.

became one of the intellectual strategies whereby contemporaries tried to cope with the relativism, cynicism or outright irrationalism in many *fin-de-siècle* cultural currents.[34]

The question "What holds society together?" seemed particularly acute in the international realm where the absence of a tangible supranational standpoint had agonised lawyers through the nineteenth century. German experience provided little constructive materials. The *Reich* had emerged from a series of wars and Bismarck's attitude on foreign affairs was openly based on *Machtpolitik*. Did not Lasson – and later Kaufmann – argue precisely that the normal condition of States was struggle, and that war remained the ultimate judge among them? A century earlier Kant had assumed that exit from this situation was a rationally dictated moral obligation that could be fulfilled by a social contract among States designed to set up a confederation.[35] This was hardly a practical option. Instead the internationalists now focused on the innumerable cultural, commercial, and other ties to which Germany was bound and to which international law – they believed – gave normative expression. Where deniers focused on the absence of a common sovereign, the internationalists responded by a cultural argument about a European community that was to be advanced by a well-administered balance of power policy.

There was something of a *dialogue des sourds* in this debate, the protagonists agreeing on much more than they were willing to concede. The hard core of the disagreement lay in the philosophical question of (the basis of) obligation. How could independent States be bound? The men of 1873 had responded by referring to a civilized conscience-consciousness whose requirements, they assumed, were transparent to everyone. This response could not withstand examination. The realm of morality and goodness was transformed into the realm of the will. Most public lawyers, especially in Germany, and especially since Kant, now theorized about social reality as the territory of supreme, rational human will. Gerber already postulated that "Die Staatsgewalt ist die Willensmacht eines persönlich gedachten sittlichen Organismus."[36] After Bergbohm's 1876 book, this view was adopted practically by every

---

[34] For a review of the partly irrationalist, partly romantic revolt against the positivism of the period, cf. H. Stuart Hughes, *Consciousness and Society. The Reorientation of European Social Thought 1890–1930* (New York, Knopf, 1958).
[35] Immanuel Kant, "The Metaphysics of Morals," in *Political Writings* (Hans Reiss ed., 2nd, enlarged edn., Cambridge University Press, 1991), p. 165 (§ 54).
[36] Gerber, *Grundzüge*, p. 19.

German internationalist. When Heinrich Triepel (1868–1949) published his widely read study on the relations of international and national law in 1899, he held it self-evident that all law was an effect of legislative will, and did not even bother seriously to consider alternatives.[37] Many international lawyers, and not only in Germany, shared his confidence. Law became psychology writ large: to know it was to see it as the effect of a human *voluntas*. Questions of morality proper – principles of right conduct dictated to individuals or communities from beyond – were translated into questions about whose will prevailed in society.[38] Relations of will became a kind of human causality (whose will worked as an effective motivation for action?) that permitted an observational study of society after the model of natural causality.

However, this implied an attitude towards (ordinary) morality and politics that was not simply skeptical but threatened to set up a superior morality under which the will to power, the subject's commitment to assert its subjectivity over others, would become the single defensible normative principle. This would have become uncomfortably close to what Nietzsche had written and would have entailed no *legal* doctrine of a social "ought." Before 1914, many German internationalists had already pointed to the logical difficulties in a purely will oriented theory of legal obligation.[39] But lawyers subscribing to a view of law as will had done so only to distance themselves from the "fictions" of natural law. Once *that* task had been undertaken, they quickly moved from pure voluntarism into something other, or more, than it. It was, they retorted, not "real" or "arbitrary" will on which they argued, but a "rational will" or will expressed in its external manifestations: actual behavior or the treaty text as pure form.[40] Or they argued that the "acceptance" of law did not always have to be express but could be inferred from the context, from the "necessary relationship that every legal rule should have with the communal principle in the international community."[41] For law as science, it was not necessary that a rule be actually declared by States for

---

[37] Heinrich Triepel, *Völkerrecht und Landesrecht* (Leipzig, Hirschfield, 1899), pp. 28–35.
[38] Cf. Paul Heilborn, *Grundbegriffe und Geschichte des Völkerrechts* (Handbuch des Völkerrechts, Erste Abteilung, Berlin, Stuttgart, and Vienna, Kohlhammer, 1912), pp. 5–8.
[39] E.g. L. von Bar, "Grundlage und Kodifikation des Völkerrechts" (1912–1913), VI *ARWP*, pp. 145–158.
[40] P. Schoen, "Zu Lehre von Grundlagen des Völkerrechts" (1914–1915), VIII *ARWP*, p. 293; Heilborn, *Grundbegriffe*, pp. 6–7.
[41] Franz von Holtzendorff, *Handbuch des Völkerrechts* (4 vols., Berlin, Habel [Parts II–IV Hamburg, Richter], 1885), I: *Einleitung in das Völkerrecht*, pp. 44, 45.

it to be law, it was – unless a contrary will was demonstrated – sufficient that it could be inferred from the social needs of the situation, including the need to protect national self-determination.

Here it is necessary to pause to consider briefly the extraordinarily important "German" idea of freedom as the sense of compulsion to will what is necessary. It was already central to Kant's critical philosophy that undogmatic knowledge was self-determined; enlightenment came from throwing off the self-imposed immaturity that came from alien guidance, typically expressed in dogmatic empiricism or rationalism, and religion.[42] This epistemological view implied autonomy as a personal and social ideal and a concept of law as self-determination: legislation by the will over itself. For Kant, freedom was not the indiscriminate realization of one's passions or interests – indeed, this was immaturity in the above sense. Freedom could exist only as a looking beyond such contingencies. To be free was to make one's will harmonious to universal reason – a reason according to which one should always act in accordance with what one can simultaneously will as universal law. Where enlightenment lay in reliance on reason, freedom consisted in the acceptance of what reason dictated as duty.

In the context of domestic society, this became covalent with the call to obey positive law and laid the groundwork for the doctrine of the *Rechtsstaat* – "Argue as much as you like, and about whatever you like, but obey!"[43] In the international realm, however, there was little positive law available. Kant had considered the case of human history – locating freedom at the level of individuals while redefining the human species as the realm of nature. To make the two compatible, Kant was compelled to assume that nature was ultimately moral (nature as realization of freedom).[44] In an analogous way, internationalists thought that national freedom could be realized only within the realm of necessity that international relations was. An implicit morality was thus read into the facts of interdependence towards which lawyers now turned – with the simple argument that these facts could always be read as the content of undeclared (but rational) will. There may be differences of opinion about what were the "necessary consequences drawn from the common will of nations" ("nothwendigen, aus dem Gemeinschaftswillen des Staaten ziehenden Schlussforderungen") – but this was normal and could be dealt

---

[42] Cf. Immanuel Kant, "What is Enlightenment?," in *Political Writings*, pp. 54–60.
[43] Kant, "What is Enlightenment?," p. 59.
[44] Immanuel Kant, "Idea for a Universal History with a Cosmopolitan Purpose," in *Political Writings*, pp. 41–53 and comment in Krieger, *The German Idea of Freedom*, p. 93.

with by interpretation.[45] Now constraint could be found in non-psychological laws: balance of power, economic interdependence or solidarity. Human will might be the immediate motivation for action but how it functioned was dependent on "deeper" social laws. Even Heilborn acknowledged this. Having defined law as self-legislation, he inferred its continued validity over "arbitrary" will from the same source: "But if the creation of a legal order is a necessary implication of human nature, then its negation is excluded by the same necessity. The intrinsic consciousness of right and duty in human beings does not allow law as arbitrary propositions [*willkürliche Satzung*] but as the just order of life."[46] The view of law as rational self-legislation gave expression to the social ideal of autonomous, self-determining legal subjects. It was a liberal idea. But it connected only with difficulty with any concrete reality. Inasmuch as the theory was not presented as one of revolution (which it was not), it tended to portray any actual social order as intrinsically rational.[47] If no importance was given to the *actual* (however "dogmatic") will, the argument collapsed into a defense of the status quo. Now surely lawyers – least of all *German* lawyers – could not just think that the present order was law by its intrinsic force. What was the relationship of psychological "will" to the more properly sociological concept of "power?" Nietzsche's concept of the will to power was suggestive but ambivalent. Which was the dominant term in the relationship: was power an instrument of will, or will a rationalization for power? Should lawyers examine political reality by reference to how some people (or States) wanted that reality to be – or should they assess the normative nature of State policies by reference to what worked in practice?

This difficulty may be illustrated by reference to the 1894 study of treaties by the Swiss liberal internationalist Otfried Nippold (1864–1938). He observed that in international relations power seemed to go before the law and that this had been nowhere more visible than in European behavior in the colonies. Treaties that were cited as proof of the beneficial expansion of international law had been imposed by brutal force on peaceful communities.[48] Rejecting *Weltstaatlich* utopias as imperialism in disguise he emphasized the centrality of treaties in a

---

[45] Holtzendorff, *Handbuch*, I, pp. 45–46.   [46] Heilborn, *Grundbegriffe*, p. 6.
[47] Kant himself was an advocate of enlightened absolutism. Cf. "The Contest of Faculties," in *Political Writings*, pp. 186–189 and comments in Krieger, *The German Idea of Freedom*, pp. 86–125.
[48] Otfried Nippold, *Der völkerrechtliche Vertrag, seine Stellung im Rechssystem und seine Bedeutung für das internationale Recht* (Berne, Wyss, 1894), pp. 4–5.

strictly consensual legal system: "Alles positive Völkerrecht ist auf den Willen der Staaten zurückzuführen."[49] The problem lay not in excess voluntarism but in the law's insufficient regard to the actual wishes of communities. Prevailing doctrines refrained from concluding that imposed treaties – including peace treaties – were invalid. They were enchanted by effective power in contradiction with their professed voluntarism. A treaty imposed by force (whether or not a peace treaty) was not voluntarily concluded and cannot be rationalized as binding under a system of co-ordinative wills.[50]

For Nippold, it was clear that treaties were the most important source of international law. Like other liberals, he imagined State will as the rational will to participate in increasing co-operation and even in the harmonization of domestic laws. A natural *Annäherung* and *Ausgleichung* were slowly leading to something like a world State.[51] Despite his sociological language, however, Nippold saw most progress in international law as a result of the work of *Wissenschaft*.[52] He proposed the establishment of an international organization of jurists with a much larger membership than that of the *Institut* as well as the setting up of an international training school for international lawyers – a proposal that culminated in the establishment of the Hague Academy of International Law in 1913. His work did not contain a serious effort to analyze the social forces that would determine the direction of future integration. It was an armchair sociology he espoused, built on the assumption that States would – when gently guided by men of science – come to understand where their real interests lay, and agree on a world federation. Here was its weakness: irrespective of its sociological language, Nippold's view emerged from a Kantian rationalism that defined internationalism as rational – and thereby undermined his criticism of the present system of imperial power. For to distinguish between beneficial internationalism and malignant imperialism one needed to have substantive criteria; in the absence of a material theory of progress, Nippold could do this only by falling back on his liberal intuitions.

Looking for a realistic law at the turn of the century, German internationalists alternated between a voluntarism that protected the right of (German) self-determination and a set of naturalist assumptions about

---

[49] Nippold, *Der völkerrechtliche Vertrag*, pp. 51, 4–6, 18–22.
[50] Nippold, *Der völkerrechtliche Vertrag*, pp. 7–8, 165–177.
[51] Nippold, *Der völkerrechtliche Vertrag*, pp. 252–282.
[52] Nippold, *Der völkerrechtliche Vertrag*, p. 13.

the international world (culture, history, society) that explained the necessity of Germany's being bound into legal relationships. It is not that the law now finally became a philosophical instrument for social engineering as Roscoe Pound (1870–1964) interpreted the latest stream in the profession.[53] Pound came from the outside and failed to understand the Europeans' view of the discipline as the bearer of a humanist tradition. What the profession sought from philosophy was reassurance that its normative project was still valid and might perhaps finally devise a correct relationship between cosmopolitan community and patriotism. A century earlier, Kant had been able to align his liberalism with the former; now the more pressing need was to defend the latter.

Between the dangerous and the illusory State

The social conflicts engendered by industrialism and mass politics in Germany in the 1890s were reflected in the political realm as a crisis of public law and the conception of the State: Wilhelminian rule conflicted with the needs and outlook of modern society. The imperial constitution of 1871 had set up a "system of skirted decisions" in which the position of the central government towards the *Länder* (Prussia in particular) remained obscure, and the monarchic principle, while formally preserved, conflicted with the powers of the *Reichstag*, creating a tension that Imperial Chancellors from Bismarck onwards did their best to exploit for conservative advantage. Struggle between these power positions had had the result "that the German Empire had already become, in principle, an almost ungovernable entity by the 1890's."[54] Under such conditions, German liberals had increasing difficulty in fitting their loyalty to the central government with liberal principles and often compromised to join with the Prussian Junkers to create a common anti-socialist front.[55] This sometimes meant a strengthening of State power by social

---

[53] Roscoe Pound, "Philosophical Theory and International Law" (1923), II *Bibliotheca Visseriana*, pp. 89–90.

[54] Wolfgang J. Mommsen, *Imperial Germany 1867–1918. Politics, Culture and Society in an Authoritarian State* (London, New York, Sydney, Auckland, Arnold, 1995), p. 147.

[55] Stolleis, *Geschichte*, II, pp. 454–455, Kaarlo Tuori, *Valtionhallinnon sivuelinorganisaatiosta*, (2 vols., Helsinki, Suomalainen lakimiesyhdistys, 1983), I, pp. 59–60. The social democrat party (SPD) espoused theoretical Marxism and was largely supported by the working class. Proscribed during 1878–1890 it grew rapidly to become the largest party in the *Reichstag* elections of 1912.

legislation and development of ideas of *"Leistungsstaat"*[56] – a strategy that prompted Max Weber's famous critique of bureaucracy and further complicated the traditional alliance between liberals and the State.

Throughout the nineteenth century, German academic public law sought to provide an Archimedean point for a politically split society by its construction of legal system from the principle of the *Volkswille* that constituted a way to attain unification in the mind even as it had been lacking in reality. In principle, the *Allgemeine Staatslehre* might have continued to provide that unifying focus in the 1890s had it not by then become politically too polarized. Natural law had been long discredited and *völkisch* Idealism hardly provided a credible basis for reflection on the condition of a deeply divided *Volk*. Legal philosophy was in a "chaotic state."[57] Advances of natural sciences in the latter half of the nineteenth century could be accommodated neither with Hegel's idealism nor with the leading school of public law positivism associated with von Gerber and Laband. A more realistic conception of the State was needed. Theorization about the public realm, too, needed to start from facts.[58] But it was not obvious what the relevant "facts" were, in what the law's positivity consisted.

A purely sociological theory reduced the State to a reflection of underlying social tendencies, sometimes, as in France, to an instrument of social solidarity (cf. chapter 4), but in Germany to an instrument of a group (a race, a class) to exercise power (*Herrschaftsinstrument*).[59] The most effective of these was the historical materialism of Karl Marx and Friedrich Engels that reduced the State to an ephemeral reflection of economic forces. But even mainstream opinion learned to think that the State was above all an institution with a monopoly of violence. The liberal internationalist Franz von Liszt (1851–1919) quite casually defined the State as: "a power that stands over individuals . . . a will to rule that is something other than the sum of individual wills, a power to rule that comprises individuals and constrains them also against their will."[60] At the opposite end stood the "free law" theories of Hermann

[56] Cf. e.g. Fritz Ringer, *The Decline of the German Mandarins. The German Academic Community, 1890–1933* (Hanover and London, Wesleyan, 1990 [1969]), pp. 130–136.
[57] Stolleis, *Geschichte*, II, pp. 423–424.
[58] Stolleis, *Geschichte*, II, p. 435; Juha Tolonen, *Stat och Rätt* (Åbo Akademi, 1986), p. 108.
[59] These were particularly Jewish theorists and it may be that the theory represented their personal experience, cf. (on Gumplowicz, Ratzenhoffer, Menger, and Oppenheimer), Stolleis, *Geschichte*, II, pp. 442–447.
[60] Franz von Liszt, *Das Völkerrecht* (5th edn., Berlin, Häring, 1907), p. 7.

Kantorowicz (1877–1940) and others that emphasized the significance of socially spontaneous *Individualrecht* and marginalized formal State law altogether.[61]

Such theories were without illusion about the State. They were also politically dangerous. Either they made the legitimacy of State power suspect as an ideological facade, or they dismissed public policy as altogether irrelevant in the determination of social order. Ludwig Gumplowicz (1858–1909) a *Staatslehrer* from Graz of Polish origin, for instance, insisted on the need to let go of the illusion of law as an expression of common will. No such will existed; the State was an aggregate of groups struggling against each other with the result that some groups were always more powerful than others and the minority invariably ruled over the majority. That science was to focus on these naked facts might make the groups that benefited from this state of affairs uncomfortable: "But it is not up to science to worry over the momentary comfort of the ruling classes."[62] Quite consistently, Gumplowicz – a denier of international law – closed the 1902 edition of his book on the social State-idea in an obituary for the *Rechtsstaat*.[63]

Brutal realism was an uneradicable part of the cultural pessimism of the 1890s. Many German readers of Nietzsche fixated on the doctrine of the will to power as a substitute for conventional morality that provided a convenient ground for unscrupulous self-assertion. The direction of pessimism was not necessarily towards revolution. Gustave Le Bon's (1841–1931) shallow but extremely popular theory of the manipulability of all groups, including electoral bodies and parliamentary assemblies had unabashedly conservative implications: "As regards the possible effects of reason on the spirit of the electorate, one would have to have never read the minutes of an electoral meeting not to have a firm view on the topic. What are being exchanged there are claims, abuses, sometimes blows, but never reasons."[64] These and comparable views

---

[61] Cf. Gnaeus Flavius (Hermann Kantorowicz), "Der Kampf um die Rechtswissenschaft" (1906), in *Rechtswissenschaft und Soziologie, Ausgewählte Schriften zur Wissenschaftslehre* (Karlsruhe, Müller, 1962), pp. 13–29.

[62] Ludwig Gumplowicz, *Die sociologische Staatsidee* (2nd edn., Innsbruck, Wagner, 1902), p. 4. Theological, rationalistic, and juridical ideas of the State were to be replaced by sociology that took its starting-point from the primal existence of social groups for which the State was an instrument and the individual a dependent, malleable material, Gumplowicz, *Die sociologische Staatsidee*, pp. 51–52.

[63] Gumplowicz, *Die sociologische Staatsidee*, pp. 219–224. Cf. also the comments in Max Seydel, *Grundzüge einer allgemeinen Staatslehre* (Würtzburg, Stuber, 1873), pp. 31–32.

[64] Gustave Le Bon, *Psychologie des foules* (Paris, PUF, 1963 [1895]), p. 109. Cf. also Gumplowicz on "social suggestion," *Die sociologische Staatsidee*, pp. 205–219. On the

about irrational forces lying at the heart of political organization not only created doubts about the legitimacy of the State but encouraged attitudes of cynicism or revolution that were diametrically opposed to the civic virtues advocated by public law.

Under such conditions, liberal lawyers were called upon to defend the State as the representative of the general interest. But they could no longer do this by conceiving of the nation as a historically determined, organic *Volkswille* or a reflection of the social contract. The former view smacked of anachronistic conservatism. The latter was vulnerable to scientific objections: the original contract was a myth.[65] So they fell back on the Hegelian view of the State as the reconciliation of the ideal and the actual, individual and the community. They adopted "a universalism whose purpose it was to ensure individual freedom and progress, by establishing a rational, impersonal, and legal framework realized through the state."[66] Where Kant had combined freedom with reason, and become vulnerable to the critique of abstract character of the latter, the liberals now substituted the concrete State in its place.[67] A strong State could be created without undermining individual freedom through democratic reform and by strengthening rational authority – that is to say, bureaucracy – in which the liberal elite would have a decisive role. In the *Rechtsstaat* the bureaucracy would rule itself "according to fixed and logical principles . . . which stood above the rulers and the ruled."[68]

This strategy produced two paradoxes whose effects would show up only later in the course of political struggles within the Weimar Republic. To conceive of the State as a form of self-rule by the bureaucracy slowly widened the gap between the public realm and the civil society that would finally break the legitimacy of the *Rechtsstaat*. Bureaucratic routinization would become a mortal threat to the freedom it had once been created to support. On the other hand, the *Rechtsstaat* imbued the State in Germany with an ethical character absent in France or Britain. As most of State law, however, continued to be produced by

---

1890s turn of sociology from its historical orientation to the problem of the crowd, cf. Stephen Kern, *The Culture of Time and Space* (Harvard University Press, 1983), pp. 221–222.

[65] Georg Jellinek, *Allgemeine Staatslehre* (3rd edn., Berlin, Springer, 1922), pp. 148–158, 204–218. Cf. also Tuori, *Valtionhallinnon*, I, p. 53.

[66] Michael Freeden, *Ideologies and Political Theory. A Conceptual Approach* (Oxford University Press, 1996), p. 210.

[67] For a more recent analysis, cf. Paul Franco, *Hegel's Philosophy of Freedom* (New Haven and London, Yale University Press, 1999), pp. 278–341.

[68] Ringer, *The Decline of the German Mandarins*, p. 9.

authoritarian means and for authoritarian purposes, the broad cultural result was that "the autocratic State thus became a moral agent charged with the realization of liberty which was not conceived as freedom from restraint, as elsewhere, but instead as the 'inner freedom' of ethical self-direction in compliance with duty as determined by the State."[69] That a State which showed itself to the naked eye as a *Herrschaftsinstrument*, vested with the monopoly of violence, could also appear as a cluster of logically related rules, principles, and legal institutions, designed to protect freedom, was an act of intellectual gymnastics by liberal lawyers made possible by the impeccably German arguments they had learned from Kant and Hegel. Yet the more democratic struggles called for an alliance between the liberals and the State, the more important became the threat posed by this strategy to the vague internationalism of those same liberals. Was it possible to support both the State and the international order?

Rechtsstaat – domestic and international: Georg Jellinek

Georg Jellinek's (1851–1911) eclectic theory of the State synthesized a number of separate trends in German public law into a comprehensive defense of the *Rechtsstaat* that also created a professionally plausible justification of international law. His *oeuvre* was at once a continuation of the formalism of the Gerber–Laband school and an overcoming of it by an explicit orientation towards social reality from neo-Kantian premises. Its political realism was reflected in the theory of law as a matter of State will while it also bound that will into a process of cultural determination.

In his dissertation to the University of Leipzig in 1872 the twenty-one-year-old Jellinek had already contrasted the metaphysical pessimism of Schopenhauer to the constructive optimism of Leibnitz and had no difficulty in agreeing with the latter. Pessimism was philosophically untenable, an attitude projected on world history by people living through unhappy times, a philosophy of quietism and death. Even in such times, however, many spirits would continue to struggle; even if nations may run their course, humanity will progress and emerge rejuvenated from the ashes of the past. In Leibnitz, individuality and conflict were reconciled at a higher level of structural harmony, and the present world was the best of possible worlds whose defects only highlighted its brilliant

---

[69] James T. Kloppenberg, *Uncertain Victory. Social Democracy and Progressivism in European and American Thought 1870–1920* (Oxford University Press 1986), p. 178.

harmony. This was a true German philosophy, the philosophy of optimism and action, struggle for progress and the perfection of the world.[70] Jellinek was educated in the family of a Viennese Rabbi in a broad "Humboldtian" way. Even his contemporaries admired his breadth of learning and he himself confessed that though he had concluded a marriage of convenience with law his real love remained with philosophy.[71] Jellinek's first legal product, *Die sozialethische Bedeutung von Recht, Unrecht und Strafe* (1878), participated in the debate about the possibility of overcoming *laissez-faire* by the ethically oriented economic and social policy that had been advocated by the influential *Verein für Sozialpolitik*.[72] In 1883 Jellinek was appointed Extraordinary Professor in Public Law at the University of Vienna but failed to attain full professorship due to a virulent anti-semitic campaign conducted by *Wiener Presse* that was scandalized over the prospect over a Jew teaching the international law of a Christian–European State community. Consequently he left Vienna and was invited to a full chair in Heidelberg in 1890 where he befriended the neo-Kantian legal philosopher Wilhelm Windelband and Max Weber, for whom he provided inspiration by his use of the concept of the ideal type and through his theory of the religious basis of human rights.[73]

Jellinek was a good specimen of the modernist wing of the German academic community that sought to respond to the uncertainties of the age by an accommodation of insights from modern science – sociology, anthropology, and psychology. These insights enabled him to construct a complex argument about the *Rechtsstaat* that ended up paradoxically espousing contradictory positions on two themes. His methodology created space for a fully autonomous public law while also basing that law firmly on sociological insights about the centrality of power in the

---

[70] Georg Jellinek, "Die Weltanschauungen Leibnitz' und Schopenhauers. Ihre Gründe und ihre Berichtigung. Eine Studie über Optimismus und Pessimismus," in *Ausgewählte Schriften und Reden* (2 vols., Berlin, Häring, 1911), I, pp. 1–41.

[71] Andreas Fijal and Ralf-René Weingärtner, "Georg Jellinek – Universalgelehrter und Jurist" (1987), 27 *Juristische Schulung*, p. 98.

[72] The *Verein* had been set up in 1872. Its leading members were the economists Gustav Schmoller and Lujo Brentano who were identified with the new "ethical direction," cf. Ringer, *The Decline of the German Mandarins*, pp. 146–147.

[73] Cf. Guenther Roth, "Introduction," in Max Weber, *Economy and Society* (2 vols., trans. Guenther Roth and Claus Wittich, University of California Press, 1978), I, p. lxxvii. A different version of Jellinek's career move is told in Willibald M. Plöchl, "Zur Entwicklung der modernen Völkerrechtswissenschaft an der Viennaer Juristenfakultät," in F. A. von der Heydte *et al.*, *Völkerrecht und rechtliches Weltbild, Festschrift für Alfred Verdross* (Vienna, Springer, 1960), pp. 43–44.

State. His law was founded on (subjective) State will – while accompanied by a sociological argument about how that will was (objectively) constrained so as to give reality to individual rights and to international law.

Although the main body of Jellinek's work was in the field of public law, and written into his *Allgemeine Staatslehre* of 1900, read widely beyond Germany,[74] its relevance for international law is direct and has been lasting. The distinction between a sociological and a legal perspective on the State made it possible to characterize diplomacy, too, as both struggle for power and the administration of a legal system. The thesis of the normative power of the factual created space for a Kantian internationalism that built on self-legislation by a will aware of the constraints under which it had to work.

Jellinek's defense of the reality of international law consisted of a demonstration that it was essentially similar to other, uncontroversial types of (public) law. It had been conventionally assumed that treaties possessed legal character only by delegation from higher-level norms of natural law, analogies from the law of obligations, or from custom.[75] This perspective had failed to create a "juristic" conception of international law. To achieve this, one needed first to ask what in general explained the law's binding force. This, Jellinek wrote, was its practical validity (*praktische Geltung*), understood in a psychological way, as a feeling or conviction of validity.[76] "The positivity of the law is based in the final analysis always on the conviction of its validity. On this purely subjective element the whole legal order is built."[77] A legal norm was felt as valid (and thus "valid") when it acted as motivation for the will of a legal subject.[78] What joined uncontroversial cases of law was that they expressed legal relationships as relations of will. Now sometimes, as in

---

[74] In a short period of time, three editions came out and the third had been reprinted six times by 1929. The book was translated into French, Spanish, Italian, Czech, Russian, and Japanese. Cf. Roland Holubek, *Allgemeine Staatslehre als empirische Wissenschaft. Eine Untersuchung am Beispiel von Georg Jellinek* (Bonn, Bouvier, 1961), pp. 3–4.

[75] Georg Jellinek, *Die rechtliche Natur der Staatenverträge. Ein Beitrag zur juristischen Construktion des Völkerrechts* (Vienna, Hölder, 1880), p. 4.

[76] Jellinek, *Die rechtliche Natur der Staatenverträge*, p. 2.

[77] Jellinek, *Allgemeine Staatslehre*, pp. 333–334. Jellinek saw only two alternatives: the law arose either from a source that was independent from human will – in which case the concept of law was "metaphysical speculation" – or as a matter of human consciousness, of human will.

[78] The relationship of such a subjectively based theory of law to Max Weber's views about legitimation is clear.

much civil law, that relationship was between a superior and an inferior will and expressed a relation of power (*Herrschaft*). It was this relationship that those had in mind who doubted the reality of international law: there was no superior–inferior relationship between States. However, all legal relations were not between two separate wills. Jellinek's proof of international law's binding force consisted in showing how in a number of uncontroversial cases law emerged from a will that limited itself. Self-legislation explained not only the State's being bound by constitutional and administrative law but the very possibility of there being subjective rights against the State in a situation where a naturalist justification of such rights was not scientifically plausible.[79]

Among later jurists, *Selbstverpflichtungslehre* has received a reputation as a disingenuous offshoot of an étatist positivism. How can a will limit itself? If a State is bound only if it so wills, does not that make obligation mere illusion? Obligation vanishes when the State changes its mind.[80] Such criticisms fail, however, to address Jellinek's (Kantian) move away from a pure voluntarism into a more genuinely sociological understanding of the law in terms of the structural constraints imposed on State will by the environment. In order to understand Jellinek's delicate oscillation between a (purely) psychological and a (purely) sociological theory of law, it is necessary to examine the way he saw law both as an autonomous scientific discipline and firmly embedded in social and psychological reality.

In accordance with the teaching of his Heidelberg colleagues Weber and Rickert, Jellinek made the distinction between natural sciences and the *Geisteswissenschaften*, locating the theory of the State firmly as part of the latter. It had no natural object – for instance, it could not be reduced to a study of the *Volk* with the view to elucidating some natural organism in which the State and the people were entangled. Nor could it be thought of in terms of ethics or teleology, for these led into metaphysics: "To grasp an objective purpose exceeds the capacity of our knowledge."[81] It was to be an empirical science – not a science of the objective being of States but of States as they appear (and, perhaps, must appear) to consciousness.[82] Like all science, *Staatslehre* was synthetic, it did not

---

[79] Jellinek, *Die rechtliche Natur der Staatenverträge*, esp. pp. 19–28.
[80] Cf. e.g. Nelson, *Rechtswissenschaft*, pp. 26–30, 57–66; von Bar, "Grundlage und Kodifikation des Völkerrechts," pp. 145–157; Hans Kelsen, *Das Problem der Souveränität und die Theorie des Völkerrechts* (2nd edn., Tübingen, Mohr, 1928), pp. 168–174.
[81] Jellinek, *Allgemeine Staatslehre*, p. 151.
[82] Cf. Holubek, *Allgemeine Staatslehre*, pp. 9–14, 23–25.

seek to present things in themselves but in light of the scholar's concepts that sought to make sense of the disparate representations in the external world.[83] The theory of the State should not ask "what is a State?" but "how do we think about States?". The State was a mental construction, existing ultimately nowhere but in our heads. It was not arbitrary for this reason, however, but a "thought-necessity," needed in order to make sense of the appearances of the social world.

A useful legal theory had to explain the variations that appear in empirical reality. This was not the case with, for instance, the prevailing theory about composite international persons, a crucial problem of public law in the wake of the American Civil War, the establishment of the Swiss Confederation (1848), and of the German *Reich* (1871). Full confusion reigned. Every new case, Jellinek wrote, had become *sui generis*. What now were needed were general legal concepts, based on induction and formulated as ideal-types under which the complexity of appearances could be managed.[84] A federal or confederal structure was not something that existed in the events themselves. It was imposed on them by the observing scientist seeking to synthesize perceptions offered by empirical reality. Such syntheses were not effects of general causes or invariable laws: in human sciences and law generalizations were possible only in the form of broad types (though different, human beings also resembled each other) that created cultural affinities between phenomena. Individual particularities were abstracted away, leaving only general and formal categories.[85]

From these premises Jellinek developed his "two sides theory" of the State – the State as a sociological and a juridical conception, a distinction that mirrored the Kantian dichotomy between the world as *Sein* and as *Sollen*. In the sociological realm, the State could be portrayed as a set of relations of will that took the appearance of *Herrschaft*, the use of power by some over others. Or it appeared as a geographically based community of individuals pursuing determined objectives. Synthesizing legal thought joined these aspects – relations of power and pursuit of purposes – together by conceiving those who exercised power in terms of organ status within the purposefully acting State.[86] Hence

---

[83] The theory of the State did not examine empirical States but aimed to group them by induction into ideal-types that would then be used as explanatory aids, *Allgemeine Staatslehre*, pp. 36–42.

[84] Georg Jellinek, *Die Lehre von den Staatenverbindungen* (Vienna, Hölder, 1882), pp. 11–16; *Allgemeine Staatslehre*, pp. 33 et seq.   [85] Jellinek, *Allgemeine Staatslehre*, pp. 29–42.

[86] This does not mean that the State is a fiction: it is an organizing principle, "eine unserem Bewusstsein notwendige form der Synthese," *Allgemeine Staatslehre*, p. 170.

the definition of the (sociological) State as a "permanent community of individuals possessing an original power to rule."[87]

This did not, however, exhaust the State's being. No social institution or event – and certainly not the State – could be reduced to one single frame of explanation. From a juridical perspective, the State could be conceived as a legal subject, in which case the sociological community (*Verbandseinheit*) appeared as a particular kind of corporation (*Körperschaft*). Again, this described no objective reality. Constructive legal thought used a category such as "*Körperschaft*" to explain its object.[88] Through it, the commands, prohibitions, and permissions by determined individuals could be imputed as acts of the State and seen as creative of legal norms. From a sociological perspective, these norms expressed the will of those in power; from a legal perspective, they were binding because they emanated from the State.[89]

Thus the theory of the State was split in two: the sociologically inclined *Allgemeine Soziallehre des Staates* and the legal–normative *Allgemeine Staatsrechtslehre*. The inclusion of both aspects as parts of a general theory enabled the taking account of the advances in sociology and history without reducing the legal State to a passive reflection of either.[90] Jellinek's psychological theory enabled him to maintain the autonomy of law from social power in a way that had been an important aspect of German public law positivism and served two purposes in the consolidation of bourgeois society. First, by treating all legal subjects as formally equal, it justified the exchange relations in the market whose functioning required that traders be abstracted from their particular situation and entitled the State to intervene in a corrective fashion without the accusation of partiality.[91] Second, by abstracting itself from teleological, historical, or "organic" explanations, it separated the formal structures of the State from the infights in the political realm and offered State organs – the Imperial Chancellor and the bureaucracy in particular – the ability to operate outside the bitter conflicts that tended to paralyze parliamentary politics.[92]

Both aspects were useful in the description of the international world,

---

[87] Jellinek, *Allgemeine Staatslehre*, pp. 180–181.
[88] Jellinek, *Allgemeine Staatslehre*, pp. 169–173, 182–183.
[89] Holubek insists that in this way, Jellinek's theory went far to justify de facto power relations, *Staatslehre*, e.g. pp. 18–19, 50–57. This is true inasmuch as State will is seen as the (arbitrary) will of the power-holders. This is not, however, the way Jellinek sees it.
[90] Jellinek, *Die Lehre von den Staatenverbindungen*, pp. 9–10.
[91] Tuori, *Valtionhallinnon*, I, pp. 41–50.
[92] For a critical view, cf. Holubek, *Staatslehre*, pp. 54–57.

too, as the realm of sovereign equality where States were abstracted from their particular qualities and not submitted to an external political or moral assessment of their activities. A sociological understanding of diplomacy as a realm of *Herrschaft* was not incompatible with a legal understanding of the international as a system of market relations between formal States that were legally bound to the extent that they consented to so being. The emergence of the legal from the sociological took place by reconceiving relations of power as relations of will. The sovereignty of the State thus became "the quality of a State to be obligated only through its own will."[93] Moreover, to say that the State is bound by its own will is nothing else than to affirm that the organs have the competence to legislate which law affords them. Or from the reverse perspective: if State law binds its organs – and this is of course the very purpose of public law – then this, too, means that State is bound by its own will. *Rechtsstaat* follows automatically from Jellinek's premises.[94]

Self-legislation is then not in conflict with international law but, on the contrary, a guarantee of its legal force.[95] It reconciles autonomy and authority within a structure of argument received from Kantian ethics:[96] only an act that comes from autonomous choice can have ethical significance. An act produced by irresistible external force has no moral value. The autonomous individual legislates for herself. Acting within the international sphere, the sovereign State is in an analogous position. It legislates for itself and its capacity to do so – its autonomy – is the exhaustive explanation for why it is bound. But this is not true only of its international obligations. The whole of the State's constitutional and public law are based on self-legislation.[97] To think self-legislation impossible is to think of the Prince as *legibus solutus*, an argument for absolutism.

---

[93] Jellinek, *Die Lehre von den Staatenverbindungen*, p. 32.
[94] This meaning is often (and sometimes tendentiously) overlooked by critics. Least of all is *Selbstverpflichtung* to be seen as a naturalist analogy from individual rights as presented e.g. by Ernst Reibstein, *Völkerrecht. Eine Geschichte seiner Ideen in Lehre und Praxis* (2 vols., Munich, Freiburg, 1963), II, pp. 40–41. Cf. also Léon Duguit, *Le droit social, le droit individuel, et la transformation de l'Etat* (Paris, Alcan, 1908), pp. 53–54 as well as Léon Duguit, *L'Etat, le droit objectif et la loi positive* (2 vols., Paris, Fontemoing, 1901), I, pp. 124–131.
[95] "Was bis jetzt nur trotz der Souveränetät und gegen die Souveränetät behauptet werden konnte, kann nun durch die Souveränetät erklärt werden." Jellinek, *Die Lehre von den Staatenbindungen*, p. 36.
[96] Cf also Jellinek, *Die rechtliche Natur der Staatenverträge*, p. 14 and Jellinek, *Gesetz und Verordnung* (Tübingen, Mohr, 1911, reprint of the 1887 edn.), p. 192.
[97] At one point Jellinek goes further, arguing that all obligation is self-assumed: even in superior–inferior relations (such as those between the State and the citizen) the decision to obey is ultimately based on the citizen's understanding of what is required of her. Jellinek, *Die rechtliche Natur der Staatenverträge*, p. 15.

International law as philosophy: Germany 1871–1933

Admittedly, such a psychological jurisprudence came close to the relativism of the *Lebensphilosophen* of the period. No external morality dictated to States what they should will. The State's only clear duty was to be true to its autonomous self. Did this not make the international world look like that "monster of energy," that "sea of forces flowing and rushing together," of which Nietzsche had spoken in a famous passage in 1885, the world as "the *will to power – and nothing besides!*"?[98] But Jellinek immediately retreated from a purely relativist, subjective understanding of will. The will was constrained through the normative power of facts, *normative Kraft des Faktischen*. Human thought vested states of things that have stood for a long time – social normality – with normative quality.[99] What exists becomes what should exist. This was no illegitimate leap from facts to norms: the relationship was mediated by consciousness. The mind vested tradition with normative sense. But the mind, too, countered its own conservatism by its tendency to rebel against states of things that failed to meet expectations of justice. In both directions, facts received normative meaning through the activity of the mind, free and constrained simultaneously.[100]

The argument about the normative force of facts combined voluntarism with social power in a way that provided a conceptual basis for a theory and critique of legitimacy. It could have functioned in the international sphere as in the domestic. In his 1880 book on the law of treaties, however, Jellinek received the force of *Selbstverpflichtung* from the purpose of the State and the nature of the international society.[101] Why can the State not free itself from an obligation by changing its mind? True, it may effectively change its mind where there is a reasonable motive for doing so. This has always been accepted by the doctrine of *rebus sic stantibus*. No compact is concluded to remain for ever in force – yet few of them contain formal termination clauses.[102] But to suggest that a State may *always* modify its obligations by a further change of mind is to think of State will as completely arbitrary. This cannot be so. The State – as we have seen – is a purposeful community. Among its purposes is the wish to engage in contacts with other States. To break one's compacts would go against this. It would make social life impossible. To

---

[98] Friedrich Nietzsche, *The Will to Power* (ed. Walter Kaufmann, New York, Vintage, 1967), p. 550 (italics in original).   [99] Jellinek, *Allgemeine Staatslehre*, p. 337.
[100] This is close to Tönnies' distinction between *Wesenwille* and *Kürwille* – the former expressing a will close to a person's nature, the latter an arbitrary choice. Cf. Ringer, *The Decline of the German Mandarins*, pp. 164–165.
[101] Jellinek, *Die rechtliche Natur der Staatenverträge*, pp. 40–45.
[102] Cf. also Jellinek, *Die Lehre von den Staatenverbindungen*, pp. 102–103.

have a purpose is to will the presence of the conditions under which the purpose may be fulfilled.[103] If a State can fulfill its purpose only by participating in international life, then it must keep its promises unless there is a reasonable motive – such as *Notrecht* – for disregarding them.[104] No State can be reasonably assumed to commit suicide! This is not to say that the "living conditions of nations" ("*Natur der Lebensverhältnisse*") under which States are compelled to seek their purposes are natural law – they are the concrete reality States have to take into account in their interaction with each other.

In his 1880 book, Jellinek countered the weaknesses of pure voluntarism by a sociological rejoinder: law is based on will, but will is constrained by the environment, conceived in a rationalistic manner. The need for co-operation compelled States to project each other as legal subjects towards which they made promises that enabled co-operation for the attainment of reciprocal and common interests.[105] Although confederations and other inter-State compacts, he argued in 1882, were based on regular treaties, and as such on *Selbstverpflichtung*, they were also a socially conditioned feature of modern life. Interdependence pushed (rational) States into co-operation: "Gemeinschaft ist überall da vorhanden, wo es Verkehr gibt."[106] This was a community of interests and purposes whose internal cohesion was constantly being strengthened by cultural development and the needs of international administration and which was expressed in legislation but based ultimately on "nature."[107]

Rationalism and politics: a difficulty

Jellinek brought public and international law together with sociology, politics, and history, combined philosophical idealism with dogmatic positivism, natural science with psychology. Such use of a technique of multiple perspectives was not dissimilar from that used in the literature

---

[103] Jellinek, *Die rechtliche Natur der Staatenverträge*, p. 44.
[104] Jellinek, *Die rechtliche Natur der Staatenverträge*, p. 62.
[105] Jellinek, *Die rechtliche Natur der Staatenverträge*, pp. 48–50. For critics, the view that the State was constrained by the environment was no legal constraint: it described a factual condition which States might or might not take account of, Nelson, *Rechtswissenschaft*, pp. 60–62.   [106] Jellinek, *Die Lehre von den Staatenverbindungen*, p. 94.
[107] Jellinek, *Die Lehre von den Staatenverbindungen*, pp. 95, 109–113. Jellinek had used an analogous argument in his discussion of the emergence of norms in primitive society in *Die sozialethische Bedeutung* in 1878, pp. 16–22, 25. There he defended a social conception of ethics against an individualist one in a way that suggested a collective determination of the contents of *voluntas*, cf. e.g. pp. 33–41. For a criticism of this as naturalism, cf. Triepel, *Völkerrecht und Landesrecht*, pp. 80–81n.

International law as philosophy: Germany 1871–1933

and art of the period: accepting different descriptive vocabularies suggested the existence of more than just one reality.[108] By opening up diverse ways of thinking about the State Jellinek was able to satisfy the need for a realistic appreciation of social power, simultaneously justifying the *Rechtsstaat*.[109] But he bought the success of his construction by an altogether unwarranted assumption of the intrinsic rationality of the European political order, a rationality that he needed in order to explain why the self-legislating freedom of States would not lead into anarchy or imperialism.

In the period after the establishment of the Empire, from 1871 to 1890, it must have seemed plausible to argue that though international law was based on State will, that will would reflect the rational necessities of the surrounding world. If the complex network of treaties with which Bismarck had managed European foreign policy could be seen as a reflection of deeper social necessities – the workings of the balance of power, for instance – then there was nothing suspicious about it. In 1890, Jellinek reflected upon the state of the international order in relatively optimistic terms. True, no legal arrangement would do away with the "unchanging nature of the human soul" that sometimes called for war in order to realize a revolutionary idea, or to bring in a better period. The possibility of war remained an index of freedom, the ability to transcend existing (irrational) power. But with the increase of interdependence and the costs of war for national societies, interest in peace would continue to grow: "Indeed, it may be said that the interest towards the maintenance of peace has now attained an unprecedented intensity."[110]

But to assume that States would continue to hold themselves bound by their agreements even against their short-term interests was to think of them as rational interest-calculators in a world where there was no doubt that everyone's long-term interest lay in co-operation. Both assumptions seemed difficult to sustain. The nationalist politics of European States seemed far from a rational process of interest-calculation. And there was little evidence that co-operation instead of decisive action would bring about the best national result. After Bismarck's fall, the Reinsurance treaty

---

[108] Cf. Kern, *The Culture of Time and Space*, pp. 139–149.
[109] Stolleis regards it as a summary of nineteenth-century German public law theory, *Geschichte*, II, pp. 451–454. But it may perhaps also be seen as a break towards an increasingly eclectic legal study.
[110] Georg Jellinek, "Die Zukunft des Krieges" (1890), in *Ausgewählte Schriften*, II, pp. 537, 515–541.

with Russia was allowed to lapse. Chancellor von Bülow's declaration of a German *Weltpolitik* ("world policy") in 1897 was accompanied by a grasp for new colonies in Africa and the Far East, the creation of economic spheres of influence, and a massive increase in naval power. What historians call "social imperialism" sought to unite German classes under an unashamed nationalism and an adversarial atmosphere in Germany was exploited in the popular mind through the image of an irreducible opposition between a (deep and creative) German *Kultur* and a (shallow and commercial) Anglo-French "Civilization." The Kaiser's eccentric and unpredictable incursions into foreign policy did nothing to assure other powers of Germany's peaceful intentions.[111] As Jellinek himself observed at the opening of the 1899 Hague Peace conference, it was a fine irony on the Emperor's part to appoint to the German delegation two lawyers one of whom (Baron von Stengel) had only recently published a pamphlet ridiculing the idea of perpetual peace and the other (Philipp Zorn) had just denied international law's quality as real law.[112]

Whatever the philosophical merits of the theory of self-legislation, its political credibility was undermined by the perception of European diplomacy in terms of an aggressive desire for hegemony. The argument from the "*Natur der Lebensverhältnisse*" would have needed a separate defense in order to act as a plausible constraint for the will to power. Merely to state that co-operation would bring about peace was to state the conclusion, not the argument. Self-legislation translated into international law the Kantian theory of freedom as the reasonable will. A formal order seems a necessary implication of the freedom of the single State: "I should exercise my freedom so that it leaves room for the equal freedom of others." But such rationalism had little to do with political reality. It either implied a fundamental critique of the present international order – or it assumed a sociology of interdependence, but failed to produce any evidence for it. Jellinek remained the optimist he declared himself in 1872, who believed that even war might have beneficial consequences, but his optimism remained grounded in a liberal faith about the intrinsic rationality of political and economic modernity that was undermined by experience.

[111] For the argument that Wilhelm II was in fact mentally ill, cf. John G. Röhl, *The Kaiser and His Court. Wilhelm II and the Government of Germany* (Cambridge University Press, 1994). On Germany's social imperialism, cf. Mommsen, *Imperial Germany*, pp. 77–100.
[112] Georg Jellinek, "Zur Eröffnung der Friedenskonferenz" (1899), in *Ausgewählte Schriften*, II, pp. 542–543, 547–548.

Drawing lines in the profession

At the turn of the century, there were no chairs specifically for international law in Germany so that the topic was usually combined with constitutional or administrative law. Even in major universities such as Heidelberg, Leipzig, and Munich, only a few courses were given in the subject, and those by public law generalists that had done little independent research into it. There was undoubtedly no other juridical discipline, the pacifist liberal Walther Schücking (1875–1935) wrote in 1913, whose representatives could be characterized as properly outsiders to the field they taught.[113] Some assumed that the situation resulted from the great codifications (particularly of the German Civil Code, the BGB) that had monopolized lawyers' attention in the past fifteen to twenty years.[114] Others felt that it was an outcome of the predominance of Bismarckian *Machtdenken* in public administration.[115]

A 1919 study commissioned by the German League of Nations Union (*Deutsche Liga für Völkerbund*) held it nothing short of scandalous that one of the members of the German delegation to the 1907 Hague Conference, an Admiral, confessed to having read nothing of international law apart from the textbooks of von Liszt and Oppenheim. The study proposed to the German ministry of education a massive increase of university positions in the subject and its inclusion in the curricula of all institutions of higher learning as well as in the entry examinations (*Prüfungsexamen*) for public administration. Before the war internationalists had argued that as a world power Germany could not afford to neglect the study of international law. Now such study seemed all the more important inasmuch as it could be used to oppose the domination of the League of Nations by the *Entente* powers.[116]

By 1919 three streams of writing on international law had emerged at German universities.[117] The public law tradition concentrated on examining treaties from the perspective of the *Reich* constitution. Another faction, led by Schücking, aligned the subject as part of its

---

[113] Walther Schücking, "Der Stand des völkerrechtlichen Unterrichts in Deutschland" (1913), VII *Zeitschrift für Völkerrecht*, pp. 375–382.
[114] Karl Strupp, "Die deutsche Vereinigung für internationales Recht: ihre Notwendigkeit, ihre Entstehung, ihre bisherige Tätigkeit" (1914), XXIV *Zeitschrift für Internationales Recht*, pp. 355–357.
[115] Moritz Liepmann, "Die Pflege des Völkerrechts an den deutschen Universitäten" (1919), 6 *Monografien der Deutschen Liga für Völkerbund*, pp. 14–15.
[116] Liepmann, "Die Pflege," pp. 5–15.   [117] Cf. also Stolleis, *Geschichte*, III, pp. 86–89.

left–pacifist sensibility and called for collaboration across professional and political boundaries. A third stream, closest to the *Institut*, combined its mild reformism with the sophistication of German *Rechtslehre*, taking seriously the argument from interdependence that promised a scientific explanation for how sovereign States could be free and still bound. Each of the three should be understood by reference to the German political context and be seen as waging a distinctly German debate about legal form and legal substance, social ideals, and the concrete reality. Public lawyers were convinced of the superior insights that the German legal tradition had developed of the workings of State and law. Self-consciously historical and *völkisch*, they could not fail to regard the international as the realm of the unhistorical and the artificial. Pacifists advocated domestic democratic reform as part of their cosmopolitanism. The textbook writers of the third stream were in something of a dilemma. Little of the positive law had emerged from German sources: the British could always argue from their colonial practices, their *ententes* and arrangements since the early seventeenth century. The French had their political *philosophes*, their universalist traditions. What the Germans had was idealist philosophy and a historical jurisprudence. Schooled in this jurisprudence, and surrounded by skeptics, German internationalists had to come up with seriously scientific explanations to demonstrate that there was an international realm with a concrete historical and cultural base and that it was actually useful for German diplomats to pay attention to it, too.

Public law and the Hague Treaties

As the German system combined international law at the universities with other branches of public law, it was natural that much of the writing in the field reflected the general preoccupations of public lawyers, followed the "juristic Method," and took the perspective of the *Reich* constitution. As Heinrich Triepel noted in 1922, whatever the internationalists had to say about this system, it did not isolate international law as Roman law did and often contributed to the depth and recognized quality of the German scholarship on it.[118] Yet, and perhaps Triepel himself was an example of this, it did create a German *Sonderweg* in which the national perspective so clearly dominated over abstract

---

[118] Heinrich Triepel, "Ferdinand von Martitz. Ein Bild seines Lebens und seines Wirkens" (1922), 30 *Zeitschrift für internationales Recht*, p. 162.

International law as philosophy: Germany 1871–1933

internationalism. This was expressed very adroitly by one of the men of this tradition, Germany's representative at the Hague Peace Conferences of 1899 and 1907, the constitutional lawyer and monarchist Philipp Zorn (1850–1928) in his Rectoral address at the University of Bonn in 1911: Germany was the leading power in Europe – but its unity was threatened internally and externally. He therefore pleaded that the unity of the German State be held as "the uppermost law of our public lives": "So too in that branch of public law which the German legal language has been accustomed to calling international law."[119]

For Triepel or Zorn – like Laband – international law was made principally of treaties, conceived as expressions of sovereign will, not as emanation from an interdependent modernity. Even if the former took a step in the internationalist direction by his *Vereinbarung* doctrine (that sought to respond to the criticisms against self-legislation), that remained a thin, intellectual construction that failed to support an autonomous, cultural sense of an international realm. For Triepel as for Zorn the international was a vacuum that was filled by the wills of States entering and exiting it more or less as they pleased. Triepel's nationalism was graphically illustrated by his resignation from the *Institut* in 1919 as a protest against the Versailles Treaty. But though everyone quoted the passage in Zorn's constitutional law book that relegated unratified treaties to the realm of morality, he was by no means against them, and later became a firm supporter of compulsory arbitration.[120]

There is no doubt that these lawyers were closest to the German government – that is to say, the Emperor – whose aversion to the *esprit d'internationalité* seemed conclusively demonstrated by the appointment of Baron von Stengel (1840–1930) and Zorn as members in the German delegation to the first Hague Peace Conference. Von Stengel was a relatively unknown Professor of Administrative and Constitutional Law from Munich whose merits included the publication of a textbook on German colonial law and a pamphlet against utopian ideas of eternal peace. In 1909 von Stengel still taught the incompatibility of sovereignty with compulsory arbitration and criticized the compromise under which Germany had "in principle" agreed to it in the Hague two years earlier. He associated it with eighteenth-century French individualist sentimentalism, pacifism and social democracy that ignored the lessons of history

---

[119] Philipp Zorn, *Das deutsche Reich und die internationale Schiedsgerichtsbarkeit* (Berlin, Rothschild, 1911), p. 6.

[120] Philipp Zorn, *Das Staatsrecht des deutschen Reiches* (2 vols., Berlin, 1883–1895), I, pp. 495–500.

and constituted mortal dangers for a Germany encircled by hostile neighbors. No world State was emerging; nations and races were simply too different. British pacifism was British imperialism in disguise. A treaty on freezing the levels of armament, for instance, would leave British naval domination intact. But sentimentalism was wrong in principle, too. War was not only an instrument of destruction. It also acted like revolution, pushing aside obsolete political forms, making room for the new and dynamic, supporting artistic and scientific creativity, heroism, and the spirit of self-sacrifice. As Japan's victory over Russia had demonstrated, von Stengel wrote, without preparedness for war, Europe would succumb to the yellow races.[121]

Von Stengel's appointment was widely criticized but his role in the Hague remained small. His 1909 tract collected many conservative themes about international politics under an assessment of the Hague Conferences. It responded to ideas prevalent in Germany but remained an isolated pamphlet within the international law community. By contrast, Zorn became an active participant in the Conferences and propagated their results with enthusiasm, publicly commending Chancellor von Bülow's change of attitude to arbitration in 1899 (in which Zorn himself seems to have played an important role) but criticizing Germany's steadfast opposition to making it compulsory in 1907.[122] He was proud of the German contribution in the drafting of the Statute of the Permanent Court of Arbitration and agreed with Jellinek's positive assessment of its importance.[123] In his Rectoral address he claimed that the initial German skepticism had been caused by inflated expectations and used the occasion to reiterate the pointlessness of its continued opposition to compulsory arbitration. It had already been adopted in a German–British arbitration treaty of 1904, and there was no reason why it could not be generalized. Even without a specific reservation, it was obvious that vital interests and national honor (*Ehrenklausel*) would limit the potential dangers.

Yet Zorn carefully distanced himself from the pacifists. Whether the conferences were organs of an "international community," as Schücking had recently argued, was not a legal question: participant States still

---

[121] Cf. Karl von Stengel, *Weltstaat und Friedensproblem* (Berlin, Reichl, 1909).

[122] On Zorn's role in settling the "arbitration crisis" created by the German government's initial rejection of all permanent arbitration, cf. Arthur Eyffinger, *The 1899 Hague Peace Conference. "The Parliament of Man, the Federation of the World"* (The Hague, London, and Boston, Kluwer, 1999), pp. 373–378.

[123] Philipp Zorn, "Moderne Legitimisten" (1908–1909), II *ARWP*, pp. 178–179.

acted as individual subjects whose will determined what was attainable.[124] In 1911, he cautioned against transforming the Court from a list of arbitrators into a standing body.[125] After 1918, however, he enthusiastically greeted the establishment of the Permanent Court and held it natural that the two bodies should be integrated into one. But he joined lawyers who preferred the Hague system to the League which he, together with practically all his German colleagues, understood as an instrument of Anglo-American imperialism.[126]

The public law perspective was not intrinsically hostile to international law. Liberal-minded lawyers such as Robert Piloty (1863–1926) pointed out that it was an aspect of the move from absolutism to republicanism that the State saw itself bound by law also in its external relations.[127] Foreign policy was not an affair of power alone, but a projection of the State's legal order beyond its boundaries – a view whose consequences were later explored in Kelsen's monism. Yet, however much sympathy public lawyers might have had for internationalism, it must have seemed awkward to them to derive the complex legal system of the Wilhelminian State from it. A preference for the international over the national – or, as Kelsen put it, for pacifism over imperialism – was by no means a culturally obvious choice within the profession.

A pacifist profession? Kohler, Schücking, and the First World War

There existed no international law journals in the German language at the turn of the century. Occasional articles on international questions (including colonial and private international law) had been published in the *Archiv des öffentlichen Rechts*, set up by Laband and Felix Störk (1851–1908) in 1885.[128] In 1906 Josef Kohler (1849–1919), a prolific

---

[124] Philipp Zorn, *Weltunionen, Haager Friedenskonferenzen und Völkerbund* (Berlin, Dummler, 1925), p. 7.
[125] Philipp Zorn, *Das deutsche Reich und die internationale Schiedsgerichtsbarkeit* (Berlin and Leipzig, Rothschild, 1911), pp. 7–8, 16–28, 44.
[126] Zorn, *Weltunionen*, esp. pp. 47–60.
[127] Robert Piloty, "Staaten als Mächte und Mächte als Staaten. Ein Wort zu den Grundlagen des Völkerrechts" (1914), VIII *Zeitschrift für Völkerrecht*, pp. 360–365.
[128] Of the 28 articles classed under these items in the *Archiv's* first 25 years, three were written by well-known international lawyers – Heinrich Lammasch (1853–1920) from Vienna, whose contribution dealt with nationality, Ferdinand von Martitz (1839–1922) from Tübingen and Berlin who, though trained in legal history, constitutional, and administrative law, was one of the German members of the *Institut*, and whose long article on the suppression of slavery and the slave trade in Africa

writer in legal philosophy, history, comparative law, and in many fields of legal dogmatics, set up the first German journal devoted to international law, the *Zeitschrift für Völkerrecht und Bundesstaatsrecht*. Kohler's interest in international law stemmed from his multidisciplinary and internationalist leanings and Hegelian idealism. He remained, however, an outsider to the profession (he never became a member or *associé* of the *Institut*), emphasizing in non-technical articles the close links between international law – including his own journal – and the pacifist movement. In 1910, for example, he attacked the standard conservative argument about war's inevitability. Even if it was impossible to cease all war immediately, this was no argument against a policy of small steps. Even if war exceptionally – as war of *liberation* – might have positive effects, such effects were now achievable on the pacific fronts of economy, technology, and science. Pacifism, he wrote, was not feminine, as its opponents claimed, but offered many outlets for the demonstration of manly vitality ("männliche Lebenskraft").[129]

Kohler was concerned over the German image as a nation of militarists. As a large power in the heart of Europe it had special reason to refrain from aggressiveness. He had no doubt that Germany and its neighbors were equally civilized and peaceful and needed to learn to talk that way, too. He believed in the cultural unity of humanity and characterized international law as a "science of peace."[130] In 1913 Kohler welcomed the opening of the Peace Palace in the Hague and of the new law school – the Hague Academy – and wrote optimistically about arbitration, the slow coming of a world federation, and a permanent world court. Though news from the Balkans was worrisome, he wrote, the Peace Palace was inaugurated under favorable circumstances.[131]

Footnote 128 (*cont.*)
remained one of the more important legal treatments of the topic, and Friedrich Geffcken (1830–1896), also a member of the *Institut*, commenting on a French–Chinese dispute. All three articles were published in the *Archiv's* first volume. In later years, most of the international law materials came from established public lawyers such as von Stengel and Störk or young doctors who edited their theses for the *Archiv*. However, the classification of an academic German jurist as an "international lawyer" is complicated. As in Germany the subject was combined with constitutional or administrative law, someone formally qualified in all these subjects was free to orient himself through his writings or his participation in professional societies. For an early positive assessment of the "German system," cf. Triepel, "Ferdinand von Martitz," p. 162.

[129] Josef Kohler, "Die Friedensbewegung und das Völkerrecht" (1910), IV *Zeitschrift für Völkerrecht*, p. 138. [130] Kohler, "Die Friedensbewegung," pp. 129–131.
[131] Josef Kohler, "Der Friedenstempel" (1913), VII *Zeitschrift für Völkerrecht*, pp. 237–240.

His optimism did not survive the war. In a joint editorial with Max Fleischmann (1872–1943, the future editor of von Liszt's *Völkerrecht*) in 1916 Kohler declared that the international law of agreements had come to an end. The war had demonstrated the enormous differences in the legal consciousness of European powers. The English total war (*Wirtschaftskrieg*) struck at civilians and was completely at odds with the German idea of war as struggle between States. It was time for a German journal to bring forward the German standpoint. It was time for a jurisprudence that would not rest content with examining the day's diplomacy: a new law should arise from the depth of the histories, lives, and interests of European societies. Dreams of peace had dispersed like soap bubbles and the Peace Palace could now open its doors for other worthy human goals. With undisguised bitterness Kohler admitted having been himself prisoner of the illusion that other nations would share his idealism; that they too would have enough to do at home. All this was error: "Treaties with liars and traitors cannot form sources of law; only peoples with a sharp moral sense may be entitled to participate in law-creation."[132] Could the British and the French be trusted, or be treated as brothers? "*Nein und dreifach nein.*" Instead of treaties, a natural law was now needed, Kohler wrote, that was progressively enveloped in culture as an idea simultaneously historical and rational; not an abstract conceptual jurisprudence but a science whose leading principles would emerge from the observation of life itself. This would be a truly German science and a legislator that would express necessary historical and rational truths. The victorious war would inaugurate the Kaiser as the guarantor of international law and justice.

Kohler's about-face led to a complete break with the pacifists – manifested in the firing of Hans Wehberg (1885–1962) from his recently attained co-editorship in the journal. Kohler himself did not survive to follow the ups and downs of the German international lawyers' relations with the League of Nations. By contrast, Wehberg, and in particular his friend Walther Schücking, became heavily involved in the post-war reconstruction. Schücking who was also a left–liberal politician (member of the Progressive People's Party and after its demise in 1918 of the German Democratic Party), a member of the German peace delegation at Versailles, and the only German judge at the Permanent Court of International Justice, alternated between positions of influence and

---

[132] Josef Kohler, "Das neue Völkerrecht" (1916), XI *Zeitschrift für Völkerrecht*, p. 7. Kohler also justified Germany's occupation of Belgium as a legitimate case of *Notrecht*. Cf. (1914–1915), 8 *ARWP*, pp. 412–449.

marginality. His career highlighted the genuine ambivalence of a legal politics hovering between pacifist internationalism and commitment to domestic democratic reform. Schücking sought a break from the political traditions of the Prussian *Machtstaat*. He advocated a German *rapprochement* with the West and interpreted his own left–liberal sensibilities as the real heritage of the German people. Among German international lawyers, his position came closest to the mainstream of the *Institut de droit international:* a naturalistically backed but pragmatically oriented reformism, an optimistic belief in the harmony of reason, peace and cooperation within permanent international institutions. It is easy to understand why Schücking became the most respected German international lawyer outside Germany – but also why his influence at home remained negligible apart from the moment after the war when the direction of his pacifism and German policy briefly coalesced.

Schücking came from a family of liberal traditions but did not engage in politics until having received a chair at Marburg's conservative law faculty in 1902.[133] The crises of the first years of the century and his contacts with left–liberal politicians, his mentor Ludwig von Bar from Marburg (1836–1913) and above all the Austrian pacifist Alfred Fried (1864–1921), led him into a political jurisprudence and alignment with the latter's "organizational pacifism" that were completely alien to German public law.[134] Like the Statute of the *Institut,* Schücking saw the international jurist as an educator of the people, a "Mentor des Volkes über alle Klasseninteressen."[135] Lawyers were not describers of but participants in international politics and had a duty not only to report on existing law but to further its development. Schücking blamed his colleagues for their backward-looking orientation, their disregard of natural law and of the socio-economic developments of the *fin-de-siècle*. Germany was stuck with nationalism at a time when everyone else was becoming internationalist.[136] In a much-read pamphlet in 1909 he repeated Bluntschli's proposal for a European confederation with the long-term objective of a World State.[137] He later had several occasions to develop his

---

[133] For Schücking's early years, cf. Detlev Acker, *Walther Schücking* (Munster, Aschendorff, 1970), pp. 4–13.
[134] He admitted having received much of his education in international law from Fried. Acker, *Walther Schücking*, p. 42.   [135] Acker, *Walther Schücking*, p. 18.
[136] Walther Schücking, *Die Organisation der Welt* (Leipzig, Kröner, 1909), p. 7.
[137] Walther Schücking, "L'organisation internationale" (1908), XV *RGDIP*, pp. 5–23, later published as "Die Idee der internationalen Organisation in der Geschichte," in *Der Bund der Völker. Studien und Vorträge zum organisatorischen Pazifismus* (Leipzig, Geist, 1918), pp. 17–34.

proposal, but its outline remained unchanged. Law, pacifism, and international institutions formed a closed trinity: without one, the other two would not be attained. The position arose from a genuine but ethnocentric faith: World State meant a gradual Europeanisation of the world.[138]

Schücking's most famous argument was his interpretation of the Hague Peace Conferences of 1899 and 1907 as a World Confederation. In a book that started with a complaint about the impoverishment of German spiritual life at the turn of the century – a point he constantly repeated – Schücking attacked his colleagues for having completely misunderstood the work of the Hague. For "in the year 1899 the Hague Conference, although not *expressis verbis*, yet *implicite* and *ipso facto*, created a World Confederation [*Weltstaatenbund*]."[139] In a long, dogmatic argument Schücking almost suggested that where there were diplomats and politicians sitting down with full powers to negotiate a law-making treaty, there was a confederation. This, he opined, followed as the necessary result of the employment of conceptual jurisprudence. " It is the task of jurists to subsume the new creation under one of the categories of public law or, if this were impossible, to create a new category for the novel structure."[140] In contrast to technical co-operation within international unions, the Permanent Court with its standing administration was a genuinely *political* body with unlimited substantive jurisdiction.[141] As the States now had (unwittingly) set up a confederation of the world, it followed – "logically" – that they recognized each other as sovereign equals, equally entitled to independence and territorial inviolability.[142] A peaceful world was created by juristic interpretation! This involved suggesting that States had set up a creation whose nature not only escaped them but, had it been expressly stated, would have been immediately rejected. The oddity of the suggestion is hardly diminished by

---

[138] Walther Schücking, "Die Annäherung der Menschenrassen durch das Völkerrecht," in *Der Bund der Völker*, pp. 59–78.

[139] Walther Schücking, *Das Werk vom Haag, Erster Band: Die Staatenverband der Haager Konferenzen* (Munich and Leipzig, Duncker & Humblot, 1912), p. 81. The book has been translated as *The International Union of the Hague Conferences* (trans. G. Fenwick, Oxford, Clarendon, 1918), in which the expression "*Weltstaatenbund*" has been inappropriately translated as "World Federation," p. 86. Throughout the book, however, Schücking takes pains to refrain from arguing that the Hague Convention of his proposal would set up a supranational form of government.

[140] Schücking, *Das Werk vom Haag*, p. 81.

[141] Schücking, *Das Werk vom Haag*, p. 74. Nonetheless, he recognized that the optional character of the process and the fact that not all States had signed the convention remained (practical) limits to its functions and deviated from its character as a *Weltstaatenbund*. [142] Schücking, *Das Werk vom Haag*, p. 280.

Schücking's oscillation between conceptual jurisprudence and politics. He even suggested that the interpretation was a historically consistent development of the public law tradition: Laband had used formalism to strengthen the structures of the young *Reich*; Jellinek had employed history and philosophy to legitimize the *Reich* against its enemies. The next step was internationalism. He proposed a thirteen-article constitution to be adopted for the Confederation at the third Hague Conference that was projected for 1915.[143]

Schücking propagated his Confederation in innumerable public speeches and at meetings of academic and political societies as well as through the establishment, in 1910 (with Jellinek, Nippold, Piloty, Liszt, and Ullmann), of an Association for International Conciliation (*Verband für internationale Verständigung*). However, none of his colleagues agreed with his proposals as such and many were strongly against them. The activity of the *Verband* was obstructed by an imperialist faction and by the difficulty of keeping a distance towards pacifist organizations. Although participation in its meetings grew constantly during 1910–1913, it failed to receive mass support and, though formally continued until 1926, lost all influence in 1914.[144]

But if Schücking's points about the "Work of the Hague" were of doubtful strength as law, they did become useful when the war drew attention to future European organization. In 1914 Schücking became member of the pacifist *Bund Neues Vaterland* which was prohibited by the military authorities during the war but re-emerged after the armistice as one of the most genuinely committed German organizations to speak for an association of nations as part of the peace.[145] Through the *Bund*, Schücking had already during the war taken part in the effort by European pacifists to initiate informal peace talks.[146] Though these

---

[143] This was a modest proposal. The confederation would have sought to preserve peace without encroaching on the independence of its members. It would have administered a judiciary and a codification process, sought to enhance the protection of individuals, and dealt with administrative and executive tasks. Its Conference would have met once every ten years with a governing council and special commissions to deal with daily affairs. Its decisions would have been subject to national ratification. Schücking, *Das Werk vom Haag*, pp. 236–271.

[144] On the *Verband*, cf. Acker, *Walther Schücking*, pp. 50–59.

[145] Christoph M. Kimmich, *Germany and the League of Nations* (University of Chicago Press, 1976), p. 17. Schücking was himself prohibited from publishing articles, corresponding with foreign colleagues, and traveling abroad. Cf. his "Der Völkerbundsentwurf der deutschen Regierung," in P. Munch, *Les origines et l'oeuvre de la Société des Nations* (2 vols., Copenhagen, 1924), II, p. 141.

[146] "The Central Organization for a Permanent Peace" was set up in 1914 first in Switzerland and then in the Netherlands. It covered peace societies from ten

attempts were unsuccessful – the British insisted that Germany first renounce all claims over Belgium – the "Minimal Programme" drafted through that co-operation contained provisions on future organization that came from Schücking's hand and closely followed his *Werk vom Haag*.[147] At the time, his pacifist colleagues were taken aback by his concentration on dogmatic questions at the expense of attention to the tactical problems of the day, sometimes interpreting it as a pro-German distraction. For Schücking opposed labeling Germany as alone responsible for the war and avoided taking positions on minority questions that might have been harmful for Germany. In general, however, he had little patience for short-term planning and tactical maneuver. In 1918, as German politicians were already groping their way towards an honorable peace, he declared that only an express alignment with pacifism would salvage international law from its present decay: "in this sea of blood through which we must wade our way, let us raise our white flag and let it flutter in the wind: even if the passion of the times may raise ever higher the hate of peoples against each other, we still believe in the greater power of love."[148] In 1918 Schücking conducted a minute analysis into the events that had led from Sarajevo to the war. What had gone wrong? Schücking had no tolerance for suggestions that nothing could be done because wars arose from irrational passion or because they were an inevitable part of the natural order. The Austro-Bosnian conflict *could* have been avoided if only more efficient procedures of settlement had been present.[149] Dealing with the July crisis as a legal conflict (for Schücking any important conflict was bound to contain legal claims) did not mean recourse to impossibly rigid methods of settlement. Flexible procedures – such as mediation – were available and their use would have provided – and should provide – time for passions to cool down and the parties to reach a settlement. Though the will of war may be there, it can be controlled by tying the parties to an efficient negotiating process.[150]

After the armistice and the November revolution Schücking bound himself increasingly with the new Germany that he hoped would develop into a properly Western democracy. His great moment came in

---

European States – five neutrals and five belligerents – and debated general issues such as post-war organization as well as concrete issues such as annexations, reparations, minorities, and democratic control of foreign policy. Cf. Acker, *Walther Schücking*, pp. 66–101.   [147] Acker, *Walther Schücking*, pp. 78–82.

[148] Walther Schücking, *Die völkerrechtliche Lehre des Weltkrieges* (Leipzig, von Veit, 1918), p. 12.   [149] Schücking, *Die völkerrechtliche Lehre des Weltkrieges*, pp. 42–51.

[150] Schücking, *Die völkerrechtliche Lehre des Weltkrieges*, pp. 202–204, 212–219.

early 1919 as news of the results of the Paris negotiations reached Berlin and it began to dawn on the government that not only would peace not be negotiated by reference to Wilson's fourteen points, as Germans had hoped, but that it would not be negotiated at all. In the previous autumn Schücking had participated in the drafting of a constitution for the League within the *Deutsche Gesellschaft für Völkerrecht*. On this basis he was asked to prepare a proposal for the German Government together with the influential head of the Legal Division of the *Auswärtiges Amt*, Walter Simons (1861–1937), a future member of the *Institut*, and the latter's follower Friedrich Gauss.[151] The result was a text that contained provision for a world Parliament, compulsory adjudication or mediation of *all* disputes, and no final right to go to war. It adopted provisions from the draft of the *Gesellschaft* on functional co-operation, freedom of the seas, protection of minorities, and the joint administration of colonies.[152] Introducing it to the German Government in April 1919 Schücking stressed that it was much more progressive than the Allied draft, a real manifestation of "liberty, equality, and fraternity among nations."[153]

The Allies included nothing of the German draft in the Covenant.[154] As one of Germany's six main delegates at the Peace Conference, misinformed like most of the population about the depth of Allied feelings against Germany, Schücking went through the worst disappointment of his career. The predominant position of the Council and of the Great Powers, the absence of a World Parliament, and the residual role of war in the Covenant fell far short of war-time plans and even of Wilson's proposals. It is of course uncertain to what extent the German Government felt committed to its own proposals. They were probably intended at

[151] Simons worked for a brief period after Ebert's death as acting *Reichspräzident* and later became President of the German *Reichsgericht*. He was expert in private international law and an active participant in international jurists' co-operation. He edited Pufendorff's *De jure naturae et gentium* for the Carnegie Series and published a brief historical essay on the development of international law since Grotius. He also gave a series of lectures at the Hague Academy of International Law: "La conception du droit international privé d'après la doctrine et la pratique en Allemagne" (1926/V), 15 *RdC*, pp. 437–529.

[152] For the text of the official German draft and a short comparative introduction, cf. Hans Wehberg and Alfred Manes, *Der Völkerbund-Vorschlag der deutschen Regierung* (Berlin, Engelmann, 1919).

[153] Kimmich, *Germany and the League of Nations*, p. 20. Cf. Schücking's comparison of the Paris draft with the German proposal in *Ein neues Zeitalter? Kritik am pariser Völkerbundsentwurf* (Berlin, Engelmann, 1919). Cf. also Acker, *Walther Schücking*, pp. 114–116.

[154] Cf. Walther Schücking and Hans Wehberg, *Die Satzung des Völkerbundes* (Berlin, Vahlen, 1921), pp. 11–12.

least as much to enlist the support of world opinion as to remedy the actual gaps of the allied draft.[155] Nonetheless, the disappointment felt by Schücking and the newly organized German international law community about the Allies' treatment of Germany was certainly genuine, and permanently infected the image of the League in their eyes. Though Schücking, among others, felt that parts of the peace treaty were outright illegal, he and Wehberg continued to campaign for early German entry into the League. Their hope was either to be able to amend those treaties from the inside, or at least to set them aside in the long-term construction of a universal and egalitarian international system.

Writing to his wife from Versailles in May 1919 while the German delegation was waiting for Allied responses, Simons referred to Schücking as "a great child, a pure heart and an incorrigible idealist."[156] Though a rather stereotyped image of a pacifist – especially from the pen of a diplomat – the description does point to a real problem that lay in Schücking's apparent denial of the complexity of the political world, including his own position. He was a nationalist who interpreted "real" Germanness as in accord with his politics, and German interest as always *a priori* identical with law and peace.[157] Yet, this made him suspect both in Germany and abroad. Despite his close contacts with the foreign ministry, and his careful taking account of German interests, he was marginalized by his academic and political colleagues as soon as they no longer needed him. And his foreign colleagues sometimes saw his dogmatism as frankly obstructive. For Schücking, the policy of revision was a "policy of law," as if it had been self-evident – and not political at all – that the Rheinland and the Saar were to be vacated as soon as possible and that the *Anschluss* should be immediately realized as a means to do away with Prussian dominance.[158] When the Allies had little sympathy for such (or other) proposals, Schücking could only interpret this as a failure by the West to live up to its own declared principles – a conclusion that made Germany the only advocate of a *Rechtsfrieden*.

In 1930 Schücking was elected as the first German judge at the Permanent Court in the Hague – a position from which the Hitler Government unsuccessfully sought to withdraw him in 1933. Although he felt the appointment a crowning point of his career, he nonetheless complained about the extent to which the judges seemed guided by

---

[155] Hajo Holborn, "Diplomats and Diplomacy in the Early Weimar Republic," in Gordon Craig and Felix Gilbert (eds.), *The Diplomats 1919–1939* (Princeton University Press, 1953), pp. 133–134. [156] Acker, *Walther Schücking*, p. 118.
[157] Acker, *Walther Schücking*, p. 171. [158] Acker, *Walther Schücking*, pp. 186–190.

national preferences and political views – particularly in the 1931 *Austro-German Customs union* case.[159] This was a puzzling but revealing admission from one who had started his career by espousing a political jurisprudence. If the Allied judges had voted against the Union, and Schücking in favor, the former position was a political aberration while the latter arose from objective legality: an idealism that sees no paradox in such a coincidence is a weak guide through the political complexities of a difficult era.

Schücking died in the Hague in 1935 as the most respected German international lawyer of the era. Yet his influence inside Germany remained small.[160] In the course of the years, he had taken an increasingly oppositional stance that sometimes verged on an unattractive form of self-importance – as when he introduced his draft disarmament treaty by claiming himself (in addition to Wehberg) as the only German ever to have favored such an idea.[161] His open defiance of the legal establishment and the public law tradition meant that he failed to gather followers during his teaching in Berlin during 1921–1926 and was ostracized by the faculty. The atmosphere of Kiel (1926–1933) was more congenial but his parliamentary membership and activities in Geneva continued to limit his intellectual influence. Not surprisingly, he was targeted by the *Gleichsschaltung* of 1933 at which point the development of pacifism in Germany finally became an impossibility.

The internationalists: between sociology and formalism

From the moment of *Reichsgründung* there had of course been professors (of whom Bluntschli, albeit a Swiss, was the most well known) who steered mid-way between public law conservatism and cosmopolitan liberalism, hoping to reconcile statehood with a working conception of the international realm. These men wrote textbooks that went into several editions, participated in the work of the *Institut*, and tried to reconcile its codification activity with the more sophisticated jurisprudence of their domestic colleagues. Among the first of them was Baron Franz von Holtzendorff (1829–1889), originally a criminalist, a friend of Cobden's

---

[159] Acker, *Walther Schücking*, p. 204.
[160] He was one of the founders of the *Deutsche Liga für Völkerbund* in December 1918 as well as of the *Deutsches Comité für europäische Cooperation* in 1928, both of which initially had important public figures as members but failed to develop into mass organizations. Cf. Acker, *Walther Schücking*, pp. 147–154, 181–186.
[161] Schücking, *Das Werk vom Haag*, p. 305n1.

International law as philosophy: Germany 1871–1933

(of whom he had written a biography), and an activist in the Protestant lawyers' movement, whose career in Berlin had been obstructed in the 1860s by the Prussian Government's aversion towards his liberal opinions. From 1873 onwards he held a chair in Munich where he made a name for himself as a legal Encyclopaedist, organizing the production of collective volumes in a number of legal fields. The first instalment of his *Handbuch des Völkerrechts* appeared in 1885, containing an almost 400-page introduction to the basic concepts, nature, sources, and early history of international law. It was written in the spirit of the *Institut* and was well received by its members: Rivier in Belgium and Fauchille in France drew heavily from it in their own textbooks. Yet it also showed traces of its background in a formalist public law, confident with historical and cultural arguments, and void of hyperbolic humanitarianism.

Holtzendorff used the organic metaphor to describe the intercourse between civilized States as a legal system, instead of just an aggregate of treaties. Like domestic law, international law had a deep-structural foundation in European consciousness (*"Kulturrecht"*). The "ethnographic basis of international law" explained why its applicability was limited to Europe and could not be extended to the "barbarians."[162] It did have its weaknesses (uncertainty of content and predominance of self-help) but the more intensive the relations between European nations became, the more these would be offset by new forms of legislation, adjudication, or enforcement. It was the task of legal science to give articulation to the social trends – the *legum leges* – that slowly created law out of cultural uniformity.[163] In the 1880s Gladstone had argued that "each train that passes a frontier weaves the web of the human federation."[164] Holtzendorff drew liberally from this commonplace assumption. No religion existed to unite Europe. Proposals for a *Weltstaat* would only turn against the individualism that animated them.[165] Instead, the Europeans would be bound in a network of social, economic, and cultural relations by the laws of modernity themselves.[166]

Such arguments explained international law analogously to the way organic theories had explained modern Germany. But they did not provide a knock-out argument against *Realpolitiker* such as Lasson who

---

[162] Holtzendorff, *Handbuch*, I, pp. 11, 45. He lamented, however, that it seemed still dominated by national approaches which sometimes differed greatly, reflecting differences of legal culture, most markedly between civil and public law, pp. 71–72.
[163] Holtzendorff, *Handbuch*, I, p. 73.
[164] Quoted in Kern, *The Culture of Time and Space*, p. 229.
[165] Holtzendorff, *Handbuch*, I, pp. 35–37.   [166] Holtzendorff, *Handbuch*, I, p. 6.

interpreted European diplomacy as struggle for power between essentially egoistic nations. To them, Holtzendorff responded by conceding their starting-point. Statehood was indeed the most important fact of European life. Instead of undermining international law, however, it was the very condition of its existence, the mechanism that held in check civil society's centrifugal forces. Like all society, the international world was ruled by the search for autonomy on the one hand, and integration on the other. Lawyers had sometimes assumed that international law could be possible only through preferring the *Universalrechtsidee* to the *Nationalitätsidee*, or individualism over community. But neither had intrinsic priority. Abstract universals always developed through concrete particulars. Every individual participated in a universal society but they all did this through their communities, their States. How nationalism and cosmopolitanism finally related to each other was determined by world history of which, in drawing the juridical limit, international law was an agent.[167] This it was to do in accordance with the requirements of "universaler rechtlicher Notwendigkeit und nationaler Freiheit."[168]

By the end of the century, however, such arguments had become suspect. Were not differences between European nations ultimately more important than their superficial similarities? What was "culture," after all, and was it possible to verify its demands? As Holtzendorff's chair in Munich was taken over in 1889 by the Viennese professor of public and criminal law, Emanuel Ullmann (1841–1913), German lawyers were moving into more sociological language. In an 1898 textbook that came to replace Heffter's old treatise and competed with that of Liszt, Ullmann stated confidently that the "power of facts and practical living conditions" in the international society had overridden the feelings of independence that emerged from formal sovereignty. In order to improve their economic performance, States were drawn to cooperation just as primitive people had once come together in organized society, limiting their freedom in their self-interest. "The real living conditions of peoples" had made them reciprocally dependent of each other. Self-limitation had become "recognized as a necessity dictated by the nature of practical relations and conditions."[169]

Ullmann's international law was a thorough description of the diplomatic system of *fin-de-siècle* Europe: a world of States, a system for protecting public interests. Individuals did enjoy freedom but not as a

[167] Holtzendorff, *Handbuch*, I, pp. 31–34, 38–40. [168] Holtzendorff, *Handbuch*, I, p. 42.
[169] Ullmann, *Völkerrecht*, pp. 3, 4.

matter of international law. The system was based on Christian morality and natural rights – but they became law only through formal recognition. Slavery was undoubtedly wrong – but it was illegal only between parties to treaties that provided so. Like any human creation, international law was only incompletely realizing the moral idea.[170] Ullmann's argument oscillated, like Jellinek's, between sociology and psychology and led into formalism. On the one hand, there was the *fact* of increasing co-operation and reciprocal dependence – especially in the welfare field – between States; new patterns of exchange and co-operation between *Kulturvölker*. On the other hand, there was a common legal consciousness, a *recognition* by European peoples of the practical necessity of international law.[171] As with Jellinek, the sociological argument upheld the binding force of the law: it was part of the criteria of positive law that it enjoyed what Ullmann called "objective determinacy" (*objektive Bestimmtheit*), an immediately knowable reflection of society. On the other hand, a norm must also be created by a recognized authority – that is, it must be explained as a purposeful human creation by someone entitled to create it, and be accepted as law by others.[172] The psychological argument explained the law's legitimacy, inserting a normative direction into the sociological one.

Holtzendorff and Ullmann had both turned to international law after a career in *Staatsrecht* and criminal law.[173] Franz von Liszt of Berlin, the author of the period's most widely used German international law textbook, had a very similar background. His fame is based not on the textbook but on his extensive work on criminal law where he had employed the methods of the natural sciences to examine the causal relations between crime and punishment. A positivist and a liberal reformer like Holtzendorff, Liszt was also an international activist in his own field but apart from a small pamphlet at the beginning of the war refrained from methodological innovation as an internationalist. Nonetheless, the naturalist–sociological perspective is very visible. For he saw a State's membership in the legal community not as an effect of choice but a:

---

[170] Cf. the discussion of individual rights in Ullmann, *Völkerrecht*, pp. 228–229.
[171] Ullmann, *Völkerrecht*, p. 13.
[172] Ullmann, *Völkerrecht*, pp. 19–22. This duality is also visible in Ullmann's view that although the emergence of States is a matter of power and fact – of sociology – and not of legitimacy, through recognition States may still organize their relations in accordance with their political priorities, pp. 64–69.
[173] Ullmann became an *associé* of the *Institut* in 1899 and a full member in 1904. Cf. Max Fleischmann, "Emanuel von Ullmann" (1913), VII *Zeitschrift für Völkerrecht*, pp. 326–331.

"necessary result of a community of interests that points out to the sovereign wills of individual States the way they *must* take in order not to be destroyed."[174] Crime and punishment, in other words. Though international law arose from self-legislation, natural causality *compelled* States to direct their (rational) will into co-operation. However, both Ullmann and Liszt moved rapidly from sociological and psychological generalities to an affirmation of the law's autonomy. The effect of the distinction both made between formal (immediate) sources of law (custom and treaty) and material (mediate) sources (social necessity and recognition, natural law, legal philosophy, and politics) was to reaffirm the independence of the legal method. The lawyer's task was limited to interpreting the formal sources and organizing them into systems. They were the accessible surface of the (sociological and psychological) materials of social life, grounded in and explained by but functionally independent from the latter.[175]

Such arguments were more modern than those by Holtzendorff, as they reached beyond the dubious concept of "culture" into sociological and psychological points about interdependence, community of interests, and social needs. Nonetheless, they were not founded on actual studies of social causality but on the need to explain how States could be sovereign and still form a society; free and yet bound. That task needed no special study and could be undertaken with a few dialectical words at the outset of a textbook. The rest of the law could then be defined in a purely formal way, as treaty and custom – the materials that everyone in any case agreed in considering as the proper stuff of the legal profession.

By contrast, in a 1908 book Heinrich Geffcken (1865–1916) from Cologne (not to be confused with Friedrich (F. H.) Geffcken [1830–1896], Heinrich's father, the compiler of the 1882 and 1888 editions of Heffter's *Völkerrecht*) suggested basing international law on a genuinely public law theory of interests. Drawing inspiration from Jhering, Geffcken drew a distinction between two kinds of social organisms: those in which members had a common perception of their interests (*Vorstellungsorganismus*) and those in which specific social techniques had been developed to realize those interests in practice (*Aktionsorganismus*). The special character of the international society lay in its having developed into the former but not (yet) into the latter.[176] Geffcken had no

---

[174] Liszt, *Völkerrecht*, p. 10.
[175] Ullmann, *Völkerrecht*, pp. 27–28; Liszt, *Völkerrecht*, pp. 12–14.
[176] Heinrich Geffcken, *Das Gesammtinteresse als Grundlage des Staats- und Völkerrechts. Prolegomena eines Systems* (Leipzig, Deickert's, 1908).

International law as philosophy: Germany 1871–1933

doubt that international law should be understood to emerge from *Selbstbindung* by States. Often, however, State wills expressed similar objectives behind which lay common interests. The scientific method would reach from what was on the surface – State will – into a more fundamental level. International law's reality was based on the interest each State had in being recognized by others as a legal subject, and in remaining bound by promises made. "What we have been accustomed to calling international law is the set of materially identical or corresponding laws modern cultural nations have passed to regulate the living conditions between their States."[177] Geffcken ended, however, as Heilborn had done, by proposing a novel systematization of the law's substance, now organized on the basis of a theory of interests. The work remained a piece of conceptual jurisprudence, enveloping a language of interests, but inflating the importance of legal doctrine and system in a manner that was anachronistic as soon as it was written.

The first serious sketch for a historical sociology of international law was published in 1910 by the Swiss lawyer Max Huber (1874–1960), Professor from Zürich, later a judge and President of the Permanent Court of International Justice.[178] Much of Huber's intellectual debt was to Germany, to the legal sociology of Ferdinand Tönnies and to Otto von Gierke's *Genossenschaft* theory. His argument also resembles Geffcken's but avoids the latter's conceptualism. As Switzerland's delegate to the 1907 Conference Huber had been bitterly disappointed about Germany's obstructionist behavior and his small book can be read in part as a reaction against the nationalism of the diplomats he saw around him. Undoubtedly, States were the concrete reality of the international. But this did not prevent the emergence of law as an effect of their economic interests and the homogenization of their cultures. International law had started out, he argued, as an instrument for national economies to collect resources first by individual exchange contracts between isolated States and then by law-making treaties regulating long-term relations between

---

[177] Geffcken, *Das Gesammtinteresse*, p. 39.
[178] Huber had been educated in Zürich, Lausanne, and Berlin where at the age of 24 he submitted his dissertation on State succession to Paul Heilborn. The strictly positivist thesis was very well received and contributed to Huber's award of the chair in Zürich in 1902. For studies on Huber, cf. Olivier Diggelmann, "Anfänge der Völkerrechtssoziologie. Die Völkerrechtskonzeptionen von Max Huber und Georges Scelle" (Dissertation, Zurich, 1998, on file with author); Jan Klabbers, "The Sociological Jurisprudence of Max Huber. An Introduction" (1992), *Österreichische Zeitung für öffentliches Recht und Völkerrecht*, p. 197. Cf also Peter Vogelsänger, *Max Huber. Recht, Politik, Humanität und Glauben* (Frauenfeld and Stuttgart, Huber, 1967).

large numbers of States. National economies could no longer extricate themselves from the network of complex dependence. None of this meant, Huber held, that States had become unimportant. International institutions were still much more frequently individualistic "parallel organs" than vertically integrated bodies of "social law."[179] Key areas of national security and economy remained outside integration while cultural factors – nationalism, imperialism, or a sense of regional solidarity – contributed to the extent to which some groups of States developed a deeper integration than others.[180]

Huber's discussion of the sociological basis of international law brought together strands of contemporary sociological theory and basic assumptions about the international realm that lawyers had entertained since the mid-nineteenth century. Pacifist internationalists such as Fried were now able to rely on scientific data (instead of moral generalization) to argue that the international world was developing from fragmentation to integration, co-ordination to subordination.[181] In Huber, they also found a theory of the international legal community that was based on long-term collective interests, separated from the aggregate of States' individual interests. When Huber linked those interests to the recent democratic changes and the increasing predominance of economic considerations over purely political ones, he received an image of the international world that fitted well the profession's liberal imagination. Old aristocratic–exclusive diplomacy was being modified by a "nüchterne Sachlichkeit" of transnational economy, public opinion, and international organization, all working as instruments of progress.[182] The book came out only late in the day. The fact that it reached its optimistic conclusion only four years before the war suggests that something was wrong in its arguments.

1914

Holtzendorff, Ullmann, Liszt, and Geffcken were university men, academic lawyers trained in Laband's "juristic method," constructing formal legal systems out of rationalistically interpreted historical and sociological facts. This program was badly hit by the war. If there was a

---

[179] Max Huber, *Die soziologischen Grundlagen des Völkerrechts* (Berlin, Rothschild, 1928), pp. 23–24. This is a republication of the essay from 1910.
[180] Huber, *Die soziologischen Grundlagen*, pp. 61–67.
[181] Huber, *Die soziologischen Grundlagen*, p. 22.
[182] Huber, *Die soziologischen Grundlagen*, pp. 58–60.

International law as philosophy: Germany 1871–1933

European cultural community, or an *Interessengemeinschaft*, it did not automatically lend itself to the construction of a legal system, analogous to domestic public law. Peace and justice were not a spontaneous outcome of economic interdependence or cultural integration, and merely to insist that rationally thinking it was so was to discredit rationality rather than a world that seemed stubbornly "irrational."

Most German lawyers took an impeccably patriotic line in the war. Liszt signed the declaration of German intellectuals completely rejecting accusations of the illegality or inhumanity of Germany's unlimited submarine war. When Albéric Rolin informed *Institut* members that owing to the impious war, the meeting scheduled for Munich had to be cancelled, Liszt responded by the observation that far from being impious the war was sacred, and sent in his resignation.[183] Inside Germany, the war gave vent to the old antagonisms about the nature of international law. Most lawyers agreed with Kohler that much of the old law had collapsed. But there was complete disagreement about what the "old" law had been like, and, consequently, what was needed by way of reform. Reading through the German wartime writings one is struck not only by the force with which the old arguments between "natural law" and "positivism" are restated but also by the way politics and history are as it were suspended for the moment of the academic struggle. Nothing demonstrates the isolation and helplessness of the German international law community better than its turn inwards, and backwards, into nineteenth-century debates about the basis of the law's binding force. These were debates about modernity and tradition between protagonists who had no idea of the implications at stake and who clung the more desperately to their narrow doctrinal world the more intensive the challenge of politics and history from the trenches became.

From the traditionalist side, lawyers such as Viktor Cathrein (1845–1931) interpreted the war as a consequence of the overheating of national passions, loss of the sense of right as well as the "naturalistic and materialistic ideas of our time." Therefore, he wrote, our solution must be "back to the old natural law, back to faith in a personal God and the principles of Natural Law."[184] In a well-rehearsed technical argument he

---

[183] Albéric Rolin, "Rapport du Secrétaire-Général" (1919), 27 *Annuaire IDI*, p. 311. After the *Institut* condemned Germany's war crimes and its violation of Belgium's neutrality, Triepel also resigned in 1920. Among the Germans, only Wilhelm Kaufmann (1858–1926) remained a member throughout. Cf. Fritz Münch, "Das Institut de droit international" (1990), 28 *Archiv des Völkerrechts*, pp. 83, 89, 104–105.

[184] Viktor Cathrein, *Die Grundlage des Völkerrechts* (Freiburg, Herder, 1918), pp. 96–100.

showed, once again, why it was logically impossible to find the law's foundation in State will – there had to be a non-voluntary reason for why will should be binding. Through a familiar dialectics, he demonstrated how positivist lawyers constantly fell back on non-positivist assumptions – and how ironic it was that it was they who kept indicting natural law as a Hydra that always grew a new head from an old wound.[185] Fear of natural law was a fear of sin, a justified fear that grew out of the secular exaggerations of Hobbes and Rousseau first, and then from the collapse to a spiritually impoverished positivism. Yet for all the radical conservatism of his language – including his proposal to set the Pope as the international appeals court – Cathrein's natural law was empty of reform. God still spoke through States and had enacted the right of self-preservation and self-perfection at the top of the system. Familiar ideas about good faith, just war, and *suum quique tribuere* formed its substance: *pacta sunt servanda* was still tempered by the *rebus sic stantibus* – and no indication was given about how (or by whom) to measure the "fundamental" character of the change.

The exact opposite was preached on the modernist side that saw not positivism but not enough positivism as the problem. Speaking in occupied Bonn in 1918 at the centennial of the University, its Rector, Ernst Zitelmann (1852–1923), the private international lawyer and legal theorist, a kindred spirit of Bergbohm's, argued that the war had demonstrated how much of international law still remained the pious wishes of writers of textbooks. The tendency to fill the gaps of positive law with political opinions and principles of morality had simply proven too great. But no *Rechtsgefühl* sufficed to create law; interdependence or cultural homogeneity might push towards but are not law in themselves. Even the fragments of formal law were often unreal (that is to say, unverifiable) as they incorporated natural law maxims that hid fundamental disagreement. Treaties were conditioned by implied clauses, provisions of *Notrecht* or *rebus sic stantibus* under which anything could be done.[186] Had not the whole of the law of war collapsed at the fundamental disagreement between the Germans and the English about the very nature of war? Was there anything else to be expected from the proposed League than a tired repetition of moral formulas to justify power policies? For the future, Zitelmann proposed little more than the recapture of the faith in the dynamism and strength of the German people, its capacity to endure the harsh peace, its *Mut und Klugheit*, and its natural leadership.[187]

There was a great tiredness about the pamphlets and talks that poured

---

[185] Cathrein, *Die Grundlage*, p. 30.
[186] Ernst Zitelmann, *Die Unvollkommenheit des Völkerrechts* (Munich and Leipzig, Duncker & Humblot, 1919), pp. 34–39. [187] Zitelmann, *Die Unvollkommenheit*, pp. 57–60.

out of Germany during the war years. Easy to understand as outlets for frustration and incomprehension in face of the enormity of the devastation, and the disappointment of the peace, these were works of reassurance, of whistling in the dark, not auguries of transformation. However much Cathrein or Zitelmann were able to identify real problems in the *Zeitgeist* or its law, they were still engaged in a philosophical debate that *defined* the public law consciousness of the nineteenth century. But neither was a key member of the international law community. Having written their cathartic works they could withdraw. For the mainstream lawyers, the liberal reformers, the problem was not about settling the naturalism–positivism controversy but the eminently more practical one of making a reality of pre-war speculation about permanent international institutions. In a touching 1917 pamphlet Liszt recapitulated the litany of the pre-war developments that had seemed to usher in a new cosmopolitan age: treaties, unions, integrating economies, and developing cultures and industries. In a rare mode of confession he wrote that he had himself believed the war impossible until the moment it was declared. This had been a mistake – a fatal error about the causal force of integration. Interest conflicts and the drive to expansion had led States into a destructive policy of shifting alliances.[188] The recipe followed the analysis: if interdependence did not automatically provide for the conditions of peace or lawfulness, then formal institutions were needed. The lingering proposals for a *Staatenbund* must be made a reality. Even if the proposed schemes were not all functional, that was a minor problem. Now it was time for practical work.

Getting organized

From German internationalist quarters at the University of Kiel came in 1914 the transformation of what since 1891 had been a journal of international private and criminal law, into the *Zeitschrift für internationales Recht (Niemeyers Zeitschrift)*.[189] The journal had published occasional articles on

---

[188] Franz von Liszt, *Vom Staatenverband zur Völkergemeinschaft: ein Beitrag zur Neuorienterung der Staatspolitik und des Völkerrechts* (Munich, Müller, 1917).

[189] Cf. Ottobert L. Brintzinger, "50 Jahre Institut für internationales Recht an der Universität Kiel" (1964), 19 *Juristenzeitung*, pp. 285–286; Stolleis, *Geschichte*, III, p. 89, and above all Ingo Hueck, "Die Gründung völkerrechtlicher Zeitschriften in Deutschland im internationalen Vergleich" in Michael Stolleis (ed.), *Juristische Zeitschriften. Die neuen Medien des 18.-20. Jahrhunderts* (Frankfurt, Klostermann, 1999), pp. 403–407. The publication of Niemeyer's *Zeitschrift* was discontinued in 1937. The Institute continued its publishing work in 1948 with the *Jahrbuch für internationales Recht* that has since then been transformed into the *German Yearbook of International Law*.

international law since 1902 but from now on devoted at least half its space to international law debates and documents. In the same year its founder, the private international lawyer Theodor Niemeyer (1857–1939), also set up a Seminar of International Law in Kiel that soon changed itself into the Institute of International Law and became the most important research institute in the field in Germany. It was headed by Niemeyer until the position was taken over by Schücking for the period 1926–1933.[190]

Niemeyer was an advocate of legal co-operation and harmonization, a pragmatic rationalist who, as member of the International Law Association, had in 1912 organized its small German faction into a national society with the intention of drawing interest from economy and public life to international law and to organize the Association's 1915 Conference in Hamburg as well as to influence the direction of its codification work.[191] In 1917 his initiatives with other academic lawyers and with the *Auswärtiges Amt* led to the establishment of the *Deutsche Gesellschaft für Völkerrecht*, of which he became the first President and which the Kiel Institute administered together with its many other international law activities.[192]

Other institutions followed suit. In 1922 Albrecht Mendelssohn-Bartholdy (1874–1936) set up an *Institut für auswärtige Politik* in Hamburg as a reaction to the Versailles Treaty and the isolation of the German international law community. Its main activities lay in the field of publication of historical and diplomatic acts and in collaboration with

---

[190] In connection with Schücking's dismissal in 1933, the Kiel University was transformed into a leading university for the study and development of Nazi law (*Stosstruppuniversität*). The Institute was handed over to the Nazi lawyer Paul Ritterbusch (1900–1945) under whom it no longer carried out significant scientific activities – apart from the one occasion at which Carl Schmitt gave a lecture on April 1, 1939 on his *Grossraumlehre*, that started a wide debate in Germany about the transformation of the subjects of international law. Cf. Mathias Schmoeckel, *Die Grossraumtheorie. Ein Beitrag zur Geschichte des Völkerrechtswissenschaft im Dritter Reich* (Berlin, Duncker & Humblot, 1994).

[191] Karl Strupp emphasizes the activities of the German contingent to oppose the Anglo-American theory of "total war" – the view that war would automatically suspend private contracts and debts, "Die deutsche Vereinigung fur internationales Recht; ihre Notwendigkeit, ihre Entstehung, ihre bisherige Tätigkeit" (1914), 24 *Zeitschrift für Internationales Recht*, pp. 360–363. For Niemeyer's reports of ILA activities, cf. (1904), 14 *Zeitschrift für Internationales Recht*, p. 152 (1906), 16 *Zeitschrift für Internationales Recht*, p. 212, and (1912), 22 *Zeitschrift für Internationales Recht*, p. 213.

[192] Cf. (1918), 26 *Zeitschrift für Internationales Recht*, p. 280; Hermann J. Held, "Das Institut für internationales Recht an der Universität Kiel" (1921), 29 *Zeitschrift für Internationales Recht*, pp. 146–149 and Stolleis, *Geschichte*, III, p. 88.

Berlin's "democracy school," the *Deutsche Hochschule für Politik*.[193] The Kiel institute received a more serious competitor in 1925 from the *Kaiser-Wilhelm Institut für Völkerrecht* in Berlin (now the Max Planck Institute of Foreign and International Law, in Heidelberg) that was set up through Heinrich Triepel's initiative and started to publish the *Zeitschrift für ausländisches öffentliches Recht und Völkerrecht* under the direction of Victor Bruns (1884–1943).[194] The Institute was well-resourced and invited lawyers such as Triepel, Kaufmann, and Rudolf Smend (1882–1975) to sit in its scientific council (*Leitungsgremium*). It gave legal opinions to government and Parliament on a regular basis and its fame was at least in part a result of the international visibility of its members.[195] However, Niemeyer's collaboration with the Foreign Ministry, his contacts abroad, the Kiel Institute's manifold activities, and the quality of its archives and libraries assured its place as the leading institution of study of international law in Germany until 1933. Thereafter, it fell in the shadow of the Berlin Institute as Bruns became a member of the national-socialist lawyers' association (though apparently never a member of the Nazi party).[196]

In his *Rektoratsrede* at the University of Kiel in 1910 and in his later writings Niemeyer attempted to advance the cause of a scientific, functionally oriented "positive internationalism" that he saw as a necessary aspect of social and political progress. International law had been limited in the past by the dogmas of an étatist positivism that took no account of the increasingly important intercourse between societies, companies, and individuals. A sociologically oriented international law should cover all such relations, becoming simply "the application of

---

[193] In 1934 the Jewish Mendelssohn-Bartholdy was compelled to emigrate to England. The Hamburg Institute was taken over in 1936 by Friedrich Berber (1898–1984), who entertained close contacts with the future Nazi foreign minister Joachim von Ribbentrop and united his institute with the *Deutsche Institut für Aussenpolitische Forschung* the latter had set up in Berlin. Stolleis, *Geschichte*, III, pp. 273–274.

[194] Schücking had been the candidate of the social-democrats and the liberal press but had been turned down by the Faculty. Wolfgang Kohl, "Walther Schücking (1875–1935). Staats- und Völkerrechtler – Demokrat und Pazifist," in Kritische Justiz (ed.), *Streitbare Juristen* (Baden, Nomos, 1988), p. 238.

[195] Ingo Hueck, "Die deutsche Völkerrechtswissenschaft im Nationalsozialismus. Das Berliner Kaiser Wilhelm Institut für ausländisches öffentliches Recht und Völkerrecht, das Hamburger Institut für auswärtige Politik und das Kieler Institut für internationales Recht" (forthcoming article, on file with author).

[196] However, despite the fact that Kaufmann was replaced by Carl Schmitt in the Institute's scientific council, it continued its activities with relatively little interference and provided at least some room for independent counseling. Hueck, "Die deutsche Völkerrechtswissenschaft"; Stolleis, *Geschichte*, III, pp. 395–396.

legal thought to international relations."[197] The international community was not an abstract–moral entity but emerged slowly from different types and levels of daily transnational co-operation. Treaty-making should not be seen as just a technical aspect of diplomacy but a purpose oriented social process that was realizing the cosmopolitan dream without practically anyone noticing. Because of this solidarity of interests, he assured his German audience, no choice needed to be made between nationalism and internationalism. Rightly conceived, the two were the same.[198]

The sociologically inclined internationalism of the Kiel Institute and the *Zeitschrift* were close to Schücking's "organized pacifism." As Niemeyer proudly (and by and large correctly) claimed in 1921, his journal had remained the only forum for scientific internationalism in Germany during the war. It might have suffered defeats but the core of positive internationalism was intact, of this the activities of the League of Nations were tangible proof.[199] Accordingly, the Kiel institute and the *Zeitschrift* continued to advocate a relatively consistent positive attitude towards the League even after Germany had left it.

The establishment of the *Deutsche Gesellschaft für Völkerrecht* in January 1917 was warmly supported by the German Foreign Ministry. Its membership ranged from economists such as Lujo Brentano (1984–1931) to the sociologists Ferdinand Tönnies (1855–1936) and Hermann Oncken (1869–1945) and the historian Friedrich Meinecke (1862–1954). Important members from the public law community included Laband, Smend, Walter Jellinek (1885–1955), and Franz Jerusalem (1883–1970). Although the war had an effect on the themes dealt with, Niemeyer was able to direct its activities to constructive objectives. The first meeting in Heidelberg in October 1917 concentrated on an analysis of the much-discussed contrast between the "German" and "English" concepts of warfare, of which the latter was understood as – unsurprisingly – illegal. Professor Mendelssohn-Bartholdy's address summarized the difference as one between a "heroic" concept of war as struggle between States and a "commercial" concept of war as struggle between peoples, the difference itself following from the contrasting ways in which statehood was

---

[197] Theodor Niemeyer, *Völkerrecht* (Berlin and Leipzig, De Gruyter, 1923), pp. 10, 6–10.
[198] Theodor Niemeyer, "Vom Wesen des internationalen Rechts" (1910), 20 *Zeitschrift für Internationales Recht*, pp. 1–15; Theodor Niemeyer. "Rechspolitische Grundlegung der Völkerrechtswissenschaft" (1924), 31 *Zeitschrift für Internationales Recht*, pp. 1–39.
[199] Theodor Niemeyer, "Vorwort" (1921), 29 *Zeitschrift für Internationales Recht*, pp. iv–v.

understood in Germany and Britain.[200] The second general meeting was devoted to economic issues, namely to safeguarding the freedom of trade after the war. Although the choice of the topic perhaps implied a criticism of the British *Wirtschaftskrieg*, the addresses were predominantly directed to the coming post-war economic order.

As war fortunes started to turn against Germany, interest in the conditions of the coming peace grew. Many Germans grasped at President Wilson's proposals as the best available basis for the coming talks. The German population was especially enthusiastic about the proposal concerning a future association of nations.[201] Many Germans were genuinely committed to the idea of an effective *Völkerbund*. Ferdinand Tönnies, for example, pleaded in favor of the League at the second meeting of the *Gesellschaft* in 1918 and, amid cries of "bravo," suggested that it was to be superior to the sovereignty of its members.[202] For others, the League's principal benefit was that it could be used as an instrument to safeguard German Great Power status after the war.

Thus it was no surprise that Simons, speaking in his capacity as the head of the Foreign Ministry's Legal Division, proposed in September 1918 that the *Gesellschaft* set up a study group to prepare a draft statute for the coming association of nations. The Ministry had already studied such proposals for some time and had come to appreciate the differences of view that reigned in the matter. It was time to be active, Simons said, in order to oppose the Anglo-Saxon concept of a League of victors – that would not be an association but a capitulation. A long applause followed his conclusion that Germany must play a leading role in this work.[203] A study commission was set up under Niemeyer's leadership which divided itself into eleven sections – two of which were headed by Schücking – that each dealt with a special aspect of the League. A large number of members participated in this work, whose outcome was a detailed draft with commentary on individual articles, adopted in January 1919. All disputes were to be submitted to arbitration or conciliation. Economic and military sanctions were to be decreed by the Executive Council "according to the rules of international law and the laws of humanity" (Art. 16). The Council would also determine whether

---

[200] Albrecht Mendelssohn-Bartholdy, "Der Gegensatz zwischen der deutschen und englischen Kriegsrechtsauffassung und seine künftige Überwindung im Völkerrecht" (1917), 1 *Mitteilungen der Deutsche Gesellschaft für Völkerrecht*, pp. 23–34.
[201] Cf. Kimmich, *Germany and the League of Nations*, pp. 6–18.
[202] 2 *Mitteilungen der deutsche Gesellschaft für Völkerrecht* 1918, p. 120.
[203] 2 *Mitteilungen der deutsche Gesellschaft für Völkerrecht* 1918, pp. 134–137.

an individual member was acting in self-defense. International unions were to be united under the League's administration. There were provisions on disarmament, freedom of international trade, and the administration of colonies.[204]

Some of the provisions of the draft found their way into the official German proposal. Otherwise, however, it was lost in the general stream of unofficial proposals on post-war organization. It had no effect on the Allied draft which remained substantially unchanged from February 1919. The Germans had been unrealistic if they had expected that the Allies would see the negotiations as other than implementation of German war guilt. The German Foreign Minister Brockdorff-Rantzau's theatrical appeal to the "law" of the fourteen points, delivered sitting down at Versailles on May 7, 1919, did nothing to assuage the Allies and created an atmosphere in which the Germans were compelled to oppose the treaty by the fatal strategy of trying to redeem their national past.[205]

Beyond Versailles: the end of German internationalism

German lawyers shared the shock and bitterness in the country about the conditions of the peace. They had never felt that German policy had alone been responsible for the war and completely rejected the war guilt clause. Nor did they think Germany the main perpetrator of war crimes, as Allied propaganda had suggested. On the contrary, they felt that the unlimited submarine war, for instance, was a justified response to the Anglo-American total war on the German population. There is no reason to think that Zorn was being insincere or eccentric when he wrote in 1925 that the war had been launched by France and Britain on Germany.[206] Some even argued that the peace was not binding on Germany because it had not been negotiated in "practical application" of Wilson's fourteen points under which Germany had concluded the armistice.[207] The League was seen as an *Entente*-dominated body in which Germany would never have full equality. Until 1923, the *Auswärtiges Amt* regarded entry useless as the League did not seem to have jurisdiction to modify the conditions in the Peace Treaty – the main objective of German foreign policy.

---

[204] Cf. Deutsche Liga für Völkerbund, "Der Völkerbundsentwurf der Deutschen Gesellschaft für Völkerrecht" (1919), 1 *Monographien zum Völkerbund*.
[205] Holborn, "Diplomats," pp. 137, 145.   [206] Zorn, *Weltunionen*, pp. 49–60.
[207] Cf. Alexander Hold-Ferneck, "Zur Frage der Rechtsverbindlichkeit des Friedensvertrages von Versailles" (1922), 30 *Zeitschrift für Internationales Recht*, pp. 110–117.

International law as philosophy: Germany 1871–1933

In this situation, the position of the German internationalists became increasingly complicated. Most German members left the *Institut*, which was felt to have taken a pro-Versailles attitude.[208] Simons resigned from his position in the Foreign Ministry. In their early commentary on the Covenant, Schücking and Wehberg did portray the League as a continuation of the development towards an organized world community. But even they had to admit that its drafting history, placement in the Peace Treaty and the powers of the Council made it fall far short of that ideal. And they, too, argued about its significance as a means of revision.[209] After 1919 the discipline of international law became indissociable from the criticisms of the Peace Treaty, and was pushed to the forefront in the German call for a *Rechtsfrieden*.[210] The only group of professional diplomats whose position was strengthened in Weimar were the members of the Legal Division who dealt with League matters and led the fight against the Peace Treaty.[211] The defenders of the League were either pushed into the camp of the pacifists – in which case they were marginalized from policy-making tasks – or fell into a strategic attitude that undermined the ideological basis of their internationalism.

Most international lawyers approved of Stresemann's policy of slow *rapprochement* with the West and membership in the League. Even when they did not condemn the Peace Treaty as outright illegal they trusted that it was so blatantly unjust that an argument in favor of revision by a well-behaved League member could not be reasonably opposed. The far-reaching arbitration treaties that Germany concluded in the 1920s, for instance, as well as the sweeping arbitration provisions in the Locarno *Westpakt* of 1925 were interpreted by the *Deutsche Gesellschaft für Völkerrecht* as additional channels to open the Versailles package.[212] After the Ruhr crisis in 1923, Britain began to solicit German membership and interest in it grew inside Germany as well. The international atmosphere resulting from the setting up of the Dawes Plan on the payment of German reparations in 1924 and the Locarno agreements made German entry into the League finally possible. But this was achieved only after a prolonged dispute about the reallocation of seats in the Council that ended in Brazil's resignation and the humiliation of Poland and its allies.[213]

---

[208] Cf. Fritz Münch, "Das Institut de droit international" (1990), 28 *Archiv des Völkerrechts (AVR)*, pp. 76–105.
[209] Schücking and Wehberg, *Satzung des Völkerbundes*, pp. 11–15, 17–18, 44–56, 76.
[210] Cf. also Stolleis, *Geschichte*, III, pp. 87–88.   [211] Holborn, "Diplomats," p. 154.
[212] Karl Strupp, *Das Werk von Locarno* (Berlin and Leipzig, de Gruyter, 1926), pp. 92–93, 113.   [213] Cf. Kimmich, *Germany and the League of Nations*, pp. 82–91.

The position of German international lawyers was summarized by Karl Strupp (1886–1940) in 1926. The acceptance of the Dawes Plan and the Locarno guarantee had made operative the obligation of the Allied powers under Article 431 of the Versailles Treaty to withdraw immediately all troops from German soil. As League member, Germany would enjoy equality and could then use Article 19 of the Covenant to argue for a revision of the rest of the Versailles obligations "that stuck like knives in the flesh of every German." This, he said, was the test of the reality of the Locarno spirit on the side of the *Entente*.[214]

Apart from the small pacifist faction, German lawyers cultivated a predominantly strategic attitude towards the League. Although its functional activities were seen as useful, its collective security and peaceful settlement tasks were understood as a half-serious smoke-screen over Anglo-American imperialism.[215] The failure of the Disarmament Conference was construed as a failure to attain German equality through playing by League rules and constituted an argument in favor of unilateral rearmament. Once *that* step had been taken, there was no reason to believe that the other provisions of Versailles would be any more resistant to determined challenge. As Carl Schmitt argued in 1932, imperialism was not only military or economic but above all conceptual: it worked through providing concrete meaning to words such as "war" and "peace," "security" and "disarmament." A conceptual imperialism controlled weak or defenseless States by controlling the meaning that formal legality received in regimes of "demilitarization" and intervention. A nation was finally vanquished by letting itself be controlled by such words: if Germany was not to fall under imperial domination, it could not let such words control its concept of international law, its ability to decide what international law, concretely, meant.[216]

Ways of escape – I: Hans Kelsen and liberalism as science

Schmitt was right, of course. The League was no *weltstaatlich* utopia. Its rules and activities were completely dominated by the decisions and

---

[214] Strupp, *Das Werk von Locarno*, pp. 110–112.
[215] The story of the drafting of the Covenant as an essentially Anglo-American project is told e.g. in Fritz Bleiber, *Der Völkerbund. Die Entstehung der Völkerbundssatzung* (Berlin, 1939), pp. 155–159.
[216] Carl Schmitt, "Völkerrechtliche Formen des modernen Imperialismus" (1932), in *Positionen und Begriffe im Kampf mit Weimar-Genf-Versailles 1923–1939* (Berlin, Duncker & Humblot, 1988[1940]), pp. 176–180.

policies of the major States. Its inactivity in the Manchurian crisis may have reflected prudent statesmanship that sought containment instead of reversal of aggression – perhaps reversal was not even attainable. But it spelled the end of a collective security based on the unexceptional duty for members to take action under Article 10 of the Covenant. When Italy attacked Abyssinia in the fall of 1935, there was no longer any serious discussion about the application of military measures and even the economic boycott was organized formally outside the League, touched only one-tenth of Italy's trade (oil was always left carefully outside), and was dropped after the conquest of Addis Ababa out of fear of leading Mussolini into Hitler's bosom.

German internationalists such as Niemeyer or Schücking had sought in international institutions the remedy for the failure of spontaneous integration to bring about peace. Their functionalism seemed increasingly implausible after the attempt to close the gaps in the Covenant by the Geneva Protocol was finally rejected and the Disarmament Conference dragged on from one unproductive session to another. After Stresemann's death in 1929, German attitudes towards the League changed into open confrontation. If the other powers were not willing to grant German equality in the League – this was how the stakes at the Disarmament Conference were seen – then it had to be forced on them from the outside. For right-wing critics such as Schmitt the inability of the League to deal with German grievances became an index of their general critique of formal constitutions. Their recipe was to give up the fictions of legality and to recognize law's dependence on the decisions of the powerful. For German internationalists, however, that would have meant giving up everything the profession had preached in the nineteenth century as well as traditions they had enlisted as precursors from much earlier times. But if social spontaneity did not lead into peace, and moral consensus within the League was only a fragile veil over political disagreements, what could be done?

Many lawyers sought to find a solution in the revaluation of statehood, defining sovereignty as the competence to carry out the purposes of a cosmopolitan order. This type of traditionalism was, however, vulnerable to critiques of natural law as ideology. Besides, as the socialist constitutional lawyer Hermann Heller (1891–1933) pointed out, many of the numerous critiques of sovereignty after the First World War engaged a straw man – no political theorist had ever espoused the absolute conception they attacked. Without a concept of sovereign authority in a concretely existing community (*eine konkrete Gemeinschaft*), they continued to move in an abstract conceptual heaven.[217] Yet, there was force to the argument that the attempt to square the circle of statehood and international law was doomed to fail on logical grounds. Either the State was sovereign – and there was no really binding international order. Or there was a binding international order – in which case no State could truly be sovereign. Hans Kelsen's (1881–1973) relentlessly consistent monism constituted an efficient critique of the German public law tradition that had tried to imagine that the national and the international could live harmoniously side by side as independent normative orders. This, as Kelsen argued, would have meant that human beings might be under different obligations at the same time: "do x" and "do not do x." This was unacceptable. It was the very point of knowledge to construct its object as a coherent whole. This was as true of the science of norms as of any other knowledge. The political unity of humanity lay on an epistemological, or *scientific* postulate ("das Postulat der Einheit der Erkenntnis") that compelled one to think either State law or international law as superior. Logic dictated two alternatives but not how to choose between them. This was a political choice, described by Kelsen as that between objectivism and subjectivism, altruism and egoism, pacifism and imperialism.[218]

With such associations, Kelsen left the reader in no doubt about which he thought the ethically worthwhile choice. Indeed, the primacy of the State legal order (a pleonasm, really, for a State did not *have* a legal order but *was* one[219]), if only pursued with logical rigor led not only to a denial of international law but also to a denial of every other national legal order apart from the speaker's. Since Laband, German public law had tried in various ways to embrace international law by deriving its validity from its incorporation or acceptance in the national legal order. But this, too, led to solipsism: every other State's legal order remained an external and potentially hostile normative world.[220] No wonder encirclement had become a collective German neurosis!

As is well known, Kelsen's project was much wider than merely to argue that logic compelled a choice between the primacy of international or State law – as he defined the sovereignty question.[221] The pure

---

[217] Hermann Heller, *Die Souveränität. Ein Beitrag zur Theorie des Staats- und Völkerrechts* (Berlin and Leipzig, De Gruyter, 1927).
[218] Kelsen, *Das Problem der Souveränität*, pp. 102–115, 120–124, 152–153, 317–319.
[219] Kelsen, *Das Problem der Souveränität*, p. 131.
[220] Kelsen, *Das Problem der Souveränität*, pp. 151–204, esp. pp. 187–190.
[221] Kelsen, *Das Problem der Souveränität*, pp. 13–16, 37–40, 102–103.

theory of law developed in the 1920s and summarized in the *Reine Rechtslehre* of 1934 constituted an altogether new opening for legal thought, and certainly a decisive closing of the search for a "juristic method" that had preoccupied German public law from von Gerber onwards. Here now was a method that did not compel the lawyer to become an amateur sociologist or a dilettante moralist.[222] The search for a "firm foundation" to legal thought from outside the law itself that had defined late nineteenth- and early twentieth-century jurisprudence had been unnecessary, even mistaken. Law's special form of existence was irreducible to social or psychological facts or moral–political desiderata. It was constituted in the "validity" of the legal norm, a property it received by delegation from another norm situated at a formally higher level. It was a characteristic of legal norms that they belonged together in systems, constituted in relationships of delegation of validity. The only properly legal question was whether this or that normative proposition was "law." And that question was conclusively answered by the demonstration that it was part of the system, the chain of validity: an administrative act was "law" if it had been in the official's competence; such competence was provided by an administrative decree which was "law" if it was passed in accordance with the relevant statute; the statute was "law" if enacted in accordance with the constitution and the constitution was "law" if it had entered into force in accordance with the first constitution. What closed the ascending chain of delegations was the famous *Grundnorm* – the basic norm that provided for the validity of the whole system, a norm that Kelsen characterized at different times in different ways but which in 1934 – and in its most plausible form – appeared as a necessary hypothesis, a norm which one *needed to believe valid* in order that everything that one already knew about the legal system should be true.[223]

Kelsen's epistemological–scientific outlook and his transcendental deduction of the basic norm were firmly embedded in his philosophical neo-Kantianism. Nonetheless, they left no stone standing of the academic conventions of German public and international law. Among the problems to which the pure theory was able to offer a logically coherent solution were those of the nature of the State and the relationship between sovereignty and international law. Since Jellinek, German

---

[222] Published in English as Hans Kelsen, *Introduction to the Problems of Legal Theory. A Translation of the First Edition of the Reine Rechtslehre or Pure Theory of Law* (trans. Bonnie Litschewski Paulson and Stanley L. Paulson, with an introduction by Stanley L. Paulson, Oxford, Clarendon, 1992). [223] Kelsen, *Introduction*, pp. 55–76.

Staatslehre had worked with a two-sided conception of statehood: one side was empirical and historical, the other normative and formal. In accordance with their *völkisch* politics, German lawyers automatically assumed the priority of the former to the latter. The really acting agency was the historical State that was the legal system's "creator" or "carrier." The State, so the argument went, was a factor in the world of *Sein* that through its will and power brought about the legal world of *Sollen*.[224]

Kelsen had followed Jellinek's seminars in Heidelberg in 1908 but had been unimpressed by them and positively put off by the atmosphere of uncritical admiration surrounding the older man.[225] For him, the two-sided theory was pure fiction, a case of a metaphor having taken on a life of its own, an effect of the deceit of *Verdoppelung* – the mechanism whereby an instrument of knowledge is reconceived as the object of knowledge. Like "ether" for physics or "soul" for psychology, "State" was used as a postulated substance behind perceived relations and qualities.[226] The doubling was twofold: first, normative relationships were conceived as the substance of a "State"; second, the State was assumed to have a natural reality to contrast with the ought-reality that norms have. It was precisely this naturalization of the State that must be fought by critical law, Kelsen held.[227]

This was not a politically innocent jurisprudence. At the stroke of a pen it redefined as ideology all the nineteenth-century historical and sociological theories that had sought to answer the question of the "real" nature of (Austrian/German) statehood as well as the attempt to derive international law from humanitarian morality or the sociology of interdependence.[228] Where sociology had claimed to provide a scientific standpoint on society, Kelsen revealed its being just as value-dependent and political as morality and theology had been. The various organic, psychological, or functional theories of statehood were not descriptions

---

[224] Kelsen, *Der soziologische und der juristische Staatsbegriff*, pp. 2–3.
[225] Rudolf Métall, *Hans Kelsen. Leben und Werk* (Vienna, Deutige, 1967), p. 11.
[226] Kelsen, *Der soziologische und der juristische Staatsbegriff*, pp. 207–210.
[227] Kelsen, *Der soziologische und der juristische Staatsbegriff*, p. 215. In a delightfully polemic passage Kelsen observed the resemblance of State theory to Christian monotheism. In both, a transcendental unity is postulated behind a perceived reality: Thou shalt have no other God . . . , Kelsen, *Der soziologische und der juristische Staatsbegriff*, p. 225. Cf. also Kelsen, *Das Problem der Souveränität*, p. 21 and Hans Kelsen, "Les rapports de système entre le droit interne et le droit international public" (1926/IV), 14 *RdC*, pp. 233–248.
[228] On Kelsen's critique of sovereignty as critique of ideology, cf. Alfred Rub, *Hans Kelsens Völkerrechtslehre. Versuch einer Würdigung* (Zurich, Schultess, 1995), pp. 129–131.

of something real but suggestions for the evaluation of social action – "ethisch-politischer Spekulation."[229] For in the "real" world, Kelsen insisted, there were simply a lot of persons behaving. Constructive legal thought projected or described their behavior as activity of the State by using legal norms such as "competence" and "duty" to characterize it.[230] It was not that this projection was a normative truth aside a sociological truth of State power. There simply was *no "State" at all outside the juridical realm*. When they spoke of "States," even sociology and history based themselves on the legal notion, however much their examination of the reality of the behavior of those individuals so identified differed from law.[231]

In other words, the State was neither a person nor a will that stood against an independent law. The two were not distinct: stripped of its ideological and metaphoric properties, the State was identical with the domestic legal order.[232] This view corresponded closely to the political reality of the decaying Danube monarchy in which it was developed. Without its form, the Empire was nothing, as Kelsen himself observed in 1918, when its fate was sealed by the defeat and Kelsen was busy drafting a plan at the request of the War Ministry for its replacement by

---

[229] Kelsen, *Der soziologische und der juristische Staatsbegriff*, pp. 46–74, 46.

[230] Kelsen, *Das Problem der Souveränität*, pp. 124–130, 143–144, 162–167. On law as a scheme of interpretation, cf. Kelsen, "Les rapports de système," pp. 240–241; Kelsen, *Introduction*, p. 10.

[231] There was no single characterization of the "reality" of States. Definitions of the material *Verband* of statehood differed as much as States did. A notion of *Wechselwirkung* was unable to distinguish between "State" and other forms of association and forgot that interaction could be towards integration and disintegration. Usually sociology referred to psychology; conceiving the State as a feeling of "belonging." But this merely posed the further question of what type of psychical relationship was involved. An internal "feeling" was an individual matter that did not ground a realm of collective statehood. The assumption of a trans-individual unity of wills or parallelism of psychological processes (common will, group feeling, common consciousness) led into social psychology – and easily collapsed into the metaphysical notion of a group soul. (Kelsen thinks Freud a distinct progress from Le Bon: the masses have no soul, libido is an individual matter, *Der soziologische und der juristische Staatsbegriff*, pp. 21–22.) A State cannot be described as a "psychological mass" – for it has a permanence that is inscribed in its institutions. The point is that the members of a group mediate their relations through a regulating order, that is to say, a system of norms, and come to think of themselves as members of a State by reference to it. But in such a case, the State's existence is a matter by definition independent of any "feeling of association": it is a juridical notion which then offers, through metaphor and *Verdoppelung*, a point of identification for the group, *Der soziologische und der juristische Staatsbegriff*, pp. 25–30.

[232] Kelsen, "Les rapports de système," pp. 234–235, 242–243; *Introduction*, pp. 99–106.

national States.[233] To speak of the State as a person or as a legal subject was metaphoric language to address the fact that it was left for the State's legal order to point out those human beings who had particular competencies to create or enforce legal norms.[234] Or, more adequately, and from the perspective of the primacy of international law, the State was a *partial* legal order which had a certain territorial and personal sphere of validity, as determined by international law. Sovereignty was not an essence which the law simply had to confront but "a bundle of legal obligations and legal rights, that is, the unity of a complex of norms" that was determined from inside the law itself.[235] What had traditionally been discussed as the problem of sovereignty was simply the question of the primacy of legal orders restated in *Verdoppelt* language.

In the "real world," legal norms – rights and obligations – acted as a specific social technique that regulated the behavior of individual human beings. To be under an obligation meant the situation where a certain (undesired) behavior was made the condition for the application of sanctions. Duties were prior to rights, the latter describing the condition where the required behavior was conditioned on the will of the right-holder.[236] To say that international law imposed obligations on States was to state that it imposed obligations on individuals indirectly, by leaving the determination of their identity to the domestic legal order. Here as elsewhere law worked as a frame of interpretation whereby the acts of individuals were endowed with the meaning of, for instance, "treaty-making," "violation," or "sanction."

This did away not only with the theory of the State as a subject of international law but also with the view of State will as the single (or most important) source of international law.[237] As a social technique, law came about in two ways: by conscious enactment (treaties) or spontaneously (custom).[238] There were, of course, psychological motives and social and political causes behind both of its sources. But law was not a science of motives or causality. From the legal perspective, the

---

[233] Cf. Métall, *Hans Kelsen*, p. 42. The Emperor seems however not to have read Kelsen's memorandum but acted under his German advisors, Métall, *Hans Kelsen*, pp. 21–22, 29.   [234] Kelsen, *Introduction*, pp. 109–111.

[235] Kelsen, *Introduction*, pp. 47, 48–49.

[236] Kelsen, *Introduction*, pp. 42–46. In this way, all rights became political inasmuch as their application was conditioned on "will."

[237] Cf. Kelsen's critique of self-legislation, in *Das Problem der Souveränität*, pp. 168–174. The very question of "source" could legally be dealt with only as a problem of where the norm received its validity – and this was always another norm, *Das Problem der Souveränität*, pp. 105–107.   [238] Kelsen, *Introduction*, pp. 66–107.

question about the "source" of law sought only to find out which directives qualified as (legally) valid. And *that* question could be answered only by examining the chain of validity. Whether law arose from someone's will or reflected a community's consciousness were like the question about its moral appropriateness: they were not answerable in a legal way, and pointed to other scales of evaluation than the legal (namely psychology, political theory, or ethics). This did not mean that these questions were wrong, or nonsensical, only that there was no legal response to them.[239]

The pure theory was by no means a *Lebensfremd* abstraction. On the contrary, as Kelsen himself stressed, it intervened in politics in the way a critique of ideology did: by revealing the political content of theories that had been thought of as neutral:

> The Pure Theory of Law exposes once and for all the attempt to use the concept of sovereignty to lend a purely political argument – which is always vulnerable to a comparable counter-argument – the appearance of a logical argument, which would by its very nature be irrefutable. And precisely by exposing the argument as political, the Pure Theory of Law facilitates development that has been stunted by mistaken notions, development in terms of legal policy – facilitates such development, but does not justify or postulate it. For that is a matter of complete indifference to the Pure Theory of Law *qua* theory.[240]

In this extraordinary passage Kelsen not only quite correctly assessed the political significance of the pure theory but also revealed its limitation, a limitation that explains something of the failure of his politics.

For Kelsen was by no means a non-political man. He made no secret of his democratic and left–liberal preferences or of his cosmopolitanism.[241] He felt no scruple participating in political polemics, revealing himself several times during his career in Austria and Germany as a firm supporter of the formal–constitutional order.[242] His book on the concept of sovereignty – written during the war though published only in the 1920s – as well as his Hague lectures of 1926 ended in a plea towards a humanistic–universalist standpoint, invocation of a *Weltrechtsordnung*: the unhappy state of international law theory was a result of the fact that

---

[239] Kelsen, *Das Problem der Souveränität*, pp. 134–139. [240] Kelsen, *Introduction*, p. 124.
[241] Kelsen was closest to Austrian socialists but never formally joined them. Métall, *Hans Kelsen*, p. 33. On Kelsen's political positions and their significance for his international legal doctrine, cf. also Rub, *Hans Kelsens Völkerrechtslehre*, pp. 75–86.
[242] Most famously in his debate with Carl Schmitt about the "guardian of the constitution." For recent analysis, cf. David Dyzenhaus, *Legality and Legitimacy. Carl Schmitt, Hans Kelsen and Hermann Heller in Weimar* (Oxford, Clarendon, 1997), pp. 102–160.

social consciousness had not (yet) developed so as to reach beyond State boundaries.[243]

A number of political positions followed from the fundamental (though in Kelsen's own view, fundamentally arbitrary) choice in favor of the primacy of the international legal system. It qualified States as organs of international law and determined their jurisdiction from an international perspective.[244] It postulated the international legal order as gapless in the sense of allowing no (logical) distinction between legal and political matters. Every dispute was amenable to legal resolution by the logical principle of the exclusion of the third: a claim could only either be justified or unjustified in law. It highlighted the role of courts and lawyers: for it was up to them to declare the individual norm that applied to the case and this norm was always underdetermined by general standards. Finally, it emphasized the role of organized coercion: if an obligation to behave in a certain way existed if the opposite behavior triggered a "coercive act," then any pretense of a legal order must be accompanied by the presence of some institutional system of constraint.

Some of these positions found expression in Austria's Federal Constitution that Kelsen drafted at the request of the Austro-Marxist *Staatskanzler* Karl Renner in 1920 and particularly in the setting up of the *Reichsgericht* as a real constitutional court.[245] They were also expressed in Kelsen's support for Stresemann's *Erfüllungspolitik* as well as his criticisms of the Covenant. Kelsen advocated the separation of the League from the Peace Treaties, criticized the absence of legislative powers within the League and the predominance of the Council over the Permanent Court of International Justice. He was especially critical of the absence of a provision for competence to the Court to order sanctions.[246] The criticisms were condensed in his 1942 revised draft of the Covenant that prohibited war (otherwise than as a sanction), provided for compulsory adjudication of all disputes by the Court, and majority voting in the Council.[247]

Many other German-language international lawyers participated in the Kelsen *Kreis* from 1911 that grew into the *Vienna School* in the 1920s.[248] Apart from Alfred Verdross (1890–1980), whose alignments

---

[243] Kelsen, *Souveränität*, p. 320; "Les rapports de système," pp. 325–326.
[244] Kelsen, *Souveränität*, pp. 257–266.   [245] Métall, *Hans Kelsen*, pp. 35–36.
[246] Cf. Rub, *Hans Kelsens Völkerrechtslehre*, pp. 278–283.
[247] Hans Kelsen, *Peace Through Law*.
[248] Particularly Verdross, Kunz, and Guggenheim. On Kelsen's "disciples," cf. Rub, *Hans Kelsens Völkerrechtslehre*, pp. 110–120; Métall, *Hans Kelsen*, p. 29.

were obscure,[249] most of them were liberals or social-democrats, openly opposed to the rise of the German extreme right and forced to leave Germany either for that reason, because of their Jewishness, or both. Whatever one thinks of the "objectivity" or "value-neutrality" of the pure theory as legal method, it is plainly wrong to think it arose in a scholar's chamber as an instrument to escape from political confrontation. It implied the *Rechtsstaat*, accepted that questions about the *content* of law were matters of political value, and sharpened the analytical skills of the political activist. Moreover, open advocacy for a juristic method was also an argument for the autonomy of the legal profession – a far from irrelevant suggestion in 1930s Germany and Austria. And yet, like every revolutionary idea, after it was institutionalized, it tended towards that fetishism of the form that Marxist lawyers always accused it of: a totalizing attitude about the limits of legal propriety, an escape from moral insecurity, an ideology, in a word.

How did that come about? The beginnings of an answer may be found in the sharpness of the dichotomy that Kelsen posed between science and politics that did much to discard politics as an altogether irrational matter of the heart's passion. In a way, Kelsen bought the success of his critique of the German legal tradition by an emasculation of his politics. The covert insincerity of the last sentence in the above quote provides a clue to the weakness of the pure theory – the claim that after theory and critique have revealed every prior doctrine as politics in disguise, their task is over: the development of World Law becomes "a matter of complete indifference to the Pure Theory of Law *qua* theory."

Pushing politics outside the realm of science and theory, Kelsen downgraded its importance in the diplomatic and constitutional struggles of the day. By casting his own cosmopolitan liberalism as a matter of subjective value, he deprived himself of a plausible language in which to defend it – visible in his excessive use of irony and pathos as styles of political argument. Preference for democracy came to seem no more than a matter of taste. It is a familiar paradox of liberal reason that methodological toleration of contrasting value-systems undermines personal faith in any. Kelsen himself was religiously indifferent and converted to Catholicism in 1905 out of the good prudential reason to secure himself a future in Vienna's notoriously antisemitic law faculty. Clearly, such relative distance from one's values provides a

---

[249] Cf. Anthony Carty, "Alfred Verdross and Othmar Spann: German Romantic Nationalism, National Socialism and International Law" (1995), 6 *EJIL*, pp. 78–97.

fruitful ground, and perhaps even good motivation, for the relentless pursuit of a "value-free," pure science. But it also undermined Kelsen's liberalism by making it seem just the cold and abstract, empty vessel for egoism that conservatives and revolutionaries accused it of. It also created a psychologically hazardous position where political conviction, where pressed by external events, might easily lapse into professional "neutrality" as a facade for cynicism, or despair. For the average lawyer, retreat to pure form must have seemed a tempting technique to deal with moral insecurity in a hostile environment. Unfortunately, even on Kelsen's premises, there was no innocent space for German lawyers to occupy in Weimar. Pure legality existed only in the realm of the transcendental.

Kelsen's political vulnerability lay in his equally "arbitrary" choice of the primacy of the international over the national. This was to state the problem, not the solution. For decades, German academics had been involved in a debate about the relative merits of German *Kultur vis-à-vis* the cosmopolitan rationalism of the French Enlightenment. The primacy debate was indissociable from that politically loaded dichotomy and Kelsen brought in nothing new to resolve it. A preference for the international on logical grounds was to invoke precisely those ideas that that German nationalists associated with the abstract superficiality of rationalist liberalism, its absence of a concrete social ideal.

As theory, *Reine Rechtslehre* was enormously powerful and it is no surprise that it was furiously attacked. It drew the rug from under the feet of a legal tradition that had devoted itself to furthering the project of the (German) nation-State. It revealed the "value-neutrality" of any substantive legal order as a myth. As the content of legal standards, law was political through and through, a forum for struggle that continued from the enactment of legislation to the determination of the content of every single administrative act or contract: legal interpretation was everywhere and interpretation was "a problem not of legal theory but of legal policy."[250] And here precisely lay the problem. Because Kelsen thought that the question of the *content* of the law was a matter of interpretation, and interpretation was a political act, *as lawyer* he had nothing to fall back on when the channel of formal legality was used to destroy that very legality. To be sure, he could go in political opposition. And he could argue that the unjust law was to be set aside. The pure theory was uncommitted to any unconditional obligation of obeying the law. But

---

[250] Kelsen, *Introduction*, p. 82.

whether one could keep the realms of objective law and subjective politics distinct, as this required, and overrule the former by the latter, put an impossible burden on the strength of the lawyer.

After having been fired from his position as Professor at the University of Cologne in 1933, Kelsen took a position at the *Institut Universitaire des hautes études internationales* in Geneva and was invited by Roscoe Pound to Harvard in 1940. Having failed to secure a position there, he settled in Berkeley where he taught until his retirement. Most international lawyers today know of his work and many continue to admire him as legal theorist. The admiration is almost without exception tempered by the rejoinder that, of course, it was just theory and therefore could never be realized in practice. This is a problematic position: that theory is right but nonetheless useless or even dangerous and that moral goodness lies in our carrying out practices on the pragmatic basis betrays an altogether objectionable admiration of the profession at its most bureaucratic, a most unreflective, most self-perpetuating form of elitism.

The challenge is to show that a legal theory that offers only a *transcendental* realm of legality – a world with no access for the legal profession – is false *qua* theory. This is not a simple task. The problems of the pure theory do not lie in its internal coherence but in its relationship to the surrounding world. Despite the critical bite of Kelsen's arguments, they still emanate from nineteenth-century German legal thought: academic, system oriented, and neurotically concerned over its status as *Wissenschaft*. What needs demonstrating is that the prejudice that sets up the strict dualism of law/politics or objectivity/subjectivity cannot, as a matter of theory, be upheld. That requires a rethinking of the premises of public law altogether, and a rejection of the assumption that knowledge and "theory" are limited to the realm of the rational, a bringing together of knowledge and politics from that analytical separation that started with Kant and grounded both the project of the *Rechtsstaat* and the social conditions in which it was destroyed.

Ways of escape – II: Erich Kaufmann and the conservative reaction

Where Kelsen criticized the League in terms of his cosmopolitan monism, Erich Kaufmann held it a useful instrument to enhance Germany's position *vis-à-vis* the victorious powers. He was, of course, a critic of the Versailles Treaty which he felt constituted a "Diktatfrieden ... die an politischen und wirtschaftlichen Sinnlosigkeiten ihresgleichen in der Geschichte nicht haben."[251] He greeted Locarno as a necessary though far from sufficient step towards German equality. Though it did not formally abrogate the Versailles settlement it did transform Germany's position from being the object of dictated duties to an equal participant in a security arrangement that recognized the legitimacy of Germany's security concerns. Kaufmann combined a rejection of liberal rationalism with a much wider acceptance of international organization than German conservatives generally did. He endorsed the conclusion of arbitration treaties as they would enable Germany to bring its many grievances against the *Entente* powers before independent organs.[252] He was disappointed at the constant misunderstandings among the Germans about the League's character either as an anti-German pact or the rudiments of a *Weltstaat*. It was both less and more than what most Germans assumed; less as its activities frequently resulted only in reports, decisions, recommendations – paper, paper, paper; more as it provided procedures for the discussion and sometimes settlement of legal and political conflicts while the unanimity principle effectively prevented intrusion in sovereignty.[253]

Though as legal theorist, Kaufmann was a determined enemy of the liberal rationalism represented by most German internationalists, this by no means classed him among the "deniers." An academic by background, he was appointed professor at Kiel in 1912 and in Königsberg and Berlin in 1917 and collaborated with Bruns at the Kaiser Wilhelm Institut from 1927 until his replacement by Schmitt in 1934. He was much used as legal adviser to the German Foreign Ministry, negotiating treaties with Germany's neighbors and representing Germany, Austria, and the Free City of Danzig at the Permanent Court of International Justice. All this time, he continued to write essays and give lectures on international and German constitutional law, legal theory, and philosophy. As a conservative (though not a member of the conservative party), he was not, unlike Kelsen, a friend of parliamentary democracy and held the Weimar constitution a *Lebensfremd* abstraction, pieced together from French and English sources and unrespectful of German legal traditions.[254] Kaufmann rejected rationalism in its sociological and formalist versions and abhorred Jellinek's and Kelsen's metaphysical

---

[251] Erich Kaufmann, "Der Völkerbund" (1932), in *GS*, II, p. 224.
[252] Erich Kaufmann, "Locarno" (1925), in *GS*, II, pp. 167–175.
[253] Kaufmann, "Der Völkerbund," pp. 229–236.
[254] Erich Kaufmann, "Die Regierungsbildung in Preussen und im Reiche und die Rolle der Partien" (1921), in *GS*, I, pp. 374–377.

skepticism. But he never joined the extreme right nor made apologies for Hitler's dictatorship or its international offshoot, the *Grossraumlehre* – although he did regard it an "eternal law of life" that some nations still had a "vital space" to fill while for others it had already become too small.[255]

Although Kaufmann's *Das Wesen des Völkerrechts und die Clausula rebus sic stantibus* (1911) had been written before the war, the war had done little to discredit its argument, perhaps to the contrary, and he continued to develop its ideas in his later writings, restating them for foreign audiences in a somewhat more polished form in his 1935 general course at the Hague Academy. Kaufmann himself regarded *Wesen* as principally a book in legal philosophy and later recognized a certain youthfulness in the delight he had taken there for paradoxical formulations. Read together with his later writings, what emerges is an *oeuvre* that seeks to escape from the superficial rationalism and paralyzing dichotomies of liberal thought and to understand – and to control – the world of public and international law as a *concrete reality*.[256]

Kaufmann's work was aimed against neo-Kantian legal theory (as represented, for example, by Jellinek and Kelsen) and specifically its internationalist variant that imagined the international world as (contractual) market relations between States that had been abstracted of their particular characteristics and whose rational will compelled them to join the system to enable the realization of their (subjective) purposes – a construction that closely resembled liberal arguments about how to justify constraint in a domestic system of initially autonomous, self-regarding individuals. This view, Kaufmann held, profoundly mistook the nature of the State and, therefore, also of the international realm. Since the mid-nineteenth century liberal lawyers had employed a domestic model of *subordination law* in their analyses of international politics, attempting to inject an "objective principle" above States – a common value, community will or economic rationality.[257] But since the

---

[255] Kaufmann, "Règles générales," p. 558.
[256] His 1932 assessment of the League was an admirably undogmatic description of its strengths and weaknesses. Created as a concert of Great Powers, it had in its practical work been able to create, if not a social ideal, at least "a special atmosphere, tradition, spirit and style": even the more important State interests could be coordinated through it. Great Powers could expound their ideals and have them criticized though it. By this means it could effectively maintain peace – for the moral isolation of Great Powers was far more dangerous than their ability to show leadership in cooperation. "Der Völkerbund," pp. 236–237.
[257] Kaufmann, *Das Wesen des Völkerrechts*, pp. 203–204.

demise of the idea of a great Christian Republic, no concrete center, or objective life-principle, had emerged to provide an effective basis for the *international* distribution of social values in the way the domestic legal order distributed values in the national society.[258] There was no community, no *Menschenzwecke* or leader with unchallenged authority in the world.[259] From the perspective of a subordination model, international law could seem only a chimera. Although many lawyers entertained a "longing for the universal monarchy of an infallible Pope,"[260] the subordination model was finally broken in theory by Hegel and Ranke and in practice by Bismarck.[261]

The liberals' mistake crystallized in their formal concept of the State that was accompanied by an image of international law that either followed the subordination model or became a playing field for the arbitrary wills of States.[262] Liberalism, Kaufmann explained, had failed to produce a conception of the State that would be anything but a passive receptacle of individual interests and purposes, a formal defender of individual rights, a cold edifice for the rule of those in power. Like Kantian ethics, such formalism could never explain why the State – the individual, concrete State – might, with good reason, command compliance, sometimes even the lives of its citizens. For the conservative view, statehood was not a matter of subsumption under a definition but a spiritual reality that represented the blood and flesh of earlier generations that present generations had the responsibility to preserve for future ones. It was stories and legends from which it was impossible to detach the interests or wills of its individual members; indeed one's individuality was always in part a reflection of them.[263]

As the centre of social reality, the State united the dichotomies that remained unresolved within formal thought. When, for example, liberal rationalism created an irreducible (and destructive) antagonism between the individual and the community, it failed to see how the two interacted and constantly constructed each other. A numerical *Einzelheit* turned into concrete *Besonderheit* through social recognition.[264] As a concrete and

---

[258] Kaufmann, *Das Wesen des Völkerrechts*, p. 136.
[259] Kaufmann, *Das Wesen des Völkerrechts*, pp. 188–189.
[260] Kaufmann, *Das Wesen des Völkerrechts*, p. 192.
[261] Kaufmann, *Das Wesen des Völkerrechts*, pp. 204–205.
[262] Kaufmann, "Vorwort," in *GS*, III, p. xxi.
[263] Erich Kaufmann, "Über die konservative Partei und seine Geschichte" (1922), in *GS*, III, p. 151.
[264] Kaufmann, *Das Wesen des Völkerrechts*, p. 145. Cf. also the argument on the functioning of the *Volksgeist* in the individual in "Zur problematik des Volkswillens" (1931), in *GS*, III, pp. 274–275.

historical matter, there was no antinomy between the individual and the community, freedom, and the State. What abstract rationalism could see only as an unbridgeable divide, historical dialectic united in concrete life. This was the meaning of Hegel's dictum about the State being the reality of concrete freedom.

Judged against the concrete State, the international was weak and superficial. The liberal imagination often projected it as a cosmopolis of abstract, unconnected individuals – a "humanity" – whose members enjoyed natural rights and belonged to their communities out of free consent. But no individual was abstract or unconnected in this way. All were products of history and parts of something international only through their States. Failure to understand this *concrete reality* was the reason for the failure of rationalism to develop a credible concept of either the law or the State.[265]

Law was a relationship, a measure, a distribution value (*Verteilungswert*).[266] Unlike morality or aesthetics, it did not speak of the value of things in themselves; it gave a perspective from which value was projected onto things. In Europe, the State had become this projective point, a *Machtentfaltung*, a single unity (will/power) that served no higher purpose but whose only desire was to assert itself in history.[267] The way the widest material and moral energies had been collected and centralized in the State had been brilliantly exemplified in Germany. Struggle against French attempts at universal monarchy had finally ended German weakness in the nineteenth century and concentrated German energies to self-assertion. Since then, the German State had become the unifying principle for the cultural life of the German nation, the central, all-encompassing reality of German modernity, the producer of a "Gesamtplan des menschlichen Kulturlebens."[268]

International law was unable to project or distribute values in this way. Unlike the State, it lacked a positive perspective, a single criterion. Peace, for example, was a purely negative and formal idea that implied no principle of distribution. A *Weltstaat* was a Utopia, and not a beneficial

---

[265] Kaufmann, *Das Wesen des Völkerrechts*, pp. 182–185.
[266] Kaufmann, *Das Wesen des Völkerrechts*, pp. 129–131.
[267] Kaufmann, *Das Wesen des Völkerrechts*, p. 135. Kaufmann shared Stahl's view that this was best realized in a monarchic constitution where the monarch became the "single nucleus" of the State – the center without which the State would disperse into an aggregate of partly conflicting wills. "Friedrich Julius Stahl als Rechtsphilosoph" (1906), in *GS*, III, p. 43.
[268] Kaufmann, *Das Wesen des Völkerrechts*, p. 137. This was so also in a liberal society where the limits of the private realm are always dependent on the decision by the State. "Règles générales," pp. 363–364.

one at that.[269] This is what it meant to say that international law existed not in the form of subordination but as co-ordination: it existed simply as agreement.[270] This was not agreement that bound – as liberal lawyers held – because there was a superior legal order that postulated it (*pacta sunt servanda*) but because of the nature of the sovereign will itself. Kaufmann's will-to-be-bound was like the promise in Nietzsche's aristocratic morality, creating an entitlement not to others but to oneself, expressing: "a proud consciousness... a special consciousness of power and freedom, a feeling of the ultimate completion of man. This liberated man, who is really *entitled* to make promises. This master of free will, this sovereign – how should he not be aware of his superiority of everything which cannot promise and vouch for itself?"[271]

Limits to international law's binding force followed from its character. Domestic contracts were binding as they fulfilled ultimately social purposes. Hence there were, for instance, no principled limits to legal subjects' ability to contract.[272] Not so in the international realm. A State could not contract out everything. A treaty that went against the State's right of self-preservation would be *ipso facto* invalid. Such right of self-preservation was the only properly fundamental right in the international system.[273] Other candidates – such as equality or *Notrecht* – presumed objective assessments (of equality or proportionality) that were alien to co-ordination law which left the ultimate assessment to States themselves.[274] Substantively, co-ordination law may cover as much as subordination law. The difference lies in the way co-ordination law leaves the parties "above" their commitments; free to renounce them if, due to changed circumstances, they go against the right of self-preservation.[275]

Although co-ordination law entailed no centralized values or common will it did reflect the presence of order in an actually existing whole ("Ordnung innerhalb eines realen Ganzen").[276] In modern international life, Kaufmann explained, not unlike other internationalists, States had a number of common or reciprocal interests and were often ready to co-operate to further them, even at the cost of short-term

---

[269] Kaufmann, *Das Wesen des Völkerrechts*, p. 135.
[270] Kaufmann, *Das Wesen des Völkerrechts*, pp. 151, 159–160.
[271] Friedrich Nietzsche, *On the Genealogy of Morals* (trans. D. Smith, Oxford University Press, 1996), p. 41.   [272] Kaufmann, *Das Wesen des Völkerrechts*, pp. 172–178.
[273] Kaufmann, *Das Wesen des Völkerrechts*, pp. 196–199.
[274] Kaufmann, *Das Wesen des Völkerrechts*, p. 199.
[275] "Der Staat muss, soll das Koordinationsrecht nicht in Subordinationsrecht umschlagen, über seiner Vertragen stehen bleiben," Kaufmann, *Das Wesen des Völkerrechts*, pp. 181, 204.   [276] Kaufmann, *Das Wesen des Völkerrechts*, p. 189.

special interests, as long as the latter were not considered vital. *Interessensolidarität* made sure that compacts were kept in such "new" areas as technical co-operation, traffic and postal connections as well as in "old" diplomatic law.[277] The need for stability and security of expectations pushed States into compliance while reprisals and retorsions made sure that no breach would be committed light-heartedly.[278] Yet, these were factual, not normative constraints. In co-ordination law, every State *may what it can*.[279] But what it can is determined by the social environment in which it acts: here lay the concrete nature of the international order, including the League.

The difficulty in accepting that these arguments ground any binding international order follows from the way the limits to State action were conceived by Kaufmann in apparently purely factual, instead of normative, terms. From the perspective of analytical jurists such as Kelsen this is unconvincing. From the existence of a need to co-operate or an obstacle to the realization of one's purposes a right or a duty cannot follow. But this is to assume the validity of a dichotomy that Kaufmann thinks typical of the rationalist positivism against which his "concrete thinking" is directed, errors of one-dimensional thought. The State and the law, facts and norms, the specific and the general – science and politics – do not stand opposed to each other but are aspects of the same (dialectical) reality. "Power" and "law" did not exist in opposition: the idea of the State presumed a historically determined transcendence. They may appear to conflict from a particular *individual* standpoint; from the perspective of the *Weltordnung* the two were indissociable, delimiting each other's sphere of validity in historically specific ways. When liberal lawyers seek a criterion with which to distinguish between a band of robbers and the State, and attempt to do this by opposing "power" to "law," they move in a circle: perhaps the law was enacted by the Mafia! The distinction can be made only by reference to the (internal) value of each concrete community concerned.[280]

Kaufmann's 1911 book became a favorite target of liberal critics. In his 1917 overview of pre-war German international theories as a "jurisprudence without a law," the neo-Kantian radical socialist Leonard Nelson (1882–1927) maintained that Kaufmann's legal philosophy

---

[277] Kaufmann, *Das Wesen des Völkerrechts*, pp. 190–191.
[278] Kaufmann, *Das Wesen des Völkerrechts*, pp. 200–201.
[279] Kaufmann, *Das Wesen des Völkerrechts*, p. 201.
[280] "Werte der konkreten Gemeinschaft," Erich Kaufmann, "Kritik der neukantischen Rechtsphilosophie" (1921), in *GS*, III, pp. 223–224.

destroyed legal concepts altogether: there had been no more consistent and brutal juridical system for justification of the right of the powerful.[281] Like other critics, he saw the book as a confused camouflage for State egoism. In his early analysis of the international law of national socialism, Eduard Bristler (John H. Herz) regarded Kaufmann's view of victorious war as the ultimate criterion of justice as the crowning theory of the imperialist *Machtstaat*. Though an outsider to national socialism, and a target of *Gleichschaltung*, Kaufmann had become an unwitting facilitator of fascism.[282]

But a more charitable reading of *Wesen des Völkerrechts* that draws upon Kaufmann's other writings is able to appreciate the effort to deal with the paradoxes and weaknesses that a purely rationalistic or a purely sociological scholarship entails – the mindless oscillation between voluntarism and naturalism that became the shared fate of variations of disenchanted turn-of-the century jurisprudence after 1918. For liberals, Kaufmann's search for the concrete and the spiritual was wrought with danger. Did it not legitimize precisely those national passions that it had been the task of modern jurisprudence to suppress? Was Kaufmann's defense of irrationalism anything but a recipe for anarchy? Were his admiration of Bismarck and the flexibility of the Wilhelminian constitution only attempts to prepare ground for a charismatic leader ready to turn charisma into an instrument of tyranny?

Kaufmann's romantic conservatism was indissociable from his nationalism.[283] After all, he held a lecture in occupied Brussels in 1915 on the duties of the occupying power in which he conveniently dismissed the German violation of Belgium's neutrality as part of "bad Hague law" while applying the "good Hague law" that provided for the creation of the conditions of lawfulness by the occupying power.[284] Yet it was not an aggressive nationalism he espoused. For him German sensitivity for the irrational and its attempt to envelop the irrational within a comprehensive understanding of the world positively prevented it from turning into imperialism. It could only respect the different forms of the irrational, wanting to see its manifoldness flourish. Imperialism

---

[281] Nelson, *Rechtswissenschaft ohne Recht*, p. 231.
[282] Eduard Bristler, *Die Völkerrechtslehre des Nationalsozialismus* (Zurich, Europa, 1938), pp. 53, 62, 170.
[283] This voice is nowhere more eloquent than in Kaufmann's 1920 talk on the history of the conservative party – an essay exploring the pervasive opposition between the conservative–romantic German *Geist* and its counterpart, the abstract rationalism of the (Western) Enlightenment, "Über die konservative Partei," pp. 133–175.
[284] Erich Kaufmann, "Das Legalitätsprinzip im Auslandsverfahren in besetztem feindlichen Gebiete" (1915), in *GS*, II, p. 6.

was the consequence of a Western rationalism that (with Hume) did recognize reason as a slave of passion but left its own particular (British or French) passion outside its formal reason while simultaneously seeking to universalize it under "sociology" and "natural law."[285]

Kaufmann's teaching could undoubtedly be used for ignoble purposes – which teaching could not be so used? But it did have a much better grasp of the dynamics that had divided the German international law community into two opposite camps – pacifists and nationalists – than members of either camp themselves had. Its orientation towards the concrete and the substantive avoided the pitfalls of formalism and abstraction into which these regularly fell. In a talk on the future of arbitration in 1932 Kaufmann lamented the sharp division of attitudes among German lawyers on this matter. An impassioned examination showed that arbitration had an important role in the settlement of international problems; but that in vital questions self-help – that is, power – still provided the *ultima ratio*. At the same time, he pointed out that a weak State – such as Germany – was in a particularly vulnerable position inasmuch as it had to comply with an unjust law – such as Versailles – but that there was nothing dishonorable if it then relied on the protective provisions that such law might contain.[286] For Kaufmann after the 1930s unlike, for instance, Carl Schmitt, the law was an autonomous set of determinate rules and institutions, with an objective and peaceful ethos, that Germany could use in order to advance its national interests. Unlike the internationalists, he refused to think of present law as inherently good only because it was formal law – but unlike the nationalists, he believed it might be used to Germany's benefit. Neither good nor bad in itself, its significance was determined in the concrete context.

After *Wesen des Völkerrechts*, the best-known of Kaufmann's international law works is his 1935 general course at the Hague. In the latter, emphasis has shifted towards a more conventional idealism. Whether because of his delicate situation at the time – he had been removed from his position at the University and was obliged to have his lectures cleared by the regime[287] – or because he was speaking in front of a non-German audience, Kaufmann now presented himself as a Platonist for whom both statehood and positive law were expressions of, or directed

---

[285] Kaufmann, "Über die konservative Partei," pp. 172–175.
[286] Erich Kaufmann, "Probleme des internationalen Gerichtsbarkeit" (1932), in *GS*, III, pp. 304–319.
[287] Detlev F. Vagts, "International Law in the Third Reich" (1990), 84 *AJIL*, p. 676.

towards, substantive ideas of justice. Starting his course by the defense of the idea of an unwritten *general* international law that he received from his general idea of law, he directed his views against both formalist and sociological positivism – against the "fetishism of the written law" and the "hubris of the will" that led into a bottomless nihilism.[288] On the basis of positive law and legal institutions it was the task of jurisprudence to find and articulate this idea:

> All profound analysis of reality leads into elements which, though they cannot be grasped by the senses, and far from having only a subjective or psychological existence, are objective and constitutive of what is real: these are real categories of general and eternal nature, substantive forms that inhere in particular and individual substances.[289]

Throughout the course, Kaufmann used dialectics to overcome objections against extreme étatism and standard naturalism: the transcendental was embedded in the immanent, the ideal accessible through the actual. The State was the most important reality of the social world and the only original subject and guarantor of international rights.[290] Yet the State was bound by the *forms of justice* that pre-existed it: distributive, retributive, and procedural, and by its assignment as the "support and guarantor of objective law."[291] State law and international law were part of the same spiritual unity, autonomous from but linked through interpretation, *refoulement* and cross-referral.[292] National sovereignty became dependent on supranational values, among which Kaufmann included individual life, liberty, and property. Quoting Bodin's view that sovereignty had no limit apart from those determined by "laws of God and nature," he defined sovereignty as an instrument or a supporter of such values. It became "supreme service and supreme responsibility."

In 1935 Kaufmann attacked formalist positivism from a much more confidently internationalist position than before – indeed, he had become a member of the *Institut de droit international* in 1931 and now spoke of the spirit of legal institutions, the idea of the law, a transcendental

---

[288] Kaufmann, "Règles générales," pp. 313–319.
[289] "Toute analyse approfondie des realités conduit à des éléments idéaux qui, bien que non palpables par les sens extérieurs et loin de n'avoir qu'un existence subjective et psychologique, sont d'ordre objectif et constitutifs des phénomènes réels: il s'agit de catégories réelles d'ordre général et éternel, de formes substantielles inhérents aux substances particulières et individuelles." Kaufmann, "Règles générales," p. 319.
[290] Kaufmann, "Règles générales," pp. 397–401.
[291] Kaufmann, "Règles générales," p. 399.
[292] Kaufmann, "Règles générales," pp. 436–458.

concept of justice that he assumed lay behind the often incomplete and sometimes unjust positive laws and institutions. If he did subscribe to the view of international law as autolimitation by States, he did that expressly in the Hegelian understanding that this meant that they were "required to realise 'freely' the commandments of the objective and eternal 'laws' that dominate the objective moral order."[293] The inverted commas around "freely" and "laws" suggest that neither could be directly spoken of. Kaufmann continued in 1935 to defend the reality of collective persons such as States and regarded the spiritual nation (and not the abstract individual) as the concrete basis of the international world. But there was no antinomy between humanity and the nation: humanity consisted of nations and individuals participated in humanity through national traditions and processes. States were not withering away; interdependence brought them together but also intensified their struggle: industries and agriculture were national assets, useful also for total wars.[294] As before, the State stood in the center of Kaufmann's law, this time defended not merely from the inside of the nation but also as an instrument of supranational values. Like legal realists, Kaufmann now saw the State as the access-point for those values, the medium whereby they were: "put in a hierarchy, controlled, enveloped, co-ordinated, organized and put in harmony with each other and with the superior interests of the national community."[295] In 1935 Kaufmann defined the (liberal) conflict between the State and the international realm away. There was international justice – but it could be accessed only through the State. Neither monism nor dualism was right: it was impossible to establish a general primacy between the international and the national. Each looked towards the other and strove for *Aufhebung*: this and the judicial techniques for avoiding contradiction were part of the dialectic and the teleology embedded in law.[296]

The 1935 lectures continued the "fundamental" critique of the formalist positivism and sociological and psychological jurisprudence. Neither they nor the rationalist neo-naturalism that became popular after the war could produce an understanding of the concrete character of States. Where liberal jurisprudence imagined the international in terms of a market rationality, Kaufmann projected it as a terrain for struggle between various dialectical poles (individual/community,

[293] Kaufmann, "Règles générales," p. 460 n1.
[294] Kaufmann, "Règles générales," pp. 335–341, 348–349.
[295] Kaufmann, "Règles générales," p. 363.
[296] Kaufmann, "Règles générales," pp. 436–437, 440–441.

state/society, national/international) whose synthesis produced the concrete order of the moment. To think of international law simply as State will was a shallow understanding, not only of the law but of the directedness of will always to an object beyond itself. Law could not be dependent on a human *Vorstellung* or *Anerkennung*. Both presume there to be something to believe or recognize that lies outside the human psyche.[297] A consciousness of law cannot be a final criterion of law because it is, by definition, a consciousness of something outside itself. This is not just a technical, epistemological mistake but an existential one. Pure voluntarism is a degenerated form of social thought, a nihilism, blind to the extent to which "will" is always a product of something; a socially constructed, historically determined entity.

Although Kaufmann's 1935 lectures constituted an elegant – even if authoritarian – compromise between the traditions of German public law conservatism and internationalism, it provided no real relief for those concerned over the constant disappointments about the ability of the inter-war diplomacy to deal with the impending international crises. The international community existed as a series of procedures, but as a spiritual reality it was empty. There was no agreement on what "peace" and "justice" under it might mean. Collective action under international organs failed to be on behalf of "humanity" and remained that by a majority against a minority.[298] Kaufmann had no more interest than Jellinek or Kelsen in examining the constraints that pushed States into co-operation, or the power of the institutions that States had set up. But unlike the liberals, he did not entertain hope that interdependence would bring about peace. He had no faith in the unspirited and abstract realm of the international – and when he revealed his faith in a transcendental natural law in his Hague lectures, this was already after the Hitler regime had expelled him from his position as professor and legal adviser. Little wonder that instead of a policy-proposal, he resorted to pathos: "World history is not, as Hegel formulated it in his *History of Philosophy*, a terrain of happiness; the pages of universal history that speak of happiness are empty. History is a tragedy that always repeats itself, that requires an attitude of heroism from its students."[299] Some of that attitude may have been visible in the philosophical debates that Kaufmann was able to continue with his students in a seminar at his private home in Berlin-Nikolassee until late 1938 when he finally had to leave for the

---

[297] Cf. also Nelson, *Rechtswissenschaft ohne Recht*, pp. 16–19, 49–50.
[298] Kaufmann, "Règles générales," pp. 557–579.
[299] Kaufmann, "Règles générales," p. 557.

International law as philosophy: Germany 1871–1933

Netherlands and hide himself – and perhaps also in his return to Germany among the first refugees in 1946.[300] But one cannot help thinking that as he assumed as international lawyer, *a priori*, that the actual was the guarantor of the ideal, and that where that did not seem to be the case, one was dealing with an inevitable historical tragedy, this was already an intellectual escape into an imaginary kingdom of dialectics; the compensation of defeat in today's world by a theological faith in victory in tomorrow's.

Break: the end of philosophy

An account of German international law in the pre-Second World War era comes to an abrupt halt in the middle of the 1930s. A dark gap stands between that moment and the reconstruction of internationalism at the universities of the Federal Republic after the war.[301] At that point, it is a serious temptation to engage in speculation about the relationship of German public law – including international law – doctrines and the rise of Nazism. Clearly, German conservatism contained strands of thought and sentiment that marched in parallel with national socialism.[302] Clearly, German liberalism was both too divided and too fragile – indeed in some ways an odd liberalism – to put up a strong defense against the Nazi tide.[303] That the legal profession so meekly collapsed in the *Gleichschaltung* ("co-ordination") of 1933 has been explained as a result of the quick elimination of its Jewish leadership (particularly important in international law) and the financial and other difficulties

---

[300] Cf. e.g. Karl Josef Partsch, "Der Rechtsberater Auswärtigen Amtes 1950–1958. Erinnerungsblatt zum 90. Geburtstag von Erich Kaufmann" (1970), 30 *Zeitschrift für ausländisches öffentliches Recht und Völkerrecht (ZaöRV)*, pp. 227–228.

[301] In 1933, there were over eighty experts on international law in Germany, of whom thirty-five taught at universities. Fifteen of them were targeted by Nazi measures by 1939, usually replaced by younger lawyers eager to develop a national-socialist international law doctrine. The Kiel Institute was taken over by the Nazi Ritterbusch in 1935, the Hamburg Institute was united with Ribbentrop's diplomatic academy in Berlin in 1936. Only the Kaiser Wilhelm Institut in Berlin could continue in relative independence under the opportunist Bruns and then the party member Carl Bilfinger (1879–1958), under whom it resettled in Heidelberg in 1948–1949. Cf. Vagts, "Third Reich," pp. 661–704; Hueck, "Völkerrechtswissenschaft." For the German journals, cf. Hueck "Gründung völkerrechtlicher Zeitschriften," pp. 403–416.

[302] Cf. e.g. Jeffrey Herf, *Reactionary Modernism. Technology, Culture, and Politics in Weimar and the Third Reich* (Cambridge University Press, 1984).

[303] Cf. e.g. James J. Sheehan, *German Liberalism in the Nineteenth Century* (Chicago University Press, 1978), esp. pp. 272–283.

into which it had entered.[304] The narrative of the coming into predominance of Nazi law has been told in terms of a radical break as well as a logical continuation of tradition and most histories contain elements of both. Naturalism and positivism, formalism, and sociological theories have each been indicted in the process. Such interpretations hinge on larger assumptions about the nature of fascism in general: dark irrationalism or the "banality of evil?" What in general is the relationship between (legal) ideas, ideologies, and political practices?

But whatever the causes, one tradition of thinking about international law came to an end. This was the tradition that dealt with international politics as a problem of philosophy, more particularly of a philosophy that was to give expression to human freedom while also being respectful of the nature of societies in which freedom could become a reality. The dialectics of that attempt is epitomized in the opposition between Kant and Hegel or, as I intimated in the last two sections, between Kelsen and Kaufmann, and every aspect of German legal thought in the period links to it in one way or another.

The Copernican revolution inaugurated by Kant in German metaphysics posited autonomy as the social ideal: the self-legislating subject was grounded in the transcendental architecture of pure reason. For Hegel, however, the particular reason advocated by Kant, and the subject that accompanied it, were not free from "dogmatism" – they were products of a way of life that had the (ideological) tendency of thinking of its own experience as universal. The kind of freedom that Kant and his followers advocated – individual autonomy of fully rational agents, attempting to co-ordinate their behavior through universaliseable maxims – was a product of an agnostic liberalism that fitted remarkably well with the social conditions of post-feudal society. The autonomous individual could never reach pure reason; reason realized itself only in world-history in which individuals were always located as already participants in some concrete reality that they could never shrug off.

Such a debate lay behind the division of German philosophy and public law in the nineteenth century into more or less individualist and communitarian streams, rationalist and historicist theories. According to the standard narrative, Savigny had reacted against the abstract rationalism of enlightenment thought and mainstream internationalism

---

[304] Kenneth F. Ledford, "Lawyers and the Limits of Liberalism: The German Bar in the Weimar Republic," in Terence C. Halliday and Lucien Karpik (eds.), *Lawyers and the Rise of Western Political Liberalism* (Oxford, Clarendon, 1997), pp. 231–233.

International law as philosophy: Germany 1871–1933

(Holtzendorff, Ullmann) against the historicism of suspected "deniers" such as Savigny and Lasson. The two cannot, however, be separated so schematically but continued life within each attempt at novel grounding: of this, Jellinek and the doctrine of the rational will provide good examples. Yet the syntheses were again torn apart by the relentless rationalism and individualism of Kelsen in one direction, and the equally relentless historicism and collectivism of Kaufmann in another.

The synthesis of Kant and Hegel in German international law takes this form: The autonomous State is the social ideal. The view of autonomy as rational self-legislation makes the ideal compatible with international order. Through self-legislation, the State takes its place in the concrete reality of the international world: free to legislate in accordance with the intrinsic rationality of its social laws. In such an argument, the State appears alternatively as history's subject and object, its freedom both negative and positive. Accordingly, the argument is vulnerable to criticisms from both perspectives: It does not provide real freedom as the (egoistic) State will inevitably create a *bellum omnium:* a sphere of fear, not autonomy. Or, it does not provide real freedom as the State is not entitled to legislate in accordance with its own interests or needs but is completely constrained by the (economic, military, etc.) structures of power in which it lives.

What made the failure of this philosophical discourse particularly dangerous in Germany was the weakness of its political structures. Where in Britain and France statehood had become second nature, an unproblematic "concrete reality" within which social ideals could compete, in Germany, the debate constantly shook the limits of the political order. Far from taken for granted, Germany's statehood was the very problem: was it real or artificial – organ or aggregate – freedom or authority? What ideals did it embed – or was it neutral? In Germany, every political debate took on a philosophical significance: and when philosophy failed to provide a resolution, no political structure proved strong enough to fall back on. There is a tragic aspect in the Kant/Hegel dichotomy, as manifested in the opposition between Kelsen's pacifism and Kaufmann's view of war as the social ideal. In Kelsen, pacifism followed from an extreme relativism: all ideals were equally subjective, and as long as the formal principle of legality was honored, the law had nothing to say about them. This implied a society of unconnected individuals, unable to produce a justification for any social ideals apart from that of the abstract market-place. In Kaufmann, the State overrode the particularity of individuals and provided a focus for collective ethical life. Hence war as the social ideal: only war constituted proof of the presence of a realm of objective value over the subjective wants of individuals. Where the Kantian–Kelsenian perspective led to an alienated moral agnosticism that was vulnerable to the critique of technical reason, the Hegel–Kaufmann outlook prepared the ground for a totalitarian State.

The Kant–Hegel debate and the various reconciliations define German modernity as insistence on the enlightenment heritage on the one hand (individual autonomy, political and economic liberty, technical and scientific progress) and profound suspicion of enlightenment on the other (alienation, economic exploitation and class rule, herd morality).[305] With Heidegger in the 1930s, a completely new set of questions was posed for philosophy that pointed beyond modernity itself. Whatever consequences his "fundamental" questions may have had for politics or philosophy, they were not questions through which international lawyers could think themselves able to understand or resolve their dogmatic or practical problems. Whether there was an international law down that road in the first place – and Heidegger himself became increasingly skeptical about the political application of his *Seinsfrage* after 1935[306] – may be doubtful. With Heidegger (and with postmodernity) the suggestion of using philosophy to resolve problems of international law and politics came to an end.

The end of philosophy also brought to an end the German project of the *Rechtsstaat* that presented itself as representative of both freedom and authority, as articulated in Kant's conception of the rational will and in Hegel's concept of the State.[307] German liberals such as Jellinek grasped at it as a defense of bourgeois freedoms and a guarantee of social order. The effort to explain freedom and order not only as compatible but defined by reference to each other lay at the heart of legal formalism of the public law tradition. Among liberals, it articulated a moderate concept of statehood directed to protection of individual rights. Among conservatives it explained individual rights as an acceptable ingredient of an authoritarian State. But the idea of positive freedom involved was inherently unstable. If freedom is nothing but the realization of and if

---

[305] In this sense, e.g. Robert Pippin, *Modernity as a Philosophical Problem. On the Dissatisfactions of European High Culture* (2nd edn., Oxford, Blackwell, 1999), pp. 160–179.

[306] Cf. e.g. Hans Sluga, *Heidegger's Crisis. Philosophy and Politics in Nazi Germany* (Cambridge, Harvard University Press, 1993), pp. 214–219.

[307] Cf. also Krieger, *The German Idea of Freedom*, pp. 458–470.

need be imposition of order, then its point is lost. Dialectics easily collapses into reductionism. After the war, German internationalists no longer hazarded the dangers of dialectics: the search for a social ideal that would be respectful of concrete reality was replaced by Western abstract humanitarianism.

This was already anticipated in the moving last chapter of the 1934 Hague lectures by Karl Strupp who had been dismissed from his position in Frankfurt in 1933, and had moved first to Istanbul and then to France where he committed suicide on the eve of the German occupation. For the positivist Strupp, the complete failure of the Codification Conference of 1930 had been a grave disappointment that left him only the avenue of natural law on which to argue – and yet, he lamented, a natural law without the real, substantive agreement of States would fall apart the moment it was needed. Between non-existent positive law and an ineffective natural law, all that was left was a hope that the ideals of natural law would become the ideal of States, their own (positive) natural law. Such oscillation between professionalism and faith by a lawyer deeply aware that "the very foundations of the law of nations were shaking by the force of attacks from outside" was vivid testimony of the dead-end into which the divided tradition of German public law had come.[308] To hope for harmony was already to have given up hope.

[308] Karl Strupp, "Les règles générales du droit de la paix" (1934/I), 47 *RdC*, pp. 581–586.

4

International law as sociology: French "solidarism" 1871–1950

"Here is a tranquil and charming village in a small peaceful State: its canals slumber in the calm of justice, interrupted only by a horizon of mountains whose snowy peaks inspire properly elevated thoughts. This is the chosen seat for elected international public power." In this setting (which is not difficult to recognize as Rousseau's imaginary Geneva) we see the Parliament of Nations, "this immense and luxurious building, with spacious galleries, rich bibliographies, numerous bureaux of commissions," together with a "smaller, though still imposing palace of the International Governmental Commission, or, more properly, of the Administrative Commission." On both sides of a large boulevard there arise the offices of the ministries: an International Administration of Finances, a Customs Commission, a Monetary and Finances Commission, the headquarters of international postal administration, railways, straits, the great international rivers . . . There is also the building of the Ministry of Colonies "for care over races under trusteeship has been confided to the Society of Nations itself." Still other facades appear: "at the end of the avenue, perpendicular to other buildings, very visible and in a much more sombre style lies that of the Directorate of International Armed Forces." "But the veritable engine of the international society is the administration of justice. Here it finds the preponderant place which it has lost in so many States . . . The International Court of Justice, chosen initially from lists of candidates proposed by States, has become thereafter completely independent. It now recruits its own personnel, as vacancies become available, from lists composed in consultation by the supreme courts of member States."[1]

[1] Georges Scelle, *Le Pacte des Nations et sa liaison avec Le Traité de Paix* (Paris, Sirey, 1919), pp. 101–102, 105–106.

International law as sociology: France 1871–1950

This romantic imagery interrupts Georges Scelle's (1878–1961) 400-page commentary on the Covenant of the League of Nations of 1919 and provides the true source of inspiration not only for that commentary but for the whole of the *oeuvre* of this late follower of solidarist radicalism. Not only do we find an international legislator, administration, adjudication and police force, situated in this local, yet cosmopolitan setting, the structure of the international society it administers has been completely transformed. Its legislative body is not composed of representatives of States, not even of geographical constituencies, but of the professions – such professions having become the centers around which members of the global electorate now construct their identities. "The representation of peoples thus became a representation by professionals, competent because chosen from among technical experts, exempt from all tyranny because the majority that would be formed over particular questions would always vary; such majority uniting the representatives of different professions in accordance with particular professional interests."[2]

In Scelle's utopia, the world is ruled by professional corporations: States – and indeed politics – have become extinct. The corporations would be represented in relation to the volume of their economic activity so as to guarantee that their relative input corresponds to their "*utilité sociale.*" Questions that interest particular nationalities may still occasionally arise, and are dealt with through co-operation between the national sections of inter-professional alliances. As the direction of this majority-formation, too, is controlled by the allocation of seats to different corporations, decision-making continues to reflect social utility.[3] To be sure, this would not have been a rapid development – the evolution to this point would have taken "centuries."[4] But there was no doubt it constituted modernity's direction, the goal of a fully rational, cosmopolitan administration of things that were by their nature economic or technical.

This global syndicalism links Scelle firmly in the stream of French radical–liberal thought, from Auguste Comte (1798–1857) and Emile Durkheim (1858–1917) to the lawyer–politician Léon Bourgeois (1851–1925) and Léon Duguit (1859–1928), the doyen of French public law, each of whom looked for the direction of policy from scientific and technical expertise. When discussing French inter-war internationalism, it is necessary to bear in mind its teleological bent, the vision of a federally organized and professionally administered global polity.

[2] Scelle, *Le Pacte des Nations*, p. 110. [3] Scelle, *Le Pacte des Nations*, p. 110.
[4] Scelle, *Le Pacte des Nations*, p. 111.

This vision separates French thought about international affairs – or politics generally – from the German tradition surveyed in chapter 3. From philosophical premises, assumptions that highlighted the existential freedom of the individual, German public lawyers came to see the State as the center of domestic and international law. Following Kant, they held that the autonomy of human will was the source of all secular normativity and, following Hegel, that rational will was concentrated in the State. Their liberal *Rechtsstaat* aimed to reconcile competing political wills by becoming thoroughly formal and bureaucratic. This created an existential void, however, in which there was constant need to buttress the State (its "legitimacy") from additional arguments about its organic nature or from public law's connection to the German *Geist*. Yet such arguments were old-fashioned: "Combine liberalism with modernism and we are left with the overthrow of authority and an endless search for its substitute," writes Max Weber's most recent biographer.[5] Weber himself feared that in Germany's atrophied political culture democracy only strengthened the bureaucracy's hand and he advocated world power and a strong and responsible plebiscitary leader as sources for the legitimacy of the German State.[6] In the course of the development of public law doctrine and practice in the Weimar period, the argument from existential autonomy (and solitude) was finally transformed into extreme authoritarianism as the German escape from freedom was completed by the spring of 1933.

It is an unexpected paradox that as we now turn to the French doctrines of public and international law in the late nineteenth and early twentieth centuries, the relationship between freedom and constraint, subjective and objective law, appears overturned. The new French doctrines assume the essential determination of individuals – what they will, the power they possess – by the moral or social laws of their collectivities.[7] For them, the State becomes an ephemeral, almost transparent form, at best an instrument or a "function" – sometimes a metaphor – for the actions of the social collectivity that encompass all aspects of the

---

[5] John Patrick Diggins, *Max Weber. Politics and the Spirit of Tragedy* (New York, Basic Books, 1996), p. 67.
[6] Cf. Wolfgang J. Mommsen, *Max Weber and German Politics 1890–1920* (trans. Michael S. Steinberg, University of Chicago Press, 1984), pp. 390–414 and *passim*.
[7] For an unequivocal statement of this, cf. Emile Durkheim, *The Division of Labor in Society*, trans. W. D. Halls, introd. Lewis Coser (New York, London, Free Press, 1997 [1893]), pp. 329–340. For Durkheim's polemical and pervasive preference for collective determination, cf. Steven Lukes, *Emile Durkheim. His Life and Work. A Historical and Critical Study* (Stanford University Press, 1973), pp. 19–22, 34–36, 79–85.

lives of individuals. To be sure, classical and revolutionary political theory in France had always had an individualist bias. The State was seen as an effect of the social contract, the product or aggregate of the activities of *citoyens:* a purely utilitarian, not an ethical idea.[8] Still in 1920 Carré de Malberg (1861–1935) held it established that the State had no interests or will of its own but that, from a realistic point of view, its interests were the interests of individuals and its will the will of those who govern.[9] But where classical political theory and the *privatisme* of the *Code Civil* had portrayed individuals as undetermined and autonomous, an increasing number of politicians and social scientists, including lawyers and legal theorists, were arguing from the 1880s and 1890s onwards – against *laissez-faire* liberalism but also to pre-empt the advance of socialism – that an irreducible social solidarity bound individuals to positions and communities that dictated to them what they should will and what their true interests were.[10]

From a traditionalist communitarianism and a sociological naturalism arguments were made that reduced formal States to instruments for external purposes and led inexorably to one kind of federalism or other. The result was – another paradox – a cosmopolitan monism that seemed liberal to the extent that it saw human collectivities as aggregates of their constituent individuals but authoritarian as it sought to reconcile the conflicting wills and interests of individuals by reference to the essential solidarity it derived from a natural morality or a more or less mechanistic theory of social determination.

The background of such ideas lay in the properly French terrain of Saint-Simonian optimism about economic and social progress, in the positivism of Comte and Durkheim, in the liberal or Catholic nationalisms of Renan or (the later) Barrès and in the civic republicanism that in France turned away from the exaggerated individualism and rationalism of the eighteenth century.[11] What united such diverse intellectual strands was their view of the State and of positive law as indicators or functions of the objective laws of the social realm, of economic or industrial development,

---

[8] Cf. Robert Redslob, "La doctrine idéaliste du droit des gens. Proclamée par la révolution française et par le philosophe Emmanuel Kant" (1921), 28 *RGDIP*, pp. 448–489.

[9] R. Carré de Malberg, *Contribution à la théorie générale de l'Etat* (2 vols., Paris, Sirey, 1920), I, pp. 25–27.

[10] For one account of the *via media* character of French "solidarism," cf. James T. Kloppenberg, *Uncertain Victory. Social Democracy and Progressivism in European and American Thought 1870–1920* (Oxford University Press, 1986), pp. 212–216, 301–305.

[11] Kloppenberg, *Uncertain Victory*, pp. 175–176.

division of labor, intellectual cultivation, the common good, and social solidarity. By itself, such a combination of ideas could have led to many types of international politics and law. With the French lawyers in the 1920s and 1930s it led to federalism – emphasis on increasing integration, economic interdependence, the League of Nations, blueprints for a European Union. That it did so was strongly supported by the Franco-German adversity, transfigured in the minds of the protagonists as an opposition between internationalism and nationalism.

French international lawyers had always stressed the indissociability of French interests from those of the world at large. After 1918, they argued for a firm European order that would guarantee French security against German aggression. But there was, as we saw in chapter 2, a larger assumption about France as the champion of universal humanitarianism. When Scelle in 1920 reflected upon the fate of the German colonies, he had no hesitation in assuming that "for cultural and social reasons" the peoples of those territories would naturally hope to be ruled by the French.[12] The League of Nations, René Brunet (1882–1951) wrote in 1921, was a product of the French political idea. Supporting it France was only being faithful to its own humanistic ideals.[13] Not all Germans conceived the international as a sphere for *Machtpolitik* – but those who did not were quite constrained in their politics. By contrast, French lawyers were inclined to see it in terms of a gradually increasing economic and cultural solidarity, and were applauded. Each spoke from the perspective of national tradition. If the strength of the Wilhelminian empire lay in the economic and military might of the German State, the *gloire* of France hardly resided in the fragile structures of the Third Republic.

Internationalism as nationalism: the idea of France

Thank God French science has not been in the habit of mixing with the courtesans of success. In many occasions, and until quite recently, it has without hesitation taken the side of the oppressed, without attention to the number or force of the oppressors.[14]

One striking aspect of French international law towards the end of the nineteenth century was its ability to connect a cosmopolitan outlook with an impeccably patriotic alignment behind French interests. This is not to

---

[12] Georges Scelle, *La morale des traités de paix* (Paris, Cadet, 1920), pp. 164–165.
[13] René Brunet, *La société des nations et la France* (Paris, Sirey, 1921), pp. 244–256, 266.
[14] A. Pillet and J. Delpech, "La question finlandaise. Le manifeste du Tsar examiné au point de vue de droit international" (1900), VII *RGDIP*, p. 405.

say that its internationalism would have been less than honest. On the contrary, since the early nineteenth century French republicans had identified the French nation through the universal principles of the Revolution – non-intervention, national autonomy, and self-determination.[15] To be sure, as pointed out by Robert Redslob (born 1882) from the University of Strasbourg, that the French themselves did not always live up to those ideals followed from their profound ambivalence: Was a people entitled to intervene in support of another people's self-determination? How come the National Assembly of 1792 made no exception to the death penalty where the entity seeking autonomy was part of the French Republic?[16] Such paradoxes – or apparent paradoxes – allow a glimpse of the cunning of the national spirit that can sometimes construct a particularist identity out of universalist principles, challenging our commonplace assumption of the fundamental character of the dichotomy between matters "national" and matters "universal."

The quote at the head of this section is from a 1900 article by Antoine Pillet (1857–1926) and Joseph Delpech (born 1872), two representatives of a first generation of international lawyers in France, defending Finland's autonomy against the Russification that had commenced a year earlier. Most of the French international law community took a firm stand in Finland's favor, defending Finnish legal institutions and culture against what was perceived as an illegal Russian policy. Finnish nationalism was constructed by French lawyers out of the universalist principles of Western enlightenment (but also its cultural self-understanding in a larger sense) against the Eastern mysticism that Russia was thought to represent.[17] In French eyes, Finland appeared special as it identified itself on the basis of the same principles as the French did.

As we saw in chapter 2, French international lawyers employed a consistently humanitarian rhetoric to defend French colonial expansion. Their positions fell in line with the general transformation of French attitudes towards expansion in the 1880s, after the first years of mourning over the defeat at Sedan. Even the great socialist Jean Jaurès (1859–1914) became an enthusiast of the French mission to "spread the Gospel of French culture, liberalism, and egalitarianism, the principles

---

[15] Michel Winock distinguishes helpfully between an "open" and a "closed" French nationalism, of which the former carried the idea of the civilizing mission, the latter demanding "France to the French," in *Nationalism, Anti-Semitism and Fascism in France* (trans. J. M. Todd, Stanford University Press, 1998), pp. 24–26.
[16] Redslob, "La doctrine idéaliste," pp. 445, 448.
[17] Cf. further Outi Korhonen, *International Law Situated: Culture, History and Ethics* (The Hague, Boston, and Dordrecht, Kluwer, 2000).

of 1789."[18] A real masterpiece in this genre is, however, the 800-page monograph of 1904 on French diplomacy under the Third Republic and international law by Frantz Despagnet from the University of Bordeaux.[19] The book consisted of a detailed commentary on all major international developments between 1873 and 1899 from the perspective of French interests and international law. It was not an apology for French diplomacy: though Despagnet commended many aspects of French policy, he had also many critical things to say about it. The reader was left in no doubt, however, that whenever France was acting reprehensibly, its failure lay in its departure from the essence of its own identity. Where British violations were a natural result of its arrogance, and German violations of its general nonchalance about law, a French violation (such as the declaration of rice as contraband during the Franco-Chinese war of 1885) was a special scandal as it was a denial by France of its own idea.[20]

The assimilation of French and international interests was facilitated by France's international position. As Despagnet repeatedly emphasized, the defeat of 1871 had made France "morally convinced of the need to protect the weak" (by way of arbitration, for instance),[21] and turned its ambition from the continent to the colonies. In the odd position of challenger in regard to Britain and an old colonial power in regard to Germany, its own policy turned almost automatically to seek support from internationalism. This was most evident in the Balkans and Africa. In the former case, the main conflict was between Russia and Britain. It thus fell upon French diplomacy to achieve the *Entente* that led to the 1878 Berlin Congress, the French thinking of themselves as only following their traditions as the representatives of Christian populations in the Orient. While Russia was looking for aggrandisement and Britain protected its route to India, and both violated the 1856 guarantee of Turkey's integrity, France's only wish, Despagnet wrote, was to have a stable system of territorial and minority rights that would guarantee respect for commitments towards Turkey.[22]

Like other French commentators, Despagnet held Brazza's African activity to be "un des examples les plus consolants pour la civilisation"

---

[18] Quoted in James J. Cooke, *New French Imperialism 1880–1910. The Third Republic and Colonial Expansion* (Paris, IN, 1973), p. 20.
[19] For a brief biography, cf. the obituary in (1906), 21 *Annuaire IDI*, pp. 480–485.
[20] Frantz Despagnet, *La diplomatie de la troisième république et le droit des gens* (Paris, Sirey, 1904), pp. 393–395.
[21] Despagnet, *La diplomatie de la troisième république*, pp. 117–119.
[22] Despagnet, *La diplomatie de la troisième république*, pp. 22–70.

and emphasized French recognition of the rights of the indigenous populations.[23] It was France that had prevented Britain and Germany from using their colonial protectorates as veiled annexations at Berlin 1884–1885. Despagnet fully endorsed the explanation that the establishment of the French protectorate over Tunisia in 1881 was carried out in self-defense to prevent hostile incursions into Algerian territory.[24] In Egypt, the problem was Britain's predominance and inconsistency: France had nothing but a wish to see the Ottoman Empire's (of which Egypt was a formal part) integrity respected. In the French Sudan, expansion was a natural necessity; resisting chiefs such as the formidable Samori were characterised as aggressors, "ambitious, cruel and treacherous."[25] In Madagascar, the Radical Government's war against the "rebel" Hovas was carried out in 1895–1896: "with a remarkable moderation by General Duchesne whose humanitarian orders were fully carried out by his troops; . . . the most flattering testimony of their humanitarian spirit and discipline was given spontaneously by foreign correspondents."[26] If the war in Madagascar – like that in Annam a few years earlier – was conducted against a protected power, these were wars of necessity, Despagnet argued, brought about by the protected power on itself. Only when it turned into de facto annexation in breach of the confidence of the Hovas, did Despagnet find reason for criticism.[27]

Despagnet's France was a politically vulnerable nation, striving to enhance its position with morally and legally justifiable action against a Britain envious of its victories in the colonies and a Germany fearful of its desire of *revanche* in Europe. If France lost – as it did in Egypt in 1882 – this was not only a tragedy for France but a blow to world peace.[28] The ambivalence of Despagnet's characterization of French policy at the Berlin Conference could be applied generally to the way French internationalists saw the relations between France and the world: "it is by advocating moral considerations at diplomatic assemblies that the vanquished France could first reconquer the position in the world that belongs to it."[29] This is to repeat the Revolutionary ethos of 1789:

---

[23] Despagnet, *La diplomatie de la troisième république*, p. 128.
[24] Had not France received a free hand from Salisbury three years earlier but held back from taking action as Tunisia was, after all, an independent country? Despagnet, *La diplomatie de la troisième république*, p. 77.
[25] Despagnet, *La diplomatie de la troisième république*, p. 403.
[26] Despagnet, *La diplomatie de la troisième république*, pp. 710–711.
[27] Despagnet, *La diplomatie de la troisième république*, pp. 714–716.
[28] Despagnet, *La diplomatie de la troisième république*, p. 294.
[29] Despagnet, *La diplomatie de la troisième république*, p. 285.

natural liberty and the general will come together in an idea that is France itself. A few years later, in reconquered Strasbourg Redslob contemplated the effect of *la Grande Guerre* on this idea. It had broken Europe in two. It had interrupted the slow recognition of the revolutionary principles. Nevertheless:

> French soldiers have carried the Gospel of human rights to the frontiers of civilized Europe. After Leipzig and Waterloo, their flags were torn from conquered monuments. But the monuments of justice and truth that they have built among peoples have stood. The France of the Revolution conquered Europe by the arms of the spirit. What the France of 1789 did for the people, the France of 1914 did for nations. The France of Valmy, of Jammapes and Fleurys fought for individual liberty, the France of Marne fought for the liberty of the Universe. She will achieve her brilliant aim. The uncertainties and detours in which today's diplomacy confounds are but a passing mist through which the people will climb to the light of summits. The idea will always triumph. *And the idea, it is France.*[30]

From civilists to functionalists 1874–1918: Renault to Pillet

"The idea of France" – in legal terms, this was certainly the *Code Civil*. No wonder that the study of law in France was dominated by the exegetic school through most of the nineteenth century. Legal doctrine consisted of textual commentary on the *Code* and even discussion of court practice was viewed with suspicion. Indeed, "[r]arely in history has a single movement been predominant for so long and so totally as was this school in nineteenth-century France and Belgium."[31] Not amenable to the methodological strictures of exegesis, and sidelined by the Napoleonic system that transformed the *Ecoles de droit* principally into training schools for judges and *avocats*,[32] international law remained a rather marginal academic topic in France until late in the century – a kind of a specialized part of natural law. When Charles Giraud retired from the chair in Paris (the only international law professorship in France at the time) in 1874 the post was temporarily and without enthusiasm filled by Louis Renault (1843–1918) from Dijon, whose previous writing and experience had been exclusively in the fields of Roman and

---

[30] Redslob, "La doctrine idéaliste," p. 456, italics in original.
[31] R. C. Van Caenegem, *An Historical Introduction to Private Law* (Cambridge University Press, 1988), p. 148. For the variants of the exegetic school, cf. also André-Jean Arnaud, *Les juristes face à la société du XIXe siècle à nos jours* (Paris, PUF, 1975), pp. 45–74.
[32] "Les études de droit international dans les facultés de droit françaises" (1962), VIII *Annuaire français de droit international* (*AFDI*), p. 1233.

commercial law.[33] Having been permanently appointed to the chair in 1881, Renault held the position for 36 years, becoming "the personification of the French conception of international law for almost a half-century."[34] Much of his career and certainly much of his fame was based on activities outside the university. In 1890 Renault was appointed *jurisconsulte-conseil* at the *Quai d'Orsay* in which capacity he wrote legal briefs for the minister and represented France at much of the diplomacy of the time, including both Hague Peace Conferences.[35] He was the most frequently used member of the Permanent Court of Arbitration, participating in seven of the fourteen cases that were brought to it during his lifetime.[36] His bearded figure towers over the development of French international law until the First World War. For those for whom the war did away with the respectability of the old diplomatic system, it was his brand of pragmatism that seemed in need of reform.

Renault's appointment came at a time when the "privatism" of the *Code Civil* had come under increasing strain. The view that the law's principal mission was to regulate relations between private individuals provided a poor basis for the development of public law and failed to account for new legislation dealing with the social problems of an emerging industrialized economy. Until the 1870s, even public law had been based on the voluntarist principles of the Napoleonic code that saw the State as a compact between mature citizens.[37] The same construction had been projected onto international law as well. The 1862 prize essay of Eugène Cauchy (1802–1877) on the law of the sea submitted to the *Académie des sciences politiques et morales,* for example, examined its subject on a purely rationalist basis. It projected States as persons who, like individuals, had rights that belonged to them by virtue of their personhood: the right to defend oneself and to work for one's perfectioning. Each State was free – just like each individual – to the extent that its freedom did not violate that of other States. The rights of States at sea were derived from natural law: the freedom of the seas, the concept of

---

[33] Cf. Paul Fauchille, "Nécrologie Louis Renault (1843–1918)" (1918), XXV *RGDIP*, pp. 8–14; Albert de Lapradelle, *Maîtres et doctrines du droit des gens* (2nd edn., Paris, Editions internationales, 1950), pp. 249–261.

[34] J. Bonnecase, *La pensée juridique française. De 1804 à l'heure présent* (2 vols., Bordeaux, Delmas, 1933), I, p. 417.

[35] For an extremely detailed review of his work at diplomatic conferences, cf. Fauchille, "Nécrologie Louis Renault," pp. 36–104.

[36] Fauchille, "Nécrologie Louis Renault," pp. 104–107.

[37] On the "privatist"–"publicist" battle in France in 1840–1880, cf. Arnaud, *Les juristes*, pp. 37–45.

the territorial sea, right of passage, and other norms were consequences of the nature of those areas, their non-appropriability and their character as ways of access to resources or other sea areas. Within this rationalist framework, Cauchy described the development of maritime history in five periods that peaked in the contemporaneous ideas of freedom of the seas, contraband, and maritime neutrality, marvellously underwriting everything the French had always argued against the British.[38]

By contrast, in 1877 Théophile Funck-Brentano (1830–1906) of the *Ecole libre des sciences sociales* and Albert Sorel (1842–1906), a diplomatic historian with the *Académie Française*, published an overview of the field without a word about natural rights or indeed about theory or method, describing international law as the practices of nineteenth-century diplomacy: formal relations between sovereigns, treaties, intervention, recognition, responsibility, war, and neutrality. Theirs was a practitioner's handbook: it discussed the advantages of protocol, the political consequences of treaty relations and excluded from the law everything that did come under reciprocal obligation or common interest. That the book came from outside the law faculties, and paid no attention to how the matter was dealt with in standard British, Italian, or German textbooks was strikingly visible in its awkward theory of political causality as international law's sanction: history, the authors suggested, will revenge illegality.[39]

So when Renault reviewed the field in 1879, he concluded that little had been written in France that was up to date. Appreciating the "often profound" reflections in Funck-Brentano and Sorel, he felt their spirit "more philosophical or political than juridical," and noted their relative ignorance of legal doctrine which they sometimes assimilated to that of the "dreamers and utopians" of the *Sociétés de la paix*.[40] Renault's writing established the subject in France in the spirit of the European mainstream as represented by the work of the *Institut de droit international*. The law was still justified by rationalist arguments and the organization of the materials was received from Justinian's *Institutes:* persons, things, obligations, and forms of action (including war!). Like civil law, the law of nations had to do with guaranteeing the widest possible liberty for States compatible with the equal liberty of others.[41] "From the simultaneous existence of equally independent nations it is possible to derive rationally

---

[38] Eugène Cauchy, *Le droit maritime international considéré dans ses origines et dans ses rapports avec les progrès de la civilisation* (Paris, Guillaumin, 1862).
[39] Th. Funck-Brentano and A. Sorel, *Précis du droit des gens* (3rd edn., Paris, Plon, 1900).
[40] Louis Renault, *Introduction à l'étude de droit international* (Paris, Larose, 1879), pp. 48–49.
[41] Renault, *Introduction*, p. 6.

rules."[42] To this extent, international law was "not a creation of will, it [was] anterior to the constitution of States and the organization of different social powers."[43] These points were accompanied, however, by sociological and economic arguments: France sent its wine and its art everywhere to receive cotton and coffee, gold, and silver in exchange. Division of labor, as well as the development of science and technology, were creating a common patrimony of humanity, expressed in increasing numbers of treaties and converging forms of State behavior.

This is why it was unnecessary to continue the dispute between the rational and historical schools, debates "aussi confuses et aussi ennuyeuses qu'inutiles."[44] For Renault, international law was an eminently practical part of the diplomatic sciences, the professional technique of men of international affairs – not an abstract derivation from the nature of the State or an instrument towards world government. Renault was completely against intervention in the internal affairs of States for humanitarian reasons, defining war as a pure fact and the laws of war a consequence of the prohibition of purposeless violence.[45] On the other hand, he lamented the lack of interest in France in international affairs: for those planning a diplomatic career, it was imperative to know the point of view of other peoples, he argued. Hence most of his 1879 *Introduction* is taken by lists of *recueils* and manuals of treaties and official acts, with comments on their usefulness, as well as instructions on how to infer general rules from them.

Although Renault did commend Bergbohm's ultrapositivistic writings to his readers,[46] there is no evidence that he would have been deeply influenced by German *Staatsrechtslehre*. His narrow doctrinal production arose from a civilist background and the domestic–rationalist analogy while the substance of his work never dwelt on the problems of such old-fashioned theory: for him, international law was not philosophy but a professional technique.[47] Renault never published a larger monograph.

[42] Renault, *Introduction*, p. 11.   [43] Renault, *Introduction*, p. 8.
[44] Renault, *Introduction*, p. 12.
[45] Renault, *Introduction*, pp. 18–19; Louis Renault "Préface," in Robert Jacomet, *Les lois de la guerre continentale* (Paris, Fournier, 1913), p. 9.   [46] Renault, *Introduction*, p. 25n1.
[47] During more than thirty years of teaching in Paris, his general course underwent only minor modifications, the most important of which was, perhaps, the replacement of a separate treatment of the position of individuals by an examination of the law of territory. For the programs of his courses at the University of Paris, at the *Ecole libre des sciences politiques* and the *Ecole supérieure de la marine*, cf. the annexes to Fauchille, "Nécrologie Louis Renault," pp. 148–229. This change may have been occasioned by the separation of matters of private international law as their own topic, and the emergence, towards the end of the century, of something like a coherent body of case-law to teach.

Practically all of his teaching and writing took the form of commentary on contemporary events, conferences, and disputes of which he often had first-hand experience.[48] In writing about international unions, unlike most jurists of the period, he refrained from speculating about whether they could be interpreted as an emerging international administration or the first steps towards federalism. He understood them as forms of technical assistance to European diplomacy whose functions were limited to co-ordination of sovereign politics.[49] Like Rolin, Westlake, and the other members of the *Institut* (whom he joined in 1878 as an associate and in 1882 as a full member), he wished to contribute to a rational diplomatic system between existing (European) States, not in undermining it. Although he was awarded the Nobel Peace Prize in 1907 for his role in the two Hague Peace Conferences, he never participated in the peace movement – indeed he would probably have seen such activities as mutually exclusive.

By the 1890s additional chairs of international law were set up in such provincial universities as Bordeaux, Grenoble, and Toulouse.[50] A significant event was the establishment of the *Revue générale de droit international public* (*RGDIP*) at Renault's initiative in 1894 that from the outset adopted a profile indicative of the extent of its mentor's influence. Where Germans continued to agonize over the existence or binding force of international law, and particularly its relationship to domestic (public) law, the *Revue* focused on on-going disputes, conferences, and conventions with large recent events and documentary sections. Its outlook was professional–technical and avowedly nationalist: that international law was a beneficial part of the conventions of diplomacy was as much a forgone conclusion as the fact that among European States

---

[48] His most important publication, however, is the two-volume *Précis de droit commercial*, published together with Charles Lyon-Caen in 1884–1885 plus a *Manuel* and a *Traité* on the same subject, each of which went into several editions in the early twentieth century. These works stressed the need to focus on practice instead of continuing commentary on the increasingly obsolete provisions of the *Code Civil* or the 1807 Commercial Code. To examine practice instead of old texts was particularly necessary in order to capture the international conditions of an enormously expanded commerce. *Traité de droit commercial* (2nd edn., 2 vols., Paris, Pichon, 1889), I, pp. vi–x, 38–63.

[49] Cf. Louis Renault, "Les unions internationales. Leurs avantages et leurs inconvénients" (1896), III *RGDIP*, pp. 14–26.

[50] A discussion of the reform of law teaching had been underway since the 1860s but only with the reforms of 1878, 1880 and 1889 did all faculties start teaching constitutional, administrative and international law as well as political economy and finance. Cf. Henri Berthélemy, *L'Ecole de droit* (Paris, LGDJ, 1932), pp. 8–11.

only France was sincerely committed to the advancement of an international rule of law. Politics entered the journal normally in connection with commentary on recent events such as the Fashoda crisis, the Egyptian debt question or events in the Far East. To the extent that the foreign policy of the Third Republic was largely a colonial policy, the *Revue* followed closely national priorities. Leafing through the first twenty volumes of the *Revue*, it almost seems as if international law's field of application was between European powers acting *outside* Europe – as if intra-European questions concerned policy and commerce, but not of law.[51] The question of Alsace–Lorraine emerged regularly but it was still a rare exception when in 1899 – the year of Fashoda – Paul Fauchille drew attention to the "Anglo-Saxon peril" he observed alongside the "yellow" one and called upon continental Europe to form a customs union with prohibitive external tariffs as well as a political–military alliance against British and American predominance.[52]

Paul Fauchille (1858–1926) was one of his two students that Renault chose as editors of the *Revue*. He was a real *flâneur* who never occupied a university or administrative position but worked at home with a wide array of publishing projects in history and international law as well as initiatives with the *Institut*. In 1919 Fauchille became one of the founders and the first Secretary-General of the *Institut des hautes études internationales* with the University of Paris. It was Fauchille who declared that the purpose of the *Revue* was to defend the rights and interests of France – a declaration that has been benevolently but not incorrectly interpreted as meaning that he associated French interest with the universal interest.[53] It was not by coincidence that Fauchille began his 1911 report to the *Institut de droit international* on the customary laws of naval warfare by the observation that the very idea of drafting such rules on the basis of humanitarian ideas could be traced back to Napoleon.[54] Fauchille was a man of facts and details and thus well suited to edit the *Revue*'s

---

[51] The recurrent anarchist attacks in Europe in the 1890s gave impetus for scholars to publicize their views on the principles of extradition for politically motivated crimes. This, too, was law in the service of the sovereign: the domestic anarchist was analogous to the colonial people – an outsider to the established order, an object of discipline.

[52] Paul Fauchille, "L'Europe nouvelle" (1899), VI *RGDIP*, pp. 1–8.

[53] De Lapradelle, *Maîtres et doctrines*, pp. 302–303 and generally pp. 263–306. Fauchille did his doctorate for Renault in Paris on the question of maritime blockade: *Du blocus maritime, étude de droit international et de droit comparé* (Paris, Rousseau, 1882). His two historical works are *Question juive en France sous le premier empire* (Paris, Rousseau, 1884) and *La diplomatie française et la ligue des neutres 1887–83* (Paris, Pedone-Lauriel 1913 [1892]).

[54] Paul Fauchille, "Rapport préliminaire et questionnaire; manuel des lois de la guerre maritime" (1912), 25 *Annuaire IDI*, p. 42.

chronique section. His articles, too, were often commentaries on recent events while his activity at the *Institut* focused on the effects of new technology, especially aviation, on international law.

In 1898 Renault chose Fauchille to compile a second edition to Henri Bonfils' (1835–1897) *Manuel de droit international public* which became perhaps the most widely used French textbook. It came out in six editions before 1914 and the eighth edition (under Fauchille's name) was published in 1926 with more than 4,000 pages. This book was an eclectic survey of all fields of international law following the initial author's *civiliste* method – in order not to disturb the habits of French students, he had once remarked. There were five sections: persons, things, peaceful relations, settlement of disputes, and redress (i.e. war). Where German lawyers examined statehood and treaties usually with the ambition of proposing a "system," Fauchille adopted civil law divisions without comment. A short introduction explained that (public) international law was the least developed of the branches of the general science of law. Its object was the study and exposition of the laws governing the coexistence and reciprocal actions of the States that formed a juridical community.[55] There was a sociological and a historical perspective: the reality of international law lay in the fact that States needed rules – to which they consented either expressly or tacitly – in accordance with the "law of sociability – a natural and necessary law, not only for individuals but also for States."[56] On the other hand, its basis lay in the shared habits and common culture of civilized nations. There was no antagonism between law and politics: compliance with the law was, in the long run, also in the interests of individual States.[57] In the great conferences of the nineteenth century the European nations had "recognized the solidarity that united them as members of an international community."[58]

Bonfils–Fauchille was throughout a practical, non-formalist book that summarized much of the teaching of other books – those of Bluntschli, Holtzendorff, and Twiss – and the diplomacy of the nineteenth century. The only full subjects of international law were States – though both individuals and the Pope had certain functional rights. Statehood depended on the social fact of the existence de facto of States – but the enjoyment of sovereign rights depended on recognition, that is, on politics. If non-Christian entities could not be treated as States, this was

---

[55] Henri Bonfils and Paul Fauchille, *Manuel de droit international public* (2nd edn., Paris, Rousseau, 1898), p. 27.   [56] Bonfils–Fauchille, *Manuel*, p. 3.
[57] Bonfils–Fauchille, *Manuel*, pp. 28–29.   [58] Bonfils–Fauchille, *Manuel*, p. 7.

simply a reflection of the fact that they did not possess "un système commun de morale, qui assure entre elles la réprocité des droits et des devoirs."[59] There was only one fundamental right – the right to existence. Every other right followed as a conceptual derivation from it. If in some cases such rights were violated – the right of non-intervention, for example, was constantly breached by the United States and Britain – Bonfils–Fauchille simply noted this as part of international law's weakness but not as a theoretical challenge.[60]

By the 1880s French lawyers had generally begun to depart from the canons of exegesis. Absolute freedom of contract or unchallenged right of property were unable to deal with the social ills of the Third Republic and to check the advance of socialist ideals.[61] The emergence of a collectivist radical–liberalism in French politics was paralleled in law schools by new anti-literalist, sociologically oriented civil and public law teaching such as François Gény's (1861–1959) influential distinction between the juridical "*donné*" and "*construit*," a theory of the juridical science as a method for finding the law embedded in actual social relations ("donné") and a technique for constructing normative principles out of the purposes of positive law.[62] But neither Gény's hermeneutics nor the sociological or institutionalist public law doctrines by Saleilles, Hauriou, or Duguit produced an immediate effect on French international law. On the other hand, the very emergence of international law in the *facultés* in the 1880s had to do with the expansion of legal culture.[63] To counter the skeptics, sociology seemed needed: *ubi societas, ibi jus*. This was Renault's strategy and followed in Bonfils–Fauchille as well. Nonetheless, it seems as if Renault and Fauchille exhausted their innovative resources by moving to international law from the legal mainstream. Speaking already from the margin, they wished to prove international law's seriousness by demonstrating that it could be practiced as technically as any other law, with as much attention to detail as in civil or criminal law – as if justifying their profession could be achieved only by a condescending nod from the legal center.

By contrast, two articles that did seek to advance the theory of international law in the first decade of the *Revue* were both written by Fauchille's co-editor Antoine Pillet, a civilist from Grenoble who

---

[59] Bonfils–Fauchille, *Manuel*, p. 106.   [60] Bonfils–Fauchille, *Manuel*, pp. 146–160.
[61] Van Caenegem, *An Historical Introduction*, pp. 150–151; Arnaud, *Les juristes*, pp. 75–86.
[62] François Gény, *Méthode d'interprétation et sources en droit privé positif* (Paris, Bibliothèque de jurisprudence civile contemporaine, 1889).   [63] Arnaud, *Les juristes*, pp. 112–113.

became Renault's adjunct in Paris in 1896. In a paper on the constitutive elements, domain, and object of international law that opened the first issue of the *Revue* Pillet foreshadowed the direction of later sociological jurisprudence.[64] Five years later he expanded on his views in a much-quoted article on the role of fundamental rights of States which both grounded international law analogously to liberal law but also defined and delimited these rights from the perspective of the society in which they were to operate.[65] Pillet – the "philosopher" among early French internationalists[66] – applied to international law precisely those criticisms that had been used to attack the individualism of the *Code Civil*.

In the former article, Pillet distinguished between "human law" that was universal but on whose practical application there was much controversy and international law proper that was a law between States – or, more accurately, between (European) States that shared similar ideas about statehood and its social functions.[67] Because the convention of the profession was then (as it has remained since) not to refer to extraneous sources for one's arguments, Pillet apologized to his readers for his brief entry into "social philosophy." International law was premised upon the existence of an international society. That such society existed followed from "interdependence, the social law of our era."[68] It was a sociological mistake to think of States as independent and to conceive this in the language of fundamental rights. Pillet dissociated himself, however, from German *Interessenjurisprudenz*. Interests were irreducibly heterogeneous and without a standpoint from which their conflict could be settled.[69] Moreover, States were no autonomous beings having independent

[64] Antoine Pillet, "Le droit international public, ses éléments constitutifs, son domaine, son objet" (1894), I *RGDIP*, pp. 1–32.
[65] Antoine Pillet, "Recherches sur les droits fondamentaux des Etats dans l'ordre des rapports internationaux et sur la solution des conflits qu'ils font naître" (1898), V *RGDIP*, pp. 66–89 (Part 1), 236–264 (Part 2), and (1899), VI *RGDIP*, pp. 503–532 (Part 3). [66] De Lapradelle, *Maîtres et doctrines*, pp. 308–310.
[67] Pillet, "Le droit international public," pp. 13–18. For Pillet as for others, non-European entities could not be treated in the same way as European States because they did not possess this idea of State functions, Pillet, "Le droit international public," p. 25. To be sure, the European ideas were a reflection of the advanced degree of European civilization and "le degré de civilisation de chaque peuple est la mesure de ses droits," Pillet, "Le droit international public," p. 24.
[68] Pillet, "Recherches sur les droits fondamentaux," 1, p. 89. No-one can live alone and for a State to try to do this was to commit suicide, Pillet wrote, with disguised reference to Durkheim whose *Suicide: Etude de sociologie*, that made precisely the point of loneliness (anomie) as a cause of suicide in modern industrial society had come out in the previous year.
[69] Pillet "Recherches sur les droits fondamentaux," 2, pp. 242 *et seq*.

International law as sociology: France 1871–1950

interests of their own but rather instruments or functions of their communities and the conflicts between them were conflicts between such functions: "the State has no other *raison d'être* than the functions it exercises towards the subjects which are under its authority."[70] International law neither emerged from, nor reflected State interests. It arose from activities whereby States in their external relations sought to realize the objectives of their national communities. Its basis was not mere consent (though consent was one of its sources) but the necessity that States coordinate their activities to fulfill their functions.[71]

What was special about international conflicts, Pillet argued further, was that in them one public interest clashed with another public interest – the realization of the functions of one State were prevented by the pursuit of its functions by another.[72] To resolve such conflicts, a theory was needed that would establish a hierarchy of functions. It was remarkable that no such theory had been so far created, Pillet wrote, and saw his own work as path-breaking in this respect.[73] In his view, the significance of functions could be assessed only in reference to their importance to the relevant national communities. The less important function should then give way to the more important one in accordance with the "law of the least sacrifice."[74]

Pillet also applied his functionalist theses in his prolific work on private international law, arguing that conflicts of law should be resolved by reference to the social purposes of the laws, by especial attention to whether they were meant as permanent or general.[75] The theses did not

---

[70] Pillet "Recherches sur les droits fondamentaux," 3, p. 505. Likewise, Pillet "Le droit international public," pp. 4–5.
[71] Pillet, "Le droit international public," pp. 10–11.
[72] Pillet, "Recherches sur les droits fondamentaux," 3, p. 503.
[73] Pillet, "Recherches sur les droits fondamentaux," 2, pp. 244–256. A State had three functions towards the national community: conservation of the community, the administration of its affairs and seeing to its progress, responding to the need of provision for internal order, freedom and justice. "Recherches sur les droits fondamentaux," 3, pp. 510–521.
[74] Pillet, "Recherches sur les droits fondamentaux," 2, p. 244. Such a view did not hold States to be subjects of rights but instruments for the fulfillment of the purposes of national communities. State sovereignty, Pillet argued, was not to be respected because it encompassed the existential freedom of the State but because it denoted respect for the State's duties towards its citizens. Thus, for example, if what was important was "function" and not formal sovereignty, then it could be explained how private individuals or companies could sometimes carry out public administration or undertake actions in the colonies that amounted to acquisition of territory. Pillet, "Le droit international public," pp. 31–32.
[75] A law intended as permanent would then overrule a territorially limited law and a law intended as general would overrule a personal status conferred by foreign law. Cf. Antoine Pillet, *Principes de droit international privé* (Paris, Pedone, 1903).

initially provoke a methodological debate in the *Revue* or elsewhere, perhaps because they reflected ideas about interdependence and solidarity that had become a commonplace in French legal and political debate in the 1890s and were anyway far from suggesting revolutionary changes to legal practice. A sort of functionalism *avant-la-lettre* had been part of the profession's cosmopolitanism from the beginning; dressing it in sociological language became necessary only when cosmopolitanism seemed endangered – that is to say, after the war.[76]

Solidarity at the Hague: Léon Bourgeois

In a series of commentaries on the First Hague Peace Conference of 1899 professors Despagnet and Aléxandre Mérignhac (1857–1927) from Toulouse proudly highlighted the central role that the French delegation had had in trying to get the best possible result out of the Russian proposals on disarmament and directing the debate to the more fruitful avenue of the setting up of a permanent body for dispute settlement. Britain, Germany, Austria, and Italy had been impossible, egoistic trouble-makers: was France not the only State that joined Russia in signing all the conventions adopted at the Hague?[77] Two members of the French delegation were accredited for having played a decisive role in preventing the Conference from failure. One of them was Louis Renault, who participated in the modest capacity as a technical delegate but became the rapporteur of the Second Commission that prepared the draft Convention on the laws and customs of war and headed the difficult negotiations of the drafting committee for the Final Act of the Conference. In fact, Renault seemed to have been everywhere during the Conference and gradually came to be considered its unofficial legal adviser. Contemporaries praised Renault's drafting technique, his legal mind and his diplomatic courtesy. This was where he made his international reputation: "Il vint à la Conférence en Français, il la quitta en citoyen du monde."[78]

But if Renault was the indefatigable drafter, the *Maître* of legal technique, Léon Bourgeois (1851–1925) was not only the chairman but also

---

[76] At that time, Pillet's views were cited as representative for a relativist or objectivist theory on sovereignty, cf. Georges Scelle, "La guerre civile espagnole et le droit des gens" (1938), XLV *RGDIP*, pp. 292–293.

[77] F. Despagnet and A. Mérignhac, "Opinion sur la Conférence de la Haye et ses résultats" (1900), VI *RGDIP*, pp. 879, 881.

[78] J. B. Scott, *Les Conférences de la paix de la Haye de 1899 et 1907* (Carnegie Endowment for International Peace (3 vols., Oxford, Clarendon, 1927), I, pp. 151–152.

the ideologist of the French delegation which he had chosen to head in 1899 instead of accepting the offer from the President of the Republic to form a new government. Bourgeois was a lawyer, active freemason, former (and future) minister, and former Prime Minister (1895–1896), one of the most influential men in turn-of-the-century France. Since Clemenceau's temporary withdrawal from the leadership of the Radical (liberal) party in 1893 Bourgeois had been its ideological leader. After the resignation of his government in 1896 he published a small pamphlet, *Solidarité*, that advocated a third way between retreating *laissez-faire* liberalism and ascendant socialism, emphasizing the duties that citizens owed to each other and suggested far-reaching social legislation to deal with the consequences of the great depression of 1873–1895. The book became an enormous success and the policy of "solidarism" it promoted "the official social philosophy of the Third Republic."[79]

At the Hague Bourgeois chose to sit in the First Commission that dealt with the Russian disarmament proposals. As is well known, the proposals came to naught. Being the politician he was, Bourgeois could not accept that no report or proposal could be adopted. Perhaps a generally worded statement might be acceptable so as to show the world that the delegations had at least tried their best. In a characteristic argument, Bourgeois pointed out to his colleagues that they were in the Conference not only to cast private votes but to give expression to general ideas. One of these was the burden that armaments put on the European national economies. And he proposed that the Conference express its opinion: "that the restriction of military charges, which are at present a heavy burden on the world, is extremely desirable for the increase of the material and moral welfare of mankind."[80] The economic argument for pacifism had been part of French liberal radicalism and socialism since Constant and Proudhon early in the century. With Bourgeois, the technique of dealing with a political difficulty by a recital of an apparently incontrovertible socio-economic fact was introduced into the conventions of multilateral diplomacy. The Conference not only agreed to express this *voeu* but repeated its gist eight years later to get away from

---

[79] J. E. S. Hayward, "The Official Social Philosophy of the French Third Republic: Léon Bourgeois and Solidarism," *VI International Review of Social History* (1961), p. 21. Cf. also Theodore Zeldin, *France 1848–1945* (2 vols., Oxford, Clarendon, 1973–1977), 1, pp. 656–658 and for a colorful description of Bourgeois, R. E. Kaplan, *Forgotten Crisis. The Fin-de-siècle Crisis of Democracy in France* (Oxford, Berg, 1995), pp. 41–43.
[80] *The Proceedings of the Hague Peace Conferences: The Conference of 1899* (Carnegie Endowment of International Peace, under the supervision of J. B. Scott, Oxford University Press, 1920), p. 319.

the analogous difficulty that arose in connection with the Second Peace Conference.[81]

Bourgeois chaired the Third Commission as well as the smaller *comité d'examen* that discussed pacific settlement and ended up proposing the establishment of the Permanent Court of Arbitration. France supported the surprise British move to set up a permanent tribunal and Bourgeois even suggested that its bureau should be given right of initiative. If commentators have credited the success of the Third Commission to Bourgeois (together with the Belgian Descamps), it is not difficult to see to what extent this must have followed from his technique of insisting on the neutrality of the provisions. Bourgeois – and French commentators – were especially proud of the success the delegation had in inserting into the draft a provision on the duty of every State to remind parties to a conflict of their obligations of peaceful settlement. To a Serbian delegate who was concerned that such a provision could be used as a means to exert pressure on weak States, Bourgeois responded: "there are neither great nor small Powers here; all are equal before the work to be accomplished . . . when it is a question of weighing rights, there is no longer any inequality, and the rights of the smaller and weakest weigh just as much on the scales as the rights of the greatest."[82]

Bourgeois was appointed to the French Senate in 1905 and became Minister of Foreign Affairs the following year. He defended the results of the Hague with great energy, interpreting them as an emanation of solidarity between civilized nations.[83] Somewhat like Schücking (though without reference to him) Bourgeois felt that the Conferences had organized the common will of participating States: "It is possible to recognize there the first features of a Society of Nations."[84] In addresses to the National Assembly and learned societies Bourgeois explained that the Conferences were a tangible illustration of solidarism in action: peace through law had become one of the "*idée-forces*" of which the solidarist philosopher Fouillée had written.[85] There now existed a large

---

[81] *The Proceedings of the Hague Peace Conferences: The Conference of 1907* (Carnegie Endowment of International Peace, under the supervision of J. B. Scott, Oxford University Press, 1920), p. 90.
[82] Third Commission, Seventh Meeting, July 20, 1889, *Proceedings 1899*, pp. 663–664.
[83] Léon Bourgeois, "Préface," in A. Mérignhac, *La Conférence internationale de la paix* (Paris, Rousseau, 1900), p. vii.
[84] Léon Bourgeois, *Pour la société des nations* (Paris, Fasquelle, 1910), pp. 214–216, 272–286.
[85] Bourgeois, *Pour la société des nations*, pp. 23–26, 167. Cf. also Bourgeois, "Discours à l'Institut de droit international" (1910), 23 *Annuaire IDI*, pp. 365–373 and e.g. Alfred Fouillée, *L'Evolutionnisme des idées-forces* (Paris, Alcan, 1890).

International law as sociology: France 1871–1950

number of conventional obligations, an arbitral court and a Prize Court as well as isolated provisions on sanctions. The new system had been seen in successful action in the dangerous Franco-German *Casablanca* affair in 1908–1909. Above all, the new provision that recognized the duty (*devoir*) of parties to remind any State in conflict of its peaceful settlement obligations was, Bourgeois opined, a manifestation of a new relationship between States "that are no longer the passive neutrals but neighbors in solidarity with the obligation to maintain general peace."[86]

Unlike his German colleagues, Bourgeois had no hesitation in referring to the increasing visibility of peace societies as evidence of the new spirit. Where classical diplomacy had sought peace in the balance of power, the work of the Hague aimed at peace through law and the creation of a "universal conscience."[87] To be sure, no progress had been made in disarmament – although the *voeu* expressed in 1899 and 1907 was not meaningless, either.[88] Compulsory arbitration and a permanent court still remained unachieved – but Bourgeois remained hopeful about the diplomatic compromise of 1907 that accepted compulsory arbitration "in principle."[89] In this he was not alone. Mérignhac's detailed study of the 1899 Conference concluded that the failures were outweighed by the fact that so many States, large and small, continental and maritime, had come together in a common effort. What had produced this, he felt, was "quite simply the sentiment of international solidarity that could be felt in all of this co-operation and that soon united those that had been previously separated by so many elements."[90]

It is hard to say how much of this enthusiasm was genuine. During the Boer War Bourgeois defended the work of the Hague by the strategy of small steps: peace could not be created overnight, the conventions were also to educate governments and peoples, cautioning against skepticism and impatience.[91] There is no doubt that the Conference atmosphere – the friendly collegiality among the delegations, a sense of historical mission – made an impression on him. Although he was sorry that little could be attained in disarmament and compulsory arbitration, he stressed the importance of the laws of war and peaceful settlement. Perhaps he was truly thinking that a sense of solidarity and good will was

---

[86] Quoted in Mérignhac, *La Conférence internationale*, p. 393.
[87] Bourgeois, *Pour la société des nations*, pp. 12–18, 166–173.
[88] Bourgeois, *Pour la société des nations*, pp. 132–133.
[89] Cf. "Rapport sur la deuxième Conference de la Paix (1907), addressé au Ministère des Affaires Etrangères," in Bourgeois, *Pour la société des nations*, pp. 193–194.
[90] Mérignhac, *La Conférence internationale*, p. 369.
[91] Bourgeois, *Pour la société des nations*, pp. 166–173.

spreading in Europe – but it is hard to understand how he failed to see the skies darkening.

The theory of solidarism

After the Hague Conferences Bourgeois was hailed as "the apostle of global harmony based upon disarmament and arbitration."[92] However, his solidarism was initially conceived for the French political environment. It is frequently overlooked that although the French Third Republic suffered from endemic governmental discontinuity (there were altogether fifty-four cabinets between 1875 and 1914) the same persons tended to re-emerge as ministers and that while elsewhere in Western Europe the electoral base of liberalism was narrowing, in France centrist (liberal–Radical) governments continued to rule on their own or with support from the socialists. This state of affairs was largely owing to the appeal enjoyed by a solidarist theory that suggested putting into effect the social reforms implied in the political program of 1789 – and to forestall the left from initiating a new political revolution.[93]

Bourgeois and his liberal radicals were steadfast opponents of *privatisme* and *laissez-faire*, arguing for increased State intervention through social legislation and support for voluntary association: from the early 1890s they had initiated various social insurance and pensions schemes, the limitation of the working day, and educational reforms, all of which were to be financed by progressive income and inheritance taxation.[94] Although governmental weakness or simple lack of nerve sometimes prevented the full realization of the Radical–left program, solidarism emerged as the title for a kind of social-democratic modernization of "liberty, equality, and fraternity" – with Bourgeois sometimes arguing all three as applications of solidarity, sometimes describing solidarity as the legal–political form for the emotionally loaded but somewhat disreputable revolutionary idea of "fraternity."[95] Solidarist vocabulary united many kinds of

---

[92] J. E. S. Hayward, "The Official Social Philosophy of the French Third Republic: Léon Bourgeois and Solidarism" (1961), VI *International Review of Social History*, p. 24.
[93] Therefore, socialist co-option was violently opposed by revolutionary syndicalists such as Georges Sorel. Cf., e.g., Norman Stone, *Europe Transformed 1878–1919* (2nd edn., Oxford, Blackwell, 1999), pp. 203–206, 220–226.
[94] On solidarism and French radicalism, cf. Zeldin, *France*, pp. 641–724; Hayward, "The Official Social Philosophy," pp. 34–41; and especially Michel Borgetto, *La notion de fraternité en droit public français. Le passé, le présent et l'avenir de la solidarité* (Paris, LGDJ, 1991), pp. 380–382 and the analysis of "solidarist" legislation 1890–1914, pp. 420–507.
[95] Léon Bourgeois, *Solidarité* (7th edn., Paris, Colin, 1912), pp. 105–106. Cf. also Borgetto, *La notion de fraternité*, pp. 345–350.

political movements.[96] Catholic conservatives, for instance, used it to oppose the liberalism that "exalts the individual" and the socialism which "crushes the individual," and sought from it a communitarian principle that could be associated with moral and religious revival.[97]

Solidarism was characterized less by a definitive agenda than by a general aversion to the absolutism of individual rights and an emotional preference for social responsibility. In the *facultés de droit* many jurists were developing sociologically oriented, collectivist, or even socialist theories to support an interventionist public realm. In this process they were often transformed, to use Arnaud's language, from the "pontiffs" of a self-confident bourgeois society into social "vigilantes" – assistants of a public power keen to reconstruct its legitimacy in the conditions of mass politics and industrialism.[98] Nonetheless, for Bourgeois the juridical sense of *solidarité* (drawn from the *Code Civil*) remained its key sense.[99] Three aspects of it were particularly significant. First, he wrote, it was: "the result of two forces that were for a long time hostile to each other but have recently approached each other and been united in all nations that have reached a superior level of evolution: *the scientific method and the moral idea.*"[100] Bourgeois now theorized solidarism as simultaneously factual and normative in the way of much natural law.[101] Its factual side

---

[96] J. E. S. Hayward describes the history of the concept in three periods. Between 1792 and 1848 it was used as a mystical idea, a "reactionary and irrationalist longing for a lost social stability and unity." In 1848 it became politicized and denoted an agenda of social reform first of a far-reaching but after 1870 of a conciliatory nature. After 1896 it became attached to the electoral program of the radicals – "a dogmatic credo, supported by detailed schemes of social reform," "Solidarity: The Social History of an Idea in Nineteenth-Century France" (1959), IV *International Review of Social History*, pp. 273, 261–284. Cf also Borgetto, *La notion de fraternité*, pp. 344 *et seq.*

[97] Cf. e.g. A. Mazel, *Solidarisme, individualisme & socialisme* (Paris, Bonhoure, 1882).

[98] Cf. Arnaud, *Les juristes*, pp. 86–125. On the activist role of French jurists, largely committed to liberalism in nineteenth-century France, cf. also L. Karpik, "Builders of Liberal Society: French Lawyers and Politics," in T. C. Halliday and L. Karpik (eds.), *Lawyers and the Rise of Western Political Liberalism* (Oxford, Clarendon, 1997), esp. pp. 108–123.

[99] André-Jean Arnaud, "Une doctrine de l'Etat tranquillisante: le solidarisme juridique" (1976), 21 *Archives de philosophie de droit*, p. 133. [100] Bourgeois, *Solidarité*, p. 6.

[101] It was criticized by many contemporaries precisely for making the illegitimate inference from empirical assertions about factual solidarity to normative ones about social justice. Bourgeois tried to deal with this problem by invoking a psychological "sense of justice" as one part of the natural drive towards association that enabled making the distinction between "solidarité de fait" and normative solidarity, "solidarité-devoir." Cf. Bourgeois, *Solidarité*, pp. 129–130, 159–176; Léon Bourgeois, "L'idée de solidarité et ses conséquences sociales," in *Essai d'une philosophie de solidarité. Conférences et discussions* (Paris, Alcan, 1902), pp. 9–17.

– its rootedness in the verifiable conditions of society – was emphasized whenever stress on its scientific basis was needed. Its normative side served as a basis of political and legal reform, for delimiting the proper scope of legislation. It thus participated in a general project of sociological thought to give an objective foundation for ethics.[102] Second, solidarism preached that humans were not born free but as debtors to society.[103] Every citizen owed something to every other citizen, including previous and future generations. This debt was not freely contracted but arose from the fact of membership in human society, and was the price everyone needed to pay for services received.[104] In fact "la Révolution a fait la Déclaration des droits. Il s'agit d'y ajouter la Déclaration des devoirs."[105] Third, Bourgeois invoked the legal concept of the quasi-contract. It was pointless to ask individuals to consent to society: no-one ever existed in an authentic pre-social state. Nonetheless, political obligation could still be linked to consent, namely rational consent to objective law that was "an interpretation and a representation of an agreement that would have been concluded between persons had it been possible to consult them under conditions of equality and freedom."[106] The State, too, was a "quasi-contrat d'association": both contractual and non-contractual, voluntary and compulsory at the same time. Although solidarist lawyers later rejected this construction that derived in part from Kant, in part from a jurisprudence (such as Gény's) that sought to justify judge-made law under the strict literalism of the *Code Civil*, such a dichotomous construction seemed – and still appears for political philosophers such as John Rawls, for instance – the only way to avoid immediate objections that a purely consensual or a purely non-consensual legal theory would encounter. If the language of the "quasi-contrat" no longer seems plausible, the ideas of rational, presumed, hypothetical or tacit consent lay at the heart of twentieth-century political theory.

It was not difficult for international lawyers to associate themselves with solidarism. Arguments about interdependence and rational

[102] Hayward, "Official Social Philosophy," p. 25.
[103] Bourgeois, "L'idée de solidarité," p. 54.
[104] "L'obligation de chacun envers tous ne résulte pas d'une décision arbitraire extérieur aux choses; elle est simplement la contre-partie des avantages que chaqu'un retire de l'état de société, le prix des services que l'association rend à chacun," Bourgeois, "L'idée de solidarité," p. 46. [105] Bourgeois, *Solidarité*, p. 120.
[106] Bourgeois, "L'idée de solidarité," p. 61. For the background of this idea in the views of social obligation of Alfred Fouillée, cf. Kloppenberg, *Uncertain Victory*, pp. 191–192.

consent had been routinely made by the profession to argue why rational States had good reason to feel bound by international law. Much of what little theory Renault had written as well as the introduction to the 1898 edition of Bonfils–Fauchille, for example, set the foundations of international law on interdependence. "Cette belle loi de l'humanité" was factual and normative, voluntary and non-voluntary in precisely the way that had made solidarism such an invaluable political asset in France.[107] Such a view was always only a step away from imagining States as transparent instruments for the advancement of social objectives that were shared perhaps not only by the citizens of the relevant State as Pillet had argued but between individuals everywhere – a conclusion later drawn by federalists such as Georges Scelle.

Yet solidarism was an open-ended term whose very generality explained its usefulness and set limits to what it could attain. Like Bourgeois himself, it was "of great charm, animated by a constant desire to please" – yet also reluctant to assume a firm course.[108] Bourgeois became one of the few anti-Dreyfusards among the Radicals, less out of antisemitism than fear of the consequences of the affair on republicanism generally. In French foreign policy, solidarism had little to say by way of innovation – apart from explaining France's actions as motivated by both national and international concerns. Despite the Radicals' anti-colonial rhetoric, the Bourgeois cabinet of 1895–1896 found itself involved in the awkward colonial war in Madagascar that led from the original aim of enforcing a protectorate to full annexation, behaving in the business, as Despagnet pointed out, with less than good faith towards the indigenous.[109]

The war of 1914–1918 and solidarism

The shock of the First World War – more than 1.5 million French soldiers dead – destroyed many Frenchmen's belief in traditional diplomacy. The violation of Belgium's neutrality as an automatic part of the Schlieffen Plan and the widely publicized violations of the Hague rules committed by German troops in occupied territory – duly enumerated in Renault's study of war crimes at an early stage of the war[110] – also

---

[107] Bonfils–Fauchille, *Manuel*, pp. 4, 3–13.   [108] Zeldin, *France*, pp. 656–657.
[109] Despagnet, *La diplomatie de la troisième république*, pp. 719–724 and e.g. Guillemin, *L'expansion*, pp. 389–392.
[110] Louis Renault, *Les premières violations du droit des gens par l'Allemagne. Luxembourg et Belgique* (Paris, Tenin, 1917).

eroded much of the plausibility of international law. As the news of the attack on Belgium and of the real and imagined atrocities against civilian populations spread in France, Pillet was among the first to conclude that this showed the illusory character of the conventional legal framework. The Hague Conventions had been a sham, a dangerous façade that created a mirage of security. People – Germans in particular – were not the fundamentally rational beings the Hague system presumed: war had been launched out of private caprice and waged without restraint. The lesson drawn by Pillet was that international law could not be created by agreement between diplomats and statesmen or through abstract discussions at conferences. It could emerge only when people and nations had grown to accept it: a civilized people behaved in a civilized way. In the absence of such – "civilized" – culture treaties would remain a hypocrisy:[111] "only the awareness and practice of Christian morality may provide the laws of war the support they need, and it is because they had forgotten this elementary fact that nations are now witnessing with stupor the unforeseen re-emergence of barbarism."[112] The Hague Conferences failed because they worked on the conditions of peace in the abstract, and not on the actual causes of war: the constitution of Poland, the Finnish question, the extermination of the Armenians, or the Balkan situation. Having avoided such "real" issues, the Hague Conferences could end only in failure.

The Versailles Treaty, Pillet wrote in 1919, was a continuation of the same hypocrisy. Instead of making future wars impossible by doing away with the German Empire (through non-recognition) and limiting Prussia's territorial ambitions it was burdened with irrelevant details and utopian aspirations. By not allowing France to occupy the left bank of the Rhine, the door to future German aggression was left open. The treaty was unjust: it should have included provision for immediate reparation, including direction to use German prisoners of war to repair French monuments and villages. Above all, he argued, the League was nonsense. If ever it did emerge it was destined to collapse: "of all the errors that have been committed, this was the worst of all as it penetrated all sections of the treaty and as it now constitutes the largest obstacle for a durable peace."[113] From all this Pillet drew a personal conclusion: apart from a few articles attacking the timidity of the peace

---

[111] Antoine Pillet, *Les leçons de la guerre présent au point de vue de science politique et du droit des gens* (Paris, Plon, 1915); Pillet, "La guerre actuelle et le droit des gens" (1915), XXIII *RGDIP*, pp. 5, 203, 462–471. [112] Pillet, "La guerre actuelle," p. 471.
[113] Antoine Pillet, *Le traité de Versailles* (Paris, Rivière, 1920), p. 37.

and the weakness of the League, he turned away from public to private international law in which he was to spend the rest of his professional life.[114]

While many lawyers pointed at the technical deficiencies of the Hague law,[115] they refrained from seeing *that* as the main problem. Most internationalists, and certainly the French elite, were convinced that war had arisen out of a German grasp at world hegemony, and its conduct had reflected German concepts of sovereignty, *raison d'Etat* (*Kriegsräson*) and *Notrecht*. The German violations had been so blatant, and the law had been so defenseless, that most French politicians felt uneasy speaking of German guilt in positive–legal terms at all; it was an almost metaphysical guilt that was thrust upon Germany, a guilt inadequately encompassed in terms of violations of the Hague treaties. This attitude – that Germany bore more than just a banal legal responsibility – was dramatically reflected in Clemenceau's brief, brutal invitation to the German delegation at Versailles on May 7, 1919 to give its (written, not oral; a discussion was out of place) comments on the draft peace Treaty in fourteen days. Now, paradoxically, it was Germany's Brockdorff-Rantzau who spoke of law and self-determination and who suggested that all powers' responsibility was to be subjected to examination by an impartial commission. Of this, nothing was heard from Clemenceau. No attention was given by the Allies to the German proposals.[116]

Clearly, a much more fundamental spiritual and political reconstruction than a mere technical adjustment of the Hague Treaties was needed. For those who could not join Pillet, the situation called for action. On the following day, as the Germans withdrew to examine the Allied draft, the legal adviser of the French delegation, the dean of the Paris law school, Ferdinand Larnaude (born 1853) invited the members of the *Institut de droit international* (apart, of course, from the German members, most of whom had anyway already resigned), present in Paris or otherwise available to a meeting to discuss the recommencing of the Institute's activities. In his welcome speech, he made no secret as to how he saw the war: "France has been the defender of law in this war, as it always has been in the course of its glorious history."[117] Already in 1917

---

[114] De Lapradelle, *Maîtres et doctrines*, pp. 319–321.
[115] Cf. especially James W. Garner, "La reconstitution du droit international" (1921), XXVIII *RGDIP*, pp. 413–440, 438.
[116] For the speeches of Clemenceau and Brockdorff-Ratzau, cf. e.g. *Der Kampf um den Rechtsfrieden* (Berlin, Engelmann, 1919), pp. 23–29.
[117] Discours de M. Larnaude (1919), 27 *Annuaire IDI*, p. 294.

the French Prime Minister and Foreign Minister Ribot had appointed Bourgeois to head the French committee to consider the setting up of a *Société des Nations*.[118] By this move, the direction of French inter-war international law was set. It was only natural that he and Larnaude became the French representatives on President Wilson's Committee on the League of Nations ("Crillon Committee") within which they advocated a standing military force (or at least a military planning committee) in the service of the League.[119] Later, as the first French representative in the League Council and the Council's first President Bourgeois continued to defend collective security and international sanctions and fully associated himself with the effort to interpret the League as a first step towards universal federation.

The draft Covenant prepared by the French and submitted to Wilson in June 1918 contained provisions for effective sanctions, supported by an international army. It also provided for a Council of Great Powers, mandated to make binding decisions e.g. on disarmament. Legal disputes were directed to a tribunal and political ones to the Council. The French had unshakeable faith that they would always be on the side of peace-loving nations and that their predominance coincided with the general interest.[120] However, Wilson's choice of the Hurst–Miller draft as the basis for discussion made the result inevitably "a triumph of Anglo-American diplomacy."[121] The British had aimed at an organization for co-operation, the Americans emphasized the territorial guarantee. The outcome was a compromise negotiated in ten three-hour sessions during February 3–13, 1919. The French were almost methodologically sidelined and their suggestion of the international army was rejected for political and constitutional reasons. Accordingly, when the League came into existence, on January 10, 1920, few Frenchmen had faith in its capacity to deter aggression. Bourgeois attributed responsibility for this state of affairs squarely to Wilson and took upon himself as the first President of the Council to examine alternatives to fill the

---

[118] The other two members of the committee were Admiral Lacaze and Jules Cambon, former ambassador to Berlin.

[119] Cf. Scelle, *La Pacte des Nations*, pp. 326–328; Léon Bourgeois, *L'oeuvre de la Société des nations, 1920–1923* (Paris, Payot, 1923), pp. 52–53. On Bourgeois' international activities, cf. Hayward, "The Official Social Philosophy," pp. 41–46.

[120] Arnold Wolfers, *Britain and France between Two Wars: Conflicting Strategies of Peace from Versailles to World War II* (New York, Norton, 1966), pp. 161–162.

[121] F. S. Northedge, *The League of Nations. Its Life and Times* (New York and London, Holmes & Meier, 1986), p. 41.

gaps.[122] Time for such proposals was, however, over. During its first years the League saw itself frequently by-passed by Great Power diplomacy carried out by the Inter-Allied Conference of Ambassadors, a left-over from wartime co-ordination. Nonetheless, the supporters did not lose faith. Bourgeois was involved in practically all of the early activities of the League: "The edifice of peace can be built on law, and law alone."[123] One of his early reports organized the Committee of Jurists that was to set up the Statute of the Permanent Court of International Justice.[124] Another worked as the basis for setting up a provisional committee of commercial and financial experts, perhaps the first universally based body to manifest the belief that international problems were best dealt with if left to technical experts.[125] In 1923, the Commission dropped the word "provisional" from its title. All of this was justified through international solidarity – a solidarity, as Bourgeois assured the skeptics at home, which proved the indissociability of France's interests from those of the international community.[126]

Bourgeois was awarded the Nobel Prize in 1920, largely for his activism at the Peace Conferences. He and Larnaude (who set up the *Union juridique internationale* for this purpose) became active propagandists for the League, interpreting it as a tangible manifestation of the union between universal humanitarianism and the French idea. They saw it as not just a League of governments but of peoples who were to be educated into internationalism through it. For the essence of the French spirit – in contrast to German – lay in:

> the vocation of sacrifice for an ideal at the same time national and human that had inspired the great movements of the French people, from the crusades at the moment when Christianity fixed its eyes on the whole of humanity to the immortal campaigns of the sons of Revolution who ran to the frontiers to save the endangered *Patrie* and carry far the flag to announce human rights to peoples.

As Heidegger was later to argue about the German language, Bourgeois highlighted the exceptional qualities of the French, the unity between the "genius of our race and the genius of Humanity – had not

---

[122] Bourgeois blamed above all Wilson's unwillingness to allow full discussion on all the proposals and his insistence to deal with the Covenant first, and only thereafter with the Peace Treaty. Bourgeois, *L'oeuvre*, p. 36.
[123] Bourgeois, *L'oeuvre*, pp. 112, 114–118.
[124] For the report and commentary, cf. Bourgeois, *L'oeuvre*, pp. 159–208.
[125] Bourgeois, *L'oeuvre*, pp. 363–394.   [126] Bourgeois, *L'oeuvre*, pp. 130–133.

Humanity found in the works of our great writers the sovereign expression that has made our language the language of all those who think and of our philosophers and orators and poets the classics of Humanity?"[127] The difficulty with solidarism, as with the radicalism that characterized the Third Republic lay in the contradiction, no secret to contemporaries, between its extravagant claims and its absence of political direction. Like the doctrines of its spiritual leader, the philosopher Alain (Emile Chartier – one central influence in the work of Georges Scelle), it was a non-doctrine for which the attribute "opportunism" fitted perfectly.[128]

By the 1920s the renewalist force of solidarism had been largely expended. In a talk in 1921 before an audience of lawyers and diplomats in Paris, Bourgeois reformulated his ideas in a series of moral commonplaces. He sketched a view of Western history as the gradual development of an international ethics, partly as a result of material interdependence, partly through the emergence of a common conscience among civilized nations. The peaceful heritage of the revolution and of the nineteenth century had been corrupted by the barbaric violence of the war for which Bourgeois saw no other explanation than "Machiavellian" German attitudes. Reconstruction meant having the law penetrated by the moral ideas of civilized society: "real peace, in a State, can only be a peace between honest people. It is necessary therefore that States, too, in their relations with each other, *become honest people.*"[129] By 1921, however, such an analogy must have sounded hollow: an appeal to return to nineteenth-century ideas about virtue. The reference to "honesty" does, however, direct attention to France's famous obsession with guarantees against Germany. Though the Peace Treaty was felt as a disappointment French politicians from all sides insisted on strict compliance – "honesty" – with its terms. Hence, they were often criticized by friends for being "over-pedantic about the legal aspects of international affairs."[130] France was waging a losing battle. Formalism did not work. Prime Minister Poincaré's attempt to give teeth to Germany's obligations by the occupation of the Ruhr in 1923 led to electoral defeat and withdrawal. Insistence on the sanctity of treaties, buttressed by military sanctions, lost its public appeal. The world gradually turned against demanding strict German compliance with a settlement widely held to have been unrealistic in some parts and unjust in

---

[127] Bourgeois, *L'oeuvre*, pp. 18–19.   [128] Cf. Bernard Halda, *Alain* (Paris, Editions universitaires, 1965), pp. 18–19.
[129] Léon Bourgeois, "La morale internationale" (1922), **XXIX** *RGDIP*, pp. 21, 5–22.
[130] Wolfers, *Britain and France*, p. 26.

others. As German rearmament began in earnest in 1935 there was no longer a realistic prospect that France or its allies could have effectively relied on the Peace Treaties.

Scientific solidarism: Durkheim and Duguit

If treaties and formal diplomacy seemed only a thin façade over the reality of Europe, many lawyers now turned to science, particularly sociology, to reimagine an international order less amenable to the kind of catastrophe the First World War had been. Particularly promising seemed Durkheimian sociology, with its relentlessly anti-individualist outlook and its emphasis on the *conscience collective* as the fundamental social fact. To answer the question about what held modern industrial society together, Durkheim had in 1893 provided a theory of "organic solidarity" that accounted for integration even in a society where there was no universal resemblance between the tasks or positions of individuals. The fact of division of labor was only superficially disintegrating: the shoemaker, the civil servant, and the factory owner might lead completely different lives; but that did not mean they were not reciprocally dependent on the distinct contribution each had to give. Even as individuals might experience modernity differently, and pathological cases (such as anomie) emerged, modern societies still cohered as functional wholes. Organic solidarity depicted the paradox that the increase of the autonomy of individuals carrying out diversified tasks deepened their dependence on each other.

Organic solidarity did not involve moral choice. Although collective consciousness existed only in the psyche of individuals, individuals could not "choose" to share or not to share it. It was a social fact and could be studied as one. The "normal method of the moralists," Durkheim wrote dismissively, had been to put forward a "general formula for morality" and to examine society through it: "Nowadays we know how little value may be attached to such summary generalizations."[131] Instead of engaging in unending controversies about the good society, scholars should focus on the laws of motion that determined the direction and intensity of social development.[132] Evidence of such laws could be found in the

---

[131] Durkheim, *The Division of Labor*, p. 44.
[132] For an excellent review of the emergence of comtist sociology in France and especially Durkheim's role in the 1880s, cf. Lukes, *Emile Durkheim*, pp. 66–86. For reviews of the emergence of sociological jurisprudence in the late nineteenth and early twentieth century (especially Savigny, Maine, and Durkheim), cf. Julius Stone, *Social Dimensions of Law and Justice* (London, Stevens, 1966), pp. 35–41, 86–163.

legal system. The mechanical solidarity of a pre-modern consciousness was reflected in the predominance of repressive sanctions and the penal law: deviation from the norm of resemblance was punished by making the culprit suffer. By contrast, organic solidarity was visible in the predominance of civil law and restitutive sanctions. Instead of punishment, the aim was to restore the situation *ex ante* (e.g. the contractual equilibrium).[133]

Durkheim's image of domestic modernity – increasing autonomy and diversification – seemed equally applicable to characterize the international modernity of the States-system. If division of labor led to increasing interdependence (organic solidarity) that produced a particular type of law, then proof of international law's reality and necessity had been given in an apparently scientific way, without the intervention of suspect moral generalizations. It was derived from the laws of international modernity themselves.

Well before the war, French public law had already used such arguments to create a conception of the State diametrically opposed to the German one. Building directly upon Durkheim's concept of *solidarité sociale*, Léon Duguit (1859–1928), Durkheim's friend and colleague at the University of Bordeaux, the most important theorist of public law of the period, argued that law was not an effect of the State but a transformation of the objective needs of interdependence. The State and the popular will were both "metaphysical fictions." Instead, (objective) law emerged directly from the fact of mutual dependence in conditions of division of labor.[134] It was distinguishable from other norms (i.e. those of morality and economics) by the recognition of the need of a social sanction; not the actual application of such sanction but the recognition that it would be desirable.[135] This was a monistic concept of law that did not recognize doctrinal distinctions between private and public or national and international law. All law expressed "ultimately," as an empirical matter, normative relations between individuals.[136]

Although Duguit never developed an express theory of international

---

[133] Durkheim, *The Division of Labor*, pp. 44–52, 68–69, 77–83.

[134] There is an ambivalence between a sociological and a psychological concept of law (interdependence/solidarity) – although Duguit is clear that the sense of solidarity is not dependent on individual psychology. On the other hand, many have read the argument from social solidarity as a neo-naturalist principle; a fact-based normativity. Cf. e.g. Paul Guggenheim, "Léon Duguit et le droit international" (1959), LXIII *RGDIP*, p. 636.

[135] Albert Brimo, *Les grands courants de la philosophie du droit et de l'état* (Paris, Pedone, 1978), p. 251.   [136] Cf. Arnaud, *Les juristes*, p. 139.

law – he died just before he was supposed to lecture on the matter at the *Ecole des hautes études internationales* in Paris – he did argue that the principles applicable between individuals applied likewise to relations between social groups – what he called "intersocial law." Here the international was neither separate nor privileged: it was just another context of collective action that competed with relations between professional or religious groups, families, companies, and so on. The State was, as it were, wiped away from reality by a conceptual *fiat*. What was real was always already cosmopolitan: the complex (but single) network of interdependencies into which individuals were born and lived their lives.

Duguit took the starting-point for his polemically written *magnum opus* of 1901 from the German public law concept of the State as a sovereign juridical person and of public law as an effect of State will. None of such concepts had any reality:

Here are the facts: Individuals with common needs and different inclinations, who exchange services, who have always lived together and have always exchanged services, who by virtue of physical constitution cannot avoid living together and exchanging services, individuals of whom some are stronger than others, and of whom the strongest have always exercised constraint on the weaker ones, individuals that act, and have consciousness of their actions. Here are the facts. Beyond them, there is only fiction.[137]

Duguit's ambition was to establish legal study firmly as an empirical social science: laws emerged spontaneously from the objective facts of interdependence and solidarity. "all individuals are obligated, because they are social beings, to obey the social rule, and every individual who violates this rule provokes necessarily a social reaction."[138] Empiricism left no room for subjective (natural) rights of individuals or the sovereignty of the State. The idea of such rights implied the superiority of one will over that of others. This was pure ideology. A will was a fact and had no antecedent superiority over any other will.[139] It could produce legal effect only if it was determined by a social objective and was in conformity with the social law of interdependence and solidarity.[140]

---

[137] Léon Duguit, *Etudes de droit public: L'Etat, le droit objectif et la loi positive* (2 vols., Paris, Fontemoing, 1901), I, p. 6.
[138] Léon Duguit, *Le droit social, le droit individuel et la transformation de l'état* (Paris, Alcan, 1908), p. 6.   [139] Duguit, *Le droit social*, pp. 14–21.
[140] Duguit, *Le droit social*, p. 71. The two notions were practically interchangeable: "Dans la solidarité je ne vois que le fait d'interdépendance unissant entre eux par la communauté des besoins et la division du travail les membres de l'humanité et particulièrement les membres d'un même groupe social." Duguit, *Le droit social*, p. 8.

Property, for instance, was a social function; its limits were not determined by a given subjective right but by objective law, by what kind of property regime the society needed. Administrative or legislative acts, too, were facts. They were not binding because they emanated from State will but to the extent that they provided a faithful translation to what was socially necessary.[141]

Like Bourgeois and Pillet, Duguit saw the State as a kind of political arm of social solidarity. Its functions were completely determined by what solidarity required. The law binds only "if it formulates a rule of [objective] law or puts it into effect, and only to the extent it does so."[142] Legislation was not creative but declaratory. This is why laws were binding on those who voted for them. There was no need to have recourse to an ingenious (but false) theory of self-legislation.[143]

Both Bourgeois and Duguit resolved the potential conflict between society and the individual by recourse to an *a priori* assumption of a harmony of interests in compliance with objective laws. Freedom meant the recognition of the necessity of solidarity with others – as articulated in binding laws that received their legitimacy from the rational objective of putting solidarity into effect.[144] Although Duguit avoided using the construction of the quasi-contract, his notion of the State amounted to materially the same: the State existed to guarantee the well-being of individuals (who thus had a rational cause to assent to it) without needing anyone's (actual) consent.[145] No wonder that critics attacked Duguit for retreating to naturalist faith in social-scientific language![146] In a curious way, individuals become both fully free and fully constrained. They were free in their position as the ultimate social reality; Duguit expressly dissociated himself from Durkheim's notion of

---

[141] They are binding if they join the conditions of *acte juridique*: "une déclaration de volonté émanant d'une personne capable, ayant pour objet une chose qu'elle peut vouloir, déterminée par un but légal et faite dans l'intention de créer une situation juridique," Duguit, *Le droit social*, pp. 70–71.   [142] Duguit, *Le droit social*, p. 52.

[143] Duguit, *Le droit social*, pp. 52–54. There is the objection that this creates anarchy: everyone can decide whether or not to obey. Duguit does not have a good response to this. First, he says, a number of laws are self-evident. Second, those that are not, need not necessarily be opposed by violence or anarchy. The solution is to set up a tribunal that consists of members of all classes that would judge the law's lawfulness, Duguit, *Le droit social*, pp. 55–58.

[144] Cf. Brimo, *Les grands courants*, pp. 250–253 and Michel Miaille, *Une introduction critique au droit* (Paris, Maspero, 1982), p. 332.   [145] Cf. Arnaud, *Les juristes*, pp. 139–140.

[146] Cf. also Lucien Sfez, "Duguit et la théorie de l'Etat," (1976), 21 *Archives de philosophie de droit*, p. 121. On the other hand, naturalists such as Truyol, for instance, welcomed him warmly into the company of Grotius and Aristotle, Antonio Truyol, "Doctrines contemporaines du droit des gens" (1951), LV *RGDIP*, p. 38.

a *conscience collective*, independent from the conscience of particular individuals.[147] But they were also fully constrained by the social laws that seemed to determine (although Duguit is not fully clear) not only how individuals should go about realizing their pursuits, but what those pursuits could be in the first place.[148]

Duguit shared the Comtean view of history as a movement from theological to philosophical to positive (scientific) regulation.[149] Like Kelsen, he argued that to speak of sovereignty – whether of Kings or the people – was like a theology that used the concept of "spirit" in order to explain psychological phenomena: "Ce ne sont là que des formules scolastiques, qui s'évanouissent au simple examen de la réalité."[150] By contrast, objective law emerged directly, without metaphysical conceptions to mediate between direct experience and action. Now it is evident that there may be a conflict between formal law and the objective conditions of society, or a conflict between political and social power. This was the case in France in 1848 and perhaps in the 1890s as well: while social power lay in the hands of the bourgeoisie, the workers held parliamentary superiority. This was the endemic problem of unitary States: threat of revolution ensued from the exercise of domination by one class over others.[151] Duguit's cure – like Durkheim's – was decentralization and syndicalism.[152] Like Bourgeois, however, Duguit distanced himself from revolutionary syndicalism and Marxism that he thought sought only violence and were fixated on the conflict between capital and labor.[153] In Duguit's view, Durkheim's "brilliant" theory on the division of labor had demonstrated how interdependence and solidarity emerged between groups of workers that carried out different types of work and provided for different types of need.[154] In the long run, the allocation of public functions to the *syndicats* would coincide with the dismantling of the

---

[147] For Durkheim, collective (or "common") conscience was constituted of the "totality of beliefs and sentiments common to the average members of a society [that] forms a determinate system with a life of its own . . . [with] specific characters that make it a distinct reality," Durkheim, *The Division of Labor*, p. 39.

[148] It is hard to see how Duguit could fully accept Durkheim's two concepts of solidarity and *still* hold individuals as the fundamental social fact. He seems to have rejected Durkheim's view of the collective as a real entity while perhaps thinking that the content of individual conscience could be socially determined, Lukes, *Emile Durkheim*, p. 103. For the oscillation in Duguit, cf. Sfez, "Duguit," pp. 122–123.

[149] *Le droit social* is full of references to Comte, cf. e.g. pp. 12, 17, 24, 149.

[150] Duguit, *Le droit social*, p. 27.   [151] Duguit, *Le droit social*, pp. 45–44.

[152] Cf. also Lukes, *Emile Durkheim*, pp. 536–541.

[153] On Georges Sorel, cf. Duguit, *Le droit social*, pp. 106–108.

[154] Duguit, *Le droit social*, pp. 115–118.

State and thus rid society of "the false and dangerous political system based on sovereignty and the personality of the State."[155]

International solidarity . . . almost: Alvarez and Politis

It is doubtful if Renault, Fauchille, and Pillet felt themselves inaugurating a new school. Only the last of the three was conversant with Durkheimian sociology. But this is how their work was characterized in 1912 by Alexandre (Alejandro) Alvarez (1868–1960), a Chilean diplomat and a Pan-Americanist who had studied under Renault in 1896–1900 and traveled back and forth between Europe and the Americas until settling down in Paris in the 1920s. Alvarez came to Europe to declare that international law was in a crisis and to preach the message of a sociologically and politically oriented renewal. The crisis concerned the way the teaching of international law had departed from the reality of international relations and was discussed through a narrow and formal conception that Alvarez expressly associated with civil law. Happily, during the last few years a new school had developed in France that was no longer prisoner to civil law and which examined international law closely "following its transformations, their causes and their results." He credited Renault as the leader of the new school and cited Bonfils–Fauchille (oddly) as its leading product.[156]

Alvarez preached the reform of international law through codification so as to make it reflect the "realities" of international life. He was well aware of the teachings of Duguit and Durkheim and stressed the need for precise articulation of what was required by the solidarity that governed the conditions of modernity. He became enormously influential in Europe and the Americas during a career that reached into the late 1950s, a figurehead of a "new" international law that spoke with a non-European voice, sought to lower the boundary between international law and international relations, and emphasized doctrine's role in adapting the law to social facts and justice. To the extent that he operated with "juridical conscience" and public opinion and was critical of an excessive emphasis on sovereignty, his writing was well in line with the views of the *Institut*. More than his future colleagues, however, Alvarez received his views from general developments in jurisprudence and was able to articulate them into a self-conscious progressivism.

[155] Duguit, *Le droit social*, p. 147.
[156] Alejandro Alvarez, *La codification du droit international – ses tendances, ses bases* (Paris, Pedone, 1912), p. 9 n1.

International law as sociology: France 1871–1950

Already in 1912 Alvarez claimed that international law had fallen into disrepute by failing to take account of the economic, technological, and cultural changes, including peoples' increasing desire for peace. Despite its avowed positivism, it reflected the ideas of a by-gone international society, "metaphysical or *a priori*" doctrines of fundamental rights, independence and sovereignty.[157] Like modern domestic society, however, the international world was no longer ruled by individualism but by "the principle of solidarity that also takes into account the interests of the social group, because individuals live in society and in a situation of mutual dependence."[158] As a result, an international "regime of solidarity" was being constructed through international unions, legislative conferences, and legal co-operation.[159] Most lawyers had failed to see this. They worked with a narrow concept of international community, restricted to Christian nations, limiting the law to formal rules. Or they looked upon the changes from an individualist perspective provided by the theory of "fundamental rights." None of this took account of the "modern tendencies": the subjects of law were no longer only the European or civilized States – all States contributed to the formation of the law. Also religious denominations, international organizations, and individuals possessed rights under it. The law's content no longer arose from Great Power policy but from different and even contrasting values that reflected the different histories of peoples and were sometimes reflected in regional systems such as that in force in the Americas.[160] Most importantly, formal law always contained gaps and obscurities. By reference to modern French hermeneutic jurisprudence (Gény, Saleilles) Alvarez emphasized the jurist's constructive role: "[t]he role of the interpreter today 'must consist in assisting openly the development of institutions to the direction of social phenomena by making new cases harmonious with them'."[161] The main enemy was legal formalism. All law grew from popular *conscience* and legal sources reflected only places where that conscience would manifest itself. There was no *a priori* reason to limit those manifestations by some formal criterion. There was thus no great divide between law and justice, law and social reality. If popular *conscience* was moving away from individualism, the lawyer had to move there, too.[162] "The idea of solidarity is thus of crucial importance for

---

[157] Alvarez, *La codification*, pp. 6–7. [158] Alvarez, *La codification*, p. 33.
[159] Alvarez, *La codification*, pp. 47, 59–62   [160] Alvarez, *La codification*, pp. 77–98.
[161] Alvarez, *La codification*, p. 160. Alvarez quoted his own earlier study on the new methods of law, *Une nouvelle conception des études juridiques* (1904).
[162] Alvarez, *La codification*, pp. 137–140.

international law. It must guide its future orientation and at the same time provide objective elements of interpretation; correctly understood, it will bring back international law's lost prestige."[163] Despite his critic's voice, Alvarez was close to the reform oriented anti-formalism of the *Institut* members, which he read in light of what he had learned from French legal theory. Using his non-European voice and his interest in a regional American law, he could pass as an innovator while ensuring ready acceptance by the mainstream. For the claim to renew legal doctrine because it has failed to reflect "social reality" is a deeply conservative technique that deflects criticism away from "reality" and those responsible for it. By directing his attack against an academic enemy that was largely a straw man, Alvarez remained unthreatening for the legal establishment and could be celebrated as a wonderful manifestation of the profession's liberality.[164] After all, Alvarez's strong view against the possession of any legal personality by indigenous tribes ("populations barbares") was a conveniently colonialist attitude to take by a Chilean jurist.[165]

It may seem odd that Alvarez was able to preach the message of transformation and "new" international law in virtually unchanging terms from 1912 to his last major work of 1959.[166] This apparent paradox is, however, quite an important aspect of Alvarez's acceptance by the profession. Even if not all lawyers shared his terminology about "crisis" and "transformation," most of his substantive ideas were adopted by *Institut* members from early on. The call for "realism" by taking account of interdependence, a critical attitude towards formalism and sovereignty, the integration of individual rights, orientation towards international organizations, peaceful settlement, and codification – all that had become quite central to liberal solidarism.

So it is no surprise that Alvarez succeeded in the 1930s in having some of the principal professional organizations – the International Law Association, the *Académie diplomatique internationale* and the *Union juridique internationale* – pass a declaration on the *Great Principles of Modern International Law*. In forty articles it laid down the principal tenets of Alvarez' solidarism: interdependence, the predominance of general over special interests, and a tighter organization of the international

---

[163] Alvarez, *La codification*, p. 128.
[164] Cf. further Martti Koskenniemi, *From Apology to Utopia. The Structure of International Legal Argument* (Helsinki, Lakimiesliiton kustannus, 1989), pp. 178–186.
[165] Alvarez, *La codification*, p. 84.
[166] Alejandro Alvarez, *Le droit international nouveau dans ses rapports avec la vie actuelle des peuples* (Paris, Pedone, 1959).

community.[167] It took up conventional points affirming sovereignty and consent on the one hand and the duty of assistance and co-operation on the other, highlighting the role of equity as a source of law, recognizing the obligation to protect core individual rights, and appealing for peaceful settlement and codification. The list of the rights and duties of States was derived from a project carried out within the American Institute of International Law after 1919.

In his *exposé des motifs* Alvarez repeated the arguments about "crisis" and "transformation" that had originated in the mid-nineteenth century and had now evolved to a moment of the greatest anxiety.[168] Yet, there was little indication in what, precisely, the crisis consisted – apart from the law's general detachment from "reality." Even a close reading indicates only two rather undramatic problems: formalism and Eurocentrism. In particular, Alvarez refrained from identifying his enemy. If law was based on interdependence, why did it now (and since the mid-nineteenth century) fail to reflect it? Was this a problem of politics or doctrine? In the former case, Alvarez should have identified the political causes (or actors) that prohibited "life" from receiving an authentic expression in law. But the impression is that he always identified the problem with an obsolete legal doctrine – thus either inflating the importance of a marginal profession, or failing to indicate why one should be concerned.

Alvarez saw the declaration of 1936 as an endorsement of his own anti-formalism: it was based on the predominance of broad "principles" that both integrated political transformation and constrained it, a step away from "strictly juridical" norms towards the taking account of social law and international justice by norms that were "plus suples, plus vivantes et en contact constant avec la réalité (l'aspect politique)."[169] The declaration looked towards international organization that would go beyond the League and often take the way of regional integration. It was an endorsement of a new, scientific law that was not only a tool of lawyers but was to be distributed everywhere so as to become an effective code for international policy.

Like Alvarez, Nicolas Politis (1872–1943), another visible proponent of full-scale reform of international law, was a foreigner (a Greek later naturalized also as French), a student of Renault's and a close reader of Duguit and solidarist literature. He too combined a life as a politician and a diplomat – as foreign minister during the war and representative

---

[167] Cf. Alejandro Alvarez, *Exposé des motifs et déclaration des grands principes du droit international moderne* (Paris, Editions internationales, 1936).   [168] Alvarez, *Exposé des motifs*, pp. 5–9.   [169] Alvarez, *Exposé des motifs*, p. 25.

of Greece in the League – with that of a scholar.[170] Much of his work, too, is written in the form of programmatic restatements of the need to complete the ongoing international "transformation" from a sovereignty-dominated law to a new system of solidarity. The gist of his proposals is contained in his early Hague lectures about the principle of "abuse of rights" as a limitation of sovereignty and two books from the 1920s and 1930s on the new tendencies of international law and on the role of neutrality.

For Politis, international law, like all law, emerged from social facts. From this he drew the three consequences of solidarist doctrine: that legislation (or codification) had only declaratory, and not constitutive, effect; that all law dealt ultimately with individual behavior; and that States possessed rights only to the extent that was functionally necessary. The use by a State of its freedom was illegal if such use was "[only] to the detriment of the collectivity's general interest."[171] Sovereignty was to be replaced by "the solidarity of human relations [which] is the great social phenomenon of today."[172] States were artificial fictions and the individual the only "real" subject of international law, situated in a historical continuum from family to tribe; tribe to nation; nation to region; region to universal community. Many lawyers, Politis claimed, such as Kelsen and Verdross, Schücking, Krabbe, and Westlake, had already understood this. And while official diplomacy was still being obstructive, it was "powerless against the realities of life."[173] In 1927 Politis reviewed four diplomatic developments that manifested the new realities: increasing acknowledgement of the position of the individual; the emergence of an international criminal law; creation of a compulsory system of international justice; and codification. To carry the changes through required both activism and prudence; for the most part, Politis believed that the League was being successful, despite occasional setbacks (such as the failure of the Geneva Protocol in the drafting of which he was personally involved) or timidity (concerning the choice of topics of codification).[174]

By the same token, he argued in 1935, taking up a matter of great concern for French internationalists, that neutrality had become irreconcilable with "the modern conditions in the lives of peoples."[175] First, in an interdependent economic system, all goods could be viewed by a

---

[170] For biography, cf. De Lapradelle, *Maîtres et doctrines*, pp. 371–403.
[171] Nicolas Politis, *Les nouvelles tendances du droit international* (Paris, Hachette, 1927), p. 14.
[172] Politis, *Les nouvelles tendances*, p. 76.   [173] Politis, *Les nouvelles tendances*, p. 61.
[174] Politis, *Les nouvelles tendances*, pp. 185–190, 215–220.
[175] Nicolas Politis, *La neutralité et la paix* (Paris, Hachette, 1937), p. 8 and *passim*.

belligerent as aiding its adversary's war effect. Second, solidarity compelled assistance to the victim. In the absence of a duty of assistance, no deterrence will work. Third, the principle of the just war implied by the Kellogg–Briand Pact was morally incompatible with the egoism of the neutral.[176] If violence takes on the character of community sanction, no room is left for neutrality. But although the Covenant had profoundly transformed the conditions of neutrality, it had not yet fully done away with it. That after 1928 the law no longer contained a place for it meant that it was "in advance of the facts." The task was to proceed step by step to make neutrality unnecessary.[177]

The argument about "transformation" was delicately poised between utopia and reality – a doctrine of the "in-between." The world was enveloped within an objective historical process – called "reality" or sometimes simply "life" – that could not be hindered by the conservative forces (that were never really identified) holding on to a political system that was, in fact, already in the past. There were difficulties in such a position. Why, for instance, lay so much emphasis on the need of codification when treaties even at best remained only declaratory of the objective law and invalid to the extent that they conflicted with it? Why did Politis need to say that in addition to the law being embedded in "life," its source was "the juridical conscience of peoples" – thereby subscribing to the dubious assumption that popular conscience was always capable of grasping "life" in its authenticity?[178]

But Politis was more interested in the diplomatic efforts in which he took an active part in the League and elsewhere than in the theoretical problems of his "in-between" doctrine. In some ways, the sense of change, of leaving some things behind while not quite attaining one's goals must have seemed a psychologically credible description of his experience in trying to close the gaps of the Covenant. Perhaps, one could say, Politis' writing came together by the assumption that while the pace and direction of legal change were determined on the grand scale, this left some room for diplomatic alternatives. The lawyer's task became the careful balancing of requirements of stability and change, the adaptation rather than full-scale transformation of tradition – such as his step-by-step strategy for the elimination of neutrality – so as to work towards the ultimate goal of universal federation.[179]

---

[176] Politis, *La neutralité*, pp. 96–99.
[177] Politis, *La neutralité*, pp. 179 et seq, 205–209, 210.
[178] Cf. e.g. Politis, *Les nouvelles tendences*, pp. 49, 62.
[179] This seems suggested e.g. by Politis' discussion of the development of international criminal law and codification, *Les nouvelles tendences*, pp. 95–137, 193–229.

In 1943, shortly before his death, Politis published his last book on "the international morality" – an analysis of the prevailing crisis in terms of Europe's (and the League's) moral breakdown. Many of the ambiguities of solidarist doctrine were in evidence: oscillation between economic determinism and moral pathos, faith in rationality, and analysis of the crisis in terms of unreason, laying the foundation of moral rules alternatively on "usage" and the gospel – with the idea that all this was somehow expressed by "science" as represented, for instance, through Spencerian evolutionism. Politis saw the war as an incident of the economic decline that had resulted from a division of Europe in two – a developed, industrial West and the large agrarian East and South.[180] Yet, apart from the suggestion for European economic reorganization, most of the book came out as a smörgåsbord of moral commonplaces – an appeal for the strengthening of five moral rules: loyalty, moderation, mutual assistance, respect, and the spirit of justice. The discussion appealed for an enlightened but empty altruism – with passing critical remarks on the nationalist right (represented by Maurice Barrès) in France, and, perhaps oddly, admiration for the morality of the Salazar Government in Portugal.[181] As moral theory, the book's greatest problems lay in its emptiness, and the ambivalence about whether the meaning of morality was defined by convention or revelation.[182] As a political blueprint, it left completely open why the European federalism suggested in its last chapter would be any more available after the war than it had been before – unless the reference to the war as moral purification in the opening pages was more than a mere slip of the pen.[183]

The strength and weakness of the solidarity advocated by Alvarez and Politis was based on its character as a hybrid, uneasily balanced between sociology and natural law. On the one hand, it grew directly from social "reality" – as such, it could be opposed against the "metaphysical" orientation of earlier doctrines, their ignorance of the interdependence and solidarity of international "life." But neither wanted to suggest that this meant full-scale acceptance of the present political or economic structures. Alvarez carefully distanced himself from the historical school that (as he thought) possessed no perspective from which to criticize present law. There had to be an element of justice as well, he wrote: "This ideal

---

[180] Nicolas Politis, *La morale internationale* (Neuchâtel, Baconnière, 1943), pp. 11–18.
[181] Politis, *La morale*, pp. 66, 79, 82.   [182] Politis, *La morale*, pp. 45–47, 81.
[183] Politis, *La morale*, pp. 24–27.

of justice consists, in summary, of the substitution of the old individualist concept with the idea of solidarity."[184] Politis agreed in the critique of individualism and his "five rules of morality" constituted an outline of a theory of social justice on partly historicist, partly religious assumptions. His writing combined fact-description with normative requirements whose fulfillment was always in the society's self-interest.[185] Hence its distinctly paternalistic tone. It became a technique to demonstrate both the positivist merits of one's science – it was a "fait social" – as well as its political virtue – it respected the "conscience of peoples" and enshrined an "ideal of justice." When Politis contemplated the possibility of eradicating war in 1935, his ultimate argument was about faith in reason, "bonne entente, respect mutuel" – an affirmation of a solidarist faith, with the arrogant implication that the varying meanings that such expressions received in social life were to be seen as "errors" to the scientific truth of one's own view.[186]

Meanwhile in Paris . . .

Alvarez and Politis were smoothly integrated into the French international law community that did not feel the least threatened by their call for transformation and renewal. After all, solidarism was a language of French origin and internationalism well in accord with the spirit of a France where, after 1919, there may still have been patriots "but somehow patriotism was dead."[187] If it was difficult for a Frenchman not to think obsessively in terms of "guarantees," one look at the League as it emerged from the Treaties seemed to underwrite the conception that a much more fundamental international transformation was needed than Versailles had even tried to effect.

So it is no wonder Fauchille and Alvarez, together with their friend professor Albert Geouffre de Lapradelle (1871–1955), Renault's successor at the Paris faculty, were able to align every French internationalist and a large number of French and international politicians from Balfour to Beneš, Hanotaux to Hymans, Poincaré to Venizelos behind the proposal for setting up the *Institut (*later *Ecole) des hautes études internationales* as a school for foreign and domestic lawyers and diplomats in Paris in 1919, an initiative that had been temporarily postponed because of the war. Funds for the Institute were received from the French government and

---

[184] Alvarez, *La codification*, p. 140.   [185] Cf. also Politis, *La morale*, p. 74.
[186] E.g. Politis, *La neutralité*, pp. 220–221; *La morale*, pp. 133–137.
[187] Eugene Weber, *The Hollow Years. France in the 1930's* (London, Sinclair, 1995), p. 17.

the Carnegie foundation while a donation by Alvarez constituted the basis for a professional library. That the purpose of the *Institut* was to "contribute to the reconstruction of international law in conformity with the contemporary requirements of the life of States" and to "develop the influence of ideas about justice and morality on the formation of international law" clearly shows the influence of Alvarez and it was hardly a coincidence that the first lecture given at the new school as it opened in 1921 was the one by Léon Bourgeois on international morality referred to above.[188]

In the course of 1919–1939, the Paris *Institut* became one of the most important institutions of teaching international law and politics in annual courses directed at a multinational audience of students, diplomats, and young professionals. The founders insisted that international law be taught in connection with history, diplomacy, and economics and they combined law teaching with regular courses in such subjects. The number of enrolled students had by 1932 risen from twelve to 130, with annual attendance reaching 150 in peak years.[189] Reflecting upon the early years of the *Institut*, Alvarez and de Lapradelle emphasized their intention to have the students learn "the profound basis of international life," including the point of view of the new world. They felt that international law

> had to be separated from its old image as a dry juridical discipline which had rightly made it fall into disgrace, that it had to be connected with the realities of contemporary life, especially the policies of States and the sentiments of nations and that it had to take into account the great transformations that had taken place.[190]

Practically every French internationalist of some renown, and a large number of foreign professors (though few Germans) gave courses at the *Institut*. On the basis of a list of those courses it cannot be said that their substance had been geared towards any particular direction: even if ideas about "transformation," interdependence, and the demise of sovereignty were much on the surface, the overall impression was that of an eclecticism whose limits were effectively set by the fact that the teachers were established professors in a period where the possession of a university chair could rarely be connected with *avant-garde* politics. That the

---

[188] Cf. "L'Ecole internationale de droit international" (1920), XXVII *RGDIP*, pp. 145–152.

[189] "Discours de M. A. de La Pradelle, Institut des hautes études internationales (Douzième anniversaire, jeudi 22 novembre 1932)" (1933), 7 *RDI* (Paris), p. 13.

[190] Alejandro Alvarez and Albert de La Pradelle, "L'Institut des hautes études internationales et l'enseignement du droit des gens" (1939), XLVI *RGDIP*, p. 666.

anniversaries of the *Institut* were attended by the French President and other high officials while Alvarez participated continuously in its direction and he and Politis were regular lecturers there speaks something of the special link that emerged between the rhetoric of solidarity and the self-understanding of French policy in those years. De Lapradelle had all reason to note that the spirit of teaching at the *Institut* would not cease to be French by the fact that it was international – "bien au contraire."[191]

Yet it would be too much to say that the French international lawyers would have felt equally comfortable with the language of solidarism. There were those like the diplomatic historian and lawyer, professor at the *Ecole libre des sciences politiques,* Charles Dupuis (1863–1939) who ridiculed the attempt to get rid of sovereignty by Duguit and Politis – this would be to attempt to get rid of police, administration, taxation, and welfare. Nobody wanted it. Instead, internationalism and nationalism should be balanced against each other. In the realist fashion, he criticized the Kellogg–Briand Pact as being both indeterminate in content and based on a presumption about the binding force of promises which, if it were true, would make the pact unnecessary.[192] He specifically attacked Politis' concept of the abuse of right which to him smacked of an "abuse of words." Either one acted within one's right or one did not. To say that one was using rights in an "anti-social" and thus abusive fashion injected a moral evaluation into what should be a legal assessment.[193] Dupuis shared the disappointment of Pillet and the French right about the conditions of Versailles: The League, he argued in 1920, had come about without taking account of the lessons of history. Of the three conditions for international order – renouncing absolute sovereignty, presence of international organization, and a spirit of internationalism – the third (which he seemed to equate with an internationalist public opinion) was a precondition for the others and remained to be created. The Pact was too abstract and unclear in a way that would not matter if the League could rely on an *esprit international*. But there was no such spirit, Dupuis argued.[194] A real law needs to be backed up by force: in the ideal world, the use of force would rely on public opinion. In its absence, the drafters of the Covenant should have taken their lesson from nineteenth-century diplomacy that showed that even if the balance of power was eminently not a legal principle, it could still be used to support law and

---

[191] "Discours de M. de La Pradelle," p. 12.
[192] Charles Dupuis, "Règles générales du droit de la paix" (1930/I), 32, *RdC*, pp. 27–31, 215–224.   [193] Dupuis, "Règles générales," pp. 88–95.
[194] Charles Dupuis, *Le droit des gens et les rapports des grandes puissances avec les autres états avant la pacte de Société des Nations* (Paris, Plon, 1921), pp. 7–11, 477–532.

whether it was so used was a function of the intelligence of the diplomats.[195] Under the League this truth had become shrouded under vacuous generalities.

And there were formalists like Jules Basdevant (1877–1968), one of the holders of the two chairs in international law at the Paris faculty (with Albert de Lapradelle) in the 1920s and 1930s, Renault's successor at the *Quai d'Orsay*, later a long-time judge at the International Court of Justice.[196] Basdevant was an expert in the law of treaties whose teaching consisted of textual commentaries undertaken in light of the jurisprudence of arbitral tribunals and the Permanent Court at which he performed regularly as counsel. Like everyone else, he paid homage in his 1936 course at the Hague to the old naturalists whose teaching he equated with international law "theory." Today, however, natural law had become an "aspect of psychology." Its usefulness was limited to an element in the interpretation of obscure treaty and customary rules.[197] Law was based on recognition; general rules existed only to the extent that States had accepted the jurisdiction of tribunals that applied general principles. Like Dupuis, Basdevant had little tolerance for arguments about the withering away of sovereignty. As a practitioner and a representative of his government, he defended the virtues of the diplomatic system. Individuals, for instance, were subjects of international law only indirectly while the sovereignty of the State was sovereignty under the law.[198]

Where men like Dupuis or Basdevant – a realist and a formalist – differed from the solidarists was in their lack of optimism about or at least their reluctance to speculate over international transformations. They were equally concerned over the weaknesses of the League and highlighted the limitations of law; but they did not advocate programs of far-reaching reform. Dupuis interpreted the League in terms of the unchanging laws of Great Power policies, and Basdevant analyzed the limited materials that codification and expanding case-law offered to

---

[195] Charles Dupuis, *Le principe de l'équilibre et le concert européen de la paix de Westphalie à l'acte d'Algéciras* (Paris, Perrin, 1909), esp. pp. 104–108 and 504–513.
[196] The second chair was set up after the war. Other internationalists taught at Paris as well. But Louis Le Fur had a professorship "without a chair" and Gilbert Gidel's position was in constitutional law. Politis had been appointed "honorary professor" at the faculty and teaching in international law (for instance, courses at the Hague Academy) was given by the public and constitutional lawyers Gaston Jèze and Joseph-Barthélemy. For the faculty in 1932, cf. Berthélemy, *L'école de droit*, pp. 66–69.
[197] Jules Basdevant, "Règles générales du droit de la paix" (1936/IV), 58 *RdC*, pp. 481, 488–491.   [198] Basdevant, "Règles générales," pp. 525–529, 577–582.

him without the ambition to blow them up into a full legal system. Dupuis was a university man who preferred observation and analysis to activism (though he, too, was a member of the *Institut de droit international* and an energetic writer of legal opinions). Basdevant was a governmental jurist who recognized the useful but limited role law could play in diplomatic affairs.[199] Neither made a secret of his distaste of the solidarists' sweeping generalizations.

Much closer in spirit to Alvarez and Politis was professor Joseph-Barthélemy (1874–1945), colleague to both Dupuis and Basdevant, "the incontestably leading constitutional lawyer in the 1930s,"[200] who received fame through his analyses of the "crisis of democracy" in Europe but glided from an idiosyncratic liberalism into the position of *garde des Sceaux* in the Vichy Government in 1941–1943.[201] In his course at the Hague in 1937 Barthélemy examined the effect of the internal politics of States on international law. With the background of the Italian attack on Abyssinia and the Spanish Civil War, he sought to tear apart "slogans" and ideologies about the international behavior of different types of government. Adopting the language of "facts," but stressing their complexity and manipulability, Barthélemy relativized the distinction between democracy and autocracy – "deconstructed" that opposition – and showed that neither was *essentially* peaceful or belligerent. However one defined one's terms, it was impossible to avoid the conclusion that sometimes it was autocracies, sometimes democracies that intervened. Léon Blum's famous oscillation between proletarian solidarism and a defense of non-intervention in the Spanish Civil War was only one (though perhaps particularly tragic) illustration of the opportunism of ideologies.[202] Political regimes were naturally drawn to co-operation with similar regimes over national frontiers; yet sometimes this led from conflict between States to an intensification of social conflict within them. Moscow's revolutionary exports were one example; another was

---

[199] Basdevant stayed as legal adviser to the Foreign Ministry at the beginning of the occupation, hoping to be able to influence the relations to the occupying power through legal argument. As the German demands for the Vichy government became excessive (as French airports were requisitioned for the German war effort), he resigned. Cf. Bohdan Winiarski, "Jules Basdevant (1877–1968)" (1969), 53/2 *Annuaire IDI*, p. 489.

[200] Dominique Gros, "Peut-on parler d'un droit antisémite?," in *Le droit antisémite de Vichy* (Paris, Seuil, 1996), p. 17.

[201] Joseph-Barthélemy, *La crise de la démocratie contemporaine* (Paris, Sirey, 1931).

[202] Joseph-Barthélemy, "Politique intérieure et droit international" (1937/I), 59 *RdC*, pp. 448, 462–486.

the International Labour Organization's (ILO) attempt to resolve issues of national social policy by an internationalist fiat.[203] The elegant complexity of Barthélemy's Hague talk, its critique of ideology and his defense of democracy as an "attitude or spirit . . . a form of behavior towards the individual" failed, however, to provide a justification for the optimism he expounded at its conclusion.[204] Basically a defense of non-intervention, and a criticism of attempts to measure legal attitudes by reference to the character of the regime of a country with which one was dealing, the article professed no faith in the League nor in diplomacy or politics generally; it looked for spiritual renewal but failed to indicate the direction from which it might be expected to arrive.

The divergence between Dupuis, Basdevant, and Joseph-Barthélemy on the one hand, and the solidarists on the other, failed to produce real controversy. The reasons must in part come from the rules of professorial *politesse*; open controversy was not encouraged. But in part, also, controversy must have seemed pointless as the language of solidarism was not in sharp political conflict with what was being preached by legal realists (with whom Barthélemy had much in common) and formalists. The teachings by Bourgeois, Alvarez, and Politis faithfully ratified French concerns about the international order. Moreover, as we have seen, solidarism did not come with a tight package of political ideas. Aside a forward-looking technologically and scientifically oriented optimism, there was an anti-individualism that sometimes – in Bourgeois' lecture of 1921, in Politis' book of 1943 – interpreted European crisis in distinctly conservative ways: as a breakdown of tradition that implied an appeal for a return to nineteenth-century religious or bourgeois values. Although the origins of solidarism might have been left of the political centre, that did not prevent Alvarez from collaborating closely with the conservative Albert de Lapradelle at the Paris *Institut* and elsewhere.[205]

---

[203] Barthélemy, "Politique intérieure," pp. 464–467.
[204] Barthélemy, "Politique intérieure," pp. 492, 519.
[205] For example, in his commentary to the jurisprudence of the mixed arbitral tribunals set up by the Treaty of Sèvres, and dealing with disputes between Romania and Hungary, de Lapradelle highlighted the fundamental role of international law in the protection of private property: "In the defense against attacking property international law occupies an exceptional position that makes it one of the bastions of civilisation," A. de Lapradelle, *Recueil de la jurisprudence des tribunaux arbitraux mixtes créées par les traités de paix* (5 vols., Paris, Documentation internationale, 1927), IV, p. 559. In 1942 he wrote polemically against Soviet diplomacy, almost portraying Hitler as Christianity's last refuge against Bolshevism: "combattre le bolchewisme, c'est défendre la civilisation chrétienne." The book labeled Stalin as the principal aggres-

International law as sociology: France 1871–1950

In the curriculum of the first year of the new *Institut*, there was also a series of lectures by the new Professor of International Law at the University of Strasbourg, Louis Le Fur (1870–1943), on the "philosophy of international law," which condemned materialism and voluntarism as parts of the breakdown of tradition that Germany had sought to accomplish. What was needed was a return to the "first foundations of a universal morality and law; to what had been called a *philosophia perennis*" that reached from Greek Antiquity to seventeenth- (but not eighteenth-) century natural law.[206] Like "solidarity," "transformation" meant different things for different people. Like many Frenchmen, Le Fur understood the war of 1914 as an externally introduced break in the natural development of European societies, produced by an intellectual attack against tradition by German *Lebensphilosophie* as realized in the policies of the Wilhelminian Empire. From this perspective, reconstruction meant the spiritual regeneration of European tradition and in particular of Christian natural law.

The French right and left agreed that the kind of diplomacy that had prevailed in 1914 had been a major cause of the war. Both held that a reformed international law was to give expression to forms of more authentic community. But where the former preached moral and religious revival, and obedience to authority, the latter sought renewal from science, technology, and institutional cosmopolitanism. Both used solidarist language to advance federalist ideas. The federalism of tradition constituted a hierarchical structure of communities whose purpose was to facilitate the renewal of Europe's spiritual energies. Modernist federalism sought to liberate the professional classes to realize the progressive laws of social interdependence. It is conventional to speak of the return of natural law in juristic thinking after the First World War. This undermines the degree to which at least French lawyers were looking both backwards *and* sideways: into tradition and history – the Spanish Scholastics, Grotius, and the teachings of the Catholic Church[207] – but also towards Rousseau and Durkheim and recent theories of public law,

---

sor on Poland and speculated about the need for a coming Finnish–German alliance in the North, A. de Lapradelle, *Le marxisme tentaculaire. La formation, la tactique et l'action de la diplomatie soviétique* (Issidou, Editions internationales, 1942), pp. 310, 202–204, 229.

[206] Louis Le Fur, "Philosophie du droit international" (1921), XXVIII *RGDIP*, p. 577.

[207] Cf. in this respect among the writings by the *Révérend Père* Yves Leroy de la Brière (1877–1941), e.g. "Evolution de la doctrine et de la pratique en matière de représsailles" (1928/II), 22 *RdC*, pp. 237–294; *Le droit de juste guerre: Tradition théologique et adaptations contemporaines* (Paris, Pedone, 1938).

to answer the question about how to provide for the coherence of an international system – a question that automatically translated itself into what would protect France from Germany. If French lawyers were keen to see in the League more than just a treaty (although they disagreed on just how much more) and frequently speculated about federalism and a European Union, solidarist vocabulary provided an effective means to do this; to move in ideas from diversity and antagonism to co-operation and harmony at some concrete level of reality. But one's solidarity is another's oppression; and there are many kinds of solidarity, including that of the master and the slave. The traditional and modernist responses to the crisis did not always lie well side by side.

L'affaire Scelle

On February 15, 1925 Georges Scelle, at the time the Professor of International Law at the University of Dijon and head of the Cabinet of the left coalition government's (*cartel des gauches*) Minister of Labor was nominated by the Minister of Public Education to hold the course of public international law at the University of Paris. This decision contradicted the faculty council's proposal that had put in first place Louis Le Fur, a Catholic–conservative international lawyer and legal philosopher who had moved from Strasbourg to Rennes in 1922. The faculty reacted strongly against such intrusion into university autonomy: irrespective of political alignment, all but one professor condemned the Minister's action.[208] Among the students as well, criticism of the violation of the university's independence – the terms in which the matter was propagated by right-wing students – was near-unanimous.[209]

On March 2 violent demonstrations and acts of "vandalism" organized by students of the *Action française*, monarchist, and other right-wing student groups took place in the course of Scelle's first lecture, with the result that the police had to be called in to secure order. The University Council was called to an urgent meeting. The demonstrations continued, however, during Scelle's second lecture in the following week with posters being distributed that attacked François Albert, the Minister of Education, for his breach of traditional norms of university–Ministry relations.

Disturbances continued, however, and on March 31, the Dean of the

---

[208] Cf. Marc Milet, *La faculté de droit de Paris face à la vie politique. De l'affaire Scelle à l'affaire Jèze 1925–1936* (Paris, LGDJ, 1996), pp. 222–224.
[209] Milet, *La faculté de droit*, pp. 29–31.

Law faculty – Professor Henri Berthélemy – was suspended from office for having refused to call in the police anew. The students were shocked and organized a new manifestation on April 2 in support of the Dean, renewing the declaration that interference in University's affairs by the government was intolerable.[210] The Ministry reacted by deciding to close the Faculty. On the following day the matter was raised in the National Assembly in which *députés* from all sides criticized the government's handling of the "*affaire Scelle*." On April 11, the Ministry gave in. The faculty was reopened on April 20 and Scelle's courses were suspended. Less than a week thereafter, however, the government fell on a budgetary vote – hostility towards it having been largely fomented by its incoherent handling of the affair.[211] Le Fur was nominated to hold the course. Almost a year after these events students still interrupted Scelle's lecture in the Café Procope. By contrast, Le Fur was appointed to the Paris faculty and held in his inaugural lecture on March 3, 1926, according to the *Action française* "in the midst of acclamations."[212]

L'affaire Scelle was mainly about university politics, and the doctrinal positions of the two protagonists did not play a visible part in it. On the other hand, it did polarize the relationship between the rightist majority in the Faculty of Law and the left-leaning jurists such as Gaston Jèze, whom we met in chapter 2 criticizing commercial colonization, the internationally well-known expert of the law of public finance who had voted for Scelle and later himself became the target of a similar series of protests for his involvement as Abyssinia's counsel against Italy in the League in 1935–1936. In Paris, Scelle must have represented not only Herriot's controversial coalition but also a step towards the unknown – novel theories about the law, interdisciplinary connections, and unabashed journalistic activity in favor of political causes. Le Fur's qualifications were impeccable so that the result was clearly no scandal even if Scelle's name today completely overshadows Le Fur's.

Solidarity with tradition: Louis Le Fur

In 1928 the Parisian essayist Julien Benda (1867–1956) published his famous tract *La trahison des clercs*,[213] attacking contemporary intellectuals for having set aside universal idealism and having turned into

---

[210] Milet, *La faculté de droit*, p. 151. [211] Milet, *La faculté de droit*, pp. 155–156.
[212] Milet, *La faculté de droit*, p. 161.
[213] Translated as *The Treason of the Intellectuals*, by Richard Aldington (New York, Norton, 1969 [1928]).

enthusiastic supporters of national causes and racial or class agitation. What he saw around him was: "a humanity which has abandoned itself to realism with a unanimity, an absence of reserve, a sanctification of its passion unexampled in history."[214] For Benda, war would be an imminent consequence. International institutions and treaties had left intact the spirit of war that prevailed in France and Germany.[215] As if hoping against hope, Benda pleaded for a "betterment of human morality," a return to traditional idealism and its standard tropes, "justice as such," "humanity as such," "universal fraternity."[216]

To react to the cultural modernism represented, for example, in Bergson's philosophical intuitionism or Gide's heroic individualism on the one hand, and to communism and nationalism on the other, by an appeal to traditional values and universal justice was a common reaction among conservative intellectuals everywhere. In France, that reaction had a concrete object in Germany whose national characteristics, history, and political ambitions were seen throughout French society as responsible for the climate of subjectivism that Benda sought to exorcize from the imagination of the clerks.[217] For some such as Joseph-Barthélemy, parliamentary democracy was mortally threatened by the absence of political authority, the growing influence of the *mutualités*, and problems of parliamentary method. Without an effective reform of the State, democracy would lose out to its competitors.[218] A few years later, Julien Bonnecase from the University of Bordeaux identified a similarly profound malaise in French legal thought that seemed connected to the metaphysical pessimism and celebration of subjectivism that he read as parts of the *Zeitgeist*. Legal thought had become uncertain about its premises and pessimistic about its meaningfulness, part of a world "without a soul" – as manifested by the prevalence of utilitarianism and conceptualism in legal doctrine.[219]

Like Benda, Louis Le Fur concentrated his energy on advocating a return to universal tradition, represented by natural law, indissociable from Christian morality. Le Fur had rejected the solidarist theories of Bourgeois as early as 1909 "si en vogue aujourd'hui." Little natural solidarity was visible between States and where it existed as a fact, it could

---

[214] Benda, *Treason of the Intellectuals*, p. 181.
[215] Benda, *Treason of the Intellectuals*, p. 184.
[216] Benda, *Treason of the Intellectuals*, p. 202.
[217] For Benda's anti-Germanism, cf. Winock, *Le siècle des intellectuels*, pp. 244–245.
[218] Joseph-Barthélemy, *La crise de la démocratie contemporaine*, esp. pp. 133 *et seq.*
[219] Bonnecase, *La pensée juridique française*, pp. 80–162.

not be used as a basis for normative conclusions. Only a superior morality could explain why solidarity was a good thing, and what it required.[220] In his criticism of the legal theories of Duguit and Scelle Le Fur stressed that instead of solidarity, moral character was the fundamental fact about human beings. The defense of legal obligation required more than reference to sociological or (in Scelle's case) biological facts. It needed a concept of the common good. Accompanied by anti-metaphysical individualism, solidarism led to anarchy. But, Le Fur held, Duguit and Scelle had both smuggled naturalist assumptions into their theories. That their naturalism was hidden, however, or sometimes expressed through reference to public opinion or sentiment of justice, made it dangerously close to the moral subjectivism against which both solidarism and traditional naturalism were poised.[221] Le Fur appreciated solidarism's critique of voluntarism and sovereignty but did not share its faith in sociology, accompanied by a neglect of tradition. But when he wrote about the crisis of majoritarian democracy and of the State, largely approving Joseph-Barthélemy's analyses, and suggested a return to the common good, it remained far from clear where the difference between that open-ended concept and the one advocated by solidarists lay.[222]

Le Fur was no more an original thinker than Benda but, like the latter, able to strike a responsive chord in his audience by finding the main culprit for the destruction of the authority of tradition in nineteenth-century German political and legal thought and *Kultur*. He explained the shocking vulnerability of pre-war internationalism as a story of sin and its wages, a loss of moral sense, and uncontrolled fall into the abyss of violence. The message bore a redemptive hope, of course, in the form of a moderate reform of the international system towards a decentralized universal federation. It is no surprise that Le Fur found himself a much-used speaker, a three-time lecturer at the Hague Academy of International Law, a member and vice-president of the *Institut de droit international*, and in 1933 the President of the *Institut international de philosophie du droit et de sociologie juridique*.

---

[220] Louis Le Fur, "La paix perpetuelle et l'arbitrage international" (1909), XVI *RGDIP*, pp. 447–448.

[221] Louis Le Fur, "Le fondement du droit dans la doctrine de Léon Duguit," in *Les grands problèmes du droit* (Paris, Sirey, 1937), pp. 389, 414–423, 432–433. Cf. also Le Fur, "Règles générales du droit de la paix" (1935/IV), 54 *RdC*, pp. 88–94, 101–103.

[222] Louis Le Fur, "La démocratie et la crise de l'Etat," in *Les grands problèmes*, pp. 530, 572–583.

Two aspects of Le Fur's writing manifest the conservative vision of international legality: an idealist identification of the ills of the *Zeitgeist* with subjectivism and positivism, and a moderate global federalism in which each hierarchical level would receive its rightful place in a "pyramidical" structure of interlocking authorities. At the time, both supported a political agenda for guarantees against Germany and strengthening the League, understood as a (rather timid) system of dispute-settlement.[223]

The critical program was outlined in a 1920 book on the just war that was prefaced by the conservative nationalist Maurice Barrès (1862–1923), describing the outcome of the war as a victory of the "French idea of law" and equating justice with the return of Alsace–Lorraine to France.[224] The attack on tradition was a distinctly German operation: "In the first rank of the systems destructive to morality and law are those elaborated by Germans . . . Things have come to the point where it is possible to say without exaggeration that present Germany has lost the notion of law, at least law in the traditional sense."[225] After Martin Luther, the largest part of the responsibility for this state of affairs lay with Kant's methodological doubt about the human ability to know the good.[226] This led to subjective idealism – the world as a projection of human consciousness – that romantic writers used for the adoration of *völkisch* nationalism.[227] The categorical imperative could only appear as an irrational escape from skepticism. And it imposed too great a demand for individuals. Breaking down under its own weight, Kantian morality left its subjects in a void that was quickly filled either by the Hegelian State as the Ersatz-center of moral lives or a Nietzschean amoralism, the "paganism of passions."[228] "The idea of liberty as a unique rule of action can only breed anarchy and in fact consecrate the triumph of the strongest."[229] Under such conditions, law was reduced to a contract to set up a sovereign to deter individuals from destroying each other. Not differentiating between good and bad laws, and seeing the State only as a system of constraint, the Kantian view became "if not the theoretical legitimation, at least the practical consolidation of despotism."[230] In the 1930s Le Fur saw these dangers in the degeneration of parliamentarism into a search for special advantages

---

[223] Louis Le Fur, *Précis de droit international* (3rd edn., Paris, Dalloz, 1937), pp. 308–309.
[224] Louis Le Fur, *Guerre juste et juste paix* (Paris, Pedone, 1920), Préface par Maurice Barrès, pp. v, vi.   [225] Le Fur, *Guerre juste*, p. 11.   [226] Le Fur, *Guerre juste*, p. 29.
[227] Le Fur, *Guerre juste*, pp. 31–33.   [228] Le Fur, *Guerre juste*, p. 38.
[229] Le Fur, *Guerre juste*, p. 20.   [230] Le Fur, *Guerre juste*, p. 23.

and support for particular interests. Without a morally informed principle of the general good the political order was powerless in face of modernity's crisis.[231]

The same applied internationally. If there was no overriding sense of the common good, States were cast in a perpetual condition of potential war and there was no point from which to challenge their decision to use force to defend themselves.[232] Self-legislation was the international equivalent of the liberal contract. To think of law in terms of State will "destroys all morality and with it, all civilization."[233] It was regression to barbarism: "Either a law superior to human will, or material force; there is no other alternative."[234]

Autonomy led to nationalism and war. For authoritarian (German) nationalism, nothing stood before the nation's imperial ambitions. But even a liberal nationalism (Mancini and Wilson) that conceived the nation as voluntary association ("a plebiscite every day" in Renan's memorable phrase) led to endless demands for secession or to the tyranny of the State that needed to combat it.[235] Hence, self-determination could be only "condemned by modern public law."[236] Even in a united nation it would so excite popular passion that it would lead to imperialism.[237]

The second way of German errors lay with positivist historicism and racism. The former taught that there was no universal moral order. But if the *Volksgeist* was not limited by something outside itself, it became a name for majority rule whose only limit was popular aspiration.[238] The organic theory mistook a biological metaphor for reality and ended up in the complete submission of individuals to the State.[239] Moreover, positivist nationalism led inescapably to racism, reducing human beings to their physical characteristics, neglecting their moral nature and opening the door for reproductive manipulation.[240]

Throughout the 1920s and 1930s Le Fur wrote with passion, and a sense of acute danger against the errors of German philosophy –

---

[231] Le Fur, "La démocratie," pp. 530–583.
[232] Cf. Immanuel Kant, "The Metaphysics of Morals" and "Perpetual Peace: A Sketch," in *Political Writings* (ed. Hans Reiss, Cambridge University Press, 1991), pp. 98, 165. Le Fur, *Guerre juste*, pp. 23–24, 27–28.   [233] Le Fur, *Guerre juste*, p. 50.
[234] Le Fur, *Guerre juste*, p. 92.
[235] Louis Le Fur, *Races, nationalités, états* (Paris, Alcan 1922), pp. 68–77.
[236] Louis Le Fur, *Nationalisme et internationalisme au regard de la morale et du droit naturel* (Paris, Chronique sociale, 1926), p. 15. His reference here is to the Åland Island case.
[237] Le Fur, *Races*, pp. 77–82.   [238] Le Fur, *Guerre juste*, pp. 48–49.
[239] Le Fur took delight in the fact that German racism was itself drawn from the writings of non-Germanic scholars such as Lamarck, Darwin, and Gobineau.
[240] Le Fur, *Guerre juste*, pp. 39–47 and *Races*, pp. 40–60.

subjectivism, voluntarism, positivism, materialism, formalism, historicism. Practically every deviation from tradition was guilty by association with a German doctrine; and every German doctrine ultimately an apology of force.[241] Jhering, Jellinek, and Triepel were branded as immoral defenders of State absolutism in theory, and German *Herrschaft* in practice. Even Kelsen stood accused for justifying the "oppression of the individual by the State."[242] Le Fur's description of the historical method reduced it to a caricature: every normative conclusion was criticized as a lapse into rationalism.[243] Apparently, a debate between two concepts of naturalism was impossible. Hence the technique of drawing the enemy as a straw man and indicting him for the sins of his nation. But Le Fur had no sympathy for the writings of Alvarez, either, that for him seemed to glorify arbitrary consensus.[244] Even the theories of Duguit and Scelle were more acceptable as they were really, despite themselves, moral doctrines in the garb of sociological language.

Le Fur's international law was a set of doctrines by philosophically minded lawyers and derivations or (unintended) effects of such doctrines. Whatever difficulties and problems there were in diplomacy or politics always followed in some way from philosophy. Consequently, the remedy too had to be philosophical: "to return, with traditional philosophy, to an objective criterion, the pursuit of happiness or the search for order."[245] This meant a return to Christian religion, the only system of thought that was built on universality.[246] However, despite tradition's roots in Christian dogma, its content could always be verified by "positive observation and universal experience" – were not intelligence and morality always regarded as values of higher order than power or riches![247] Despite his partiality to philosophy, Le Fur insisted that his natural law could be demonstrated by reference to social necessity, "la loi sociale des Etats." Even proof of God's existence was empirical, the fact of belief in God being "almost universal."[248]

Such a mixture of philosophical and empirical arguments usefully expressed the various ambivalences that constituted the conservative spirit. Le Fur condemned racism, for instance, at a philosophical level.

---

[241] Louis Le Fur, "Le droit et les doctrines allemandes," in *Les grands problèmes*, pp. 312, 378–388. [242] Le Fur, "Règles générales," p. 44.
[243] Cf. e.g. Le Fur, *Précis*, pp. 190–198 and "Règles générales," pp. 147–152.
[244] Le Fur, "Règles générales," pp. 45–71, 124–144. [245] Le Fur, *Guerre juste*, p. 19.
[246] Louis Le Fur, "L'église et le droit des gens," in *Les grands problèmes*, pp. 502–529.
[247] Le Fur, *Guerre juste*, pp. 94–95.
[248] Louis Le Fur, *Nécessité d'un droit international pour coordonner les diverses activités nationales* (Paris, Chronique sociale, n/d), pp. 5, 19.

As a defense of the German *Vollkulturstaat*, it was pure ideology.[249] But racism's unscientific character remained limited to its application between European races that were completely mixed, and none more so than the German.[250] There was no doubt, he argued in 1935, that there existed "peoples that were really inferior, situated at a different level of civilization" to whom international law could not be applied.[251] Nor was he a pacifist. On the contrary, the absence of a judge between States meant that they sometimes had to go to war to defend justice. But in so doing they had to comply with natural law.[252] In fact, Le Fur claimed, the view that war was not a sovereign privilege but the enforcement of justice was shared everywhere apart from Germany. Even old German theory (Klüber, Heffter, Bluntschli) – to which the new sometimes gave hypocritical acceptance – shared it.[253] To the objection that the criteria for just war were open to political misuse Le Fur responded that to reason this way was to reason in a world of absolutes; man lives in a world of relativity. That people may disagree is not an argument against natural law but an incident of the weakness of human reason.[254] It was the very reason for which law and the State were needed and for which suggestions "from some Catholic corners" that international law could be replaced by Catholic doctrine could not be accepted.[255]

Central to Le Fur's writing was the transposition of the philosophical argument to the reality of international politics. The struggle between objectivism and subjectivism, morality and arbitrariness was re-enacted in the opposition of France and Germany. The war had been a struggle between two fundamentally opposed conceptions: "the concept of civilized world which is nothing other than the Christian concept . . . and . . . the concept of pagan antiquity – its best elements apart – adopted and aggravated by people that have used all the resources of a cultivated dialectics to ensure the triumph of the passions over the superior elements of humanity, law morality and reason."[256] Le Fur associated himself with the disappointment of the French right over the conditions of the peace: too much heed had been given to manifestations in favor of Germany. The left and high finance had united to protect their commercial interests by advocating minimal obstacles to rapid German

---

[249] Le Fur, *Races*, pp. 27, 28.
[250] It was impossible to identify racial unity: language, ethnic background, and cultural form were completely mixed between European peoples, Le Fur, *Races*, pp. 25, 27–39. [251] Le Fur, "Règles générales," p. 10.
[252] Le Fur, *Guerre juste*, pp. 6–8, 75–79. [253] Le Fur, *Guerre juste*, pp. 70–71.
[254] Le Fur, *Guerre juste*, pp. 77–78. [255] Le Fur, "L'église," pp. 518–519.
[256] Le Fur, *Guerre juste*, p. 164.

recovery. Sovereignty went with responsibility and William II should have been brought to justice in France. The claim for natural frontiers at the Rhine having been discarded, even the military occupation of the left bank was limited to a maximum of fifteen years. With the weakness of the League, France was left unprotected.[257]

Yet his naturalism failed to indicate ways of concrete renewal. In the 1930s he affirmed the absurdity of holding States bound by treaties if conditions had fundamentally changed – a problem at the heart of the German call for revision. True, "an obsolete law that is contrary to the social order is a bad law." However, unilateral repudiation was unacceptable. It was best if the parties would agree but war could not be overruled as *ultima ratio*. Art. 19 of the Covenant had mandated the League Assembly to advise the reconsideration of treaties that had become inapplicable. But the Assembly's powers were only recommendatory and needed to include the votes of the parties. Hence, today's form prevailed over social or moral necessity – but did so only as a result of prudential evaluation. Revision by international decision would now be too dangerous.[258]

Le Fur defended the State against the extremes of individualism and imperialism. The State was an indispensable instrument of the common good, "le juste milieu, le moyen terme."[259] It could not be reduced to a contract between free individuals or to an empty shell over the free nation.[260] It was a political synthesis of conflicting wills which overcame this conflict by aiming towards the common good. This was the State as *Patria*, the historical and empirical "will to live together."[261] The supreme territorial authority was received from and limited by the moral law: "The last word must always belong to justice and reason." [262] The State was the "reason" for the "passion" that was the nation,[263] a public law *association* whose co-ordinative functions were limited by the co-ordination tasks of other associations, families, *syndicats*, international organizations, and so on. It was not a formal (Kantian) system of co-ordination as it aimed towards the common good that looked for humans' spiritual capacities and limited the search for (economic) efficiency by moral principle.[264]

---

[257] Le Fur, *Guerre juste*, pp. 117, 138, 139–162.
[258] Le Fur, "Règles générales," pp. 217–29, 233, 242–244.
[259] Le Fur "La démocratie," pp. 582–583.
[260] Le Fur, *Races*, p. 91 and Le Fur, "Le fondement de droit," in *Les grands problèmes*, pp. 43–44.   [261] Le Fur, *Races*, pp. 97–103.   [262] Le Fur, *Races*, pp. 115, 110–132.
[263] Le Fur, *Nationalisme et internationalisme au regard de la morale et du droit naturel* (Paris, Chronique sociale, 1926), p. 8.
[264] Le Fur, "Le fondement du droit," pp. 38–65.

International law as sociology: France 1871–1950

The nature of Le Fur's authoritarian federalism can be gleaned in his 1926 argument about the harmony between "beneficial" forms of nationalism and internationalism.[265] "Reason" compelled one to think in terms of an ascending way: from the family to the nation; the nation to the State; from States to the international society.[266] Every association at every level had its own purpose; each purpose linked to the purpose of the whole, determined by objective law. Everywhere the search was for the common good "which is the same for all, for the society and its members, individuals and intermediate groups . . . there is no opposition between the honest and reasonable objectives of individuals and the State."[267] There was a natural development to this structure, evolving to the fourth and "final stage": "internationalism is nothing but a continuation of the expansion of human societies that dates back to the beginning of history; it is the normal result of a development of many thousands of years."[268] No conflict existed between science and reason: disagreement was always proof of error, normally the error of egoism, fed by individualist theory. The pyramidical structure – "une synthèse harmonieuse . . . une construction hiérarchisée"[269] – encapsulated the truth of the unity of the human race. In articulating and protecting this structure international law "rests on two great scientific facts: one ethical, the profound unity of the human species; the other economic, the presence of a certain international solidarity, the interdependence of nations."[270] Such harmony reflects the normative unity that leads via natural law – including the objective law of solidarity – ultimately to the one God. As the errors of individualism, racism, and unhealthy nationalism were set aside, the world would regain the unity it had lost in the Reformation and the Enlightenment. Individuals are free; but as such

---

[265] A sane nationalism was a social necessity, not an absolute but a relative (natural) preference for one's nation and the well-being of one's compatriots. The two errors that led to its being incompatible with internationalism were the doctrine of the inequality of nations and absolute sovereignty, Le Fur, *Nationalisme et internationalisme*, pp. 9–16. A sane internationalism, again, is based on the theory of economic interdependence and moral unity of humankind.

[266] Le Fur, *Nationalisme et internationalisme*, pp. 21, 23–24, 28 ("En réalité, la société – et la future société universelle des Etats comme les autres – est une pyramide . . . cette pyramide à base large dont le couronnement est la Société des Nations").

[267] Le Fur, *Nationalisme et internationalisme*, p. 26.

[268] Le Fur, *Nationalisme et internationalisme*, p. 18.

[269] Le Fur, *Nationalisme et internationalisme*, p. 27.

[270] "[R]epose sur deux grands faits scientifiques: l'un d'ordre ethique, l'unité profonde de l'éspèce humaine; l'autre d'ordre économique, l'existence d'une certaine solidarité internationale, d'une interdépendance économique des nations," Le Fur, *Nationalisme et internationalisme*, p. 5.

they are ("en un certain sens") submitted to society: they must consent to what is necessary for social peace, above all to an effective authority.[271] The key words are "reason" and "authority": reason compels submission to society, the pyramidical structure, the two rules of international society: that no one may cause harm unjustifiably to others, and that there must be sanction. This latter supposes a juridical authority, legislative authority but also "a spiritual power, the only guardian of morality, and with it, of the notions of order and justice" – the independent Catholic church.[272]

Le Fur's arguments gave expression to a widely felt sense in France and elsewhere that the problems of industrial modernity, including war, followed from a neglect of tradition – and associated the challenge to tradition with German industrial, political, and intellectual predominance, as well as the spread of electoral democracy "that was leading certain States to ruin."[273] However, there was no clear sense what "tradition" meant, apart from a sense of moderation, of good will, kindness, piety towards authority, even "love."[274] Le Fur did not propose legal or institutional reforms that would have differed from standard reforms of the League and guarantees against Germany. His federalism was a moderate structure for which more important was the sense of order and hierarchy than any particular arrangement in which the elements would fall. What was lacking now, he wrote in 1935, was proper authority: to renew international politics was to do away with private justice among States.[275] That authority would determine the jurisdiction of particular associations, and define what the "common good" meant in particular contexts. Just as Le Fur's worst fear was always "anarchy," the standard remedy was authority.[276]

Le Fur was decidedly anti-positivist but when called upon to defend some particular view, always took care to produce a positivist defense: natural law was right because . . . most lawyers now seemed to think so; federalism was needed because . . . the world had become interdependent. Law was like other sciences, he said in an argument against Kelsen, based on generalization from facts.[277] He saw the economy as a funda-

---

[271] Le Fur, *Nationalisme et internationalisme*, p. 20.
[272] Le Fur, *Nationalisme et internationalisme*, p. 29.
[273] Le Fur, "Règles générales," p. 133.
[274] Le Fur, "Le fondement du droit," pp. 65–71.
[275] Le Fur, "Règles générales," pp. 191–193.
[276] Cf. e.g. Le Fur, "La démocratie," pp. 536–537, 560–583.
[277] Le Fur, "La démocratie," p. 564.

mental social fact but refrained from advocating either free trade or protectionism. In sum, "tradition" here was less a material doctrine about the way the world should be governed or organized than an attitude of human nature, about authority and community. Here lay its weakness: it was an attempt to renew the nineteenth-century concept of virtuous conscience – moral sense and honesty[278] – at a time when the very idea of virtue had been undermined by the developments against which it was stated. It saw the world in terms of philosophical doctrines confronting each other; as if how people behaved were determined by them. Le Fur was eclectic because tradition was so; because that was a tradition born in another age and for other kinds of *problématique*; a tradition that was silent about how to resolve the problems of a non-traditional age.

The solidarity of fact: Georges Scelle

Where Le Fur looked for tradition in order to respond to modernity's crisis, Georges Scelle harnessed modernity in a battle against the problems caused by tradition. From the 1919 commentary of the League Covenant to the late 1950s, he never departed from his idiosyncratic legal monism that held law a translation of sociological and ultimately biological processes that led inexorably to federalism. From the outset, Scelle's writing followed a direction different from that of the mainstream internationalists in France.[279] His first published work was on legal history – an exposé of the *oeuvre* of Richard Zouche (1590–1660) – and his 1906 dissertation in Paris dealt with the economic history of Spanish imperialism.[280] The social–historical method was consciously

---

[278] Cf. e.g. Le Fur, "Règles générales," pp. 151–152, 159–160.
[279] After his dissertation in 1906 Scelle for the first time took part in the *agrégation* – unsuccessfully. Thereafter he attained practical experience as the Secretary of the Brazilian delegation at the second Hague Conference and to the US delegation in the *Orinoco Steamship Co.* case. He was Professor of International Law at the University of Sofia in Bulgaria in 1908–1910. After teaching in Lille and Dijon, he passed his *agrégation* at the third try in 1912 and was appointed to the University of Dijon. He was mobilized and ordered to the front in August 1914, participating in combat duty and acting as "officier jurisconsulte" to the French Eighth Army. He was demobilized in November 1918, taking up again his appointment in Dijon. During 1929–1933 he also taught at the University of Geneva as well as the Graduate School of International Studies. In 1932 he was invited to a chair in Paris. Cf. Charles Rousseau, "Georges Scelle (1878–1961)" (1961), LXV *RGDIP*, pp. 5–8; Oliver Diggelmann, "Anfänge der Völkerrechtssoziologie. Die Völkerrechtskonzeptionen von Max Huber und Georges Scelle im Vergleich" (unpublished PhD thesis, on file with author, Zürich, 1998), p. 120.
[280] Georges Scelle, *La traité négrière aux Indes de Castilles – Contrats et traités d'assiento* (2 vols., Paris, Larose & Tenin, 1906).

chosen by Scelle to depart from standard histories that focused on kings, captains, and dramatic events. He wanted to express the needs and interests of "anonymous crowds," together with the geographic, economic, and social conditions in which they lived, the true causes, he wrote, of political events.[281] The forms of de facto colonial domination by the United States in Central America was the subject of two early articles, while other brief works came out as case studies on aspects of sovereignty, recognition, and arbitration, with the main point lying in a political or otherwise anti-formalist assessment – though still through conventional language.[282]

By 1928 Scelle had gained enough self-confidence to write a long analysis on the basis of his solidarist method on the status of Vilna after the Polish occupation had been accepted by the Allied Conference of Ambassadors in March 1923. The article turns out to be a defense of the decision of the Ambassadors and an indictment of the obstruction of the (right-wing) Lithuanian Government in the League-led negotiations. The relevant legal criterion was whether the decision corresponded to the situation of fact and to what was required by "international solidarity." On both scores, Lithuania's unwillingness to accept a decision on the basis of self-determination (it had refused to accept a plebiscite in this largely Polish-inhabited region) and the interests of European peace tilted the scales against it. In Scelle's eyes, Lithuania was invoking an anti-social concept of sovereignty while the Poles had been ready to accept the Allied verdict (which of course underwrote the main Polish claim). In fact, Scelle concluded, it was doubtful if Lithuania merited to have been constructed as a State in the first place; autonomy or internationalization might have produced a result better in accord with the ethnic and historical solidarities and requirements of equitable administration.[283] Scelle's views in the matter went on all points contrary to those of Le Fur, from whom Lithuania had requested an opinion. The Ambassadors, Le Fur had argued, had no jurisdiction to effect a de facto transfer of Vilna to Poland without

---

[281] Scelle, *La traité*, p. vii.
[282] Cf. Georges Scelle, "L'Affaire de la Orinoco Steamship Company" (1911), XVIII *RGDIP*, p. 201; "Le contrôle financier américain au Honduras et au Nicaragua" (1912), XIX *RGDIP*, p. 128; "La ratification de la Convention du Gothard du 13 octobre 1909" (1913), XX *RGDIP*, p. 497; and "Les Etats-Unis d'Amérique et les révolutions méxicaines" (1914), XXI *RGDIP*, p. 128.
[283] Georges Scelle, "La situation juridique de Vilna et de son territoire. Etude sur le différend polono-lithuanien et la force obligatoire de la décision de la Conférence des Ambassadeurs du 15 Mars 1923" (1928), XXV *RGDIP*, pp. 730–780.

Lithuania's consent.[284] It was not an insignificant part of Scelle's argument that he viewed the Lithuanian government a dictatorship.[285] If politics and law were both about putting solidarity into effect, there was little point in insisting on a distinction. Even if the acts of a government de facto might be credited with prima facie legality, such legality could be set aside in favor of more pressing considerations.

Scelle was a thoroughly political animal. As a social radical, he followed Bourgeois and later solidarists in taking an active interest in the development of labor legislation and syndicalist solutions to the social problems of the day. In 1924 he wrote of labor legislation in very advanced terms in a collective volume that contained articles by radicals such as Charles Bouglé, Lucien Lévy-Bruhl, and Gaston Jèze.[286] In the same year, as we have seen, he entered the Cabinet of Justin Godart, the Minister of Labor in Herriot's left coalition in which he participated in the drafting of the laws that set up the *Conseil Nationale de l'Economie* that sought to co-ordinate French economic policies by integrating representatives from labor, employers, and government. In 1927 he published a book for the *licence en droit* on French and international industrial legislation, endorsing the progressive steps that had been taken in France in the past few years.[287] Though he supported the claims of labor unions for progressive industrial and labor legislation – including female suffrage – he opposed communism and was critical of Soviet policy.[288] From the 1920s onwards Scelle published regularly articles and commentaries in the leftist *Depêche de Toulouse, Quotidien*, and in other papers, often with a much more polemical tone than in his scientific work.[289] He admired the writings of the radical philosopher Alain (Emile Chartier) and received from him a skeptical attitude towards political oligarchies and nationalist rhetoric. He was an active member of the committee of the *Paix par le droit* and of the French and international League of Nations Associations and, after a brief period of hesitation, a staunch

---

[284] Cf. *Consultations de M. A. de Lapradelle, Louis Le Fur et André Mandelstam de la décision de la Conférence des Ambassadeurs du 15 mars 1923* (Paris, Editions internationales, 1928), pp. 41–80. [285] Scelle, "La situation juridique de Vilna," p. 777.
[286] Georges Scelle, *La politique républicaine* (2 vols., Paris, Alcan, 1924).
[287] Georges Scelle, *Précis élémentaire de législation industrielle* (2 vols., Paris, Sirey, 1927).
[288] On Scelle's political views, cf. also Diggelmann, "Anfänge der Völkerrechtssoziologie," pp. 122–125.
[289] He argued, for instance, that instead of adopting a position of cold neutrality, the International Labour Organization should defend the claims of the working class. Cf. Antoine-Jean Leonetti, "Georges Scelle; Etude d'une théorie juridique" (unpublished *Thèse de doctorat d'Etat*, Université de Nice-Sophia Antipolis, January 1992, on file with author), p. 294.

supporter of the idea (though not always the practice) of the League of Nations.[290]

Like many others, Scelle was profoundly influenced by the war experience in which he saw in part a distinctly German folly but to a greater extent a consequence of the anti-social ideas of sovereignty. In this, he was firmly in the camp of Alvarez and Politis at home and, for instance, Kelsen in Germany and Hugo Krabbe (1857–1936) in the Netherlands. His developed views were for the first time clearly laid down in a 1923 course at Fauchille's *Institut* in Paris at which Le Fur had expounded his "philosophy" of international law two years earlier.[291] Scelle argued that the First World War had broken sovereignty in favor of methodological individualism. It was now realized that like all societies the international society was composed of individuals and nothing but them – to ignore this was to remain trapped in an anti-scientific collectivism. However, Scelle agreed with Rousseau or Bourgeois that individuals were not the independent atoms of rationalist liberalism. They were linked by innumerable solidarities that varied in intensity and extent. Such solidarities formed the substratum of social life, thus marking a de facto regionalism that it would be unscientific to ignore.[292] If States held a predominant place among human collectivities this was just a historical accident. There was nothing particular about them: they, too, were only a means to realize individuals' solidarity.

The State and its government constituted the main international administrative organs, increasingly accompanied by properly international bodies. International commissions, unions, and technical organizations were multiplying. Public international law was to co-ordinate these developments. Its principles formed the unwritten constitutional law of the international society. In this way, international law reflected the international social milieu: individuals and collectivities were given to it as social facts. The rest of its substance was divided into constitutional principles (principles of public authority, legislation, and sanctions), administrative law (the administrators, their sphere of competence, public services), the law of contracts, and international penal law.[293]

---

[290] Rousseau, "Georges Scelle," p. 9.
[291] Georges Scelle, "Essai de systematique de droit international (Plan d'un cours de droit international public)" (1923), XXX *RGDIP*, pp. 116–142.
[292] Scelle, "Essai de systematique," p. 119.
[293] Scelle, "Essai de systematique," pp. 124–141. Constitutional law was above all a sociological law – without it, society would dissolve. It distributed personal and collective

International law as sociology: France 1871–1950

Most of Scelle's mature ideas were present in this early sketch and further elaborated in his general course at the Hague Academy of 1933, in the two-volume *Précis* that came out in 1932 and 1934 and in an extensive report to the *Institut international de droit public* of 1935.[294] Many of those ideas – monism, the significance of *traités-lois*, and the role of the *dédoublement fonctionnel* – are quite well known but it may be convenient to summarize them in four points.

First, positive law was a (more or less successful) translation of the objective laws of social solidarity. Scelle followed Durkheim in explaining social cohesion as an effect of mechanical and organic solidarity, grounded in the biology of human needs.[295] From these emerged an implicit constitution that organized the government of common affairs through procedures for legislation, jurisdiction, and enforcement. None of this was a matter of choice. It was impossible to live in society without those functions being dealt with in some way.[296] Legislation involved an essentially *scientific* task:[297]

> the legislator has no other mission than to translate the laws of existence ["lois de l'être"] into normative laws. It is their coincidence that is the intrinsic foundation of the law's validity, its extrinsic validity residing in the regularity through which possession and exercise of legislative competences is carried out. As the legislator wills the law, he cannot but will what the law wills.[298]

This led into *monism*: like social reality, law, too, was one. Distinctions between State law and international law, private and public law were perhaps useful for exposition but without normative difference. The bonds of solidarity (solidarity as fact, not as a "feeling" or a moral principle) formed innumerable groups or societies, within and between which different needs give basis to different laws. Such societies were hierarchically related so that the more inclusive ones overrode the less inclusive ones. For example, treaties automatically overrode conflicting national law (although their reception had a practical value in that it

---

status as well as providing for a judicial function. For analysis and criticism, cf. Leonetti, "Georges Scelle," pp. 304–312. In addition, private international law (the sphere of which, however, was determined by public law) was divided into international civil, commercial and labor laws, Scelle, "Essai de systematique," pp. 141–142.

[294] Georges Scelle, "Théorie du gouvernement international" (1935), *Annuaire de l'Institut international de droit public*, pp. 41–112.   [295] Scelle, *Précis*, I, pp. 2–5.

[296] Scelle "Théorie du gouvernement international," pp. 50–52.

[297] This did not mean that anyone who disapproved of particular legislation could ignore it. Legislation enjoyed the presumption of being in accordance with the objective law (*hypothèse de bien légiféré*), cf. Scelle, *Précis*, II, pp. 297–299.

[298] Georges Scelle, *Théorie juridique de la révision des traités* (Paris, Sirey, 1936), p. 47.

made it easier for national administrators to apply them).[299] The law of humanitarian intervention, being a law of the international society, overrode national sovereignty, that is to say, the constitutional competence of the administrators of national societies.[300] Local solidarity cannot be opposed to a global one. This is the foundation of Scelle's "federal phenomenon," the slow integration of smaller units into larger ones (but also the break-up of empires). It was visible in the development from national to international to supranational administration, from governmental to international guarantee of legality, from diplomatic protection to international intervention. Though international bodies were still mostly composed of governmental representatives, secretariats had increasingly independent representation, and sometimes, as in the ILO, even professional interests.[301]

Second, like Duguit's, Scelle's social world consisted ("ultimately") of relationships between individuals.[302] The individual was the only *real* legal subject, endowed by society with "essential competencies" and a sphere of discretion that grounded her freedom, conceptualized – somewhat oddly – as the right to life, liberty, movement, trade, and economic establishment.[303] To be sure, individuals entered into different types of social relations of which the State was only the most intensive one. Alongside it, the international milieu organized individuals also into supra-State societies (international organizations, particularly the League of Nations) and extra-State societies (such as the Catholic church or the Jewish Council).[304] But like all social conglomerates the State was in the end a mere fiction: at the level of reality, there were only individuals, either as subjects of liberties, objects of behavioral regulation, or as administrators (*gouvernants*), nothing more.

Third, law's function was to distribute competencies to individuals who appeared either as private individuals exercising subjective rights (or liberties) or as agents or administrators of particular societies.[305] Every new obligation was, somewhat as in Kelsen, a modification of some person's competencies.[306] In the exercise of competencies, individuals were not normally expected to realize their own will but to act in the pursuit of public functions: legislation, adjudication, and enforcement –

---

[299] Scelle, *Précis*, II, pp. 349–364. [300] Scelle, *Précis*, II, pp. 50–54.
[301] Scelle, "Théorie du gouvernement international," pp. 77–79. For the social-scientific basis of Scelle's federalism, cf. Leonetti, "Georges Scelle," pp. 268–301.
[302] Cf. Scelle, "Théorie du gouvernement international," pp. 42–44.
[303] Scelle, "Théorie du gouvernement international," p. 66.
[304] Scelle, *Précis*, I, pp. 288–312. [305] Scelle, *Précis*, I, pp. 9–14.
[306] Scelle, *Précis*, II, p. 347.

conceived not in terms of the exercise of "rights" but doing what was necessary (in the contract, however, the law had delegated the determination of what is necessary to individuals).[307] Hence followed the famous doctrine of the *dédoublement fonctionnel* – the situation where an individual has been put in a position of agent or administrator of two or more societies, e.g. where a national Parliament in approving a treaty legislated both for the national and the international society. In the same way – and controversially – national governments are also put in a position to administer international society.[308]

Fourth, legal technique used material and procedural regulation (*droit normatif/droit constructif*) to attain its objective (*but*) – the satisfaction of social need. This was not necessarily identical with the legislator's subjective aim (*motif*).[309] Normative law had to do with the content of the behavioral obligation, constructive law contained the procedures whereby it was legislated and administered and violations were reacted to. The core of constructive law was society's (implicit) constitution.[310] While juridical stability and material security were in national society guaranteed by the State's monopoly of force, the corresponding international procedure – collective intervention – was poorly developed. From Scelle's perspective, for instance, Article 10 of the Covenant constituted a mutual guarantee by governments of the territorial extension of their competencies – yet, the Council had only limited powers to enforce them.[311] In the wake of the Manchurian crisis it had become evident, however, that those competences had to be regarded as binding, and not restrained absurdly by the requirement of unanimity that would include the vote of the parties.[312] Scelle received this conclusion from a thoroughly functional interpretation of the Covenant – in fact a constitutionalization of the objectives of the foreign policy of French liberals; a continuation of the struggle Bourgeois had waged in favor of the standing military force at the Hôtel Crillon in 1919.

Scelle's language was idiosyncratic and repetitive – as befits a sociological monism that reduced politics to an expression of non-political necessities. The redescription of society through methodological

---

[307] Scelle, *Précis*, I, pp. 18–20; "Théorie du gouvernement international," pp. 49–52, 60.
[308] Cf. Scelle, "Théorie du gouvernement international," pp. 54–57 as well as Leonetti, "Georges Scelle," pp. 340–385 and Antonio Cassese, "Remarks on Scelle's Theory of 'Role Splitting' (*dédoublement fonctionnel*) in International Law" (1990), 1 *EJIL*, pp. 210–234. [309] Scelle, *Précis*, I, p. 16; II, pp. 336–368.
[310] Scelle, "Théorie du gouvernement international," pp. 49–50.
[311] Scelle, "Théorie du gouvernement international," pp. 57–59, 62–65.
[312] Scelle, "Théorie du gouvernement international," pp. 87–90, 92.

individualism and social solidarity – speaking not of State sovereignty, for instance, but of the competence of national administrators – opened social reality to an apparently less ideological analysis than traditional language. Under it, governments did not have a "right" to govern nor States a "reserved domain."[313] These were distorted expressions for the duty of governments to provide for the welfare of their communities. There were no open references to moral or political value: Scelle thought ideas about justice subjective and unverifiable.[314] The concept of just war, for instance, was always "too easy to criticize" because it was based on subjective notions.[315] War was not illegal because it was "wrong" but because it was anti-social. Scelle avoided "evaluation" that would have been independent from an analysis of what solidarity required – an analysis that was never mere exposition of facts or of the positive law (i.e. of the reaction of international legislators).[316] This was the language of a sociological positivism that fell on the side of the modernist reaction to the breakdown of nineteenth-century political systems – the project (initiated by Durkheim) of replacing morality by sociology and thinking of social problems from the perspective of their scientific resolution. Where Le Fur had combated individualism by seeking a revival of Christian tradition, Scelle accepted individualism but moved away from it by the assumption that its effects could be controlled by constraining arguments drawn from modern (social) science.

Scelle had no sympathy for nationalism or other non-functional principles of social association. Although it was necessary that the law protect (racial or religious) minorities, this was ultimately "artificial subjectivism": objective law knew neither majorities not minorities, and made no distinction between religious or ethnic principles that did not possess "objective social validity" and would transcend them on the way to federalism.[317] Scelle had little tolerance for claims of self-determination by colonized peoples. Colonization was a method of administration of backward territories whose inhabitants were unable to put their resources to active use. No nation had a right to enclose itself; the control of territory implied the obligation to use it to further international solidarity. The developed nations had an obligation of trusteeship over the

---

[313] Scelle, "Théorie du gouvernement international," p. 60.
[314] Scelle, *Précis*, I, p. 41.
[315] Georges Scelle, "Quelques reflexions sur l'abolition de la compétence de guerre" (1955), LVIII *RGDIP*, p. 6.
[316] Cf. especially Georges Scelle, "La situation juridique de Vilna," pp. 730–780.
[317] Scelle, "Théorie du gouvernement international," p. 70.

less developed ones, only partially recognized in the mandates system. As a form of public service, it should turn into direct international governance.[318]

Scelle hoped to provide a resolution to problems of international politics by applying the solidarist framework – which invariably turned out to prefer a slightly left-leaning liberalism with little distance from the preferences of French diplomacy. Methodological individualism entailed that freedom of trade, movement, and commercial establishment became central principles of the international order. To limit such freedoms a special justification was always needed.[319] Intervention was recast as a normal feature of a system in which all government by definition was intervention in somebody's competence. Its lawfulness could be determined only by reference to whether some action (the establishment of customs duties, the treatment of individuals, occupation of a territory) was in fact in that person's competence – this again being a function of social utility with the proviso that de facto administration constituted only a prima facie presumption of competence.[320] The law of territory was recast as the "law of the public domain." Areas of non-exclusivity were constantly expanding: the coastal State, for instance, might have servitude over coastal waters but no sovereignty.[321]

For Scelle, international law was about learning the scientific truth about how society was to be administered so as to best secure the attainment of social utility. The view had no limit: the international milieu was merely one and a rather arbitrarily limited aspect of a monistic world. Disagreement about the law appeared as truth and error about (social and biological) facts; not as struggle over interests or values. It is not difficult to see how such theory might seem appealing to deal with international conflict. Already formulating the problem provided a solution: there was no irreducible antagonism between interests; every conflict demonstrated error on somebody's part and it was the point of juridical technique to find out on whose part. War, for example, could only be lawful or not; neither a matter of privilege nor of formal definition, war was either anti-social violence or enforcement, *tertium non datur*.[322] Law and politics turned into sociology with a normative task, just as

---

[318] Scelle, *Précis*, I, pp. 143–145. For Scelle's arguments about the need to open China and Japan for foreign trade – forcibly if necessary, cf. Leonetti, "Georges Scelle," pp. 314–315.   [319] Scelle, *Précis*, II, pp. 64–89.
[320] Scelle, "Théorie du gouvernement international," pp. 71–77, 81–85.
[321] Cf. in more detail the discussion in Leonetti, "Georges Scelle," pp. 325–335.
[322] Scelle, "Théorie du gouvernement international," pp. 101–106.

Durkheim had thought it might. Comte's prediction (and Weber's fear) of the vanishing of the political class would become a reality; politics became administration by experts.

The central weakness of Scelle's objectivism was manifested in the intangibility of the "reality" it postulated – a problem that left it balancing between an inconsequential positivism and revolution, accompanied by the hope that federalism will one day make this problem disappear. This may be illustrated by his 1936 treatment of the revision of treaties, a pressing question of League diplomacy at the time. A contractual theory had been unable to develop a workable doctrine of *rebus sic stantibus*, possessing neither a criterion for identifying a relevant change nor a procedure to put it into effect. To argue that the *rebus* was an implied clause in the treaty or an inference from justice necessitated recourse to psychological studies or moral principles on which anything could be proved. The theory of contractual equilibrium failed to see that many treaties – peace treaties, in particular – reflected no balance at all. Lacking a criterion, traditional theory was compelled to relegate the question of revision to politics, to be resolved by power.[323]

By contrast, for Scelle treaties did not create the law but only declared it.[324] This appeared to make the problem of revision disappear: a change of necessity would automatically transform the legal situation as well. But what to do if a State was using the *rebus* doctrine so as to escape from unwanted obligations or obstructing a much-needed change in defense of the status quo? For such eventualities, Scelle conceded that formal law did enjoy a presumption of validity (*hypothèse de bon légiféré*) – as a court judgment enjoyed validity until overturned by a superior court.[325] After all, then, formal law was constraining, and independently of disagreement about the demands of social necessity.

Scelle denied that his 1936 book was intended as a contribution to the struggle over Versailles. However, he did stress that territorial and peace treaties were not exempt from effect by change of circumstances, and his

---

[323] Scelle, *Théorie juridique de la révision*, pp. 14–29.
[324] That the international legislature consists of national legislatures was reflected in the way draft treaties were presented to parliaments, voted and entered into force through national legislative processes. Though some treaties resemble contracts, most lay down general rules and establish competencies for administrators. Of course, the rule concerning third States does not apply, inasmuch as there are no third States in regard to objective situations! In practice, too, treaties often express a wider solidarity and end up affecting State behavior far beyond the limited circle of parties. Scelle, *Précis*, II, pp. 367–368; *Théorie juridique de la révision*, pp. 44–45, 50–52.
[325] Scelle, *Théorie juridique de la révision*, p. 47; *Précis*, II, pp. 336–368.

views had clear consequences for that debate.[326] The political dilemma was this: a credible opponent of Hitler's unilateralism needed to show that there was some mechanism whereby Germany's legitimate grievances could be dealt with. Otherwise the wide recognition of the obsoleteness of Versailles might have enabled Hitler to portray himself as an executor of solidarity. But unilateral revision could not be allowed. However, there was no specific mechanism for treaty-revision that would have been independent from that provided in the treaty itself. And it was absurd (and anti-social) to think that in the absence of specific provision no revision was possible. So revision had to be sometimes possible by way of *acte contraire*. If a discrepancy existed and was widely recognized, it might ultimately lead to revolution – the institution of a "government of fact" that would carry out the necessary legislative change by force – such as the Allied government over Germany in 1918.[327]

This was, Scelle admitted, weak. Although the international legislator had to consider proposed changes in good faith, there was no guarantee that a legislator enjoying benefits from the status quo would be ready for modifications. Absent effective institutions for legislative change, politics would remain a battle between opposing forces. Proposals to transfer revision to courts or to mediation were implausible. Legislative change involved the translation of natural laws into human laws, "a task at the same time scientific and social in which judgments of compromise, equity and utility are harmoniously married."[328] Only the Assembly had, under Article 19, such competence. This was not a competence to revise but to declare with binding force that the fact of obsoleteness was present and that the treaty had to be revised.[329] For Scelle, it was inconceivable

---

[326] To exempt territorial treaties from the *rebus* rule is to fall back on the old idea of State territory as property, inherent in the sovereign – whereas as social function, it is properly analyzed as a territorial delimitation of the competence of the national government, understood as performing a dual role as a national and an international administrator. If the peace treaty is analyzed by voluntarist theory, its continued maintenance cannot be sustained: it was concluded under duress. But duress for Scelle was a social fact with legislative consequences. Owing to its primitive character, the international system sometimes allows bullets to replace ballots, Scelle, *Théorie juridique de la révision*, pp. 57–58.

[327] In France, for instance, the revolution of 1848 had been needed to start the development that led to the institution of labor law and finally the act on accidents of 1898 that set aside the individualist principles that had governed the subject under the *Code Civil*, and enacted the revolutionary principle of responsibility for risk. It is the same internationally. If governments persist in upholding obsolete law, the ultimate means of change is unilateral repudiation that may involve war, Scelle, *Théorie juridique de la révision*, p. 50.   [328] Scelle, *Théorie juridique de la révision*, p. 67.

[329] Scelle, *Théorie juridique de la révision*, pp. 79–80.

– that is, against the social meaning ("sens social nécessaire") of the Covenant – that the Assembly's view could be lawfully overridden. But only a future supranational legislation would do away with the danger of war as a last recourse. The future international legislator should be entitled to directly modify national law, thus spelling the end of sovereignty. In a social environment, nobody had the right to an individual morality. With a veiled reference to the Nazi regime Scelle concluded his 1936 book with the wish that tyranny and violence would be eradicated from society by legislation. Today, however, everything still hung on the presumption of the binding force of present, formally valid law – a presumption that fatally weakened Scelle's objectivism, making it appear just another politics of reform, among others.

The imposing architecture of Scelle's 1919 federal utopia was invulnerable to experience: in 1950 Scelle described the international system as he had done thirty years earlier, as an aggregate of individuals, living through varying solidarities, administered through the *dédoublement fonctionnel*, with a residual international administration, the United Nations, compromised by the right of veto but once again carrying the hope of global federation.[330] By the onset of the Cold War such a view had lost political force. Its combination of realism and utopia seemed insufficient under both headings, too abstract to ground a realistic program for renewal and far from independent of the political struggles that it hoped to overcome. Scelle's international world remained the world of public diplomacy, Locarno Treaties, League of Nations, and the International Labour Organization. That he was sidelined from the preparation of the Schuman Declaration of May 9, 1950, the century's most significant federalist move, betrays the sense in which his *Droit des gens* must have seemed to the cultivators of the new pragmatism as old wine in yesterday's bottles.

Which solidarity? Whose tradition? The Spanish Civil War

Le Fur and Scelle described the law as a translation of social or moral necessities, anterior to the political society. Their objectivisms were responses from the right and the left to the inability of party politics to deal with the deepening problems of the period.[331] Finding a field of

---

[330] Georges Scelle, "Le droit public et la théorie de l'Etat," in Georges Scelle *et al.*, *Introduction à l'étude de droit* (2 vols., Paris, Rousseau, 1951), I, pp. 96–106.
[331] Cf. Le Fur, "La démocratie," pp. 530–583.

normativity outside politics, both hoped to contribute to the creation of social life that would rely on something stronger than the artificial structures of the liberal State. Yet the languages of tradition and solidarity deviated in ways that far from transcending political conflict reproduced it in the language of legal theory. Both were aware of the problem in their adversary's position: As Le Fur argued against Scelle, mere reference to "biology" hardly transformed politics into science. Whose "biology" was meant? At least in Dr. Spencer's sense, biology led to war, not solidarity: an anterior moral choice was needed.[332] On the other hand, as Scelle pointed out, such a choice was always somehow arbitrary, moral preferences being "essentially subjective and varying in every particular case."[333] The attempt to postulate an objective–scientific legal order outside politics remains a persistent trait in the internationalist imagination; irrespective of the embarrassing ease with which it bent to support political positions.

The Spanish Civil War (1936–1939) divided European intelligentsias for the first time in uniformly right–left positions. Correspondingly, Le Fur characterized the Phalangist action in terms remarkably similar to those he had used to describe the Franco-German adversity in the Great War. It was a "struggle between the Christian civilization and atheistic communism or, more briefly, as Unamuno has said, between civilization and barbarism."[334] For Le Fur, Franco led a popular uprising against an illegitimate government. Despite his stress on order and authority, and his criticism of nationalist agitation in the 1920s, he now turned the tables of the law against the formal government: the left had forfeited its right to govern. Although it had come to power through elections, the electoral system itself had worked illegitimately by bringing a slight de facto majority into the government. The Phalangists were no rebels but exercised a right of resistance, as consecrated in Christian theology. In any case, he added, they were in possession of more than two-thirds of Spanish territory.[335]

Hence, foreign States and the League were duty-bound to recognize the Phalangists as belligerents and to refrain from assisting the government or from allowing their nationals to do so.[336] On the other hand, the German and Italian intervention on Franco's side constituted a lawful reaction to communist attacks on foreign ships and a permissible

---

[332] Le Fur, "Règles générales," pp. 96–97.   [333] Scelle, *Précis*, I, p. 35.
[334] Louis Le Fur, "La guerre de l'Espagne et le droit," 2 (1938), 21 *RDI* (Paris), p. 98.
[335] Louis Le Fur, "La guerre de l'Espagne et le droit," 1 (1937), 20 *RDI* (Paris), pp. 348–352.   [336] Le Fur, "La guerre," 2, pp. 61–67.

counter-measure against the "massive" Soviet assistance to the government.[337] The bombing of Guernica by white air forces was a tragic but understandable reprisal against the government troops' earlier attacks and the communist strategy to locate military targets in the middle of civilian areas.[338] In any case, he wrote, much of Guernica had already been destroyed by communist and anarchist bombings on the ground. Proof of the justice of Franco's cause was that wherever territories were "liberated," people enthusiastically joined him.[339]

Pleading full objectivity and non-partisanship, Scelle came in each point to an opposite conclusion. There was no equality between the parties: one was a lawful, elected government, the other a rebel force. The numerous nationalizations and requisitions which the loyalists had carried out were lawful exercises of governmental competencies, bound to incur respect from other States.[340] In principle, intervention on the governmental side was perfectly legitimate. Moreover, in this case, non-interference was strictly illegal because it amounted to de facto intervention in favor of the rebels in view of the "massive" clandestine involvement of Italy, Germany, and Portugal already on Franco's side.[341]

Le Fur argued that League members had a duty of non-intervention inasmuch as the Covenant had created a system of solidarity between States and Art. 10 spoke only of action against *external* aggression.[342] For Scelle, however, non-intervention was incompatible with any legal order and particularly with the Covenant. First, it isolated States and was thus in conflict with the needs of solidarity. Second, the history of diplomacy was a history of constant interference. There was nothing new in this; also non-intervention is intervention on the side of the status quo power. Third, under Art. 11 of the Covenant, the Council had a duty to intervene where the domestic situation constituted a threat to the peace. Intervention was also allowed under Arts. 16 and 17 as the situation in Spain could be analyzed as war of aggression against the lawful government.[343]

The contrasting analyses of the Spanish Civil War by Le Fur and Scelle followed naturally from the way they understood the events in opposite ways. For one, this was a struggle by the Spanish people against

---

[337] Le Fur, "La guerre," 2, pp. 65, 70–73.   [338] Le Fur, "La guerre," 2, p. 95.
[339] Le Fur, "La guerre," 1, pp. 366, 363–364.
[340] Georges Scelle, "La guerre civile espagnole et le droit des gens," 1 (1938), XLV *RGDIP*, pp. 272–279.
[341] Georges Scelle, "La guerre civile espagnole et le droit des gens," 3 (1939), XLVI *RGDIP*, p. 197.   [342] Le Fur, "La guerre," 2, pp. 62–63.
[343] Scelle, "La guerre civile," 3, pp. 201–228.

Eastern barbarism; for the other it manifested the lawful government's effort to put down a rebellion sustained by foreign intervention. There was no objective or innocent realm of pure description: the effective solidarities could not even be identified irrespective of political positions, in this case, either in favor of electoral democracy and a functional concept of government, or "a Christian corporatism and nationalist syndicalism."[344] Already the identification of what counted as "order" was politics-dependent. Thus, for Le Fur, "everywhere where Marxist communism is established, it brings with it disorder and general ruin."[345] Even where "communism" installed and consolidated, it failed to qualify as "order" because of its intrinsic barbarism. Le Fur pushed his material notion of order so far that it turned into its formal opposite: even if the governmental "order" had not been the overt barbarism it was, it would still have had to yield to "the dynamism of the nation," carried out by revolution if necessary.[346] For Scelle, again, "order" was constituted of the exercise by the elected government of its lawful competencies under the constitution. His formalism was substantively based: even if the new law of the Covenant dealt with governmental legitimacy, this was only in connection with international war. In civil war, the *nécessité sociale* to provide for the protection of outside interests necessitated the detachment of the de facto government's position from assessments of legitimacy.[347]

Le Fur and Scelle were both advocates of anti-formalist legal theory. For Le Fur, this meant that only relative value should be given to the government's status as such. The "barbarism" of the government or the "dynamism of the nation" were the operative principles.[348] For Scelle, again, intervention on the government's side was received from the material principle of solidarity: Spain's abstract sovereignty constituted no bar against intervention.[349] While emerging from apparently anti-formalist premises, both positions enshrined one or other type of formalism as well: either the formalism of non-intervention by a denial of League competence and an affirmation of sovereignty (Le Fur) or the formalism of the government and an affirmation of League competence by reference to Covenant provisions and the loyalist status (Scelle).

---

[344] Le Fur, "La guerre," 2, p. 98. [345] Le Fur, "La guerre," 1, p. 368.
[346] Le Fur, "La guerre," 2, p. 59. [347] Scelle, "La guerre civile," 1, pp. 271–274.
[348] It was clear for Le Fur, for instance, that the Franco government was more respectful of international obligations (it had showed its willingness to restore foreign property that had been subjected to nationalizations) and to carry out a policy of national and international reconciliation, Le Fur, "La guerre," 1, pp. 81, 84–87.
[349] Scelle, "La guerre civile," 1, pp. 266, 273.

In the end, both positions predictably reflected the positions of right and left intellectuals. They did nothing to support the view that law had to do with the expression of scientific or moral necessities. To the contrary, the political nature of the arguments was revealed in the way neither lawyer could simply have "found out" that the law in fact supported his opponent. Both positions were overdetermined: the preferred outcome was argued correct from every conceivable standpoint, even contradicting standpoints, to the extent that it was no longer credible. Despite its objectivist and scientist pretensions, the international law practiced by Le Fur and Scelle was an inextricable part of inter-war politics and not an overcoming thereof.

The European Union

In 1929 France's foreign minister Aristide Briand (1862–1932) proposed to the League Assembly the creation of a European Union to deal with the economic crisis in Europe. This proposal was reflected in a French Memorandum of May 1, 1930 that suggested the establishment of a "régime permanent de solidarité conventionnelle pour l'organisation rationnelle de l'Europe."[350] According to the proposal, the Union would seek to deal with economic problems through political agreements (an approach that was reversed in the 1950s). It would not seek to replace the League but to complement its activities. It would consist of a general conference connected to the League Assembly, an Executive Council, and a permanent Secretariat. Most States agreed in principle but put forward a number of reservations concerning its proposed institutional form as well as the subordination of economy to politics. The League Assembly set up a Commission to study the proposals which, however, ended its activity after Briand's death and German exit from the League in 1933.

The proposal, de Lapradelle later noted, had been inspired by an idea by Alvarez.[351] Both Scelle and Le Fur took a positive view on it, pointing at the indisputable historical fact of European solidarity. "Sociology teaches us that federalism is a constant law of evolution in

---

[350] Briand Memorandum, Georges Scelle, "Essai relatif à l'Union européenne" (1931), XXXVIII *RGDIP*, p. 528 n7. See also B. Mirkine-Guetzewitch and Georges Scelle (eds.), *L'Union européenne* (Paris, Delagrave, 1931), pp. 59–70. This collection also contains, apart from the memorandum, the responses of 25 European governments to it and excerpts from the discussion in the League Assembly in 1929 and 1930.

[351] A. de Lapradelle, *La paix moderne (1899–1945). De la Haye à San Francisco* (Paris, Editions internationales, 1947), p. 89.

human communities," Scelle had written.[352] Though Le Fur observed that the histories and interests of European nations differed and that they lacked a common juridical framework, he emphasized the "common morality" that united European peoples.[353] Scelle felt such differences rather superficial in view of the sociologically based European solidarity. He had no doubt that European federalism was on the way and praised Briand's intuitive genius in making the proposal precisely at the right moment when the League had shown its inefficiency in dealing with European problems and outside States were increasingly using the League to intervene in Europe.[354]

Both Scelle and Le Fur held the federal phenomenon ultimately universal, not regional. However, both recognized the many ways in which the League fell short of that ideal: the obstructive linkage between the Covenant and the Peace Treaties,[355] the predominance of the Great Powers and the unanimity requirement,[356] loopholes in the dispute settlement and sanctions provisions.[357] Scelle and Le Fur agreed that the League's most promising achievements were in functional integration. Setting up the International Labour Conference had been an "excellent" means to decentralize the powers of the League into co-operation that slowly expanded to other fields.[358] The territorial and commercial provisions of the Peace Treaties and the organization of traffic in international rivers further expanded international administration. The

---

[352] Scelle, *Précis*, I, p. 188.
[353] Scelle, "Essai," p. 522. Louis Le Fur, "Les conditions d'existence d'une Union européenne" (1930), 6 *RDI* (Paris), pp. 78–82.   [354] Scelle, "Essai," pp. 528–529.
[355] Neither Scelle nor Le Fur seriously believed that a universal federation had been created at Versailles. Law being a translation of the state of social forces, Scelle wrote, no more could be attained than what those forces permitted. Universal solidarity was only twenty years old and hardly ready for federation. He thus accepted that the League was also a provisional de facto regime over Germany, a *Sainte Alliance Démocratique*. But once the threat of German aggression was removed, the provisions of the Covenant would allow a progressive transformation. Scelle, *Pacte des Nations*, pp. 85–88, 125–150, Scelle, *La morale*, p. 17.
[356] In due course, Scelle thought, the League needed to be thoroughly democratized and composed of representatives of nations and professions, not of governments "too much inclined to apply obsolete formulas and career diplomats' doubtful political maneuvers." Scelle, *Pacte des Nations*, p. 376. Now it was for public opinion to bring this work to conclusion in accordance with the "principles of liberalism and science." Scelle, *La morale*, pp. 14, 273–275. Citing Jaurès, Scelle proposed a system of decision-making that would allow each community to participate in accordance with its social usefulness. However difficult it was to determine this, it was the only means to lay a basis for the development of the organization in accordance with the needs of solidarity.   [357] Le Fur, *Précis*, pp. 261–309.
[358] Scelle, *Pacte des Nations*, pp. 268–276.

League's activities for the protection of women and children and preventing drug traffic, mandates, and the minorities treaties had significantly strengthened its federal ethos and pointed in the direction of future activism.[359]

However, these achievements had been outweighed by political disappointments. The crisis over Germany's entry in the League in 1926 that resulted in the withdrawal of Brazil and the creation of semi-permanent seats in the Council for Poland and Spain, made Scelle draw the conclusion that the League needed to be regionalized. Members should participate in League organs as representatives of their regions. He advocated a kind of subsidiarity: those matters should be treated regionally for which this was the most effective or natural context. But in the long run, he always saw this decentralization taking place in a functional, not geographical way.[360] For Le Fur, regional integration fitted nicely with his "pyramidical" federalism, the objective of a balanced, hierarchical order in which intermediate levels would have distinct competencies appropriate to each.[361]

Yet both also saw difficulties in the proposal. The relationship between the Union and the League was left obscure: might the Union empty the League of its substance? Both also thought the proposal timid: it maintained the sovereignty of its members.[362] Le Fur emphasized an additional, fundamental problem in the proposal. How should "Europe" be defined? Russia, for instance, was only half-European and Turkey only one-tenth so. The Soviet Union had nothing whatsoever in common with Western civilization.[363] Nonetheless, despite such problems, Scelle stressed the historical significance of the proposal as a strategy for peace. For peace could not be attained only by diplomacy. An organization was needed. The League had been created for this purpose. Although it still

---

[359] Scelle, *Pacte des Nations*, pp. 380–395; *La morale*, p. 8; Le Fur, *Précis*, pp. 610, 278–282. For Scelle the League's technical bodies constituted an *international public service* that formed the roots of his supranational corporatism. Inasmuch as they – like the Permanent Court – sometimes involved non-League members, they acted through the *dédoublement fonctionnel* as organs of a world community, Scelle, *Précis*, I, pp. 267–270.

[360] He agreed with the proposal of the French Union of League of Nations Associations that had used solidarist language in order to defend the creation of groups of nations inside the League and suggested that one of them be a European Union. Cf. Georges Scelle, *Une crise de la Société des nations* (Paris, PUF, 1927), pp. 227–231, 247–248.

[361] Cf. Le Fur, *Précis*, pp. 308–309 and especially Le Fur, "Le développement historique du droit international de l'anarchie international à une communauté internationale organisée" (1932/III), 41 *RdC*, pp. 548–556.

[362] Scelle, "Essai," p. 532; Le Fur, "Conditions d'existence," pp. 76–77.

[363] Le Fur, "Conditions d'existence," pp. 74–75.

remained a contact point for foreign offices, many of its minor aspects manifested a supranational, federal ethos. But one of the mistakes of its founders had been the neglect of regionalism: "the League could not become universal in any other way than becoming regional."[364]

For Scelle, the main merit of the proposal for a European Union was that it contained an organization. Through it, the sharpness of interest conflicts would diminish and European solidarity would be strengthened. Again, Le Fur was more skeptical and warned against "Anglo-Saxon" faith in the enlightened power of public opinion. To work, the Union needed not only common principles but effective institutions and sanctions. Chauvinist propaganda should no longer be allowed. There should be a *tribunal ou jury d'honneur* to watch over European journalists and education and to suggest, or possibly to command, the suppression of activities that insulted other States. In addition to the setting up of a European Court and a legislative assembly, he suggested the creation of a European air force, situated at equal distance from main capitals and having the capacity to reach, by way of reprisal, the industrial centers of potential aggressors.[365]

In April 1950, Jean Monnet (1888–1979) was preparing the proposal that was to become known as the Schuman Plan that led to pooling of the heavy industries of France and Germany within the European Coal and Steel Community (ECSC) and eventually, in 1957, to the Rome Treaty that established the European Economic Community (EEC). Contemplating the details of the plan Monnet requested the young Professor of International Law from the University of Aix-en-Provence, Paul Reuter (1911–1990), whom he knew from Reuter's previous association with the French Government, to provide an opinion on certain territorial issues relating to the delimitation of the plan. Monnet noticed Reuter's sharpness and enthusiasm and involved him in the small group of advisers who then drafted the proposal that the French Foreign Minister Robert Schuman made on May 9, 1950 and among France's negotiators for the Treaty that resulted from it.[366]

Reuter's involvement in this process was, it seems, purely accidental. Monnet had not consulted Georges Scelle or the other inter-war lawyers

---

[364] Scelle, "Essai," p. 524.   [365] Le Fur, "Conditions d'existence," pp. 92–94.
[366] Cf. Jean Monnet, *Mémoires* (trans. Richard Mayne, London, Collins, 1978), pp. 294–295; Paul Reuter, "Aux origines du plan Schuman," in *Mélanges Fernand Dehousse* (2 vols., Paris, Nathan, 1979), II, *La construction européenne*, pp. 65–68; François Duchêne, *Jean Monnet. The First Statesman of Interdependence* (New York and London, Norton, 1994), p. 200.

despite (or because of?) having himself been a Deputy Secretary-General of the League under Eric Drummond in 1919–1923 and having had much experience in dealing with international lawyers in connection with the Upper Silesian and the Saar questions. Politically, too, Monnet had been close to Léon Bourgeois with whom he co-operated during those early years and with whom he had been antagonized by the rightist Poincaré's inflexibility over the German debt question. Moreover, one of his collaborators testifies that he was constantly surrounded by lawyers – though also that he kept them on the sidelines, feeling that their subtle literalism was sometimes an obstacle to creative policy: "To envisage the final form of the European Community today, when we have wanted it to be a kind of process of change is a contradiction in terms. Anticipating the result blocks the spirit of invention."[367]

That the inter-war lawyers played no role in the initiation of European unification constitutes an ironical gloss on the nature of their federalism. Wanting to do away with sovereignty they in fact wanted to do away with the discipline in which they were professionals. Le Fur's natural law, just like Scelle's sociological objectivism, were escapes from the political dilemmas that daily diplomacy had to grapple with. To believe that the problems of international policy could be thought of in terms of moral correctness and error – this was also the way Politis put it in 1943 – was counter-intuitive and unhelpful. It was to assume that the problems of the day were always already solved in some jurist's heaven – although nobody had access to it – and that the task was not so much to settle and compromise than to try to get there. Scelle's sociology and his Rousseauan idea of citizenship were no different in this respect. The assumption was that freedom and community were not only reconcilable but dependent on each other; that free will and individual interest were in harmony with general will and interest. This was the heritage of French republicanism – that legal problems were really resolved outside the law, namely in sociology and in the various technical and functional disciplines Scelle advocated. Like Comte, Scelle had no argument to explain why lawyers might have something useful to do in the scientifically administered bureaucracy that was the logical outcome of his views.

It would be wrong to think that as the European Union today imagines itself as a new legal order, it only draws the conclusions earlier

---

[367] François Fontaine, "Forward with Jean Monnet," in Douglas Brinkley and Clifford Hackett (eds.), *Jean Monnet: The Path to European Unity* (Basingstoke, Macmillan, 1991), p. 55.

preached by the critics of sovereignty.[368] That critique was part of a rationalist optimism that was impossible to sustain as a basis of credible reform after the final demise of the inter-war system. If there was to be federalism, it could not be seen as a realization of a blueprint conceived at some academic's desk. Paul Reuter, for instance, was constantly on guard against "general ideas and abstract formulas through which one often seeks to deal with situations that have nothing in common" and the assessment that he was "extremely hostile, not to 'theory' in its veritable sense but to the *a priori* of theorists" suggests that he might not have looked too kindly upon the kinds of speculation with which inter-war jurists such as Scelle and Le Fur felt themselves at home.[369] The new generation had been profoundly influenced by the experience of the 1930s, described later by Raymond Aron (1905–1983) as the experience of an oncoming storm, and a difficulty in doing anything about it: "I am still marked by this experience which inclined towards an active pessimism. Once and for all, I ceased to believe that history automatically obeys the dictates of reason and the desires of men of good will."[370] In an ironic twist, the teaching of the "men of good will" and pessimists converged in that neither was able to find much for international lawyers to achieve. The rationalists took their lesson from Comte and Durkheim and saw federation as a scientific necessity: only technical administration would remain – politicians, soldiers, and lawyers were recast as survivals from feudal or theological ages. Pessimists such as Aron would look towards Weber and the irreducibility of power and interest and lay their stakes with a statesmanship of prudence – such as Monnet's – as the only alternative to tragedy.

In the 1950s, the movement towards a European Union turned Briand's strategy on its head: instead of dealing with economics through politics, it chose to deal with a political problem – the security of Europe – through economic solutions.[371] In so doing, it effectively set aside federalist views that were based on political or moral axioms, generalizations about human nature or the good society. It became a thoroughly functional enterprise, somewhat like Scelle had in 1919 imagined the

---

[368] Although the ideas of direct effect and supremacy were of course central in Scelle's federalism, cf. also Leonetti, "Georges Scelle," pp. 298–301.

[369] The quote and characterization of Reuter are from Jean Combacau, "Paul Reuter, Le Juriste" (1989), XXXV *AFDI*, pp. xvii, xviii.

[370] Raymond Aron, "On the Historical Condition of the Sociologist," in *Politics and History* (New Brunswick and London, Transaction, 1984), p. 65.

[371] For the dynamism written into the plan, cf. Paul Reuter, "Le plan Schuman" (1952/II), 81 *RdC*, pp. 531–537.

host city of his federal utopia. It was not for nothing that René-Jean Dupuy (1918–1997) characterized the High Authority of the Coal and Steel Community in 1957 as "le premier exemple historique de l'avènement internationale des technocrates" and linked its origins to the suggestions by Saint-Simon and Proudhon to employ technical experts to advance corporate interests overriding those of States.[372]

The twilight of the idea of France: between politics and pragmatism

Charles Rousseau (1902–1993) explained in his 1944 textbook on the general principles of international law that he had aimed to follow a "strictly positive" method purged of all naturalism – if not indeed of all theory. For the vice of natural law lay in its being "all theory," which meant it had no practical application. By contrast, Rousseau would concentrate on the law immediately given through the work of legal sources and the practice of States, international organizations, and tribunals. In a rhetorical gesture that became a standard trope of post-war legal pragmatism Rousseau explained that the problem of the basis of international law's binding force – its "foundation" – was an extralegal one and could therefore be safely dismissed from positive legal study. For most purposes, the materials that international lawyers were to deal with were sufficiently identified by legal practice – a position whose circularity was scarcely hidden by Rousseau's statement of his conviction that this was not at all "un point de vue théorique" but a fact confirmed by practice itself.[373]

The new spirit was also visible in the establishment of the *Annuaire français de droit international* in 1955 for the purpose of following and commenting upon the events of international relations on an annual basis with the stated purpose of "avoiding the construction of useless and dangerous systems, detached from the realities of international life." Affirming that the studies and chronicles that were to be published in the *Annuaire* would not neglect the "social context," its statement of purpose reflected a modest idea about international law not as a field for speculation about world government or eternal peace but a technical instrument of the diplomacy of the day.[374] This did not mean that

---

[372] René-Jean Dupuy, "L'organisation internationale et l'expression de la volonté générale" (1957), LX (*sic!*) *RGDIP*, p. 564 and for his prescient analysis of the Community's democratic deficit, Dupuy, "L'organisation," pp. 566–579.
[373] Charles Rousseau, *Principes généraux du droit international public* (Paris, Pedone, 1944), pp. 42, 52–53.   [374] "Avant-propos," (1955), I *AFDI*, p. xiii.

international law would become increasingly marginalized at the universities. On the contrary, in 1954 a course of international institutions was for the first time made compulsory for the first year of law studies in Paris and courses in international law topics were offered in increasing numbers, usually with a historical or "international relations" orientation, so as to allow easy access to non-lawyers, taking up a sizeable part of the audience. In the 1960s, the institutional aspect of international law teaching increased with a predominance on European organizations and, after 1968, with the conscious effort to become "more sociological."[375] The profession continued to be concerned about its practical relevance, however, worrying about the up-to-date quality of its teaching materials and seeking closer contacts with the *Quai d'Orsay*. It was for this reason that the *Société française pour le droit international* was set up in 1967 and specialized centers on international human rights law and the law of peace and development were inaugurated at the universities of Strasbourg and Nice the following year.

A well-attended colloquium on the teaching of international law that took place in Geneva in 1956 expressly repudiated inter-war approaches to the topic and called for a "more objective and realist study of the international milieu." Study of international law must provide adequate room for the underlying realities of positive law.[376] Oddly enough, what those preceding doctrines were charged with was "formalism" – when in fact much of the French international legal tradition from Renault and Pillet to Le Fur and Scelle had been decidedly anti-formalist, Alvarez even having made a career out of preaching against formalism. Yet already at this time concern was voiced about the proliferation of methods and disciplines around international law and international relations and that the increasing technical specialization of the field led to a loss of "une vue synthétique et sainement équilibrée" in its education.[377]

This oscillation as well as the finding of the enemy in the formalist camp (which was in fact empty) testified to a certain malaise about the pragmatic turn. Surely international law had to be connected to something grander than the day-to-day problems of diplomacy. Although as

---

[375] Cf. "L'enseignement du droit international public en France" (1956), II *AFDI*, pp. 981–985; "Les études de droit international dans les facultés de droit françaises" (1962), VIII *AFDI*, pp. 1233–1234; "L'enseignement et la recherche en droit international en France face aux besoins de la pratique" (1967), XIII *AFDI*, pp. 1157–1158; "La société française pour le droit international" (1968), XIV *AFDI*, p. 1172.

[376] Paul de Visscher, "Colloque sur l'enseignement du droit international," Rapport (1956), LX *RGDIP*, pp. 570, 572.   [377] De Visscher, "Colloque," p. 569.

René-Jean Dupuy pointed out in his early critique of the European institutions, pragmatism in fact followed from strands of French political thought, it failed to highlight what earlier lawyers had expressed in terms of *l'idée de France*, active pursuit of universal enlightenment, humanitarianism, and liberty. In 1945 Albert de Lapradelle still addressed the French delegation that was preparing to depart to the San Francisco Conference in the grand tradition, observing that it belonged to France, "before any other nation, to put to the service of humanity the clarity of its thought, the generosity of its genius, and the memory of its pains."[378] Such language was gravely undermined by the difficulties which the delegation would have in obtaining a Security Council seat for France, its most pressing concern. The age when universal humanitarianism and the French self-image coalesced was over. Paul Reuter saw this clearly as he confessed that the finding of the solution to the problems of European politics from the construction of a common market for large French and German steel companies – that is to say, "taking Europe seriously" – would mean to give up *un certain idée de France*.[379]

It would be wrong to say that no effort was made at French universities after the war to recreate a "synthetic view" with the help of theory – only that those efforts had no success whatsoever. The two articles in the 1950s *Revue générale* that engaged in doctrinal abstraction both attacked sociology as the founding discipline of international law, repeating the point about the impossibility of drawing norms out of social facts. Truyol y Serra and Smyrniadis (was it a coincidence that both were foreigners?) decried the spiritual poverty of positivism and advocated a turn to metaphysics and morality – yet failing to answer the pragmatist's objection about the arbitrary or non-consequential nature of what one came up with as one's fundamental principles.[380] When the latter claimed that this morality was "anchored in the conscience of human beings" he seemed to be echoing Marcel Sibert's (1884–1957) 1951 textbook which based the necessity of international law on the fact that "[l]a conscience des peuples honnêtes la proclame." Sibert at least was able to translate his moral generalizations into a theory of *ordre public* that had some technical–professional meaning for lawyers; whereas Smyrniadis' "international morality" was left floating in a conceptual

---

[378] His originally anonymous analyses and appeals having been collected in Lapradelle, *La paix moderne*, pp. 141, 136–138.   [379] Reuter, "Aux origines," p. 66.

[380] Antonio Truyol, "Doctrines contemporaines du droit des gens" (1950), LIV *RGDIP*, pp. 415–416; Bion Smyrniadis, "Positivisme et morale internationale en droit des gens" (1955), LIX *RGDIP*, pp. 110–120.

heaven that already accommodated the equally intangible abstractions of Politis and Le Fur.[381] The genuine difficulty about doctrine is perhaps best illustrated in the fact that French international lawyers did nothing to follow Roberto Ago's (1907–1995) quite brilliant distinction between "positive law" that was actually legislated into existence and "positive law" that was spontaneously followed irrespective of whether it could be traced back to a legislative will or legal procedure.[382] Here would have been a sociologically based articulation of something like a modern theory of natural law with a concrete content. But it was one thing to declare it as part of an academic debate about doctrines and traditions – in which it fared quite well – and another to suggest that lawyers could in their practical work dispense with formal sources or arguments about State will. In the final analysis, perhaps it was genuinely irrelevant what the "basis" of international law was; perhaps there was neither need nor possibility for a theoretical justification for the practices in which lawyers engaged; perhaps they were best thought of as the kind of *bricolage* of which Lévi-Strauss had written, the haphazard collection of bits and pieces from available argumentative techniques so as to deal with practical problems as they emerge in the routines in which international lawyers participate.

Perhaps it was the imperative need to decide between Scelle and Le Fur, and the impossibility of making that choice, that explained the move to pragmatism. Both lawyers were critics of diplomacy who advocated a central place for international law in the administration of international society. Both rejected formalism and constructed their law so as to express ideas, principles or facts outside the legal system; either in a pre-existing social solidarity (Scelle) or the tradition of Christian humanism (Le Fur). But how could one choose? For, as innumerable critics of solidarism pointed out – and as Duguit acknowledged in his later years – one needed a conception of justice so as to give normative direction to one's sociological generalizations. Le Fur knew this, but sought justice from a particular (and controversial) tradition. Somehow, the door to the universalism of 1789 and the related *idée de France* had been closed. Every justice had become either so general as to be meaningless, or was revealed as ideology. The choice between "solidarism" and "tradition" revealed aspects of both. On the one hand, there was the ease with which solidarity as an *abstract* doctrine could be turned to buttress

---

[381] Marcel Sibert, *Traité de droit international de la paix* (2 vols., Paris, Dalloz, 1951), II, pp. 8, 14–18.

[382] Roberto Ago, "Droit positif et droit international" (1957), III *AFDI*, pp. 14–62.

Christian humanitarianism and tradition invoked to defend individual rights. On the other hand, these apparently endlessly flexible terms did have a concrete, culturally fixed meaning in the France of the 1920s and 1930s as signifiers for radical syndicalism and conservative authoritarianism. What went on behind the academic façade was a thoroughly political controversy. And it is at least to some extent the utter helplessness of those doctrines on the eve of the war that made it impossible for post-war lawyers to espouse them anew. The new generation did not turn to pragmatism because it was theoretically unsophisticated. On the contrary, as Peter Sloterdijk has shown, it had learned all the critical lessons of the Enlightenment, and that everything is relative, even its own idea: and that the recognition of this fact has left it only the outlet of lowering its expectations, of becoming profoundly, and unreflectively "real."[383]

[383] Peter Sloterdijk, *Critique of Cynical Reason* (trans. M. Eldred, foreword A. Huyssen, University of Minnesota Press, 1987).

5

Lauterpacht: the Victorian tradition in international law

Tradition in modernity

Less than two months after the capitulation at Munich, on November 16, 1938, Hersch Lauterpacht delivered an address to the League of Nations Union of his new academic home, Cambridge University, on the general subject of the League. He started the address by confiding to his audience that this was a topic on which he felt so strongly as to be unable to trust the "freely spoken word" and that in order to maintain restraint and deliberation, he would read from a manuscript, as was not his custom.[1] Nonetheless, the address departs from Lauterpacht's customary, detached and complicated, somewhat dry English at several points, most notably when, slightly after the middle, he switches over to the first person plural. The address opens with the argument that the events of the 1930s – the Manchurian and Abyssinian Wars, the Munich accords – and the attitudes taken by key League members have meant that the Covenant's collective security provisions, the territorial guarantee (Art. 10) and the obligation of collective response (Arts 15 and 16), have fallen into desuetude. In the fulfillment of its principal objective, the League has failed. All that remains is the hope – asserted without conviction – "that the true spirit of man will assert itself in the long run." Then follows the abrupt and uncharacteristic jump into informality and engagement:

---

[1] "The League of Nations," in *International Law, being the Collected Papers of Hersch Lauterpacht* (4 vols., systematically arranged and edited by Elihu Lauterpacht, Cambridge University Press, 1970–1978), 3, p. 575.

But what have we to do in the meantime? Ought we to abandon the League and start afresh as soon as the obstacles disappear? Ought we to maintain it and to adapt it to the needs of a retrogressive period? Ought we to pursue the ideal of universality by reforming the League so as to make it acceptable for everyone? Ought we to admit that if peace cannot be achieved by collective effort, there are other good things that can be achieved through it?[2]

The questions are asked in a rhetorical, anxious mood, at least as much to highlight the urgency of the situation as to indicate alternative ways of response. Should the law be abandoned, or modified, should its content or scope be adjusted in accordance with political realities? The questions are familiar to international lawyers continuously managing the distance between ought and is, law and fact. Here the issues at stake seem to be exceptionally great, however. They concern the intrinsic rationality of federalism and its concomitant, law and order through collective security: "progress in things essential has been arrested and the clock turned back."

Lauterpacht's address posits a cultural or political community that feels estranged from the course of inter-war politics – the politics of national over common interests, of the reign of "short-sighted benefits" over stable and balanced growth, and the rise of dictatorships "on a scale unprecedented in history."[3] There is little doubt about the principles which identified Lauterpacht's Cambridge audience as a community. To invoke those principles Lauterpacht chooses to look into the past – like Grotius once did in seeking authority from the customs of the Romans, "better peoples and better times."[4] Traveling beyond the immediate past, the nationalisms and disorder of the *fin-de-siècle*, his gaze stops at the words of the Prince Consort at the 1851 International Exhibition in London: "Nobody who has paid any attention to the peculiar features of our present era will doubt for a moment that we are living a period of the most wonderful transition which tends rapidly to accomplish that great end to which indeed all history points – the realization of the unity of mankind."[5] And in a tone of unmitigated Victorian nostalgia: "How

---

[2] Lauterpacht, "The League of Nations," p. 583.
[3] Lauterpacht, "The League of Nations," pp. 580–582.
[4] Hugo Grotius, *De jure belli ac pacis. Libri tres* (translation, F. W. Kelsey, 3 vols., Carnegie Endowment for International Peace, 3, *Classics of International Law*, 1925), Prolegomena para. 46 (p. 25).
[5] Lauterpacht, "The League of Nations," p. 587. In his monumental history of the nineteenth century, Peter Gay links this statement to the Lord Mayor's Banquet of 1850, predating the Exhibition. *The Bourgeois Experience. Victoria to Freud: The Education of the Senses* (5 vols., Oxford University Press, 1984–1999), I, p. 46 and generally, pp. 45–56.

immeasurably far backwards do we seem to have travelled from those days of unbounded optimism?"[6]

To find a place for law in a dangerous time, Lauterpacht looks back into the middle of the nineteenth century and hopes to resuscitate its liberal rationalism and its ideal of the rule of law, its belief in progress, its certainty about the sense and direction of history – Proust's *bon ange de la certitude*. For him, Munich seemed deadly because it was an un-Victorian, anti-traditionalist attack on the political ideals – and the political system – that had become entrenched during the heyday of the bourgeois century. The way to combat it was to engage the public opinion for the defense of the idea of the League of Nations as a world federation, the "culmination of the political and philosophical systems of leading thinkers of all ages . . . the final vision of prophets of religion."[7]

This was no sudden turn in Lauterpacht's thought. Throughout the 1920s and 1930s he had critiqued a "positivism" that had extolled the virtues of statehood and sovereignty and, allying itself with aggressive nationalism, been responsible for the catastrophe of the First World War. This was to be replaced by a gapless and professionally administered system of cosmopolitan law and order in the image of the liberal State. Historians debate over the "modernist" and "traditional" understandings of the effects of the First World War on European consciousness.[8] In this optic, I see Lauterpacht as a traditionalist for whom the war

---

[6] Lauterpacht, "The League of Nations," p. 587. Examples of nostalgia abound. For example, Lauterpacht thinks that Westlake's doctrines could be accepted today with only "minor alterations" owing to supervening political changes, "Westlake and Present Day International Law" (1925), *Collected Papers*, 2, p. 400. Discussing in 1959 the 1871 London Protocol Lauterpacht notes that "[i]n comparison of what was to follow, this was a law-abiding age," "International Law and the Colonial Question 1870–1914," *Collected Papers*, 2, p. 99.

[7] Lauterpacht, "The League of Nations," pp. 583, 585. Lauterpacht's general lectures in the Lent Term of 1938 founded international law under the Covenant on the peace schemes of Dubois (1305), Sully (1603), and William Penn (1693), and invited students to read inter-war commentary on them. It then presented the "legal organization of peace" in five parts: (1) The duty not to resort to force; (2) the duty of peaceful settlement; (3) the duty to accept arbitral or judicial settlement; (4) the duty to enforce collective decisions; and (5) the duty to participate in the machinery of peaceful change. This was a complete constitutionalization of international affairs, a system of Rule of Law writ large. *Syllabus of Six Lectures by Professor Lauterpacht on the Legal Organization of Peace in the Lent Term, 1938* (unpub. syllabus, on file with author).

[8] For the modernist view, cf. Paul Fussell, *The Great War and Modern Memory* (Oxford University Press, 1975). For the traditionalist interpretation, cf. Jay Winter, *Sites of Memory, Sites of Mourning. The Great War in European Cultural History* (Cambridge University Press, 1995).

of 1914–1918, together with its causes in aggressive nationalism as well as the twenty-year crisis that followed it, constituted an irrational rupture in the peaceful and inherently beneficial international developments associated with the nineteenth century. Lauterpacht always characterized the inter-war years as a period of "retrogression."[9] It was retrogression from the cosmopolitanism that had inspired Wilson in Paris in 1918–1919 but which owed its origin to the high liberalism of half a century before.[10] Lauterpacht never gave up Victorian ideals, liberalism and progress. On the contrary, he reasserted them in response to the experience of the Second World War in a famous 1946 article on the "Grotian Tradition in International Law" as well as in his post-war writings on human rights, rooting them expressly in the rationalist philosophy of the Enlightenment.[11]

Lauterpacht's traditionalism sets him apart from his Viennese teacher and contemporary Hans Kelsen, a legal modernist *par excellence*. Although Lauterpacht did hold Kelsen in the greatest esteem (and is reputed to have had a photo of Kelsen on the wall of his study, together with the photo of his mentor Arnold McNair (1885–1975) and an engraving of Grotius) and was impressed by the constructivist imagination at play in the Pure Theory of Law, he differed strongly in regard to the place of natural law for legal construction. Where Kelsen, in a pure modernist fashion, sought refuge from a politics gone wrong in pure form, Lauterpacht insisted on the need to incorporate by reference fundamental (Victorian) values as the only guarantee against the politics of irrationalism.[12]

---

[9] Cf. e.g. Hersch Lauterpacht, "International Law after the Covenant" (1936), *Collected Papers*, 2 (1936), p. 145.

[10] For Lauterpacht's early enthusiasm about Wilson and the League of Nations, cf. "The Mandate under International Law in the Covenant of the League of Nations" (1922), *Collected Papers*, 3, p. 40.

[11] McNair remembers Lauterpacht telling him that the article on the Grotian tradition "contained more of his essential thinking and faith than anything else he had written," "Memorial Article" (1960), *Annals of the British Academy* (hereafter McNair), p. 379. Cf. also *International Law and Human Rights* (London, Stevens, 1950) and the discussion under Nuremberg and Human Rights below.

[12] Hersch Lauterpacht, "Kelsen's Pure Science of Law" (1933), *Collected Papers*, 2, pp. 404–430, especially pp. 424–429, where Lauterpacht argues that Kelsen's rejection of a natural law basis for his system was "unnecessary." My reading of Kelsen as a legal modernist is slightly more elaborated in "The Wonderful Artificiality of States" (1994), 88 *American Society of International Law (ASIL) Proceedings*, p. 22 et seq. In a survey Alfred Rub has, however, piled Kelsen together with the other 1920s reconstructivists that aimed to combine naturalist with positivist aims, *Hans Kelsens Völkerrechtslehre. Versuch einer Würdigung* (Zurich, Schultess, 1995), p. 19.

However, had Lauterpacht been *simply* a naturalist critic of nationalism and sovereignty, there would be little reason to distinguish him from the mainstream of the reconstructive scholarship that arose during the 1920s in Europe and elsewhere, was branded "Utopianism" in the 1940s and 1950s and is now practically forgotten. True, he does confess to a utopian federalism, liberal humanism, and the associated values of cosmopolitan individualism. Kant (together with Grotius) is his acknowledged spiritual father. But the liberal legacy is ambiguous and in his professional work Lauterpacht treads a more complex path that could not have been taken by such traditionalist inter-war figures as, for instance, Politis in France or Schücking in Germany – names that, unlike Lauterpacht, enter legal texts only to mark the discipline's historical continuity and pedigree, like ancestral portraits in the house of legal pragmatism, irrelevant beyond decorative purpose.[13]

Lauterpacht belongs to the modernist camp in that he, like Kelsen, shares a non-essentialist epistemology. He is skeptical about the ability of interpretative methods to safeguard against arbitrariness. Hence, for example, his emphatic and repeated criticism of judicial recourse to the doctrine of "normal meaning," which assumes what is to be proved and simplifies out of recognition the constructive aspects of judging.[14] Principles of interpretation "are not the determining cause of judicial decision, but the form in which the judge cloaks a result arrived at by other means."[15] Nor are pure facts impartial arbitrators of normative disputes. Whether an entity is a State is not imposed on the observer through an "automatic test" but the result of construction, undertaken, of course, "in good faith and in pursuance of legal principle."[16]

Law is how it is interpreted. Lauterpacht's modernity lies in his constant stress on the primacy of interpretation to substance, of process to rule in a fashion that leads him into an institutional pragmatism that is ours, too. Such nominalism liberates lawyers to create international

---

[13] Unlike his ultra-traditionalist Viennese contemporary, Alfred Verdross, Lauterpacht did not assume that the unity of mankind could realize itself by an incessant repetition of its intrinsic rationality. Where Verdross relied on the self-evidence of natural law, Lauterpacht stressed the constructive role of judicial practice in fixing its meaning, cf. e.g. Lauterpacht, *International Law and Human Rights*, pp. 103–111.

[14] Hersch Lauterpacht, "The Doctrine of Plain Meaning," *Collected Papers*, 4, pp. 393–403. Likewise *The Development of International Law by the International Court* (2nd edn., New York, Praeger, 1958), pp. 49–60, 116–141.

[15] Hersch Lauterpacht, "Restrictive Interpretation and the Principle of Effectiveness in the Interpretation of Treaties," *Collected Papers*, 4, p. 410.

[16] Hersch Lauterpacht, *Recognition in International Law* (Cambridge University Press, 1947), pp. 48–51.

order by imagining that it already exists. However, it raises the further question of *power*, about who it is that is vested with the interpreting, meaning-giving authority? Thereby it creates what for Lauterpacht became the single most important problem of the existing international legal order, the problem of *self-judging obligations*, the State's ability to interpret for itself what its obligations are.

Now Lauterpacht is able to dispose of this difficulty only by returning to a liberal historicism that sees in public opinion, interdependence, common interests, and the indivisibility of peace compelling causes for a federalism that will dispose of self-judgment. As the international community outgrows the temporary phase of State sovereignty, a system of public administration will emerge that fulfills the ideal of the Rule of Law. Interpreting the law becomes the task of impartial and responsible public officials, in particular lawyers. Even as the League was struggling with the Abyssinian fiasco, and neutrality and alliances surfaced to replace collective security, Lauterpacht continued to profess "faith in the ultimate assertion of reason in the relations of man [from which] conceptions like the League of Nations and collective security must be regarded as manifestations of a permanent and ever recurring purpose, and their eclipse must be regarded as temporary and transient."[17]

Finally, Lauterpacht always saw, and frequently characterized himself as, a challenger of orthodoxy, a "progressive."[18] His main works open up as criticisms of doctrines and theories that marginalize international law as a "primitive" law or seek to limit its application by recourse to concepts such as "political" or "non-justiciable disputes." Situating international law within a historical trajectory of European thought towards a Kantian, cosmopolitan law, he attacked entrenched substantive doctrines about the nature of recognition of States and governments, the position of the individual in international law, the criminal responsibility of States, State immunity, etc. that in one way or another appeared as obstacles to the law's great passage to universalism.

It is important to be clear about the sense of these critiques. The "progressivism" from which they emanate is not in conflict but perfectly compatible with nineteenth-century liberal sentiments – as, indeed, the quote

---

[17] Hersch Lauterpacht, "Neutrality and Collective Security" (1936), *Politica*, p. 154.
[18] He does this most frequently in an indirect way, by praising the progressive spirit of scholars with whom he agrees. Cf. e.g. Hersch Lauterpacht, "The Grotian Tradition in International Law" (1946), *Collected Papers*, 2, pp. 359–363; "Westlake and Present Day International Law," p. 402; "Brierly's Contribution to International Law" (1955), *Collected Papers*, 2, p. 431. Cf. also *International Law and Human Rights*, pp. 103–111.

from Prince Albert's speech makes clear. The target is not (European) tradition *per se*, nor even the main current of that tradition, Enlightenment thought. Lauterpacht's critical posture is *internal* to its cosmopolitan and rationalist mainstream and directed at the margins, against the "metaphysical" or outright "mystical" doctrines of nationalism, statehood, and sovereignty. Thus, for example, Lauterpacht criticizes Spinoza's doctrine of the reason of State and his separation of individual and State morality as an illogical deviation from the healthy rationalism of his general political philosophy. Somehow, when dealing with international relations, "a fatalistic determinism took the place of reliance upon the power of reason ... the master's hand lost its cunning."[19]

As I will argue more fully later on, Lauterpacht's critique emanates from, or at least can be understood against the background of, the Austrian liberalism that had its heyday in the 1860s but disintegrated under the pressure of the nationalist, antisemitic mass movements of the *fin-de-siècle* years. For Lauterpacht, "Hegelian" philosophy as well as the associated code names, "Hobbes" and "Machiavelli" assume the role of respectable scholarly representatives for those anti-liberal sentiments, the separation of law and statehood from the rationally right.[20] From such posturing, Lauterpacht's critique extends to "politics" in general, branded as irrational, egotistic, short-sighted, and certainly "unscientific." All of this follows from the aim to liberate history's intrinsic rationality by a legal ordering of international affairs.

Lauterpacht's ambivalence towards colonialism may illustrate the direction and limits of his liberalism. On the one hand, Lauterpacht regards the nationalist, exploitative face of imperialism as "the most ruthless economic exploitation of native peoples, maintained by the despotic rule of military administration."[21] On the other hand, he admires the "liberal tradition in British foreign policy" that abolished slavery and the Independent State of the Congo and led to treaties to protect the natives. Lauterpacht saw these activities marking a progressive turn in

[19] Hersch Lauterpacht, "Spinoza and International Law" (1927), *Collected Papers*, 2, pp. 374, 375.
[20] Lauterpacht, "Spinoza and International Law," pp. 366–384. Thus as "totalitarianism and its denial of fundamental human freedoms drew their mystical inspiration from the philosophical revolt against reason – one of the most characteristic manifestations of the German National-Socialistic and Italian Fascistic doctrines – it was inevitable that the drive to vindicate human rights should, once more, ally itself with the rationalist foundations, truly laid by Locke, Newton and Jefferson, of the philosophy of natural law," *International Law and Human Rights*, p. 112.
[21] Hersch Lauterpacht, "The Mandate under International Law in the Covenant of the League of Nations" (1922), *Collected Papers*, 3, p. 39.

the doctrine of the subjects of international law that became concrete in the League's Mandates system.[22] The differentiation works on the basis of humanitarian sentiments that were quite central to the mid-Victorian liberal consciousness. Awareness of complexity, ulterior motives, the powers of desire, and the effects of its repression – essential to modern mentality and especially its (tragic) realism – are non-existent. Where Kelsen, for instance, was quite conversant with Le Bon's theories of the irrational behavior of the masses, it would have been unthinkable for Lauterpacht to integrate such disturbing evidence into his ordered world. For Lauterpacht, even at the worst of times, the world remains a whole, united in the rational pursuit of liberal ideals. Here he is in 1941, defending the "reality of the law of nations" before the Royal Institute of International Affairs, Chatham House:

> The disunity of the modern world is a fact; but so, in a truer sense, is its unity. Th[e] essential and manifold solidarity, coupled with the necessity of securing the rule of law and the elimination of war, constitutes a harmony of interests which has a basis more real and tangible than the illusions of the sentimentalist or the hypocrisy of those satisfied with the existing *status quo*. The ultimate harmony of interests which within the State finds expression in the elimination of private violence is not a misleading invention of nineteenth century liberalism.[23]

Today, international law remains one of the few bastions of Victorian objectivism, liberalism, and optimism. After realism, however, we may no longer feel comfortable in speaking the (paternalistic) language of the "harmony of interests." When called upon to defend our nineteenth-century doctrines, irony may remain our only weapon: "so what better have you got?" Not so with Lauterpacht. His seriousness is warranted by his faith and his faith by a temporal displacement. Even if irrationality is here today, rationality prevails tomorrow. For me, Lauterpacht's main contribution to international law is to have articulated the theoretical and historical assumptions on which the practice of international law is based in a fashion of exceptional clarity. If we want to continue those practices, but feel embarrassed when we try to express their premises, I see only two ways out. Either the practice must be changed (to reflect our modern/post-modern theory) or we have to engage the theory. But it is no longer possible to proclaim prophetic certainties in order to

---

[22] Hersch Lauterpacht, "International Law and the Colonial Question 1870–1914," *Collected Papers*, 2, pp. 101–109.

[23] Hersch Lauterpacht, "The Reality of the Law of Nations," *Collected Papers*, 2, p. 26.

defend having societies' foundational questions squeezed into the form of legal disputes, to be managed in bureaucratic routines by the only remaining group of Victorian gentlemen, international lawyers.

This is why Lauterpacht's work feels historical and contemporary simultaneously. We have been able to add little to the analysis of the relationship of law and politics after the debates between Lauterpacht, E. H. Carr (1892–1982), and Julius Stone (1907–1985).[24] We still regard as authoritative his writings on the Permanent Court or its successor or on any substantive international law problem. Still after his hundredth birthday, Lauterpacht remains interesting as he belongs to the era of our fathers and grandfathers, bridging the gap between the liberal rationalism of the nineteenth and the functional pragmatism of the late twentieth century. Close and distant at the same time, he is uniquely placed to provide an understanding of why it is that we stand now where we do. Whatever Oedipal urge may be satisfied by a recounting of his work will, I hope, be excused by the fact that we, too, are historically situated in a project that is not only an abstract ideational exercise but a continuum of political, moral, and professional choices.

A complete system

That law is an effect of lawyers' imagination is nowhere clearer than in the development of international law from isolated diplomatic practices of the nineteenth century into a legal order some time early in the twentieth. Professional jurists took upon themselves to explain international affairs in the image of the domestic State, governed by the Rule of Law. For that purpose, they interpreted diplomatic treaties as legislation, developed a wide and elastic doctrine of customary law, and described the State as an order of competences, allocated to the State by a legal order.[25] A culture of professional international law was created through the setting up of the first international associations of jurists (such as the *Institut de droit international* and the International Law Association in 1873), doctrinal periodicals (such as the *Revue de droit international et de*

---

[24] Cf. E. H. Carr, *The Twenty-Years' Crisis 1919–1939* (2nd edn., 1981 [1946], esp. chs. 10–13), and Julius Stone, *Legal Controls of International Conflict* (New York, Rinehart, 1954), and from Lauterpacht, e.g. his "Some Observations on the Prohibition of 'Non Liquet' and the Completeness of the Law," *Symbolae Verzijl* (1958), pp. 196–221 as well as Stone's response "Non Liquet and the Function of Law in the International Community" (1959), XXXV *BYIL*, pp. 124–161.

[25] Anthony Carty, *The Decay of International Law? A Reappraisal of the Limits of Legal Imagination in International Affairs* (Manchester University Press, 1986), esp. pp. 13–39.

législation comparée and the *Revue générale de droit international public*) as well as the publication of many-volumed presentations of State practice in the form of systematic legal treatises.[26]

It was not a simple task to imagine diplomatic correspondence and a few arbitration cases as manifestations of an autonomous legal order. In 1935 a skeptic still described the situation as follows: "There is in fact, whatever the names used in the books, no system of international law – and still less, of course, a code. What is to be found in the treatises is simply a collection of rules which, when looked at closely, appear to have been thrown together, or to have accumulated, almost at haphazard."[27] Two strategies seemed possible. Either one could take whatever materials – treaties and cases – one could find that bore some resemblance to domestic law and explain the inevitable gaps in the system as a result of the "primitive" character of international law.[28] Or one could try to expand the law's scope by arguing as Grotius had done, from Roman and domestic law, general principles, and ideas about a common morality.[29] Although in fact both avenues were followed, the former seemed to realize better the statism and the objective of the "scientification" of law that was the great aim of late nineteenth-century jurisprudence.[30]

However, such a "primitive" law proved unable to prevent the First World War, or even to regulate its conduct. Whereas in many aspects of intellectual life the shock of the war was expressed by a turn away from traditionalism, mainstream reconstructive thought in international law sought to bring to a completion the project of creating an international public order on the same principles that had underlain the domestic, peaceful order of European States during most of the preceding

---

[26] Cf. generally Martti Koskenniemi, *From Apology to Utopia. The Structure of International Legal Argument* (Helsinki, Lakimiesliiton kustannus, 1989), pp. 98–100, 106–127; Antonio Truyol y Serra, *Histoire de droit international public* (Paris, Economica, 1995), pp. 115–129.

[27] Sir Alfred Zimmern, *The League of Nations and the Rule of Law 1918–1935* (London, Macmillan, 1935), p. 98.

[28] "International law does not conform to the most perfected type of law. It is not wholly identical in character with the greater part of the laws of fully developed societies, and it is even destitute of the marks which strike the eye most readily of them." W. E. Hall, *A Treatise on International Law* (4th edn., Oxford, Clarendon, 1895), p. 15 and (comparing international law with primitive Teutonic law of self-help), p. 16.

[29] For arguments about international law's basis in Roman law, cf. H. S. Maine, *International Law, The Whewell Lectures* (London, Murray, 1887), pp. 16–20.

[30] Cf. Koskenniemi, *From Apology to Utopia*, ch. II. For this interpretation of nineteenth-century jurisprudence, cf. also Boaventura de Sousa Santos, *Toward a New Common Sense. Law, Science and Politics in the Paradigmatic Transition* (New York, Routledge, 1995), pp. 56 *et seq.*, 72–76.

century.[31] Hence, Lauterpacht's early work is written in the form of a doctrinal polemic against a voluntarist and State-centered "positivism," castigated as the main obstacle on the way to universal legal organization.[32] That the critique was doctrinal, and not directed against diplomacy, follows from the view of politics (and diplomacy) as the rational application of doctrines. In order to constrain politics one had to develop better doctrines.[33] The problem, Lauterpacht held, was the low level of ambition in pre-war doctrine, its readiness to compromise with aggressive nationalism and to leave a large field of activity – such as the right to wage war – outside legal regulation. Lauterpacht's constructive work was directly aimed at such self-amputation. This work begins by his 1925 dissertation in the London School of Economics, *Private Law Sources and Analogies in International Law* (1927), comes to fruition with his most important doctrinal work *The Function of Law in the International Community* (1933) and is conveniently summarized in his 1937 Hague lectures, *Règles générales de la droit de la paix*.[34]

Lauterpacht's thesis is that the law that regulates the affairs of States is neither "special" nor "primitive," but like any other branch of the law. He critiques the "tendency of international lawyers to treat fundamental questions of international law apart from the corresponding phenomena in other fields of law."[35] While international law does have "imperfections" (the absence of a doctrine on the vitiating effect of duress, the wide scope left for the doctrine of *rebus sic stantibus*, the voluntary character of third-party dispute solution) these are merely transient difficulties that the inevitable development of economic interdependence, democracy, and enlightened public opinion will do away with.[36]

The form of Lauterpacht's argument is important. It reconstructs the

---

[31] This was, of course, the Wilsonian ideal, enthusiastically shared by the international law establishment.

[32] For him, "positivism" was a kind of pedestrian Hegelianism, nationalism with a legal face, the doctrinal defense of the *raison d'état*. It was divided into a seriously philosophical strand, associated, for example, with the work of Kaufmann, Anzilotti, and Jellinek, and a technically oriented pragmatism, building on the primacy of sovereignty or State will to law and prevalent, for example, in the writings of Hall.

[33] As he points out in 1927: "the relationship between international law and political theory is of a more pervading character than is commonly assumed. It is the ultimate results of the theory of the state which are resorted to by international lawyers in the foundations of their systems," "Spinoza and International Law," p. 368.

[34] (1937/IV), 62 *RdC*, pp. 99–419, published in English as "General Rules of the Law of Peace," *Collected Papers*, 1, pp. 179–444. The references are to the translation.

[35] Lauterpacht, *Function of Law*, p. 248.

[36] Lauterpacht, *Function of Law*, pp. 403–407, 431–434.

law's unity as a *scientific* postulate. Law no less than physics shares a *horror vacui*: it detests a vacuum.[37] For scientific evaluation, a topic must be construed as a totality. This can be done by legal analogy that is "an application to the domain of law of that conception of analogy which logicians and scientists necessarily apply in their respective disciplines."[38] Though more uncertain, and prone to misuse for special pleading, analogy is the lawyer's means of supplementing fragmentary or contradictory materials so as to ensure law's systemic unity.

In the liberal fashion, Lauterpacht's attack was conducted in the name of the universal principles of science: logical consistency and correspondence with facts. Positivism failed in both. It was logically incoherent: State will cannot be the ultimate source of the law. From where comes the rule that says that will binds? To avoid circularity, the *pacta sunt servanda* or an equivalent metanorm must be assumed to exist as a non-consensual norm.[39]

More importantly, positivism is at variance with "facts." *Private Law Sources and Analogies* shows that judges and arbitrators use maxims of municipal jurisprudence and general principles of law (equity, justice) to fill gaps between consensual norms.[40] States acquire and dispose of territory in a manner analogous to transactions with private property.[41] Domestic notions of occupation and possession structure controversies in the law of the sea.[42] Practice concerning state servitudes, succession, and responsibility is based on the application of private law concepts.[43] Treaties are applied, interpreted, and terminated like private contracts.[44] Rules of evidence and procedure (such as estoppel or the *res judicata*) have no special international sense.[45] Positivists, however, have

---

[37] Hersch Lauterpacht, "Succession of States with Respect to Private Law Obligations" (1928), *Collected Papers*, 3, p. 126.

[38] Lauterpacht, *Private Law Sources*, p. 83. It is not absolute but an "inductive and experimental method subject to correction," p. 84.

[39] Lauterpacht, *Private Law Sources*, pp. 54–59; *Function of Law*, pp. 416–420. In Lauterpacht's own reformulation it becomes, however: *voluntas civitatis maximae est servanda*, "Règles," *Collected Papers*, 1, p. 233.

[40] Cf. especially the series of case analyses in Lauterpacht, *Private Law Sources*, pp. 215–296.   [41] Lauterpacht, *Private Law Sources*, pp. 91–104.

[42] Lauterpacht, *Private Law Sources*, pp. 108–116.

[43] Lauterpacht, *Private Law Sources*, pp. 119–151.

[44] Lauterpacht, *Private Law Sources*, pp. 155–202. The admissibility of duress (i.e. the validity of peace treaties) does not compel a conceptual distinction between treaties and municipal contracts but follows from the "shortcomings of international law as a system of law," pp. 156–167. However, the analogy concerns only general principles of municipal contracts, not individual rules, pp. 176–180.

[45] Lauterpacht, *Private Law Sources*, pp. 203–211.

failed to notice these facts and use "ingenious reasoning" to protect their "arbitrary dogma[s]."[46] Lauterpacht uses expressions such as "metaphysical" and "mystical" in their modern sense, as synonymous for unreal or unscientific, to challenge the special position given by positivists to statehood or sovereignty.[47]

Here as elsewhere, scientism is accompanied by methodological individualism, a liberal political theory. Statehood cannot set up a permanent veil between the international legal order and individual human beings. Being "an artificial personification of the metaphysical State,"[48] sovereignty has no real essence: it is only a bundle of rights and powers accorded to the State by the legal order. Therefore, it can also be divided and limited.[49] Nor is territory in any mystical relationship to the State (as part of its identity) but an object of powers analogous to ownership.[50] Furthermore, "[t]reaties are contracts made by human beings acting as representatives of groups of human beings called States."[51] All law has to do with regulating human behavior; analogy is really but an aspect of the law's wholeness.[52] Therefore, contrary to the received view, States can also be punished and subjective fault remains an element of their responsibility.[53]

By conducting his study in the form of an examination of practice, Lauterpacht is able to attack voluntarist positivism on its own terrain of scientific factuality without having to resort to the moralizing rhetoric of naturalism or the formalism of the pure theory of law. The same terrain enables him to set up a "progressive" political program that puts the individual into the center and views the State as a pure instrumentality. Behind nationalism and diplomacy the world remains a community of individuals and the rule of law is nothing else than the state of peace among them: "Peace is pre-eminently a legal postulate. Juridically, it is a metaphor for the postulate of the unity of the legal system."[54] This double program – scientism and individualism – was as central to interwar cosmopolitanism as it had been to Victorian morality. It was shared,

[46] Lauterpacht, *Private Law Sources*, pp. 75, 74. The ingenuity being the use of "principles of general jurisprudence," which in fact cloak natural law arguments or generalizations from municipal laws, Lauterpacht, *Private Law Sources*, pp. 31–37.
[47] Lauterpacht, *Private Law Sources*, pp. 74, 79, 299; *Function of Law*, p. 431 ("the sanctity and supremacy which metaphysical theories attach to the State must be rejected from any scientific conception of international law").
[48] Lauterpacht, *Private Law Sources*, p. 299.   [49] Lauterpacht, "Règles," pp. 367–377.
[50] Lauterpacht, "Règles," pp. 367–372.   [51] Lauterpacht, "Règles," p. 361.
[52] Lauterpacht, *Private Law Sources*, pp. 71–79.
[53] Lauterpacht, "Règles," pp. 391–397, 401–402.
[54] Lauterpacht, *Function of Law*, p. 438.

among others, by the equally reconstructive doctrines of Verdross and Kelsen. Like them, Lauterpacht accepts the postulate of a community of human beings as a necessary consequence of the existence of an international legal order.[55] But unlike Verdross, he refrains from deriving the latter from the former. The equation works the other way: the community is not a condition but the *effect* of the legal order.[56] This sounds very Kelsenian and in fact Lauterpacht shares much of Kelsen's neo-Kantian constructivism. But instead of relying on the *Grundnorm*, he emphasizes his independence from his teacher by proving his point by means of empirical, rather than logical, argument, labeling his a "critical and realistic monism."[57]

Private Law Sources and Analogies set up international law as a complete system on a par with domestic law. *The Function of Law* argued that there is no valid reason to challenge this completeness by the division of international disputes into two types – legal and political – as expressed in the (positivist) doctrines of non-justiciability.[58] Such division "is, first and foremost, the work of international lawyers anxious to give legal expression to the State's claim to be independent of law."[59] This is an argument about the slippery slope: as the division between the political and the legal cannot be carried out by a determinate rule, it leaves it always open for the State to opt out from the law's constraint by insisting on the "political" nature of the case. Here we meet the problem of self-judgment, Lauterpacht's *mala malaficiorum*, for the first time. Non-justiciability is merely another side of self-judgment and leads international law beyond the vanishing point of jurisprudence. But Lauterpacht challenges the distinction between two types of disputes. For him "all international disputes are, irrespective of their gravity, disputes of a legal character in the sense that, so long as the rule of law is recognized, they are capable of an answer by the application of legal rules."[60] *The Function of Law* goes through each

---

[55] Cf. e.g. Lauterpacht, *Function of Law*, p. 421.
[56] Lauterpacht, "Règles," p. 263. There could hardly be a more express statement of the importance of doctrine's reconstructive task!
[57] Here Lauterpacht expressly formulates his cosmopolitanism: international law as the law of a community of mankind, individuals as its ultimate subjects, States as the instruments of the (overriding) legal order, "Règles," pp. 193–196. His self-portrait is of a challenger to the "orthodox conception," p. 197. The positioning in respect of Verdross and Kelsen and the label "critical and realistic monism" appears on p. 214.
[58] *Function of Law* is structured to refute four versions of the non-justiciability thesis, namely that disputes are political when: (1) legal rules are absent; (2) important issues are at stake; (3) judicial involvement would conflict with the needs of justice or peace; and (4) at issue are conflicts of interest rather than disputes over rights.
[59] Lauterpacht, *Function of Law*, p. 6.   [60] Lauterpacht, *Function of Law*, p. 158.

non-justiciability doctrine showing how they become apologies for the unlimited freedom of action of States. As in *Private Law Sources and Analogies*, Lauterpacht shows that a view that there are "gaps" in law fails to reflect international practice. Courts and tribunals constantly decide cases by analogy, general principles of law, balancing conflicting claims or having recourse to the needs of the international community or the effectiveness of treaty obligations.[61] The "political" nature of a dispute has never prevented a tribunal from giving a legal answer to it.[62]

But he goes further, arguing that the completeness of the rule of law "is an *a priori* assumption of every system of law, not a prescription of positive law."[63] Though particular laws or particular parts of the law may be insufficiently covered, "[t]here are no gaps in the legal system as a whole."[64] This is not a result of a formal completeness of the Kelsenian type, meaning that in the absence of law, the plaintiff has no valid right and his claim must be rejected.[65] The very notion of "law's absence" is suspect as it presumes that law consists of isolated acts of State will. But if law is thought of in terms of general principles, judicial balancing, and social purposes, then "gaps" connote only *primae impressionis* difficulties to decide cases. Legal argument is always able to fill the gap in the end.[66] Even "spurious gaps" may be filled: an unsatisfactory single rule may be by-passed to give effect to a major principle of law, the intention of the parties, or the purposes of the legal system as a whole. In this way, even legal change is regulated by the law.[67]

That the legal order is unable to recognize the existence of gaps results from its inability to limit their scope. In particular, there is no method to distinguish between "essentially" important (political) and non-important (legal) issues.[68] Whether a matter touches on the State's "vital interests" or "honor" cannot be decided in abstraction from the State's own view of it: "the non-justiciability of a dispute . . . is nothing else than the expression of the wish of a State to substitute its own will

---

[61] Lauterpacht, *Function of Law*, pp. 110–135.
[62] But I am not sure that the *Alabama* (1871), *British Guiana* (1897), *Alaska* (1903), and *North Atlantic Fisheries* (1910) cases suffice as proof of this, Lauterpacht, *Function of Law*, pp. 145–153. [63] Lauterpacht, *Function of Law*, p. 64.
[64] Lauterpacht, *Function of Law*, p. 64.
[65] Lauterpacht, *Function of Law*, pp. 77–78, 85–104.
[66] Hence McNair's apt characterization of Lauterpacht's writing as "constructive idealism," McNair, "Memorial Article," p. 378.
[67] Lauterpacht, *Function of Law*, pp. 79–87, 254–257 and *passim*. Cf. also "The Absence of an International Legislature and the Compulsory Jurisdiction of International Tribunals" (1930), XI *BYIL*, pp. 134, 144–154.
[68] Lauterpacht, *Function of Law*, pp. 139–241.

for its legal obligations."[69] Nor is a distinction between "disputes as to rights" and "conflicts of interest" any more successful. If the determination is left to the State itself, then it becomes an unlimited right to opt out from third-party settlement. If such determination is left to the tribunal, then it is tantamount to calling for a decision on the merits of the claim – and thus fails to serve the original purpose of providing *the* criterion through which the distinction could be made.[70]

Arguments about the clash between law, on the one hand, and justice or peace, on the other, are equally vacuous.[71] Critics mistake complexity for conflict. Problems of the unjust rule may always be tempered by reference to the larger purposes of the law, *rebus sic stantibus*, abuse of rights or equity.[72] The needs of realism are incorporated in the State's undoubted right to determine the conditions of self-defense and in the exception to the vitiating effect of duress in the law of treaties.[73]

The refutations of the distinction between legal and political disputes in *The Function of Law* turn on what appears as a sophisticated modern *interpretativism*: no international event is by its "essence" legal or political, its character as such is the result of projection, interpretation from some particular standpoint. If the distinction were to be upheld, it would always allow a State to present its unwillingness to submit to the legal process as a result of the "application" of this distinction. The constraining force of obligations would be left to the obligated. But: "An obligation whose scope is left to the free appreciation of the obligee, so that his will constitutes a legally recognized condition of the existence of the duty, does not constitute a legal bond."[74] That the question of self-judging obligations becomes the central problem of his later doctrinal work follows from Lauterpacht's *nominalism*, the view that the law is always relative to interpretation. In *The Function of Law*, this view leads him to focus on the impartiality of judges and arbitrators and to examine their ability to interpret the law so that everybody's vital interests are secured.[75] To us, such an enquiry into judicial honesty and com-

---

[69] Lauterpacht, *Function of Law*, p. 159.   [70] Lauterpacht, *Function of Law*, pp. 353–361.
[71] Lauterpacht, *Function of Law*, pp. 245–345.
[72] Lauterpacht, *Function of Law*, pp. 270 *et seq.*
[73] "It is not sufficiently realized that fundamental rights of States are safe under international judicial settlement, for the reason that they are fundamental legal rights," Lauterpacht, *Function of Law*, p. 173, and generally pp. 177–182, 271.
[74] Lauterpacht, *Function of Law*, p. 189. This is, paradoxically, the very point E. H. Carr makes against Lauterpacht. Precisely because there can be no distinction between law and politics, the latter will always prevail, *The Twenty-Years' Crisis*, p. 195.
[75] Lauterpacht, *Function of Law*, pp. 202–241.

petence seems a somewhat facile solution for world peace, naïve and old-fashioned. But Lauterpacht's nominalism is ours, too. Our own pragmatism stands on the revelation that it is the legal profession (and not the rules) that is important: "There is substance in the view that the existence of a sufficient body of clear rules is not at all essential to the existence of law, and that the decisive test is whether there exists a judge competent to decide upon disputed rights and to command peace."[76] *The Function of Law* puts forward the image of judges as "Herculean" gap-fillers by recourse to general principles and the law's moral purposes that is practically identical with today's Anglo-American jurisprudential orthodoxy.[77] Moreover, it heralds the end of jurisprudence and grand theory in the same way legal hermeneutics does, by focusing on the interpretative practices of judges. This ensures it a measure of "realism" while its sophisticated interpretative approach avoids the pitfalls of voluntaristic positivism. Simultaneously, however, it remains hostage to and is limited by the conventions and ambitions of that profession. In this sense, *The Function of Law* is the last book on international theory – the theory of non-theory, the acceptable, sophisticated face of legal pragmatism.

Between Zionism and assimilation

Lauterpacht was born in 1897 in the small Jewish village of Zolkiew outside the town of Lwów in Galicia, at the time a part of the Austro-Hungarian Empire. His parents had been "extremely orthodox" but he himself was not very devout. He was, however, given full instruction in the Torah, spoke Yiddish and Hebrew with ease and could chant the Passover service in the Ashkenazi style.[78] In Lwów he had been active in the *Zeirei Zion* movement (a collection of youth groups that, although not strictly socialist "expressed intense social concern and advocated the nationalization of land")[79] and had worked for the establishment of a Jewish Gymnasium. Antisemitism and in particular the *numerus clausus* for Jewish students at the University of Lwów compelled his move to Vienna in 1918 where he became the first President of the newly established

---

[76] Lauterpacht, *Function of Law*, p. 424.
[77] I have argued about the essential similarity of Lauterpacht's constructivism and Ronald Dworkin's jurisprudence in my *From Apology to Utopia*, pp. 35–38.
[78] "Note by Eli Lauterpacht" (Lauterpacht Archives, Cambridge).
[79] Howard M. Sachar, *A History of Israel. From the Rise of Zionism to our Time* (2nd edn., New York, Knopf, 1996), p. 146.

World Federation of Jewish Students.[80] According to his son, Professor Elihu Lauterpacht, "He was neither 'Austrian' nor 'Polish'. His identification was 'Jewish.'"[81]

The rise of Zionism as a political movement in the Habsburg realm at the close of the nineteenth century was closely connected with the pogroms and the unprecedented rise of overt, politically active antisemitism. Taking a Zionist position was a natural and common reaction among Jewish intellectuals against Czech and German nationalisms and Christian-socialist politics and provided more generally a shield for the Jewish population captured between the Ukrainian–Polish antagonism in Galicia.[82] Historically, however, this constituted a departure from the traditional Jewish loyalty to the Empire and its close association with Austrian liberalism whose heyday had been from 1860 to 1895.[83] When liberalism as well as the Empire started their terminal decline and became unable to answer the challenges of nationalism, socialism, and antisemitism, Zionism must have seemed at least as tempting an alternative to Jewish traditionalism as assimilation had previously.

During the war, Lauterpacht stayed at his father's timber mill that had been requisitioned by the Austrian Government as part of the war effort. Galicia was several times overrun by foreign – especially Russian – military forces pillaging the countryside and sometimes armed with orders for the "purification" of Jewish "subversives." Although antisemitism had been far from absent before the war, the grave economic difficulties thereafter gave rise to a plague of persecution in Galicia, resulting in an overall 20 percent decrease in the religious Jewish population during 1910–1921. In many locations the Jewry was effectively halved. "Poland was reborn in Galicia in 1918–1919 to pogrom music."[84]

---

[80] Of which Einstein in Berlin was the Honorary President. For some of this biographical data cf. McNair, "Memorial Article," pp. 371–373. Lauterpacht was one of the Federation's founding members. He had drafted its statute and participated in its establishment Conference on September 1–3, 1922. The Federation had several national societies as members and Lauterpacht's activity seems to have required much diplomatic wrangling between their positions, particularly in regard to the question of Zionism. He seems to have advocated as wide a representation of the interests of Jewish students as possible.   [81] "Note by Eli Lauterpacht."

[82] Cf. Carl E. Schorske, *Fin-de-Siècle Vienna. Politics and Culture* (New York, Vintage, 1989), pp. 5–7, 127–133, 163 *et seq*.

[83] Apart from the classic by Schorske above, cf. Shmuel Almog, *Nationalism & Antisemitism in Modern Europe 1815–1945* (Oxford, Pergamon, 1990), pp. 37–40; Steven Beller, *Vienna and the Jews 1867–1938* (Cambridge University Press, 1989), pp. 122–143.

[84] William O. McCagg, *A History of the Habsburg Jews 1670–1918* (Bloomington, Indiana University Press, 1989), p. 203 and generally pp. 182–187, 202–207.

Although moving to Vienna provided a much-used exit from the persecution surrounding the *shtetl*, even the University was unable to maintain its traditional policy of openness. As Kelsen recalls, Lauterpacht's Jewish background was "under the circumstances which actually existed in Vienna at the time, a serious handicap" and may have contributed to his receiving no more than a pass grade for his Doctorate in the Faculty of Law.[85]

It may be conjectured that Lauterpacht wrote his Viennese dissertation on the topic of Mandates in the Covenant as an offshoot of his Zionist interests, although Palestine did not – perhaps for reasons of prudence – figure prominently in it. Nonetheless, the general argument of the thesis, namely that the Mandates system did not constitute a camouflaged cession or annexation, clearly supports the wish to develop it into a Jewish homeland – as indeed he expressly argued.[86]

In 1923, Lauterpacht moved to Britain. Not much of his early Zionist politics is visible in later years. He did give two lectures to the British society of Jewish Students in 1924 on the character and policy of the World Federation as there had been a division of opinion about whether membership in the Federation necessitated taking a Zionist political position: apparently, it did not. Lauterpacht also appealed for a statement against the *numerus clausus* in Polish universities and contemplated action in the League of Nations by the World Federation on this matter.[87] But soon he allowed his Zionism to lapse and fell back on the more traditional Jewish association with liberal rationalism and individualist – hence cosmopolitan – ethics.[88] From now on, he assimilated with post-war liberal internationalism, letting his Jewish background resurface only incidentally – in an article on the persecution of Jews in Germany in 1933,[89] in legal opinions given to the Jewish Agency in

---

[85] Hans Kelsen, "Note" (1961), 10 *International and Comparative Law Quarterly*, pp. 2, 3–6. The convert Kelsen himself was advised not to take up a university career because of his Jewish background. On this and antisemitism in Vienna at the time generally, cf. Beller, *Vienna and the Jews*, pp. 188–206.
[86] Lauterpacht, "The Mandate under International Law," p. 84.
[87] Texts of two lectures, Lauterpacht Archives.
[88] On the individualist ethics of Austrian and Polish Jewry, cf. Beller, *Vienna and the Jews*, pp. 106–121.
[89] Copy of manuscript available with author. It is not clear where the article was published if indeed it ever was. The manuscript will be published in *Collected Papers*, 5. This constituted an appeal for a condemnation by the Council of the League of all racial persecution, arguing that the matter falls under Council jurisdiction as it affects peace and good order among nations (Art. 4 of the Covenant) and is connected with the League's humanitarian and legal objectives. Lauterpacht suggested that a draft

Palestine or the Agency's permanent UN mission in New York in the late 1930s and 1940s,[90] and in a small *divertissement* on some Biblical problems of the laws of war.[91]

The argument for the completeness and unity of the law must have seemed important enough to enable Lauterpacht to establish himself in Britain and to overcome possible suspicions British lawyers might have had against him. Hence in 1931, still working with *The Function of Law*, he sought to refute the widely held British view that a fundamental difference existed between the Anglo-American and Continental schools of legal thought. Lauterpacht finds no such fundamental divide.[92] More importantly, assuming its existence would be undesirable from a humanitarian point of view and "question that ultimate uniformity of the sense of right and justice which is the foundation of the legal ordering of the relations between states." It will hinder the (inevitable) development of international law into a "common law of mankind."[93]

Lauterpacht's first article, published in 1925, on the contemporary significance of John Westlake – the most prominent British international

---

Footnote 89 (*cont.*)
    resolution should avoid expressly mentioning Germany and should be presented by the representatives of neutral countries (e.g. Spain or Norway). It should have an Annex detailing the facts of persecution from original German sources. Lauterpacht's proposed draft recognized that persecution is contrary to the "public law of Europe" (but apparently not of universal import!) and appealed to League members for a scrupulous non-discrimination in their treatment of minorities.

[90] These concerned matters such as the application of differential customs tariffs and the Imperial Preference under Art. 18 of the Mandate for Palestine, *Collected Papers*, 3, pp. 85, 101.

[91] This paper, dated in 1932, is a 21-page manuscript dealing, on the one hand, with the apparent conflict between Israeli atrocities during the conquest of Canaan and the restraints on warfare in the Ten Commandments and, on the other, with the influence of Jewish concepts on the distinction between just and unjust wars. The manuscript bears no indication of whether it was published. Lauterpacht Archives, copy on file with author.

[92] Hersch Lauterpacht, "The So-Called Anglo-American and Continental Schools of Thought in International Law" (1931), *Collected Papers*, 2, p. 452. To do this, he analyzes substantive doctrines of the law of peace or war, rules of procedure (evidence and recourse to *travaux préparatoires*) and legal philosophy. He claims that continental jurists are not so idealistic, philosophical or system-bound as British prejudice believes. In fact, positivism and the rigid separation of law/justice was developed as a continental approach (Ross, Jhering, pp. 50–51). Also, the strongest criticisms of formalism were developed there (Gény against the *école d'exégèse*; Jhering against *Begriffsjurisprudenz*). The law/*Recht* distinction, too, is illusory: Law = subjective plus objective *Recht*. Where British sense adds Equity to law, the continental *Recht* includes equitableness within the law without the need for special jurisdiction (p. 49n4).

[93] Lauterpacht, "The So-Called Anglo-American," p. 62.

lawyer of the nineteenth century – performed a double feat in this respect. On the one hand, it enabled Lauterpacht to make the point that what was needed was not the rejection of tradition by a full-scale acceptance of either naturalism ("pious wish") or skeptical realism. The best of tradition, as in Westlake's work, combined idealism and political fact in a progressive historical vision that saw contemporary imperfection in terms of progress towards an "organized government of States." Because Westlake's teaching on the subjects and sources of international law and State sovereignty carried this (Victorian) vision, the supervening changes in international politics ("greater than anyone could foresee") required only "alterations of detail" in his work to make it fully applicable in post-war conditions.[94] On the other hand, the argument enabled Lauterpacht to associate "tradition" with the particular tradition of his new home, Britain. This is an enduring feature of his work.[95] Inasmuch as the challenge to the international order was a challenge to Britain's dominant position in it, Lauterpacht's clear preference for British international law against German ("Hegelian") jurisprudence aligned his assimilative strategy with the on-going cultural battle of tradition against revolution.[96]

Lauterpacht's early self-positioning in Britain as a champion of a legal

---

[94] Lauterpacht, "Westlake and Present Day International Law," pp. 385–403; quotes are from p. 400.

[95] It is nicely present not only in Lauterpacht's early and extensive use of Roman law in *Private Law Sources* but in his expressed view that this accords with "British-American jurisprudence" that has "never completely discarded the historical connection of international law and the law of nature [and] regards Roman law as a subsidiary source of international law," p. 298. Later on, he supports British policy in regard to colonies, the illegality of Iran's nationalization of its oil industries, and the jurisdiction of British courts in war crimes and immunities cases. For him, humanitarian ideals and especially human rights emerged from a specifically British tradition. Lauterpacht, *International Law and Human Rights*, pp. 127–141.

[96] Lauterpacht presented "positivism" – the principal object of his criticism – as a particularly German tradition. Cf. e.g. *Private Law Sources*, pp. 43–50. On the related German theory of international law as a law of "co-ordination," cf. *The Function of Law*, pp. 407–416 and "Spinoza and International Law," pp. 379–383. The only (slight) nostalgia that he seems to have felt for his Central European origins appears in a preference for the wider scope of law studies and especially of the philosophy of law as compared to legal studies and "general jurisprudence" in Britain. Cf. Hersch Lauterpacht, "The Teaching of Law in Vienna" (1923), *Journal of the Society of Public Teachers in Law*, pp. 43–45 (on the other hand, he regards British written exams as infinitely better than the Austrian viva voce examination).

The interpretation of Germany as the modernist challenger to British-dominated traditionalism is presented e.g. in Modris Eksteins, *Rites of Spring. The Great War and the Birth of the Modern Age* (New York, etc., Anchor, 1989), pp. 55 *et seq*, 80–94.

cosmopolitanism can also be understood as an *assimilative strategy*[97] in relation to a British academic elite that by 1933 in a famous vote in Oxford had by a large majority declared its unwillingness to die for King and Country.[98] In his writings on statehood and jurisdiction, the constant playing down of the significance of national boundaries works to the same effect, as indeed does his 1928 article on the duties of States in relation to revolutionary activities of private individuals abroad.[99] There being no obligation on States to guarantee each other's legal or political systems, there is no legal justification for curtailing the political activities of émigrés either. The argument creates space for politics on a cosmopolitan scale, particularly important in an era of dictatorships, and supports the widespread inter-war phenomenon of revolutionary politics carried out from abroad.

Lauterpacht's newly found cosmopolitanism as an assimilation strategy is also suggested by the fact that his Viennese dissertation of 1922 had "reject[ed] private law analogy in any form."[100] A year before disembarking in Britain he had argued that international law's development towards autonomy was undermined by a positivist jurisprudence that had constant recourse to private law analogy under the guise of "general law concepts" to fill *lacunae* in positive law – a method that "endangers the independence of international law and fails to recognize its peculiarity."[101] The special meaning of the private law concept distorts the inter-State relationship to which it is applied. "The differences between legal systems are disregarded and the fact forgotten that legal institutions must be construed within the context of their own legal systems."[102] It is only when, in an exceptional case, "[p]ositive international law itself adopts concepts and institutions which have already

---

[97] On the equivocal effects of cosmopolitan distancing as a strategy of assimilation, cf. Zygmunt Bauman, *Modernity and Ambivalence* (Cambridge, Polity, 1991), pp. 78–90 (discussing its use by Jewish intellectuals in the inter-war period), pp. 102 *et seq.*

[98] This is the vote of February 1933 taken among members of the Oxford Union, the University's prestigious debating society.

[99] Hersch Lauterpacht, "Revolutionary Activities by Private Persons Against Foreign States," *Collected Papers*, 3, pp. 251–278 (short of armed transboundary excursions, States have no duty to suppress hostile private activity carried out by other States).

[100] Lauterpacht, "The Mandate under International Law," pp. 29–84, p. 61 and generally pp. 51–61.

[101] Lauterpacht, "The Mandate under International Law," p. 57. ("Rules governing inter-State relationships, which are in fact laid down by treaty or custom are, for the sake of order and categorization and for easier understanding and interpretation, attributed ex post facto to an already existing and well-developed private law concept.") [102] Lauterpacht, "The Mandate under International Law," p. 58.

specific implications in one or more legal system" that we can speak of analogy – for instance, when Art. 22 of the Covenant adopts the term "Mandate."[103] The argument is not quite clear, however. At another place Lauterpacht notes that even if international law appropriates by treaty private law concepts, "its own special nature transforms these concepts and even robs them of their content. In practical terms, therefore, there is no analogy."[104]

Three years later, his British dissertation makes precisely the contrary point: "A critical examination shows that the use of private law analogy exercised, in the great majority of cases, a beneficial influence upon the development of international law."[105] True, Lauterpacht's argument here is different from the Viennese dissertation to the extent that he now sees in Art. 38(3) of the Statute of the Permanent Court of International Justice – "general principles of law" – the vehicle through which private law concepts may penetrate into international law. That provision had been adopted only recently (in 1920) and was therefore not mentioned in his dissertation.[106] Nonetheless, one cannot fail to be struck by the transformation of the outlook on international law implied by this change of heart. Now the door was open definitively to lift international law from its isolation as a marginal, or a special law, a collection of fragmented pieces of State will, and to argue that it constituted a whole system, a single, unified legal order.

Three practical activities to that same effect were Lauterpacht's editorship of the *Annual Digest of Public International Law* cases (that became the *International Law Reports* in 1950) from 1929 to 1956, his editorship of four consecutive editions of *Oppenheim's International Law* from the fifth edition (1937) onwards, and the editorship of the *British Year Book of International Law* between 1944 and 1954. Taken together, these activities demonstrate not only the external success of Lauterpacht's assimilative pursuit but also the seriousness with which he took the argument in

---

[103] Lauterpacht, "The Mandate under International Law," pp. 58–59.
[104] Lauterpacht, "The Mandate under International Law," p. 55. The impression is that Lauterpacht's teachers in Vienna would not have accepted a general argument from analogy and that because he wanted to argue that in the case of Mandates (especially Palestine), no covert annexation was involved, and that as this was in conformity with the private law notion of "mandate," the argument had to be done by way of exception. [105] Lauterpacht, *Private Law Analogies*, p. viii.
[106] For the drafting history, cf. Alfred Verdross, "Les principes généraux du droit dans la jurisprudence internationale" (1935/II), 52 *RdC*, pp. 207 *et seq*; Géza Herzcegh, *General Principles of Law and the International Legal Order* (Budapest, Akadémiai Kiadó, 1969), pp. 11–33.

Private Law Sources and *The Function of Law*. Here there were now all the materials from which international lawyers could construct a working system to resemble the domestic legal order: cases, commentary and a doctrinal forum, henceforth available in most major libraries and (in the case of *Oppenheim*) even on the shelves of Foreign Offices.

A political commitment

By 1927 Lauterpacht had settled in Britain. He was married (since 1923), his son was born and he had received a lectureship at the London School of Economics (recommended by Harold Laski, Arnold McNair, and N. C. Gutteridge). His relations with his early supervisor McNair had developed into a friendship. In 1931 he was naturalized as a British subject. The following year he became Reader in Public International Law at the University of London and was called to the Bar by Gray's Inn in 1936. Lauterpacht was now relatively free to express his view on various aspects of international and British policy. And because, according to the argument in *The Function of Law*, every event of international policy was amenable to legal analysis, it seems logical that he should think it important to undertake public analyses of contemporary international events from a legal perspective.

Consistent with his domestic analogy, Lauterpacht saw the League Covenant as a "fundamental charter of the international society."[107] Its character as a constitution was formally expressed in Art. 20 that set up "the absolute primacy of the Covenant over any other treaty engagements of Members of the League *inter se*."[108] Conflicting posterior treaties between Members were null and void, as were those with third parties that "knew or ought to have known" of the Member's conflicting prior engagement.[109]

This view led Lauterpacht to deny that the League was merely a coordinative body of diplomatic conciliation and to emphasize the provisions on collective security whose importance both contemporary critics and enthusiasts often belittled as a consequence of their "realism" or in their effort to combat it by focusing on the League's functional activities.[110]

---

[107] Hersch Lauterpacht, "Japan and the Covenant" (1932), 3 *Political Quarterly*, p. 175.
[108] Hersch Lauterpacht, "The Covenant as the Higher Law" (1936), XVII *BYIL*, p. 55.
[109] Lauterpacht, "The Covenant as the Higher Law" pp. 63–64, 60.
[110] Hersch Lauterpacht, "International Law after the Covenant" (1936), *Collected Papers*, 2, pp. 156–157.

For Lauterpacht, however, "collective security is, upon analysis, nothing else than the expression of the effective reign of law among States, just as its absence is the measure of the deficiency of international law as a system of law."[111] A series of writings in the 1930s and 1940s defend this view in face of the League's successive failures to influence the course of world events and to keep aggression at bay. The problem in the Manchurian or Abyssinian crises concerned neither the basic idea of the Covenant nor its substantive provisions but the procedural framework that allocated to States themselves the competence to interpret it. He was able to maintain faith in a comprehensive order of legal substance by locating the problems of world peace at the level of a jurisdictional difficulty that would be overcome as the intrinsic rationality of federalism was revealed to everyone.

What, for example, was the significance of the claim made by the principal signatories to the 1928 Kellogg–Briand Pact that they themselves remained the sole judges of the application of the right of self-defense? In a language familiar from *The Function of Law*, and later from his period at the Court, Lauterpacht wrote: "An interpretation which leaves to the interested States the right to decide finally and conclusively whether they have observed the Treaty probably deprives the Pact of the essential *vinculum juris* and renders it legally meaningless."[112] The "principal weakness" was not one of substance but of interpretative competence. Because lawyers were not entitled to assume that the Pact was meaningless it had to follow, in the absence of provision for third-party determination, that it was the legal profession's collective (if decentralized) duty to do this – for instance, by agreeing on a definition of aggression.[113]

While opposing realist skepticism about collective security, Lauterpacht was equally opposed to idealist attempts to explain away interpretative problems by accepting as self-evident particular understandings of the contested provisions and by holding States bound by something they had clearly not accepted. The fact was that the Covenant, the Locarno Treaties, and the Pact of Paris were self-judging. If this might have rendered them under domestic law legally non-existent, in the international society it had to be accepted as the result of its (provisionally) insufficient

---

[111] Hersch Lauterpacht, "Neutrality and Collective Security" (1936), *Politica*, p. 133.
[112] Hersch Lauterpacht, "The Pact of Paris and the Budapest Articles of Interpretation" (1934), 20 *Transactions of the Grotius Society*, p. 198.
[113] Lauterpacht, "The Pact of Paris," pp. 199–201.

degree of integration.[114] The attempt to constitutionalize politics under these instruments did not, then, make politics disappear but relocated it within the inevitable "discretion" that was available to interpret the status of actions contested under their broad terms.

Lauterpacht's discussion of the League's inability to take effective action to counter the Japanese aggression in China during January 1931–April 1933 follows this understanding. As is well known, member States and the League Assembly refrained from qualifying the Japanese invasion as "resort to war" under Art. 16 of the Covenant – and thus maintained their freedom of action (while a contrary determination would, under the strict terms of that Article, have signified the presence of an "act of war" against all members). Lauterpacht was concerned to avoid the interpretation that Members' reluctance to act had been in breach of the Covenant – a view that would only have vindicated the realist point by demonstrating the "illusory value of its fundamental aspect."[115] Whether a use of armed force constituted "resort to war" called for interpretation on which opinion might legitimately be divided: "[T]he assembly's failure to recognize that the action of Japan constituted 'resort to war' was due to the way in which the members of the League, availing themselves of their discretion, interpreted the Covenant."[116] The Covenant was not being breached, it was being interpreted. However, the self-judging character of the provision did not preclude lawyers from taking a critical view on the way in which interpretative discretion was being used.[117] Lauterpacht's preference was to reject both of the extreme views – namely that *any* use of armed force constituted "resort of war" or that only hostilities which the belligerents themselves consider to bring about a "state of war" qualified as

[114] Lauterpacht held it clearly undesirable "that the lawyer should endow such instruments with an authority and content which they do not possess and which their signatories never intended them to have . . . By doing that he may contribute to the predominance of the atmosphere of befogging unreality and artificiality created by such treaties." "The Pact of Paris," p. 196.
[115] Hersch Lauterpacht, "'Resort to War' and the Interpretation of the Covenant During the Manchurian Crisis" (1933), 28 *AJIL*, p. 43.
[116] Lauterpacht, "'Resort to War,'" p. 55. By this means, Lauterpacht candidly observed, "the matter of securing peace . . . was left to a large extent to what is essentially a political decision," p. 58.
[117] Self-judgment followed the absence of compulsory third-party settlement. It did not mean that everybody must accept as final and conclusive the State's own view. A completely self-judging obligation would be no obligation at all. As the principle of effectiveness excluded the interpretation of legal instruments as meaningless, it must be assumed that the State's view may be subjected to critical scrutiny. "The Pact of Paris," pp. 187–189.

such. Literal and purposive interpretations needed to be balanced against each other. This allowed him to opt for the *via media* of a "constructive state of war," dependent on a contextual assessment of the scale and intensity of actual fighting.[118]

By this argument, Lauterpacht was able to maintain the constitutional character of the Covenant and the primacy of law over politics, as the argument in *Private Law Sources* and *The Function of Law* required, while at the same time "realistically" admitting that what the Covenant required was a matter of interpretation in which politics had a large though not an unlimited role to play. The legal question focuses away from the substance to procedure. Discussing the early phase of the Manchurian crisis, Lauterpacht felt that the "crucial question" was "of course"[119] the effect of Japan's dissenting vote in the adoption of the resolution by the Council of October 24, 1931 that required Japan to commence troop withdrawal as soon as possible. While normal voting rules required unanimity, Lauterpacht argued that the votes of the parties were to be discounted where the matter had a "judicial nature." In such case, *nemo judex in sua causa* was to applied. As it was applicable to the determination of Japan's duties, Japan's vote was not to be counted and the resolution was legally binding on it.[120]

The tension between collective security and neutrality likewise implicated self-judgment. In principle, a gapless collective security system left no room for neutrality.[121] But the Covenant was not such a system, not even if the obligations under the Pact of Paris of 1928 were added to it.[122] This was owing to the absence of a League competence to interpret the Covenant authoritatively. Art. 16 left it to the Members to determine if one of them had resorted to war in breach of its obligations (or whether its actions constituted "resort to war") and thus triggered the sanctions mechanism. But even if a Member made such a determination this still did not automatically result in a state of war between it and the Covenant-breaker – hence neutrality became applicable.[123] True, Members could not consistently charge each other with "resort to war" and fail to take economic measures. Non-participation in military action, however, and hence neutrality in a military sense, was always

---

[118] Lauterpacht, "Resort to War," p. 52.
[119] Lauterpacht, "Japan and the Covenant," p. 179.
[120] Lauterpacht, "Japan and the Covenant," pp. 179–185.
[121] Lauterpacht, "Neutrality and Collective Security," p. 149.
[122] Lauterpacht, "The Pact of Paris," pp. 191–194.
[123] Lauterpacht, "Neutrality and Collective Security," pp. 140–141.

available.[124] "The vital part of the Covenant was thus made to repose on the edge of a legal dialectics of a limited but destructive subtlety."[125] Though in conflict with the substance of the Covenant, neutrality continued to exist as a function of this self-judging competence, qualified by the duty of non-recognition – "the ineffective apology of guilty conscience."[126]

This situation reflected the undeveloped state of the law which it was the jurist's duty to disclose (instead of hiding it under ingenious but unrealistic interpretations).[127] The rational solution, however, was to propose "the conferment of a power of *decision* upon a qualified majority of the Council including all the Great Powers but excluding the disputants."[128] In fact, Lauterpacht argued, inasmuch as the *nemo judex* principle is accepted as governing the interpretation of the Covenant, no formal amendment was necessary.[129] By these arguments Lauterpacht was able to keep collective security and the constitutional character of the League intact. Neutrality becomes a de facto position derived from a temporary procedural difficulty, not a principled right or fundamental feature of the system itself.

Neutrality involves political choice and freedom of action. Hence the difficulty of finding a place for it under a legally based international order. At the outset of the Second World War Lauterpacht's views were strongly affected by the interest not to interpret the Lend Lease and US economic assistance to the Allies as a violation of neutrality. After Pearl Harbor, however, he no longer felt constrained in this way. In a 1942 talk in the United States, Lauterpacht observed that there had been no agreed law on the matter in the inter-war era and that no such law was visible then.[130] The old law on neutrality was "glaringly archaic,"[131] a "function of the legal admissibility of war."[132] In a total war – such as world war – neutral trade with the enemy was an "incongruous anachronism" and any rights of neutrality "precarious and illusory."[133] This

[124] Cf. e.g. Lauterpacht, "Japan and the Covenant," p. 187.
[125] Lauterpacht, "Neutrality and Collective Security," p. 137.
[126] Lauterpacht, "Neutrality and Collective Security," p. 149.
[127] Lauterpacht, "Neutrality and Collective Security," pp. 148 *et seq*; "The Pact of Paris," pp. 191–197.
[128] Lauterpacht, "Neutrality and Collective Security," p. 138 (emphasis in original).
[129] Lauterpacht, "Japan and the Covenant," pp. 189–190.
[130] Lauterpacht, "The Future of Neutrality" (unpublished manuscript, Lauterpacht Archives, copy on file with author).
[131] Lauterpacht, "The Future of Neutrality," pp. 3, 8.
[132] Lauterpacht, "The Future of Neutrality," p. 7; "Neutrality and Collective Security," p. 146.   [133] Lauterpacht, "The Future of Neutrality," pp. 4, 5.

was not a conflict where a State could remain neutral for it was fought for "the purpose of vindicating the rule of law among nations."[134] Nor did there exist any place for neutrality in the Allied-conceived future legal order. To the contrary, there would be a legal duty on "all mankind" to make war upon the aggressor.[135] The principles of collective security and the indivisibility of peace would be parts of the new law.

Lauterpacht understood the problems of the 1930s as a measure of the absence of legal constraint on the conduct of foreign policy. In this, he was not alone. Since the First World War, the British public had been particularly suspicious of diplomacy and the diplomatic establishment.[136] In July 1933 Arthur Henderson (1863–1935), the former Foreign Secretary of the Labour Government and the Chairman of the Disarmament Conference, published a pamphlet on "Labour's Foreign Policy" in which he proposed the incorporation of Britain's international obligations on the avoidance of war and peaceful settlement into British law.[137] In response to a request to elaborate a proposal to this effect Lauterpacht drafted a Peace Act which provided that the Covenant, the Pact of Paris, the 1928 General Act for the Pacific Settlement of Disputes, as well as the British acceptance of the compulsory jurisdiction of the Permanent Court, "shall have the force of law." Under the Act it was to be unlawful for a British Government to terminate any of these undertakings, to threaten or to declare war or resort to force, as well as to "order the invasion or occupation of any part of the territory of a foreign State." Any contrary act or Order in Council was to be considered null and void. No defense of superior orders would be applicable for the servants of the Crown implementing such a decision.[138]

---

[134] Lauterpacht, "The Future of Neutrality," p. 1.
[135] Lauterpacht, "The Future of Neutrality," p. 9.
[136] Cf. Gordon A. Craig, "The British Foreign Office from Grey to Austen Chamberlain," in Gordon A. Craig and Felix Gilbert (eds.), *The Diplomats 1919–1939* (Princeton University Press, 1994 [1953]), pp. 22–25, 47.
[137] Arthur Henderson, *Labour's Foreign Policy* (London, The Labour Party, 1933). The booklet reaffirmed the traditional Labour view that "war in any circumstances should be made a crime in international law" (p. 4) and argued that the only way to peace was to agree on compulsory settlement of disputes.
[138] Hersch Lauterpacht, "The Peace Act, a draft" (unpublished, Lauterpacht Archives, copy on file with author). The Act goes further than the instruments as it covers use of force short of "war" and binds Britain not to withdraw its unilateral declaration of compulsory jurisdiction. The duty to respect foreign territory was, however, limited to the extent that there is "instant and grave danger to the life and person of British subjects." Such humanitarian intervention could, however, continue beyond 21 days only by an authorization by the League Council (para. 4).

Where Henderson's original proposal was motivated by the will to "make clear to all the world exactly where the Great Britain stands"[139] the Act could, according to Lauterpacht, in fact achieve "much more." It could "secur[e] a substantial measure of unity of international and municipal law in a matter of paramount importance" as well as, more concretely, "subject . . . to the examination by English courts the hitherto exclusive prerogative of the Crown in the domain of foreign affairs."[140] The draft aimed at domestic enforcement of international obligations in the absence of adequate international guarantees of observance. It reflects the view of international and domestic affairs as a single normative system and limits political discretion in foreign affairs by judicial *fiat*.

The proposal was, of course, never adopted. Finally Lauterpacht reacted to the events of the 1930s by the twin defense of the wounded idealist, abstraction and displacement. In a discussion of peaceful change, he observed that the problem was much more significant than a mere revision of the Peace Treaties – the terms in which it was usually discussed. It related to the establishment of a true international legislature with compulsory membership, majority voting, and effective enforcement. Whatever setbacks the League had suffered, or might suffer, this objective – federalism – remained intact and would one day be realized owing to its intrinsic rational force.[141]

The constitutionalization of politics and the solution of problems of peace by a temporal displacement is given a general form in *Recognition in International Law*, Lauterpacht's first major work after the war (1947). Ostensibly a book on a relatively minor technical topic, its argument condenses the *problématique* of Lauterpacht's inter-war "political" period and establishes the priority of law to political will and political fact. In Lauterpacht's own words, the aim was to "introduce an essential element of order into what is a fundamental aspect of international relations . . . [and to] prevent it from being treated as a purely physical phenomenon uncontrolled by legal rule and left entirely within the precarious orbit of politics."[142] Far from a mere technical rule, recognition is "a task whose implications and potential consequences are of capital political signifi-

---

[139] Henderson, *Labour's Foreign Policy*, p. 19.
[140] "Memorandum on the Draft of the Peace Act" (Lauterpacht Archives, copy on file with author). Lauterpacht explains the basic idea here as an attempt to overcome the "dualism of moral standards which in modern times has been typical of the conduct of the affairs of nations within and outside their borders."
[141] Hersch Lauterpacht, "Peaceful Change. The Legal Aspect," in C. A. W. Manning, *Peaceful Change* (London, Macmillan, 1938), pp. 143–145.
[142] Lauterpacht, *Recognition*, p. 73.

cance."[143] It is the vehicle for removing international status from the precarious realm of politics: statehood, governmental authority, belligerency, and insurgency. Recognition becomes the master technique for establishing the connection between abstract rule and its concrete manifestation. For example: "A lawful acquisition would be meaningless unless it were accompanied by the right to have it acknowledged and respected."[144] The shift of perspective from the rule to its recognition, from the abstract formulation of status to the duty to give effect to it, is a significant step towards making a reality of the legal order. If the order is a complete whole (as was argued in *Private Law Sources* and *The Function of Law*), and if each of its rules is accompanied by the duty to recognize the rights which it establishes (and not to recognize a status brought about by violation) then indeed foreign policy can always be redescribed as the administration of the law. Where politics used to be central and law marginal, the relation of the two now becomes reversed. Governmental freedom of action is reconceived as limited "discretion" in the administration of the law. True, such decentralized administration reflects the undeveloped character of international law – a reflexion itself of the undeveloped integration of international society. Pending the establishment of collective, impartial organs to undertake this task, however, comprehending the process of recognition in terms of legal duty is "not a source of weakness of international law but a substantial factor in its development to a true system of law."[145]

Recognition is a consistent and far-reaching attempt to imagine international law as a complete and self-regulating normative system. What first appears as an act of political will is revealed as an exercise of interpretative discretion. Today, however, the constitutivist view expounded in *Recognition* enjoys no more adherence than it did fifty years ago. It seems too bold in suggesting that legal statehood is dependent on whether the world of diplomacy is prepared to grant it. It seems too weak in failing to explain why rules about statehood could effectively constrain diplomacy in this task. Lauterpacht's redescription relocates policy but does not diminish its centrality.

According to Lauterpacht, were the widespread (positivist) view that the recognition of States and governments is a matter of policy, and not of law, correct, it would constitute as glaring a gap "in the effective validity of international law" as the admissibility of war did prior to the

---

[143] Lauterpacht, *Recognition*, p. 69. [144] Lauterpacht, *Recognition*, p. 409.
[145] Lauterpacht, *Recognition*, p. 78.

1928 Pact of Paris.[146] Such a situation would also be ethically intolerable as it would fail to uphold the right of human communities to constitute themselves as political entities: "the right of recognition follows from the overriding principles of independence of States and of prohibition of intervention."[147] Again, Lauterpacht's target is a mistaken doctrinal view. And again, the attack is conducted in terms of scientific factuality: "the view that recognition is not a function consisting in the fulfillment of an international duty but an act of national policy ... has the further result of divorcing recognition from the scientific bases of fact on which all law must ultimately rest."[148] Accordingly, the book is written as an extensive survey of the diplomatic and recognition practice of the most important States (Britain and the United States, in particular). In Lauterpacht's view, States have not regarded recognition as a matter of arbitrary political will but have consistently argued that granting or withholding it was a matter of duty, relative to the ascertainment of facts. That this method entrenches the statism of an international system which he elsewhere held as its main defect remains invisible as factuality is here used to buttress a normativist view against deviating "realisms." But it does make it necessary for him to argue in terms of a historical trajectory in which the present is only a temporary stage to be superseded by a collectivization of recognition through the integration of the international community "which, in the long run, is the absolute condition for the development of the potentialities of man and humanity in general."[149]

The factual argument is weak. It is easy to believe that States do not argue that when they grant or withhold recognition, they are doing it as a matter of political will. It is in the nature of diplomacy to defend one's position by reference to external "objective necessities." If Canning argued that the British recognition of South American colonies in 1823 followed from their actual fulfillment of the conditions of statehood,[150] is this not a typical diplomatic move to justify one's political position in as uncontroversial terms as possible in order to forestall the counter-reaction of one's adversary (Spain in this case)? Surely the same is true of most situations where the grant of status is a matter of political controversy. A "realist" has no difficulty in interpreting Canning's policy as a political maneuver against Spanish predominance and an attempt to extend British influence in the Western hemisphere.

---

[146] Lauterpacht, *Recognition*, pp. 3–6. [147] Lauterpacht, *Recognition*, pp. 142, 158–165.
[148] Lauterpacht, *Recognition*, p. 5, also p. 91. [149] Lauterpacht, *Recognition*, p. 78.
[150] Lauterpacht, *Recognition*, pp. 13–17.

Lauterpacht: the Victorian tradition in international law

The book's factual claims comply with the expectations of the reading public but fail to provide a conclusive demonstration of a historical thesis. Much more important are arguments according to which the declarativist view is epistemologically naïve while (pure) constitutivism is ethically unacceptable. The modernity and consequence of *Recognition* lies above all in Lauterpacht's successful repudiation of the naïve realism that clung to the "scientific" character of political facts and sought respectability from an entrenchment of power. The epistemological and the ethical are brought together in *Recognition* by insisting on that which lies between, interpretation.

Declarativism is naïve as it assumes that the emergence of political entities endowed with legal rights and duties, and in particular of States (or governments, or belligerents), is a question of pure fact. Recognition not only fails to create status, it is reduced to a formality and we must remain in constant doubt about why it should have any significance at all. But in fact statehood is not a physical fact that would be able to disclose itself mechanically for all the world to see, or whose presence or absence can be determined by some "automatic" test, as shown by the extreme variety of actually existing States.[151] Statehood is a conceptual construct which refers back to the presence (or absence) of a set of criteria for the attainment of the relevant status. What those criteria are and whether they are present depends on acts of human cognition. If that act of cognition is not there, i.e. if nobody recognizes an entity as a "State," then there is little point in insisting that the status still exists. Only through recognition can a fact transform itself into a "juridical fact."[152] A State or a government whose existence is acknowledged by nobody cannot successfully claim to be treated as such. Its status has reality only within its own solipsist universe.[153]

The constitutive view acknowledges the complexity of the social world and the ensuing primacy of the *interpretation* of facts over facts in their "purity." Inasmuch as it holds recognition to be an act of "pure politics," however, it goes too far in the opposite direction. From the existence of a gap between "facts" and their cognition it draws the consequence that

---

[151] Lauterpacht, *Recognition*, pp. 45–51.   [152] Lauterpacht, *Recognition*, p. 75.
[153] This may seem obvious as regards statehood. Its significance is highlighted in relation to the frequent assertions by States that they do not recognize foreign governments. In normal cases no express recognition is needed because the matter is clear. Recognition asserts its constitutive significance, however, when there are rival factions: in such cases a state wishing to maintain some kind of relations with the State concerned is bound to give some kind of recognition – implicit or de facto – to one such faction. Lauterpacht, *Recognition*, pp. 156–157.

the two are wholly independent from each other, that recognition is an act of pure, unconstrained political will. But in fact nobody treats it as such. If statehood is a matter of fulfilling some antecedent criteria, then surely recognition must comply with such criteria – and that it is so regarded is evident, for example, in the generally accepted view that holds premature recognition as a violation of the law[154] and that tests governmental authority by reference to its effectiveness; to hold otherwise would allow intervention in the internal affairs of the State.[155]

The only open question that remains is what the legal criteria of attaining the relevant status are, and how they are to be interpreted. Here there is, of course, much debate and discretion. On the one hand, a legal view is incompatible with politically loaded criteria, such as legitimacy of origin, religion, political orientation, or even the willingness to abide by international law.[156] On the other hand, such criteria cannot be purely factual, without violating the principle of *ex injuria non jus oritur*. The effectiveness of government cannot be just a matter of power, but must be accompanied by a degree of legitimacy.[157] Non-recognition of illegally attained title is not the consequence of a specific doctrine to that effect but of the general principle that no one may profit from his own wrong. True, there is always a "political element" in appreciating such criteria.[158] But discretion is not free, at least it cannot be exercised for the advancement of one's own interests. In exercising it, States are fulfilling the function of administering international law.

Lauterpacht's modernist, neo-Kantian epistemology combines constitutivism and declarativism. Recognition is "declaratory of facts and constitutive of rights."[159] Such a construction takes a strong view on interpretation. Facts do exist as the (absent) referents of the criteria for recognition. But they appear only in interpretation. As facts cannot interpret themselves "there must be *someone* to perform that task."[160] That someone is each State. Interpretation is not a political act of will, however. As its ultimate reference is a fact, it must be held an act of cognition. We notice here the central paradox of modernist epistemology: though knowledge (unlike will) is universal, it appears (like will) only in partial truths. Lauterpacht accepts relativism, but only as a temporary condition, a consequence of the present world's fragmented nature.

---

[154] Lauterpacht, *Recognition*, pp. 9–12.   [155] Lauterpacht, *Recognition*, pp. 98 *et seq.*
[156] Lauterpacht, *Recognition*, pp. 31–32, 102–104.
[157] Lauterpacht, *Recognition*, pp. 115 *et seq.*   [158] Lauterpacht, *Recognition*, pp. 26–37.
[159] Lauterpacht, *Recognition*, p. 75.
[160] Lauterpacht, *Recognition*, p. 55, italics in original.

The problem is not only that interpretation is difficult (indeed, the complexity of international life is acknowledged in the intermediate doctrine of de facto recognition)[161] but also that we cannot be assured that it is always undertaken in good faith. Lauterpacht believes that accepting the legal character of recognition will to some extent diminish the likelihood of divergent findings.[162] To dispose finally of the unacceptable situation of self-judgment, however, recognition must be collectivized, allocated to an "impartial international organ."[163] This can, however, be undertaken only when international integration arrives at its final form of universal organization with compulsory membership.[164]

Recognition illustrates the problems of modern law. Facts are needed to constrain (arbitrary) political will. However, facts need to be interpreted. In the act of interpretation political will reasserts itself. "Criteria" or "methods" are needed to control interpretation – and we must struggle about finding *them* a normative basis and a determinate content. *Recognition*, like post-formalist law in general, seeks an exit from the circle of interpretative problems by a turn to process: focusing away from facts and criteria to the qualities of (future) procedure. For Lauterpacht, recognition – the meaning of facts and allocation of status – must ultimately become the function of democratic debate: (interpretative) wills must try to find each other in search of a collective consensus. The relocation of the resolution in a future process, however, seems undermined by the description of the present. Why would such collectivization take place if, in fact, recognition is important and States disagree on the meaning of facts? Why would collectivization of a political decision any better protect the rights of individual entities than its decentralization; why would adding up more wills come to establish the cognitive correctness of the conclusion?

In *Recognition*, too, Lauterpacht's gaze looked into the nineteenth century as an era when diplomacy was orderly and honored the consent of the governed:[165] *Imperium et Libertas*.[166] It was his last "political" work. It offered a redescription of diplomacy as the administration of the law which at the stroke of the pen wiped away the political "retrogression" of the inter-war years. Its legal utopia relied not only on diplomats' willingness to understand their job accordingly but – much more crucially

---

[161] Lauterpacht, *Recognition*, pp. 329 *et seq.* [162] Lauterpacht, *Recognition*, p. 58.
[163] Lauterpacht, *Recognition*, pp. 55 and generally 67–78, 165–174, 253–255.
[164] Lauterpacht, *Recognition*, pp. 77–78. [165] Lauterpacht, *Recognition*, pp. 130–140.
[166] Cf. Harold Temperley, *The Victorian Age in Politics, War and Diplomacy* (Cambridge University Press, 1928), pp. 14–21.

– on their ability to clear the inevitable (interpretative) disagreements through democratic debate which, if it were present, would render the redescription unnecessary. Lauterpacht's utopia was not unworkable because diplomats were unwilling to imagine themselves as judges but because, to judge wisely, they needed to be good diplomats!

Nuremberg and human rights

Whatever may have been the reaction of Lauterpacht's Cambridge audience in the autumn of 1938 to his plea for the revival of Victorian tradition, international politics took a different course. The absolute powerlessness of law in face of a political and military logic completely discredited the idea of simply resuscitating the League.[167] Despite the infinitely greater horrors of the Second World War compared to those of its predecessor, however, no great movements of revival or rejection followed in its wake. The establishment of the United Nations took place as a pragmatic necessity, an outcome of technical realism and sense of duty rather than political inspiration, as if no formal reaction could possibly have matched the enormity of the sufferings caused by the war.

Lauterpacht's whole family, his parents, his brother and sister and their children, with the exception of one niece, were murdered in the Holocaust, presumably as early as 1940. It is not clear when he learned of the fate of his family. Nothing is visible of this tragedy in his writings – although it seems evident that the turn from "politics" to "human rights" must have been influenced by it. Lauterpacht himself spent the war years in Britain, teaching in Cambridge as Whewell Professor of International Law after 1938, and making two lecturing trips to the United States and providing services to the British Government. In 1945–1946 he became a member of the British War Crimes Executive, in which capacity he went to Nuremberg and wrote drafts for Britain's Chief Prosecutor, Sir Hartley Shawcross (born 1902).

Lauterpacht's drafts for the opening and closing speeches of the British prosecutor are characteristic in their absence of emotion and

---

[167] This was what Lauterpacht had proposed as late as 1939–1940 in a talk that avoided taking a straightforward federalist stand and that is among those rare writings in which he shows some understanding of statehood as "an expression of actual diversity of interest, economic and other, and of disparities of wealth, culture and standards of life between States," Hersch Lauterpacht, "Sovereignty and Federation," *Collected Papers*, 3, pp. 13, 5, 14–25.

concentration on doctrinal detail.[168] He keeps in check his Jewish background and writes about the Shoah as the killing or extermination of "civilians" and "non-combatants." The closing draft begins with a slightly defensive discussion of the competence of the Tribunal and of the fairness of its procedures, its impartiality and independence. Lauterpacht stressed the Tribunal's function as an administrator of general, not victors', international law. The substantive part of the draft defends the notions of a State's as well as individuals' international responsibility as parts of already existing law and draws upon Lauterpacht's earlier views.[169] The discussion is technical – an analysis of a 1935 arbitration between Canada and the United States being strangely out of place in this connection. Sometimes Lauterpacht gets carried away by his academic views, directing his attacks not only against German policy but statehood as such: "[t]he mystical sanctity of the sovereign State . . . is arraigned before the judgment of the law."

The extreme restraint and formality of Lauterpacht's drafts is understandable. Of all British international lawyers, he was most vulnerable to the charge of special pleading. Only parts of his drafts found their way into the passionate, even angry, speeches of the British prosecutor. As Shawcross noted, "the sentiment in Nuremberg" required concentration on the facts rather than on the law.[170] Nonetheless, the full story of Lauterpacht's role in Nuremberg remains untold and Shawcross expressed his gratitude on several occasions, sometimes very generously, noting at the end of the process, that "I hope you will always have the satisfaction in having had this leading hand in something that may have a [lasting?] influence on the future conduct of international relations."[171]

During the war Lauterpacht had already participated in the debates concerning the future of world organization. Inspired by an American debate in 1942–1943, he drafted a scheme for an international rule of

---

[168] Lauterpacht Archives, copies of parts of the draft for the closing speech on file with the author. Shawcross had contacted Lauterpacht in May–June 1946 asking for assistance in the preparation of these statements and specifically directing him to concentrate on the legal and historical aspects of the case.

[169] These themes – the advocacy for a War Crimes tribunal, the elaboration of the basis of its jurisdiction, as well as the law applicable and a discussion of a neutral State's duty to extradite suspects – are also dealt with in "The Law of Nations and the Punishment of War Crimes" (1944), XI *BYIL*, pp. 58–95 (an article based on a Memorandum Lauterpacht prepared for a Committee set up by the Department of Criminal Science at Cambridge University).

[170] Shawcross to Lauterpacht, November 27 and November 30, 1945 (Lauterpacht Archives). [171] Shawcross to Lauterpacht, July 11, 1946 (Lauterpacht Archives).

law that reproduced in ten principles his liberal, cosmopolitan credo.[172] The organization was to be universal, its continuity with the League should be recognized (thus symbolically recognizing continuity with the "greatest political advance made by the society of nations"[173]), and it should be independent from the peace settlement. There were to be a prohibition of war, a compulsory rule of law, systems of collective security, peaceful change, majority voting, human rights protection, and international adminstration. Courts were to be allocated major tasks, e.g. the determination of the existence of "war," as well as setting the limits of international legislation.[174] There would also be a system of effective enforcement of judgments.[175]

In 1944, Lauterpacht also participated in a discussion initiated by the American Society of International Law (ASIL) on the future of world organization. He was critical of the text produced for this purpose by Manley Hudson for the relevant ASIL Committee,[176] regarding it a "rather timid and uninspired document."[177] Its rhetoric was too general, giving the "impression of somewhat pretentious embellishment." It failed to propose a binding system of international legislation, contained no provision for the protection of human rights, applied the unanimity principle in important matters, and maintained the legal/political disputes distinction which, as Lauterpacht had demonstrated in *The Function of Law*, allowed States to opt out from legal procedures at will. Writing to his British colleagues, Lauterpacht noted that "there is room for a parallel and perhaps better effort in this country."

The proposal led to an exchange of written drafts and comments between members of a British International Law Committee, in which in addition to Lauterpacht, at least Hurst, McNair, and Brierly participated.[178] In this correspondence Lauterpacht consistently took a

---

[172] Undated memorandum, 1942/43, *Collected Papers*, 3, pp. 462–503.
[173] Undated memorandum, 1942/43, p. 474.
[174] Undated memorandum, 1942/43, pp. 481, 483.
[175] These ideas were not generally shared among the British international law community. Professor Brierly, for instance, took a very critical view of the proposals – especially of the implied aim of forcing democracy as the internal form of government – and remarked drily that the "proposals might be more effective if they were less ambitious." Brierly to Lauterpacht December 15, 1943 (Lauterpacht Archives).
[176] Cf. 38 *AJIL* (Supplement), pp. 44–139.
[177] Memorandum (undated, presumably spring or early summer 1944). From Lauterpacht to Sir Cecil Hurst, "Notes on the Postulates, Principles and Proposals," Lauterpacht Archives, copy on file with author.
[178] The full composition or general activities of the Committee are not known, cf. note by Eli Lauterpacht in *Collected Papers*, 3, p. 461.

Lauterpacht: the Victorian tradition in international law

federalist position, advocating, as in his inter-war writings, universal and compulsory membership in the future organization (with temporary non-admission of former "Axis Powers and their Allies"), binding international legislation in matters of international concern (and generally, though not without exception, through majority vote), binding and compulsory settlement of disputes, collectivization of recognition, and enforcement jurisdiction bestowed on the organization, with special (but not sole) responsibility on the four major Powers.[179]

Some of Lauterpacht's proposals that were controversial or absent from other drafts presented to the Committee (such as a unitary budget for the various bodies, the non-use of force principle, the trusteeship system, a provision on the protection of human rights, and registration of treaties) ended up in the UN Charter. Nonetheless, in an assessment of the state of international law given at the Hebrew University in Jerusalem in May 1950,[180] Lauterpacht did not hide his dissatisfaction. In his view, the situation was worse now than it had been in 1919. The inter-war years had been a period of regression to which the peace of 1945 had brought no significant relief. Modernity had failed him. He attributed this to four rather different causes: lawlessness in the conduct of warfare, the suppression of normal conditions by the Allies in occupied Italy and Germany, the prevailing atmosphere of admiration of power, and the requirement of unanimity of the permanent members of the Security Council.[181] Even recent progress in some areas (the growth of international organization, the acceptance of the principles of enforcement and human rights) "has been obscured by the tangible and menacing reality of the division of the world into two opposing groups of States."[182]

After the sombre assessment of the state of the post-war world, Lauterpacht's writing takes a new turn. Instead of trying to develop better doctrines on traditional textbook subjects Lauterpacht now focuses directly on individual human rights and advocates institutional

---

[179] Cf. International Law Committee: "The Nature of International Law – Draft by Professor Brierly, Observations by Professor Lauterpacht" (June 12, 1944); International Law Committee on the Hudson Document: "Sir Cecil Hurst's Draft of a Revised Covenant. Observations by Professor Lauterpacht" (July 15, 1944), Mimeo, Lauterpacht Archives, copies on file with author.

[180] Lauterpacht represented Cambridge University at the 25th anniversary of the Hebrew University and gave two lectures there, one in English, one in Hebrew.

[181] "International Law after World War II," *Collected Papers*, 2, pp. 159–170.

[182] "International Law after World War II," p. 167. Cf. also "The Grotian Tradition in International Law," p. 1 n 2.

means of protection at universal and regional levels. He explains that there has been "widespread conviction" that the "major purpose of the war" had been the creation of effective institutions to protect human rights, in particular the establishment of an International Bill of the Rights of Man.[183] Much of his late 1940s work is written as a polemic in favor of such an instrument, the subject of a pamphlet of 1945, of a number of public lectures, and of the main work of his human rights period, *International Law and Human Rights* (1950).

However, although Lauterpacht's subject-matter focus is now different from his pre-war concerns, the traditionalist impulse seems even more prevalent than before. *Human Rights* takes on a language of grave formality. He now speaks of the "majestic stream of the law of nature."[184] Words such as "fundamental," "inalienable," and "sanctity" abound, underlining the ahistorical, quasi-religious seriousness of human rights. The book's revivalist argument is this: natural rights (that is, individual human rights) are rooted in (Western) legal and political thought, from Greek philosophy to modern Western constitutions.[185] These rights are supported and "enforced" by natural and international law, the two having developed together from Grotius and Vattel to the doctrine of humanitarian intervention,[186] and, finally, the UN Charter which places human rights "on the enduring foundations of the law of nature."[187] To make matters more concrete and to make no mistake about where the tradition is to be found, Lauterpacht identifies it with the "English sources," the "powerful tradition of freedom conceived, in the words of the Act of Settlement, as the 'birthright of the English people.'"[188]

This revivalist argument feels like Walter Benjamin's famous image of the "Angel of History." Lauterpacht is propelled forwards with his gaze fixed firmly in the receding past in which history's pile of debris seems always highest when nearest.[189] The invocation of Greek philosophy and Enlightenment thought seemed necessary in order to re-establish the credibility of European liberal political culture – of which many assimilated Jews had good reason to feel they were the real bearers[190] –

---

[183] Lauterpacht, *International Law and Human Rights*, p. 79.
[184] Lauterpacht, *International Law and Human Rights*, p. 79n15.
[185] Lauterpacht, *International Law and Human Rights*, pp. 73–93.
[186] Lauterpacht, *International Law and Human Rights*, pp. 114–126.
[187] Lauterpacht, *International Law and Human Rights*, p. 145.
[188] Lauterpacht, *International Law and Human Rights*, p. 139.
[189] Walter Benjamin, *Illuminations* (ed. and with an introd. Hannah Arendt, New York, Schocken, 1968), pp. 257–258.   [190] Beller, *Vienna and the Jews*, pp. 142–143.

and to explain the immediate past as an externally imposed distortion and not a logical consequence of the tradition.[191] Only an openly philosophical stance could make the traditional project seem credible in face of increasing popular cynicism about international law and organization, reflected in the academic turn from international law to international relations and in the journalistic predominance of a new, dynamic realism.

Beyond the celebratory recounting of Western intellectual history, *Human Rights* conveys no interpretation of the cultural or political meaning of the inter-war era, or of the causes and vicissitudes of the Second World War. In particular, the book fails to examine the relationship between the optimistic legalism of the League era and the collapse of the political order. The only reference to the Holocaust appears in a footnote that quotes Earl Russell from 1946![192] The book's naturalist part (section II, chapters 5–8) remains a separate, historico-moral treatise with little connection to what went before (the description of the erosion of statehood as the organizing principle of the law) and what comes after (a discussion of the place of human rights in the Charter and the project for an International Bill of Rights). The isolation of the book's three parts from each other suggests that Lauterpacht did not succeed in attaining a satisfactory reconciliation of traditionalist morality with modernist legality. The result is a work that either reproduces the liberal canon and the primacy of individual rights over a potentially hostile public power; or becomes a partisan plea for a particular institutional arrangement (public power!) to support individual rights as effectively as possible.

Human Rights explains itself again as a critique of "[t]he orthodox positivist doctrine . . . that only States are subjects of international law."[193] The curious impression is being conveyed that the problems of world order depend on a mistake about the proper listing of legal subjects. This somewhat absurd feeling is strengthened by the rest of the book's first part that counters this (academic) dogma by reference to the emergence of international organizations as legal subjects[194] and the recognition of the position of the individual as protected or rendered

---

[191] "[T]he menacing shape of unbridled sovereignty of the State in the international sphere [created the] urge to find a spiritual counterpart to the growing power of the modern State," Lauterpacht, *International Law and Human Rights*, p. 112.
[192] Lauterpacht, *International Law and Human Rights*, p. 71n 22.
[193] Lauterpacht, *International Law and Human Rights*, p. 6.
[194] Lauterpacht, *International Law and Human Rights*, pp. 12–26.

responsible by international treaties.[195] The result is an implicit suggestion that the problems of post-war reconstruction do not lie in diplomacy or politics but in legal doctrine's inability to reflect the (increasingly beneficial) facts of international life. The issue is (only) "one of not permitting the dead hand of an obsolete theory to continue to lie heavily upon the development of international organisation."[196] Such doctrinal focus, however, deprives the work of critical force. Who would be interested in adjusting the insights of a marginal theoretical preoccupation if diplomatic facts (as well as the law) have already been transformed to reflect the politically desirable?

The same problem emerges in the discussion of the place of human rights in the UN Charter, the section that follows the philosophical excursus into Western naturalism. Lauterpacht insists that Arts 1(3) and 55(c) of the Charter, dealing with "promoting . . . respect for human rights," are not simply programmatory postulates but create enforcible legal obligations. By recourse to the principle of effectiveness, he interprets the reference to human rights in the Charter in the broadest possible terms while the scope of "domestic jurisdiction" in Art. 2 (7) is given the narrowest feasible understanding.[197] Lauterpacht reads the whole liberal agenda into those provisions: they provide protection for individuals against the government and its subdivisions as well as other intrusions in the private realm.

Just as in the "political" writings of the 1930s, it turns out that the substance of the rights is less important than the procedures, the key problem being "what shall be the international machinery for securing the rights after they have been recognized."[198] Lauterpacht was disappointed by the early jurisdictional decision by the Commission on Human Rights not to take action on individual petitions and responded by the argument that human rights were not merely an incidental decoration but an underlying theme of the Charter. It would therefore have been possible for the Commission in accordance with the principle of effectiveness to examine individual complaints.[199] He urged as the essential part of the future International Bill of Rights – what became the two

---

[195] Lauterpacht, *International Law and Human Rights*, pp. 27–47.
[196] Lauterpacht, *International Law and Human Rights*, p. 19.
[197] Lauterpacht, *International Law and Human Rights*, pp. 145–154.
[198] Talk on the BBC in October 1949, *Collected Papers*, 3, p. 413.
[199] "State Sovereignty and Human Rights" (1950), *Collected Papers*, 3, pp. 419–421; *International Law and Human Rights*, pp. 229–251.

Covenants in 1966 – the inclusion of a mechanism of individual (and not only State) complaints. To deny such right would be "tantamount to a withdrawal, to a large extent, of the principal benefit conferred by the Bill."[200]

The most interesting part of *Human Rights*, however, is the criticism of the "deceptive" or "concealing"[201] character of the 1948 Universal Declaration on Human Rights. Even during the drafting of the Declaration Lauterpacht had warned against not rushing ahead so as not to end up in vacuous generalities.[202] This had been to no avail, however. The provisions of the Declaration became too general and open-ended to be applicable. No institutional safeguards or mechanisms for implementation were attached to it. States were unanimous and emphatic in their denial of the legal character of the Declaration.[203] And they were right – any attempt to interpret it as a legal instrument were bound to fail. Retreating to formalism Lauterpacht stressed the "duty resting upon the science of international law to abstain from infusing an artificial legal existence into a document which was never intended to have that character."[204] Lauterpacht viewed the Declaration as mere decoration; not only unnecessary but counter-productive, a *substitute* for effective action. Even attempts to endow the Declaration with moral value were futile: what moral value has a commitment that States are openly entitled to disavow? It thus became legal doctrine's task to create a living sense of the Declaration's insufficiency and to quicken the pace of negotiations for an effective Bill of Human Rights.[205]

There is a tension between the invocation of the tradition of natural rights in the second part of the book and the critique of the 1948 Declaration in the third. For if the tradition is correct, Lauterpacht should not be too worried about the effects of the Universal Declaration that seems, after all, to have rhetorically incorporated much of its substance. On the other hand, surely the critique of the Declaration as mere "façade" or "substitute" is equally applicable to the human rights tradition that Lauterpacht seeks to revive. The absence from Lauterpacht's

---

[200] "State Sovereignty and Human Rights," p. 423.
[201] Lauterpacht, *International Law and Human Rights*, p. 421.
[202] Letter to the Times, July 26, 1947, *Collected Papers*, 3, pp. 408–409.
[203] Lauterpacht, *International Law and Human Rights*, pp. 397–408.
[204] Lauterpacht, *International Law and Human Rights*, p. 417.
[205] Cf. also Lauterpacht's talk of 1949, *Collected Papers*, 3, p. 413.

revivalist argument of a serious account of the relationship between the liberal tradition and diplomatic history makes it just as vulnerable to a criticism of bad faith as the Declaration in its purely rhetorical formulation.

The problem lies in Lauterpacht's unwillingness to pinpoint the politics he finds unacceptable. Instead, the focus of his criticism falls always on the abstract and formal conception of statehood, viewed in the standard liberal fashion as mere "administrative convenience"[206] that had degenerated into an "insurmountable barrier between man and the law of mankind."[207] The critique of statehood is the counterpart of Lauterpacht's cosmopolitan individualism. But whether that critique is the unequivocal consequence of the tradition may be open to doubt. Surely Lauterpacht would have conceded that at least in some cases – perhaps quite a few cases – statehood functions as a protective device over the freedoms that tradition seeks to uphold.[208] In 1947 Lauterpacht participated in the drafting of the Declaration of Independence of the State of Israel. Surely he could not have refused to take part in the creation of the Jewish State because of his principled view about the malignant character of statehood![209]

The point here is that the relationship between the tradition and the institutional proposals is more complex than Lauterpacht is willing to acknowledge. Tradition (natural law) and modernity (institutional experience) refuse to lie comfortably in the same bed. A reliance on the former may sometimes support statehood, sometimes federalism. Everything depends on the circumstances and the relevant question becomes less whether to prefer statehood or integration but *what* States,

---

[206] Lauterpacht, *International Law and Human Rights*, p. 68 and generally pp. 67–72.
[207] Lauterpacht, *International Law and Human Rights*, p. 77.
[208] As indeed he does by recognizing "a certain duality" about statehood: on the one hand its only justification is the protection of individual rights, on the other, it appears also as "the absolute condition of the civilized existence of man [sic]," Lauterpacht, *International Law and Human Rights*, p. 80. This duality disappears, however, as Lauterpacht moves to prophesy: there is no regret for the loss of these benefits on the route to federalism. Lauterpacht's federalism has been strengthened from the more careful realism of 1939–1940 in "Sovereignty and Federation," *Collected Papers*, 3, pp. 14–25.
[209] In fact, when defending British jurisdiction on the treasonable activities of aliens abroad (through a wide formulation of the "effects" doctrine) or on the scrutiny of the international lawfulness of acts of other States, Lauterpacht has no difficulty in defending British sovereignty to the extent that it can be used to attain his preferred outcomes. Cf. "Allegiance, Diplomatic Protection and Criminal Jurisdiction over Aliens" (1946), *Collected Papers*, 3, esp. pp. 234–239 and "Testing the Legality of Persian Policy" (1952), *Collected Papers*, 3, pp. 242–244.

or integration *on which terms* to prefer.[210] But these are issues of substantive politics that Lauterpacht is not willing to face directly.

The tension between ethics and institutions (or tradition and modernity) is visible in post-war internationalism more generally. On the one hand, there is the need to be able to relate contemporary law to a tradition of progressive thought so as to demonstrate its critical distance from an unacceptable political present: "better times and better peoples." The rhetorical formulation of the tradition, however, remains indeterminate to the degree that the accusation of façade legitimation is always applicable and can be dealt with only by reference to the effects, actual or expected, of the advocated norms in social reality. This leads to the demand for and discussion of institutional proposals that function at the level of empirical sociology: who is constrained and by what means, who decides, controls, implements? Are the norms self-judging, or is there a third party to decide on their application? What is its jurisdiction? Who elects its members? And so on.

Once focus is shifted to these latter issues, however, it becomes increasingly difficult to see on what basis the various institutional solutions can be assessed. If the institutions are invoked in order to defend (or criticize) tradition, then the tradition cannot, without circularity, be invoked to to defend (or criticize) institutions. The result will be a purely institutional–pragmatic, technical discourse in which an autonomous super-criterion of "effectiveness" or "binding force" will determine the acceptability of particular outcomes. Normative politics becomes institutional technique. This is pure modernity.

Lauterpacht's discussion of human rights crystallizes in his critique of

---

[210] A similar ambiguity is evident also in the idealism/realism discussion of the era. Where historians such as E. H. Carr used existing institutional practices to challenge the "utopian" views of lawyers such as Lauterpacht, their conclusions were – as Lauterpacht perceptively noted – conditional on a particular interpretation of the character and logic of those institutions. Where the two disagreed was not on whether one should rely on hard "facts" or the liberal "tradition," but how the two were to be interpreted. This is why Carr's self-characterization as a "realist" appeared to Lauterpacht as a dishonest debating strategy. "On Realism," *Collected Papers*, 2, pp. 57–58. Why should not the view that "the ultimate interest of States is peace" be equally "realist" as any other statement about their interests? There is a distinction here between the short term and the long term, but whichever one chooses is not consequent on one's "realism" or "idealism" but on one's understanding of human nature. For Lauterpacht, the ultimate distinction is between optimism and tragedy: do people learn from mistakes or do they not? This is much more a distinction of style and culture than of epistemological commitment. In a conclusive refutation of realist naïveté, Lauterpacht notes that "in the realm of human action, ideas are facts," p. 65.

the ineffectiveness of the Universal Declaration and in his proposal for a legally binding and enforcible Bill of Rights. The invocation of the tradition of liberal Enlightenment becomes concrete in a bureaucratic structure. Natural law is transformed into twenty-nine draft articles that define the rights to be protected, oblige States parties to incorporate individual rights into their domestic law "by appropriate constitutional means," and set up a machinery of international supervision. There would be a nine-member Human Rights Council with broad powers to consider petitions, to set up investigative Commissions, and conduct enquiries. States would be entitled to appeal from the Council's findings to the International Court of Justice (ICJ). In cases of non-compliance, the General Assembly could take "such action as may be appropriate in the circumstances."[211]

The Bill of Rights is Lauterpacht's response to the ineffective Universal Declaration and foreshadows the 1966 International Covenants. Where Lauterpacht's "political" writings in the inter-war era crystallized in a proposal for the collectivization of recognition – and thus in an effective constitutionalization of the inter-state system – his "human rights" writings seek an institutional solution to the moral and political dilemmas of the age. And the teleological framework is constantly present. The function of law is to bring about "the gradual integration of international society in the direction of a supra-national Federation of the World – a development which must be regarded as the ultimate postulate of the political organization of man."[212] Lauterpacht reacted to the Second World War by an express invocation of the liberal–humanist tradition that had been the target of defeated dictatorships. As he could no longer trust the transparency or immediate plausibility of the tradition, however, the focus of his writings turned to more effective institutions, control, and constraint. The theory of liberal humanism and the associated principles of human rights and the Rule of Law are supplemented by and finally submerged in institutional

---

[211] For the text of Lauterpacht's proposed Bill, cf. Lauterpacht, *International Law and Human Rights*, pp. 313–321 and commentary 325–393.

[212] Lauterpacht, *International Law and Human Rights*, p. 46. Lauterpacht was quite express about federalism. In his 1950 talk in Jerusalem, he urged his audience to see world federation "not as an infinite ideal but as an object of a moral duty of positive action and as a practical standard of human endeavour." Two features of such federation are important: the dissolution of the international personality of members and the direct relation between individuals and the federation. For that purpose the State of Israel was called to contribute its "proper and appointed share." "State Sovereignty and Human Rights," p. 430.

proposals. Political critique is neutralized in a critique of statehood as such – with the result that tradition becomes increasingly abstract while the problems of peace appear overwhelmingly as issues of institutional competence.

The birth of pragmatism

After the war, Lauterpacht compensated his disappointment in the lawlessness of the politics of international security by trying to revive the humanitarian tradition in European political philosophy in a new law of human rights. The other track he now followed was an increasing emphasis on the importance of enlightened international law practice. He aimed to grasp the problem of world peace – always a problem of legal order to Lauterpacht – from two sides: the postulation of a cosmopolitan ethic and a stress on legal activism. Each acted so as to support the other: the cosmopolitan ethic was concretized in enlightened judicial practice; judicial practice received its legitimacy from progressive cosmopolitanism. The two were brought together in a constructive conception of the legal order as a function of judicial imagination.

To carry out this task it did not suffice to remain in the university. Lauterpacht had learned the limits to which academics could imagine an international legal order into existence. In April 1948 he arrived in New York to serve for three months as an adviser to the UN Secretariat on the codification of international law. In that function, he prepared a draft program of work including suggested topics for codification of which a substantial part was adopted by the newly established International Law Commission as its first program.[213]

However, laying down a program for the codification of international law did not satisfy Lauterpacht's desire to enter legal practice. After all, the nucleus of the law was less in its substance than in its interpretation and application. Having served as Counsel to the British Government in

---

[213] Hersch Lauterpacht, "Survey of International Law in Relation to the Work of Codification of the International Law Commission," *Collected Papers*, 1, pp. 445–530. Lauterpacht's suggestions included the codification of the recognition of States, jurisdictional immunities, extradition, right of asylum, State succession, the regime of the High Seas and territorial waters, nationality, the law of treaties, diplomatic and consular intercourse, State responsibility, and arbitration procedure. Nearly all of these topics were included in the Commission's 1949 work program. For the adoption of the program, cf. UNGA Res. 373 (IV) of December 6, 1949. Cf. also H. W. Briggs, *The International Law Commission* (Ithaca, New York, Cornell University Press, 1965), pp. 169–176.

the *Corfu Channel* case, he wrote a letter in May 1949 to the British Legal Adviser, expressing an interest "in advising private clients and foreign governments . . . mainly for the reason that it brings [him] in touch with the practical side of international law."[214] And he affirmed his loyalty by expressing his readiness to exclude cases that would interfere with his teaching or be "clearly contrary" to the views of the British Government – with the characteristic reservation that unless he thought it useful that such opinion be given by him instead of somebody else.

Before he retired from the bar and replaced Brierly in the International Law Commission in 1952, he had participated as counsel or advisor in a number of international cases, including *Anglo-Iranian Oil Company* and *Nottebohm*.[215] During 1952–1954 he served as a member of the Commission, where his principal achievement consisted in the preparation of two reports on the law of treaties.[216] What is noteworthy in those reports is the central role, again, allocated to the judicial function in curtailing the liberty of parties to interpret or apply a treaty. A party asserting the invalidity of a treaty on the ground of its having been imposed by the use or threat of force or otherwise in violation of the principles of the UN Charter must bring its claim to the International Court of Justice.[217] The same applied also to other grounds of invalidity, a unilateral determination never enabling a State to free itself from a treaty provision.[218]

Lauterpacht returns repeatedly to the problem of the freedom of the State to interpret for itself what the law was – and his omnibus solution remains the transfer of interpretative competence to international bodies, in particular courts. This followed from his nominalism: the law is how it is read and the crucial issue is who is entitled to read it. Already in 1930 he had criticized the wide formulations of the British Declaration of acceptance of the compulsory jurisdiction of the Permanent Court under the Optional Clause. For instance, the exclusion of disputes that

---

[214] Lauterpacht to Sir Eric Beckett, K. C., Foreign Office, May 16, 1949 (Lauterpacht Archives).

[215] For Lauterpacht's Draft of Legal Submissions to the ICJ in the *Anglo-Iranian Oil Company* case, cf. *Collected Papers*, 4, pp. 23–89. His memoranda for the Government of Liechtenstein in the *Nottebohm* case (1950) as well as for the Swiss Government in the case concerning the proceedings against a Romanian consular officer in Switzerland (*re Solvan Vitianu*, 1949) have been reproduced in *Collected Papers*, 4, pp. 5–19 and *Collected Papers*, 3, pp. 433–457.

[216] The two reports supplement each other and have been edited and reprinted in *Collected Papers*, 4, pp. 101–388.

[217] Draft Art. 12 of the 1953 Report, *Collected Papers*, 4, p. 273.

[218] Cf. e.g. Draft Art. 11(5) and 15, *Collected Papers*, 4, pp. 257, 296.

had arisen before the ratification of the declaration was of a "highly subjective character" – for when is a dispute not related to anterior facts, sometimes to facts quite far away in time?[219] During his brief period at the Court (1955–1960), his most memorable statements related precisely to the self-judging reservations made by States to their declarations of acceptance of the Court's jurisdiction that enabled them arbitrarily to foreclose the Court's involvement. Unlike the majority of the judges, Lauterpacht felt that such a reservation made the whole declaration invalid *ab initio*: no compulsory jurisdiction was in fact created at all.[220]

To combat self-judgment, *The Function of Law* had presented the law as a limitless repository of argumentative practices through which judges could decide individual cases even where it had first seemed that the matter was "political" or where there did not seem to be any law at all.[221] Such an anti-metaphysical and practice oriented approach was in line with Anglo-American pragmatism. It is also skeptical about the ability of the juristic method to "find" the law. Lauterpacht viewed the discussion about the methods of treaty interpretation as "sterile"[222] and advocated a "flexible approach" to the ascertainment of customary law.[223] Everything is geared towards finding the *opinio juris*.[224] His criticism of State responsibility is typical. Standard doctrines had invested it with "a degree of rigidity which has hindered the development of international

---

[219] Hersch Lauterpacht, "The British Reservations to the Optional Clause" (1930), *Economica*, pp. 152, 137–172.

[220] Cf. ICJ, *Norwegian Loans* case, Reports 1957, p. 34; *Interhandel* case, Reports 1959, p. 95.

[221] The notes Lauterpacht had prepared during 1958–1960 for the second edition of the book show that his view remained unchanged. There still appeared no reason to make a distinction between justiciable and non-justiciable disputes – although, Lauterpacht now was prepared to concede, the faculty to *decide* every case did not necessarily mean that judges could *settle* every dispute. The political usefulness of the law was a question to which there could be no properly legal answer. This was a matter of faith. Cf. fragments of additions that were to be inserted in a planned second edition of *Function of Law*, manuscript for a new paragraph 11a, Lauterpacht Archives, to be published in *Collected Papers*, 5 (part IX.3). Cf. also "Some Observations on the Prohibition of 'Non Liquet'," pp. 200–201.

[222] Lauterpacht, "Règles," p. 364. Cf. also "The Doctrine of Plain Meaning," pp. 393–446. Thus, in an opinion given in 1939 to the Jewish Agency in Palestine, Lauterpacht rejected a "purely formal interpretation" of the equality clause in Art. 18 of the Mandate for Palestine in order to justify commercial discrimination on the basis of reciprocity inasmuch as it was not the text of the Mandate but "the well-being of the population [that was] the decisive test," *Collected Papers*, 3, pp. 89, 91.

[223] Hersch Lauterpacht, "International Law – The General Part," *Collected Papers*, 1, pp. 66–67. "Many an act of judicial legislation may in fact be accomplished under the guise of the ascertainment of customary law," *Development of International Law*, p. 368.

[224] Lauterpacht, "Règles," pp. 239–241.

law by . . . [the] limitation of the sources of State responsibility to a definite category of delicts defined in advance." Instead, what is needed is a "reasonable adjustment of conflicting considerations."[225] Typically, to attain this flexibility Lauterpacht envisions a large scope of application for the equitable doctrine of abuse of rights, closing the system by means of trust in enlightened judges: the inherent dangers in such a flexible standard ("the abuse of abuse of rights") is checked by international tribunals themselves.[226] The bottom line of the argument, never seriously put in question, is the assumption that international jurists are able to check the injustice at the national level and that they do this not through the "automatic" application of fixed rules but by balancing the various contextual determinants involved.[227]

Lauterpacht's pragmatic constructivism is nicely manifest in a 1950 article on the law applicable to the continental shelf. Here there was a question in which a number of States had resorted to unilateral acts to influence their legal position. Many argued that this was permissible because no rule had crystallized and the *Lotus* principle – the presumption of liberty of action – would therefore have to be applied. However, consistent with the teaching in *The Function of Law*, Lauterpacht discarded the possibility of *non liquet* and instead constructed the applicable law by the relevant legal principles available. There were two such opposing principles: geographical contiguity and effective occupation. Both were too extreme, however, and could not be used to dictate particular solutions. To the contrary: "the conceptions of effective occupation and contiguity, being relative, are but a starting point. It is within the legitimate province of the judicial function – and of statesmanship – to use them with such discretion as the equities of the case and considerations of stability require."[228] Everything hinged on the "decisive

---

[225] Lauterpacht, "Règles," p. 383.

[226] Lauterpacht, *Function of Law*, pp. 282–306; "Règles," pp. 383–386, *Development of International Law*, pp. 162–165.

[227] For example, applying the laws passed by the Allied occupation authority in Germany after the war, French courts had restored the German nationality of Jewish stateless persons whose nationality had been illegally removed by the Nazi regime. This, however, placed them perversely in the position of "enemy aliens." To check the manifest injustice involved, Lauterpacht advocated recourse to the ICJ either under a 1938 Convention or under the advisory procedure. There was no question in his mind about enlightenment not residing at the international level. Hersch Lauterpacht, "The Nationality of Denationalized Persons," (1949), *Collected Papers*, 3, pp. 383, 401–404.

[228] Hersch Lauterpacht, "Sovereignty over Submarine Areas," (1950), *Collected Papers*, 3, p. 200.

test of reasonableness," more particularly on the "judicial ascertainment of reasonableness."[229] Where texts (treaties) and facts (custom) remained indeterminate, and the possibility of autointerpretation was ruled out as a matter of legal principle, authority could reside only in courts, those enlightened organs of "socially attainable justice."

Lauterpacht's mature views on the constructive tasks of judges are laid down in *Development of International Law by the International Court* the second edition of which came out in 1958, only two years before his death. In comparison to *Function*, Lauterpacht seems more reserved: the Court has not been a significant instrument for peace. The "state of international integration" has not allowed it to attain the goals which the drafters of the Statute had set.[230] However, where politics is fixed, law is creative. The book is a celebration of judicial creativity. It is precisely because of the absence of general legislative machinery that it falls upon international courts (i.e. international lawyers) to take on the task of legislation, e.g. by stating their views on as many legal points as possible in connection with individual cases.[231]

For Lauterpacht, judicial legislation exists everywhere, although law finds no clear articulation for it. It is treated by recourse to "the fiction that the enunciation of the new rule is no more than an application of an existing legal principle or an interpretation of an existing text."[232] But this fiction, like the controversy about whether judges create law or merely "reveal nascent rules" is "highly unreal."[233] That decisions of the Court are not legal sources but only evidence of the law turns on an equally unreal distinction. For practical purposes, those decisions are treated as authoritative.[234] In the absence of such formal, doctrinal obstacles, the way is open for creativity and imagination by lawyers.

The greatest part of *Development of International Law* – like its companion article on the prohibition of *non liquet* – is an exposé of the argumentative techniques that have enabled the Court to "legislate" or speak in favor of such activism. Arguments from general principles, such as the

---

[229] Lauterpacht, "Sovereignty over Submarine Areas," pp. 184, 185, 217.
[230] Lauterpacht, *Development of International Law*, pp. 3–5.
[231] Lauterpacht, *Development of International Law*, pp. 37–47. The suggestion that international courts might be used as legislative avenues by providing non-binding opinions on desirable law was, of course, already made in *Function of Law* and especially in "The Absence of an International Legislature and the Compulsory Jurisdiction of International Tribunals" (1930), XI *BYIL*, pp. 134, 144–154.
[232] Lauterpacht, *Development of International Law*, p. 155.
[233] Lauterpacht, *Development of International Law*, p. 21.
[234] Lauterpacht, *Development of International Law*, pp. 20–25.

nemo judex in sua causa or abuse of rights,[235] have not been limited to a technical application of Art. 38(3) of its Statute but have aimed to attain – with frequent reference to estoppel or good faith – a "socially realizable morality."[236] The Court may itself have formulated such principles by reference to parallel developments in adjacent rules or fields of the law.[237] Sometimes it has done this after having expressly excluded the existence of an antecedent law in the matter.[238] A very frequent strategy has been to aim at maximal effectiveness of the law – typically to curtail the "artful devices" of the State burdened by the obligation.[239]

In a thoroughly realist vein, Lauterpacht dismissed the view of judicial practice as the simple application of rules, for "those rules are often obscure or controversial"[240] – and yet, shunning realism, he took care to qualify that this was not to give the Court a license to replace the law, or party intention, if ascertainable, and to allow a "rule of thumb" to replace a "flexible, critical and discriminating" application of the law.[241] This duality of freedom and constraint, creation and repetition, is a part of Lauterpacht's Victorian morality that always links liberty with responsibility and set clear limits to what he allowed himself to put forward. Everything depends on the enlightened responsibility of judges that enables them to see how far they can go and at what point deference to diplomacy and State will becomes necessary. Indeed, a complete freedom is unthinkable also from a scientific point of view: "It is to a large extent this practical aspect of its operation, namely in the ability of the lawyer to attempt to predict the nature of the decision, that law is a science."[242] In fact, Lauterpacht's utopia is a world ruled by lawyers. The three reasons for judicial caution that he discusses are reasons of conjecture, linked to the present, temporary, and intrinsically unsatisfactory character of international society. According to Lauterpacht, judges should not legislate because they would then lose the confidence of the governments; there would then be no cases submitted to them;

---

[235] Lauterpacht, *Development of International Law*, pp. 158–165.

[236] Lauterpacht, *Development of International Law*, p. 172. Cf. also "Some Observations on the Prohibition of 'Non Liquet,'" pp. 205–208.

[237] E.g. by expanding the scope of legal subjects or basing the rule on the vitiating effect of duress on the outlawry of war. Lauterpacht, *Development of International Law*, pp. 173–185.

[238] As in the *Anglo-Norwegian Fisheries* and *Reservations* cases, Lauterpacht, *Development of International Law*, pp. 186–199.

[239] Lauterpacht, *Development of International Law*, pp. 227–293.

[240] Lauterpacht, *Development of International Law*, p. 165.

[241] Lauterpacht, *Development of International Law*, p. 283.

[242] Lauterpacht, *Development of International Law*, p. 21.

Lauterpacht: the Victorian tradition in international law

and there would be no guarantee that their decisions would be implemented.[243] Every reason is connected to the statist character of politics, and to self-judgment. None of them would be present in Lauterpacht's federalist utopia, as we have seen. There, national governments would have no sovereign right of veto, the jurisdiction of courts would be compulsory, and the implementation of their decisions would fall upon effective administration. In other words, judges should exercise caution because of reasons of prudence, relative to the present nature of the international world, not because of any principled objections against judicial legislation. If indeed (as Lauterpacht assumes) the international bar is a collection of enlightened cosmopolitan liberals, what reason would there be for thinking otherwise?

In *The Function of Law*, Lauterpacht demonstrated the unacceptable consequences of any doctrine of "inherent limitation" of the judicial task. In *Development of International Law* he examines the practice of the International Court of Justice and its predecessor, showing how the unlimited and constructive nature of judicial activity has presented itself. None of the incidents of judicial caution that Lauterpacht takes up is portrayed in a positive or even less progressive light. Some appear as "disappointments."[244] Other incidents of apparent judicial caution in fact turn out as bold attempts to curtail State freedom.[245] Yet other examples of the exercise of caution are merely apparent.[246] In advisory jurisdiction, there is no reason for caution inasmuch as the Court is acting in its capacity as the principal judicial organ of the United Nations.[247] Throughout "caution" is characterized negatively, at best as a prudent device not to antagonize governments.

The problem of world order arises from the ability of States to interpret for themselves the law to which they claim they are bound. The need for an independent legal process arises from the wish to curtail such self-judgment. The legal process, however, is not an automatic application of rules. Claims presented by States are never fully right or wrong but have "varying degrees of legal merit."[248] The judge's task becomes

---

[243] Lauterpacht, *Development of International Law*, pp. 75–76.
[244] Lauterpacht, *Development of International Law*, p. 100.
[245] Thus the discussion of the Court's attempt to limit the application of *rebus sic stantibus* speaks less about judicial caution than about the Court's willingness to affirm the law's binding force in face of governmental attempts to circumvent it. Lauterpacht, *Development of International Law*, pp. 84–87.
[246] Lauterpacht, *Development of International Law*, pp. 142–152.
[247] Lauterpacht, *Development of International Law*, pp. 109–110.
[248] Lauterpacht, *Development of International Law*, p. 398.

that of the pragmatic manager of conflicting interests. Everything is dependent on the judge's professional ability and good sense. With a subtle shift, the final resting-place of Lauterpacht's argument lies in the enlightened responsibility of judges and lawyers, their ability to manage the world order by equitable compromises, by overruling unjust laws, and suggesting desirable legislative changes. As Lauterpacht once noted: "[I]n the sphere of action, ideas may not be more potent than the individual human beings called upon to realize them."[249] The image of progress is no longer (as in the inter-war "political" period) that of diplomats arguing about collective security in Geneva, nor (as it was after the Second World War) that of UN bodies administering human rights. Nor is progress fixed in legal rules and principles. Now it resides in the judicial profession, in its ability to construct a world of legal constraint by a pragmatic attitude towards its task.

A Grotian tradition?

Austrian liberalism of the *fin-de-siècle* was, Carl Schorske has written, a "garden-variety Victorianism . . . secure, righteous and repressive; politically it was concerned for the rule of law, under which both individual rights and social order were subsumed. It was intellectually committed to the rule of the mind over the body and to latter-day Voltairism: to social progress through science, education and hard work."[250] Its backbone was the "legalistic, puritanical culture of both bourgeois and Jew."[251] However, in the period of nationalist agitation and class conflict in late nineteenth-century Europe, "the only social group which seemed to represent the state were the Jews."[252] The Habsburg Jewry in particular had manifested a "total dedication to liberalism."[253] From this perspective, it is possible to understand why the ideals of rationalism and progress became so firmly embedded in Lauterpacht's work – just as they characterized the oeuvre of his more famous colleagues Jellinek and Kelsen. Lauterpacht's legal utopia seeks to revive on a cosmopolitan scale the Victorian liberalism that failed to survive the offensives of nationalism and socialism in Central and Eastern Europe.[254]

It might seem curious that an active Zionist during the second decade

---

[249] Lauterpacht, "Brierly's Contribution," p. 451.
[250] Schorske, *Fin-de-Siècle Vienna*, p. 6.
[251] Schorske, *Fin-de-Siècle Vienna*, p. 7.
[252] Hannah Arendt, *The Origins of Totalitarianism* (2nd edn., 1958), pp. 25 and generally 11 *et seq.*   [253] Beller, *Vienna and the Jews*, p. 123.
[254] For the utopia of a united humanity as part of the Jewish enlightenment, cf. Beller, *Vienna and the Jews*, pp. 141–143.

of the twentieth century was transformed into a cosmopolitan individualist during the third. However (at least part of) Jewish nationalism had been essentially reactive and had arisen to combat German and Austrian antisemitism. What Viennese Zionists such as Theodor Herzl – or Lauterpacht – wished to create was a secular, liberal–democratic State; in this they were opposed by the rabbis and the religious right.[255] When the protective need for a national Jewish State no longer seemed pressing – after Lauterpacht came to Britain – Zionism could transform back into a cosmopolitan ethos that was the natural home of the Jewish enlightenment.[256] It was not until the oppression of German Jewry began that an extreme protective need arose anew. At that point, notwithstanding his critical posture towards statehood, Lauterpacht was prepared to lend his efforts to support the establishment of the State of Israel.

Where late nineteenth-century Viennese culture moved from the ideal of the man of reason to the search for the psychological, feeling man, Lauterpacht never followed suit. His utopianism remained grounded in the idea of the rational man, convinced that peace and social order through law were inescapable rational necessities and political passion an external distortion. Even in 1946, almost absurdly, Lauterpacht's Victorian faith remained unshaken:

> The modern state is not a disorderly crowd given to uncontrollable eruptions of passion oblivious of moral scruples. It is, as a rule, governed by individuals of experience and ability who reach decisions after full deliberation and who are capable of forming a judgment on the ethical merits of the issues confronting them.[257]

It was the legal profession's task to protect the powers of reason – universal by definition – against a modernist *Gefühlskultur*, the "collective passion,"[258] the politics of the crowd, short-sighted positivism, national interest, and in particular the "crime," the "ruthless egotism," and the "ideology" of the *raison d'état*.[259] This rationalism was the driving force behind "progressive" proposals such as those to do away with State immunity,[260] to establish the criminal responsibility of States, and a

---

[255] Aside from the above work by Schorske, cf. McCagg, *A History of the Habsburg Jews*, pp. 198–199.   [256] Beller, *Vienna and the Jews*, pp. 140–143.
[257] Lauterpacht, "The Grotian Tradition," p. 338.   [258] Lauterpacht, "Spinoza," p. 9.
[259] Lauterpacht, "The Grotian Tradition," pp. 344, 345, 346.
[260] In 1950, Lauterpacht wrote a memorandum to a British Interdepartmental Committee on State Immunity that ended in a proposal to do away with a substantial part of immunity and to put the foreign sovereign in a situation analogous to that of the domestic sovereign. "The Problem of the Jurisdictional Immunity of Foreign States," (1951), *Collected Papers*, 3, pp. 315–373. Here, as elsewhere, progress seemed to reside in a submission of States to the legal process.

collective system of humanitarian intervention.[261] It was indissociable from a liberalism that sought to guarantee maximum political freedom for the individual in the economic and political realms and to limit respectively the legitimate field of State activity.[262]

Internationally, sovereignty was often manifested in the faculty of self-judgment, and the problem of world order for Lauterpacht became how to control self-judgment. This was a question of institutional competence and jurisdiction, the exercise of constraint over States. Paradoxically, the liberal argument that had in the nineteenth century been used to buttress the State against the forces that had threatened it, was in the twentieth turned against the State that had succumbed to those forces. That argument received force and direction, as well as being limited, by a strong background morality that forms the key to the specifically Victorian outlook of Lauterpacht's liberalism.

Contemporary assessments often highlight the importance of *morality* for Lauterpacht. Jenks, for instance, speaks about the "essentially moral foundation" of Lauterpacht's work but extends that attribute even deeper by the observation that "[t]he outstanding quality of the man was his moral stature."[263] Of course, Lauterpacht himself repeatedly insisted that a conception of international law as derived from State will was insufficient and that there was constant need "for judging its adequacy in the light of ethics and reason."[264] Where law might be lacking, unclear, contradictory, or unjust – and it was often precisely that – morality came to the rescue, ensuring the law's completeness and acceptability, sometimes in the guise of general principles, sometimes as domestic law analogy, always through the constructive mediation of judicial practice. This was the Grotian tradition, to satisfy "the craving, in the jurist and layman alike, for a moral content of the law."[265] The question, however, is: what does "morality" mean in this connection?

---

[261] Cf. e.g. "Règles," pp. 302–304; "Book Review. Karl Lowenstein, Political Reconstruction" (1946), XXIII *BYIL*, pp. 510–511.

[262] Cf. Hersch Lauterpacht, "Revolutionary Actitivies by Private Persons against Foreign States" (1928), *Collected Papers*, 3, pp. 251–278 (an argument against State involvement in peaceful transboundary political subversion) and "Boycott in International Relations" (1928), *Collected Papers*, 3, pp. 297–311 (an argument in favor of the freedom of non-public entities to engage in collective commercial countermeasures). Cf. also Hersch Lauterpacht, "Revolutionary Propaganda by Governments" (1928), *Collected Papers*, 3, pp. 279–296 ("revolutionary propaganda, when originating from the Government itself, constitutes a clear international delinquency," p. 281).

[263] C. Wilfried Jenks, "Hersch Lauterpacht – The Scholar as Prophet" (1960), XXXVI *BYIL*, pp. 101, 102.   [264] Jenks, "Hersch Lauterpacht," p. 330.

[265] Lauterpacht, "The Grotian Tradition," p. 364.

Lauterpacht: the Victorian tradition in international law

It is possible to examine Lauterpacht's moral rationalism by contrasting it to the post-Victorian modernisms of Kelsen and E. H. Carr. In his otherwise positive assessment of the *Reine Rechtslehre*, Lauterpacht swept aside Kelsen's rejection of a natural law basis for his system, a rejection Lauterpacht saw as a "theory superadded to the main structure of his doctrine – principally for the sake of argumentative advantage, but ultimately to the disadvantage of the whole system."[266] The almost *ad hominem* character of this view reveals Lauterpacht's inability to appreciate the critical force of Kelsen's moral agnosticism. Lauterpacht doubts whether Kelsen in fact succeeded in keeping his theory uncontaminated by morality and suggests that the success of his work lies in that he did not.[267] Kelsen would not have disagreed with Lauterpacht's point that morality enters the law through its application and interpretation, but would have insisted only that how they do it is not a properly legal question – though no less important for that reason. Kelsen did not deny the place of values in law (and for legal study) but insisted on the need for openness in "value-choices" – e.g. the choice between dualism and monism.[268] Such relativism was not part of Lauterpacht's world: the Eternal Verities could not be subjected to "choice," but were embedded in the teleological framework of history and expressed in the best works of the liberal philosophical tradition.

Where in Kelsen Lauterpacht found too little morality, in Carr he found too much. Building upon the primacy of States and State power realism accepted a double morality – one morality for individuals, another for States – in which the reason of the State always finds a justification to override the individual – but universal – ethic. From the perspective of methodological individualism,[269] State morality – as expressed, for example, in the Hoare–Laval pact[270] – was a vicious distortion, a metaphysical mistake, that blinded realists from grasping that the world was united in the search for a single human good that could be understood only as the good of individuals, similar in their nature as social animals.

---

[266] Hersch Lauterpacht, "Kelsen's Pure Science of Law" (1933), *Collected Papers*, 2, pp. 424, 428–429.   [267] Lauterpacht, "Kelsen's Pure Science of Law," pp. 428–429.
[268] Hans Kelsen, *Das Problem der Souveränität und die Theorie des Völkerrechts* (2nd edn., Tübingen, Mohr, 1928), pp. 257–266.
[269] "The analogy – nay, the essential identity – of rules concerning the conduct of states and of individuals... is due to the fact that states are composed of individual human beings; it is due to the fact that behind the mythical, impersonal, and therefore necessarily irresponsible personality of the metaphysical state there are actual subjects of rights and duties, namely individual human beings." Lauterpacht, "The Grotian Tradition," p. 336.
[270] "Professor Carr on International Morality," *Collected Papers*, 2, pp. 67–73. See also "The Grotian Tradition," pp. 333–346.

In Lauterpacht's individualist world the (realist) tragedy of irreducible conflict, of incompatible goods, is defined away. Morality and enlightened self-interest always point in the same direction. The general good is "identical with" national interest, conceived as the interest of the individuals forming the nation.[271] The optimistic belief in the parallel interests of the rich and poor, weak and powerful, seeks to restore a pre-Dickensian or perhaps a Pre-Raphaelite world of justice and harmony – the "tradition of idealism and progress"[272] – in which man's essential nature is social and where the deepest truths are the simplest ones, that Grotian "law of love, the law of charity, of Christian duty, of honour and of goodness."[273]

The starting-point of the realist critique had been "the collapse of the whole structure of utopianism based on the concept of the harmony of interests."[274] Lauterpacht responds by repeating the axiom of the harmony of interests that is precisely what Carr put in question. He can only remain puzzled by the incomprehensibility of somebody not taking for granted the Truth for which "man" is by nature endowed by "an ample measure of goodness, altruism, and morality."[275] Between tragedy and optimism no rational argument can take place. Only the way of indignant rejection remains open.[276]

The reactions towards Kelsen and Carr reveal the nature of Lauterpacht's Victorianism. It relies on the interlocutor's willingness to take for granted the intrinsic rationality of a morality of sweet reasonableness, the non-metaphysical doctrine of the golden middle. It relies not on general principles or logical deductions as would a Thomistic, religious morality. It is a morality of attitude at least as much as substance, a morality of putting one's foot down when everybody's arguments have been given a hearing. Among the many virtues of Grotius, Lauterpacht admired his "atmosphere of strong conviction, of reforming zeal, of moral fervor."[277] It is an individualist morality controlled by the attempt to balance right with duty and freedom with reason.[278] It is

[271] Lauterpacht, "Professor Carr," p. 90.
[272] Lauterpacht, "The Grotian Tradition," pp. 359–363.
[273] Lauterpacht, "The Grotian Tradition," p. 334.
[274] Carr, *Twenty-Years' Crisis*, p. 62.   [275] Lauterpacht, "The Grotian Tradition," p. 24.
[276] Lauterpacht's response to E. H. Carr remains unpolished and it was not published before inclusion in *Collected Papers*.
[277] Lauterpacht, "The Grotian Tradition," p. 361.
[278] For the former point, cf. Lauterpacht's argument in favor of the criminal jurisdiction of British courts against "Lord Haw-Haw," or William Joyce, an American citizen domiciled in Britain at the service of Germany's propaganda during the war. Hersch Lauterpacht, "Allegiance, Diplomatic Protection and Criminal Jurisdiction against Aliens" (1946), *Collected Papers*, 3, pp. 221–241.

a morality of control and self-control for which the greatest desire is the end of desire. Lauterpacht accepts Spinoza's dictum: "[t]he man is free who lives, not according to the right of nature but according to reason. And it is liberty achieved through obedience to reason which is the ultimate object of the state."[279]

Coda

I have interpreted Lauterpacht's work in terms of a movement that started as a theoretical–doctrinal effort to imagine an international legal order resembling the structures of the liberal State and ended up in celebrating the virtues of a legal pragmatism that is alien to theory and doctrine. For me, Lauterpacht's oeuvre and career constitute a striking illustration of an international legal consciousness that sought to resuscitate the rationalism of the nineteenth century in the aftermath of the First World War but used up its emancipatory potential in the doctrinal struggles of the 1930s; became eclectic after the Second World War and was institutionalized as the normal discourse of law and diplomacy in the 1960s.

In his main theoretical work, *The Function of Law in the International Community* (1933), Lauterpacht elaborated the doctrine of a gapless international legal order to defend in legal terms the unity of a world that seemed to be heading from fragmentation to catastrophe, from the League of Nations to the Holocaust. It was in line with the ideas of nineteenth-century Jewish enlightenment and prevailing pacifist sentiments, and helped Lauterpacht to assimilate within a cosmopolitan elite that constructed its identity from rationalist, anti-nationalist sentiments and an individualist cultural outlook.

During his career, Lauterpacht applied this projected legal order to politics, morality, and professional practice. I see these moves as corresponding to three orientations in twentieth-century liberal jurisprudence. First, there was the attempt in the 1930s and 1940s to construe international law as a scientifically based, operative constraint on the conduct of foreign policy. This strand in Lauterpacht's writing ended with the collapse of the inter-war peace system and the establishment of the United Nations on "realist" principles. The central thesis in *Recognition in International Law* (1947) (namely that nationalism can be tempered by a rational legal order) is the most ambitious outcome of this effort. Second was a move to replace legal politics by an attempt to articulate in ethical terms the political unity that had seemed lost as the juggernaut of modernity crashed into

---

[279] Lauterpacht, "Spinoza and International Law," p. 374.

Auschwitz. The high point of this effort is the publication of *Human Rights in International Law* (1950), a celebration of rationalist naturalism that ended in a practical proposal. The third move was towards increasing emphasis on enlightened judicial practice – that is, legal pragmatism – as an instrument for peace, and culminates in the publication in 1958 of the second edition of the *Development of International Law by the International Court* – an articulate defense of judicial practice's ability to reconcile the demands for order and justice in international life. Where *The Function of Law* completed the work of theoretical reimagination, *Recognition* hoped to bridge the gap between that theory and practice, *Human Rights* instituted an abstract justification for the legal project, and *Development of International Law* inaugurated pragmatism as the culture of future generations of international lawyers.

My interest in this narrative lies in what it tells us about what happened to international law as political commitment during the twists and turns of a particularly tragic half-century that came to rest in a pragmatism of the 1960s which by now may have spent whatever creative force it once had.[280] But I do wish to stress the biographical aspects of this interpretation as well. The significance of a story that begins in 1897 in a small Jewish community in Galicia and traces the successive transformations of an active Zionist student in Vienna into a university lecturer in London in the 1920s, into the holder of the Whewell Chair of International Law in Cambridge in the year of the *Anschluss* (1938), into a member of the British War Crimes executive in 1945, and finally into a judge at the International Court of Justice in 1955, is bound to transcend its purely individual aspects. I have wished to situate Lauterpacht in a biographical and historical context in order to expel the sense that his doctrine was merely a free-floating academic play, an intellectual's pastime or at best a move in a sealed-off utopian discourse. I see it as a consistent attempt to maintain, through projection, the wholeness of a social world and personal identity when none of the competing projects (of science, politics or economy) had been up to the task. Lauterpacht was a Victorian liberal in a time when the dialectic of the enlightenment is only slowly asserting itself. That he had no doubt about the universal and intrinsically beneficent character of legal reason defines him as an historical agent whose defense of legal reason maps out for us a large field of our shared professional past.

---

[280] Cf. my "International Law in a Post-Realist Era" (1995), 16 *Australian Yearbook of International Law*, pp. 1–19.

6

Out of Europe: Carl Schmitt, Hans Morgenthau, and the turn to "international relations"

On April 28, 1965 President Lyndon B. Johnson disclosed that 400 US marines had landed in the Dominican Republic "to give protection to the hundreds of Americans who are still in the Dominican republic and to escort them back to the country." In a few days with the ostensible support of the Organization of American States (OAS) the evacuation turned into a large-scale invasion by more than 20,000 troops to prevent an elected leftist government from taking power. In May President Johnson justified the operation by the need to "prevent the emergence of another Cuba in the Western hemisphere." As he later remarked, "the danger of a Communist take-over in the Dominican republic was a real and present one . . . a communist regime in the Dominican republic would be dangerous to the peace and security of the hemisphere and the United States."[1] In connection with the Cuban situation, the United States had already earlier been able to persuade the OAS that the adherence of any of its members to "Marxism–Leninism" would trigger the right of self-defense, interpreting "communism" as equivalent to "armed attack" under Art. 51 of the UN Charter. As the marines were landing in the Dominican Republic, the Legal Adviser of the State Department, L. C. Meeker, asserted a general right to use military force by the United States in the Western hemisphere against "foreign ideologies."[2] Later that same June, he addressed the American Foreign Law Association, drawing the attention of his audience to the

---

[1] Quoted in Max Harrelson, *Fires all around the Horizon. The UN's Uphill Battle to Preserve the Peace* (New York, Praeger, 1989), p. 182.
[2] Quoted in Thomas M. Franck, *Nation against Nation. What Happened to the UN Dream and What the US Can Do About It?* (Oxford University Press, 1985), p. 71.

artificiality of reliance on absolutes for judging and evaluating the events of our time . . . [B]lack and white alone are inadequate to portray the actuality of a particular situation in world politics and . . . fundamentalist views on the nature of international legal obligation are not very useful as a means for achieving practical and just solutions of difficult political, economic and social problems.[3]

Soon thereafter Wolfgang Friedmann (1907–1972) of the Columbia Law School published a fierce criticism of this argument and especially the Legal Adviser's dismissal of what he had described as the "legal fundamentalism" of the critics of the intervention. Friedmann was a legal theorist and an international lawyer of German origin who had been dismissed from his positions by the Nazi government in 1934 and had settled in the United States in 1955. What he had to say was this:

> The Legal Adviser's argument is one of policy, not of law, and it seeks to justify what is patently, by standards of international law, an illegal action, in terms of the ultimate policy objectives of the United States. By using the language of legal rather than political justification, the argument comes unintentionally close to the attempts made by Nazi and Communist lawyers to justify the interventionist and aggressive actions of their respective governments in terms of the legal order of the future. Nazi lawyers spoke of the *Völkerrechtliche Grossraumordnung* (international legal order of wide spaces) . . . Surely, the legal as well as the political style of the United States should remain unmistakably different from that of its totalitarian opponents.[4]

Friedmann connected these arguments to the US involvement in Vietnam and wondered whether it had come to the melancholy conclusion "that it can no longer afford to abide by international law, that it must counter the imperial aspirations of the Soviet Union, and especially of Communist China, by similar means." This, he concluded, would mean "the absorption of the great majority of world's states as vassals or subjects in the few remaining empires" – something he observed had been forecast after the end of the First World War in Oswald Spengler's *Decline of the West* and George Orwell's *1984*: "The abandonment of the principles of national integrity and the distinction between civil and international war – both cardinal to the present structure of international law – is the legal corollary of imperial power struggle."[5] As if he had not made his concerns clear enough, Friedmann drew

---

[3] Quoted in Wolfgang Friedmann, "United States Policy and the Crisis of International Law. Some Reflections on the State of International Law in 'International Co-operation Year'" (1965), 59 *AJIL*, p. 868.

[4] Friedmann, "Crisis," p. 869. The same point is made as the central argument in Thomas M. Franck and Edward Weisband, *Word Politics: Verbal Strategy among the Superpowers* (Oxford University Press, 1971).   [5] Friedmann, "Crisis," p. 871.

a parallel between his critique and that made by Julien Benda in the *Trahison des Clercs* forty years earlier, concluding the article by the observation that "Freedom is today threatened from many sides. It has never survived the abandonment of intellectual independence."[6]

Friedmann's critique is interesting not only because of its exceptionally anxious tone but also because of the references to the inter-war debates that it contained. He was himself well placed to suggest the parallel of the *Grossraumordnung*. But in fact, the theory of the *Grossraumordnung* had been presented as a generalization of the Monroe Doctrine and the connected idea of a single-power supremacy in the Western hemisphere. While Friedmann was writing, the main protagonist of that theory had still not said his last word about the legal significance of the profound transformations that had taken place in the world order after the Second World War.

A 1950 retrospective

Already in 1950 Carl Schmitt (1888–1983) had published his last large work with the intriguing title *Der Nomos der Erde* which dealt with the end of the "European era," the closing of the *ius publicum Europaeum* that had regulated world order for the past 300 years.[7] That Schmitt chose to speak of *nomos* where he might as well have spoken of the "law" of the world was burdened with meaning. The word "*nomos*," usually translated as "order" (or sometimes "law," "rule," or even "decision"), came into Schmitt's political vocabulary in 1933–1934 via German Protestant theology and signified a substantive or concrete (spatial) order or determination, in contrast to the formal notion of *Gesetz* that Schmitt linked with the degenerated normativism of nineteenth-century jurisprudence.[8] Where a people (such as the Jewish) without land or State might well identify itself by reference to a formal law, the German substance – as indeed the substance of Europe itself – was based on principles of identification the most important among which was the original act of land-taking (*Landnahme*).[9]

---

[6] Friedmann, "Crisis," p. 871.
[7] Carl Schmitt, *Der Nomos der Erde im Völkerrecht des Jus Publicum Europaeum* (Berlin, Duncker & Humblot, 1950).   [8] Schmitt, *Der Nomos der Erde*, pp. 36–51.
[9] On the antisemitic connotations of the contrast *nomos* – *Gesetz* (to which Schmitt was no alien), cf. e.g. Wolfgang Palaver, "Carl Schmitt on Nomos and Space" (1996), 106 *Telos*, pp. 105–127 and Rafael Gross, "'Jewish Law and Christian Grace' – Carl Schmitt's Critique of Hans Kelsen," in Dan Diner and Michel Stolleis (eds.), *Hans Kelsen and Karl Schmitt. A Juxtaposition* (Gerlingen, Bleicher, 1999), pp. 105–107. For a useful summary of Schmitt's antisemitism cf. Heinrich Meier, *The Lesson of Carl Schmitt*.

The Gentle Civilizer of Nations

According to Schmitt, the European *nomos* had originated in the discovery of the new world and the organization between European imperial powers of that *Landnahme* – the "last great heroic deed of the European peoples"[10] that had replaced the *respublica Christiana* in a first global, secular principle of ordering. Like every *nomos*, European public law had had an internal and external aspect: it had organized European space into nation-States that recognized each other as sovereign; and it had distinguished between a non-European land space that was free for appropriation and the High Seas that remained open. The great achievement of this *nomos* had been the limitation of European warfare: abolishing of civil and religious wars and creating a non-discriminatory concept of (European) war as a "duel" between formally equal sovereigns and its humanization by conceptualizing the enemy as a *justus hostis*.[11]

But this (concrete) order, Schmitt argued, had collapsed in 1890–1918 in face of a sea-based, economically driven Anglo-American universalism that was slowly doing away with earlier spatial distinctions and the centrality of sovereignty. A "discriminatory concept of war" had emerged that depicted the enemy no longer as a public law opponent but as an enemy of "humanity" *tout court* against which no measures were excessive. The 1885 Berlin Act had marked a watershed: a last great all-European *Landnahme* – but also the first expression of a decadent civilizing mission that was a mere façade for irreparable European division. The corruption of the old *nomos* was strikingly illustrated in the fiction of the "Independent State of the Congo" and its adoption as a colony by Belgium in 1909 – when even twenty-five years later there was no idea whether the colony consisted of 14 or 30 million inhabitants![12]

By the end of the nineteenth century, Schmitt argued, European

---

Footnote 9 (*cont.*)
Four Chapters on the Distinction between Political Theology and Political Philosophy (University of Chicago Press, 1998), pp. 151–158. Among a burgeoning secondary literature, this work is among the more interesting. On Schmitt's notion of *nomos*, cf. G. L. Ulmen, "The Concept of Nomos: Introduction to Schmitt's Appropriation/Distribution/Production" (1993), 95 *Telos*, pp. 39–51 and Mathias Schmocckel, *Die Grossraumtheorie. Ein Beitrag zur Geschichte der Völkerrechtswissenschaft im Dritten Reich, insbesondere der Kriegzeit* (Berlin, Duncker & Humblot, 1994), pp. 34–37.

[10] Carl Schmitt, "Nomos-Nahme-Name," in *Staat, Grossraum, Nomos. Arbeiten aus den Jahren 1916–1969* (Berlin, Duncker & Humblot 1995), p. 585; Schmitt, *Der Nomos der Erde*, pp. 69–109.   [11] Schmitt, *Der Nomos der Erde*, pp. 112–183.

[12] Schmitt, *Der Nomos der Erde*, pp. 188–200. The Berlin Conference was also significant in that non-European powers – particularly the United States – now for the first time played a significant role.

lawyers had lost consciousness of a concrete spatial order underlying the law, having started to speak in increasingly abstract and universal terms, naïvely interpreting the expansion of common diplomatic vocabulary as a European advance. In truth, Europe had lost its centrality; the *ius publicum Europaeum* no longer existed. This was not only owing to the emergence of new States. The almost universally accepted ideology of free trade was forging a global economy that undermined European States, not least by compelling them to work out a constitutional separation between the public realm and the realm of property, trade, and industry, the latter silently expanding into a countervailing cosmopolitan order.[13] Professional lawyers took no notice of the new ordering principles – such as universalism vs. particularism or politics vs. economy. An era of empty normativism began; international law was reduced to a collection of precedents, applied without distinction, and of treaties that were accepted all the more enthusiastically as their application was disputed.[14] Neither such law nor its only explicit ordering principle – the distinction between "civilized" and "non-civilized" – was powerful enough to prevent the slide into the abyss of 1914.

From his vantage-point of post-war Germany, Schmitt concluded that international law had been reduced in 1890–1939 to an "empty formalism of rules" that were apparently generally accepted and thus hid from peoples' consciousness the reality that a concrete order of recognized powers had gone under and nothing had been found to replace it.[15] Versailles was no longer a European settlement; on the contrary, in the League "delegates from Paraguay, Uruguay and an Indian Maharaja . . . lectured to Europe on World Unity."[16] The League was a confused mélange of regional and universal pursuits and antagonisms. Debates on peaceful change had failed to touch the principal territorial or economic aspects of Europe's division. Nothing had been done to resolve the striking conflict between the permanent neutrality of some members and their collective security obligations. The League was neither a political subject nor a substance: every important political act either took place outside it (for instance, in the Allied Conference of Ambassadors) or was veiled in an apparently neutral process (such as the Permanent Court's opinion in the *Mosul Boundary* case). It could not be a political unit as it had neither a determined guarantee (for Versailles remained just a continuation of the Western alliance) nor a

---

[13] Schmitt, *Der Nomos der Erde*, pp. 208–209. Cf. also Schmoeckel, *Die Grossraumtheorie*, pp. 24–31.   [14] Schmitt, *Der Nomos der Erde*, pp. 211–212.
[15] Schmitt, *Der Nomos der Erde*, p. 200.   [16] Schmitt, *Der Nomos der Erde*, p. 217.

homogeneous membership.[17] All this was illustrated by the position of the United States. As a formal sovereign, it was outside; as the greatest economic power it was involved in every political discussion – through its South American dependencies in the League and through its private citizens (Young and Dawes) in the settlement of the German debt. The official ideology separated economy from politics – subordinating the latter to the former and thus guaranteeing the political superiority of the United States in every matter having to do with Europe.[18]

Finally, Schmitt drew attention to a silent transformation in the concept of war, inaugurated by the war guilt clause in the Versailles Treaty. The indictment of William II had been based not on law but on the commission of a supreme offense against international "morality." The US entry in the war had transformed it from a confrontation between "just enemies" into one where justice and morality were assumed to be on one side, injustice and immorality on the other.[19] This discrimination became inextricable from a new, moral approach to war, which continued in the League debates over aggression as the supreme international evil, was declared in the Kellogg–Briand Pact (1928), and finally codified in the London Protocol of August 8, 1945 that set up the Nuremberg tribunal.[20] From that point on, war could only be a "crime" on one side, and enforcement of morality on the other.

Vision of a new order

Throughout the 1930s Schmitt had written about American imperialism – the imperialism of free trade, of the "open door," the Stimson Doctrine, and the elastic and unilateral Monroe Doctrine – as the most obvious substitute for the Eurocentric *nomos*, even if the United States seemed trapped in a nervous back-and-forth between isolationism and

---

[17] For these arguments at length, cf. Carl Schmitt, *Kernfrage des Völkerbundes* (Berlin, Dümmler, 1926).   [18] Schmitt, *Der Nomos der Erde*, pp. 216 *et seq.*, 228–231.
[19] Schmitt, *Der Nomos der Erde*, p. 242.
[20] Schmitt, *Der Nomos der Erde*, p. 255. In 1945 Schmitt wrote a lengthy legal opinion (*Gutachten*) on the concept of aggression, in which he criticized the indictment of aggressive war as an international crime, claiming that while many of the "monstrous atrocities" of the Hitler regime deserved to be solemnly condemned (though even they did not become classifiable under "usual positive law") the concept of "criminalization" should not be used in international law (it would break the citizen's duty of loyalty to his State) and was particularly inappropriate for the characterization of aggression that had not by 1939 become illegal. Cf. Carl Schmitt, *Das internationalrechtliche Verbrechen des Angriffskrieges und der Grundsatz "Nullum crimen, nulla poena sine lege"* (Berlin, Duncker & Humblot, 1994), p. 81.

interventionism. The core of US policy lay in economic expansion which it interpreted as a non-political process – thereby asking the world to agree to a profoundly political "Anglo-Saxon" understanding of the social role of economy and private property. This was sometimes accompanied by the formalization of American control (especially in the Western hemisphere). More often, however, especially in Europe and the Far East, the United States pledged political non-intervention and free economic expansion, devising informal modes of control, economic pressure, and its proxies in Geneva, to bring recalcitrant States into line.[21]

Moralism was an essential part of the emerging *nomos*. It was reflected in the slow abolition of neutrality and the abstract condemnation of aggression – with the caveat carefully inserted into the Kellogg–Briand Pact that allowed the United States to decide for itself what might count as aggression and how to combat it.[22] An empire would hardly wage war on a non-discriminatory basis; it would in fact wage no war at all – it would engage in police action for the punishment of "criminals."[23] The remarkable coincidence between universalism and the interests of American foreign policy was visible in the new law of recognition. Granting or withholding belligerent status to domestic rebels could be used as a means of intervention or isolation, and the recognition of governments (Tobar and Estrada Doctrines) or (non-)recognition of territorial title (Stimson Doctrine) offered themselves as internationally effective techniques of intervention.[24] When these changes were linked with the presence of mass-destruction weapons, it seemed clear for Schmitt in 1950 that the new *nomos* would target large populations in remote areas in a fashion that could not be conceptualized in terms of traditional war. It would bring into existence – in fact allow only the existence of – wars on behalf of humanity, wars in which enemies would enjoy no protection, wars that would necessarily be total.[25]

In 1955 Schmitt conceded that the fluctuations of American policy reflected an uncertainty about the future and he saw three alternatives

---

[21] Cf. Carl Schmitt, "Völkerrechtliche Formen des modernen Imperialismus" (1932), in Schmitt, *Positionen und Begriffe im Kampf mit Weimar-Genf-Versailles, 1923–1939* (Berlin, Duncker & Humblot, 1988 [1940]), pp. 162–180 and "Grossraum gegen Universalismus" (1939), *ibid.* pp. 295–302.
[22] Cf. e.g. "Das neue Vae Neutris" (1938), in Schmitt, *Positionen und Begriffe*, pp. 251–255.
[23] Schmitt, "Völkerrechtliche Formen," pp. 176–178.
[24] Schmitt, *Der Nomos der Erde*, pp. 274–285.
[25] Schmitt, *Der Nomos der Erde*, pp. 298–299.

for the coming global order.[26] One was a universal empire under one great power – the United States. This, of course, he saw as a tragedy, a final victory of the dominance of economy and technology (and those possessing them) over the rest of the world. A second alternative was for the United States to take over England's place in the old territorial equilibrium as the "balancer," the external guarantor of Europe's internal peace, accompanied by unquestioned primacy in the Western Hemisphere. The third alternative – clearly preferred by Schmitt and perhaps seen by him as the one most likely to emerge – was a structure of territorial division between a limited number of large blocks (*Grossräume*) that mutually recognized each other and excluded external intervention: the image of Spengler and Orwell, and the focus of Friedmann's anxiety in 1965.

In his last important article, published in 1978, Schmitt considered that the first alternative was most likely to realize itself in terms of an industrial world appropriation, the subjugation of all the industries of the world under one power. His negative assessment was unrelenting: "The day *world politics* comes to the earth, it will be transformed into *a world police power*."[27] Yet he thought that it was the third alternative that had so far realized itself: ideological and economic struggle had led to the formation of three *Grossräume:* the United States, the USSR, and China, each of which was capable of excluding external intervention, with a fourth sphere of the developing States, still – at the time – enjoying "a certain political freedom of movement." As regards Europe, Schmitt confessed himself "deeply pessimist." Forces of globalization overrode European unity.[28] This assessment (though he did not make it express in 1978) was also an assessment about the state of European law. In an intellectual "testament" Schmitt had written in the course of 1943 and 1944, in face of imminent German collapse, he had identified European jurisprudence as the foundation of the European spirit and the *ius publicum Europaeum*. In the absence of a legislature, Europe's predominance in the world had been articulated by European lawyers who

---

[26] "Der neue Nomos der Erde," (1955), in Schmitt, *Staat, Grossraum, Nomos*, pp. 518–522. Cf. also commentary in Jean-François Kervégan, "Carl Schmitt and World Unity," in Chantal Mouffe (ed.), *The Challenge of Carl Schmitt* (London, Verso, 1999), pp. 68–69 and Wolfgang Palaver, "Carl Schmitt on Nomos and Space" (1996), 106 *Telos*, pp. 111–112.
[27] Carl Schmitt, "Die Legale Weltrevolution: Politischer Mehrwärt als Prämie auf juridische Legalität" (1978), 3 *Der Staat*, pp. 321–339. Trans. G. L.Ulmen, as "The Legal World Revolution" (1987), 72 *Telos*, pp. 73–89, p. 80 (italics in original). The references are to this translation. [28] Schmitt, "The Legal World Revolution," p. 85.

had drawn from Roman law and whose last great name had been Savigny. Since 1848 this jurisprudence had been gradually instrumentalized in the service of national legislatures and parties. It had become part of "an untrammelled technicism which uses state law as a tool" and lost its role as the "last refuge of legal consciousness."[29] A quarter of a century later he had no reason to change this assessment. That the forces for European unity were no match to an economically and technologically driven globalization paralleled the inequality of strength between a doctrinal–technical *Europäisches Gemeinschaftsrecht* and what he called "ideologies of progress."[30]

Though Schmitt developed his *Grossraumlehre* chronologically close to Hitler's declarations about the need for German *Lebensraum* (from 1939 onwards) and though it undoubtedly served German foreign policy goals, its content was independent of them.[31] Schmitt did not conceive his "large space" on racial grounds and he generalized it as a historical type of regional predominance. Schmitt connected the demise of the *ius publicum Europaeum* with the demise of the formal State and the formal equality between belligerents. For him, the Monroe Doctrine illustrated a first case of a new type of informal domination by one power over a region, something Japan had earlier aimed at in the Far East and Germany in Central and Eastern Europe. The merit of the *Grossraum* principle lay in the realistic recognition it implied that some powers radiated their culture, economy and influence beyond their formal boundaries.[32] A positivist law – such as Versailles – inevitably failed to counteract its dynamic force. Whether or not one appreciated the advantages of the old *nomos* (and Schmitt's attitude towards it was nostalgic), its time was over. It was powerless in face of expanding American economic and cultural influence. To counter the universalizing pull of a capitalist *Grossraum* would have required the presence of a confident political entity. From his 1920s writings to his article on world revolution in 1978,

---

[29] Carl Schmitt, "Die Lage der europäischen Rechtswissenschaft" (1943/44), trans. G. L. Ulmen as "The Plight of European Jurisprudence" (1990), 83 *Telos*, pp. 35–70, 64, 66.

[30] Schmitt, "The Plight," p. 76. In the 1978 article Schmitt chose as the paragon for Europe's unity "the more than 1,000 pages of the standard work on European common [i.e. Community] law by Ipsen," Schmitt, "The Legal World Revolution," p. 85.

[31] On the other hand, Schmitt's later admirers overstate their case when they write that the two concepts had "nothing to do with each other," Julien Freund, "Schmitt's Political Thought" (1995), 102 *Telos*, p. 36.

[32] Carl Schmitt, "Grossraum gegen Universalismus," pp. 299–301.

Schmitt had no doubt that this required a clear perception of where the enemy lay. For: "everywhere in political history, in foreign as well as domestic politics, the incapacity or the unwillingness to make this distinction [i.e. the distinction between friend and enemy] is a symptom of the political end."[33]

The ambivalences of a *Katechon* (restrainer)[34]

By 1950 Schmitt had become an intellectual pariah owing to his association with the national-socialist regime in 1933–1936. Although he had been blacklisted by the SS thereafter, and lost all influence with the regime, moving from constitutional law and political theory to international law, his enthusiasm for Hitler's dictatorship after 1933, his reputation as a *Kronjurist* of the Nazi government and his (continued) antisemitism kept him a *persona non grata* within West German political society until his death (at the age of 95) in 1983. He had been arrested by the Allies in August 1945 and held in an interment camp until 1947. He had also been brought to Nuremberg as a potential defendant in the war crimes trials but was released without charges.[35] Schmitt continued writing, however, until the 1970s and had a large circle of admirers within and beyond Germany. He has usually been held as one of the sharpest critics of political liberalism but it is unclear what his precise relationship to liberalism was. For many, he was an external enemy, while others regard him an internal critic. There is no doubt that he was conservative (though probably not a conservative revolutionary). That his relationship to liberalism remains an enigma speaks at least as much about the occasional obscurity of his writing and his frequent changes

---

[33] Carl Schmitt, *The Concept of the Political* (trans. and introd. by George Schwab, with a new foreword by Tracy B. Strong. 1st edn. 1927, trans. from 2nd edn. of 1932, Cambridge, Mass. and London, MIT Press, 1996), p. 68.

[34] Schmitt later characterized himself as a *Katechon*, that is a retarder or restrainer. The expression has a religious origin, signifying an earthly power that restrains the secular advance of the Antichrist. For Schmitt, this original sense mixes comfortably with his mission of restraining the "total functionalization" of law in the service of social or economic policies. Cf. Paul Piccone and G. L. Ulmen, "Schmitt's Testament and the Future of Europe" (1990), 83 *Telos*, pp. 19–20.

[35] Cf. Joseph Bendersky, "Carl Schmitt at Nuremberg" (1987), 72 *Telos*, pp. 91–96 and the "Interrogation of Carl Schmitt by Robert Kempner," *ibid.*, pp. 97–129. A key point in the interrogation was the prosecutor's question about whether Schmitt had engaged in a theoretical grounding of Hitler's *Lebensraum* policy. Schmitt of course denied this, claiming that his was a historically and scientifically based concept that he would defend at any time.

of position as of the variations and contradictions of that cluster of views usually associated with "liberalism."[36]

Most of the recent Schmitt revival concentrates on him as a political thinker – a "political theologian," ironically but understandably appropriated by left critics of liberalism. However, Schmitt's contribution to German constitutional law has always been appreciated, as testified to by the regular publication of new editions of his 1928 *Verfassungslehre*.[37] But Schmitt was also a significant international lawyer. Or, perhaps better, arguments about international law arose naturally from his political and legal theory. While many political theorists have commented extensively on Schmitt's 1950 book on the eclipse of the European *nomos*, rather few international lawyers have done so.[38] This may not be surprising. The ethos of post-1946 international law has been – not least in Germany – uniformly universalistic and humanitarian, and thus in principle vulnerable to Schmitt's acerbic critiques. Failing to address those critiques, however, and continuing to construct their normative systems

[36] The literature on Schmitt is too voluminous to be fully reflected here. The standard English-language biography is Joseph Bendersky, *Carl Schmitt: Theorist for the Reich* (Princeton University Press, 1983). Also very useful is George Schwab, *The Challenge of the Exception. An Introduction to the Political Ideas of Carl Schmitt between 1921 and 1936* (2nd edn., with a new introd., New York, Greenwood, 1989). Both of these contain relatively positive assessments that are now countered by the very polemical study by William E. Scheuerman, *Carl Schmitt: The End of Law* (Lanham, Boulder, New York and Oxford, Rowman & Littlefield, 1999). The best English-language study, however, is Gopal Balakrishnan, *The Enemy: An Intellectual Portrait of Carl Schmitt* (London, Verso, 2000). Renato Cristi, *Carl Schmitt and Authoritarian Liberalism* (Cardiff, University of Wales Press, 1998), makes the useful point about Schmitt being a liberal in the sense of advocating a liberal economy outside a strong State. Two collections of essays shed light on the various aspects of Schmitt's work in the English language, Chantal Mouffe (ed.), *The Challenge of Carl Schmitt* (London, Verso, 1999), and David Dyzenhaus (ed.), *Law as Politics. Carl Schmitt's Critique of Liberalism* (Duke University Press, 1998). Brief accounts of Schmitt's biography are also contained in the English translations of his major works.

[37] The left appropriation of Schmitt is reflected in particular in the pages of the US periodical *Telos* that has devoted several extensive studies and special issues to Schmitt and published translations of his key writings. Cf. e.g. the articles by Piccone, Ulmen, Hirst, Bendersky, and Söllner in "Symposium: Carl Schmitt: Enemy or Foe?" Special Issue (1987), 72 *Telos* as well as the articles by Ulmen, Böckenförde, Slade, and Bendersky in "Carl Schmitt Now" (1996), 109 *Telos*. The ambivalence of the left in regard to Schmitt is also usefully discussed in the essays contained in Mouffe, *Challenge of Carl Schmitt*.

[38] The best work is Schmoeckel, *Die Grossraumtheorie*. For useful discussions by non-lawyers, cf. Paul Piccone and G. L. Ulmen, "Schmitt's 'Testament' and the Future of Europe" (1990), 83 *Telos*, pp. 3–34 and Kervégan, "Carl Schmitt and World Unity," pp. 54–74. A useful analysis is also Peter Stirk, "Carl Schmitt's Völkerrechtliche Grossraumordnung" (1999), 20 *History of Political Thought*, pp. 357–374.

through the thinnest sociological generalizations, international lawyers have been compelled to witness the growth of a neighboring discipline – "international relations" – that has incorporated Schmittian insights as parts of its professional identity. Schmitt's reprehensible association with the Nazis and his blatant antisemitism throw a well-founded shadow on his life as well as on some of his writings from that period. But they fail to undermine the force of many of his insights about law and the new political order. To deal with Schmitt is necessary, as many have argued, to understand the complex relationship between political utopias and struggles; and international lawyers do owe an explanation for the fact that while there has never been as much talk about international law and morality as in the twentieth century, never have atrocities on such wide scale been committed in the name of political utopias. Under such circumstances, the choice between writing another 1,000-page textbook on humanitarian law and trying to deal with Schmitt's critiques of universal moralism should not be too difficult.

A discipline transforms itself: Schmitt on Scelle and Lauterpacht

Before the war Schmitt had found the academic articulation for the end of the *ius publicum Europaeum* as well as the contours of its successor in the writings of Georges Scelle and Hersch Lauterpacht, two lawyers whose separate lines of argument converged in the view of international law as the law of a "*communauté universelle.*"[39] In Scelle's *Droit des gens* Schmitt saw the so far most consistent application of radical liberal–democratic ideas to the international system. Employing the French concept of the legislative State, Scelle's federalism may have oscillated insecurely between individualism and collectivism, but relegated formal State law definitely into the realm of the metaphysical and the unscientific. Where Scelle was expressly dismissive of the *lex lata/lex ferenda* distinction, Lauterpacht developed a more limited common law analysis of international cases

---

[39] Carl Schmitt, *Die Wendung zum diskriminierenden Kriegsbegriff* (Berlin, Duncker & Humblot, 1988 [1938]), pp. 1–8. The pamphlet is based on a paper given to the Association of German Jurists in October 1937, as Schmitt had been expelled from political positions and feared for his safety. But he did not turn his back on Nazi policy and remained supported by Göring and Hans Frank. Nonetheless, the paper may be seen as an attempt to move to a less politically contentious realm and to participate in a wider European scholarly debate. In this, he had little success. Foreign Minister Ribbentrop congratulated him for expressing so well the German position. Balakrishnan, *The Enemy*, pp. 207, 228–231.

that nonetheless crystallized into a gapless world law. Scelle saw international institutions as the instruments of federalism; Lauterpacht allocated that function to the judiciary.

Schmitt's discussion of Scelle and Lauterpacht is nuanced and even to an extent admiring. He saw the two less as full-scale representatives of a new system than as perceptive analyzers of the gaps and inconsistencies of the old formalism behind Versailles, unable to sustain a new *nomos*. Coming from the tradition of Constant and Proudhon, Scelle worked towards a strong federal institution as a representative of mankind with the right – even the duty – to intervene if particular States violated the freedoms that underlay the system.[40] Nationality became a matter of free choice and minority regimes and mandates forms of international administration, detached from the States-system of a traditional European law. All citizens had a right to resist if their State violated international law. With his rejection of the traditional concept of war, Scelle transformed every international violence into a global civil war with crime on one side, police action on the other. Lauterpacht's more conventional starting-point led to the same result: the activities of judges and arbitrators became "an international constitutional machinery."[41] Peace became a postulate of order and war of the absence of order: war had a place in the system only as breach. The view of the Covenant as "higher law," combined with the territorial guarantee and the sanctions under Art. 16 led to the same point that Scelle had reached: the aggressor was thrust outside as a violator against whom all the rest of humanity would take defensive action.

If the Covenant was mankind's constitution and sanctions community action against a law-breaker, then neutrality had room only as a limited, technical exception from the collective obligations – such as the historically based Swiss neutrality – but not a free foreign policy alternative. There can be no neutrality between the policeman and the thief. The concept of *collective action*, Schmitt held, was a key to the emerging *nomos*.[42] It reintroduced the notion of the just war into international law – with the significant twist that the power to decide where justice lay was now arrogated to the League Council. This development bore, for Schmitt, three corollaries. First, it did not merely re-state the Christian concept of the just war. Although American authors such as James Brown Scott (1866–1943) propagated the "Catholic conception of international law,"

---

[40] Schmitt, *Die Wendung*, pp. 16–17. [41] Schmitt, *Die Wendung*, p. 22.
[42] Schmitt, *Die Wendung*, pp. 26–36.

no turn to religion was possible. The new just war existed in a wholly secular environment. The justice of the just war referred only to the "values" of the participants, allowing them to characterize themselves as the enforcers of a de-nationalized normative truth. It returned Europe to the civil war from which the *ius publicum Europaeum* had tried to save it.

Second, instruments such as the Kellogg–Briand Pact abolished war – but only at the level of *concepts*: by labeling violence either as crime or as enforcement. Far from limiting violence, this merely lifted the restraints that had been the most valuable achievement of the old European *nomos*, and allowed extreme measures against the adversary. This is how Schmitt interpreted the Allied action against Germany: the blockade, the war guilt clause, the indictment of the Kaiser, and the reparations. These were not parts of a "duel" between States but of a total war – a war of annihilation – against Germany seen as the criminal who could not apply to sovereignty for its protection. Against such an enemy – just as against the pirate – any measures could be taken as enforcement, and restraint was a matter only of the enforcer's private conscience. Statehood was abolished as the basis of the system. The illegal belligerent was divided into two parts: the regime that had commenced the war (of aggression) and was to be treated as a group of gangsters, and the rest of the population that was to be "protected" and enlisted as co-fighters. The State enjoyed no protection but was to be treated as a "rogue State" ("*Räuberstaat*").[43]

Third, this transformation implied a program of imperial expansion by the powers in charge of the decision-making in League organs. Both Scelle and Lauterpacht aimed to explain the Covenant as a constitution of a world community. If the League was a federation, then there could of course be no war among its members: all violence became a matter of criminal law. But if in addition to being a federation, the League also saw itself in universal terms, then it became an Empire in the precise sense that the way it treated third States was determined by its *internal* laws. Here was the heart of the emerging *nomos* and the significance of the transformations of legal doctrine as well as those of international reality itself.[44]

Against liberal neutralizations and depoliticizations

In his 1938 essay and in his other writings on the Geneva League Schmitt was applying positions that he had first formulated in regard to

---

[43] Schmitt, *Die Wendung*, p. 46.   [44] Schmitt, *Die Wendung*, pp. 47–52.

the constitutional problems of the Weimar republic and liberal democracy's principles of operation. His discussion of the universalizing tendencies of international law cannot be detached from his critique of the all-encompassing search for depoliticization and neutralization that had characterized Western liberal thought since the end of the religious era. Since then, liberalism had reduced all problems either into the realm of a romantic aestheticism or chosen to treat them as exclusively economic and technological.[45] The end of European public law at the end of the nineteenth century came about as a result of the blurring of the notion of politics that had been a "presupposition" behind the concept of the state.[46]

This argument was a central part of Schmitt's early analysis of political romanticism (1919) that depicted nineteenth-century bourgeois sentimentality as an aesthetic and subjectivist attitude towards the political world, and withdrawal from active participation.[47] The romantic sensibility conceptualized every social event in relationship to the self that perceived it and projected on it an esthetic value that it took as the object of its interminable discussions. The political romanticists, Schmitt argued, had been endless contemplators of their own feelings about the world, but never willing to engage in action about it. We have encountered this type already:

> They made speculations, plans and bold promises. They made intimations and held out prospects. They responded to every expectation of a fulfillment of their promises with new promises. But the enormous possibilities that they had opposed to reality never became a reality. The romantic solution to this difficulty lay in representing possibility as a higher category. In commonplace reality, the romantics could not play the role of the ego who creates the world. They preferred the state of eternal becoming and possibilities that are never consummated to the confines of concrete reality.[48]

Another technique for escaping politics, Schmitt argued in his *Political Theology* (1922), lay in a normativism that sought to replace the State by its law and to rid politics from the notion of sovereignty. In the late nineteenth century, liberalism and secular jurisprudence had started to

---

[45] Carl Schmitt, "Das Zeitalter der Neutralisierungen und Entpolitisierungen" (1929), in Schmitt, *Positionen und Begriffe*, pp. 123–132.
[46] "The concept of the state presupposes the concept of the political." Schmitt, *The Concept of the Political*, p. 19.
[47] Carl Schmitt, *Politische Romantik* (1919/1925), trans. Guy Oakes as *Political Romanticism*, Cambridge, Mass. and London, MIT Press, 1986).
[48] Schmitt, *Political Romanticism*, p. 66.

downplay the conflictual character of the political realm. The legitimacy of State authority was received not from its ability to maintain peace but from the application of an impartial and objective, democratically based legal system. "All significant concepts of the modern theory of the state are secularized theological concepts."[49] The legislator was now conceived in the image of the omnipotent God, possessing a response to every question, having resolved every conflict in advance. State law was like the law of nature: all-pervading, omnipotent, and without an exception.

There could hardly have been a more striking gap between this kind of liberal jurisprudence and the struggle against political collapse that was the reality of Weimar. The situation itself seemed to prove that order did not emerge from the spontaneous love of one's neighbors but had to be created by the political system. In a famous debate between Kelsen and Schmitt about who is the "guardian" of the constitution, Kelsen pointed to the supreme federal court while Schmitt observed that this might be so as long as things stay normal, but not if there is an extreme emergency – defined as the inability of the regular legal process to control the situation. Here Schmitt expounded his radical definition of the sovereign as "he who decides on the exception," that is to say, on "whether there is an extreme emergency as well as what should be done to counter it."[50] The state of exception performed in politics the same task that miracle did in theology: it reaffirmed and proved the authority of the normal. How this was done cannot be legally circumscribed; no law can foresee the exception and the conditions for suspending itself. And more: every normality owes its existence to a *pouvoir constituant* that once formed an exception: "The exception is more interesting than the rule. The rule proves nothing; the exception proves everything: It confirms not only the rule but also its existence, which derives only from the exception."[51] Legal normality hid political conflict from sight but did not make it disappear. Conflict re-emerged every time the law was to be applied. "In every transformation there is present an *auctoritatis interpositio*."[52] The legal system relied on decisions by those in authoritative positions: Kelsen had been able to construct a depoliticized law only by emptying it of its content and ignoring implementation, the all-important question *Quis judicabit?*

[49] Carl Schmitt, *Political Theology. Four Chapters on the Concept of Sovereignty* (1922, 2nd edn., 1934; trans. George Schwab, Cambridge, Mass. and London, MIT Press, 1985), p. 35.   [50] Schmitt, *Political Theology*, pp. 5–7.
[51] Schmitt, *Political Theology*, p. 15.   [52] Schmitt, *Political Theology*, p. 31.

Carl Schmitt, Hans Morgenthau and "international relations"

Of course, everyone is for law, morality, ethics and peace; no-one will want to commit injustice; but *in concreto* the relevant question is always who shall decide what in this case is law, what counts as peace, what is a threat or disturbance of peace, with what means it shall be restored, when a situation has become normal or "peaceful" and so on.[53]

Against abstract normativism Schmitt posed his own anti-formalism. Only by focusing on law as decisions (and not as an abstract normativity) can the conflictual reality of politics be fully appreciated, and the means conceived whereby conflict does not escalate into civil war. Even in 1932 Schmitt was ready to support the enactment of an emergency law that would have banned the political activities of forces hostile to the Republic, including the Nazi party. As Hindenburg recoiled, Schmitt threw in his lot with the new regime in 1933 – with disastrous results for his reputation.

The argument about liberalism's failure to take determinate decisions had been extensively discussed in Schmitt's *Crisis of Parliamentary Democracy* (1923).[54] Here Schmitt revealed his ambivalent relationship to democracy. On the one hand, democratic legitimacy was the only form of legitimacy on which the modern nation-State could draw. On the other hand, democracy often conflicted with liberalism's procedural principles. Democracy ideally meant identity between the people and the State. Liberalism intended to bring about that identity through parliamentary representation and the principles of discussion and openness. But parliaments had everywhere degenerated to factions representing special interests and forums for inter-party compromise. Discussion had become an empty formality. Liberal relativism made it unable to articulate the principle of identity on which its constitution was based: who constituted the *demos* and against whom it did so.[55]

---

[53] Carl Schmitt, "Zu Friedrich Meinecke's 'Idee der Staatsräson' (1926)," in Schmitt, *Positionen und Begriffe*, p. 50.

[54] Carl Schmitt, *Die geistesgeschichtliche Lage des heutigen Parlamentarismus* (1923/1926), trans. Ellen Kennedy as *The Crisis of Parliamentary Democracy*, Cambridge, Mass. and London, MIT Press, 1988).

[55] This was particularly visible in the reluctance of liberals to enforce the homogeneity that was of the essence of democracy. It meant not only the inclusion of the similar but also the exclusion of the different. Without principles of exclusion, democracy would turn into an undiscriminating cosmopolitanism. No democratic country, Schmitt argued, practiced such, even if some claimed they did, and it was doubtful if any could. For there was no absolute equality: equality always existed in regard to some criterion (status, merit, age, nationality, etc.) – and though parliaments do not often discuss that criterion (because they take it as self-evident), this does not mean it does not exist. Cf. "Die Gegensatz von Parlamentarismus und moderner Massendemokratie" (1926), in Schmitt, *Positionen und Begriffe*, pp. 59–66.

As the Parliament was taken over by interest-groups, State power was undermined in two contrasting ways. In the nineteenth century, the State had become a *pouvoir neutre*, its tasks limited to resolving interest conflicts between economic and social actors. This was the classical liberal model of the weak State. In the twentieth century it became completely enmeshed with society, or, as Schmitt called it, a "total State" out of weakness; a "self-organization of society" with innumerable welfare, economic, or cultural tasks. But when everything becomes "politics," no scope is left for "the political."[56] This was the condition of Weimar. The State no longer had any independent power to maintain order. Against the weakness of the liberal (total) State, Schmitt emphasized the position of the Reich President in maintaining the constitution and theorized the office of the President – instead of the Parliament – as the democratic representative.[57] Central to this construction was the distinction between the "fundamental principles" of the constitution and its procedural provisions that enabled Schmitt to argue that the President, as guardian of the constitution's fundamental principles, could put its procedural provisions in abeyance in order to safeguard the substance of the political order.[58] Only a ridiculous positivism, he argued, could assume that the constitution allowed its own destruction.

Schmitt's anti-formalism was connected to his emphasis on the significance of the political which, for him, was crucial for the State's function in maintaining order. Liberalism fused the State with economy, technology, and ultimately "society," in a way that lost sight of the political. It was a delusion to think that political problems could be solved by technology: even as technology was neutral as such, it was completely political in its uses. The characterization of the era as "technological" could be only preliminary: we can give a final verdict only after we have seen what kind of politics it advanced.[59] But it is likely that, like Hannah Arendt, Schmitt appreciated politics not only for its instrumental usefulness but also for

---

[56] Carl Schmitt, "Die Wendung zum totalen Staat" (1931), in Schmitt, *Positionen und Begriffe*, pp. 146–157.

[57] Thus in his study on dictatorship Schmitt put forward the concept of commissarial dictatorship that was limited by its purpose of maintaining the core of the constitution, a dictatorship, in other words, in which the will of the people was reflected. For Schmitt, there was no essential contradiction between democracy and (communist or fascist) dictatorship; inasmuch as democracy was best expressed in the concept of the *volonté générale*, it was not a procedural but a substantive principle. Cf. also "Die Gegensatz," pp. 64–66.

[58] This is the gist of his book *Legalität und Legitimität* (1932, 4th edn., Berlin, Duncker & Humblot, 1988). Cf. also Schmitt, "The Legal World Revolution," pp. 75–76.

[59] Carl Schmitt, "Das Zeitalter der Neutralisierungen und Entpolitisierungen," p. 131.

existential reasons. Politics as struggle defined something essential in what it is to be a human being "and that those who would diminish the political diminish humanity."[60]

Schmitt's most famous thesis was undoubtedly the definition of the political in terms of the irreducible opposition between the friend and the enemy: "The specific political distinction to which political actions and motives can be reduced is that between friend and enemy."[61] The core sense of the political as struggle lies in this definition. If the State is a political body, then the definition of its enemy constitutes its principle of identity. Hence it is the task of the State to be clear about who its internal and external enemies are. To the extent that the State is "depoliticized" or reduced to a social association among others, it has lost this capacity and, no longer able to recognize its enemies, will not be able to maintain order, will no longer be a real State at all.

The friend–enemy distinction as the meaning of the political cannot be reduced to a mere metaphor. The enemy, Schmitt writes, "is not merely any competitor or just any partner of a conflict in general." Nor is the enemy "the private adversary whom one hates. An enemy exists only when, at least potentially, one fighting collectivity of people confronts a similar collectivity."[62] The enemy is the public enemy in whose concept belongs the ever-present possibility of real combat to the death. This need not become reality, indeed would normally not appear: "But it must nevertheless remain a real possibility for as long as the concept of the enemy remains valid."[63] As in the case of the exception here, too, the marginal situation completely overshadows and determines the

---

[60] Tracy B. Strong, "Foreword: Dimensions of the New Debate around Carl Schmitt," in Schmitt, *The Concept of the Political*, p. xv. Whether Schmitt should be credited with such a version of humanism is uncertain. One plausible line of argument draws from Schmitt's fervent Catholicism the thesis of the inextricability of politics and the struggle between faith and sin that seems to be a central part of what Schmitt called "political theology." From this perspective, conceiving of the "end of politics" or the replacement of politics by a harmonious social life, reduced to the administration of common matters, would constitute the heresy of an earthly paradise that would deny the reality of the original sin and the work of the Antichrist in secular society. When Schmitt says that "all genuine political theories presuppose man to be evil," this recharacterizes liberalism as not really a political theory at all but an attempt to get away from it. In this sense all political theory stands on a profession of anthropological faith, Schmitt, *The Concept of the Political*, pp. 57–58. For Schmitt, the resulting "peace and security" will inaugurate the reign of the Antichrist, as announced by St Paul in 1 Thessalonians. Cf. in particular, Meier, *The Lesson of Carl Schmitt*, pp. 160–165. [61] Schmitt, *The Concept of the Political*, p. 26.
[62] Schmitt, *The Concept of the Political*, p. 28.
[63] Schmitt, *The Concept of the Political*, p. 33.

sense of what appears as the tranquil normality. The struggle to the death with the enemy is the exception that confirms the order of normality. Schmitt's critique of Weimar liberalism focused on the blurring of a clear sense of the republic's internal enemies. But the principal application of the friend–enemy distinction was received by Schmitt in international politics.

"Whoever invokes humanity wants to cheat"

As in the sphere of politics, it belongs to the State to "decide in a concrete situation upon the enemy and the ability to fight him with the power emanating from the entity."[64] In international relations, the prospect of war to the death was an ever-present potentiality. Schmitt's awareness of and emphasis on this potentiality by no means meant that he regarded war as a social ideal, and he had no sympathy with the heroic notion of war espoused by his friend, the novelist Ernst Jünger (1895–1998).[65] The significance of war did not lie in its provision of existential meaning to the lives of individuals or in its aesthetic qualities. The readiness to fight was not to grow from a warlike attitude but from a correct perception of the role of the State: as long as a people exists in the political sphere, it must have a clear view who its enemies are. Otherwise, the State will cease to exist. What is left may be a set of collective economic or cultural pursuits – sooner or later to dissolve in civil war or by the force of external aggression.[66]

It had been the great merit of the *ius publicum Europaeum* that it had limited war into a public law duel between formal States. As we have seen, in Schmitt's view, it was being replaced by a universalistic "moralism" that far from doing away with conflict lifted all restraint on how it would be waged. In the first place, it became outright impossible to distinguish between conflict and its opposite. As war ceased to be a formal status, what came in its stead was an amorphous *status mixtus*, a grey zone of informal control and pressure by those who had the means. This, Schmitt argued in the 1920s, had happened in the protectorates outside Europe that fell short of formal annexation but guaranteed full control, as well as in the innumerable forms of supervision, occupation, and investigation over European (particularly German) territory established

[64] Schmitt, *The Concept of the Political*, p. 45.
[65] Cf. Meier, *The Lesson of Carl Schmitt*, pp. 38–39.
[66] Schmitt, *The Concept of the Political*, pp. 45–48.

by the Versailles Treaty. As new States were formed under the rhetoric of self-determination, nationalism and democracy, but simultaneously subsumed under far-reaching regimes of economic and political intervention, words such as "sovereignty" or "independence" transformed into slogans.[67] The legalization of the status quo perpetuated and normalized the mixed status of informal intervention.[68]

Secondly, and far more dangerously, moralism lifted all limits from international violence. The renunciation of war as a matter of "national policy" in the 1928 Kellogg–Briand Pact was deeply deceptive: "The solemn declaration of outlawing war does not abolish the friend–enemy distinction, but, on the contrary, opens new possibilities for giving an international *hostis* declaration new content and new vigor."[69] In practice, the declaration was accompanied by specific reservations concerning war in self-defense – reservations that were, Schmitt correctly observed, no mere exceptions to the norm of peacefulness but "gave the norm its concrete content . . . in dubious cases." As sovereignty meant the right to determine whether the enemy had attacked (or would attack unless deterred), and what was needed to counter the foreseeable attack, no change occurred in political reality. It was still the friend–enemy distinction, and the ability to draw the extreme consequences from it, that determined the political identity of States.[70]

This reality was blurred by the universalistic rhetoric that became part of the diplomatic game. Of course, Schmitt wrote, it might be possible to conceive a world where there were no States. In such world, "[w]hat remains is neither politics nor state, but culture, civilization, economics, morality, law, art, entertainment, etc." But nothing seemed further from reality:

Humanity as such cannot wage war because it has no enemy, at least not on this planet . . . When a state fights its political enemy in the name of humanity, it is not a war for the sake of humanity, but a war wherein a particular state seeks to usurp a universal concept against its military opponent. At the expense of its opponent, it tries to identify itself with humanity in the same way as one can misuse peace, justice, progress, and civilization in order to claim these as one's own and to deny the same to the enemy.[71]

---

[67] Cf. Carl Schmitt, "Die Rheinland als Objekt internationaler Politik" (1925), in Schmitt, *Positionen und Begriffe*, pp. 28–33.
[68] "Der Status Quo und der Friede" (1925), in Schmitt, *Positionen und Begriffe*, pp. 40–42.
[69] Schmitt, *The Concept of the Political*, p. 51.
[70] Schmitt, *The Concept of the Political*, pp. 50–51.
[71] Schmitt, *The Concept of the Political*, p. 54.

The language of humanity had always been a favorite tool of imperial expansion, particularly of economic imperialism. A world policy is an imperial policy, a policy whose scope is the whole of humanity. Such policy had been adopted during the inter-war era in the diplomatic language of the two principal non-European powers, the Soviet Union and the United States. Yet: "To confiscate the word humanity, to invoke and monopolize such a term probably has certain incalculable effects, such as denying the enemy the quality of being human and declaring him to be an outlaw of humanity; and war can thereby be driven to the most extreme inhumanity."[72] Is it a coincidence that the twentieth century saw the most widespread use of the concept of humanity in warfare; and the most atrocious destruction of lives ever carried out under the pretense of war? For Schmitt, it was clear that "humanity" had no political content; that no political entity, ideal or status, corresponded to it. It had been invoked in the eighteenth century against the divine right of Kings and in the nineteenth century against aristocratic or capitalist privileges. Here it had a political meaning: it identified an enemy. But if used by the League or by the Great Powers, it merely veiled the politics of those entities, the friend–enemy distinctions on which their identities were based, liberating them from restraint against dealing with the enemy. The League was not "humanity" – it did not abolish war. On the contrary: "It introduces new possibilities for wars, permits wars to take place, sanctions coalition wars, and by legitimizing and sanctioning certain wars it sweeps away many obstacles to war . . . this establishment is not a league, but possibly an alliance."[73] The humanitarian war becomes a war of annihilation (*Vernichtungskrieg*), a global civil war where the enemy does not have the dignity of a State and resistance will appear as "the illegal and immoral resistance of a few delinquents, troublemakers, pirates and gangsters."[74]

Nothing of this had changed for Schmitt in fifty years. In 1978 "humanity" was still no political subject. It remained, he wrote with reference to the argumentative practices of the United Nations, an asymmetrical concept, containing "the possibility of the deepest inequality." The implied contrast "human"/"inhuman" was like the familiar oppositions between Greek and barbarian, Christian and heathen, even superman and subhuman. The "linguistic potential for argumentation gained from the terms human and humanity" lifted all reason for

---

[72] Schmitt, *The Concept of the Political*, p. 54.
[73] Schmitt, *The Concept of the Political*, p. 56.   [74] Schmitt, *Die Wendung*, p. 43n45.

restraint in a struggle where the adversary was excommunicated from humanity altogether.[75]

It was against all this that Schmitt devised his concept of the *Grossraum* in 1939 and in 1950: as a space of politics to replace the obsolete neutralism of formal States and as a restraining instrument against the appropriation of the language of humanity by the *clercs* of a single, industrially based *nomos*. *Cuius industria, eius regio*. In a world-scale economy, this would mean not *Landnahme* but *Weltraumnahme*.[76] Because this process was conceptually identical with the demise of the *ius publicum Europaeum*, it seems natural that Schmitt did not see international law as an effective restraint on it. From his Weimar writings as well as from his "testament" of 1943–1944, however, it is possible to extract a sense about what he thought of the law's role in the struggle between single empire and *Grossräume*. Two types of legal thought were responsible for the erosion of the European jurisprudence since the nineteenth century. One was positivist formalism, identified with neo-Kantian philosophy, and, in particular, Kelsen.[77] Later, however, Schmitt changed his principal target to legal "instrumentalism" that viewed jurisprudence as a "mere craft" of legislative commentary, "an instrument of arbitrary prescriptions and endless enactments" by the "motorized legislator" of the welfare State. As a contrast to both he invoked the rationalist jurisprudence of the thirteenth- and fourteenth-century *legists*, the humanistic jurisprudence of the sixteenth century, and, in particular, the work and figure of Savigny. Possibly in view of his own catastrophic misjudgment of 1933 he wrote ten years later:

We cannot choose the changing rulers and regimes according to our own tastes, but in the changing situations we preserve the basis of a rational human existence that cannot do without legal principles as such: a recognition of the individual based on mutual respect even in conflict situation; a sense for the logic and consistency of concepts and institutions; a sense for reciprocity and the minimum of orderly procedure, due process, without which there can be no law.[78]

In his testament Schmitt advocated a historically sensitive and institutionally oriented jurisprudence that would look beyond formal laws and legislative projects or intentions and would not succumb to the temptation

---

[75] Schmitt, "The Legal World Revolution," pp. 87–88.
[76] Schmitt, "The Legal World Revolution," pp. 79–80.
[77] Cf. e.g. Schmitt, *Political Theology*, pp. 18–22.   [78] Schmitt, "The Plight," p. 67.

of an abstract humanitarianism.[79] But he remained skeptical of its existence in Europe.

Schmitt and Morgenthau: the primacy of the political

Schmitt modified his discussion of the limits of the political between the first (1927) and the second (1932) editions of *Der Begriff des Politischen*. In the first edition, the "political" had existed alongside such other realms as economy, morality, law, culture, etc. in an apparently equal position as one of the aspects of a community's life, distinct from its other aspects. In the second (and third) editions, the political stood out, however, from such delimitations so as to potentially encompass all of them. Now politics had no intrinsic limit: every aspect of life could manifest the friend–enemy opposition and thus transform itself into political struggle. Politics had no substance, it described the "*intensity* of association or dissociation of human beings."[80] This increased the need to ensure that the State had the ability to prevent that struggle from leading into an all-out civil war or indeed an all-out international war – something it could do only through a concentration of overwhelming power in the hands of a "guardian."

Now this idea of politics as an *intensity* concept did not exist in the earlier edition of the book. By contrast, it was centrally present in the 1929 doctoral dissertation to the Faculty of Law at the University of Frankfurt by the 25-year-old Hans Morgenthau, titled *Die internationale Rechtspflege. Ihr Wesen und ihre Grenzen* (The International Judicial Function. Its Nature and Limits). Morgenthau had specifically taken issue with Schmitt's influential 1927 work by reference to which he developed his own notion of the political as a quality and not a substance, capable of penetrating every realm of international life. This was the reason, the young Morgenthau claimed, that international law had been such a weak structure. Morgenthau sent his dissertation to Schmitt and received in exchange a complimentary letter. When the second edition of Schmitt's *Der Begriff des Politischen* came out in 1932, it included the new definition of the political as an intensity concept – without due acknowledgment, as Morgenthau later bitterly remarked.[81]

---

[79] Schmitt, "The Plight," pp. 54–64, 68; Schmitt, *Political Theology*, pp. 2–3.
[80] Schmitt, *The Concept of the Political*, p. 38 (italics MK).
[81] This story is made the basis of an argument about another "hidden dialogue" (besides the better known one that took place between Schmitt and Leo Strauss) between Schmitt and Morgenthau. Cf. Scheuerman, *Carl Schmitt*, pp. 225–237.

Morgenthau continued his engagement with Schmitt in the 1930s but after emigration to the United States in 1937 set Schmitt together with most of his other European baggage aside. As he received tenure at the University of Chicago in 1949 he had already laid the basis for an extraordinarily influential career in international relations by the publication of two books: *Scientific Man vs. Power Politics* (1946) and *Politics Among Nations. The Struggle for Power and Peace* (1948). His third book from that prolific period, *In Defense of the National Interest* (1951) analyzed the world situation in terms that were strikingly similar to those expressed by Schmitt.

Another retrospective

Morgenthau's 1951 book was a critique of American foreign policy but also an end-of-an-era analysis. The Second World War, Morgenthau wrote, had made the destructive effects of three "revolutions of our age" fully plain. A political change had led to "the end of the state system which has existed since the sixteenth century in the Western world." That system had been based on the balance of power between formally sovereign European nations. The non-European world had been related to it either through isolation or subordination. "Of this state system," Morgenthau wrote, "nothing is left today."[82] The end of the European age had been consummated by the emergence of two superpowers – the United States and the Soviet Union – whose power and ambition outweighed anything remaining in Europe. The adversity between these powers was total: each animated by a crusading spirit, ready to strike at first instance of possibility: "Total victory, total defeat, total destruction seem to be the alternatives before the two great powers of the world."[83]

A second, technological revolution had created a new, total concept of war. Like Schmitt, Morgenthau wrote nostalgically of a military past when "contests proceeded generally according to strict rules."[84] The mechanization of warfare and the atomic bomb had transformed modern war "into the actuality of total war" that could follow no rules, indeed that was irrational in its essence. Technology now made the destruction and the conquest of the world possible by a single power. When this transformation was linked to Morgenthau's third revolution

---

[82] Hans Morgenthau, *In Defense of the National Interest. A Critical Examination of American Foreign Policy* (New York, Knopf, 1951), pp. 41, 42.
[83] Morgenthau, *In Defense of the National Interest*, p. 52.
[84] Morgenthau, *In Defense of the National Interest*, p. 54.

– the moral transformation – this alternative started to seem almost a likelihood. Throughout modern history there had been a European "family of nations" that, despite internal dissension, had shared a common civilization and a way of life. The moral and political consensus had coincided with the restraining influence of the shared state system and stationary technology.[85] Its place had been taken by "political religions" whose ambitions knew no limits. Pointing at the "tendency towards world-wide salvation" Morgenthau echoed Schmitt's writings – without due acknowledgement on his part this time. This sentimentalism was a perversion; it was not morality but moralism, a hypocritical dressing of the national interest in the garb of morality, leading to an intensification of political conflict. For:

> The appeal to moral principles in the international sphere has no concrete universal meaning. It is either so vague as to have no concrete meaning that could provide rational guidance for political action, or it will be nothing but a reflection of the moral preconceptions of a particular nation and will by the same token be unable to gain the universal recognition it pretends to deserve.[86]

The Cold War was the final stage in the dismantling of what Schmitt had called the *ius publicum Europaeum*, its place taken by two crusading superpowers, assisted by proxies in Europe and Asia. Bolshevism and US foreign policy were both crafted into a moralistic frame they had inherited from the Second World War as a war against the absolute evil that must be compelled to unconditional surrender.[87]

Morgenthau's intention in 1951 was to defend the dignity of national interest against the utopian or legalistic detractors. In a morally agnostic world it was immoral to act on the basis of utopian ideas. If such ideas had an application, it was only to the extent "they had been given concrete content and have been related to political situations by society."[88] Like Schmitt, Morgenthau held that moralism, utopianism, sentimentalism, and legalism were not simply ineffectual guides of foreign policy but positively harmful in providing an ideological justification for a limitless crusading politics. Only the national interest was concretely rooted in a nation's experience and power, and thus a reliable guide for foreign policy. To look after one's interest – self-preservation – became both political necessity as well as moral duty: "In the absence of an integrated international society, the attainment of a modicum of order and the

---

[85] Morgenthau, *In Defense of the National Interest*, p. 61.
[86] Morgenthau, *In Defense of the National Interest*, p. 35.
[87] Morgenthau, *In Defense of the National Interest*, p. 31.
[88] Morgenthau, *In Defense of the National Interest*, p. 34.

realization of a minimum of moral values are predicated upon the existence of national communities capable of preserving order and realizing moral values within the limits of their power."

"[W]ithin the limits of their power." This was Schmitt's *nomos*, the concrete order. Morgenthau's 1951 book indicted American utopianism, sentimentalism, legalism, and neo-isolationism as fatal disregard of the need to determine clearly the (US) national interest and to keep focus on it while one was acting. The "real issue" in the cold war, for instance, was not an ideological confrontation but a desire for power that transformed the revolutionary rhetoric of the Soviet State into an instrument of Russian imperialism.[89] Morgenthau agreed with Schmitt in his critique of US utopianism. It led either into a completely unrealistic expectation that one's political contenders would feel bound by agreements concluded – the shock at Soviet dismissal of the Yalta agreement on East European democracy[90] – or it resulted in the understanding of war as moral struggle by "peace-loving nations" against the forces of evil; the branding of the enemy as a "war criminal" having committed an "act of aggression" (the inverted commas are Morgenthau's). The only policy directive can then be the extreme one: "Crush the enemy; force him into unconditional surrender; re-educate him in the ways of democratic, peace-loving nations... a United Nations provides the finishing touch for the brave new world from which war and, in the words of Mr Cordell Hull, power politics itself will have been banished."[91] Like Schmitt, Morgenthau interpreted this development as an attempt to get away from politics, intrinsic to the liberal world. Unlike Churchill or Stalin, Americans had failed to understand the nature of the political. The United Nations and international law were imagined as substitutes for power politics – while in fact they were simply new forums for it. The related opposition between peace-loving and aggressor States was only a step away from the juxtaposition of law-abiding and criminal ones. Such "legalistic exercises" were outright harmful: "At best, they have left the political issues where they found them; at worst, they have embittered international relations and thus made a peaceful settlement of the great political issues more difficult."[92]

By 1951, Morgenthau had thoroughly adapted to the American context, writing confidently in the first person plural about the virtuous realism of the foreign policy of the founding fathers – particularly Alexander Hamilton – and the disappointing policies of the "present

---

[89] Morgenthau, *In Defense of the National Interest*, pp. 69–81.
[90] Morgenthau, *In Defense of the National Interest*, pp. 105–113.
[91] Morgenthau, *In Defense of the National Interest*, p. 94.
[92] Morgenthau, *In Defense of the National Interest*, p. 102.

administration" in Europe and China. Now he showed himself both an *enfant terrible* and an unflinching patriot,[93] a conservative through and through with deep suspicion against public opinion and control of foreign policy. By contrast, the national leader appears almost like Schmitt's commissarial dictator whose position was not contrary to but a confirmation of the substance (if not the process) of general will.[94] The analysis did not have any significant room for law: the "vital objective" of US foreign policy had to be the restoration of the balance of power.[95] Law, if needed, would come later: to uphold the status quo.[96] The concrete order – balance of power – had first to be set up. And this was an irreducibly political task.

International law and politics: an asymmetrical relationship

Morgenthau confessed that his 1929 dissertation had been conceived partly as a reply to the first edition of Schmitt's *Der Begriff des politischen*. Its ostensible purpose was to conduct an enquiry into the limits of the judicial and arbitral function in the international field – a rather standard object of scholarly interest in the 1920s. Behind the legal–dogmatic surface, however, it is not difficult to detect a somewhat anxious attempt to come to terms with the relationship between law and politics in international life and, particularly, to develop an explanation for what it was that made international law such a fragile structure.[97]

Morgenthau's thesis revolved around the apparent paradox that though there were no objective reasons for why the legal process could not be used for the resolution of any kinds of international conflicts, in practice only a very small number were submitted to it.[98] Although

---

[93] Alfons Söllner, "German Conservatism in America: Morgenthau's Political Realism" (1987), 72 *Telos*, p. 169.
[94] Morgenthau, *In Defense of the National Interest*, pp. 229 et seq, 241–242.
[95] Morgenthau, *In Defense of the National Interest*, p. 159.
[96] Morgenthau, *In Defense of the National Interest*, p. 144.
[97] My reading has been much influenced by Pekka Korhonen, *Hans Morgenthau. Intellektuaalinen Historia* (Jyväskylän yliopisto, valtio-opin laitos; *Julkaisuja*, 43, 1983), pp. 12–39 as well as the very useful Christoph Frei, *Hans J. Morgenthau. Eine intellektuelle Biographie* (2nd edn., St. Galler Studien zur Politikwissenschaft, Berne, Stuttgart, and Wien, Haupt, 1994).
[98] Hans Morgenthau, *Die internationale Rechtspflege, ihr Wesen und ihre Grenzen* (Leipzig, Noske, 1929), pp. 56–57. The original manuscript bore a longer title: *Die internationale Rechtspflege, das Wesen ihrer Organe und die Grenzen ihrer Anwendung; insbesondere der Begriff des politischen im Völkerrecht*. Frei, *Hans J. Morgenthau*, p. 130n45.

scholarship and practice had long attempted to provide a criterion for the definition of questions that were suitable for legal settlement, no definite criterion had emerged. From a formal perspective, as Kelsen, Lauterpacht, and others had insisted, it was always possible for a tribunal to proceed to a decision: if the claimant had no right (that is to say, even in the absence of an applicable norm), then her claim was to be dismissed. In this sense, there were no limits to justiciability. But in practice, States refused to bring their grievances to third-party settlement – in particular if they appeared to deal with their "vital interests" or "national honor." The problem that worried lawyers was whether it was possible to define such notions – and hence the notion of the "political" – in a way that would be opposable to the State making such claim. For otherwise there seemed to exist no binding third-party settlement at all. Morgenthau's contribution to this debate was to show that no such delimitation was possible.

For instance, it was often suggested that a dispute was "political" if it related to the personality or the individuality of the State. But these perceptions were completely phenomenological, determined by the State's own self-image. It seemed impossible to oppose to a State a deviating conception of its identity. Nor could a definition be attained by reference to "vital interests" or "national honor": these, too, were dependent on what the State happened to hold important.[99] Nor, finally, did the mere fact that regulation was lacking in some area ("gap in law") define it as "political": nothing prevented States from agreeing to submit disputes about such questions to equitable settlement. This showed that the political had no fixed substance. Instead, it was better thought of as a quality that could be attached to *any* object, and no object was *essentially* free from becoming political in this sense. To say that something was "political" was to describe it in terms of the degree of intensity with which that object was linked to the State, to give it "a certain coloring, a determined nuance in contrast to anything substantial."[100] Anything might be, and nothing was necessarily political, including any question over which a court might possess jurisdiction.[101] The "political" and "legal" were not symmetrically related to each other:

---

[99] Morgenthau, *Die internationale Rechtspflege*, pp. 105–107, 119 *et seq.*
[100] Morgenthau, *Die internationale Rechtspflege*, p. 70.
[101] Morgenthau, *Die internationale Rechtspflege*, pp. 62–72. For Morgenthau, the concept of the political and the concept of national "honor" covered an identical space, *ibid.* pp. 127–128.

The "legal" and the "political" are not at all an adequate pair of concepts that could enter into a determinate contrast. The conceptual counterpart of the concept of political is formed by the concept of the non-political but not by the concept of "legal question" which, for its part, can be both political or non-political.[102]

Absence of symmetry meant that the political always loomed large over any legal substance, prepared to overtake it in case the State started to feel intensely enough about it. This conclusion showed that Schmitt's attempt in the first edition of *Der Begriff des Politischen* to work with an autonomous sphere of "the political" had been flawed. Questions initially having to do with morality, economy, or culture became political as soon as the protagonists started to feel strongly about them. In a way, Morgenthau understood Schmitt better than Schmitt himself: the relationship of the political to the legal in his 1929 dissertation came quite close to how Schmitt had conceived the relationship between the sovereign and the constitution in his *Political Theology*, or the (political) exception that prevailed over (legal) normality while remaining uncontrolled by it.

These arguments led Morgenthau to distinguish between two kinds of international conflicts: "disputes" (*Streitigkeiten*) that could be expressed in legal claims and "tensions" (*Spannungen*) that cannot be so expressed because they seek a transformation of legal rights and duties.[103] While the former could usefully be dealt with by legal methods, the latter could not. This was not owing to any intrinsic impossibility: even tensions involved positive rights and duties that could be declared by a tribunal. But those rights and duties are overwhelmed by the intensity of the feelings of the participant States about them or about the context of which they were a part. For example, there was no doubt that the Versailles settlement constituted positive law. But its being so was completely overshadowed by the intensity of the feelings (especially in Germany) concerning its injustice. The controversy between the Allied and Associated powers on the one hand and Germany on the other could never be resolved by a tribunal. The "tension" was not about what positive law said but whether and how it should be changed.

From such a notion of politics it also followed that to which class a conflict belonged could not be determined by pre-existing criteria. Like Kaufmann in his work on *rebus sic stantibus*, Morgenthau dismissed the

---

[102] Morgenthau, *Die internationale Rechtspflege*, p. 62.
[103] Morgenthau, *Die internationale Rechtspflege*, pp. 73–84.

possibility that the political could be reduced to a legally circumscribed notion of *Notrecht*.[104] Moreover, disputes and tensions may also develop into each other. A long-standing dispute may become a symbolic incident in a tension – and the dispersal of a tension may be accompanied by its transformation into one or more disputes, amenable to legal resolution.[105] But no general definition could be given. Everything depends on how the matter was viewed by the national community itself.[106] But, Morgenthau also argued, although tensions cannot be successfully dealt with by formal dispute settlement, the legal system might nonetheless take account of them – or as he put it in the language of anti-formal legal theory: the law should change from a static to a dynamic order.[107] It should develop a mechanism that would reflect underlying political transformations and integrate new values and power relations while simultaneously limiting the right of resort to war.[108]

Morgenthau's intention was not to defend increasing recourse to third-party settlement. On the contrary, in his view the fact that disputes often referred to or developed into political tensions made them frequently inappropriate for such settlement: the judges' (unconscious) bias would do away with their trustworthiness; or it would appear that a large issue was being decided by reference to its marginal aspects.[109] In both cases, the essential precondition of justiciability – trust in the settlement organ by the parties – would be absent.[110] Moreover, the scope of tensions inappropriate for legal settlement could be broadly identified only in regard to particular situations. Therefore it was useless to strive for a universal arbitration treaty. Third-party settlement was not – as suggested by the "Schiboleth der Schiedsgerichtsbewegung" – a precondition for peace but a consequence thereof.[111] Nor could tensions be dealt

---

[104] Morgenthau, *Die internationale Rechtspflege*, pp. 102–104.
[105] Morgenthau, *Die internationale Rechtspflege*, pp. 80–83 and for a more elaborated account, cf. Hans Morgenthau, *La notion du "politique" et la théorie des différends internationaux* (Paris, Sirey, 1933), pp. 72–85.
[106] Morgenthau, *Die internationale Rechtspflege*, pp. 126–127.
[107] Morgenthau, *Die internationale Rechtspflege*, p. 27.
[108] Thus disputes about *Lebensinteressen* could be integrated into the law only by their exclusion from third-party settlement. Interestingly, like Schmitt, Morgenthau applied such exclusion, for example, to the Monroe Doctrine, whose content he, too, saw completely dependent on unilateral decision by the United States. As a leading power, the latter had extended it to include increasing US intervention in Europe and Asia, Morgenthau, *Die internationale Rechtspflege*, pp. 107–109.
[109] Morgenthau, *Die internationale Rechtspflege*, pp. 84–97.
[110] Morgenthau, *Die internationale Rechtspflege*, p. 84.
[111] Morgenthau, *Die internationale Rechtspflege*, pp. 95, 97.

through mediation or conciliation: their limits lay in exactly the same place as the limits of arbitration or adjudication, in the phenomenological world of politics. Though Morgenthau ended his dissertation by expressing the hope that a "system of values and norms" would develop that would enable the articulation of "tensions," too, in the language of legal claims, he refrained from speculating when such time might come, and left the reader in some doubt about his own faith in it.[112]

The dissertation was very well received. Morgenthau's Frankfurt supervisor Karl Strupp praised its scientific value and positive reviews were written by Lauterpacht as well as Paul Guggenheim from Geneva.[113] The book's originality lay in Morgenthau's employment of a psychologically oriented social theory. What "law" or "politics" meant could not be detached from the feelings that human beings had about them. Those "feelings," again, arose from a basic psychological drive: the desire for self-expression in and recognition by community.[114] This is why he identified the scope of "national honor" with that of the political.[115] Both resided in the realm of emotional projection; and could therefore not be delimited by legal–technical language. No external standards were authoritative and conflicts could be resolved only by struggle. Nonetheless, the institutionalization of drive-fulfillment was not outside the realm of the possible. In domestic society, there was a large consensus on how the societal changes brought about by the desire for self-expression and recognition should be reflected in law. But there was no such consensus – nor any such institutions – at the international level. Here lay international law's special weakness. A shift in power will always be accompanied by threat of violence: as with Schmitt, war remained an ever-present potentiality.[116]

It is not easy to see how, in the absence of formal legislation, law might "take account" of the vicissitudes of politics, understood in terms of a theory of drives, without ceasing to be law. In an admiring memorial article on Gustav Stresemann, Germany's influential foreign minister from 1923 to 1929, Morgenthau made the point that Stresemann's success lay in his ability to conduct a genuinely German *Völkerrechtspolitik*

---

[112] Morgenthau, *Die internationale Rechtspflege*, pp. 148–152.
[113] For reviews, cf. Paul Guggenheim (1929), 35/36 *Juristische Wochenzeitschrift*, p. 3469; Hersch Lauterpacht (1931), 30 *BYIL*, p. 229.
[114] "nach Selbsterhaltung und nach Geltung innerhalb des Gemeinschaft, kurz, von dem Triebe nach Erhaltung und Durchsetzung des Persönlichkeit." Morgenthau, *Die internationale Rechtspflege*, p. 74.
[115] Morgenthau, *Die internationale Rechtspflege*, pp. 119–128.
[116] Morgenthau, *Die internationale Rechtspflege*, p. 77.

vis-à-vis the Versailles settlement while at the same time strengthening the structures of international peace. Morgenthau agreed with the majority of Germans. The settlement – including the League of Nations – had been "in its original spiritual and political function alien to the German nature."[117] By securing Germany's membership in the League Stresemann had been able to transform the organization in accordance with the new European situation and to end Germany's spiritual isolation through means that did not involve the use of violence, indeed were opposed to it

This may have been a weak consolation, however, and certainly a doubtful argument for proving the law's importance. Later on, Morgenthau no longer saw the League as an effective instrument for guaranteeing the law's realism. Were Germany's successes in Geneva not precisely proof of the weakness of international law which, as he argued in his dissertation, lay in the fact that it was constantly penetrated by politics? "From that discovery there was but one step to the conclusion that what really mattered in relations among nations was not international law but international politics."[118]

The formation of a German thinker: between law and desire

On the basis of the positive reviews of his 1929 dissertation Morgenthau finally opted for the university. Until that point he had been uncertain about his future, having, as he recounts, chosen to study law not because he was interested in it but because his father would not let him study literature. Law was a second best as it "appeared to make the least demands on special skills and emotional commitment."[119] Although his dissertation dealt with a much-discussed international law topic, and his writing technique was completely in the style of the German legal academy, its main point deviated from (and was in part directed against) the type of legal formalism represented by the works of his supervisor Strupp. The originality of the thesis lay in its psychological understanding of power – a point of view Morgenthau never gave up. The view of social behavior determined by the desire for power became one of the

---

[117] ("in seiner ursprünglichen geistigen und politischen Funktion den deutschen Wesen fremd"), Hans Morgenthau, "Stresemann als Schöpfer der deutschen Völkerrechtspolitik" (1929), 5 *Die Justiz*, p. 176.
[118] Hans Morgenthau, "An Intellectual Autobiography" (1978), 15 (January/February), *Society*, p. 65.   [119] Morgenthau, "An Intellectual Autobiography," p. 63.

hallmarks of the "Realism" for which Morgenthau became the leading academic representative in United States after the war. That view is rooted in a specifically German intellectual trajectory which combines Morgenthau's personal experience with themes of discussion prevalent in the surrounding academic and political environment.

Morgenthau was born in Coburg, Northern Bavaria, in 1904 to an authoritarian father, a Jewish doctor and a German patriot, Ludwig Morgenthau. Three experiences – he himself recalls – conditioned his development. One was the antagonism to his father; nothing young Hans could do would satisfy him and they would always remain distant, even hostile. Hence Morgenthau's life-long aloofness, even timidity. This was not unconnected to a pervasive loneliness which he later theorized into an existential condition, an aspect of human imperfection. To seek friendship was to engage in a futile search for a perfection that belonged only to God. The inevitable frustration defined human life as tragedy.[120] Morgenthau's loneliness was not only attributable to his personal timidity, however. Coburg had suffered greatly from the post-war economic slump and had by 1922 become ready for Hitler. Antisemitism was pervasive in town and at school – the Gymnasium Casimirianum – and Morgenthau often later referred to the unhappiness of his school years as he was repeatedly ostracized and mocked by his schoolmates. One incident was particularly striking. As the first of his class, on April 11, 1922 he received the honor of delivering a speech to the graduates leaving the school and to lay a laurel on the statue of the Gymnasium's founder, Duke Johann Casimir. A photograph shows how during the address another Duke, Carl Eduard von Saxe-Coburg Gotha, sat in the front row holding his nose to show his contempt for the stinking Jew.[121]

A third important aspect of his youth was an intellectual ambition that translated not only to an almost neurotic desire to get the highest marks at every subject but also to a wish to counter the surrounding, predominantly hostile world by an unflinching hardness that he tried to attain by adopting the position of an outside observer, seeking to under-

---

[120] Hans Morgenthau, "The Significance of Being Alone" (Unpublished and undated paper, Morgenthau archives, Library of Congress, Washington, copy on file with author).

[121] The story is recounted in Frei, *Hans J. Morgenthau*, pp. 24–25 and in Kenneth W. Thompson, "Hans J. Morgenthau. Principles of Political Realism," in Thompson, *Masters of International Thought. Major Twentieth-Century Theorists and the World Crisis* (Baton Rouge and London, Louisiana State University Press, 1980), p. 81.

stand the world in its naked reality, and not though the superficial (religious, ethical, political) ideas through which it publicly justified itself. For this purpose, science seemed a necessary instrument – not just any science but one that would provide direct access to the existential condition of social life. Already Morgenthau's school essays manifest this determination.[122] It prompted him to study philosophy for his first semester at the University of Frankfurt in 1923; but he left it after half a year, disappointed with the superficially rationalist scientism *en vogue* there. Turning to law was hardly a better choice in that respect, but at least it provided the basis for a future livelihood.

It was not until after graduation in 1927, when he had taken the position of assistant to the notable socialist lawyer Hugo Sinzheimer (1875–1945), a former participant in the Weimar Assembly, the owner of a law firm specializing in labor law, and through him had come to know some of the most important legal and political thinkers in Germany, that Morgenthau was introduced into an intellectual *milieu* in which he felt that matters of existential and political significance were being discussed.[123] Among a predominantly socialist group of lawyers and philosophers, Morgenthau remained, however, a conservative. Although he visited the famous *Institut der Sozialforschung* in Frankfurt several times, and came to know its leading figures, he was frustrated by what he felt as the irrelevance of their abstract Marxist hair-splitting in face of the coming Nazi tide.[124]

Morgenthau had commenced writing his doctorate with Karl Neumeyer (1869–1941), a private international lawyer and a developer of "international administrative law" in Munich immediately after graduation. Despite his admiration for Neumeyer's realist teaching methods and ethical–cosmopolitan aspirations,[125] it was only after the new contacts he had received through Sinzheimer that his work started proceeding well. In his autobiography Morgenthau credits Max Weber as his intellectual father; and Weberian themes run through his writings, including the emphasis on power and the concern with the non-rational

---

[122] Frei, *Hans J. Morgenthau*, pp. 25–30.
[123] Those people included, for instance, Franz Neumann, Otto Kahn-Freund, Paul Tillich, and Martin Buber.
[124] Morgenthau, "An Intellectual Autobiography," pp. 66–67; Frei, *Hans J. Morgenthau*, pp. 42–43.
[125] For Morgenthau's assessment, cf. the obituary note he wrote after the Jewish Neumeyer had committed suicide with his wife in Munich at the age of 71 (1941), 35 *AJIL*, p. 672.

in social life. His biographer has, however, recently been able to find through his personal notebooks a life-long engagement with Nietzsche – an engagement of which Morgenthau chose to remain silent after his entry into the United States in 1937. During a period of depression about his future as a Jew in Germany in the winter semester 1925–1926, he had read Nietzsche's *Untimely Meditations*. "It belongs to the greatest pieces of good luck in one's spiritual life to bump into the right books at the right moment," he wrote in his diary later. It took Morgenthau forty months to read, with careful annotation, through Nietzsche's collected works. It is impossible here to try to assess Nietzsche's influence on Morgenthau's writing in detail. I find no reason to challenge, and much to support, the biographer's conclusion according to which Nietzsche's effect on Morgenthau is strongest as the image or ideal of a Promethean hero, a private justification for an intellectual attitude developed during the Coburg years but until the late 1920s without a style of public expression. What he admired in Nietzsche was his "*Blick des Sehers*," the clear vision of the analytic, the free spirit with the courage to look into the bottom of the soul.[126]

This had been the perspective that Morgenthau had employed – however timidly – in the analysis of the political in his dissertation. As an intensity concept, the political referred to the human psyche, more specifically to the innate desire for self-assertion whose relationship to that other primordial notion – the lust for power – was still undeveloped. The psychological perspective led Morgenthau to study Freud and the result of that confrontation the following year was a more than 100-page manuscript *On the Derivation of the Political from Human Nature*.[127] The text, written without scientific notation and almost without references, in a didactic style as if reality itself spoke through it, sought to ground the political in individual psychology: "Individuals are always the sole carriers of social forces."[128] In a section titled "Of the basic facts of psychical life" Morgenthau found the most basic of such facts to be 'life' itself.[129] However, "life" had no form of presence that would be independent from the drives that gave expression to it. There were two basic drives: the more primitive one that looked for self-preservation

---

[126] Frei, *Hans J. Morgenthau*, pp. 101–111.
[127] "Über die Herkunft des Politischen aus dem Wesen des Menschen" (Morgenthau Archive, Library of Congress, HJM-B-151, copy on file with author).
[128] "Träger aller gesellschaftlichen Kräfte sind immer nur Einzelmenschen," "Über die Herkunft des Politischen," p. 4.
[129] Morgenthau, "Über die Herkunft des Politischen," p. 5.

Carl Schmitt, Hans Morgenthau and "international relations"

(*Erhaltungstrieb*) and existed in humans and animals alike, and the drive for self-assertion (*Bewährungstrieb*), a higher-level drive that worked on the surplus of energy produced by the successful fulfillment of the self-preservation drive.

The drive to self-assertion worked, like all drives, under what Morgenthau chose to call the principle of desire (*Lustprincip*), a limitless source of energy that in social life looked for satisfaction through the establishment of a relationship of power: the ability of a psyche to be the cause of motivations in another.[130] The most sublime form of satisfaction for the drive to self-assertion, Morgenthau wrote, was constituted by psychological superiority (*Herrschaft*), as manifested in one's ability to be the cause of the behavior of another person. Often this could not be attained without resistance. In social life, the drives of individuals collided against each other; hence the permanent condition of struggle.[131] But if power was a necessary instrument for prevailing in struggle, it was not its main objective. The objective at an individual level remained the satisfaction of the drive and at a metaphysical level, life's becoming conscious of itself.

The manuscript was never published. Morgenthau later added a five-page preface to it, connecting it to the law/politics dichotomy that had been the object of his dissertation. The manuscript could be read as an attempt to elucidate just in what the "intensity" that defined politics lay; namely in the realm of drives and the desire principle. In an autobiographical note from 1978 Morgenthau distanced himself from the Freudian language of his early paper: its reductionism could not account for the "complexities and varieties of political experience."[132] But although the desire principle does not appear in his later writings, the notion of power remains psychologically grounded: the limits of law and rationality remain set by what Morgenthau continues to assume as the existential condition of an unending quest for power.

The period in Frankfurt after 1929 was for Morgenthau one of extraordinary activity. In carrying out his *Referendariat* as Sinzheimer's assistant Morgenthau had the occasion to acquaint himself professionally with the ambivalences of the fragile Republic. He sometimes pleaded on Sinzheimer's behalf before the Frankfurt labor court and occasionally attended it as a temporary member. He recounts of that experience: "What was decisive was not the merits of legal interpretation, but the

---

[130] Morgenthau, "Über die Herkunft des Politischen," p. 17.
[131] Morgenthau, "Über die Herkunft des Politischen," pp. 31–35, 43.
[132] Morgenthau, "An Intellectual Autobiography," p. 67.

distribution of political power. Most of the judges were passionately and sometimes openly hostile to the Republic and to the political parties and social structure supporting it."[133] Or, in another context: "The judges were generally very conservative, if not reactionary, and they hated, first of all they hated Jews."[134] Such experiences must have convinced Morgenthau about the futility of confidence in a formal law, however rational its principles of organization or however liberal its political ethos. Writing almost twenty years afterwards, Morgenthau had not the slightest hesitation to characterize Weimar, the Rule of Law and the liberal internationalism associated with the League of Nations, as forms of a *decadent* liberalism – in contrast to the "heroic" liberalism of the nineteenth century – that lacked the courage to see the truth of human society as an unending struggle for power.[135]

Although Morgenthau published little during that period, many of his later ideas can be found in a series of manuscripts and notes from that time. Aside from the derivation of the political from human nature, conceived as a function of innate drives, and inspired by a proto-existentialist *Lebensphilosophie*, Morgenthau also prepared a polemical fifty-page review of German pacifism and the "new war philosophy" popularized in the writings of Ernst Jünger. The review was submitted for publication in January 1931 but was rejected – perhaps for the reason that the engagement with Jünger revealed a fascination with the latter's dramatic style and his exaltation of the war experience that was not effectively offset by the suggested sublimation in more constructive social activities.[136] The essay was prefaced by a quotation from Nietzsche's *Gay Science* that explained its title: war is but a suicide, but a suicide with good conscience. The title was a gloss on Jünger and reveals the asymmetrical interest the author has for his two subjects.

Morgenthau dismissed the "organized pacifism" of Alfred Fried, Walther Schücking and others lightly, and perhaps unjustly, as unable to understand the irrationality of politics. The war, he wrote, had demonstrated that society was no machine. Peoples did not want peace. In 1914, they desired the excitement of the war and enjoyed the passion and the distance from their grey everyday lives it promised. Moreover,

[133] Morgenthau, "An Intellectual Autobiography," p. 65.
[134] Frei, *Hans J. Morgenthau*, p. 41.
[135] Hans Morgenthau, *Scientific Man vs. Power Politics* (University of Chicago Press, 1946), pp. 41 *et seq*, 68–71.
[136] Hans Morgenthau, "Der Selbstmord mit guten Gewissen. Zur Kritik des Pazifismus und der neuen deutschen Kriegsphilosophie" (Morgenthau Archive, Library of Congress, HJM-B-96, copy on file with author).

pacifism was itself an instrument of irrationality by providing justifications for war – namely war as "sanction" by the League of Nations. Like Schmitt, Morgenthau tried to penetrate through humanitarian rhetoric: war for humanitarian purpose was no less war and no amount of tinkering with definitions ("sanction") could alter this. In the absence of effective mechanisms of legislative change, war will have to remain a present possibility, the ultimate means to fight injustice. In fact, Morgenthau quipped, pacifism and war philosophy differed only in which values they invoked to justify war.[137]

Morgenthau's lengthy quotations from Jünger align his text with the latter's powerful expressionism. The attempt to come to terms with the irrational by embracing it with full force was not too alien to what Morgenthau saw himself doing. To create distance from Jünger, Morgenthau espoused a rationalism that was at odds with the rest of the article but surfaced constantly in his later writings, too, creating the sense of contradiction that has so puzzled later commentators. He agreed with Jünger that the official justifications for war were really nothing; war was sought for the inner experience it provided, the experience of energy, danger, "life" in an authentic non-bourgeois sense. Where Jünger's vitalism failed, Morgenthau claimed, was in providing no explanation for why it still contradicted human conscience. By not treating that contradiction, but dismissing it, Jünger was pushed into extreme subjectivism. Only the inner experience became important. Like the pacifists, Jünger failed to understand that politics is always inter-subjective, a social relationship. Although expressed as a vindication of "life," Jünger's vitalism became an escape from (social) life, into death.[138] Subjective experience became a stand-in for reality – and war a "suicide with good conscience." But modern, technological warfare was doing away with struggle as Jünger admired it. Mass murder on an industrial scale provided little room for *Kampf als inneres Erlebnis*: the bomb falls and you die.[139] Morgenthau sought a solution in the Freudian theory of sublimation: even if drives determine behavior, they can be directed into constructive purposes.[140] Contrary to what was suggested in Jünger's Gothic escapism, or Spengler's popular legends, Europe was not (quite) dead yet; there was room for spiritual growth. The real battlefield, Morgenthau ended by observing, was not provided by war but by culture, politics, and

---

[137] Morgenthau, "Der Selbstmord mit guten Gewissen," pp. 2–13.
[138] Morgenthau, "Der Selbstmord mit guten Gewissen," pp. 23–25.
[139] Morgenthau, "Der Selbstmord mit guten Gewissen," pp. 23, 30.
[140] Morgenthau, "Der Selbstmord mit guten Gewissen," pp. 32–35.

economy that enabled the satisfaction of the drives without contradicting "life itself."

The two unpublished essays from 1930 examined politics as an effect of drives embedded in human nature and employed a theory of sublimation to account for enlightenment. No doubt, such an apparatus made it possible to understand some of the developments in the surrounding society. As Morgenthau's *Referendariat* came to an end in 1931, it turned out impossible for him to secure a university post in Frankfurt or elsewhere in Germany. This may not have been exclusively caused by his ethnic background. The economic situation had gone from bad to worse and large numbers of young academics were competing for diminishing opportunities. Through Sinzheimer's contacts, Morgenthau was finally invited to take a position as teacher of German public law at the University of Geneva.

For his trial lecture, Morgenthau chose to speak on the *Struggle of German Theory of the State over the Reality of the State*.[141] Here he had the opportunity to evaluate – and of course, mostly to criticize – the tradition in which he was educated. The result was an extremely ambitious thirty-page lecture that linked three phases of German public law theory from Jellinek to Kelsen and finally to Schmitt to developments in German politics and culture. The leading thread was a move from idealism to reality – that is to say, to an increasingly "realist" theory of the State. In Morgenthau's account, Jellinek's humanistic eclecticism was a clear advance over Laband's formalism; his theory of ideal types, his use of the history of ideas, and the doctrine of the "normative power of the factual" each constituted a step towards a coherent and descriptively accurate conception of the State. Unfortunately, Bismarckian reality did not lend itself to classification by typology or principles. If Kelsen went beyond Jellinek in his recognition of the contradictory character of the reality of Wilhelminian politics, his response – to withdraw from this reality altogether – could not be sustained: "pure law" did not provide solutions to actual problems. Only recently had lawyers focused on the political as the central reality of the State, even if so far in an unsystematic way. Morgenthau appreciated Rudolf Smend's (1882–1975) theory of social integration as the core reality of statehood – but criticized its

---

[141] The original French lecture bore simply the title "La doctrine et l'évolution de la théorie de l'Etat en Allemagne." The title of the German translation which closely reflected its contents was "Der Kampf der deutschen Staatslehre um die Wirklichkeit des Staates" (Morgenthau Archive, Library of Congress, HJM-B-110. Copies of the French lecture as well as the German translation are both on file with author).

insufficient grounding. If the State was torn apart by political antagonism, what point was there in restating the theoretical principle of unity? Morgenthau shared Schmitt's anti-formalism and admired his "uncommon spiritual intensity and certainty of instinct." But Schmitt's insights and critiques had never amounted to more than fragments. He had gone only half way, failing to see that what lay at the heart of the political was the unchanging psyche of the human being, the lust for power.[142] Morgenthau ended his lecture with a call for a new, psychologically based theory of the State – the theory he was working on.

The engagement with Schmitt peaked in Morgenthau's second book that was published in Paris in 1933 under the title *La notion du "politique" et la théorie des différends internationaux*. Written in a tangled French, it applied his new ideas to the subject-matter of his dissertation. The first half recapitulated the criticism of the alleged opposition between "legal" and "political" disputes and the definition of the political as an intensity concept. The positivist attempt to produce a clear line between "political" and "legal" disputes had failed.[143] In a twenty-page critique Morgenthau disputed Schmitt's theory of the friend–enemy distinction as what defined politics in a way that was analogous to the distinctions good–bad that characterized morality or beautiful–ugly that was the basis of aesthetics. The latter oppositions were derived from the quality of the relevant sphere: goodness and evil were tautologically related to morality like beautiful and ugly defined aesthetic value. In politics, the parallel opposition was between political–non-political or, possibly, politically valuable–politically non-valuable. The friend–enemy distinction was merely a personalized derivation from the more fundamental distinction between political worth and absence of such worth. Friends were politically worthy but friendship did not exhaust political worth. Enemies were undoubtedly harmful but there were other harmful things besides them.[144] Morgenthau saw the friend–enemy opposition as ultimately metaphysical, and as such beyond rational debate. The critique was not completely beside the point – but it did reflect a limited reading of the friend–enemy distinction. More significant is what unites the two Weimar lawyers: the sense of the political as a struggle that knew no intrinsic limits. Where Schmitt's understanding of this reality was ultimately religious,

---

[142] Frei, *Hans J. Morgenthau*, p. 124. On Morgenthau's wish to inaugurate a psychological theory of the State, cf. *ibid.* p. 125 and on Freud's influence, cf. Morgenthau, "An Intellectual Autobiography," p. 67.
[143] Morgenthau, *La notion du "politique,"* pp. 10–42.
[144] Morgenthau, *La notion du "politique,"* pp. 44–61.

Morgenthau chose to describe it in psychological terms. Far from a radical opposition, the engagement seemed more like sectarian struggle over orthodoxy.

The 1933 book explained the problems of international law from a psychologically based social theory. The political was of course a sociological fact. But "[w]hat is common to such sociological facts is that they all have their basis, as a psychological factor, in the will to power [volonté de puissance]."[145] Facts about States, too, are ultimately determined by the psychology of individuals.[146] In social life the principle of desire is translated into the lust for power that has three political forms of expression: the politics of the status quo (use of power in order to preserve a state of affairs advantageous to oneself); the politics of imperialism (the use of power to effect a change to one's advantage); and the politics of prestige (the use of power to manifest power, to assert oneself).[147] This threefold schema – included in Morgenthau's 1948 textbook and today the stuff of introductory courses at international relations departments – comes directly from the unpublished 1930 essay on *Herkunft des Politischen*.

Law sought to respond to the politics of the status quo by delimiting domains of power into spheres of jurisdiction and to the politics of imperialism through its rules of change. On both scores, international law was deficient. Although it did possess rules of delimitation, it was powerless to enforce them. And it was almost totally devoid of rules of change. Though all law had a preference for the status quo, international law had a real obsession to this effect.[148] Therefore it became unrealistic when status quo powers were not winning. As pressure for change increases, international law will break down. There is no magic formula for coping with such situations. True, sometimes a tension may be successfully converted into a (legal) dispute – the *Alabama* arbitration (1871) was one example. On the other hand, it may also happen that an originally legal dispute changes into (the symbol of) a political tension. In such case, it no longer can be dealt with by reference to law but involves a challenge to it.[149] At the end of his book, Morgenthau gave up the nor-

---

[145] Morgenthau, *La notion du "politique,"* p. 43.
[146] "Les constatations que nous avons pu faire dans le domaine de la vie humaine en général trouvent leur vérification dans le domaine de la vie des Etats," Morgenthau, *La notion du "politique,"* p. 61.
[147] Morgenthau, *La notion du "politique,"* p. 61. The irrationality of politics is, of course, most apparent in the third category: here subjective feelings dominate.
[148] Morgenthau, *La notion du "politique,"* pp. 66–71.
[149] Morgenthau, *La notion du "politique,"* pp. 79–85.

mative concerns and expressly refrained from a policy proposal – a rare thing for him to do.[150] It may not be a surprise that in 1933, Morgenthau saw much less prospect for a reform towards a "dynamic" law than four years earlier.

The guardian of international law: sanctions

Morgenthau's last legal book – his *Habilitationsschrift* in Geneva – *La réalité des normes. En particulier des normes du droit international* (1934) – was heavily influenced by Kelsen, though his attitude towards formalism remained unrepentantly Schmittian. Neokantianism was "the faithful expression of the decadence of philosophical thought at German universities at the end of the last century."[151] Morgenthau adopted from Kelsen a stress on "validity" as the distinguishing property of legal (as against moral or social) norms, but conceived it in psychological terms as the norm's abstract ability to determine the content of someone's will.[152] Normative relations became – like any other social relations – relations of will: the creator of the norm sought to impose his will on that of the addressee. Whether or not this succeeds is dependent on the existence of sanction: "human will can only be determined by the expectation of pleasure or fear of pain [déplaisir]."[153] Instead of pure ought Morgenthau wanted to examine the reality of the legal ought, the *Sein* of Kelsen's *Sollen*.

This was no longer a study *in* law but a study *of* law: Morgenthau now became the external observer in regard to law as well, the anthropologist or the analyst of law, instead of its practitioner. The *Sein* of law could be only psychological or physical. Through sanctions, it could be both. The fear of sanction was the psychological reality of norms that brought about conformity as the physical reality. If the expectation of sanction is missing, then the norm lacks reality: "We have today come to the conclusion that the essential problem must be seen in the nature of sanctions."[154] The essential question is whether someone can in fact send in the police.

Morgenthau's views of human nature and motivation left no space for a law that would be anything but an instrument of causality whereby one

---

[150] Morgenthau, *La notion du "politique,"* pp. 86–90.
[151] Hans Morgenthau, *La réalité des normes. En particulier des normes du droit international* (Paris, Alcan, 1934), p. xi.
[152] Morgenthau, *La réalité des normes*, pp. 25–29. Also Kelsenian are his emphasis on the analytical distinction between "le point de vue sociologique et le point de vue normatif" as well as the view of the State as the sphere of validity of State law, pp. 214–216. [153] Morgenthau, *La réalité des normes*, p. 46.
[154] Morgenthau, *La réalité des normes*, p. 242.

will determines the content of another will. Such (Nietzschean) outlook finds no social reality for morality, or natural law, beyond hypocrisy.[155] An invocation of natural law is to throw an ideological veil over the relations of will thus justified. Such justification may be an indispensable element of social stability, or for overcoming constitutional crises.[156] But it is never the ultimate reason, or guarantor, of the constitution. This guarantor is the executive body that has the power to put the sanctions into effect – an executive power that is internationally constituted by the balance of power.

Morgenthau's analysis resembles the discussion between Kelsen and Schmitt over the validity of the (Weimar) constitution, or who is its "guardian."[157] He distinguishes between the "guardian" of the international legal system *in toto* and that of its individual norms. As the former is the person that holds executive power, he comes to the apparently inevitable, yet odd suggestion that the international legal system is "ultimately" guaranteed by the Heads of State of the members of the international community.[158] The sanction of the rest of international law is determined by the public opinion: "the totality of the people that belong to the international community would then be the carriers of the norm's validity."[159] Such a defense by Morgenthau of international law's reality was at best only half-hearted.[160] That his discussion

---

[155] Which is not to say, however, that Morgenthau would join Nietzsche in going "beyond good and evil." He seems to grant the existence of natural law but locates it beyond political discourse. Morality's "validity" is always relative to the individual's conscience, *La réalité des normes*, p. 53. If natural law can express itself only through voluntary law, it is relative to the community's view and the possibility of ideology or "error" can never be excluded, Morgenthau, *La réalité des normes*, pp. 41–43.

[156] Morgenthau, *La réalité des normes*, pp. 43–44.

[157] Cf. David Dyzenhaus, *Legality and Legitimacy. Carl Schmitt, Hans Kelsen and Hermann Heller in Weimar* (Oxford, Clarendon, 1997), pp. 70–85, 108–123. In *Politics among Nations. The Struggle for Power and Peace* (New York, Knopf, 1948) the same theme is discussed in connection with sovereignty. Here Morgenthau moves from a Kelsenian conception of "sovereignty" as "supreme *legal* authority" (p. 248, italics mine) to a Schmittian notion under which such supremacy is a function of struggle between contending forces that lies normally dormant but asserts itself "in times of crisis" (p. 261).

[158] Morgenthau, *La réalité des normes*, pp. 217–219. Morgenthau holds this situation analogous to the Middle Ages when the Emperor was the secular arm of the Church, pp. 222–223n2. Possibly under Kelsen's influence Morgenthau describes States as aggregates of individuals, united in States that, when carrying out sanctions, "remplissent ici une fonction internationale déterminée," p. 233.

[159] Morgenthau, *La réalité des normes*, p. 220.

[160] The chapter on sanctions in international law is expressly written in the form of a defense against the "deniers," Morgenthau, *La réalité des normes*, pp. 223–224.

remained – paradoxically – wholly conceptual and made no reference to examples from international life emphasizes its fragility. And he conceded that the fact that normative validity ("the abstract capacity of the norm to determine the will of a person") in international law is highly relative meant that the number of its valid norms was significantly smaller than the number exposed in standard treatises.[161]

Morgenthau had difficulty in having his book accepted as a *Habilitation*. Only after the setting up of a second examination board, chaired by Kelsen, and Kelsen's unreservedly positive assessment, did Morgenthau finally receive his *Habilitation* in the spring of 1934.[162] At that time, however, his financial and professional situation in Geneva had become unbearable. After several attempts to find a teaching job in Europe – Germany was already out of the question – Morgenthau received a position at a recently established research institute for international studies in Madrid (*Instituto de Estudios Internacionales y Económicos*), teaching and publishing on international law with an emphasis on matters relative to Spain. This period came to an abrupt end in the summer of 1936 as the Morgenthaus found out that the civil war prevented their return to Madrid from a holiday abroad. They were left stranded first in Italy and then in France and Switzerland, with practically all their property left back in besieged Madrid, their valuables confiscated by the republican government as (German) enemy property. After a year's odyssey around Europe, and successive failures to get a visa to the United States, the Morgenthaus finally boarded a steam ship on July 17, 1937 from Antwerp to New York, with a visa received on the strength of the declarations by a second cousin to Frau Morgenthau, Samuel Rothschild.[163]

During his Spanish period Morgenthau updated and summarized the themes of his *Habilitation* in a two-part article on the theory of international sanctions. Although the article was written for an audience of international lawyers, it was targeted against ideas about morality and public opinion as bases for international lawfulness. The article was composed of a general theory of sanctions (a very detailed classification of elements and types of sanctions) which was applied in the international realm. A norm was a "prescription of will," its validity the

---

[161] Morgenthau, *La réalité des normes*, p. 227.
[162] Cf. Frei, *Hans J. Morgenthau*, pp. 51–56. Morgenthau was particularly disappointed at the sharp criticism from a Jewish colleague and a friend, Paul Guggenheim.
[163] Cf. Frei, *Hans J. Morgenthau*, pp. 65–70.

"abstract capacity of the norm to determine someone's will," and its effectiveness its power to do so *in concreto*. The reality of a legal norm was determined by its being accompanied by a sanction (a "measure of constraint that intervenes when the norm is violated") that was actually effective, that is to say, capable of "breaking the recalcitrant will."[164] From this definition Morgenthau arrived at a critique of pacifism and a stress on the balance of power as the condition for the reality of international law.

The critique of pacifism followed from the insistence that sanctions be not only enacted but actually effective for legal rules to have reality. It was a paradox, of course, that States had to prepare to use force in order to prevent force – "to pursue civilization by barbaric means."[165] In the absence of centralized sanctions–employment organs, however, no other conclusion was possible. The Anglo-American opposition to sanctions and reliance on public opinion was undermined by the degree to which public opinion was a fragile, manipulable aspect of democratic life. It may have significance in parliamentary democracies – even there its whimsicality was notorious – but remained absolutely useless in autocracies.[166] For a sanction to be effective, it must be able to break the resistance of its target. For national criminal law, that was normally no problem and if it is, then revolution was at hand. Internationally, the presence of overwhelming public force was an exception, however, and in the normal situation different interpretations confronted each other with some amount of force on each side. Like Kelsen, Morgenthau described international conflict as the clash of two effective national systems of sanctions whose relationship can only show their relative power:[167] "The functioning of sanctions in international law is thus of the simplest kind: everyone defends his legal position against everyone else, and reprisals serve as sanction."[168] The establishment of a balance of power marks the movement from anarchy to order. The hope of the anti-sanction school of relying on principles of justice or the harmony of interests was but "an unrealizable dream": "The justice of one is necessarily the injustice of another." To struggle for absolute justice was to lose both relative justice and peace. Such an attitude may be proper for moralists or revolutionaries, but not for the jurist for whom belongs the "tragic task" to argue not on moral or political legitimacy but on what is actually

---

[164] Hans Morgenthau, "Théorie des sanctions internationales" (1935), 3/16 *RDI*, pp. 478–483, 490. [165] Morgenthau, "Théorie," p. 496.
[166] Morgenthau, "Théorie," pp. 812–820.
[167] Morgenthau, "Théorie," pp. 493–495. [168] Morgenthau, "Théorie," p. 825.

there.[169] The Covenant or the Locarno Treaty had changed nothing: power remained in the hands of States and the legal order of the treaties was guaranteed only by the relative equilibrium between them.[170]

Schmitt and Morgenthau: the pedigree of anti-formalism

Morgenthau wrote his legal swan song from his position as lecturer at the University of Kansas City – the famous 1940 article that criticized the way international law was "paying almost no attention to the psychological and sociological laws governing the actions of men in the international sphere."[171] From the safety of across the Atlantic he described inter-war formalism as an "attempt to exorcize social evils by the indefatigable repetition of magic formulae."[172] Like German public law positivists, international lawyers had grasped at an illusion. Like the Weimar constitution, international law had become alien to "rules of international law as they are actually applied." Formalism's error lay in its dogmatic reliance on a notion of "validity" that qualified as law rules that were not actually applied, and failed to include all rules that were.

Morgenthau called for interdisciplinarity: lawyers should no longer remain blind to the "sociological context of economic interests, social tensions, and aspirations of power, which are the motivating forces in the international field."[173] They should also develop a better understanding of the relationship between law and ethics. For law made constant reference to ethical principles and "the successful search for these principles is as essential for the scientific understanding of international law as of any legal system."[174] The 1940 article was written as a prelude for an anti-formalist jurisprudence that would hark back to sociology and ethics. Such jurisprudence would not receive the meaning of a treaty, for

---

[169] Morgenthau, "Théorie," pp. 829, 830. This was very close to Weber's famous argument against an ethics of ultimate ends and for an ethics of responsibility in "Politics as Vocation," in *From Max Weber: Essays in Sociology* (trans., ed. and with an Introd. by H. H. Gerth and C. Wright Mills, London, Routledge, 1967), esp. pp. 117–128.

[170] Morgenthau, "Théorie," pp. 830–833. For Morgenthau, the modification of this situation – and the creation of an international community – would require three steps: the establishment of an international morality, the suppression of State sovereignty, and the conviction among the most influential members of this "international community" that the legal system created by it is actually legitimate, "Théorie," pp. 833–834.

[171] Hans Morgenthau, "Positivism, Functionalism and International Law" (1940), 34 *AJIL*, p. 283.

[172] Morgenthau, "Positivism," p. 260   [173] Morgenthau, "Positivism," p. 269.

[174] Morgenthau, "Positivism," p. 268.

instance, from its words but from the social context and the objective the treaty was to fulfill.[175] It would anchor legal validity not to formal legislation but to the likelihood of effective sanction and predict when sanctions might follow.[176]

But Morgenthau never developed such anti-formalist jurisprudence. Instead, he stopped writing about international law and became the theorist of power with idiosyncratic views about responsible statesmanship who is now known as the father of "Realism" in international relations. By contrast, Schmitt continued to speculate about the new international law that he saw taking the place of decadent formalism. At that point the intellectual paths of the two Weimar lawyers separated. While Schmitt saw the new *nomos* articulate a "legal world revolution," Morgenthau depicted the principal aspects of the post-war order as a realm of (pure) power, and of politics, but not of law. In order to determine where precisely the two differed, and what choices were opened to international lawyers by their shared anti-formalism, it is convenient to summarize the five points at which their paths did converge.

First, for both, an era – the European era – had come to an end. A political, technological, and moral revolution had undermined the balance of power that had dominated Victorian normality. Inter-war formalism had collapsed in face of the realities of "power." The informal opposition between the blocs now set the absolute conditions for international co-operation, diplomacy and law. It also provided an atmosphere of crisis that threatened to collapse into a full-scale nuclear destruction. The liberals had conceived technology as an instrument of peace. Schmitt and Morgenthau saw it as a means for political control, total war, and world domination.[177] Legal normality was formed by reference to the extreme situation – the nuclear catastrophe – that dictated the conditions under which lawyers could work.[178]

---

[175] Morgenthau, "Positivism," p. 282.
[176] Morgenthau, "Positivism," pp. 276–280. Morgenthau acknowledged his debt to Legal Realism, p. 274n43. But he was otherwise closer to Schmitt than to the American anti-formalists.
[177] Morgenthau, *Politics among Nations*, pp. 292–305. Cf. also Hans Morgenthau, "The National Socialist Doctrine on World Organization" (1943), Proceedings of the Seventh Conference of Teachers of International Law and Related Subjects, Washington DC, April 23–25, 1941, p. 107.
[178] For example, Morgenthau argued that a fundamental distinction was to be made between international law that dealt with stable interests (diplomatic privileges, jurisdiction, extradition of criminals, and maritime law) and the "political law" that was subservient to the play of shifting interests. This in fact repeated the distinction between important and unimportant matters and relegated international law firmly into the latter, Morgenthau, "Positivism," pp. 278–280.

Second, both Weimar lawyers saw the international order determined by a concrete distribution of power that automatically undermined sovereign equality. For Morgenthau, power was an incident of resources and foreign policy had to do with the constant redefinition of the national interest by reference to the resources available to the State. From the perspective of international order, what counted was whether a breach would be followed by a reaction. And this was a function of interest and resources, not of legislation.[179] Whatever international order may be attainable was: "predicated upon the existence of national communities capable of preserving order and realizing moral values within the limits of their power."[180] Moreover, "social force" could lie within States, but it could also lie with groups of States, or concentrations of ideological, economic, or military interest. A "competitive quest for power will determine the victorious social forces, and the change of the existing legal order will be decided, not though a legal procedure . . . but through a conflagration of conflicting social forces which challenge the legal order as a whole."[181]

Third, Morgenthau followed Schmitt in interpreting international law as part of the liberal strategy of depoliticization. Liberalism, both argued, saw international conflict as an atavistic residue of primitive ages that was to be replaced by the rational management of the States system, economics, and the harmony of interests.[182] International law would channel political tensions into committees, assemblies, and formal dispute settlement mechanisms. All of this was illusion. Depoliticization was a politics by the status quo powers to consolidate their advantages. Economy and free trade were instruments of the middle classes against old privileges, or the United States towards the world at large.[183] What Morgenthau had to say about the League Assembly echoes what Schmitt said about the Weimar Parliament: "political problems were never solved but only tossed about and finally shelved according to the rules of the legal game." This was repeated in the UN's dealing with the crises in Greece, Spain, Indonesia and Iran: "These cases have provided opportunities for exercises in parliamentary procedure, but on no occasion has even an attempt been made of facing the political issues of which these situations are surface manifestations."[184] To think of the Versailles Treaty as "law," Schmitt had argued, was to fail to understand

---

[179] Morgenthau, "Positivism," pp. 276–278.
[180] Morgenthau, *In Defense of the National Interest*, pp. 38, 117–121.
[181] Morgenthau, "Positivism," p. 276. [182] Morgenthau, *Scientific Man*, pp. 41–71.
[183] Morgenthau, *Scientific Man*, pp. 77–81, 83–84.
[184] Morgenthau, *Scientific Man*, p. 119.

its role in buttressing Anglo-American hegemony.[185] To have expected the Soviet Union to abide by its Yalta commitments, Morgenthau wrote later, was to have no understanding of its political objectives or of its readiness to repudiate the agreement.[186] Both empires, the American and the Soviet, subscribed to non-intervention – yet both intervened constantly and as soon as their interests seemed threatened. The only relevant principle was "selectivity" – the assessment of intervention and non-intervention through the careful balancing of the pros and cons in light of available resources.[187]

Fourth, the use or moralizing and legalistic language intensified international conflicts. "Peace-loving nations," Morgenthau claimed, would be in constant war against "criminal" ones. The new just war would distinguish between "belligerents whose participation is justified in ethics and law, and those who are not considered to have the legal and moral right to take up arms."[188] The result would be a "fight to the death or to 'unconditional surrender' of all those who adhere to another, a false and evil, 'ideal' and 'way of life.'"[189] In the total wars of modern ideologies, there was no longer any "framework of shared beliefs and common values." National "ethical systems" had come to present themselves as universal in a way that rendered compromise and accommodation impossible.[190]

Fifth, the critiques of legal and moral principles shifted attention to the decisions in which they received meaning in the context of political struggle. Schmitt had already undertaken a critique of the idea of

---

[185] Schmitt, *Kernfrage*, pp. 37–42.
[186] Morgenthau, *Scientific Man*, p. 105. Despite its rationalist aura, collective security, for instance, had been "simply a rationalization of the French desire for security, that is, the rationalization of French foreign policy in a certain period of history." Morgenthau, "The National Socialist Doctrine," p. 104. The use of moralistic language had become banally accepted through the American rhetoric during its involvement in the two world wars. Yet, this had not led to a world of formal legality or moral politics – only a "battle over the minds of men." Morgenthau, *In Defense of the National Interest*, pp. 208–210.
[187] Hans Morgenthau, *A New Foreign Policy for the United States* (New York, Washington, and London, Praeger, 1969), pp. 111 *et seq.* 113, 128.
[188] Morgenthau, *Politics among Nations*, p. 289.
[189] "The moral duty to spare the wounded, the sick, the surrendering and unarmed enemy, and to respect him as a human being an enemy only by virtue of being found on the other side of the fence, is superseded by the moral duty to punish and to wipe off the face of the earth the professors and practitioners of evil," Morgenthau, *Politics among Nations*, pp. 182–183. Cf. also Greg Russell, *Hans J. Morgenthau and the Ethics of American Statecraft* (Baton Rouge, Louisiana State University Press, 1990), pp. 207–209.   [190] Morgenthau, *Politics among Nations*, pp. 193, 195.

neutral interpretations in his early enquiry into the judicial function. A judicial decision was in accordance with the law when judicial practice chose to treat it so.[191] In the 1930s he had applied his "decisionism" in acerbic analyses of Weimar and the League of Nations. Though Morgenthau shared Schmitt's rule-skepticism, he still retained the ideal of the rule of law in a domestic context. But this would not work internationally. In domestic society, situations were typical; in the international world, they were unique. Hence, "only a strictly individualized rule of law will be adequate to it."[192] By recourse to a paradox – "individualized rule of law" – Morgenthau in fact adopted Schmitt's decisionism.

In Morgenthau's view, legal formalism isolated aspects of a general situation in order to make it a legal "case" to be decided on its "merits." Where this might work in a domestic context where the "social forces of integration" guaranteed that even legal decisions felt to be unjust were implemented, in international life, missing the larger context was always a scandal. Every international case was always a part of a larger situation, ramifying beyond the legal terms under which it was being considered. The relevant question then was not what the law was but what it should be "and this question cannot be answered by the lawyer but only by the statesman. The choice is not between legality and illegality but between political wisdom and political stupidity."[193] Like Schmitt, Morgenthau saw the international as a context where strategically placed individuals made choices that determined the fate of their nations and the quality of the international order. Such choices came out not as "applications of the law" but as individual assessments of the situation. The liberal attempt to attain democratic control of foreign policy was thoroughly misplaced: the popular mind could not understand the "fine distinctions of the statesman's thinking" and therefore reasoned "more often than not in the simple moralistic terms of absolute good and absolute evil."[194] By contrast, statesmanship was the prudence of the wise individual that could not be squeezed into a method or a procedure, even less a science. It had to do with the sensibility and acuteness of judgment of particular decision-makers: the

[191] Carl Schmitt, *Gesetz und Urteil. Eine Untersuchung zum Problem der Rechtspraxis* (Berlin, Liebmann, 1912).
[192] Morgenthau, "Positivism," p. 271. In regard to the principles of the UN Charter such as self-determination or justice, he claimed that "it is the concrete political situation which gives these abstract terms a concrete meaning and enables them to guide the judgments and action of men," *Politics among Nations*, p. 383.
[193] Morgenthau, *Scientific Man*, p. 120; *Politics among Nations*, p. 441.
[194] Morgenthau, *In Defense of the National Interest*, p. 223.

"extraordinary moral and intellectual qualities which all the leading participants must possess."[195]

In other words, Schmitt and Morgenthau were both led from a critique of formalism, through sociology and morality into a decisionism that no longer provided space for legal constraint beyond physical possibility and the statesman's conscience. Unlike Schmitt, however, Morgenthau did not draw from this the consequence that a new legal order was emerging that would become the instrument of a bipolar *nomos*. But that is precisely where his functional jurisprudence would have led him. He never followed up his 1940 suggestion but chose to write about international law in traditional terms because he was profoundly critical of the transformations and, unlike Schmitt, refused to see in law *merely* a ratification of the concrete order. "Power," he wrote, "engenders that revolt against power, which is as universal as the aspiration of power itself." This revolt was expressed in "ethics, mores, and law" – all three constituting the substance of which political ideologies were "but a reflection": "Superior power gives no right, either moral or legal, to do with that power all that it is physically capable of doing."[196]

Unlike Schmitt, Morgenthau held that these restraints – including international law – would continue to play a modest but definite role in co-ordinating international relations outside the key issues of foreign policy, in matters such as "the limits of territorial jurisdiction, the rights of vessels in foreign waters, and the status of diplomatic representatives."[197] Although Morgenthau lost his interest in international law after 1940, his later writings occasionally refer to it, and always in traditional terms. On the one hand, he remained critical of the decadent idealism of Geneva and inflated expectations about the United Nations. International law's lack of precision was a "debilitating vice" that created unsupported claims of rights. On the other hand, he continued to see a role for law as one aspect of the prudent statesmanship that sought to advance the national interest but also pushed the international order slowly towards a global federation that remained Morgenthau's normative ideal.[198] The result of his argument was a privileging of power and politics in the determination of international order, and a secondary, restraining character for law as an instrument of enlightened statesmanship. No doubt, Morgenthau failed to bring

[195] Morgenthau, *Politics among Nations*, p. 444.
[196] Morgenthau, *Politics among Nations*, pp. 169, 170.
[197] Morgenthau, *Politics among Nations*, p. 211.
[198] Morgenthau, *Politics among Nations*, pp. 211, 229–230.

the two together in an overarching theory – hence the sense of self-contradiction that many have found in the "realist" and "idealist" passages in his *Politics among Nations*. No doubt, Schmitt's reduction of law as an external articulation of the concrete order constituted a more consistent anti-formalism. At the time, only Morgenthau's ambivalence could provide a room for a new academic discipline: international relations. It was only later – by the time of the intervention in the Dominican Republic – that considerations of argumentative rigor would move both political scientists and international lawyers to a more confidently Schmittian anti-formalism.

From international law to international relations

It is a well-known fact that "international relations" is a predominantly Anglo-American discipline whose origins lie in the academic activities of refugees – often with a legal background – from the German *Reich* in the United States during the early years of the Cold War.[199] One of them was Hans Morgenthau, whom Stanley Hoffmann has called, bluntly, "the founder of the discipline"[200] and who was listed (with Hannah Arendt, Leo Strauss, and Herbert Marcuse) among "the four most influential of [the] refugee intellectuals" in the development of political theory in the United States.[201] Morgenthau's influence as the founder of international relations follows from his conscious departure from (legal) formalism on the one hand, but, crucially, of his steadfast refusal to collapse the field into mainstream sociology or ethics, on the other. He did not found the discipline *despite* the contradiction between realism and idealism in *Politics among Nations*. He founded it *on* that contradiction.

Before the war, the study of international relations in the United

---

[199] Cf. Alfons Söllner, "Vom Völkerrecht zum science of international relations. Vier typische Vertreter des politikwissenschaftlichen Emigration," in Ilja Srubar (ed.), *Exil, Wissenschaft, Identität. Die Emigration deutscher Sozialwissenschaftler 1933–1945* (Frankfurt, Suhrkamp 1988), pp. 164–180 (discussing Kelsen, Morgenthau, John Herz, and Karl Deutsch as typical representatives of this emigration). Out of the at least sixty-four German social scientists who emigrated from Germany, more than half had a legal background and over 90 percent took positions in American universities – in most cases in the field of international relations, p. 165.

[200] Stanley Hoffmann, "An American Social Science: International Relations," in Stanley Hoffmann, *Janus and Minerva. Essays in the Theory and Practice of International Politics* (Boulder and London, Westview, 1987), p. 6.

[201] Peter Graf Kielmansegg, "Introduction," in Peter Graf Kielmansegg, Horst Mewes, and Elisabeth Glaser-Schmidt (eds.), *Hannah Arendt and Leo Strauss. German Emigrés and American Political Thought after World War II* (Cambridge University Press, 1995), p. 1.

States had been dominated by Wilsonian legalism. Scholars with a legal background, connected with the Carnegie Endowment for International Peace, had been prominent in the field.[202] For example, Elihu Root (1845–1937) and Charles Evans Hughes (1862–1948) had been Secretaries of State and Presidents of the American Society of International Law simultaneously. State Department jurists had taken an active role in the Harvard Research in International Law that prepared the background for the 1930 League Codification Conference and continued its activities until 1949.[203] In 1930, eighteen of the twenty-four professors of international relations at American universities taught international law and organization.[204] Their idealism – whether in a formalist or natural law version – was completely discredited after the war.[205]

Morgenthau's arguments provided a much more credible basis for understanding the violence and irrationality of the international world, as well as a more effective guide for foreign policy. At the same time, they provided identity and substance for the academic discipline of international relations that had so far existed somewhat insecurely on the boundaries of law and political science. At the heart of those arguments was the claim of an essential distinction between the domestic and the international context. Morgenthau later quoted Martin Wight's succinct statement: "Political theory and law are maps of experience or systems of action within the realm of normal relationships and calculable results. They are the theory of the good life. International theory is the theory of survival. What for political theory is the extreme case (as revolution or civil war) is for international theory the regular case."[206] The distinction between a tranquil domestic normality and the struggle for survival in the international realm came about through a projection at

---

[202] Among the most visible of them were James Brown Scott (1866–1943), Pitman Potter (born 1892), and James T. Shotwell (1874–1965).

[203] The atmosphere among American internationalists during the inter-war era can be usefully gleaned in Arthur K. Kuhn, *Pathways in International Law: A Personal Narrative* (New York, Macmillan, 1953), e.g. pp. 95 *et seq.*, 144–146.

[204] Jack Donnelly, "Realism and the Academic Study of International Relations," in James Farr, John S. Dryszek, and Stephen T. Leonard (eds.), *Political Science in History. Research Programs and Political Traditions* (Cambridge University Press, 1995), p. 178.

[205] Cf. David Kennedy, "When Renewal Repeats: Thinking against the Box" (2000), 32 *New York University Journal of International Law and Politics*, pp. 378–380.

[206] The citation is from Martin Wight, "Why is There no International Theory?," cited in Morgenthau, *The Decline of Democratic Politics* (University of Chicago Press, 1969), p. 64. Cf. also Hans Morgenthau's critique of the idea of the World State, in *Politics among Nations*, pp. 391–406.

the international level of a distinct sensibility that the German refugees brought from Weimar about matters political, a sensibility which in Schmitt's case has been aptly described as an "aesthetics of horror"[207] and which in Morgenthau appears in a thoroughly pessimistic outlook on human nature and society. In order to understand international relations it was necessary to accept that iron laws governed the field transforming even good-intentioned policies into struggles for power and prestige. The liberal Kelsen scholar John H. Herz (born 1908) – another refugee from Weimar and Geneva – depicted this existential fact in 1951 in terms of the "security dilemma" that led States (even liberal States) and statesmen to seek security by accumulating their power – and thus to create a feeling of insecurity in their neighbors.[208] The "Realism" that German jurists such as Morgenthau, Herz or Karl Deutsch (1912–1992) inaugurated in the international relations academia, espoused a Hobbesean anthropology, an obsession with the marginal situation, the pervading sense of a spiritual and political "crisis" in the (liberal) West, and constant concern over political collapse.[209]

These arguments created space for an academic discipline that would be neither an extension of international law nor simply an exotic variation of sociology or ethics. "International relations" received substance and identity from Morgenthau's twin movement between 1940 and 1950: anti-formalism on the one hand, and consistent refusal to take the premises of anti-formalism too seriously, on the other. In the first place, all behavior was determined by the eternal laws of human nature, among them the principle of desire that Morgenthau had theorized in his 1930 manuscript and which in his published writings led to the description of social life – in particular, social life among States – in terms of a relentless pursuit of power. In the second place, everything also always depended on the qualities of foreign policy leaders, their ethical sensibility and acuteness of judgment. Behind Morgenthau's call for "sociology" was no properly sociological theory at all. All his social laws followed as generalizations about the individual psyche. "Society" was not an automaton but the outcome of actions by individuals seeking

---

[207] Richard Wolin, "Carl Schmitt. The Conservative Revolutionary Habitus and the Aesthetics of Horror" (1992), 20 *Political Theory*, pp. 424–447.

[208] John H. Herz, *Political Realism and Political Idealism. A Study in Theories and Realities* (University of Chicago Press, 1951).

[209] Cf. Jürgen Gebhardt, "Leo Strauss: The Quest for Truth in Times of Perplexity," in Kielmansegg, Mewes, and Glaser-Schmidt, *Hannah Arendt* (linking this attitude to the general outlook of the German academic elite – including the émigrés in the United States), pp. 84–89.

to fulfill their desires. The decisive actor in international politics was the statesman who had to rise above the masses to realize the national interest: to be, in a way, human and superhuman simultaneously.

This perspective led Morgenthau to become a determined opponent of the reigning school of American political science, associated with the teachings of Charles Merriam (1874–1953) and Harold Lasswell (1902–1978) in Chicago in the 1930s and 1940s. These scholars aimed to establish a behavioralist study of society that would employ quantitative measurements and hypothetical laws to be tested by methods of falsification. Morgenthau's 1946 book *Scientific Man vs. Power Politics* was an extended critique of precisely such efforts. They provided no understanding of the existential meaning of politics as struggle in which, as he had written in 1930, "life" attained consciousness of itself. On the contrary, behavioralism was part of that depoliticization that infected the liberal mind and made it incapable of taking determined action. If international relations was to be an independent and policy-relevant study, it needed to rely on the same intuitive insights as statesmen did.[210] Even if politics had a unique source in human nature, there was no predetermined way in which it influenced international behavior, and hence no single method of "power politics," either, that could simply be applied to reach one's objectives.[211] Even an anarchic international system could differ between periods or locations of more or less cooperation and confrontation, as both Henry Kissinger and Raymond Aron would readily concede. The idea of social engineering oversimplified and distorted the perception of the international world, creating inflated hopes about the solution of its problems – and was "bound to be disappointed over and over again."[212] Each situation called for an idiosyncratic response that could be deduced from a "scientific" model just as little as it could be received by a legalistic interpretation of a collective security pact.

In this way, Morgenthau avoided reducing international relations to a branch of scientific sociology. Instead, it came to involve an existential–decisionist understanding of politics in terms of the decisions taken by the statesman under a prudential, situational ethics, "forever condemned to experience the contrast between the longings of his mind

---

[210] Cf. Stefano Guzzini, *Realism in International Relations and International Political Economy* (London and New York, Routledge, 1998), p. 37; Söllner, "German Conservation in America," pp. 163–168.

[211] "No formula will give the statesman certainty, no calculation eliminate the risk, no accumulation of facts open the future," Morgenthau, *Scientific Man*, p. 221.

[212] Morgenthau, *Scientific Man*, p. 219.

and his actual condition as his personal, eminently human tragedy."[213] And precisely because Morgenthau's ethics, like Weber's, was situational, it provided no basis for a foreign policy guided by ethical principles, indeed was against such absolutism.[214] For Morgenthau was nothing if not critical of a morally loaded Cold War crusade against communism and the ideological aspects of the policy of containment in 1947–1968. On the contrary, his argument was directed against the ideological and "moralistic" excesses of the foreign policies of Wilson or Roosevelt which he interpreted as fundamentally hypocritical: "what the moral law demanded was by a felicitous coincidence always identical with what the national interest seemed to require."[215] Morgenthau advocated limited objectives (which he often associated with the lesser evil) with attention focused on one's main interest, and an interpretation of Soviet policy not in terms of revolutionary rhetoric but through its traditional position as an imperial power that felt itself isolated. Global commitment to intervene against communism wherever it arose was for him a fatal, ideologically induced mistake that could lead only to failure. Here lay the affinity between Morgenthau's academic work and the political realism of diplomats such as George Kennan or Henry Kissinger. Morgenthau never supported the role of an international "guarantor" for any single State (in fact, he favored world government with an effective international police force)[216] and insisted on the ultimately moral justification of a limited national interest.[217] His stress on the idiosyncratic and often tragic choices available in each situation aimed to educate foreign policy decision-makers to face up to the existential truth about human conduct – including the conduct of States – being determined by an all-encompassing *Lustprincip*.[218]

The conditions of the Cold War – particularly the threat of a nuclear catastrophe – and the emerging global ambitions of the United States provided a uniquely suitable context for the cultivation of such a spirit. So it was no wonder that there was, to quote Hoffmann again, "a

---

[213] Morgenthau, *Scientific Man*, p. 221.
[214] Compare in this regard, e.g., Morgenthau, *Scientific Man*, pp. 201–203 and Weber, "Politics as Vocation," pp. 125–126.
[215] Morgenthau, *In Defense of the National Interest*, p. 19.
[216] Cf. e.g. Hans Morgenthau, *Truth and Power. Essays of a Decade 1960–1970* (London, Pall Mall, 1970), pp. 306–314.
[217] For an early formulation, cf. Morgenthau, *In Defense of the National Interest*, pp. 33–39 and *passim*.
[218] An analogous interpretation of the "contradiction" in Morgenthau's thought about determinism and free will is in Martin Griffiths, *Realism, Idealism and International Politics; A Reinterpretation* (London, New York, Routledge, 1992), pp. 71–72.

remarkable chronological convergence between [the needs of policy-makers in Washington] and the scholars' performances."[219] An argument against isolationism and in favor of global involvement, intervention in the national interest, and the accumulation of power could not have been planted in a more fertile soil. After all, who else but the United States could think of itself as the "guardian" of the international political order – and thus find a justification to bring its force to bear if that seemed needed. This must have strengthened Morgenthau's resolve never to shun from normative statements – and thus helped to inaugurate the instrumentalist approach to international relations that still today sees scientific work justified primarily if it ends up in policy proposals.

Morgenthau's arguments led beyond law as the banal application of (formal) rules but also beyond sociology and ethics as scientific disciplines or bureaucratic techniques. Instead, they brought into existence international relations as an academic discipline that would deal "realistically" with the functioning of eternal human laws in a condition of anarchy. Already the problem-setting involved a contradiction. Realism claimed to be based on science; yet its argument was anti-scientific. The "eternal laws" of politics claimed the status of deep insights into social and psychological life. But the polemics against the behavioralists had been directed precisely against the idea that the field could be reduced to scientific laws. On the one hand, everything was always already determined by the fundamental laws of politics. On the other, everything also depended on the sensitivity of the foreign policy decision-maker to the interests of his country and the requirements of the situation. This ambivalence was completely embedded in a Weberian value-relativism: if the absence of a constraining law or morality left individuals free (and alone, as Morgenthau would write), might they still be constrained by their political sensitivity and willingness to accept responsibility?

The simultaneous affirmation of constraint and freedom was crucially important as the foundation for Morgenthau's polemical technique.[220] It made it possible for him to argue against legal positivism and in favor of a sociological emphasis on power while yet taking a traditional view on the ethics of statesmanship against attempts to reduce

---

[219] Hoffmann, "American Social Science," p. 10. For an elaboration, cf. also Steve Smith, "Paradigm Dominance in International Relations: The Development of International Relations as a Social Science" (1987), 16 *Millennium: Journal of International Studies*, pp. 189–206.

[220] Cf. also Guzzini, *Realism in International Relations*, pp. 15–31.

foreign policy to the application of scientific laws. This was a powerful technique that took account of the difficulties in applying the principles of study of domestic societies to international affairs. But it was also unstable and arbitrary. There was something suspicious in a fundamental critique of foreign policy decision-making that always ended up idolizing the most traditional values of personal character. Speakers of truth to power, possessors of historical wisdom and sensitivity for the national interest, Morgenthau's Prometheus, like Schmitt's Katechon, were mythical figures that worked as cultural metaphors originating in a world that was rapidly receding into history.[221]

Political science departments at US universities received from the German refugees an image of international law as Weimar law writ large, formalistic, moralistic, and unable to influence the realities of international life. "The real relationship between international law and the actual behavior of states," John Herz wrote, "has been that between utopian ideology and reality."[222] Having published an exposition and critique of national socialist international law in his native Germany in 1938 (under a pseudonym), Herz came to the States, like Morgenthau, to characterize international law as an overoptimistic ideology which even in its best proponents, Kelsen and Scelle, failed to take account of the "competition for power and security" that was the essence of international politics.[223] The dangerous and unpredictable conditions of international politics made it imperative that decision-makers be freed from formal rules or dogmatic moral principles that tied their hands when prudence and innovation – Morgenthau's "wisdom" – were called for. They were in full agreement with Kennan's 1951 critique of US inter-war foreign policy as having failed to understand that the "function of a system of international relationships is not to inhibit [the] process of change by imposing a legal strait jacket upon it."[224]

However, Herz and Morgenthau also reserved a limited role for law in situations where the balance of power or common interests were working. Both conserved a traditional court and case oriented image of law. Legal rules and institutions were sometimes useful as instruments for

---

[221] This is accepted by Morgenthau as he writes with undiguised nostalgia about the virtues of the aristocratic internationalism of the nineteenth century. Cf. Morgenthau, *Politics among Nations*, pp. 184–187. Not without reason, Griffiths labels Morgenthau a "nostalgic idealist," *Realism*, pp. 35, 72.
[222] Herz, *Political Realism*, p. 204. [223] Herz, *Political Realism*, pp. 96–102.
[224] George Kennan, *American Diplomacy* (expanded edn., University of Chicago Press, 1984), p. 98.

the advancement of State interests that every now and then converged to create a stable normality. The residual role they reserved for international law was an inseparable part of their traditionalism that focused on the cultivated sensibilities of foreign policy decision-makers who would understand the value of the experiences that were condensed in legal rules even if they were not "binding" or enforceable in the straightforward fashion like rules of national law.

This kind of traditionalism – that law could contribute as Kennan's "gentle civilizer of the national self-interest" – found no room within the discipline of international relations that had been created out of a critique of formalism but was left oscillating between empiricism and behavioralism on the one hand, and search for policy-relevance on the other.[225] Conceived in terms of science, international relations could not accommodate that kind of culturally embedded propositions of which "prudence" or "wisdom" consisted. It is no surprise that the only reference to "laws" in Kenneth Waltz's (born 1927), influential neo-Realist *Theory of International Politics* of 1979 were to the laws of logical relation and scientific explanation.[226] On the other hand, developed as propositions about an American foreign *policy*, international relations was too busy trying to find a foothold for the articulation of the national interests of a Great Power, engaged in an ideological struggle, not to shy away from the complacent internationalism that sought to argue – as it had done before the war – for the essential identity of US interests with that of international institutions.[227]

Elsewhere, the relations between international law and international relations have organized themselves differently. In France (with the possible exception of Raymond Aron) and many other European countries, international relations was, and continues to be, largely enmeshed with the study of diplomatic history and international organization. Positive legal rules – especially treaties and constitutions of international organizations – have a modest but useful role in structuring international life. Nor have the British (apart from, perhaps, E. H. Carr, Georg Schwarzenberger, and F. H. Hinsley) discussed international law with the sense of impending doom that has been a part of the Weimar–realist

---

[225] Cf. e.g. Donnelly, "Realism," pp. 175–197.
[226] Kenneth Waltz, *Theory of International Politics* (Reading, London, and Amsterdam, Addison-Wesley, 1979).
[227] For a recent attempt to build upon Morgenthau's "pragmatic realism" and the positivist–empirical "concessional realism" by re-integrating ethical concerns within the latter, cf. Roger D. Spegele, *Political Realism in International Relations Theory* (Cambridge University Press, 1996), esp. pp. 83 *et seq*.

Carl Schmitt, Hans Morgenthau and "international relations"

genre. To some extent, this may follow as a matter of academic tradition. International relations came about as an academic discipline as an express reaction to the shock of the war with the setting up of the Woodrow Wilson Professorship at the University College of Wales at Aberystwyth in 1919. The mandate of the chair included the promotion of world government and its first holders (K. C. Webster and Sir Alfred Zimmern) were policy oriented pragmatists with a special interest in the League of Nations.[228] Though E. H. Carr perhaps killed their type of traditionalism, the later representatives of the "English School" continued to reserve a place for international law in their analyses. Martin Wight (1913–1972) saw international law as a historical tradition that like theories about international relations was divided into "rationalist," "realist," and "revolutionist" streams, and confessed himself to have moved increasingly into the rationalist camp – with all that this meant regarding the adoption of a Grotian legal morality.[229] Hedley Bull (1932–1985) credited international law with a number of essential (albeit limited) "functions" in relation to an international order which paradoxically reflected the nature of "society" and "anarchy" simultaneously[230] while his arguments about international law as one of its institutions (alongside war, balance of power, and diplomacy) capture a rather formalistic understanding of the law. International law is – and should be – rules and the role of the lawyer should be "to state what the rules of international law are."[231] Against the interdisciplinary ambitions of the post-war American scholars he retorted that to think of international law as a "process of authoritative decision . . . deprives international law of its essential focus and leads to its disappearance as a distinct branch of international studies."[232]

Where European students of international relations have largely accepted the presence of different vocabularies within their discipline – and a rather quaint formalism in their writings about international

---

[228] For brief but useful chronologies of the definitions and delimitation of international relations as a doctrine and a set of theories (as well as canons of books), cf. e.g. William Olson and Nicholas Onuf, "The Growth of a Discipline Reviewed," in Steve Smith (ed.), *International Relations. British and American Perspectives* (Oxford, Blackwell, 1985), pp. 1–28 and Steve Smith, "The Self-Images of a Discipline: A Genealogy of International Relations Theory," in Ken Booth and Steve Smith (eds.), *International Relations Theory Today* (Cambridge, Polity, 1995), pp. 1–37.

[229] Martin Wight, *International Theory. The Three Traditions* (Gabriele Wight and Brian Porter eds., Leicester University Press, for the RIIA, 1994), pp. 233–258, 268.

[230] Hedley Bull, *The Anarchical Society. A Study of Order in World Politics* (London, Macmillan, 1977), pp. 140–145.   [231] Bull, *The Anarchical Society*, p. 150.

[232] Bull, *The Anarchical Society*, p. 160.

law,[233] Americans had internalized Morgenthau's anti-formalism as a foundational part of their discipline. Even if it might have been possible to unlearn Realism as a set of academic propositions, the interests of United States policy-makers and the outlook of a Great Power guaranteed that the critiques of legal formalism would remain an ineradicable part of the profession. Realists or liberal institutionalists, structuralists, postmodernists, or advocates of a new normativism, international relations scholars have dismissed international law on the basis of critiques they received from Weimar but which originated in a critique of German and French public law positivism in the last two decades of the nineteenth century.

The heritage of realism in American international law

The atmospheric change in the United States brought about by the Weimar refugees was no less striking in the field of international law itself. Like Morgenthau and Herz, Josef Kunz (1890–1970), Kelsen's disciple from Vienna, came to the United States and wrote through the 1950s about a crisis in international law that was a "partial phenomenon of the total crisis of the whole occidental culture."[234] Kunz, too, saw the crisis as having its roots in the First World War and peaking in the juxtaposition of the two superpowers and the consequent destruction of European values. "The decline of Europe" and "the total crisis of our occidental culture" were not independent, of course, but (although Kunz refrained from quite formulating this sentence) the second was a consequence of the first.[235] Many Americans agreed. "[T]he shadow of possible catastrophe hangs with increasing common apprehension over all our heads," Myres S. McDougal (1906–1998) from Yale told his students at the Hague Academy in 1953 in a course that outlined the task of international lawyers as anti-communist policy advisers.[236]

---

[233] On this "pluralism," cf. e.g. Richard Little, "The English School's Contribution to the Study of International Relations" (2000), 6 *European Journal of International Relations*, pp. 395–422.

[234] Josef Kunz, "The Changing Science of International Law," in *The Changing Law of Nations: Essays on International Law* (Ohio State University Press, 1968), p. 158.

[235] Josef Kunz, "The Changing Law of Nations," in *The Changing Law of Nations*, pp. 10, 35, 50.

[236] Myres S. McDougal, "International Law, Power and Policy. A Contemporary Conception" (1953/I), 82 *RdC*, p. 138. Post-war American legal thought seems in general to have been less anxious about "totalitarianism" than political thinking generally. Carl Landauer derives this from the confidence scholars such as McDougal had in the US government's ability to deal with the threat, fostered by their closeness to that government, "Deliberating Speed: Totalitarian Anxieties and Postwar Legal Thought" (2000), 12 *Yale Journal of Law and the Humanities*, pp. 171, 230–234.

Carl Schmitt, Hans Morgenthau and "international relations"

McDougal's and Harold Lasswell's Yale School was only the most visible but perhaps among the least influential of the new approaches that grew up in the United States in the 1950s and 1960s. During those years, American international lawyers were faced with three responses to the decline of inter-war formalism.[237] First, legal realism was overwhelming domestic academic law and cultivated an image of the lawyer as a policy-maker relatively free to choose the direction of legal advice. Its most important legacy consisted of "its challenge to the orthodox claim that legal thought was separable and autonomous from moral and political discourse."[238] Second, domestic social science was being instrumentalized into "policy science" in part as a result of the role of social scientists in the war effort, in part through the continuing use of the discipline to defend American policy in the cold war.[239] Third was the activity of the German émigré internationalists working on international relations as well as international law. Among the effects that this convergence of realism from three sides brought to international law in the United States two were particularly important.

One was a pervasive rule-skepticism that turned the attention of academic lawyers from exegetic work with treaties, cases, and formal diplomacy to broader aspects of international co-operation and conflict. The legal profession re-imagined itself as a participant in international policy as advisers and decision-makers in governments, international organizations, and businesses, pursuing a variety of interests and agendas. Public international lawyers increasingly conceived international law from the perspective of a world power, whose leaders have "options" and routinely choose among alternative "strategies" in an ultimately hostile world. The combination of rule-skepticism and policy orientation had already led McDougal and Lasswell in 1943 to declare that "much of what currently passes for instruction in law schools is a waste of time."[240] Formal rules were disappointing. On the one hand, they were "inconsistent, ambiguous, and full of omissions." Principles came with counter-principles and

---

[237] Of course, formalism remained in the margins, with the leading work being Grenville Clark and Louis Sohn, *World Peace Through World Law* (2nd edn., Cambridge, Mass., Harvard University Press, 1960).
[238] Morton Horwitz, *The Transformation of American Law 1879–1960: The Crisis of Legal Orthodoxy* (Oxford University Press, 1992), p. 193.
[239] Cf. Bent Rosenthal, *Etude de l'oeuvre de Myres Smith McDougal en matière de droit international* (Paris, LGDJ, 1970), pp. 40–44 and *passim*.
[240] Myres S. McDougal and Harold Lasswell, "Legal Education and Public Policy: Professional Training in the Public Interest" [1943], in Myres S. McDougal and Associates, *Studies in World Public Order* (New Haven and Dordrecht, New Haven Press and Nijhoff, 1987), p. 57.

facts failed to subsume themselves neatly under legal categories. Literal meanings or drafter intentions remained out of reach of interpreters who were engaging in "policy choices."[241] On the other hand, rules were in any case only "trends of past decision," insufficient for the needs of democratic society in an era when freedom was threatened by totalitarianism and human dignity was at stake. Legal education should become "training for policy-making."[242] In an ironic turn of the tables, the view of the jurist as the legal conscience of the civilized world reappeared. Like the men of 1873, McDougal had a political agenda, an anti-formalist outlook, and little doubt about the ability of his moral sensibility to capture people's law in its authenticity.

A second contribution of realism was the emphasis on interdisciplinarity as a crucial aspect of academic work, accommodation of insights from sociology and ethics, as Morgenthau and McDougal had suggested, but also from economics, international relations, policy analysis, political theory, anthropology, systems theory, phenomenology, and so on – an almost interminable list of more or less exotic specializations. In a 1967 overview Richard Falk (born 1930) from Princeton identified several new strands of study that aimed to "move beyond the impressionism of earlier approaches" so that they would "begin to acquire a scientific character."[243] "Functionalism" saw an international legal system emerge from day-to-day low-level political work in international institutions, governments and civil associations. Systems theory identified "strategic variables" to enable an accurate description and prediction of international behavior. Functional equivalents of domestic legal institutions had been canvassed, precedent-formation and reciprocity had been explored; communication study and game theory had become parts of the legal curriculum.

None of the individual schools came to dominance over the field. The Yale School had a powerful voice in McDougal and his associates who grasped the proposal for a functional jurisprudence in Morgenthau's 1940 article but were critical of what they interpreted as his retreat to "pure power policy."[244] But their repetitive lists of variables of policy analysis failed to protect their postulated goal values from a critique of being either an old-fashioned naturalism in disguise or a smoke screen for a defense of American foreign policy. Inasmuch as they failed to

---

[241] McDougal and Lasswell, "Legal Education," pp. 82–83.
[242] McDougal and Lasswell, "Legal Education," p. 46.
[243] Richard Falk, "New Approaches to the Study of International Law" (1967), 61 *AJIL*, p. 487.   [244] McDougal, "Contemporary Concepts," pp. 157–164.

answer the question "is this law or not?," the usefulness of their proposals appeared doubtful (and certainly not worth the trouble it took to learn their language) to lawyers whose lay colleagues persisted in asking precisely *that* question.

The Yale scholars were rivaled by the more conventionally internationalist liberals around Columbia University, such as Friedmann, Louis Henkin (born 1917), or Oscar Schachter (born 1915). Unlike McDougal and his associates the Columbia scholars were not obsessed by Great Power antagonism but worked to develop what C. Wilfred Jenks (1909–1973) termed a "common law of mankind" through social and international welfare activities. They focused on peacekeeping and resource administration through UN agencies and other functional organizations, work in human rights and economic development.[245] Friedmann's slogan about a transformation from a law of co-ordination to a law of co-operation, associated with the move from formal sovereign consent to a common interest-based system that relied on informal persuasion to reach compliance, demonstrated the continuity between the Columbia scholars and the pluralists and interdependence theorists of the inter-war. Many traditional scholars such as Charles Fenwick (1880–1973) agreed in their enthusiasm about the "extension of international law in new areas of economic and social co-operation."[246] The Columbia scholars had, however, integrated the realist teaching and were insistent to leave the kind of naturalism and formalism that were projected as the shared mistakes of inter-war lawyers.[247] They linked their institutional faith with behavioral studies about the causes of international conflict and co-operation and, somewhat like Fried or Niemeyer in Germany half a century earlier, hoped to make international law a technically sophisticated instrument for managing the tension between sovereignty and community.[248] They sometimes articulated their theoretical views in terms of the (American) "legal process" school that had been the leading successor to legal realism in the 1950s and had accepted much of the realists' emphasis on discretion but sought control by focusing on negotiating behavior, competence, and

---

[245] Wolfgang Friedmann, *The Changing Structure of International Law* (New York, Columbia University Press, 1964), esp. pp. 60–71, 82–95.
[246] Charles G. Fenwick, "International Law: The Old and the New" (1966), 60 *AJIL*, pp. 481–483.   [247] Kennedy, "When Renewal Repeats," pp. 380–387.
[248] Friedmann's law of co-operation was designed precisely to deal with Morgenthau's problem about international law always supporting the status quo. Here was the "flexible" and responsive law that overcame the rigidities of formal co-ordination, *The Changing Structure*, pp. 58–59.

restraint inside formal and informal institutions.[249] The argument by Abram Chayes (1922–2000) about the role of international law in the Cuban conflict constituted a liberal alternative to McDougal's confrontational policy analyses.[250]

McDougal argued that a conception of law as fixed "rules" seemed irrelevant unless it was accompanied by power to control and enforce and counter-productive inasmuch as it limited the choices available to those who have the means to enforce them. If Friedmann, Chayes, and others were less inclined to use the language of power they, too, worried about international law's instrumental character, believing in rather softer manners of influencing "how nations behave."[251] Everyone wanted to expand the law's scope beyond formal diplomacy, to include not only new substances such as welfare and human rights issues but also new actors such as international organizations, companies, even transnational political parties.[252] Some lawyers occupied a political middle ground. Richard Falk, for instance, regarded Morgenthau's views as "simplistically cynical" and took an expressly eclectic position between Kelsen and McDougal, suggesting that "each of these enquiries reflects a genuine intellectual need."[253] He was politically much closer to the Columbia scholars but admired the methodological rigor of McDougal and his associates. But he, too, saw the only hope for international law in learning from social sciences and became (with Saul Mendlowitz) a founder of the "World Order Models Project (WOMP)," that projected desired futures of the international system and promoted causal techniques through which they could be reached.

The one theme that connected the different strands of US interna-

---

[249] Horowitz, *The Transformation*, p. 254 and Mary Ellen O'Connell, "New International Legal Process" (1999), 93 *AJIL*, pp. 334–351.
[250] Abram Chayes, *The Cuban Missile Crisis* (New York, Oxford University Press, 1974). Cf. also Abram Chayes, *International Legal Process. Materials for an Introductory Course* (Boston, Little, Brown, 1968–1969).
[251] Cf. Louis Henkin, *How Nations Behave. Law and Foreign Policy* (2nd edn., New Haven, Columbia University Press, 1979).
[252] E.g. McDougal, "International Law," pp. 227–258.
[253] Richard Falk, *The Status of Law in the International Society* (Princeton University Press, 1970), p. 9; Richard Falk, "International Legal Order. Alwyn Freeman vs. Myres S. McDougal" (1965), 59 *AJIL*, p. 66. Cf also Richard Falk, "The Relevance of Political Context to the Nature and Functioning of International Law: An Intermediate View," in Karl W. Deutsch and Stanley Hoffmann (eds.), *The Relevance of International Law. Essays in Honor of Leo Gross* (Cambridge, Schenkman, 1968), pp. 133–152.

tional law scholarship after the realist challenge was its *deformalized* concept of law. Whatever political differences there were between McDougal and Columbia scholars, they agreed that international law was not merely formal diplomacy or cases from the International Court of Justice but that – if it were to be relevant – it had to be conceived in terms of broader political processes or techniques that aimed towards policy "objectives." A relevant law would be enmeshed in the social context and studied through the best techniques of neighboring disciplines.[254] This would mean a shift of emphasis from formal obligations to informal understandings and "regimes," with the acknowledgement that violations could be of different degrees. Such policy pragmatism received support from the negotiations leading up to the defusing of the Cuban missile crisis and the period of détente that followed. What now seemed needed was "avoiding all temptation to the adoption of single, high-level code of the law of Soviet–Western relations" and "any Western insistence on a postulated 'World Rule of Law'" in favor of an "essentially modest, low-level, empirically-based, step-by-step approach."[255] Policy pragmatism to the core.

In more recent years, Realism in the international relations departments has been challenged by a "fundamentally non-idealist" branch of liberal internationalism.[256] Realist insights have been used to project an interdependent world of co-operation beyond the nation-State. As a consequence, an intellectual alliance has been proposed between international lawyers and international relations scholars advocating regime theory – that is, a theory about the effects of informal norms in constructing collaborative "regimes."[257] It is no wonder that such approaches have

---

[254] For a full statement, cf. e.g. Falk, *The Status of Law*, pp. 9–37.
[255] Edward McWhinney, "Changing International Law Method and Objectives in the Era of Soviet–Western Détente" (1965), 59 *AJIL*, pp. 10, 11, 4n48.
[256] Donnelly, "Realism," p. 189. The influential work is Robert D. Keohane, *After Hegemony: Cooperation and Discord in the World of Political Economy* (Princeton University Press, 1984), esp. pp. 65–109 (aiming to create a theoretical frame for studying international co-operation in regimes on explicitly realist premises about States as rational egoists; every such State, Keohane argues, would have reason to collaborate in regimes that tend to remain even if no longer supported by a hegemon that helped to create them).
[257] A regime is then defined as "sets of implicit or explicit principles, norms, rules and decision-making procedures around which actors' expectations converge in a given area of international relations," Stephen D. Krasner, "Structural Causes and Regime Consequences: Regimes as Intervening Variables," in Krasner (ed.), *International Regimes* (Ithaca, New York, Cornell University Press, 1983), p. 2.

become popular in the United States. The language of "governance" (in contrast to government[258]), of the management of "regimes," of ensuring "compliance," that has become rooted in much American writing about international law, is the language of a powerful and a confident actor with an enviable amount of resources to back up its policies.[259]

Empire's law

The invasion of the Dominican Republic in 1965 was an undoubtedly imperial act. As Friedmann pointed out, it affirmed the concrete order of US predominance in the Western Hemisphere precisely in the way that Schmitt had characterized his exemplary case of the *Grossraum*. Its point was both to reassert and to enforce: intervention by outside powers – "communism" – was out of the question. It was part of a transition from what Schmitt and Morgenthau had with more or less nostalgia seen as the classical European *nomos* of sovereign equality (between European powers), via an impoverished formalism, to a new period of imperial *Landnahme* by non-European powers, radiating their culture and power beyond their formal boundaries. In Schmitt's conceptual world, the intervention was part of the world's territorial order, an act of power, of course, but precisely because it was an act of effective power, it was also an act of law, and, manifesting the opposition between the industrial and developing world, even a kind of a constitutional act.[260]

Morgenthau's attitude towards the legal meaning of the intervention was much more ambivalent. He approved of the intervention as a political act, of course, but only if it came about not through the application of "the simple slogan 'Stop Communism'" but met the "empirical test" of being actually in accordance with US interests.[261] This position followed from his repeated stress on the primacy of the national interest,

---

[258] Anne-Marie Slaughter, Andrew S. Tulumello, and Stepan Wood, "International Law and International Relations Theory: A New Generation of Interdisciplinary Scholarship" (1998), 92 *AJIL*, pp. 370–371.

[259] This, I guess, is the flip side of Oppenheim's dictum that respect for international law has been greatest in balance-of-power systems. If such balance is lacking, legal formalism gives way to the enforcement of the hegemon's morality. Cf. Stanley Hoffmann, "International Systems and International Law," in Hoffmann, *Janus and Minerva*, pp. 157–164.

[260] Cf. Carl Schmitt, "Die Ordnung der Welt nach dem Zweiten Weltkrieg" (1962), in *Staat, Grossraum, Nomos*, pp. 600–607 (identifying the developing–developed States opposition as "die wirkliche Verfassung der Erde," p. 605).

[261] Morgenthau, *New Foreign Policy*, pp. 124–125.

480

understood realistically as acting within the limits of the power that one has. Unlike Schmitt, however, Morgenthau did not immediately conclude that a new legal order was being established. Instead, he left the legal question open. The relations between the superpowers were "politics" and not law. Or, perhaps better, to think of them as law would be to move within a rationalist utopianism. What was at issue in the Bay of Pigs invasion, the Cuban quarantine, the intervention in Vietnam, or the Dominican Republic was not whether they were lawful or not but whether they were in accordance with the national interest. Two aspects of that position are noteworthy.

First, Morgenthau revealed his traditionalist, "European" attitude towards international law by assuming that it could not and should not be applied in situations that were essentially political. He did not say that there was no law on the matter of intervention, but argued that whatever that law was it was irrelevant for an intelligent assessment of the events. There was no trace of the "functional jurisprudence" of his 1940 article. Unlike most other American lawyers who were arguing about the lawfulness of the intervention in one way or the other, he refrained from taking sides on the legal controversy and especially from following Schmitt or McDougal, for whom the events were part of a process whereby a legal order was being created and reaffirmed.

Second, however, he shared with Schmitt a negative attitude about the way the United States was carrying out a morally based anti-communist crusade. And it is precisely because he was critical about it that must have made it impossible for him to interpret it through the law. For he was here between two unappealing alternatives. To have publicly criticized the intervention as illegal would have put him in the group of "legal fundamentalists" that the State Department legal adviser attacked in providing his thoroughly functional justifications. He could not now take on the role of the formalist lawyer – the "legal fundamentalist" – without becoming vulnerable to the arguments he had so often made against others. But, significantly, he could not follow the alternative adopted by Schmitt and McDougal, either, namely to replace the traditional notion of international law as a framework for formal inter-sovereign relationships by a new, flexible, policy-dependent instrument for US decision-makers. The reasons for why he could not do so are worth quoting *in extenso*:

Traditional international law and organization derive from a pluralistic, relativistic conception of the state system. Divergent as well as parallel and identical national interests are codified in international law, and it is the main political purpose of international organization to harmonize the divergent interests. Accommodation and compromise are therefore the necessary political earmarks of such legal system.

The international legal order appropriate to the globalism of American foreign policy would be monistic and absolutistic rather than pluralistic and relativistic. For American globalism assumes the existence of one valid legal order whose content is defined by the United States and which reflects the objectives of American foreign policy. Thus American globalism of necessity culminates in a pax Americana or American imperium in which the political interests and legal values of the United States are identified with universal ones.[262]

In other words, to have responded to his own call for a "functional jurisprudence" would only have legitimized a *pax Americana* of which he was profoundly critical. To have taken into account also the call for ethics would either have pushed Morgenthau into McDougal's camp of the anti-communist crusade – or it would have necessitated an ethical debate with McDougal and the crusaders about conflicting objectives and values that he could not, on his own Nietzschean premises, think could be rationally resolved. There was nothing left for him as a (European) lawyer but to retreat to the position of the outsider. Imperialism was a political, not a legal matter. Thereby he could at least preserve his nostalgic attachment to the traditionalism he had tried to exorcize in his 1940 article but which kept haunting him throughout his later career. Among the many complexities in Morgenthau's thought is that he remained a moral critic of American foreign policy. But his moral positions never emerged from large principles or utilitarian calculations. They did not take the form of naturalist or deontological argument. They were existential choices, fragmented glimpses of grand truths whose full revelation always fell short of the human capacity. The ethics of Morgenthau's idealized statecraft was a combination of prudence, historical wisdom, and a sense of tragedy, that belonged only to few statesmen. From his own pen, they came about as series of intuitively grasped truths projected upon political events by someone whom fate had accidentally but irrevocably cast as an outsider

After the Second World War, American international lawyers largely gave up the "utopian" hopes of their inter-war predecessors. The critiques of formalism rehearsed by Morgenthau and Schmitt became part

---

[262] Hans Morgenthau, "Emergent Problems of United States Foreign Policy," in Deutsch and Hoffmann, *The Relevance of International Law*, pp. 55–56.

of their renewed self-understanding. The discipline faced the choice of either accepting the marginalization of law from the center of political decision-making or adopting a functional jurisprudence that recast the lawyer as adviser for the political decision-maker. Where Morgenthau had accepted the former option, as it were, tragically, Schmitt's legacy was to inaugurate a dynamic and deformalized concept of law that would show its usefulness as the symbol of the concrete order that American power was able to produce.[263]

We have seen how McDougal and his associates on the one hand, and the Columbia and legal process scholars on the other, applied the functional understanding. They used a flexible concept of international law that would serve their preferred values by facilitating decision-making in contexts where they thought they were dominant. Interdisciplinary orientation, as Richard Falk pointed out in 1967, was a central aspect of this technique. The concern for the relevance of international law arose as the shared obsession of the profession, "relevance" being defined as instrumental usefulness whose measurement seemed to call for complex sociological and policy oriented analyses.

Today, many lawyers in the United States persist in calling for an integration of international law and international relations theory under a "common agenda." This is an American crusade. By this, I do not mean only that some of the crusaders have chosen to argue for an increasing recourse to US principles of domestic legitimacy in the justification of its external behavior,[264] nor that nearly all of the relevant literature comes from North America.[265] (Indeed, an early review of legal responses to the "realist challenge" found no significant examples

---

[263] For the argument in a domestic context, cf. Ingeborg Maus, "The 1933 'Break' in Carl Schmitt's Theory," in Dyzenhaus, *Carl Schmitt's Critique of Liberalism*, pp. 197–212. The argument for this change of self-image is stated with great clarity in Michael W. Reisman, "International Incidents: A New Genre of Study of International Law," in Michael W. Reisman and Andrew Willard (eds.), *International Incidents: The Law that Counts in World Politics* (Princeton University Press, 1988), where the author distinguishes between law as a "myth system" and an "operational code." Today, he writes "much of the . . . international legal description is patently out of step with elite expectations." Only an operational, incident oriented study will "inform about expectations of those who are politically effective in the world community." The author's criterion for legal relevance is enchantingly present in his confident indictment of formalism: "Small wonder that political advisors rarely use their international lawyers," pp. 4, 12, 15.

[264] Lea Brilmayer, *Justifying International Acts* (Princeton University Press, 1989).

[265] Slaughter, Tulumello, and Wood, "International Law and International Relations Theory," pp. 393–397 (Bibliography).

beyond the universities of the American East.[266]) Nor am I relying on the fact that the concepts of "liberalism" or "democracy" in this literature refer back to an American understanding that links them with determined (Western) liberal institutions.[267] What I want to say, instead, is that the interdisciplinary agenda itself, together with a deformalized concept of law, and enthusiasm about the spread of "liberalism," constitutes an academic project that cannot but buttress the justification of American empire, as both Schmitt and McDougal well understood. This is not because of bad faith or conspiracy on anybody's part. It is the logic of an argument – the Weimar argument – that hopes to salvage the law by making it an instrument for the values (or better, "decisions") of the powerful that compels the conclusion.

A review in 1998 of interdisciplinary approaches identified a number of ways in which international lawyers today "used" international relations theory.[268] The review also argued that international lawyers had contributed to international relations by examining the legal process as a causal mechanism, by showing how legal norms "constructed" the international system and by drawing attention to the effects of domestic and transnational law on the international scene.[269] It then mapped a "joint discipline" that would study the design of international regimes and processes, that would create specific analyses of the law's "constructive" effects, provide an account of structural transformations, and look into the disaggregation of States and the embeddedness of international institutions in domestic societies.[270]

Such an argument about "collaboration" implies a thoroughly deformalized image of international law. The relevant literature is obsessed with questions such as how and why States use international institutions

---

[266] That is to say, Yale (McDougal), Princeton (Falk), Harvard (Chayes), and Columbia (Henkin). The absence of NYU (Franck) must have been a simple oversight on the author's part. Anne-Marie Slaughter Burley, "International Law and International Relations: A Dual Agenda" (1993), 87 *AJIL*, pp. 209–214.

[267] Susan Marks, "The End of History? Reflexions on Some International Law Theses" (1997), 8 *EJIL*, pp. 449–477, esp. 471–475.

[268] That is to say, "(1) to diagnose international policy problems and to formulate solutions to them; (2) to explain the function of particular international legal institutions; and (3) to examine and reconceptualize particular institutions of international law generally," Slaughter, Tulumello, and Wood, "International Law and International Relations Theory," p. 373.

[269] Slaughter, Tulumello, and Wood, "International Law and International Relations Theory," pp. 379–383.

[270] Slaughter, Tulumello, and Wood, "International Law and International Relations Theory" pp. 384–393.

"to manage interstate co-operation or conflict,"[271] and when it might be useful for States to choose formal and when informal agreements to realize their purposes.[272] An international relations scholar has outlined two "optics" for examining international law that could be used by lawyers and international relations theorists alike, instrumentalism and normativism.[273] This was Morgenthau's appeal for sociology and ethics, in today's language. Few of these writings sustain a concept of international law that would be other than an idiosyncratic technique for studying either what works (instrumentalism) or what would be good if it should work (normativism), in other words, a special kind of sociology or morality of the international.[274] The two aspects of the argument are indissociable: under the dual agenda instrumentalism and normativism complement each other in a necessary, yet profoundly ambivalent way.

Instrumentalism proposes a law that is relevant for policy-makers by indicating the technical avenues through which they can reach their objectives. It speaks about functions and effectiveness, or, in the words of a recent study by the American Society of International Law, of "commitment and compliance."[275] For instrumentalism, law is a functional technique and legal problems are technical problems. If formal law shows itself inflexible or empty, it can always be replaced by a wider standard, policy guideline, informal mechanism of compliance control, soft law, or indeed the values of liberal democracy. For a decision process to be called "law," it would suffice that it is "authoritative" and "controlling," in McDougal's language: if it works let it be law, and let it be law as long as and to the extent that it does work. This allows turning attention away from the relative absence of formal legislation, and of the problems with the interpretation of rules that do exist. For focus on compliance silently assumes that the political question – what the objectives *are* – has already been resolved. Such focus intervenes in precisely the

---

[271] Kenneth W. Abbott and Duncan Snidal, "Why States Act through Formal International Organizations" (1998), 42 *Journal of Conflict Resolution*, p. 8.
[272] Charles Lipson, "Why are Some Agreements Informal?" (1991), 45 *International Organization*, pp. 495–538.
[273] Robert O. Keohane, "International Relations and International Law: Two Optics" (1997), 38 *Harvard International Law Journal*, p. 487.
[274] This is quite expressly stated in Keohane's article, where he observes that causality (i.e. what works) cannot provide the sole perspective from which to look at international law and adds that "the function of moral judgment" is "fundamental," Keohane, "International Relations and International Law," pp. 488–489. No other alternative is considered. Law is either sociology or morality.
[275] Cf. Dinah Shelton (ed.), *Commitment and Compliance. The Role of Non-Binding Norms in the International Legal System* (Oxford University Press, 2000).

way sociology has always done: transforming the debate about the ends of action to the means of action, from normative *praxis* to instrumental *techne*. It was this aspect of instrumentalism and the turn to "science" to which Morgenthau and Schmitt drew attention in their critiques of the liberal depoliticization and neutralization of political choices.[276]

An instrumentalist culture, however, creates the danger of administrative abuse. If law is only about what works, and pays no attention to the objectives for which it is used, then it will become only a smokescreen for effective power. Moreover, as Weber has shown, recourse to deformalized standards (such as "democratic" or "equitable") transforms law into an instrument for the power that has control over the executive. Every administrative act becomes a value-judgment by the authority in position to take the decision. In this process, benevolent jurisprudential intentions may sometimes be enlisted for dubious causes – a process that both Schmitt and Morgenthau witnessed around their professional milieu. To insist that the Weimar judge should set aside formal rules and apply directly the social interests that lay "behind" the law may have seemed a welcome reaction to the hair-splitting of Wilhelminian *Begriffsjurisprudenz*. Schmitt's early decisionism, as well as the "free law" school of Kantorowicz and others, worked with a much more sophisticated awareness of social and linguistic theory than formalistic jurisprudence had ever been able to attain. Nonetheless, Ernst Bloch comments on that experiment: "In Germany, juridical liberalism was marked by progressive intentions, but the existing relations were not at all progressive. And so the Nazi as a judge, servile through and through, but free from juridical measures, demonstrated what he could do."[277] As Schmitt and others criticized the false formality of general legislation in Weimar,

---

[276] The great virtue of technical norms – norms about effectiveness, persuasion, compliance, and so on – lies in the way their validity can be proved by scientific measurements: this (instrumental) norm (N) is valid because it can be proved to attain the objective (O) in a fashion that is valid for everyone accepting the standard of scientific measurement. The objective (O), however, is not addressed by this technique. It is simply taken as a given and often ritually restated by code expressions through which the professional context is identified such as "peace," "clean environment," "right to life," "humanitarian intervention," and so on. The political conflict regarding the meaning of such general notions in the particular context – what claims should be supported, what overridden, how scarce resources should be distributed, and so on – is hidden and attention is turned from them to problems in the technical efficiency of the implementation of whatever agenda it is the decision-maker thinks has to be implemented.

[277] Ernst Bloch, *Natural Law and Human Dignity* (trans. Dennis J. Schmidt, Cambridge, Mass., MIT Press, 1987), pp. 132, 149–152.

an odd intellectual alliance was forged between Kelsenian formalists and the Marxian left, both insisting on the need to maintain the rule of law against the use of the executive for the enforcement of Nazi decrees.[278]

In other words, if the "dual agenda" were only about what works, it would achieve a thoroughly function-dependent, non-autonomous law, an ingenious justification for a world Leviathan. Aside from sociology, ethics is needed. This was precisely what McDougal and his associates tried to attain by reference to their "goal values" of "human dignity." They were not "decisionists" in Schmitt's sense. They believed that their ethics would control decision-making by more or less automatically vindicating the "free society" that coalesced with US foreign policy goals. But that kind of naturalism could not sustain the critiques of ethics that had become part of the agnostic modernity of the profession. The lawyers on the left fared no better. Institutionalism and legal process relied on assumptions about interdependence and rational behavior that had been effectively discarded by the Realists. They were of course right to think that decision-makers in international institutions shared a basic commitment to liberal internationalism that would by and large reflect the preferences of American internationalists as well. But the scarcity of resources and conflicts of interest between States imposed choices upon institutions that were difficult to justify by the argument about long-term harmony of interests. Such choices made these institutions – the United Nations especially – vulnerable to the charge of political partiality. A moderate internationalism proved just as little controlling in the debates in the 1970s and 1980s on a new international economic order, or on how to decide between environmental and economic preferences in the 1990s, as it had been able to produce collective security in the 1930s.

Morgenthau's attempt to create constraint over foreign policy decision-making in an anarchic international environment by focusing on prudent statesmanship resembles Weber's recourse to an ethic of responsibility as a substitute for the controlling force of determining formal rules or binding ethical principles. In both, there is a tragic aspect to their proposal, and it is hard to tell whether they had much faith in its realization. Moreover, in Morgenthau "prudence" turned inwards, to the national community (national interest), and could work as an argument about acceptable international order only by a further assumption

---

[278] For a review, cf. William E. Scheuerman, *Between the Norm and the Exception. The Frankfurt School and the Rule of Law* (Cambridge, Mass., MIT Press, 1997), pp. 74–76, 93–96, 140–147, and generally.

about an invisible hand that could not be sustained by his anthropological pessimism.[279]

Today, interdisciplinary scholars in American academia hope to control the dangers of instrumentalization by accompanying it by a normative optic received from "democracy" and "liberalism." The argument still starts with a sociological point about the emergence of a new world order in which formal sovereignty, diplomacy, and law are being replaced by more fluid actors and processes such as "transgovernmental networks" (of courts, regulatory agencies, executives, even legislatures) within which judges, government officials, company executives, and members of governmental and non-governmental organizations (NGOs) and interest groups meet to co-ordinate their policies in a fashion which, by comparison with formal inter-State co-operation is "fast, flexible, and effective."[280] The argument draws inspiration from a sociology that sees sovereign equality as a formalistic obstacle against the dynamic of "real life" that leads automatically (albeit invisibly) from a "dual agenda" to a "liberal agenda."[281] That this sociology is normatively tinged is an absolutely central part of it: "The most distinctive aspect of Liberal international relations theory is that it permits, indeed mandates, a distinction among different types of States, based on their domestic political structure and ideology." As sovereignty breaks down and globalization becomes the order of the day, the dynamic of a politically oriented law will no longer tolerate formalism: "The resulting behavioral distinctions between liberal democracies and other kinds of States, or more generally between liberal and non-liberal States, cannot be accommodated within the framework of classical international law."[282] In other words, the interdisciplinary call cannot be divorced

---

[279] The tension between Morgenthau's theory of power and his faith in a controlling morality is highlighted in Jan Willem Honig, "Totalitarianism and Realism: Hans Morgenthau's German Years," in Benjamin Frankel (ed.), *Roots of Realism* (London and Portland, Cass, 1996), pp. 307–310. For the argument that an application of the Weberian ethic of responsibility in international affairs requires a conception of moral community (of individuals and of States), cf. Daniel Warner, *An Ethic of Responsibility in International Relations* (Boulder and London, Rienner, 1991), esp. pp. 107–116.

[280] Anne-Marie Slaughter, "The Real New World Order" (1997), 76 *Foreign Affairs*, pp. 193, 183–197.

[281] Anne-Marie Slaughter, "International Law and International Relations: A Dual Agenda" (1993), 87 *AJIL*, pp. 205–239.

[282] Anne-Marie Slaughter, "International Law in a World of Liberal States" (1995), 6 *EJIL*, p. 504. For (a rather conservative) argument about the threat posed by globalization to formal rules and contstraint, cf. William E. Scheuerman, "Globalization and the Fate of Law," in David Dyzenhaus (ed.), *Recrafting the Rule of Law: The Limits of the Legal Order* (Oxford, Hart, 1999), pp. 252–266.

from the *kinds* of sociology and ethics that are being advocated. The suggested sociology is always already normatively loaded, and loaded so as to underwrite the constellation already produced through power.

In Morgenthau as well as in today's liberal deformalized jurisprudence interdisciplinarity comes with two sides: an argument about sociology and an argument about ethics. The sociological argument makes law indistinguishable from the preferences of the persons whom fate and power have put in decision-making positions. The ethical argument seeks to avoid the critique that this makes law *simply* a collection of the prejudices of the decision-makers, seeking to replace the constraint rules failed to offer. But if the ethics of "prudence" in Morgenthau, "human dignity" in McDougal, or "interdependence" in Friedmann failed to create that constraint, today's interdisciplinary enthusiasts seek refuge from positions often associated with a moral doctrine adopted from Immanuel Kant. It is the particular configuration of interdisciplinarity, deformalization, and Kantian morality that inevitably comes to support a liberal Empire. Why?

Initially, the call for a new morality to constrain the international decision-maker seems hardly different from the naturalism of the inter-war lawyers, or the arguments from the civilized conscience–consciousness of the men of 1873. As such, it would be vulnerable to the critique of the manipulability of the postulated moral sensibilities, their being just the prejudices of a narrow class of internationally minded Western lawyers. But the advocates of deformalization now claim that their moral norms enjoy a special character that enables them to transgress the preferences of single individuals, clans, or nations. The force of their norms lies, they maintain, in the peculiar universality of those norms that results from their having been derived through a purely formal system of reasoning, or perhaps more accurately, from our ability to reason about them, or from reason *tout court*. Because reason (in contrast to preference) is universal, these commands enjoy universal validity. That is to say, every thinking person, State, or people would choose them – or would have reason to choose them – from behind a "veil of ignorance" about what kind of a person, group or State one is.[283] This is what it means to say, these lawyers claim, that they constitute a rational choice for all, an effective and legitimate constraint over otherwise deformalized decision-making, as well as an objective (and legal) guide for foreign policy.

---

[283] For a reformulation, cf. John Rawls, *The Law of Peoples: with the "Idea of Public Reason" Revisited* (Cambridge, Mass., Harvard University Press, 1999), pp. 32–33.

It follows that a person, group, or a State that does not share them is not only of another opinion (or preference) but has made a mistake about something that that person, group, or State should think rational for itself, too. Universalizability in theory leads automatically to expansion as practice. If my principle is valid because it is universal, then I not only may but perhaps must try to make others accept it as well. In any case, I can rest confident that I know what principles apply not only to me and my group but to any person or any group. If I engage in contacts with them, I need not face them as equals. I need not be open to their preferences because I already know that mine are universally valid, for me as well as for them, too. I may (or perhaps must) be kind towards and patient with them, but the object of my encounter can only be the transformation of the way they see the world, having them accept my principles, too (because they are not really "mine" but universally good).[284]

But this is, as many critics have argued, an impossible position. No actual person, State or people lives in abstraction from particular histories, contexts, and qualities.[285] Irrespective of whether it is possible hypothetically to make an argument about rules to which everyone has reason to agree, that position has never been open to anyone and it is doubtful whether the principles thus invented would actually be persuasive.[286] If, however, one persists in thinking that this is what one must assume as right, in order to avoid the otherwise compelling conclusion that in a deformalized environment one is simply imposing one's own preferences on others, then the temptation emerges to interpret actual decision-making in this light. That temptation becomes particularly strong if one is oneself the decision-maker. In such a case, one casts one's own views and preferences with the quality that this theory demands. But if no particular decision can claim the kind of validity that this theory regards as the only justifiable norm, then the result is imperialism in either of two alternative forms.

[284] This is the objective of the foreign policy of "liberal peoples" in Rawls, *The Law of Peoples*, pp. 92–93.

[285] The argument from a hypothetical choice situation must build on the dubious assumption that the individual self can exist in abstraction from its (historically contingent) properties or the ends it pursues. Cf. Michael Sandel, *Liberalism and the Limits of Justice* (Cambridge University Press, 1982), pp. 50–65.

[286] Michael Walzer, for instance, argues plausibly against the use of invented moral principles to apply to the lives of situated persons: a minimal morality such as offered by the hypothetical choice will be unresponsive to the concerns and aspirations of any actual ("dense") culture with a sense of belonging "there." Cf. Michael Walzer, *Interpretation and Moral Criticism* (Cambridge, Mass., Harvard University Press, 1987), pp. 11–18.

Carl Schmitt, Hans Morgenthau and "international relations"

First case is the one where the decision-maker (State, legal adviser) believes that his preferences fulfill the criteria postulated by the theory about universal (rational) norms. In such a case, every deviating position will appear as irrational, or at least partial, subjective, historically conditioned, political bias. It may be taken into account, of course, if that leads to the most effective overall realization of the decision-maker's own non-contextually valid preference. But it enjoys no independent normative validity *vis-à-vis* the decision-maker. It may be treated as an atavistic residue from political, religious, ethnic, or other such particular moralities. In due course, with increasing enlightenment (defined as gradual acceptance of the non-contextual position), it would be given up or at least loosen its obsessive hold on those who still cling to it. In a deep sense, having such preference either demonstrates ignorance and error when measured against the norms or policies that are accepted as universally valid, or results from the evil manipulations of the leaders of that other community. These positions might be called *rational imperialism*.[287]

In the second alternative, the decision-maker shares the view that the only legitimate norm is one that enjoys non-contextual validity but does not think that he (or anyone else) is now in possession of it. Every empirical position is contextually and historically based. Nonetheless, the decision-maker persists in making justifications that refer back to the non-contextual assumption. This will produce the same outcome as the

---

[287] This was the position of Christian missionaries and theologians such as Bartoloméo de Las Casas, whose defense of the Indians was based on his unquestioning faith in a single, universally valid religion. Though emerging from *love*, this view erased the Indian's particularity. Cf. chapter 2 above. Today, this position gives no independent normative standing for sovereignty, or the effective control of a government over a population. It deduces the unacceptability of a regime immediately from its having not been instituted by determined rituals of popular consultation. Often it concludes that there must be a right (or even a duty) of intervention by others to oust such a regime from office. For two critical discussions of "liberal triumphalism," cf. Brad Roth, *Governmental Illegitimacy in International Law* (Oxford, Clarendon, 1999), esp. pp. 34–35, 413–430 and Susan Marks, *The Riddle of All Constitutions* (Oxford University Press, 2000). Both suggest that to posit a "right to democracy" may raise more problems than it resolves, inasmuch as "[s]uch a 'right' either is indeterminate or entails the imposition of specific liberal–democratic worldview that has yet to find general acceptance," Roth, *Governmental Illegitimacy*, p. 424. Where Roth's analysis is predominantly descriptive and analytical, Marks hopes to juxtapose a transformative and critical notion of democracy to the "low intensity democracy" or "pan-national democracy," associated with specific Western institutions. Both focus on the *imperialist* character of the internationalist discourse of democracy in the 1990s (without using *that* word, however).

former alternative, with the significant twist, however, that the decision-maker is now acting in bad faith. He does not think that his policy enjoys the non-contextual validity that his theory of legitimate decision-making requires. But he still overrules deviating preferences, and does this by claiming that it does. This leads to what could be called *cynical imperialism*.[288]

Now both of these positions are distinctly *imperialist* in the sense that other positions are overruled not because of their content but because they do not enjoy the same kind of validity as that of the decision-maker. They do not compete on their merits, but are overruled at the outset as lacking some special character (non-contextuality) of the norms the decision-maker holds. They are not just different but at a different level of seriousness or justifiability altogether: "irrational" where the decision-maker's is "rational," "subjective" or "passionate," against his "objective" or "reasonable" position.[289] Because they are so, there never

---

[288] In Tzvetan Todorov's classic study, the distinction between rational and cynical is expressed in the opposition of Las Casas and Cortès, the former being a colonialist out of love, the latter using the language of love in search of private gain. *The Conquest of America. The Question of the Other* (trans. Richard Howard, New York, Harper-Collins, 1984), pp. 174–176. Moral universalism as a psychological trap imposing excessive demands on its proponents – and thus eventually leading to brutalization and cynicism – is a consistent theme in critiques of Kant. For a controversial argument about morality as "the last refuge of Eurocentrism," cf. Hans Magnus Enzensberger, *Civil War* (London, Granta, 1994), pp. 59, 61. This is not too far from Schmitt's arguments against universalism. The defense is taken up by Jürgen Habermas: if moralization is mediated through a legal order, no brutalization will occur. This is, as Habermas readily admits, a liberal response that assumes the presence of "an authority that judges impartially and fulfills the conditions of neutral criminal punishment." Jürgen Habermas, "Kant's Idea of Perpetual Peace, with the Benefit of Two Hundred Years' Hindsight," in James Bohman and Matthias Lutz-Bachmann (eds.), *Perpetual Peace. Essays in Kant's Cosmopolitan Ideal* (Cambridge, Mass., MIT Press, 1997), p. 147. But this seems to assume what was to be proved, namely the existence of a determining positive law or procedure that could mediate between moral beliefs and public enforcement. But if the critiques of legal formality are right, then this presumption cannot be upheld. Habermas, too, accepts that a "deception" follows from unmediated moralism, for instance in the form of a "fundamentalism of human rights." From the perspective of Schmitt and Morgenthau, every universalism involves at least internationally (that is to say, in the absence of a social cohesion sufficient to support one's interpretations) the danger of "deception": the Empire will project its internal morality to the world at large. *Perpetual Peace*, pp. 145–149. To avoid this, a more determined defense of formalism and legal autonomy would seem needed.

[289] Framed in such a way, the opposition enacts the Enlightenment story of reason against myth. The exclusion of the unreasonable preference becomes then less a political maneuver than a necessary step towards truth and progress, a pre-political operation that simply clears the ground for (rational, universal) politics. What the

is – and can never be – dialogue between the decision-maker and those with different preferences. Equality is excluded. Only imperialism remains, as Schmitt wrote more than sixty years ago, describing the new order through the discriminatory concept of war. The different-thinking Other becomes not just my adversary, but an enemy of humanity because he fails to accept what I know is true of all humanity. Therefore, as John Rawls writes today, the non-liberal, non-decent State is the *outlaw* State.[290]

A world where decision-makers learn that one is entitled to think one's preferences justified only if they are justified for everyone else, too, is bound to tragedy, or imperialism, or both. Gliding from a "continuous discomfort of a perpetually uneasy conscience" involved in acting upon preferences that one knows others do not (necessarily) share, to identifying those preferences as universal is, as Morgenthau observed, the most human of inclinations.[291] If nobody's positions are justifiable in the way demanded by the theory of rational coercion, and that, because of this, nobody has a justifiable claim for allegiance, then all decision-making in a deformalized context will always appear as the use of power to impose arbitrary preferences over others. Morgenthau's arguments about the *Lustprincip* came close to providing just such an explanation of international politics. States are obsessed by a desire for power that could be controlled only by the exceptional statesman who recognized this fact. Only that individual can rise above hypocrisy or cynicism who can accept the tragedy of life as struggle between incompatible but equally valid (because equally arbitrary) preferences.

But most interdisciplinary lawyers are led to another intellectual itinerary. Once the critique of formalism has freed the lawyer from the constraint of rules, and the Weberian problem of administrative abuse has emerged, the lawyer is encouraged to begin a quest for the fabled moral norms that dictate what are rational choices for everyone, in other words, to re-imagine the law's job as having to do with the resolution of

---

depiction fails to accept is that myth might be only another form of reason. Cf. Vincent Descombs, *The Barometer of Modern Reason. On The Philosophies of Current Events* (Oxford University Press, 1993), p. 144 and generally the discussion of the "profound ambiguity of the French Revolution . . . when a particular community [i.e. the French] presumed to speak for humanity as a whole," p. 134. Descombs' discussion builds on themes in Jean-François Lyotard, *The Differend: Phrases in Dispute* (trans. Georges van den Abbeele, University of Minnesota Press, 1988), pp. 145–147. Lyotard points out, in a Schmittian vein, that "[a]fter 1789, international wars are also civil wars," p. 146.   [290] Rawls, *The Law of Peoples*, p. 90.
[291] Morgenthau, *Politics among Nations*, p. 193.

the 3,000-year old enigma about objective morality.[292] Or the lawyer may turn away from that task in frustration and fall back on intuition – justifying this nonetheless as if it had been produced by contemplation of a moral theory that everyone has reason to accept. To escape the megalomania of the first path, and the cynicism awaiting at the end of the second, the tempting alternative is to turn back to the interdisciplinary scholars, and to accept as correct, and controlling, not only their critique of formalism but also the policies and preferences they suggest to replace it by. Do not their complex moral ponderings, multi-factor calculations, dependent and independent variables, graphs, or quixotic discourses suggest an altogether deeper mode of understanding than do the lawyer's banal antics? In this way, the anti-formalist technique, and the interdisciplinary call, in fact lead to an invitation for the lawyer to accept as authoritative the styles of argument and substantive outcome that the international relations academia has been able to scavenge from the moral battlefield. Behind the call for "collaboration" is a strategy to use the international lawyer's "Weimarian" insecurity in order to tempt him or her to accept the self-image as an underlaborer to the policy agendas of (the American) international relations orthodoxy.

A culture of formalism?

Since Kelsen, lawyers have looked for professional identity in a middle ground between that which is sociological description (of what works) and that which is moral speculation (of what would be good). This is not because lawyers would have dismissed sociology or ethics as unworthy enterprises but because neither one nor the other is able to answer the question that lawyers are called upon to answer; namely the question

---

[292] Thus Tesón, for instance, suggests that international law problems about humanitarian intervention should be answered by recourse to philosophy: "I will suggest that moral philosophy is necessarily a part of the articulation of legal propositions." This then leads him to the position where the "ultimate justification of the existence of a state is the protection and enforcement of the natural rights of the citizens." If they fail, then "foreign armies are morally entitled to help victims of oppression in overthrowing dictators, provided that the intervention is proportionate to the evil which it is designed to suppress." Ferdinand Tesón, *Humanitarian Intervention: An Inquiry into Law and Morality* (Dobbs Ferry and New York, Transnational, 1988), pp. 6, 15. The replacement of legal argument by philosophy here seems both empty and superfluous. Surely the references to "natural rights," "victims of oppression," and "proportionality" have failed to deal with the lawyer's professional insecurity; surely it is precisely the vagueness of those notions where the lawyer's problem lies – and it can hardly be resolved by restating them.

about (valid) law. There may be disagreement about the significance of that question – and some of the Weimar critics, including Schmitt and Morgenthau, certainly felt that it was . . . uninteresting. Its significance depends on what view one takes on the proper place of formal law (including lawyers, courts, legal arguments, etc.) in society, a question that emerges – as it did in Weimar – especially in face of demands for increasing legislative intervention to support particular interests or values.[293]

Sometimes there is a need for exceptional measures that cannot be encompassed within the general formulation of the formally valid rule. And there may be a time for revolution and the throwing off of valid law (and the profession that sustains it) altogether. But none of this detracts from the need to know about valid law – indeed is premised upon our ability to know it. And that need cannot be satisfied by seeking to answer the causal or the moral question. On the contrary, these latter questions can be meaningfully asked only once we share an image of law as something that is – for want of a better word – "valid." The absence of this image is a product of the Weimar heritage in American international relations theory.

Answers to questions about (valid) law are conditioned upon the criteria for validity that a legal system uses to define its substance. These criteria do refer to social facts and moral ideas but cannot be reduced to them – without doing away with the legal question (by interpreting it as "in fact" a question about what works, or what is good) and the profession that was tasked to answer it. Yet we know, of course, that questions of valid law do not admit of a single right answer. Even if there may be agreement on a form, that often vanishes when we seek to establish its meaning: States may undoubtedly not cause harm to each other. But when asked *what is "harm"?* we are led to interminable interpretative arguments, juxtapositions of rules with exceptions, principles with counter-principles. All this does little to facilitate sociological analyses about effectiveness, implementation and compliance. But that is not the lawyer's problem – unless the lawyer has internalized the self-image of the political decision-maker's little helper.

The way back to a Kelsenian formalism, a formalism *sans peur et sans reproche* is no longer open. The critique of rules and principles cannot

---

[293] For a famous argument about the dangers in the dilution of legal formality (and the emergence of a kind of "Khadi justice") in complex modern society, cf. Max Weber, *On Law in Economy and Society* (ed. with introd. and annot. by Max Rheinstein, New York, Simon & Schuster, 1954), pp. 305–315.

be undone. And even if it could be, there is hardly reason to hope for its resuscitation. Formal rules are just as capable of co-existing with injustice as informal principles. There may be a workable concept of legal validity that is independent from social facts and moral choices but it is a concept that fails to identify any particular substance as definitely legal or illegal. Kelsen and Schmitt agreed that no decision could be automatically inferred from a pre-existing norm, but that each decision set down a new individual norm, an obligation that did not exist before.[294]

Much of the appeal of functional jurisprudence has emerged from a disappointment with formalism's failure to fulfill the expectation that rules and processes would contain ready-made solutions to social conflict, and the apparent arrogance of a profession that refused to acknowledge this failure. So it has been swept aside as a petrified mysticism, unable to assist in the fulfillment of modernity's great projects: political justice, efficient and equitable economy, sustainable development, human rights. By contrast anti-formalism dressed its professionalism in a *culture of dynamism*. Why bother with rules and forms? Did they not support the past over the future, and did they not do this in an ignoble way, behind a veil of impartiality? Now it was time to reach beyond rules and the interminable controversies they occasioned. It was time to realize legislative purposes, community interests, and to balance the equities. There was to be an unmediated, perhaps even "authentic" relationship to social conflict. The professionals should speak directly to the values, interests, and passions involved – and they could do this by the technical languages of effectiveness, optimization, compliance.[295]

---

[294] Cf. Schmitt, *Gesetz und Urteil*, pp. 108–119; Hans Kelsen, *Introduction to Problems of Legal Theory. A Translation of the First Edition of the Reine Rechtslehre or Pure Theory of Law* (trans. Bonnie Litchewski Paulson and Stanley L. Paulson, with an introd. by Stanley L. Paulson, Oxford, Clarendon, 1992), pp. 77–89, and for a more elaborate account, cf. Hans Kelsen, *General Theory of Norms* (trans. Michael Hartney, Oxford, Clarendon, 1991), pp. 226–251.

[295] The discourse of "compliance" (in contrast to "breach") is one technique in the international relations' struggle against formalism. The problem with formalism, from an international relations' perspective, is that it is able to dispose with normative ambiguity only in formal dispute settlement procedures. Such procedures, however, do not rank highly within a culture of dynamism. So "compliance" is defined as a problem of technical management: conflicting participant interpretations about what might count as breach are set aside by technical measurements that are able to give a direct answer to questions about compliance irrespective of normative disagreements – but of course only under the assumption that the rule is *known* independently of such disagreements. The discourse of compliance – heavily meshed in the language of American political science – locates this knowledge in the international relations

All such notions appeared in a discussion organized by the Association of the Bar of New York City on May 2, 1966 on the US intervention in the Dominican Republic. Among invited speakers were Professor A. J. Thomas of the Southern Methodist University, the co-author of a background paper for the discussion, Professor Adolf A. Berle from the Columbia Law School, former Assistant Secretary of State, and Wolfgang Friedmann, also from Columbia. Professors Thomas and Berle were staunch defenders of the intervention. The infiltration of the revolution in the Dominican Republic by Cuban-trained communists constituted a clear and present danger, as President Johnson had said, to values that the United States projected over the Western Hemisphere. They made their arguments largely through deformalized reasoning. Professor Thomas held that "under basic legal theory... a legal rule can never be explained in terms of itself without reference to its purpose." The purpose of the rule against intervention was to protect "the liberty and self-determination of a people." But "[o]nce the communists control a government, liberty and self-determination are no longer possible." Hence, the intervention must have been justified.[296] It was also justified as self-defense against "armed attack" or "indirect aggression": if communists had successfully infiltrated the rebellion, their activities could be considered an armed attack against the territorial inviolability, the sovereignty and the independence of the Dominican Republic."[297]

There was, however, always also another tack in the arguments of Professors Thomas and Berle. To the claim that the OAS could not have been understood to take "enforcement action" in the absence of a proper authorization under Article 53 (1) of the UN Charter, Berle responded: "In old common law pleading, 'the man with the soundest

---

academy. As "breach" becomes "non-compliance," "law" becomes "regime," and peaceful settlement turns into management, the culture of dynamism inaugurates political science as a world tribunal.

[296] A. J. Thomas and Ann Van Wynen Thomas, "The Dominican Republic Crisis 1965. Legal Aspects," in *The Dominican Republic Crisis*, pp. 26–27.

[297] Thomas and Thomas, "The Dominican Republic Crisis," p. 30 and remark by A. J. Thomas, *The Dominican Republic Crisis*, pp. 96–97. In this argument, deformalization accomplishes two tasks that a formal argument could not accomplish. First, it presumes to know the *purpose* of the non-intervention rule in an unmediated fashion, irrespective of any interpretative disagreement that might exist between the parties or within legal doctrine about it. Neither are addressed: the purpose is *known*, not argued, and projected as part of the transcendental (and thus universal) condition of the argument. Second, the dissociation of liberty and communism is likewise not argued but known, again in an unmediated way, assumed as universally valid and thus in no need of (formal) defense.

case in the world was thrown out of court because his lawyers had forgotten to put in the right words of art.' I suggest that we cannot leave the rights of peoples, the safety of nations, to that kind of technicality."[298] In other words, as if in an afterthought, perhaps as an intuitive reflection of the awkwardness of the more formal – yet completely deformalized – reasoning, the proponents of the intervention sought to discard the relevance of the legal arguments altogether. Not without impatience, Berle took the floor, making it clear that the legal debate was somehow altogether beside the point: "We here deal seriously with international affairs, where life and death are at stake and not with interminable Byzantine legalistics without point or outcome."[299] Later on he added the rhetorical question, reminiscent of what Schmitt and Morgenthau had written: "in international crises, do you want action, or do you want merely words? We can have all manner of delay and debate. We can have all kinds of reference from this body to that body, to the Security Council, to the Powers having veto and back again. Is that international law or international mockery?"[300]

Faced with such arguments Professor Friedmann confessed he felt "a little like Alice in Wonderland," particularly in view of the "incredible suggestion that the revolution that took place was an act of attack against the United States, which justified self-defense." He then took on the anti-formalist legal theory of his interlocutors. They had suggested that black and white could not adequately portray the situation in world politics: "We all know that many legal situations are open and subject to different interpretations, but law is ultimately a matter of black and white, or we should have no business to sit here and profess to be lawyers . . . I submit we must find an answer in terms of right and wrong."[301] To the argument made by Mr Berle to think in terms of action, not words, Friedmann responded: "I think that as a legal argument this is perilous, because whether we like it or not, law is based on words, words formulated in statutes, in treaties, in conventions, in customary law."[302]

Now it is true, of course, that the way back to formalism was no more open to Friedmann in 1966 than it is for us today. If we think about the debate only in terms of deformalized reasoning vs. formal rules, we can have no reason to feel sympathy with Friedmann. But I think many

---

[298] Remark by Berle, *The Dominican Republic Crisis*, pp. 109–110.
[299] Remark by Berle, *The Dominican Republic Crisis*, p. 87.
[300] Remark by Berle, *The Dominican Republic Crisis*, p. 107.
[301] Remark by Friedmann, *The Dominican Republic Crisis*, p. 112.
[302] Remark by Friedmann, *The Dominican Republic Crisis*, p. 113.

Carl Schmitt, Hans Morgenthau and "international relations"

lawyers do feel sympathy for him – though they are perhaps uncertain about how to articulate that sympathy into a professionally respectable position. The first step in doing that is to realize that of all the protagonists in the debate, Friedmann – author of the widely used *Legal Theory* and *Law in Changing Society* as well as the posthumous recipient of the Phillips Prize of the American Philosophical Society – was the least vulnerable to the argument about the lack of awareness of the complexity of legal positions. Opening his remarks by pointing out that "many legal situations are open and subject to different interpretations," he wished, of course, to convey precisely the message that he was not just an impossible "Byzantine" formalist but well aware of the shades of grey in all legal argumentation. Nonetheless, in this debate the point of his critique is directed against the anti-formalist reasoning of Thomas and Berle. He says: "But there are norms of international law. If we wish to ignore them, then let us say frankly that international law is of no concern to us. But don't let us pretend that we argue in terms of international law, when in fact we argue in terms of power or of ideology."[303] Notice how Friedmann follows Morgenthau's traditionalism: law might be relevant or irrelevant but it should not be argued "in terms of power or ideology." Himself sometimes characterized as "realist," Friedmann finds much less offensive the setting aside of law from considerations of policy than the pretense that one's position of power is also supported by (suspect) legal arguments.[304] This is an argument about the somehow unacceptable arrogance of the position of Thomas and Berle. Can that arrogance be more clearly defined? Perhaps what Friedmann finds objectionable is the nonchalance with which Thomas and Berle treat his profession, the (to him) self-evident hypocrisy that accompanied their reasoning and that seemed to fatally undermine the profession's faith and integrity. Indeed, it may have seemed to him that what Thomas and Berle were doing was not part of that discourse at all.

Thomas and Berle spoke the language of moral universalism – but a universalism that showed itself as imperialism. They claimed to know what is good not only for the United States but for the citizens of the Dominican Republic (and everyone else), too. Because that was the starting-point (or condition of possibility) of their argument, they were never open to alternative views. That is what so enraged Friedmann: the implicit suggestion that the meaning of the rule of non-intervention or

[303] Remark by Friedmann, *The Dominican Republic Crisis*, p. 113.
[304] Cf. Wolfgang Friedmann, "The Reality of International Law – A Reappraisal" (1971), 10 *Columbia Journal of Transnational Law*, pp. 47–50.

the status of communism as aggression were so self-evident as to require no defense at all, and were projected as *conditions* of the debate, not as outcomes of it. Friedmann's arguments could never receive a hearing. They were overruled at the outset by the technical argument about the nature of the conversation that excluded Friedmann's "Byzantine" formalism. Friedmann felt that he was like Alice in Wonderland because the rules imposed on the debate by Thomas and Berle barred him from articulating his concerns by laying the conclusion he wanted to contest as its condition.

I suggest that the opposition between Thomas and Berle on the one hand, and Friedmann on the other, was not about "deformalized standards" and "formal rules," but about two cultures: the culture of dynamism and what could be called a *culture of formalism*. Even if formalism may no longer be open as a jurisprudential doctrine of the black and white of legal validity (a position perhaps never represented by anyone), nothing has undermined formalism as a culture of resistance to power, a social practice of accountability, openness, and equality whose status cannot be reduced to the political positions of any one of the parties whose claims are treated within it. As such, it makes a claim for universality that may be able to resist the pull towards imperialism. To be sure, we often think of formalism in terms of Kantian ideas about a (universal) reason – and in so doing fall into the trap of generalizing a European particularism: this is the stuff of the civilizing mission. The important task is to avoid that kind of imperialism while at the same time continuing the search for something beyond particular interests and identity politics, or the irreducibility of difference. This is what the culture of formalism hopes to achieve, and what was at issue in the debate in New York on May 2, 1966.

The decisive moment at which formalism's virtue was revealed was when Thomas and Berle retreated from rationalism to cynicism, moving from deformalized legal arguments about the purpose of non-intervention and the status of communism as aggression to invoking the ultimate irrelevance of law, including, of course, their own initial positions. Rational imperialism turned out to be a façade for cynical imperialism. What remained were hermetically sealed-off (subjective) "value-systems" whose clash could be resolved only by power. Deviating views received no treatment because the premises of Thomas and Berle allowed only the acceptance of their own conclusions. "Law" had no normative place. It may be used as a strategic instrument to ensure victory but it has no claim as against their material views and may be discarded as soon as victory by other means has been assured.

Now this is precisely what a culture of formalism cannot tolerate – the transformation of the formal into a façade for the material in a way that *denies the value of the formal as such*. There is an extremely important dissonance in the debate. Teasing out its implications will reveal that at issue was not only the good faith of the interlocutors or a professional "ethic of civility,"[305] even less any jurisprudential clash. The dissonance had to do with the conditions of democratic politics and progressive transformation in an era that had lost its faith in anything universal and, wary of being betrayed, has become accustomed to interpreting every potential universal as a disguised particular. Where Thomas and Berle were playing a game of power between firmly delimited political positions, Friedmann was trying to keep open the possibility of universal community, as mediated by his formalism. Thomas and Berle did not simply happen to have another substantive position from Friedmann's: the dissonance between their views related to how they saw the conditions of the debate. Thomas and Berle saw politics as a clash of incompatible particularities – "identity politics," in a word, while Friedmann kept open the space for something beyond the merely particular.

The culture of formalism represented by Friedmann may be characterized in a familiar way as a practice that builds on formal arguments that are available to all under conditions of equality. It seeks to persuade the protagonists (lawyers, decision-makers) to take a momentary distance from their preferences and to enter a terrain where these preferences should be justified, instead of taken for granted, by reference to standards that are independent from their particular positions or interests. Members of such a culture might be more interested in the generality of their arguments, their repercussions beyond the actual case, than in how that case will finally be resolved. Defenders of such culture may take their cue from Kant and insist on the need to base the outcome on some general principle, and frequently have a rather obsessive-looking interest in the procedural conditions imposed on the debate. They do this so as to distance the protagonists from their preferences and teach them openness to what others have to say. To be sure, the culture of formalism accepts that the translation of every voice to the professional

---

[305] An interesting defense of the Rule of Law in terms of an ethic of civility is made by Christine Synopwich, "Utopia and the Rule of Law," in Dyzenhaus, *Recrafting the Rule of Law*, pp. 178–195.

idiolect so as to give it a fair hearing may not always succeed. But it insists that absent the possibility of building social life on unmediated love or universal reason, persuading people to bracket their own sensibilities and learn openness for others, is not worthless.

All of this is familiar language. And it must be immediately granted that like any culture, formalism may often have become bureaucratic and worked as a smokescreen for apathy and disinterest. It may frequently have failed to live up to its promises and it has certainly sometimes been enlisted to support dubious or outright abominable causes. None of this, however, abolishes the value of the political message that its rituals, traditions, and documents express sometimes more, sometimes less adequately. What is this message? To put it simply, and, I fear, through a banality it may not deserve, the message is that there must be limits to the exercise of power, that those who are in positions of strength must be accountable and that those who are weak must be heard and protected, and that when professional men and women engage in an argument about what is lawful and what is not, they are engaged in a politics that imagines the possibility of a community overriding particular alliances and preferences and allowing a meaningful distinction between lawful constraint and the application of naked power.

Something like that was part of the political faith of the men of 1873 who projected international law as a professional practice to give effect to their complex of liberal rationalism and Victorian moral verities. It was involved in the concept of the *Rechtsstaat* as it was espoused by the (often Jewish) professors in Germany and Austria at the turn of the century that would hold in check the autocratic tendencies and disruptive forces of their fragile societies. It was the ideal of those who spoke of the rights of individuals – but also of those who defended a right of self-determination of human groups under a protective statehood. It helped to produce all the federalist proposals, blueprints for peace, disarmament and the public, international administration of the colonies in the League of Nations. And it returned from the Second World War as the unarticulated premise of a legal pragmatism that invoked "the development of international law by the international court," looked towards increased codification, the functional activities of international organizations, human rights, and the narrowing down of the domestic jurisdiction of States.

A *culture of formalism* – the story of international law from Rolin to Friedmann does have coherence. Of course, there have been twists and turns, large disappointments and small victories, starting-points that have led nowhere as well as results produced by external causes. There has been stupidity, unwarranted ambition, careerism, and much hypocrisy. But there has also been some political wisdom, and a little courage, times when faith was lost, but also stubborn refusal to admit defeat. Like any culture, formalism has oscillated ambivalently between a bright and a dark side: activism, belief in progress, rational administration on the one hand, careerism, indifference, advancement of special interest on the other. It has never been terribly sophisticated in terms of philosophical defenses and often outright disappointing when it has tried to find them. But it does have coherence and a distinct *feel* that we recognize as we read the debates in New York in May 1966. For those who feel sympathy towards Friedmann, but find it hard to express why they feel so, I suggest that the sympathy is directed towards the culture of formalism that is so conspicuously presented in his arguments.

There are two important objections to such a positive appraisal. First, it may seem that it merely rehearses a standard liberal defense of the Rule of Law – and ignores the extent to which the Rule of Law has been undermined by the realist critique that every legal position is a "politics of law." Second, it may also, or alternatively, appear that to side with Friedmann is to accept a conservatism that privileges the policy of the status quo over the interests that Thomas and Berle seek to advance, a policy equally particularist as theirs, though opposite. In other words, it may be objected that what I have called the "culture of formalism" is merely another expression for a rather worn-out form of legalism that betrays a systematic conservatism.

I do not think so. There is room for a culture of formalism even after the critique of rules has done its work. It is precisely because the critique is correct that formalism cannot be permanently associated with any of the substantive outcomes it may have co-existed with. Of course, formalism may occasionally have supported good, occasionally evil policies. It cannot replace political commitment or responsibility. Formalists may sometimes have claimed that their policies were "good" or "legitimate" because they were produced or supported by formalism. In such cases they made a monster of it. Such defenders ignore the critique of rules, and the fact that they could have acted otherwise, too. To assess the culture of formalism by reference to its substantive alignments is, as Kelsen well knew, to mix up categories that should be held distinct. A bad policy is (and should be criticized as) bad as policy and not because of whether or not it was supported by impeccable legal arguments. The emancipatory core, and the universalism of the culture of formalism, lies precisely in its resistance to subsumption under particularist causes.

But the culture of formalism cannot be reduced to a jurisprudential doctrine, either. To assume that Friedmann's position in the debate on May 2, 1966 may be translated into a defense of legal positivism or a sociological generalization about the effects of the Rule of Law is, again, to remain blind to the dissonance in the arguments: the closed world of fixed identities (we vs. the communists) in Thomas and Berle, Friedmann's openness to the possibility of community between different-thinking particularities. Alvarez, Le Fur, Kaufmann, Scelle, Lauterpacht, Morgenthau, and many other lawyers did dress their reformism in jurisprudential positions, suggesting that international problems could be resolved only after the adoption of one or another theory as the "basis" for one's legal practice. This was academic hubris. As I have argued elsewhere, resolutions to social problems cannot be derived from legal theories.[306] Theories may make us see new things and articulate experiences more sharply, and they may make us better practitioners. But they do not, and can not, contain ready-made blueprints of the good society. As Schmitt and Morgenthau correctly pointed out, international lawyers (among other liberals) have tried to do away with the irreducibly conflictual character of politics by presuming that the good society can be derived from ethically, sociologically, or scientifically constructed laws. But the fact that they cannot be so derived is an essential condition of democratic politics.

So I come finally to the value of the culture of formalism in trying to account for the possibility of democratic politics in an era deeply suspicious both of universalist ideologies and the bureaucratic management of social conflict by bargaining between interest groups. Between the Scylla of Empire and the Charybdis of fragmentation, the culture of formalism resists reduction into substantive policy, whether imperial or particular. It represents the possibility of the universal (as Kant well knew) but it does this by remaining "empty," a negative instead of a positive datum, and thus avoids the danger of imperialism. Instead, it tries to induce every particularity to bring about the universality hidden in it. Let me explain. We have become accustomed to thinking of the (postmodern) political world in terms of separate identities seeking recognition. No particular identity, however, can make a claim without doing this in universal terms, albeit, as Ernesto Laclau has shown, in terms that

---

[306] Martti Koskenniemi, "Letter to the Editors of the Symposium" (1999), 93 *AJIL*, pp. 351–361.

are necessarily negative, instead of positive, in terms of a lack – for instance lack of voice, lack of resources, lack of education, etc.[307] To make itself heard, the particular must apply to something that is universal: perhaps a right of self-determination, fair distribution of resources, equality of opportunity, and so on. No group – especially no group in a vulnerable position – can claim a right merely in terms of its separate "value-system." But even Thomas and Berle were invoking something other than the US constitution, namely the (universal) right to security and assistance against armed aggression. The particular and the universal are related through paradox: the articulation of the particular can be carried out only by reaching towards the universal. In this way, the universal also remains inseparable from the particular claims from which it emanates: no automatic application to others – imperialism – is implied.

History – and European history, in particular – is full of examples of cases where a particular actor has claimed to take on the body of that which is universal. The Christian church claimed this in the Middle Ages, the French nation in 1789, "European civilization" at the end of the nineteenth century, the working class and the market in the twentieth century. Each of them was accompanied by a law that claimed universality – and each fell, predictably, when the asserted universality revealed itself as disguised particularity. This experience has fundamentally affected today's hopes of political transformation. On the one hand, every norm or institution appears always as only partial, subjective, ideological – with the result, finally, that none of them is any longer vulnerable to critique. This has been a part of the paralysis of democratic politics. If there is no truth, there is no ideology. Politics becomes only a clash of incommensurate "value-systems" none of which can be rationally preferred. No distinction can be made between the discourse of the oppressor and the discourse of the oppressed. Only a reversal of power is possible but *never the form of that power itself*. The decolonized will use terror against the master that had terrorized it in the past. Positions are reversed but terror remains.[308]

This image of modern politics fails to account for the dependence of every particularity on a universality that defines it, and constitutes the ground from which it may experience itself as unfulfilled, devoid of some aspect without which it cannot fully realize itself. Through attention to

---

[307] Ernesto Laclau, "Universalism, Particularism and the Question of Identity," and "Subject of Politics, Politics of Subject," in *Emancipation(s)* (London, Verso, 1996), pp. 20–35, 48–51. [308] Laclau, "Universalism," pp. 29–32.

that "lack," that absence of what a particular feels it should possess in order to be fully itself, focus is directed to its universal aspect: its alleged right to self-determination, a fair distribution of resources, etc. By directing attention to that universality, the particular is opened up, and its communal lien, its shared property or value with other particularities, is revealed. But unlike in imperialism, it is not opened by a positive principle but a negative one: what is it that we lack? *The ability to articulate this lack, and to do this in universal terms, is what the culture of formalism provides.* Such articulation remains always relative to the particularity from which it emerges, and vulnerable to critique as such. Universality here is neither a fixed principle nor a process but a *horizon of possibility* that opens up the particular identities in the very process where they make their claims of identity.[309] This is why a culture of formalism that insists on articulation in terms of a universal principle, such as Friedmann's, when assessed against that of his opponents, is also premised on a need for democracy's constant expansion. Instead of repeating the structure of power by accepting this or that particularity's subjective value – through which the other would then be coerced – the very structure of power is now put in question by questioning the universality that it takes for granted. The decolonized does not merely take on the instruments of its colonial master, and turn those against it, but seeks to articulate the lack of security it experienced under colonial rule as the universal violation committed by its former ruler and make the eradication of that lack the principle of its future rule.

In other words, the political dissonance in the arguments between Thomas and Berle on the one hand, and Friedmann on the other, had to do with the possibility of a non-imperialist universality, together with a critique of the particular way universality had been defined in the arguments of Thomas and Berle. Their universalism was one of complete difference: the communist as the aggressor became the object of full exclusion: it was us *against* them. Friedmann's formalism would have required an open articulation of this principle and thus its subjection to critique that would have integrated Thomas and Berle in a single universe with the communists – thus undermining the imperialist effect of their

---

[309] To the objection that such notion of the universal reproduces Kant's regulative ideal and invites cynicism as the objective can never be realized, Laclau retorts that the actual aims remain always all that the actors fight for; here universality is incorporated as an aspect of their aims, not a good beyond it, "Structure, History and the Political," in Judith Butler, Ernesto Laclau, and Slavoj Žižek, *Contingency, Hegemony, Universality. Contemporary Dialogues on the Left* (London, Verso, 2000), p. 196.

Carl Schmitt, Hans Morgenthau and "international relations"

dichotomous world. Against the full closure of the American professors Friedmann was invoking the possibility of an open area of politics – the possibility that the principle of legal community projected by international law be articulated, reaffirmed, or perhaps redefined in the course of the debate. This may seem a rather strange way of putting a familiar idea: the Rule of Law. But it is not. The Rule of Law hopes to fix the universal in a particular, positive space (a law, a moral or procedural principle, an institution). A culture of formalism resists such fixation. For any such connection will make the formal appear merely a surface for something substantive or procedural, and thus destroys it. In this sense universality (and universal community) is written into the culture of formalism as an idea (or horizon), unattainable but still necessary. That it may appear as a culture of resistance comes from its suspicion of being harnessed for substantive causes that have only rendered themselves invisible by becoming internalized, or "second nature." To rid itself of its suspicion, it must remain open for other voices, other expressions of "lack" (or injustice) that, when given standing under it, redefine the scope of its universality. In the case of the Dominican Republic, this might have involved looking into the claims of the local factions, giving effect to the results of the election, and examining the meaning of "communism" in the conditions of social deprivation that had existed in the country. Of course, the result of the argument would have been uncertain. It would probably have polarized the debate along the same lines. But the point is not in the immediate result but in the formal standing which the aspirations of universality inscribed in the claims of the various particular groups would have received. International law would not have been reduced into "anti-communism" but would have recognized the legitimacy of the claims made even by "communists" inasmuch as these claims would have presumed universal validity.

What this means, also, is that a culture of formalism is recognizable, or indeed has identity, only in terms of its opposition to something that it is not. Here I have defined it in contrast to the culture of dynamism represented by the American anti-formalists. But it has no essence, and its techniques are constantly redefined in the context of political struggle: what the particular lacks cannot be decided once and for all.[310] If the claims of women, for instance, cannot be heard in a public law oriented system of representation, then that system has become an aspect of the process of silencing. However formal its language may appear, it

[310] Laclau, "Subject of Politics," pp. 56–60.

is betrayed as particularist, and substantive, in its remaining closed to that particular call for recognition of identity. But it is equally closed if it fixates on a particular understanding of "woman," or gender, and fails to articulate differences within those categories. And so on. In this way, formalism projects the universal community as a standard – but always as an unachieved one. The number or nature of claims of identity – and thus articulations of universal lack – remain undefined and changing. Thus every decision process with an aspiration to inclusiveness must constantly negotiate its own boundaries as it is challenged by new claims or surrounded by new silences. Yet because it is unachieved, it can sustain (radical) democracy and political progress, and resist accepting as universal the claims it has done most to recognize in the past.

As a *culture*, formalism is certainly not a substance or a theory, but straddles such frontiers as well as other dichotomies such as the social and the individual, constraint and freedom, even past and future. Although every (legal) decision is constitutive, and not just a reproduction of some underlying structure, each decision also acts as a kind of surface on which the horizon of universality becomes visible. Formalism's utopian moment lies in its resistance towards being reduced to structure (which is anyway indeterminate) or pure subjectivity (Schmitt's "decision"), and in its identifying itself as a practice of decision-making that persists in time and through which the aspirations of self-determining communities remain alive – even as (or perhaps precisely because) the universal they embody remains only a "horizon."[311] By contrast, anti-formalism is reductionist. In seeing law as determined by external objectives, structures or necessities, or making it seem the infinitely flexible instrument of the political decision-maker, it kills the possibility of politics, and of freedom, that lies in the gap between the two.

As with any culture, more and less authentic representations appear, superficial and "deep" variants, together with occasional cases of fraud, the appropriation of outward symbols without internal conviction, for purposes of manipulation. It was perhaps this special violation that explains Friedmann's anxiety at the meeting on May 2, 1966. For fraud here was the ultimate transgression, the cynicism of letting the ideal of

---

[311] Laclau speaks of a "chain of equivalences": while each decision or event remains particular, non-identical with others, the structure of political struggle may throw them on the same side of a constitutive antagonism. In such a case they become, irrespective of their differences, individual symbols or carriers of what are universal claims, "Subject of Politics," pp. 56–57, 63–65.

universality fall the moment when something about the realization of one's particular preferences is obstructed by it: "if this is to be the law of nations, then I do not see how I can continue to teach international law at Columbia, or anywhere else."[312]

[312] Remark by Friedmann, *The Dominican Republic Crisis*, p. 112.

Epilogue

There once was a professional gentleman, a barrister who divided his leisure between educating his two sons and furthering the welfare of his people. As he grew older, he saw progress divide its fruit very unevenly around himself. On the one hand, it offered marvellous opportunities for political liberation and personal autonomy; on the other hand it undermined familiar truths and traditions. The virtues of character that had seemed such reliable guides for personal and public lives – charity, reasonableness, courage in the face of adversity – were increasingly ridiculed as the symbols of the corruption of an ancient world.

He decided to learn philosophy and the new sciences of society so as to understand what tradition and experience had failed to teach him. Why were people prepared to go to such lengths in defense of extreme views on matters that had earlier been thought to have been regulated by reason and good sense? He did not precisely wish to become a philosopher or a sociologist but hoped to find intellectual reassurance and perhaps a more efficient platform from which to continue his civilizing activities.

As the sons grew up, they learned that none of this had really worked. The father had to quit his welfare activities, partly because they seemed to have no effect on his clients who were either joining extremist causes or sinking deeper into apathy, partly because they threatened his own livelihood. In an increasingly difficult economic situation, he retired a poor man. The sons loved their father dearly but reacted in opposite ways to his misfortune. One promised him that he would bring the father's project to a conclusion. The good son shared the father's ideals and would teach himself to avoid his mistakes so that he could one day come home with proof that the father had been right all along. Then they would sit down and everything would be well, as it had been. The

Epilogue

rebel son loved his father equally. But because it broke his heart to think how unjustly the world had treated his father, he reacted by rejection. "You failed because you were *wrong*," he shouted just before he slammed the door behind him.

Both sons had successful, even very successful careers, and many people admired them and tried to learn from them although what they taught were the exact opposites. But it often seemed that they were followed less because of the depth of their teaching than their ability to give powerful expression to something that many people felt intuitively right though somehow always only partially convincing. As they were saying the opposite things, well, then perhaps it was not so tragic that the listeners were believing those incompatible things as well. In the end, it was not what the two said, but the strength of their commitment that mattered most to their acolytes: how few people nowadays *really* say that in the end all that matters is either love and charity or the lust for power! "Now *we* of course know that it is *both* love and power because the world is a dreadfully complex place – but isn't it nice to know that there are some who still commit their lives to a religion of love or a religion of power as if there still existed clear alternatives to choose from?"

An empty space separates the end of the foregoing chapters from today. What happened to international law after 1960? The *Institut de droit international* continued to meet but with little sense that its members might represent the juridical *conscience* of the civilized world or that anything about international progress might depend on what took place in its closed sessions. The idea of a scientific restatement to guide the development of international relations had never been terribly successful. By 1960, the very languages of conscience–consciousness and civilization had become either inappropriate or meaningless as the articulation of the sense of legal activity.

At that time, the profession did not yet feel the implications of this fact. Many of the last representatives of international law's heroic period left the scene (Kaufmann retired in 1958, Alvarez and Lauterpacht died in 1960, Scelle in 1961, Morgenthau had already quit writing about international law in 1940) but their presence was still concretely felt. The vision of a public law oriented federalism as an instrument for liberal–humanitarian reform still seemed to bear a liberating potential. Speaking in his capacity as the President of the *Institut* to his colleagues in Brussels in 1963, Henri Rolin (1891–1973), the son of Albéric Rolin, nephew of Gustave Rolin-Jaequemyns, identified four factors that were now having a significant effect on his Institute as well as the profession more generally: technological progress, the expansion of international organization, the Cold War, and decolonization. The first two were progressive developments that gave international lawyers much to do in the management of the world order. The harnessing of technology by public international institutions opened encouraging prospects for the control and direction of social change. On the other hand, the Cold War provided a convenient explanation for why a full realization of the internationalist hopes was still impossible. If the Charter had not become an effective constitution of mankind, this must have resulted from the antagonism between the Great Powers: the Rule of Law would have to wait for the coming of a more enlightened age. Meanwhile, the way of peaceful compromise would have to be followed. But the most significant fact of the surrounding political reality was decolonization which Rolin interpreted in accordance with the profession's universalist hopes. The expansion of sovereignty and the increasing access to resources for the world's population would bring international law's expansion to a conclusion. In this regard, Rolin observed, there was still much to do. The developed States had not taken seriously their responsibility towards the poor countries of the Third World. And he ended his talk by proposing the inclusion of a *devoir d'assistance* in the Institute's declaration of rights and duties from 1929.[1]

Reading this talk from the perspective of today, our assessment is different. Technology is no longer seen predominantly as a promise but often rather a threat. The ability of public international organizations to manage technological change has been very limited. Formal decolonization did not turn out to create a just international system. Initiatives within the United Nations, such as the New International Economic Order, failed to bring about a noticeable transformation in the global distribution of resources. On the contrary, when the regulative objectives of the 1982 UN Convention on the Law of the Sea were watered down in a 1994 implementation agreement, this was done under the language of "securing the universality of the Convention" that in fact underwrote the Western policy of creating a cost-effective market for private enterprise in the deep seabed.[2] Receiving the benefit of sove-

---

[1] "Discours inaugural de M. Henri Rolin, Président de l'Institut" (1963), 50/II *Annuaire IDI*, pp. 38–47.
[2] Cf. Martti Koskenniemi and Marja Lehto, "The Privilege of Universality: International Law, Economic Ideology, and Seabed Resources" (1996), 65 *Nordic Journal of International Law*, pp. 533–555.

reignty did not do away with conflict in the Third World, though it may have localized much of it as civil war. The end of the Cold War did bring about a significant expansion of the electoral process. Yet, today's democratic melancholy suggests that progressive transformation requires more than the export of a determined set of public institutions – but just what this might require and what role international law might play in the future remains obscure. Whatever globalization may mean, it has certainly not strengthened international public policy. Nothing may have undermined the need for a middle ground between the Empire and the tribe, capitalism and identity politics. But whether it is possible to articulate and uphold such a space, without repeating the tired antics of statehood, the Rule of Law, and a State-centered international system remains an open question.

In 1963, international lawyers could still think the civilizing project valid as such, partly under way, partly obstructed by external causes. Like Henri Rolin, they would call forth a change of vocabulary in this respect, but at the same time reaffirm their faith in the public law institutions that provided the context of their professional activity. It is much less clear whether such faith can be sustained today. The acceptance by the developed States of a legal obligation to eradicate poverty in the Third World is no longer seriously expected. Indeed, the very idea that economic injustice might be usefully dealt with by States, and public law, may now seem altogether old-fashioned, and politically ambivalent. Legal internationalism always hovered insecurely between cosmopolitan humanism and imperial apology, revealing itself as either one or the other the moment it was enlisted to support a particular institutional or normative arrangement. In the conditions of the Cold War, it may still have been possible to think that this resulted from the political interpretations that the protagonists in that struggle projected on to the law. Today, it has become much harder to believe that there is a rationality embedded in international law that is independent from the political perspectives from which it is seen. On the contrary, a Security Council sanctions regime or a multilateral trade arrangement within the World Trade Organization appear as completely legal and completely political at the same time, rather like Wittgenstein's image of the duck–rabbit. If there is no perspective-independent meaning to public law institutions and norms, what then becomes of international law's universal, liberating promise?

From the outside, little may have changed between 1960 and 2000. Choosing international law at law school may still seem more than a banal career choice among others. It still implies a commitment to a mild cosmopolitan progressivism: human rights, protection of the environment, peaceful settlement, preference for the universal over the particular, integration over sovereignty. That the choice is commonly described as *commitment* highlights its existential character, its being about more than cold calculation of personal gain or the interests of one's clan. An aspect of heroism may be involved: there will be difficulties, even risk in the way ahead, and no guarantee of final victory. Courage against adversity, speaking truth to power — such images still make up a large chunk of the profession's psychological imagery. However subdued the sense of commitment to a universal normative system may appear in the daily activity of legal professionals, it is hard to think how their routines could exist for a second without some such background explanation bridging the gap between recurrent reform projects and blueprints about "governance" and control, and the reality of picking up the *per diem* from the latest caucus meeting in Geneva or New York.

Yet commitment is fragile and hard to sustain.[3] Although international governance through public law institutions continues to occupy the professional imagination, little has been done to respond to the challenges of contingency and the market. Invoking the name of Kant may go some way towards a justifying explanation but perhaps more by way of a cultural *vignette* than a serious piece of argument. Faith in progressive internationalism may have become impossible to articulate in an intellectually respectable fashion. Power and law have been entangled in much more complex relationships than the conventional imagery would allow: if collective security in the League failed because it lacked the support of power, the United Nations seems to have suffered from its becoming indistinguishable from power. Critique of sovereignty — as central to the profession in 1873, 1923, or 1963 as now — is not proof of the beneficial nature of one's proposed politics. Intervention may still emerge from solidarity and superiority and it is hard to tell which alternative provides the better frame of interpretation. As the debate on Kosovo has suggested, there may be very little law in that direction anyway. And the doubt must remain that the abstract subject celebrated as the carrier of universal human rights is but a fabrication of the disciplinary techniques of Western "governmentality" whose only reality lies

---

[3] I have discussed this further in Martti Koskenniemi, "Between Commitment and Cynicism. Outline of a Theory of International Law as Practice," in *Collection of Essays of Legal Advisers of States, Legal Advisers of International Organizations and Practitioners in the Field of International Law* (New York, United Nations, 1999), pp. 495–523.

in the imposition on social relations of a particular structure of domination. Universality still seems an essential part of progressive thought – but it also implies an imperial logic of identity: I will accept you, but only on the condition that I may think of you as I think of myself. But recognition of particularity may be an act of condescension, and at worst a prelude for rejection. Between the arrogance of universality and the indifference of particularity, what else is there apart from the civilized manners of gentle spirits?

What is the meaning of the *esprit d'internationalité* today? The verities of the men of 1873 did not survive the critiques developed by the modernity they helped to inaugurate. But neither did the *Ersatz* moralities of philosophy or sociology in the 1920s or 1930s. The vision of a single social space of "the international" has been replaced by a fragmented, or kaleidoscopic understanding of the world where the new configurations of space and time have completely mixed up what is particular and what universal. Today, the question is not whether to be cosmopolitan or not but what kind of cosmopolis one should prefer, against what particularity should one be poised today. Should there be free trade – or should some values be imagined as cultural in a deep sense, without expression in international law's political economy? Or how should one think of the global regime of cyberspace: in the struggle between Nokia and Microsoft, on the one hand, to protect commercial confidentiality, and the CIA and the Pentagon, on the other, to receive access codes for the pursuit of international criminality, which side should international lawyers take?

Because no position or policy may be identified with the international spirit as such, and even if it were, there would be no guarantee of its beneficiality, taking on the "international" as the space for one's commitment is meaningless – apart from the sense in which it may provide a political identification whose significance comes from its opposition to some contrasting pattern in the patchwork of political antagonism: I am for trade, you are for the environment. Yet environmental and trade regulators may find themselves aligned against the deregulators of the World Bank or a powerful department of trade. If particularity is the only universal characteristic we have, then every universal idea will reveal itself as particularism. None of this is to say that international law could not remain useful as a diplomatic language and an honorable aspect of professional education at law schools. But its self-understanding must now be permanently affected by the ease with which it is relativized into the rituals of a tribe living somewhere between First and

Second Avenues, around 45th and 50th street, New York, and compelled to negotiate with other tribes in a terrain that remains a no-man's land.

Like the men of 1873, international lawyers today stress the pragmatic functions of their profession. Blueprints for world order have been taken over by technical sub-disciplines and specializations. Environmental or human rights regimes are created and the legal aspects of the European Union's foreign and security policy debated without the need for an overarching theory. Writing commentary on the Statute of the International Criminal Court or a critique of the latest round of talks at the World Trade Organization offer platforms for political engagement and the demonstration of technical skill. Debates about institutional reform and reconceptualization of, say, Security Council decision-making as enforcement of human rights and democracy sustain back-up narratives that link counseling or article-writing to larger visions, grasped by private intuition rather than public discourse. Where Rolin, Scelle, or Lauterpacht derived their pragmatism from a commitment to international law as part of the cosmopolitan reason, and projected it as always *already* containing the project of their ideal society, and only a shadow of a doubt blocked the optimism of the 1960s, today's lawyers are not entitled to wallow in such reveries. This may sound all to the good – but there is a paradox here. In the absence of an overarching standpoint, legal technique will reveal itself as more evidently political than ever before. But precisely at this moment it has lost the ability to articulate its politics: when everything is politics, Schmitt wrote, nothing is. Without the ability to articulate political visions and critiques, international law becomes pragmatism all the way down, an all-encompassing internalization, symbol, and reaffirmation of power.

But maybe the time of synthesis is not yet here. Maybe it is now a time to listen, and to learn. And in the process one could do worse than remember that however one imagines what one is doing, and how that relates to other people's being, history has put the international lawyer in a tradition that has thought of itself as the "organ of the legal conscience of the civilized world." I still think international law cannot be reconceived all the time, and that doing it is at least as important as thinking about doing it. But I agree that there must be a standpoint for critique that is not just an idiosyncratic "decision" by the occasional Weberian jurist but can be articulated by reference to the ideal of universal emancipation, peace, and social progress. It is not enough to isolate these as "regulative ideals" – an all-too-convenient justification for complacency. International law's energy and hope lies in its ability to articulate existing transformative commitment in the language of rights and duties and thereby to give voice to those who are otherwise routinely excluded. This can not mean fixing the law's content permanently to definite institutional or normative structures. It is a formal ideal that seeks community by understanding that every community is based on an exclusion and that therefore it must be a part of an acceptable community's self-definition that it constantly negotiates that exclusion, widens its horizon.

Bibliography

Abbott, Kenneth and Duncan Snidal, "Why States Act through Formal International Organizations" (1998), 42 *Journal of Conflict Resolution*, pp. 3–32

Abrams, Irwin, "The Emergence of the International Law Societies" (1957), 19 *Review of Politics*, pp. 361–380

Acker, Detlev, *Walther Schücking* (Münster, Aschendorff, 1970)

Adam, Robert, "Völkerrechtliche Okkupation und deutsches Kolonialstaatrecht" (1891), 6 *Archiv des öffentlichen Rechts*, pp. 234–240

Ago, Roberto, "Droit positif et droit international" (1957), III *Annuaire français de droit international*, pp. 14–62

Alexandrowitz, Charles Henry, *The European–African Confrontation* (Leiden, Sijthoff, 1973)

Almog, Shmuel, *Nationalism & Antisemitism in Modern Europe 1815–1945* (Oxford, Pergamon, 1990)

Alvarez, Alejandro, *La codification du droit international – ses tendences, ses bases* (Paris, Pedone, 1912)

  Le droit international nouveau dans ses rapports avec la vie actuelle des peuples (Paris, Pedone, 1959)

  Le droit international nouveau; son acceptation – son étude (Paris, Pedone, 1960)

  Exposé des motifs et Déclaration des grands principes du droit international moderne (Paris, Editions internationales, 1936)

  "La méthode du droit international à la veille de sa codification" (1913), XX *Revue générale de droit international public*, pp. 725–747

  Une nouvelle conception des études juridiques (Paris, 1904)

Alvarez, Alejandro and Albert de la Pradelle, "L'Institut des hautes études internationales et l'enseignement du droit des gens" (1939), XLVI *Revue générale de droit international public*, pp. 666–669

Anghie, Antony, "Finding the Peripheries: Sovereignty and Colonialism in Nineteenth-Century International Law" (1999), 40 *Harvard International Law Journal*, pp. 1–80

Bibliography

"Francisco de Vitoria and the Colonial Origins of International Law" (1996), 5 *Social and Legal Studies*, pp. 321–336

"Time Present and Time Past: Globalization, International Financial Institutions and the Third World" (2000), 32 *New York University Journal of International Law and Politics*, pp. 243–290

Anstey, Roger, *King Leopold's Legacy: The Congo under Belgian Rule 1908–1960* (Oxford University Press, 1966)

Arendt, Hannah, *The Origins of Totalitarianism* (new edn., with added prefaces, San Diego and New York, Harcourt, 1973)

Arnaud, André-Jean, "Une doctrine de l'état tranquillisante: le solidarisme juridique" (1976), 21 *Archives de philosophie de droit*, pp. 131–151

Les juristes face à la société du XIXe siècle à nos jours (Paris, PUF, 1975)

Arnold, Matthew, "Culture and Anarchy," in *Culture and Anarchy and Other Writings*, Stefan Collini (ed.) (Cambridge University Press, 1993 [1859]), pp. 53–211

Arntz, Egide, "Le Gouvernement portugais et l'Institut de droit international" (1883), XV *Revue de droit international et de législation comparée*, pp. 537–546

Aron, Raymond, "On the Historical Condition of the Sociologist," in *Politics and History*, pp. 62–82

Politics and History (New Brunswick and London, Transaction, 1984)

Asser, T. M. C., "Droit international privé et droit uniforme" (1880), XII *Revue de droit international et de législation comparée*, pp. 5–22

"Fondation de la Revue" (1902), 2/IV *Revue de droit international et de législation comparée*, pp. 109–20

Bade, K. J., "Imperial Germany and West Africa: Colonial Movement, Business Interests, and Bismarck's 'Colonial Policies,'" in Förster, Mommsen, and Robinson, *Bismarck, Europe, and Africa*, pp. 121–147

Balakrishnan, Gopal, *The Enemy: An Intellectual Portrait of Carl Schmitt* (London, Verso, 2000)

Bar, L. von, "Grundlage und Kodifikation des Völkerrechts" (1912–13), VI *Archiv für Rechts und Wirtschaftsphilosophie*, pp. 145–158

Barreau, Marc, *Précis du droit de la nature et des gens* (Paris, Ladvocat, 1831)

Basdevant, Jules, "Règles générales du droit de la paix" (1936/IV), 58 *Recueil des cours de l'Académie de droit international*, pp. 471–692

Bauman, Zygmunt, *Modernity and Ambivalence* (Cambridge, Polity, 1991)

Baumgart, Winfried, *Imperialism: The Idea and Reality of British and French Colonial Expansion 1880–1914* (Oxford University Press, 1982)

Beaud, O. and Wachsmann, P. (eds.), *La science juridique française et la science juridique allemande de 1870 à 1918* (1990), 1 *Annales de la faculté de droit de Strasbourg*

Beller, Steven, *Vienna and the Jews 1867–1938* (Cambridge University Press, 1989)

Benda, Julien, *The Treason of the Intellectuals*, trans. Richard Aldington (New York, Norton, 1969 [1928])

Bendersky, Joseph, "Carl Schmitt at Nuremberg" (1987), 72 *Telos*, pp. 91–96

Bibliography

Carl Schmitt: Theorist for the Reich (Princeton University Press, 1983)
"Interrogation of Carl Schmitt by Robert Kempner" (1987), 72 *Telos*, pp. 97–129
Benjamin, Walter, *Illuminations: Essays and Reflections*, Hannah Arendt ed. and with an introd. by (New York, Schocken, 1968)
Bentham, Jeremy, "Principles of International Law," in *The Works*, published under the superintendence of John Bowring (9 vols., Edinburgh, 1843), II, pp. 537–560
Bergbohm, Carl, *Staatsverträge und Gesetze als Quellen des Völkerrechts* (Dorpat, Mattiessen, 1876)
Berthélemy, Henri, *L'Ecole de droit* (Paris, LGDJ, 1932)
Best, Geoffrey, *Humanity in Warfare* (London, Weidenfeld & Nicolson, 1980)
Bisschop, W. R., "Die Haager Völkerrechtsakademie" (1913), 1 *Jahrbuch des Völkerrechts*, pp. 1363–1374
Blanchard, Georges, "L'affaire Fachoda et le droit international" (1899), VI *Revue générale de droit international public*, pp. 380–430
Bleiber, Fritz, *Der Völkerbund. Die Entstehung der Völkerbundssatzung* (Berlin, Kohlhammer, 1939)
Bloch, Ernst, *Natural Law and Human Dignity*, trans. Dennis J. Schmidt (Cambridge, Mass., MIT Press, 1987)
Bluntschli, Johann Caspar, "Arische Völker und arische Rechte," in *Gesammelte kleine Schriften*, I, pp. 63–90
  Beuterecht im Krieg (Nördlingen, Beck, 1870, reprint in Amsterdam by Rodopi, 1970)
  "Le Congrès de Berlin et sa portée au point de vue de droit international" (1879), XI *Revue de droit international et de législation comparée*, pp. 1–44, 411–430
  Denkwürdiges aus meinem Leben (3 vols., published by Rudolf Seyerlen, Nördlingen, Beck, 1884)
  "Eigenthum," in *Gesammelte kleine Schriften*, I, pp. 181–232
  "Die Einwirkung der nationalität auf die Religion und kirchlichen Dinge," in *Gesammelte kleine Schriften*, II, pp. 132–147
  "Die Entwickelung des Rechtes und die Recht der Entwickelung," in *Gesammelte kleine Schriften*, I, pp. 44–55
  Gesammelte kleine Schriften (2 vols., Nördlingen, Beck, 1879)
  "Geschichte des Rechtes der religiösen Bekenntnisfreiheit," in *Gesammelte kleine Schriften*, I, pp. 100–133
  Das moderne Kriegsrecht der civilisierten Staaten (Nördlingen, Beck, 1866)
  Das moderne Völkerrecht der civilisierten Staaten als Rechtsbuch dargestellt (2nd edn., Nördlingen, Beck, 1872)
  "Die nationale Statenbildung und die moderne Deutsche Staat," in *Gesammelte kleine Schriften*, II, pp. 70–113

Bibliography

"Die Organisation des europäischen Staatenvereines," in *Gesammelte kleine Schriften*, II, pp. 279–312

"Person und Persönlichkeit, Gesammtperson," in *Gesammelte kleine Schriften*, I, pp. 91–100

"Der Rechtsbegriff," in *Gesammelte kleine Schriften*, I, pp. 7–20

"Das römische Papstthum und das Völkerrecht," in *Gesammelte kleine Schriften*, II, pp. 236–255

"Der Staat ist der Mann," in *Gesammelte kleine Schriften*, I, pp. 260–286

"Zur Revision der staatlichen Grundbegriffe," in *Gesammelte kleine Schriften*, I, pp. 287–317

Bohman, James and Matthias Lutz-Bachmann (eds.), *Perpetual Peace. Essays in Kant's Cosmopolitan Ideal* (Cambridge, Mass., MIT Press, 1997)

Bond, Brian, *War and Society in Europe 1870–1970* (London, Fontana, 1983)

Bonfils, Henri and Paul Fauchille, *Manuel de droit international public* (2nd edn., Paris, Rousseau, 1898)

Bonnecase, J., *La pensée juridique française. De 1804 à l'heure présent* (2 vols., Bordeaux, Delmas, 1933)

Booth, Ken and Steve Smith (eds.), *International Relations Theory Today* (Cambridge, Polity, 1995)

Borgetto, Michel, *La notion de fraternité en droit public français. Le passé, le présent et l'avenir de la solidarité* (Paris, LGDJ, 1991)

Bourgeois, Léon, "Discours à l'Institut de droit international" (1910), 23 *Annuaire de l'Institut de droit international*, pp. 365–373

"L'idée de solidarité et ses conséquences sociales," in *Essai d'une philosophie de solidarité*, pp. 9–17

"La morale internationale" (1922), XXIX *Revue générale de droit international public*, pp. 5–22

L'oeuvre de la société des nations, 1920–1923 (Paris, Payot, 1923)

Pour la société des nations (Paris, Fasquelle, 1910)

Solidarité (7th edn., Paris, Colin, 1912)

Bouvier, Bernard, *Gustave Moynier* (Geneva, Imprimérie du Journal de Genève, 1918)

Brière, Yves Leroy de la, *Le droit de juste guerre: Tradition théologique et adaptations contemporaines* (Paris, Pedone, 1938)

"Evolution de la doctrine et de la pratique en matière de représsailles" (1928/II), 22 *Recueil des cours de l'Académie de droit international*, pp. 237–294

Brierly, James, "The Shortcomings of International Law" (1924), V *British Year Book of International Law*, pp. 4–30

Briggs, H. W., *The International Law Commission* (Ithaca, New York, Cornell University Press, 1965)

Brilmayer, Lea, *Justifying International Acts* (Ithaca, New York, Cornell University Press, 1989)

Bibliography

Brimo, Albert, *Les grands courants de la philosophie du droit et de l'état* (Paris, Pedone, 1978)

Brinkley, Douglas and Clifford Hackett (eds.), *Jean Monnet: The Path to European Unity* (London, Macmillan, 1991)

Brintzinger, Ottobert L., "50 Jahre Institut für internationales Recht an der Universität Kiel" (1964), 19 *Juristenzeitung*, pp. 285–286

Bristler, Eduard (John H. Herz), *Die Völkerrechtslehre des Nationalsozialismus* (Zurich, Europa, 1938)

Brunet, René, *La société des nations et la France* (Paris, Sirey, 1921)

Bull, Hedley, *The Anarchical Society. A Study of Order in World Politics* (London, Macmillan, 1977)

Bulmerincq, August, "La politique et le droit dans la vie des états" (1877), IX *Revue de droit international et de législation comparée*, pp. 361–379

  Die Systematik des Völkerrechts von Hugo Grotius bis auf die Gegenwart (Dorpat, Karow, 1858)

Burrow, J. W., *Evolution and Society. A Study of Victorian Social Theory* (Cambridge University Press, 1966)

Butler, Judith, Ernesto Laclau, and Slavoj Žižek, *Contingency, Hegemony, Universality: Contemporary Dialogues on the Left* (London, Verso, 2000)

  "Restating the Universal," in Butler, Laclau and Žižek, *Contingency, Hegemony, Universality*, pp. 11–43

Caenegem, R. C. van, *An Historical Introduction to Private Law* (Cambridge University Press 1988)

Carr, E. H., *The Romantic Exiles* (Serif, London, 1998 [1933])

  The Twenty-Years' Crisis 1919–1939 (2nd edn., London, Macmillan, 1981 [1946])

Carré de Malberg, R., *Contribution à la théorie générale de l'état* (2 vols., Paris, Sirey, 1920)

Carty, Anthony, "Alfred Verdross and Othmar Spann: German Romantic Nationalism, National Socialism and International Law" (1995), 6 *European Journal of International Law*, pp. 78–97

  The Decay of International Law? The Limits of Legal Imagination in International Affairs (Manchester University Press, 1986)

Castonnet des Fosses, H., "Les droits de la France sur Madagascar" (1885), XVII *Revue de droit international et de législation comparée*, pp. 413–446

Catellani, Enrico, "Le droit international au commencement du XXe siècle" (1901), VIII *Revue générale de droit international public*, pp. 385–413, 567–586

  "Les droits de la France sur Madagascar et le dernier traité de paix" (1886), XVIII *Revue de droit international et de législation comparée*, pp. 151–158

  "La politique coloniale de l'Italie" (1885), XVII *Revue de droit international et de législation comparée*, pp. 218–240

  "Les possessions africaines et le droit colonial de l'Italie" (1895), XXVII *Revue de droit international et de législation comparée*, pp. 417–462

Bibliography

Cathrein, Victor, *Die Grundlage des Völkerrechts* (Freiburg, Herder, 1918)
Cattier, Félicien, "L'Etat indépendent du Congo et les indigènes" (1895), XXVII *Revue de droit international et de législation comparée*, pp. 263–281
  Etude sur la situation de l'Etat indépendent du Congo (Brussels and Paris, Laicier and Pedone, 1906)
Cauchy, Eugène, *Le droit maritime international considéré dans ses origines et dans ses rapports avec les progrès de la civilisation* (Paris, Guillaumin, 1862)
Chadwick, Owen, *The Secularization of the European Mind in the Nineteenth Century* (Cambridge University Press, 1995 [1975])
Challine, Paul, *Le droit international public dans la jurisprudence française de 1789 à 1848* (Paris, Loviton, 1934)
Chayes, Abram, *The Cuban Missile Crisis* (New York, Oxford University Press, 1974)
  International Legal Process. Materials for an Introductory Course (Boston, Little, Brown, 1968–1969)
Chowdhury, R. N., *International Mandates and Trusteeship Systems. A Comparative Study* (The Hague, Nijhoff, 1955)
Clark, Grenville and Louis Sohn, *World Peace Through World Law* (2nd edn., Cambridge, Mass., Harvard University Press, 1960)
Collini, Stefan, *Public Moralists. Political Thought and Intellectual Life in Britain 1850–1930* (Oxford, Clarendon, 1991)
Combacau, Jean, "Paul Reuter, le juriste" (1989), XXXV *Annuaire français de droit international*, pp. vii–xix
Comte, August, *La sociologie*, résumé par Emile Rigolage (Paris, Alcan, 1897)
Conklin, Alice, *A Mission to Civilize. The Republican Idea of Empire in France and West Africa 1895–1930* (Stanford University Press, 1997)
Constant, Benjamin, *Political Writings*, Biancamaria Fontane (ed.) (Cambridge University Press, 1988)
  "The Spirit of Conquest and Usurpation and their Relation to European Civilization," in *Political Writings*, pp. 51–83
Consultations de M. A de Lapradelle, Louis Le Fur et André Mandelstam de la décision de la Conférence des Ambassadeurs du 15 mars 1923 (Paris, Editions internationales, 1928)
Cooke, James J., *New French Imperialism 1880–1910: The Third Republic and Colonial Expansion* (Newton Abbot, Archon, 1973)
Coquery-Vidrovitch, Catherine, *Le Congo au temps des grands compagnies concessionaires 1898–1930* (Paris and the Hague, Mouton, 1972)
Cotelle, L. B. *Abrégé d'un cours élémentaire du droit de nature et des gens* (Paris, Gobelet, 1820)
Cotterell, Roger, *The Politics of Jurisprudence: A Critical Introduction to Legal Philosophy* (London, Butterworth, 1989)
Craig, Gordon A., "The British Foreign Office from Grey to Austen Chamberlain," in Craig and Gilbert, *The Diplomats 1919–1939*, pp. 15–48

Bibliography

Craig, Gordon A. and Felix Gilbert (eds.), *The Diplomats 1919–1939* (Princeton University Press, 1994 [1953])

Cristi, Renato, *Carl Schmitt and Authoritarian Liberalism* (Cardiff, University of Wales Press, 1998)

Crowe, S. E., *The Berlin West African Conference 1884–1885* (London, Longmans, 1942)

Davidson, Basil, *The Black Man's Burden. Africa and the Curse of the Nation-State* (New York, Times, 1992)

Delpech, Joseph and Antoine Marcaggi, "Le transfert à la Belgique de l'Etat indépendent du Congo" (1911), XVIII *Revue générale de droit international public*, pp. 105–163

Der Kampf um den Rechtsfrieden; Die Urkunden der Friedenshandlungen (Berlin, Engelmann, 1919)

Descamps, Le Chevalier, "Le différend anglo-congolais" (1904), 2/VI *Revue de droit international et de législation comparée*, pp. 233–259

Descamps, Edouard, *L'Afrique nouvelle* (Paris, Hachette, 1903)

Descombs, Vincent, *The Barometer of Modern Reason. On the Philosophies of Current Events* (Oxford University Press, 1993)

Despagnet, Frantz, *Cours de droit international public* (2nd edn., Paris, Sirey, 1899, 4th edn. 1910)

   La diplomatie de la troisième république et le droit des gens (Paris, Sirey 1904)

   Essai sur les protectorats (Paris, Larose, 1896)

Despagnet, Frantz and P. Mérignhac, "Opinion sur la Conférence de la Haye et ses resultats" (1899), VI *Revue générale de droit international public*, pp. 859–883

Deutsch, Karl W. and Stanley Hoffmann (eds.), *The Relevance of International Law. Essays in Honor of Leo Gross* (Cambridge, Schenkman, 1968)

Deutschen Liga für Völkerbund, *Der Völkerbundsentwurf der Deutschen Gesellschaft für Völkerrecht*, Heft 1, Monographien zum Völkerbund (Berlin, Engelmann, 1919)

Dicey, A. V. "His Book and His Character," in *Memories of John Westlake*, pp. 17–42

Diggelmann, Oliver, "Anfänge der Völkerrechtssoziologie. Die Völkerrechtskonzeptionen von Max Huber und Georges Scelle im Vergleich," unpublished PhD. thesis (Zurich, 1998, on file with author)

Diggins, John Patrick, *Max Weber. Politics and the Spirit of Tragedy* (New York, Basic Books, 1996)

Diner, Dan and Michael Stolleis (eds.), *Hans Kelsen and Karl Schmitt. A Juxtaposition* (Gerlingen, Bleicher, 1999)

Donnelly, Jack, "Realism and the Academic Study of International Relations," in Farr, Dryszek, and Leonard, *Political Science in History*, pp. 175–197

Doyle, Michael, *Empires* (Ithaca, New York, Cornell University Press, 1986)

   Le droit antisémite de Vichy (Paris, Seuil, 1996)

Bibliography

Duchêne, François, *Jean Monnet. The First Statesman of Interdependence* (New York and London, Norton, 1994)
Duguit, Léon, *Le droit social, le droit individuel et la transformation de l'état* (Paris, Alcan, 1908)
  Etudes de droit public (2 vols., Paris, Fontemoing, 1901)
Dumont, Georges Henri, *Léopold II* (Paris, Fayard, 1990)
Dupuis, Charles, *Le droit des gens et les rapports des grandes puissances avec les autres états avant la pacte de Société des Nations* (Paris, Plon, 1921)
  Le principe de l'équilibre et le concert européen de la paix de Westphalie à l'acte d'Algéciras (Paris, Perrin, 1909)
  "Règles générales du droit de la paix" (1930/II), 32 *Recueil des cours de l'Académie de droit international*, pp. 5–289
Dupuy, René-Jean, "L'organisation internationale et l'expression de la volonté générale" (1957), LX *Revue générale de droit international public*, pp. 527–579
Durand, André, "The Role of Gustave Moynier in the Founding of the Institute of International Law (1873)" (1994), 34 *ICRC Review*, pp. 543–563
Durkheim, Emile, *The Division of Labor in Society*, trans. W. D. Halls, introd. Lewis Coser (New York and London, Free Press, 1997 [1893])
Dyzenhaus, David (ed.), *Law as Politics: Carl Schmitt's Critique of Liberalism* (Durham, MD and London, Duke University Press, 1998)
  Legality and Legitimacy: Carl Schmitt, Hans Kelsen and Hermann Heller in Weimar (Oxford, Clarendon, 1997)
  (ed.), *Recrafting the Rule of Law: The Limits of the Legal Order* (Oxford, Hart, 1999)
Eagleton, Terry, *The Idea of Culture* (Oxford, Blackwell, 2000)
Eksteins, Modris, *Rites of Spring. The Great War and the Birth of the Modern Age* (New York, etc., Anchor, 1989)
Engelhardt, Edouard, "Considérations historiques et juridiques sur les protectorates" (1892), XXIV *Revue de droit international et de législation comparée*, pp. 349–383
  "Le droit d'intervention et la Turquie" (1880), XII *Revue de droit international et de législation comparée*, pp. 363–388
  "Etude de la déclaration de la Conférence de Berlin relative aux Occupations" (1886), XVIII *Revue de droit international et de législation comparée*, pp. 433–441, 573–586
  Les protectorats. Anciens et modernes, étude historique et juridique (Paris, Pedone, 1896)
Enzensberger, Hans-Magnus, *Civil War*, trans. Piers Spence and Martin Chalmers (London, Granta, 1994)
Errera, Paul, "Le Congo belge" (1908), 28 *Revue de droit public et de la science politique en France et à l'étranger*, pp. 730–753
  Essai d'une philosophie de solidarité. Conférences et discussions (Paris, Alcan, 1902)
Eyffinger, Arthur, *The 1899 Hague Peace Conference. "The Parliament of Man, the Federation of the World"* (The Hague, London, and Boston, Kluwer, 1999)

Bibliography

Falk, Richard, "Casting the Spell: The New Haven School of International Law" (1995), 104 *Yale Law Journal*, pp. 1991–2008

"International Legal Order. Alwyn Freeman vs. Myres S. McDougal" (1965), 59 *American Journal of International Law*, pp. 66–71

"New Approaches to the Study of International Law" (1967), 61 *American Journal of International Law*, pp. 477–495

"The Relevance of Political Context to the Nature and Functioning of International Law: An Intermediate View," in Deutsch and Hoffmann, *The Relevance of International Law*, pp. 133–152

The Status of Law in the International Society (Princeton University Press, 1970)

Farr, James, John S. Dryszek, and Stephen T. Leonard (eds.), *Political Science in History: Research Programs and Political Traditions* (Cambridge University Press, 1995)

Fauchille, Paul, *Du blocus maritime, étude de droit international et de droit comparé* (Paris, Rousseau, 1882)

La diplomatie française et la ligue des neutres 1887–83 (Paris, Pedone, 1913[1893])

"L'Europe nouvelle" (1899), VI *Revue générale de droit international public*, pp. 1–8

"Nécrologie Louis Renault (1843–1918)" (1918), XXV *Revue générale de droit international public*, pp. 1–253

Question juive en France sous le premier empire (Paris, Rousseau, 1884)

"Rapport préliminaire et questionnaire: Premier rapport et projet de manuel (manuel des lois de la guerre maritime)" (1912), 25 *Annuaire de l'Institut de droit international*, pp. 41–122

Fenwick, Charles G. "International law: The Old and the New" (1966), 60 *American Journal of International Law*, pp. 475–483

Ferro, Marc, *Colonialism: A Global History* (London and New York, Routledge, 1997)

Fijal, Andreas and Ralf-René Weingärtner, "Georg Jellinek – Universalgelehrter und Jurist" (1987), *Juristische Schulung*, pp. 97–100

Fiore, Pasquale, *Le droit international codifié et sa sanction juridique* (Paris, Pedone, 1890)

"Du protectorat colonial et de la sphère d'influence (hinterland)" (1907), XIV *Revue générale de droit international public*, pp. 148–159

"La science de droit international. Horizons nouveaux" (1909), XVI *Revue générale de droit international public*, pp. 463–481

Fisch, Jörg, "Africa as *terra nullius*. The Berlin Conference and International Law," in Förster, Mommsen, and Robinson, *Bismarck, Europe, and Africa*, pp. 437–476

Die europäische Expansion und das Völkerrecht (Stuttgart, Steiner, 1984)

Fischer Williams, Sir John, *Chapters on Current International Law and the League of Nations* (London, Longmans, 1929)

"Introduction," in *Memories of Westlake*, pp. 1–16

Flavius, Gnaeus (Hermann Kantorowicz), "Der Kampf um die Rechtswissenschaft" (1906), in Kantorowicz, *Rechtswissenschaft und Soziologie*, pp. 13–39

Bibliography

Fleischmann, Max von, "Emanuel von Ullmann" (1913), VII *Zeitschrift für Völkerrecht*, pp. 326–331

Flint, J., "Chartered Companies and the Transition from Informal Sway to Colonial Rule in Africa," in Förster, Mommsen, and Robinson, *Bismarck, Europe, and Africa*, pp. 69–84

Fontaine, François, *Forward with Jean Monnet*, in Brinkley and Hackett, *Jean Monnet*, pp. 1–66

Förster, Stig, Wolfgang J. Mommsen and Ronald Robinson (eds.), *Bismarck, Europe, and Africa: The Berlin Conference and the Onset of Partition* (London, Oxford University Press for The German Historical Institute, 1988)

Fouillée, Alfred, *L'évolutionnisme des idées-forces* (Paris, Alcan, 1890)

Franck, Thomas M., *Nation against Nation. What Happened to the UN Dream and What the US Can Do About It?* (Oxford University Press, 1985)

Franck, Thomas M. and Edward Weisband, *Word Politics: Verbal Strategy among the Superpowers* (Oxford University Press, 1971)

Franco, Paul, *Hegel's Philosophy of Freedom* (New Haven and London, Yale University Press, 1999)

Frankel, Benjamin (ed.), *Roots of Realism* (London and Portland, OR., Cass, 1996)

Freeden, Michael, *Ideologies and Political Theory. A Conceptual Approach* (Oxford University Press, 1996)

Frei, Christoph, *Hans J. Morgenthau. Eine intellektuelle Biographie* (2nd edn., St. Galler Studien zur Politikwissenschaft, Bern, Stuttgart and Vienna, Haupt, 1994)

Freidel, Frank, *Francis Lieber. Nineteenth-Century Liberal* (Baton Rouge, Louisiana State University Press, 1940)

Freund, Julien, "Schmitt's Political Thought" (1995), 102 *Telos*, pp. 11–42

Friedmann, Wolfgang, *The Changing Structure of International Law* (New Haven, Columbia University Press, 1964)

"The Reality of International Law – A Reappraisal" (1971), 10 *Columbia Journal of Transnational Law*, pp. 46–60

"United States Policy and the Crisis of International Law. Some Reflections on the State of International Law in 'International Co-operation Year'" (1965), 59 *American Journal of International Law*, pp. 857–871

Friedrich, Carl Joachim, *The Philosophy of Law in Historical Perspective* (2nd edn., Chicago University Press, 1963)

Funck-Brentano, Théodor and Albert Sorel, *Précis du droit des gens* (Paris, Plon, 1877, and 3rd edn., 1900)

Fussell, Paul, *The Great War and Modern Memory* (Oxford University Press, 1975)

Gagern, Charles E., *Kritik des Völkerrechts. Mit practischer Anwendung auf unsere Zeit* (Leipzig, Brockhaus, 1840)

Gann, L. H. and Peter Duignan, *The Burden of Empire. An Appraisal of Western Colonialism in Africa South of the Sahara* (Stanford University Press, 1971)

Bibliography

Garner, James W., "La reconstitution du droit international" (1921), XXVIII *Revue générale de droit international public*, pp. 413–440

Gay, Peter, *The Bourgeois Experience. Victoria to Freud* (5 vols., Oxford University Press, 1984–1999)

Gebhardt, Jürgen, "Leo Strauss: The Quest for Truth in Times of Perplexity," in Kielmansegg, Mewes, and Glaser-Schmidt, *Hannah Arendt and Leo Strauss*, pp. 81–104

Geffcken, F. H., "L'allemagne et la question coloniale" (1885), XVII *Revue de droit international et de législation comparée*, pp. 105–131

"Le traité Anglo-Allemand de 1er juillet 1890" (1890), XXII *Revue de droit international et de législation comparée*, pp. 587–602

Geffcken, Heinrich, *Das Gesammtinteresse als Grundlage des Staats- und Völkerrechts. Prolegomena eines Systems* (Leipzig, Deickert's, 1908)

Geiss, Immanuel, "Free Trade, Internationalization of the Congo Basin, and the Principle of Effective Occupation," in Förster, Mommsen, and Robinson, *Bismarck, Europe, and Africa*, pp. 263–280

Gény, François, *Méthode d'interprétation et sources en droit privé positif* (Paris, Bibliothèque de jurisprudence civile contemporaine, 1889)

Gerber, Carl Friedrich von, *Grundzüge des deutschen Staatsrechts* (3rd edn., Leipzig, Tauchnitz, 1880)

Geuss, Raymond, *Morality, Culture, and History. Essays on German Philosophy* (Cambridge University Press, 1999)

Girault, Arthur, "Chronique coloniale" (1897), VIII *Revue de droit public et de la science politique en France et à l'étranger*, pp. 91–121

"Chronique coloniale. L'expansion de la France dans l'Afrique centrale et vers le Haut-Nil" (1898), X *Revue de droit public et la science politique en France et à l'étranger*, pp. 460–463

Gong, Gerrit W., *The Standard of "Civilization" in International Society* (Oxford, Clarendon, 1984)

Grewe, Wilhelm, *Epochen des Völkerrechts* (Baden-Baden, Nomos, 1983)

Griffiths, Martin, *Realism, Idealism and International Politics; A Reinterpretation* (London and New York, Routledge, 1992)

Gros, Dominique, "Peut-on parler d'un droit antisémitiste?," in *Le droit antisémite de Vichy*, pp. 13–44

Gross, Rafael, "Jewish Law and Christian Grace – Carl Schmitt's Critique of Hans Kelsen," in Diner and Stolleis, *Hans Kelsen and Karl Schmitt*, pp. 101–113

Grotius, Hugo, *De jure belli ac pacis. Libri tres* (translation, 3 vols., F. W. Kelsey, Carnegie Endowment for International Peace, 3 *Classics of International Law*, Oxford, Clarendon, 1925)

Guggenheim, Paul (1929), review of "Morgenthau, Die internationale Rechtspflege," 35/36 *Juristische Wochenzeitschrift*, p. 3469

"Léon Duguit et le droit international" (1959), LXIII *Revue générale de droit international public*, pp. 629–638

Bibliography

Guillen, Pierre, *L'expansion 1881–1898* (Paris, IN, 1984)
Gumplowicz, Ludwig, *Die sociologische Staatsidee* (2nd edn., Innsbruck, Wagner, 1902)
Guzzini, Stefano, *Realism in International Relations and International Political Economy* (London and New York, Routledge, 1998)
Habermas, Jürgen, "Kant's Idea of Perpetual Peace, with the Benefit of Two Hundred Years' Hindsight," in Bohmann and Lutz-Bachmann, *Perpetual Peace*, pp. 113–153
Halda, Bernard, *Alain* (Paris, Editions universitaires, 1965)
Hall, W. E. *A Treatise on International Law* (4th edn., Oxford, Clarendon, 1895)
Halliday, Terence C. and Lucien Karpik (eds.), *Lawyers and the Rise of Western Political Liberalism* (Oxford, Clarendon, 1997)
Hargreaves John, "The Berlin Conference, West African Boundaries, and the Eventual Partition," in Förster, Mommsen, and Robinson, *Bismarck, Europe, and Africa*, pp. 313–320
Harrelson, Max, *Fires all around the Horizon. The UN's Uphill Battle to Preserve the Peace* (New York, Praeger, 1989)
Hartigan, Richard Shelly, *Lieber's Code and the Law of War* (Chicago, Precedent, 1983)
Hautefeuille, L. B., *Des droits et devoirs des nations neutres en temps de guerre maritime* (3rd edn., Paris, Guillaumin, 1868)
Hawthorn, Geoffrey, *Enlightenment and Despair. A History of Social Theory* (2nd edn., Cambridge University Press, 1987)
Hayward, J. E. S. "The Official Social Philosophy of the French Third Republic: Léon Bourgeois and Solidarism" (1961), VI *International Review of Social History*, pp. 19–48
  "Solidarist Syndicalism: Durkheim and Duguit" (1960), 8 *The Sociological Review*, pp. 17–36, 185–202
  "Solidarity: The Social History of an Idea in Nineteenth-Century France" (1959), IV *International Review of Social History*, pp. 261–284
Hegel, G. W. F., *Philosophy of Right*, trans. by S. W. Doyle (London, Prometheus 1996 [1896])
Heilborn, Paul, *Grundbegriffe und Geschichte des Völkerrechts, Handbuch des Völkerrechts*, Erste Abteilung (Berlin, Stuttgart, and Leipzig, Kohlhammer 1912)
  Das System des Völkerrechts aus den völkerrechtlichen Begriffen (Berlin, Springer, 1896)
  Das völkerrechtliche Protektorat (Berlin, Springer, 1891)
Heimburger, Karl, *Der Erwerb der Gebietshoheit* (Karlsruhe, Braun, 1888)
Held, Hermann J., "Das Institut für internationales Recht an der Universität Kiel" (1921), XXIX *Zeitschrift für internationales Recht*, pp. 146–149
Heller, Hermann, *Die Souveränität. Ein Beitrag zur Theorie des Staats- und Völkerrechts* (Berlin and Leipzig, De Gruyter, 1927)
Henderson, Arthur, *Labour's Foreign Policy* (London, The Labour Party, 1933)

Bibliography

Henkin, Louis, *How Nations Behave. Law and Foreign Policy* (2nd edn., New Haven, Columbia University Press, 1979)

Herf, Jeffrey, *Reactionary Modernism. Technology, Culture, and Politics in Weimar and the Third Reich* (Cambridge University Press, 1984)

Hertslet, Edward, *The Map of Africa by Treaty* (3rd edn., 3 vols., London, HMSO, 1909)

Herz, John H., *Political Realism and Political Idealism: A Study in Theories and Realities* (University of Chicago Press, 1951)

Herzceqh, Géza, *General Principles of Law and the International Legal Order* (Budapest Akadémiai Kiadó, 1969)

Hinde, Wendy, *George Canning* (Oxford, Blackwell, 1989)

Hinsley, F. H., *Power and the Pursuit of Peace. Theory and Practice in the History of Relations between States* (Cambridge University Press, 1963)

Historicus (Sir Vernon Harcourt), "The Territoriality of a Merchant Vessel," in *Letters by Historicus on Some Questions of International Law* (London, Macmillan, 1863), pp. 201–212

Hobsbawm, Eric, *The Age of Empire 1875–1914* (London, Abacus, 1989 [1987])

The Age of Revolution 1789–1848 (London, Abacus, 1997 [1962])

Nations and Nationalism since 1870: Programme, Myth, Reality (Cambridge University Press, 1990)

Hochschild, Adam, *King Leopold's Ghost. A Story of Greed, Terror and Heroism in Colonial Africa* (Boston, Mifflin, 1998)

Hoffmann, Stanley, "An American Social Science: International Relations," in *Janus and Minerva*, pp. 3–24

"International Systems and International Law," in *Janus and Minerva*, pp. 149–177

Janus and Minerva. Essays in the Theory and Practice of International Politics (Boulder and London, Westview, 1987)

Holborn, Hajo, "Diplomats and Diplomacy in the Early Weimar Republic," in Craig and Gilbert, *The Diplomats 1919–1939*, pp. 123–171

Hold-Ferneck, Alexander, "Zur Frage der Rechtsverbindlichkeit des Friedensvertrages von Versailles" (1922), 30 *Zeitschrift für internationales Recht*, pp. 110–117

Holtzendorff, Franz von, "Examen des derniers publications sur le système pénitentiaire" (1869), I *Revue de droit international et de législation comparée*, pp. 50–82

Handbuch des Völkerrechts, auf Grundlage europäisches Staatenpraxis (4 vols., I: *Einleitung in das Völkerrecht*, Berlin, Habel and Hamburg, Richter [vols. II–IV], 1885)

Holubek, Roland, *Allgemeine Staatslehre als empirische Wissenschaft. Eine Untersuchung am Beispiel von Georg Jellinek* (Bonn, Bouvier, 1961)

Honig, Jan Willem, "Totalitarianism and Realism: Hans Morgenthau's German Years," in Frankel, *Roots of Realism*, pp. 283–313

Bibliography

Hornung, Joseph, "Civilisés et barbares" (1885), XVII *Revue de droit international et de législation comparée*, pp. 1–18, 447–470, 539–60; (1886), XVIII *Revue de droit international et de législation comparée*, pp. 188–206, 281–298

"Quelques vues sur la preuve en histoire, comparée avec la preuve judiciaire, sur les documents de l'histoire contemporain et sur l'importance historique de l'actualité" (1884), XVI *Revue de droit international et de législation comparée*, pp. 71–83

Horwitz, Morton J., *The Transformation of American Law 1870–1960. The Crisis of Legal Orthodoxy* (Oxford University Press, 1992)

Huber, Max, *Die soziologischen Grundlagen des Völkerrechts* (Berlin, Rothschild, 1928 [1910])

Hueck, Ingo, "Die deutsche Völkerrechtswissenschaft im Nationalsozialismus. Das Berliner Kaiser-Wilhelm-Institute für ausländisches öffentliches Recht und Völkerrecht, das Hamburger Institut für auswärtige Politik und das Kieler Institut für internationales Recht" (forthcoming article, on file with author)

"Die Gründung völkerrechtlicher Zeitschriften in Deutschland im internationalen Vergleich," in Stolleis, *Juristische Zeitschriften*, pp. 379–420

Hughes, H. Stuart, *Consciousness and Society. The Reorientation of European Social Thought 1890–1930* (New York, Knopf, 1958)

Hyam, Ronald, *Britain's Imperial Century 1815–1914. A Study of Empire and Expansion* (London, Macmillan, 1976)

Institut de droit international, *Livre de centenaire: évolution et perspectives du droit international* (Basle, Karger, 1973)

International Law Committee (Britain) on the Hudson Document: "Sir Cecil Hurst's Draft of a Revised Covenant. Observations by Professor Lauterpacht" (July 15, 1944, mimeo, LA, copies on file with author)

International Law Committee (Britain): "The Nature of International Law – Draft by Professor Brierly, Observations by Professor Lauterpacht" (June 12, 1944, mimeo, LA, copies on file with author)

Isambert, François André, *Tableau historique des progrès du droit public et du droit des gens, jusqu'au XIX siècle* (Paris, Paulin, 1833)

Jacomet, Robert, *Les lois de la guerre continentale* (Paris, Fournier, 1913)

Jellinek, Georg, *Allgemeine Staatslehre* (3rd edn, ed. Walter Jellinek, Berlin, Springer, 1922)

Ausgewählte Schriften und Reden (2 vols., Berlin, Häring, 1911)

Gesetz und Verordnung (Tübingen, Mohr, 1911, reprint of the 1887 edn.)

"Johann Caspar Bluntschli" (1908), in *Ausgewählte Schriften*, I, pp. 284–293

Die Lehre von den Staatenverbindungen (Vienna, Hölder, 1882)

Die rechtliche Natur der Staatenverträge. Ein Beitrag zur juristischen Construktion des Völkerrechts (Vienna, Hölder, 1880)

Die sozialethische Bedeutung von Recht, Unrecht und Strafe (Hildesheim, Olms, 1967, reprint of the 1878 edn.)

Bibliography

"Die Weltanschauungen Leibnitz' und Schopenhauers. Ihre Gründe und ihre Berichtigung. Eine Studie über Optimismus und Pessimismus" (1872), in *Ausgewählte Schriften*, I, pp. 1–41

"Die Zukunft des Krieges" (1890), in *Ausgewählte Schriften*, II, pp. 515–541

"Zur Eröffnung der Friedenskonferenz" (1899), in *Ausgewählte Schriften*, II, pp. 542–558

Jenks, C. Wilfried, "Hersch Lauterpacht – The Scholar as Prophet" (1960), XXXVI *British Year Book of International Law*, pp. 1–103

Jennings, Sir Robert and Sir Arthur Watts, *Oppenheim's International Law* (1 vol, parts 1–4, 9th edn., Harlow, Longman, 1992)

Jèze, Gaston, *Etude théorique et pratique sur l'occupation comme mode d'acquérir les territoires en droit international* (Paris, Giard & Brière, 1896)

Jhering, Rudolf, *Der Kampf um's Recht* (Berlin, Philo, 1925)

Jones, Dorothy, *License for Empire: Colonialism by Treaty in Early America* (University of Chicago Press, 1982)

Joseph-Barthélemy, *La crise de la démocratie contemporaine* (Paris, Sirey, 1931)

"Politique intérieure et droit international" (1937/I), 59 *Recueil des cours de l'Académie de droit international*, pp. 429–520

Jouanjan, Olivier, "Carl Friedrich Gerber et la constitution d'une science du droit public allemand," in Beaud and Wachsmann, *La science juridique française*, pp. 11–63

Kaltenborn von Stachau, Karl, *Kritik des Völkerrechts* (Leipzig, Mayer, 1847)

"Zur Revision der Lehre von internationalen Rechtsmitteln" (1861), 17 *Zeitschrift für Staatswissenschaft*, pp. 69–124

Kant, Immanuel, "An Answer to the Question 'What is Enlightenment?'," in *Political Writings*, pp. 54–60

"The Contest of Faculties," in *Political Writings*, pp. 176–190

"Idea for a Universal History with a Cosmopolitan Purpose," in *Political Writings*, pp. 41–53

"The Metaphysics of Morals," in *Political Writings*, pp. 131–175

Political Writings (2nd enlarged edn., Hans Reiss ed., Cambridge University Press, 1991)

Kantorowicz, Hermann, *Rechtswissenschaft und Soziologie. Ausgewählte Schriften zur Wissenschaftslehre* (Karlsruhe, Müller, 1962)

Kaplan, R. E., *Forgotten Crisis. The Fin-de-Siècle Crisis of Democracy in France* (Oxford, Berg, 1995)

Karpik, Lucien, "Builders of Liberal Society: French Lawyers and Politics," in Halliday and Karpik, *Lawyers and the Rise of Western Political Liberalism*, pp. 108–123

Kaufmann, Erich, "Friedrich Julius Stahl als Rechtsphilosoph" (1906), in *Gesammelte Schriften*, III, pp. 1–45

Gesammelte Schriften (3 vols., Göttingen, Schwartz, 1960)

Bibliography

"Kritik der neukantischen Rechtsphilosophie" (1921), in *Gesammelte Schriften*, III, pp. 176–245

"Locarno" (1925), in *Gesammelte Schriften*, II, pp. 167–175

"Das Legalitätsprinzip im Auslandsverfahren in besetztem feindlichen Gebiete" (1915), in *Gesammelte Schriften*, II, pp. 1–12

"Probleme des internationalen Gerichtsbarkeit" (1932), in *Gesammelte Schriften*, III, pp. 304–319

"Die Regierungsbildung in Preussen und im Reiche und die Rolle der Partien" (1921), in *Gesammelte Schriften*, I, pp. 374–387

"Règles générales du droit de la paix" (1935/IV), 54 *Recueil des cours de l'Académie de droit international*, pp. 313–615

"Über die konservative Partei und seine Geschichte" (1922), in *Gesammelte Schriften*, III, pp. 133–175

"Der Völkerbund" (1932), in *Gesammelte Schriften*, II, pp. 224–237

Das Wesen des Völkerrechts und die Clausula rebus sic stantibus (Tübingen, Mohr, 1911)

"Zur problematik des Volkswillens" (1931), in *Gesammelte Schriften*, III, pp. 272–284

Kaufmann, Wilhelm, "Die modernen nicht-staatlichen internationalen Verbände und Kongresse und das internationale Recht" (1908), II *Zeitschrift für Völkerrecht*, pp. 419–440

Keay, John, *The Honourable Company. A History of the English East India Company* (London, HarperCollins, 1991)

Kelsen, Hans, *General Theory of Norms*, trans. by Michael Hartney (Oxford, Clarendon, 1991)

Introduction to Problems of Legal Theory. A Translation of the First Edition of the Reine Rechtslehre or Pure Theory of Law, trans. from *Reine Rechtslehre* (1934) Bonnie Litchewski Paulson and Stanley L. Paulson, with Introd. by Stanley L. Paulson (Oxford, Clarendon, 1992)

"Note" (1961), 10 *International and Comparative Law Quarterly*, pp. 2–6; also published in (1997), 8 *European Journal of International Law*, pp. 309–310

Peace Through Law (Chapel Hill, University of North Carolina Press, 1944)

Das Problem der Souveränität und die Theorie des Völkerrechts (2nd edn., Tübingen, Mohr, 1928)

"Les rapports de système entre le droit interne et le droit international public" (1926/IV), 14 *Recueil des cours de l'Académie de droit international*, pp. 233–329

Der soziologische und der juristische Staatsbegriff (2nd edn. Tübingen, Mohr, 1927)

Kennan, George, *American Diplomacy* (expanded edn., University of Chicago Press, 1984)

Kennedy, David, "The Move to Institutions" (1987), 8 *Cardozo Law Review*, pp. 841–988

"When Renewal Repeats: Thinking against the Box" (2000), 32 *New York University Journal of International Law and Politics*, pp. 335–498

Keohane, Robert, *After Hegemony. Cooperation and Discord in the World Political Economy* (Princeton University Press, 1984)

"International Relations and International Law: Two Optics" (1997), 38 *Harvard Journal of International Law*, pp. 487–502

Kern, Stephen, *The Culture of Time and Space* (Harvard University Press, 1983)

Kervégan, Jean-François, "Carl Schmitt and 'World Unity,'" in Mouffe, *The Challenge of Carl Schmitt*, pp. 54–74

Kielmansegg, Peter Graf, "Introduction," in Kielmansegg, Mewes, and Glaser-Schmidt, *Hannah Arendt and Leo Strauss*, pp. 1–10

Kielmansegg, Peter Graf, Horst Mewes, and Elisabeth Glaser-Schmidt (eds.), *Hannah Arendt and Leo Strauss: German Emigrés and American Political Thought after World War II* (Cambridge University Press, 1995)

Kiernan, V. G., *Imperialism and Its Contradictions*, ed. and introd. Harvey J. Kaye (New York and London, Routledge, 1995)

Kimmich, Christoph M., *Germany and the League of Nations* (University of Chicago Press, 1976)

Klabbers, Jan, "The Sociological Jurisprudence of Max Huber. An Introduction" (1992), *Austrian Journal of Public and International Law*, pp. 197–213

Kloppenberg, James T. *Uncertain Victory. Social Democracy and Progressivism in European and American Thought 1870–1920* (Oxford University Press 1986)

Klüber, Johann Ludwig, *Droit des gens moderne de l'Europe* (Stuttgart, J. G. Cotta, 1819)

Europäisches Völkerrecht (2nd edn., by Carl Morstadt, Schotthausen, Hurter, 1851)

Kohl, Wolfgang, "Walther Schücking (1875–1935). Staats- und Völkerrechler – Demokrat und Pazifist," in Kritische Justiz, *Streitbare Juristen*, pp. 230–242

Kohler, Josef, "Die Friedensbewegung und das Völkerrecht" (1910), IV *Zeitschrift für Völkerrecht*, pp. 129–139

"Der Friedenstempel" (1913), VII *Zeitschrift für Völkerrecht*, pp. 237–240

"Das neue Völkerrecht" (1916), XI *Zeitschrift für Völkerrecht*, pp. 5–10

"Notrecht" (1914–1915), 8 *Archiv für Rechts und Wirtschaftsphilosophie*, pp. 412–449

Korhonen, Outi, *International Law Situated: Culture, History and Ethics* (The Hague, Boston, and Dordrecht, Kluwer, 2000)

Korhonen, Pekka, *Hans Morgenthau. Intellektuaalinen Historia* (Jyväskylän yliopisto, valtio-opin laitos, *Julkaisuja*, 43, 1983)

Koskenniemi, Martti, "Between Commitment and Cynicism: Outline for a Theory of International Law as Practice," in *Collection of Essays by Legal Advisers of States, Legal Advisers of International Organizations and Practitioners in the Field of International Law* (New York, United Nations, 1999), pp. 495–523

From Apology to Utopia. The Structure of International Legal Argument (Helsinki, Lakimiesliiton kustannus, 1989)

"International Law in a Post-Realist Era" (1995), 16 *Australian Yearbook of International Law*, pp. 1–19

"Letter to the Editors of the Symposium" (1999), 93 *American Journal of International Law*, pp. 351–361

"The Wonderful Artificiality of States" (1994), 88 *ASIL Proceedings*, pp. 22–28

Koskenniemi, Martti and Marja Lehto, "The Privilege of Universality. International Law, Economic Ideology and Seabed Resources" (1996), 65 *Nordic Journal of International Law*, pp. 533–555

Krasner, Stephen D. (ed.), *International Regimes* (Cornell University Press, 1983)
  "Structural Causes and Regime Consequences: Regimes as Intervening Variables," in Krasner, *International Regimes*, pp. 1–21

Krauel, A., "Applicabilité du droit des gens à la Chine" (1877), IX *Revue de droit international et de législation comparée*, pp. 387–401

Krieger, Leonard, *The German Idea of Freedom. History of a Political Tradition* (Boston, Beacon, 1957)

Kritische Justiz (ed.), *Streitbare Juristen* (Baden-Baden, Nomos, 1988)

Kuhn, Arthur S., *Pathways in International Law: A Personal Narrative* (New York, Macmillan, 1953)

Kunz, Josef, "The Changing Law of Nations," in *The Changing Law of Nations*, pp. 3–12
  The Changing Law of Nations: Essays on International Law (Ohio State University Press, 1968)
  "The Changing Science of International Law," in *The Changing Law of Nations*, pp. 158–176

"L'école internationale de droit international" (1920), XXVII *Revue générale de droit international public*, pp. 145–152

"L'enseignement du droit international public en France" (1956), II *Annuaire français de droit international*, pp. 981–985

"L'enseignement et la recherche en droit international en France face aux besoins de la pratique" (1967), XIII *Annuaire français de droit international*, pp. 1157–1158

"La société française pour le droit international" (1968), XIV *Annuaire français de droit international*, p. 1172

Laband, Paul, *Das Staatsrecht des Deutschen Reiches* (4 vols., 5th edn., Tübingen, Mohr, 1901, 1911–1913)
  Deutsches Reichstaatsrecht (5th edn., Tübingen, Mohr, 1909)

Laclau, Ernesto, *Emancipations* (London, Verso, 1996)
  "Identity and Hegemony: The Role of Universality in the Construction of Political Logics," in Butler, Laclau, and Žižek, *Contingency, Hegemony, Universality*, pp. 44–89

Bibliography

"Structure, History and the Political," in Butler, Laclau, and Žižek, *Contingency, Hegemony, Universality*, pp. 189–212

"Subject of Politics, Politics of the Subject," in *Emancipations*, pp. 47–65

"Universalism, Particularism and the Question of Identity," in *Emancipations*, pp. 20–35

Landauer, Carl, "Deliberating Speed: Totalitarian Anxieties and Postwar Legal Thought" (2000), 12 *Yale Journal of Law and the Humanities*, pp. 171–248

Lapradelle (also La Pradelle), Albert de, "Les accords Franco-Anglais" (1904), XI *Revue générale de droit international public*, pp. 621–750

"Chronique internationale" (1899), XI *Revue du droit public et de la science politique en France et à l'étranger*, pp. 277–308

"Discours à l' Institut des hautes études internationales (Douzième anniversaire, jeudi 22 novembre 1932)" (1933), 11 *Revue de droit international et de législation comparée* (Paris), pp. 11–17

Maîtres et doctrines du droit des gens (2nd edn., Paris, Editions internationales, 1950)

Le marxisme tentaculaire. La formation, la tactique et l'action de la diplomatie sovietique (Issidou, Editions internationales, 1942)

La paix moderne (1899–1945). De la Haye à San Francisco (Paris, Editions internationales, 1947)

Recueil de la jurisprudence de tribunaux arbitraux mixtes crées par les Traités de paix (5 vols., Paris, Documentation internationale, 1927)

Lasson, Adolf, *Das Culturideal und der Krieg* (Berlin, Hertz, 1868)

Princip und Zukunft des Völkerrechts (Berlin, Hertz, 1871)

Lasson, Georg, "Adolf Lasson" (1918–1919), XII *Archiv für Rechts und Wirtschaftsphilosophie*, pp. 1–10

Lauterpacht, Elihu, "Note" (Lauterpacht Archive, Cambridge, hereafter LA, on file with author); a shorter version was published in "Sir Hersch Lauterpacht: 1897–1960" (1997), 8 *European Journal of International Law*, pp. 313–315

Lauterpacht, Hersch, "The Absence of an International Legislature and the Compulsory Jurisdiction of International Tribunals" (1930), XI *British Year Book of International Law*, pp. 134–157

"Allegiance, Diplomatic Protection and Criminal Jurisdiction over Aliens" (1947), 9 *Cambridge Law Journal*, pp. 330–348, *Collected Papers*, 3, pp. 221–240

"Book Review: Karl Lowenstein, Political Reconstruction" (1946), XXIII *British Year Book of International Law*, pp. 510–511

"Book Review: Hans Morgenthau: Internationale Rechtspflege, ihr Wesen und ihre Grenzen" (1931), XII *British Year Book of International Law*, pp. 229–230

"Boycott in International Relations" (1933), XIV *British Year Book of International Law*, pp. 125–140, *Collected Papers*, 3, pp. 297–311

Bibliography

"Brierly's Contribution to International Law" (1955–1956), XXXII *British Year Book of International Law*, pp. 1–19, *Collected Papers*, 2, pp. 431–451

"The British Reservations to the Optional Clause" (1930), *Economica*, pp. 137–172

"The Covenant as the Higher Law" (1936), XVII *British Year Book of International Law*, pp. 54–65, *Collected Papers*, 4, pp. 326–336

The Development of International Law by the International Court (2nd edn., New York, Praeger, 1958)

"The Doctrine of Plain Meaning," (1950–1952), *Collected Papers*, 4, pp. 393–446

"Draft of Legal Submissions to the International Court of Justice in the Anglo-Iranian Oil Company case" (1951), *Collected Papers*, 4, pp. 23–89

The Function of Law in the International Community (Oxford, Clarendon, 1933)

"The Future of Neutrality" (unpublished manuscript, LA, copy on file with author)

"The Grotian Tradition in International Law" (1946), XXIII *British Year Book of International Law*, pp. 1–53, *Collected Papers*, 2, pp. 307–365

International Law: Being the Collected Papers of Sir Hersch Lauterpacht (4 vols., ed. Elihu Lauterpacht, Cambridge University Press, 1970–1978)

"International Law after the Covenant" (1936), *Collected Papers*, 2, pp. 145–158

"International Law after the Second World War" (1950), *Collected Papers*, 2, pp. 159–170

"International Law and the Colonial Question 1870–1914," (1959), *Collected Papers*, 2, pp. 95–144

"International Law – The General Part," *Collected Papers*, 1, pp. 1–177

International Law and Human Rights (New York, Praeger, 1950)

"Japan and the Covenant" (1932), 3 *Political Quarterly*, pp. 174–194

"Kelsen's Pure Science of Law," in *Modern Theories of Law* (Oxford University Press, 1933), pp. 105–138, *Collected Papers*, 2, pp. 404–430

"The Law of Nations and the Punishment of War Crimes" (1944), XXI *British Year Book of International Law*, pp. 58–95

"The League of Nations" (1938), *Collected Papers*, 3, pp. 575–588

"The Mandate under International Law in the Covenant of the League of Nations" (1922), *Collected Papers*, 3, pp. 29–84

"Memorandum on the Draft of the Peace Act" (LA, copy on file with author)

"The Nationality of Denationalized Persons" (1949), *Jewish Year Book of International Law*, 1948, pp. 164–185, *Collected Papers*, 3, pp. 383–405

"Neutrality and Collective Security" (1936), *Politica*, pp. 133–155

"On Realism. Especially in International Relations" (1953), *Collected Papers*, 2, pp. 52–66

"The Pact of Paris and the Budapest Articles of Interpretation" (1934), 20 *Transactions of the Grotius Society*, pp. 178–204

Bibliography

"The Peace Act, A Draft" (LA, copy on file with author)

"Peaceful Change. The Legal Aspect," in Manning, *Peaceful Change*, pp. 135–168

Private Law Sources and Analogies of International Law (with Special Reference to International Arbitration) (London, Longmans, 1927)

"The Problem of the Jurisdictional Immunity of Foreign States" (1951), XXVIII *British Year Book of International Law*, pp. 220–272, *Collected Papers*, 3, pp. 315–373

"Professor Carr on International Morality" (1941), *Collected Papers*, 2, pp. 67–91

"The Reality of the Law of Nations" (1941), *Collected Papers*, 2, pp. 22–51

Recognition in International Law (Cambridge University Press, 1947)

"Règles générales du droit de paix" (1937/IV), 62 *Recueil des cours de l'Académie de droit international*, pp. 99–419, published in English as "General Rules of the Law of Peace," *Collected Papers*, 1, pp. 179–444

"'Resort to War' and the Interpretation of the Covenant During the Manchurian Crisis" (1933), 28 *American Journal of International Law*, pp. 43–60

"Restrictive Interpretation and the Principle of Effectiveness in the Interpretation of Treaties" (1949), XXVI *British Year Book of International Law*, pp. 48–85, *Collected Papers*, 4, pp. 404–446

"Revolutionary Activities by Private Persons against Foreign States" (1938), 22 *American Journal of International Law*, pp. 105–130, *Collected Papers*, 3, pp. 251–278

"Revolutionary Propaganda by Governments" (1928), *Transactions of the Grotius Society*, pp. 143–163, *Collected Papers*, 3, pp. 279–296

"The So-Called Anglo-American and Continental Schools of Thought in International Law" (1931), XII *British Year Book of International Law*, pp. 31–62, *Collected Papers*, 2, pp. 452–486

"Some Observations on the Prohibition of 'Non Liquet' and the Completeness of the Law," *Symbolae Verzijl*, pp. 196–221

"Sovereignty and Federation in International Law" (1939/1940), *Collected Papers*, 3, pp. 5–28

"Sovereignty over Submarine Areas" (1950), XXVII *British Year Book of International Law*, pp. 376–433, *Collected Papers*, 3, pp. 143–206

"Spinoza and International Law" (1927), VIII *British Year Book of International Law*, pp. 89–107, *Collected Papers*, 2, pp. 366–384

"State Sovereignty and Human Rights" 1950, *Collected Papers*, 3, pp. 416–431

"Succession of States with Respect to Private Law Obligations" (1928), *Collected Papers*, 3, pp. 121–141

"Survey of International Law in Relation to the Work of Codification of the International Law Commission" (1948), *Collected Papers*, 1, pp. 445–530

Bibliography

Syllabus of Six Lectures by Professor Lauterpacht on the Legal Organisation of Peace in the Lent Term, 1938 (unpublished syllabus, on file with author)

"The Teaching of Law in Vienna" (1923), *Journal of the Society of Public Teachers in Law*, pp. 43–45

"Testing the Legality of Persian Policy" (1952), *Collected Papers*, 3, pp. 242–244

"Westlake and Present Day International Law" (1925), 5 *Economica*, pp. 307–325, *Collected Papers*, 2, pp. 385–403

Laveleye, Emile de, *Des causes actuelles de la guerre en Europe et l'arbitrage* (Brussels and Paris, Muquart, Guillaumin, 1873)

"La neutralité du Congo" (1883), XV *Revue de droit international et de législation comparée*, pp. 254–262

De la propriété et de ses formes primitives (Paris, Baillière, 1874)

Le socialisme contemporain (Paris, Baillière, 1881)

Lawrence, T. J., *A Handbook of Public International Law* (8th edn., London, Macmillan, 1913)

Lawson, F. H., *The Oxford Law School 1850–1965* (Oxford, Clarendon, 1968)

Le Bon, Gustave, *Psychologie des foules* (new edn., Paris, PUF 1963 [1895])

Le Fur, Louis, "Les conditions d'existence d'une union européenne" (1930), 6 *Revue de droit international* (Paris), pp. 71–96

"La démocratie et la crise de l'état," in *Les grands problèmes*, pp. 530–583

"Le développement historique du droit international de l'anarchie internationale à une communauté internationale organisée" (1932/III), 41 *Recueil des cours de l'Académie de droit international*, pp. 505–601

"Le droit et les doctrines allemandes," in *Les grands problèmes*, pp. 312–377

"L'église et le droit des gens," in *Les grands problèmes*, pp. 502–529

"Le fondement du droit dans la doctrine de Léon Duguit," in *Les grands problèmes*, pp. 389–435

"Le fondement de droit," in *Les grands problèmes*, pp. 7–71

Les grands problèmes du droit (Paris, Sirey, 1937)

"La guerre d'Espagne et le droit" (1937), 20 *Revue de droit international* (Paris), pp. 347–367, part 2 (1938), 21 *Revue de droit international* (Paris), pp. 53–100

Guerre juste et juste paix (Paris, Pedone, 1920)

Nationalisme et internationalisme au regard de la morale et du droit naturel (Paris, Chronique sociale, 1926)

Necessité d'un droit international pour coordonner les diverses activités nationales (Lyon, Chronique sociale, n/d)

"La paix perpetuelle et l'arbitrage international" (1909), XVI *Revue générale de droit international public*, pp. 437–463

"Philosophie du droit international" (1921), XXVIII *Revue générale de droit international public*, pp. 565–603

Précis de droit international (3rd edn., Paris, Dalloz, 1937)

Races, nationalités, états (Paris, Alcan 1922)

"Règles générales du droit de la paix" (1935/IV), 54 *Recueil des cours de l'Académie de droit international*, pp. 5–307

League of Nations, *The Mandates System; Origin – Principles – Applications* (Geneva, League of Nations Publications, 1945)

Ledford, Kenneth F., "Lawyers and the Limits of Liberalism: The German Bar in the Weimar Republic," in Halliday and Karpik, *Lawyers and the Rise of Western Political Liberalism*, pp. 229–264

Leonetti, Antoine-Jean, "Georges Scelle. Etude d'une théorie juridique" (unpublished *Thèse de doctorat d'état*, Université Nice-Sophia Antipolis, January 1992, on file with author)

"Les études de droit international dans les facultés de droit françaises" (1962), VIII *Annuaire français de droit international*, pp. 1233–1234

Lewis, David Levering, *The Race to Fashoda. Colonialism and African Resistance* (New York, Holt, 1987)

Lieber, Francis, *On Civil Liberty and Self-Government* (Philadelphia, Lippincott, 1859)

Fragments of Political Science on Nationalism and Inter-Nationalism (New York, Scribner, 1868)

Liepmann, Mauritz, "Die Pflege des Völkerrechts an den deutschen Universitäten" (1919), 6 *Monografien der Deutschen Liga für Völkerbund*

Lindley, M. F., *The Acquisition and Government of Backward Territory in International Law* (London, Longmans, 1926)

Lipson, Charles, "Why are Some Agreements Informal?" (1991), 45 *International Organization*, pp. 495–538

Liszt, Franz von, "Gegenwart und Zukunft des Völkerrechts" (1914–1915), 8 *Archiv für Rechts und Wirtschaftsphilosophie*, pp. 449–451

Vom Staatenverband zur Völkergemeinschaft: ein Beitrag zur Neuorientierung der Staatspolitik und des Völkerrechts (Munich, Müller, 1918)

Das Völkerrecht. Systematisch dargestellt (5th edn. Berlin, Häring, 1907)

Little, Richard, "The English School's Contribution to the Study of International Relations" (2000), 6 *European Journal of International Relations*, pp. 395–422

Lorimer, James, "La doctrine de la reconnaissance. Fondement du droit international" (1884), XVI *Revue de droit international et de législation comparée*, pp. 333–359

Institutes of International Law. A Treatise of the Jural Relations of Separate Political Communities (2 vols., Edinburgh and London, Blackwood, 1883)

"Prolégomènes d'une système raisonné du droit international" (1878), X *Revue de droit international et de législation comparée*, pp. 339–356

Lucas, C. P., "The Working Men's College," in *Memories of Westlake*, pp. 130–137

Bibliography

Lukes, Steven, *Emile Durkheim. His Life and Work. A Historical and Critical Study* (Stanford University Press, 1973)

Lyotard, Jean-François, *The Differend. Phrases in Dispute*, trans. Georges van den Abbeele (Minneapolis, University of Minnesota Press, 1988)

Macalister-Smith, Peter and Joachim Schwietzke, "Literature and Documentary Sources Relating to the History of International Law: An Annotated Bibliographical Survey" (1999), 1 *Journal of the History of International Law*, pp. 136–212

Maine, Henry Sumner, *International Law. The Whewell Lectures* (London, Murray, 1887)

Mancini, Stanislao, "De l'utilité de rendre obligatoire, sous la forme d'un ou de plusieurs traités internationales, un certain nombre de règles générales du droit international privé pour assumer la décision uniforme des conflits entre les différentes législations civiles et criminelles (1874), 5 *Journal de droit international privé et de la jurisprudence comparée*, pp. 221–238

Mandere, H. Ch. G. J. van der, "L'académie de droit des gens de la Haye" (1923), 1 *Revue de droit international et des sciences diplomatiques et politiques*, pp. 123–134

Manning, C. A. W. (ed.), *Peaceful Change. An International Problem* (London, Macmillan, 1937)

Marks, Susan, "The End of History? Reflexions on Some International Law Theses" (1997), 8 *European Journal of International Law*, pp. 449–477

The Riddle of All Constitutions: International Law, Democracy, and the Critique of Ideology (Oxford University Press, 2000)

Martens, F. de, "La Conférence du Congo à Berlin et la politique coloniale des états modernes" (1886), XVIII *Revue de droit international et de législation comparée*, pp. 113–150, 244–280

"Le fondement du droit international" (1882), XIV *Revue de droit international et de législation comparée*, pp. 244–256

"La Russie et l'Angleterre dans l'Asie centrale" (1879), XI *Revue de droit international et de législation comparée*, pp. 227–301 and (1880), XII *Revue de droit international et de législation comparée*, pp. 23–46

Martens, G. F. de, *Précis du droit des gens moderne de l'Europe, précédé d'une Introduction et complété par l'exposition des doctrines des publicistes contemporains et suivi d'une Bibliographie raisonnée du droit des gens par M. Ch. Vergé* (2 vols., 2nd French edn., Paris, Guillaumin, 1864)

Maus, Ingeborg, "The 1933 'Break' in Carl Schmitt's Theory," in Dyzenhaus, *Law as Politics*, pp. 196–216

Mazel, A., *Solidarisme, individualisme & socialisme* (Paris, Bonhoure, 1882)

McCagg, William D., *A History of the Habsburg Jews 1670–1918* (Bloomington, Indiana University Press, 1989)

McCalmont Hill, S., "The Growth of International Law in Africa" (1900), LXIII *Law Quarterly Review*, pp. 249–268

Bibliography

McDougal, Myres S., "International Law, Power and Policy. A Contemporary Conception" (1953/I), 82 *Recueil des cours de l'Académie de droit international*, pp. 137–259

McDougal, Myres S. and Harold Lasswell, "Legal Education and Public Policy: Professional Training in the Public Interest" (1943), in McDougal and Associates, *Studies in World Public Order*, pp. 42–154

McDougal, Myres S. and Associates, *Studies in World Public Order* (New Haven and Dordrecht, New Haven Press and Nijhoff, 1987)

McLynn, Frank, *Hearts of Darkness* (London, Pimlico, 1993)

McNair, Arnold, "Memorial Article" (1960), *Annals of the British Academy*, pp. 371–385

McWhinney, Edward, "Changing International Law Method and Objectives in the Era of Soviet–Western Détente" (1965), 59 *American Journal of International Law*, pp. 1–15

Meier, Heinrich, *The Lesson of Carl Schmitt. Four Chapters on the Distinction between Political Theology and Political Philosophy* (University of Chicago Press, 1998)

Mélanges Fernand Dehousse (2 vols., Paris, Nathan, 1979)

Memories of John Westlake (London, Smith & Elder, 1914)

Mendelssohn-Bartholdy, Albrecht, "Der Gegensatz zwischen der deutschen und englischen Kriegsrechtsauffassung und seine künftige Überwindung im Völkerrecht" (1917), 1 *Mitteilungen der Deutsche Gesellschaft für Völkerrecht*, pp. 23–34

Mérignhac, A., *La Conférence internationale de la paix* (Paris, Rousseau, 1900)

Traité de droit public international (3 vols., Paris, LGDJ, 1905)

Merle, Marcel, *Pacifisme et internationalisme* (Paris, Colin, 1966)

Métall, Rudolf, *Hans Kelsen. Leben und Werk* (Vienna, Deutige, 1967)

Miaille, Michel, *Une introduction critique au droit* (Paris, Maspero, 1982)

Milet, Marc, *La faculté de droit de Paris face à la vie politique. De l'affaire Scelle à l'affaire Jèze 1925–1936* (Paris, LGDJ, 1996)

Millot, Albert, *Les mandats internationaux. Etude sur l'application de l'article 22 du Pacte de la Société des Nations* (Paris, Larose 1924)

Mirkine-Guetzewitch, B. and Georges Scelle (eds.), *L'Union européenne* (Paris, Delagrave, 1931)

Mohl, Robert von, *Staatsrecht, Völkerrecht, und Politik* (3 vols, Tübingen, Laupp, 1860)

Mommsen, Wolfgang J., *Imperial Germany 1867–1918. Politics, Culture and Society in an Authoritarian State* (London etc., Arnold, 1995)

Max Weber and German Politics 1890–1920, trans. Michael S. Steinberg (University of Chicago Press, 1984)

Monnet, Jean, *Memoires*, trans. Richard Mayne (London, Collins, 1978)

Montesquieu, Baron de, *The Spirit of the Laws*, trans. T. Nugent, introd. F. Neumann (New York and London, Hafner & Collier, 1949 [1748])

Bibliography

Moore-Gilbert, Bart, *Postcolonial Theory. Context, Practices, Politics* (London, Verso, 1997)

Morgenthau, Hans, *The Decline of Democratic Politics* (University of Chicago Press, 1969)

In Defense of the National Interest. A Critical Examination of American Foreign Policy (New York, Knopf, 1951)

"La doctrine et l'évolution de la théorie de l'état en Allemagne" (Morgenthau Archive, Library of Congress, HJM-B-110, copy on file with author)

"Emergent Problems of United States Foreign Policy," in Deutsch and Hoffmann, *The Relevance of International Law*, pp. 69–79

"An Intellectual Autobiography" (1978), 15 (January/February), *Society*, pp. 63–68

Die internationale Rechtspflege, ihr Wesen und ihre Grenzen (Leipzig, Noske, 1929)

"Der Kampf der deutschen Staatslehre um die Wirklichkeit des Staates" (Morgenthau Archive, Library of Congress, HJM-B-110, copy on file with author)

"National Socialist Doctrine on World Organization" (1943), Proceedings of the Seventh Conference of Teachers of International Law and Related Subjects, Washington, DC, 23–25 April, 1941, pp. 103–108

A New Foreign Policy for the United States (New York, Washington, and London, Praeger, 1969)

La notion du "politique" et la théorie des différends internationaux (Paris, Sirey, 1933)

Politics among Nations. The Struggle for Power and Peace (New York, Knopf, 1948)

"Positivism, Functionalism and International Law" (1940), 34 *American Journal of International Law*, pp. 261–284

La réalité des normes: En particulier des normes du droit international. Fondements d'une théorie des normes (Paris, Alcan, 1934)

Scientific Man vs. Power Politics (University of Chicago Press, 1946)

"Der Selbstmord mit guten Gewissen. Zur Kritik des pazifismus und der neuen deutschen Kriegsphilosophie" (Morgenthau Archive, Library of Congress, HJM-B-96, copy on file with author)

"The Significance of Being Alone" (unpublished and undated paper, Morgenthau Archive, Library of Congress, HJM-B-110, copy on file with author)

"Stresemann als Schöpfer der deutschen Völkerrechtspolitik" (1929), 5 *Die Justiz*, p. 176

"Théorie des sanctions internationales" (1935), 3/XVI *Revue de droit international et de législation comparée*, pp. 473–503 and 809–836

Truth and Power. Essays of a Decade 1960–1970 (London, Pall Mall, 1970)

"Über die Herkunft des politischen aus dem Wesen des Menschen" (Morgenthau Archive, Library of Congress, HJM-B-151, copy on file with author)

Bibliography

Morris, Jan, *Farewell the Trumpets: An Imperial Retreat* (Orlando, Fla., Harcourt, 1978)
Mouffe, Chantal (ed.), *The Challenge of Carl Schmitt* (London, Verso, 1999)
Moye, Marcel, *Le droit des gens moderne. Précis élémentaire à l'usage des étudiants des facultés de droit* (Paris, Sirey, 1920)
Moynier, Gustave, "Mémoire à l'Institut de droit international, à Munich, le 4 septembre 1883," in *La question du Congo*, pp. 7–25
　La question du Congo devant l'Institut de droit international (Geneva, Schuchardt, 1883)
Münch, Fritz, "Das Institut de droit international" (1990), 28 *Archiv des Völkerrechts*, pp. 76–105
　"L'Institut de droit international: Ses debuts comme organe collectif de la doctrine," in *Estudios de derecho internacional. Homenaje a.g. Antonio de Luna* (Madrid, C.S.I.C., 1968), pp. 385–396
Munch, P. (ed.), *Les origines et l'oeuvre de la Société des Nations* (2 vols., Copenhagen, Gyldendanske Boghandel, 1923)
Mutua, Makau Wa, "Why Redraw the Map of Africa? A Moral and Legal Inquiry" (1995), 16 *Michigan Journal of International Law*, pp. 1113–1176
Nelson, Leonard, *Rechtswissenschaft ohne Recht* (Leipzig, von Veit, 1917)
Newsome, David, *The Victorian World Picture* (London, Fontana, 1997)
Niemeyer, Theodor, "Rechspolitische Grundlegung der Völkerrechtswissenschaft" (1924), 31 *Zeitschrift für internationales Recht*, pp. 1–39
　Völkerrecht (Berlin and Leipzig, DeGruyter, 1923)
　"Vorwort" (1921), 29 *Zeitschrift für internationales Recht*, pp. iii–vi
　"Vom Wesen des internationalen Rechtes" (1910), 20 *Zeitschrift für internationales Recht*, pp. 1–15
Nietzsche, Friedrich, *On the Genealogy of Morals*, trans. D. Smith (Oxford University Press, 1996)
　The Will to Power, ed. Walter Kaufmann (New York, Vintage, 1967)
Nippold, Otfried, *Der völkerrechtliche Vertrag, seine Stellung im Rechssystem und seine Bedeutung für das internationale Recht* (Berne, Wyss, 1894)
Northedge, F. S., *The League of Nations. Its Life and Times 1920–1946* (New York and London, Holmes & Meier, 1986)
Nova, Rodolfo di, "Pasquale Stanislao Mancini," in Institut de droit international, *Livre de centenaire*, pp. 3–10
Nussbaum, Arthur, *A Concise History of International Law* (2nd rev. edn., New York, Macmillan, 1954)
Nys, Ernest, "Alphonse Rivier, sa vie et ses oeuvres" (1899), XXXI *Revue de droit international et de législation comparée*, pp. 415–431
　Le droit international (3 vols., new edn., Brussels, Weissenbrich 1912)
　"L'état indépendant du Congo et les dispositions de l'acte générale de Berlin" (1903), 2/V *Revue de droit international et de législation comparée*, pp. 315–332

Bibliography

"L'état indépendant du Congo et le droit international" (1903), 2/V *Revue de droit international et de législation comparée*, pp. 333–379

"François Lieber" (1902), 2/V *Revue de droit international et de législation comparée*, pp. 683–687

"Notice sur Rolin-Jaequemyns" (1910), *Annuaire de l'Académie royale des sciences, des lettres et des beaux-arts de Belgique*, Brussels, Hayez, pp. 53–87

"La science de droit des gens," in *Memories of Westlake*, pp. 43–58

O'Connell, Mary Ellen, "New International Legal Process" (1999), 93 *American Journal of International Law*, pp. 334–351

Oertzen, Peter von, *Die soziale Funktion der Staatsrechlichen Positivismus* (Frankfurt, Suhrkamp, 1974)

Okafor, Obiora Chinedu, "After Martyrdom: International Law, Sub-State Groups, and the Construction of Legitimate Statehood in Africa" (2000), 41 *Harvard International Law Journal*, pp. 503–528

Olsen, William and Nicholas Onuf, "The Growth of a Discipline Reviewed," in Smith, *International Relations*, pp. 1–28

Oppenheim, Lassa, *International Law. A Treatise. Vol. I – Peace*, 4th edn., ed. Arnold McNair (London, Longmans, 1928)

Osterhammel, Jürgen, *Colonialism. A Theoretical Overview*, trans. from the German S. L. Frisch (Princeton, Wiener, 1997)

Pakenham, Thomas, *The Scramble for Africa 1876–1912* (New York, Random House, 1991)

Palaver, Wolfgang, "Carl Schmitt on Nomos and Space" (1996), 106 *Telos*, pp. 105–127

Partsch, Karl Josef, "Der Rechtsberater Auswärtigen Amtes 1950–1958. Erinnerungsblatt zum 90. Geburtstag von Erich Kaufmann" (1970), 30 *Zeitschrift für ausländisches öffentliches Recht und Völkerrecht*, pp. 223–236

Paternostro, "La revision des traités avec le Japon au point de vue du droit international" (1891), XVIII *Revue de droit international et de législation comparée*, pp. 5–29, 176–192

Penrose, E. F. (ed.), *European Imperialism and the Partition of Africa* (London, Cass 1975)

Penwith, Courtney of, "Public Affairs," in *Memories of Westlake*, pp. 50–70

Perrinjaquet, J. "Des annexations déguisées de territoires" (1909), XVI *Revue générale de droit international public*, pp. 316–367

Piccone, Paul and G. L. Ulmen, "Schmitt's 'Testament' and the Future of Europe" (1990), 83 *Telos*, pp. 3–34

Pillet, Antoine, "Le droit international public, ses éléments constitutifs, son domaine, son objet" (1894), I *Revue générale de droit international public*, pp. 1–32

"La guerre actuelle et le droit des gens" (1916), XXIII *Revue générale de droit international public*, pp. 5–31, 203–243, 462–471

Les leçons de la guerre présent au point de vue de science politique et du droit des gens (Paris, Plon, 1915)

Principes de droit international privé (Paris, Pedone, 1903)

"Recherches sur les droits fondamentaux des états dans l'ordre des rapports internationaux et sur la solution des conflits qu'ils font naître" (1898), V *Revue générale de droit international public*, pp. 66–89, 236–264 and (1899), VI *Revue générale de droit international public*, pp. 503–532

Le traité de Paix de Versailles (Paris, Rivière, 1920)

Pillet, A. and J. Delpech, "La question finlandaise. Le manifeste du Tsar examiné au point de vue de droit international" (1900), VII *Revue générale de droit international public*, pp. 402–420

Piloty, Robert, "Staaten als Mächte und Mächte als Staaten. Ein Wort zu den Grundlagen des Völkerrechts" (1914), VIII *Zeitschrift für Völkerrecht*, pp. 360–365

Pippin, Robert, *Modernity as a Philosophical Problem. On the Dissatisfactions of European High Culture* (2nd edn., Oxford, Blackwell, 1999)

Plöchl, Willibald M., "Zur Entwicklung der modernen Völkerrechtswissenschaft an der Wiener Juristenfakultät," in *Völkerrecht und rechtliches Weltbild*, pp. 31–53

Politis, Nicolas, *La morale internationale* (Neuchâtel, Baconnière, 1943)

La neutralité et la paix (Paris, Hachette, 1937)

Les nouvelles tendances du droit international (Paris, Hachette, 1927)

Porter, Andrew, *European Imperialism 1860–1914* (London, Macmillan, 1994)

Pound, Roscoe, "Philosophical Theory and International Law" (1923), II *Bibliotheca Visseriana*, pp. 71–90

Pradier-Fodéré, P., "La question des capitulations" (1869), I *Revue de droit international et de législation comparée*, pp. 118–137

Traité de droit international public européen et americain (9 vols., Paris, Pedone-Lauriel, 1885–1906)

Proceedings of the Hague Peace Conferences, Translation of the Official Texts, the Conference of 1899 (Carnegie Endowment of International Peace, under the supervision of J. B. Scott, Oxford University Press, 1920)

Protocoles de la Conférence de l'Afrique occidentale réunie à Berlin, du 15 novembre 1884 au 26 février 1885, De Martens, *Nouveau Recueil Général* (2ème série, tôme X, 1885–1886), pp. 199–427

Proudhon, P.-J., *La guerre et la paix. Recherches sur la constitution du droit des gens* (Oeuvres complètes, nouvelle édition, Paris, Rivière, 1927)

Rawls, John, *The Law of Peoples: with the "Idea of Public Reason" Revisited* (Cambridge, Mass., Harvard University Press, 1999)

Rayneval, Gérard de, *Institutions du droit de la nature et des gens* (Paris, Leblanc, 1803)

Reddie, James, *Inquiries in International Law* (Edinburgh, Blackwood, 1842)

Redslob, Robert, "La doctrine idéaliste du droit des gens. Proclamée par la révolution française et par le philosophe Emmanuel Kant" (1921), XXVIII *Revue générale de droit international public*, pp. 441–456

Bibliography

Histoire des grands principes du droit des gens depuis l'antiquité jusqu'à la veille de la grande guerre (Paris, Rousseau, 1923)

Reeves, Jesse S., "The Origin of the Congo Free State, Considered from the Standpoint of International Law" (1909), 3 *American Journal of International Law*, pp. 99–118

Reibstein, Ernst, *Völkerrecht. Eine Geschichte seiner Ideen in Lehre und Praxis* (2 vols., Munich, Freiburg, 1963)

Reisman, Michael W., "International Incidents: A New Genre of Study in International Law," in Reisman and Willard, *International Incidents*, pp. 3–24

Reisman, Michael and Andrew Willard (eds.), *International Incidents: The Law that Counts in World Politics* (Princeton University Press, 1988)

Renault, Louis, *Introduction à l'étude de droit international* (Paris, Larose, 1879); also published in *L'oeuvre internationale de Louis Renault* (Paris, Editions internationales, 1932), pp. 1–68

Les premières violations du droit des gens par l'Allemagne, Luxembourg et Belgique (Paris, Tenin, 1917)

"Les unions internationales. Leurs avantages et leurs inconveniants" (1896), III *Revue générale de droit international public*, pp. 14–26

Renault, Louis and Charles Lyon-Caen, *Traité de droit commercial* (2nd edn., 2 vols., Paris, Pichon, 1889)

Reuter, J. N. "Finland," in *Memories of Westlake*, pp. 116–129

Reuter, Paul, "Aux origines du plan Schuman," in *Mélanges Fernand Dehousse, 2, La construction européenne*, pp. 65–68

"Le plan Schuman" (1952/II), 81 *Recueil des cours de l'Académie de droit international*, pp. 519–629

Ringer, Fritz, *The Decline of the German Mandarins. The German Academic Community, 1890–1933* (Hanover and London, Wesleyan, 1990 [1969])

Rivier, Alphonse, *Lehrbuch des Völkerrechts* (Stuttgart, Enke, 1889)

Robinson, Ronald and John Gallagher, with Alice Denny, *Africa and the Victorians. The Official Mind of Imperialism* (2nd edn., London, Macmillan, 1981)

Robinson, Ronald, "The Conference in Berlin and the Future in Africa, 1884–1885," in Förster, Mommsen, and Robinson, *Bismarck, Europe, and Africa*, pp. 1–32

Roeben, Betsy, "Johann Caspar Bluntschli, Francis Lieber und das moderne Völkerrecht" (unpublished PhD thesis, University of Frankfurt, on file with author, 2000)

Rolin, Albéric de, *Les origines de l'Institut de droit international, 1873–1923. Souvenirs d'un témoin* (Brussels, Vromant, 1923)

"La repression des attentats anarchistes" (1894), XXVI *Revue de droit international et de législation comparée*, pp. 126–152

Rolin, Henri, "Le système des mandats coloniaux" (1920), III/1 *Revue de droit international et de législation comparée*, pp. 329–363

Rolin-Jaequemyns, Gustave, "L'année 1888 au point de vue de la paix et du droit international" (1889), XXI *Revue de droit international et de législation comparée*, pp. 77–103, 167–208

"Chronique de droit international: L'année 1877 et les debuts du 1878 au point de vue de droit international" (1878), X *Revue de droit international et de législation comparée*, pp. 1–59

"Communications relatives à l'Institut de droit international" (1874), VI *Revue de droit international et de législation comparée*, pp. 167–176

"La conférence de Berlin sur la législation du travail, et le socialisme dans le droit international" (1890), XXII *Revue de droit international et de législation comparée*, pp. 5–27

"Le droit international et la phase actuelle de la question de l'Orient" (1876), VIII *Revue de droit international et de législation comparée*, pp. 293–385

"De l'étude de la législation comparée et du droit international" (1869), I *Revue de droit international et de législation comparée*, pp. 1–17, 225–245

"Fondation, à Bruxelles, d'une société politique et sociale" (1889), XXI *Revue de droit international et de législation comparée*, pp. 501–505

"De la nécessité d'organiser une institution scientifique permanente pour favoriser l'étude et les progrès du droit international" (1873), V *Revue de droit international et de législation comparée*, pp. 463–491

"L'oeuvre de l'exploration et de civilisation de l'Afrique centrale" (1877), IX *Revue de droit international et de législation comparée*, pp. 318–321

Rolland, Louis and Pierre Lampue, *Précis de législation coloniale* (2nd edn., Paris, Dalloz, 1936)

Rosenthal, Bent, *Etude de l'oeuvre de Myres Smith McDougal en matière de droit international* (Paris, LGDJ, 1970)

Roth, Brad, *Governmental Illegitimacy in International Law* (Oxford, Clarendon, 1999)

Roth, Guenther, "Introduction," in Weber, *Economy and Society*, pp. xxxiii–cx

Rousseau, Charles, "Georges Scelle 1878–1961" (1961), LXV *Revue générale de droit international public*, pp. 5–19

Principes généraux du droit international public (Paris, Pedone, 1944)

Rousseau, Jean-Jacques, *A Discourse on Inequality*, trans. with introd. M. Cranston (London, Penguin, 1984 [1755])

Rub, Alfred, *Hans Kelsens Völkerrechtslehre. Versuch einer Würdigung* (Zurich, Schultess, 1995)

Rubin, Alfred B., *Ethics and Authority in International Law* (Cambridge University Press, 1997)

Russell, Greg, *Hans J. Morgenthau and the Ethics of American Statecraft* (Baton Rouge, Louisiana State University Press, 1990)

Russell, Lord, of Killowen, "International Law" (1896), XLVIII *Law Quarterly Review*, pp. 311–329

Saalfeld, Friedrich, *Handbuch des positiven Völkerrechts* (Tübingen, Ostander, 1833)

Bibliography

Sachar, Howard M., *A History of Israel. From the Rise of Zionism to our Time* (2nd edn., New York, Knopf, 1996)

Saïd, Edward, *Orientalism. Western Conceptions of the Orient* (London, Penguin, 1995 [1978])

Salomon, Charles, *L'occupation des territoires sans maître. Etude de droit international* (Paris, Giard, 1889)

Sandel, Michael, *Liberalism and the Limits of Justice* (Cambridge University Press, 1982)

Sanderson, G. N., "The European Partition of Africa: Coincidence or Conjecture?," in Penrose, *European Imperialism*, pp. 1–54

Savigny, Friedrich Carl von, *System des heutigen römischen Rechts* (8 vols., Berlin, Veit, 1840)

Vom Beruf unserer Zeit für Gesetzgebung und Rechtswissenschaft (Reprint of the 3rd edn. [1840], Freiburg, Mohr, 1892)

Sayre, Francis B, "Legal Problems Arising from the United Nations Trusteeship System" (1948), 42 *American Journal of International Law*, pp. 262–298

Scelle, Georges, "Le contrôle financier américain au Honduras et au Nicaragua" (1912), XIX *Revue générale de droit international public*, pp. 126–135

Une crise de la Société des nations (Paris, PUF, 1927)

"Le droit dans le conflit Sino-Japonais," in Le Conflit Sino-Japonais, no. 8, *Brochures de l'Association suisse pour la Société des Nations* (Glaris, Tschudy, 1932)

"Le droit public et la théorie de l'Etat," in Scelle *et al.*, *Introduction à l'étude de droit*, I, pp. 96–106

"Essai relatif à l'Union européenne" (1931), XXXVIII *Revue générale de droit international public*, pp. 521–563

"Essai de systematique de droit international (Plan d'un cours de droit international public)" (1923), XXX *Revue générale de droit international public*, pp. 116–142

"Les Etats-Unis d'Amérique et les révolutions méxicaines" (1914), XXI *Revue générale de droit international public*, pp. 117–132

"La guerre civile espagnole et le droit des gens," Part 1 (1938), XLV *Revue générale de droit international public*, pp. 265–301; part 2 (1938), XLV *Revue générale de droit international public*, pp. 649–657, part 3 (1939), XLVI *Revue générale de droit international public*, pp. 197–228

"Une instance en revision devant la cour de la Haye: L'Affaire de la Orinoco Steamship Company" (1911), XVIII *Revue générale de droit international public*, pp. 164–202

La morale des traités de paix (Paris, Cadet, 1920)

Le Pacte des Nations et sa liaison avec Le Traité de Paix (Paris, Sirey, 1919)

La politique républicaine (Paris, Alcan 1924)

Précis de droit des gens (2 vols., Paris, Sirey, 1932–1934)

Bibliography

Précis élémentaire de législation industrielle (Paris, Sirey, 1927)

"Quelques reflexions sur l'abolition de la compétence de guerre" (1954), LVIII *Revue générale de droit international public*, pp. 5–22

"La ratification de la Convention du Gothard du 13 octobre 1909" (1913), XX *Revue générale de droit international public*, pp. 484–505

"La situation juridique de Vilna et de son territoire. Etude sur le différend polono-lithuanien et la force obligatoire de la décision de la Conférence des Ambassadeurs du 15 Mars 1923" (1928), XXV *Revue générale de droit international public*, pp. 730–780

"Théorie du gouvernement international" (1935), *Annuaire de l'Institut international de droit public*, pp. 41–112

Théorie juridique de la révision des traités (Paris, Sirey, 1936)

La traité négrière aux Indes de Castilles – Contrats et traités d'assiento (2 vols., Paris, Larose & Tenin, 1906)

Scelle, Georges *et al.*, *Introduction à l'étude de droit* (2 vols., Paris, Rousseau, 1951)

Scheuerman, William E., *Between the Norm and the Exception. The Frankfurt School and the Rule of Law* (Cambridge, Mass. MIT Press, 1997)

Carl Schmitt: The End of Law (Lanham, MD, Boulder, New York and Oxford, Rowman & Littlefield, 1999)

"Globalization and the Fate of Law," in Dyzenhaus, *Recrafting the Rule of Law*, pp. 252–266

Schmitt, Carl, *The Concept of the Political*, trans. from *Das Begriff der Politischen* [2nd edn. 1934] and with an introd. George Schwab, with a new foreword by Tracy B. Strong (Cambridge, Mass. and London, MIT Press, 1996)

The Crisis of Parliamentary Democracy, trans. from *Die geistesgeschichtliche Lage des heutigen Parlamentarismus* [1923/1926] Ellen Kennedy (Cambridge, Mass. and London, MIT Press, 1988)

"Die Gegensatz von Parlamentarismus und moderner Massendemokratie" (1926), in *Positionen und Begriffe*, pp. 52–66

Gesetz und Urteil. Eine Untersuchung zum Problem der Rechtspraxis (Berlin, Liebmann, 1912)

"Gespräch über den neuen Raum" (1955/1958), in *Staat, Grossraum, Nomos*, pp. 552–572

"Grossraum gegen Universalismus" (1939), in *Positionen und Begriffe*, pp. 295–302

Das internationalrechtliche Verbrechen des Angriffskrieges und der Grundsatz "Nullum crimen, nulla poena sine lege" (published with annotations by Helmut Quaritsch, Berlin, Duncker & Humblot, 1994)

Kernfrage des Völkerbundes (Berlin, Dümmler, 1926)

"Die Lage der europäischen Rechtswissenschaft" (1943/44), trans. G. L. Ulmen as "The Plight of European Jurisprudence" (1990), 83 *Telos*, pp. 35–70

Bibliography

"Die Legale Weltrevolution: Politischer Mehrwärt als Prämie auf juridische Legalität" (1978), 3 *Der Staat*, pp. 321–339; trans. G. L. Ulmen, as "The Legal World Revolution" (1987), 72 *Telos*, pp. 73–89
Legalität und Legitimität (1932, 4th edn., Berlin, Duncker & Humblot, 1988)
Nationalsozialismus und Völkerrecht (Berlin, Dünnhaupt, 1934)
"Der neue Nomos der Erde" (1955), in *Staat, Grossraum, Nomos*, pp. 513–518
"Das neue Vae Neutris"(1938), in *Positionen und Begriffe*, pp. 251–255
Der Nomos der Erde im Völkerrecht des Jus Publicum Europaeum (Berlin, Duncker & Humblot, 1950)
"Nomos-Nahme-Name" (1959), in *Staat, Grossraum, Nomos*, pp. 573–591
"Die Ordnung der Welt nach dem Zweiten Weltkrieg" (1962), in *Staat, Grossraum, Nomos*, pp. 592–617
Political Romanticism, trans. from *Politische Romantik* [1919/1925] Guy Oakes (Cambridge, Mass. and London, MIT Press, 1986)
Political Theology. Four Chapters on the Concept of Sovereignty, trans. from *Politische Theologie: Vier Kapitel zur Lehre von der Souveränität* [1922/1934] George Schwab (Cambridge, Mass. and London, MIT Press, 1985)
Positionen und Begriffe im Kampf mit Weimar – Genf – Versailles 1923–1939 (Berlin, Duncker & Humblot, 1988 [1940])
"Die Rheinland als Objekt internationaler Politik" (1925), in *Positionen und Begriffe*, pp. 26–33
Staat, Grossraum, Nomos. Arbeiten aus den Jahren 1916–1969 (Berlin, Duncker & Humblot, 1995)
"Der Status Quo und der Friede" (1925), in *Positionen und Begriffe*, pp. 33–42
"Völkerrechtliche Formen des modernen Imperialismus" (1932), in *Positionen und Begriffe*, pp. 162–180
Völkerrechtliche Grossraumordnung mit Interventionsverbot für raumfremde Mächte (Berlin, Deutscher Rechtsverlag, 1939)
Die Wendung zum diskriminierenden Kriegsbegriff (Berlin, Duncker & Humblot, 1988 [1938])
"Die Wendung zum totalen Staat" (1931), in *Positionen und Begriffe*, pp. 146–157
"Das Zeitalter der Neutralisierungen und Entpolitisierungen" (1929), in *Positionen und Begriffe*, pp. 120–132
"Zu Friedrich Meinecke's 'Idee der Staatsräson'" (1926), in *Positionen und Begriffe*, pp. 45–52
Schmoeckel, Mathias, *Die Grossraumtheorie. Ein Beitrag zur Geschichte des Völkerrechtswissenschaft im Dritter Reich, insbesonderes der Kriegzeit* (Berlin, Duncker & Humblot, 1994)
Schoen, P., "Zur Lehre von dem Grundlagen des Völkerrechts" (1914–1915), VIII *Archiv für Rechts und Wirtschaftsphilosophie*, pp. 287–321

Bibliography

Schorske, Carl E., *Fin-de-Siècle Vienna. Politics and Culture* (New York, Vintage, 1989)

Schou, August, *Histoire de l'internationalisme* (3 vols., Publications de l'Institut Nobel Norvégien, Oslo etc., Aschehoug, 1963)

Schücking, Walther, "Die Annäherung der Menschenrassen durch das Völkerrecht" (1911), in *Der Bund der Völker*, pp. 57–78

Der Bund der Völker. Studien und Vorträge zum organisatorischen Pazifismus (Leipzig, Geist, 1918)

Ein neues Zeitalter? Kritik am pariser Völkerbundsentwurf (Berlin, Engelmann, 1919)

"L'organisation internationale" (1908), XV *Revue générale de droit international public*, pp. 5–23, later published as "Die Idee der internationalen Organisation in der Geschichte," in Schücking, *Der Bund der Völker*, pp. 17–34

Die Organisation der Welt (Leipzig, Kröner, 1909)

"Der Stand des völkerrechtlichen Unterrichts in Deutschland" (1913), VII *Zeitschrift für Völkerrecht*, pp. 375–382

Das Werk vom Haag, Erster Band: Die Staatenverband der Haager Konferenzen (Munich and Leipzig, Duncker & Humblot, 1912)

"Der Völkerbundsentwurf der deutschen Regierung," in Munch, *Les origines et l'oeuvre de la Société des Nations*, II, pp. 138–160

Die völkerrechtliche Lehre des Weltkrieges (Leipzig, von Veit, 1918)

Schücking, Walther and Hans Wehberg, *Die Satzung des Völkerbundes* (Berlin, Vahlen, 1921)

Schwab, George, *The Challenge of the Exception. An Introduction to the Political Ideas of Carl Schmitt between 1921 and 1936* (2nd edn., with a new intro., New York, Greenwood, 1989)

Scott, James Brown, *Les Conférences de la paix de la Haye de 1899 et 1907* (3 vols., Carnegie Endowment for International Peace, Division of International Law, 1932)

The Reports to the Hague Conferences of 1899 and 1907 (Oxford, Clarendon, 1917)

Senn, Marcel, "Rassistische und antisemitische Elemente im Rechtsdenken von Johann Caspar Bluntschli" (1993), 110 *Zeitschrift der Savigny-Stiftung für Rechtsgeschichte*, pp. 372–405

Seydel, Max, *Grundzüge einer allgemeinen Staatslehre* (Würzburg, Stuber, 1873)

Sfez, Lucien, "Duguit et la théorie de l'Etat" (1976), 21 *Archives de philosophie de droit*, pp. 111–130

Sheehan, James J., *German Liberalism in the 19th Century* (Chicago University Press, 1978)

Shelton, Dinah (ed.), *Commitment and Compliance. The Role of Non-Binding Norms in the International Legal System* (Oxford University Press, 2000)

Sibert, Marcel, *Traité de droit international de la paix* (2 vols., Paris, Dalloz, 1951)

Sidgwick, Henry, *Philosophy. Its Scope and Relations. An Introductory Course of Lectures* (London, Macmillan, repr. by Thoemmes, 1998 [1902])

Bibliography

Simons, Walther, "La conception du droit international privé d'après la doctrine et la pratique en Allemagne" (1926/V), 15 *Recueil des cours de l'Académie de droit international*, pp. 437–529

Slaughter Burley, Anne-Marie, "International Law and International Relations: A Dual Agenda" (1993), 87 *American Journal of International Law*, pp. 205–239

Slaughter, Anne-Marie, "International Law in a World of Liberal States" (1995), 6 *European Journal of International Law*, pp. 503–538

"The Real New World Order" (1997), 76 *Foreign Affairs*, pp. 183–197

Slaughter, Anne-Marie, Andrew S. Tulumello, and Stepan Wood, "International Law and International Relations Theory: A New Generation of Interdisciplinary Scholarship" (1998), 92 *American Journal of International Law*, pp. 367–397

Sloterdijk, Peter, *Critique of Cynical Reason*, trans. M. Eldred, foreword A. Huyssen (Minneapolis, University of Minnesota Press, 1987)

Sluga, Hans, *Heidegger's Crisis. Philosophy and Politics in Nazi Germany* (Cambridge, Mass., Harvard University Press, 1993)

Smith, Steve (ed.), *International Relations. British and American Perspectives* (Oxford, Blackwell, 1985)

"Paradigm Dominance in International Relations: The Development of International Relations as a Social Science" (1987), 16 *Millennium: Journal of International Studies*, pp. 189–206

"The Self-Images of a Discipline: A Genealogy of International Relations Theory," in Booth and Smith, *International Relations Theory Today*, pp. 1–37

Smyrniadis, Bion, "Positivisme et morale internationale en droit des gens" (1955), LIX *Revue générale de droit international public*, pp. 99–120

Söllner, Alfons, "German Conservatism in America: Morgenthau's Political Realism" (1987), 72 *Telos*, pp. 161–172

"Vom Völkerrecht zum science of international relations. Vier typische Vertreter des politikwissenschaftlichen Emigration," in Srubar, *Exil, Wissenschaft, Identität*, pp. 164–180

Sousa Santos, Boaventura de, *Toward a New Common Sense. Law, Science and Politics in the Paradigmatic Transition* (New York, Routledge, 1995)

Spegele, Roger D., *Political Realism in International Relations Theory* (Cambridge University Press, 1996)

Srubar, Ilja (ed.), *Exil, Wissenschaft, Identität. Die Emigration deutscher Sozialwissenschaftler 1933–1945* (Frankfurt, Suhrkamp 1988)

Stengel, Karl von, "La constitution et l'administration des colonies allemandes" (1895), III *Révue de droit public et de la science politique en France et à l'étranger*, pp. 275–292

Weltstaat und Friedensproblem (Reichl, Berlin, 1909)

Bibliography

Stengers, Jan, "Leopold II and the *Association Internationale du Congo*," in Förster, Mommsen, and Robinson, *Bismarck, Europe, and Africa*, pp. 229–244

Stirk, Peter, "Carl Schmitt's Völkerrechtliche Grossraumordnung" (1999), 20 *History of Political Thought*, pp. 357–374

Stolleis, Michael, *Geschichte des öffentlichen Rechts in Deutschland* (3 vols., Munich, Beck, 1992–1999)

Stolleis, Michael (ed.), *Juristische Zeitschriften. Die neuen Medien des 18.-20. Jahrhunderts* (Frankfurt, Klostermann, 1999)

Stone, Julius, *Legal Controls of International Conflict* (New York, Rinehart, 1954)

"Non Liquet and the Function of Law in the International Community" (1959), XXXV *British Year Book of International Law*, pp. 124–161

Social Dimensions of Law and Justice (London, Stevens, 1966)

Stone, Norman, *Europe Transformed 1878–1919* (2nd edn., Oxford, Blackwell, 1999)

Strupp, Karl, "Die deutsche Vereinigung für internationales Recht: ihre Notwendigkeit, ihre Entstehung, ihre bisherige Tätigkeit" (1914), 24 *Zeitschrift für internationales Recht*, pp. 355–363

"Les règles générales du droit de la paix" (1934/I), 47 *Recueil des cours de l'Académie de droit international*, pp. 263–595

Das Werk von Locarno (Berlin and Leipzig, de Gruyter, 1926)

Symbolae Verzijl (The Hague, Nijhoff, 1958)

Symposium "Alfred Verdross" (1995), 6 *European Journal of International Law*, pp. 32–115

Symposium, "Carl Schmitt Now" (1996), 109 *Telos*

Symposium, "Carl Schmitt: Enemy or Foe?," Special Issue (1987), 72 *Telos*

Symposium "Dionisio Anzilotti" (1992), 3 *European Journal of International Law*, pp. 92–168

Symposium "Georges Scelle" (1990), 1 *European Journal of International Law*, pp. 193–249

Symposium "Hans Kelsen" (1998), 9 *European Journal of International Law*, pp. 287–400

Symposium "Hersch Lauterpacht" (1997), 8 *European Journal of International Law*, pp. 215–320

Synopwich, Christine, "Utopia and the Rule of Law," in Dyzenhaus, *Recrafting the Rule of Law*, pp. 178–195

Temperley, Harold, *The Victorian Age in Politics, War and Diplomacy* (Cambridge University Press, 1928)

Tesón, Ferdinand, *Humanitarian Intervention: An Inquiry into Law and Morality* (Dobbs Ferry and New York, Transnational, 1988)

The Dominican Republic Crisis, 1965, Background Paper and Proceedings (Dobbs Ferry, the Bar of the City of New York and Oceana, 1966)

Thomas, A. J. and Ann Van Wynen Thomas, "The Dominican Republic Crisis 1965. Legal Aspects," in *The Dominican Republic Crisis*, pp. 3–39

Bibliography

Thompson, Kenneth W., "Hans J. Morgenthau. Principles of Political Realism," in Thompson, *Masters of International Thought*, pp. 80–91
Masters of International Thought. Major Twentieth-Century Theorists and the World Crisis (Baton Rouge and London, Louisiana State University Press, 1980)
Thomson, Robert Stanley, *Fondation de l'Etat indépendant du Congo* (Brussels, Office de publicité, 1933)
Todorov, Tzvetan, *The Conquest of America. The Question of the Other*, trans. Richard Howard (New York, Harper, 1984)
The Morals of History, trans Alyson Waters (Minneapolis and London, University of Minnesota Press, 1995)
Tolonen, Juha, *Stat och Rätt* (Åbo Akademi, 1986)
Torres Campos, M., "L'Espagne en Afrique" (1892), XXIV *Revue de droit international et de législation comparée*, pp. 441–475
Triepel, Heinrich, "Ferdinand von Martitz. Ein Bild seines Lebens und seines Wirkens" (1922), 30 *Zeitschrift für internationales Recht*, pp. 155–172
Völkerrecht und Landesrecht (Leipzig, Hirschfield 1899)
Truyol, Antonio, "Doctrines contemporaines du droit des gens" (1950), LIV *Revue générale de droit international public*, pp. 373–416 (1951), LV *Revue générale de droit international public*, pp. 23–40, 199–236
Truyol y Serra, A., *Histoire du droit international public* (Paris, Economica, 1995)
Tuck, Richard, *The Rights of War and Peace. Political Thought and the International Order from Grotius to Kant* (Oxford University Press, 1999)
Tuori, Kaarlo, *Valtionhallinnon sivuelinorganisaatiosta* (2 vols., Helsinki, Suomalainen lakimiesyhdistys, 1983)
Twiss, Sir Travers, "Le congrès de Vienne et la conférence de Berlin" (1885), XVII *Revue de droit international et de législation comparée*, pp. 201–217
The Law of Nations Considered as Independent Communities (2nd edn., 2 vols., Oxford, Clarendon, 1884)
"La libre navigation du Congo" (1883), XV *Revue de droit international et de législation comparée*, pp. 436–442, 547–563 (1884), XVI *Revue de droit international et de législation comparée*, pp. 237–246
Two Introductory Lectures on the Science of International Law (London, Longman, 1856)
Tylor, E. B., *Primitive Culture: Researches into the Mythology, Philosophy, Religion, Language, Custom, and Art* (7th edn., New York, Brentano, 1924 [1871])
Ullmann, Emanuel, *Völkerrecht* (Freiburg, Mohl, 1898)
Ulmen, G. L., "The Concept of Nomos: Introduction to Schmitt's Appropriation/Distribution/Production" (1993), 95 *Telos*, pp. 39–51
Uzoigwe, G. N., "The Results of the Berlin West Africa Conference: An Assessment," in Förster, Mommsen, and Robinson, *Bismarck, Europe, and Africa*, pp. 541–552

Vagts, Detlev F., "International Law in the Third Reich" (1990), 84 *American Journal of International Law*, pp. 661–704

Verdross, Alfred, "Les principes généraux du droit dans la jurisprudence internationale" (1935/II), 52 *Recueil des cours de l'Académie de droit international*, pp. 195–251

Vergé, Charles, "Le droit des gens avant et depuis 1789," in G. F. de Martens, *Précis de droit des gens moderne de l'Europe*, pp. i–lv

Vinogradoff, Sir Paul, "Historical Types of International Law" (1923), I *Bibliotheca Visseriana*, pp. 3–70

Visscher, Paul de, "Colloque sur l'enseignement du droit international," Rapport (1956), LX *Revue générale de droit international public*, pp. 569–583

Vogelsänger, Peter, *Max Huber. Recht, Politik, Humanität und Glauben* (Frauenfeld and Stuttgart, Huber, 1967)

Völkerrecht und rechtliches Weltbild. Festschrift für Alfred Verdross, F. A. von der Heydte ed. (Vienna, Springer, 1960)

Walker, T. A., *The Science of International Law* (London, Clay, 1893)

Waltz, Kenneth, *Theory of International Politics* (Reading, London, and Amsterdam, Addison-Wesley, 1979)

Walzer, Michael, *Interpretation and Moral Criticism* (Cambridge, Mass., Harvard University Press, 1987)

Warner, Daniel, *An Ethic of Responsibility in International Relations* (Boulder and London, Rienner, 1991)

Weber, Eugene, *The Hollow Years. France in the 1930s* (London, Sinclair, 1995)

Weber, Max, *Economy and Society. An Outline of Interpretative Sociology*, eds. Guenther Roth and Claus Wittich (University of California Press, 1978)

On Law in Economy and Society, ed. with introd. and annot. Max Rheinstein (New York, Simon & Schuster, 1954)

"Politics as Vocation," in *From Max Weber: Essays in Sociology*, trans., ed. and with an intro. H. H. Gerth and C. Wright Mills (London, Routledge, 1967), pp. 77–128

Wehberg, Hans and Alfred Manes, *Der Völkerbund-Vorschlag der deutschen Regierung* (Berlin, Engelmann, 1919)

Wesseling, Henri, *Le partage de l'Afrique 1880–1914*, traduit du néerlandais par Patrick Grilli (Paris, Denoël, 1996)

Westlake, John, "L'Angleterre et la République Sud-Africaine" (1896), XXVIII *Revue de droit international et de législation comparée*, pp. 268–300

Chapters on the Principles of International Law (Cambridge University Press, 1894)

The Collected Papers of John Westlake on Public International Law, L. Oppenheim (ed.) (Cambridge University Press, 1914)

"Le conflit Anglo-Portugais" (1891), XVIII *Revue de droit international et de législation comparée*, pp. 243–265 (1892), XXIV *Revue de droit international et de*

Bibliography

législation comparée, pp. 170–205 (1893), XXV *Revue de droit international et de législation comparée*, pp. 58–71

"Introduction au droit international privé" (1880), XII *Revue de droit international et de législation comparée*, pp. 23–46

"Introductory Lecture on International Law," in *Collected Papers*, pp. 393–413

International Law. (2 vols., 2nd edn., Cambridge University Press, 1910)

"The Native States of India," in *Collected Papers*, pp. 620–632

"Relations between Public and Private International Law," in *Collected Papers*, pp. 285–311

"The Transvaal War," in *Collected Papers*, pp. 419–460

A Treatise on Private International Law, or the Conflict of Laws, with Principal Reference to its Practice in the English and Other Cognate Systems of Jurisprudence (London, Maxwell, 1858)

Wheaton, Henry, *Elements of International Law. With a Sketch of the History of the Science* (2 vols., London, Fellowes, 1836)

Histoire de progrès du droit des gens en Europe depuis la paix de Westphalie jusqu'à nos jours (2 vols., 3rd edn., Leipzig, Brockhaus, 1853)

White, Hayden, *Tropics of Discourse. Essays in Cultural Criticism* (Baltimore and London, Johns Hopkins University Press, 1985 [1978])

Wieacker, Frantz, *A History of Private Law in Europe. With Particular Reference to Germany*, trans. Tony Weir (Oxford, Clarendon, 1995)

Wight, Martin, *International Theory. The Three Traditions*, Gabriele Wight and Brian Porter eds. (Leicester University Press for the RIIA, 1994)

Wildman, Richard, *Institutes of International Law* (2 vols., London, Benning, 1849)

Wilson, H. S., *African Decolonization* (London and New York, Edward Arnold, 1994)

Winock, Michel, *Nationalism, Anti-Semitism and Fascism in France*, trans. J. M. Todd (Stanford University Press, 1998)

Winter, Jay, *Sites of Memory, Sites of Mourning. The Great War in European Cultural History* (Cambridge University Press, 1995)

Wolfers, Arnold, *Britain and France between Two Wars. Conflicting Strategies of Peace from Versailles to World War II* (New York, Norton, 1966)

Wolin, Richard, "Carl Schmitt. The Conservative Revolutionary Habitus and the Aesthetics of Horror" (1992), 20 *Political Theory*, pp. 424–447

Wood, Frances, *No Dogs and Not Many Chinese. Treaty Port Life in China 1843–1943* (London, Murray, 1998)

Woolsey, T. D., *Introduction to the Study of International Law* (5th edn., London, Sampson, 1879)

Zeldin, Théodore, *France, 1848–1945* (2 vols., Oxford, Clarendon, 1973)

Ziegler, Karl-Heinz, *Völkerrechtsgeschichte. Ein Studienbuch* (Munich, Beck, 1994)

Zimmern, Sir Alfred, *The League of Nations and the Rule of Law 1918–1935* (London, Macmillan, 1935)

Bibliography

Zitelmann, Ernst, *Die Unvolkommenheit des Völkerrechts* (Munich and Leipzig, Duncker & Humblot, 1919)

Zorn, Philipp, *Das deutsche Reich und die internationale Schiedgerichtsbarkeit* (Berlin & Leipzig, Rothschild, 1911)

'"Moderne Legitimisten"' (1908–9), II *Archiv für Rechts und Wirtschaftsphilosophie*, pp. 163–179

Das Staatsrecht des deutschen Reiches (2 vols., 2nd edn., Berlin, Guttentag, 1895–1897)

Weltunionen, Haager Friedenskonferenzen und Völkerbund (Berlin, Dümmler, 1925)

Index

absolutism, 18, 22–23
abuse of rights, 311, 402, 404
Abushiri Rebellion, 147
Act of Algeçiras, 155
Action française, 316, 317
Adam, Robert, 128
Africa, 101, 111, 116–178
aggression, 340, 378, 381, 419, 425
Ago, Roberto, 351
Alabama arbitration, 40, 62, 454
Alain (Emile Chartier), 329
Algeria, 110, 142
Allied Conference of Ambassadors, 328
Allied Supreme Council, 171
Alvarez, Alejandro, 302–305, 308–309, 310, 311, 313, 314, 322, 330, 342, 349, 511
American Society of International Law, 390, 466, 485
analogy, 364, 374–375
anarchism, 69
Anderson, Percy, 118
Anghie, Antony, 174
Anglo-Iranian Oil Company case, 400
Annam, 117
annexation
  symbolic, as basis of title, 137
Annuaire français de droit international, 348
Annual Digest of Public International Law Cases (later *International Law Reports*), 375
anthropology, 101, 455
anti-formalism, 52, 467, 475–476, 479–480, 482–489, 508
  in Alvarez, 304–305
  in Scelle and Le Fur, 341–342
  in Schmitt and Morgenthau, 459–465
  in post-war French law, 349
antisemitism, 104, 199, 359, 369–371, 407, 422, 424, 446–447, 450

arbitration, 212–213, 237, 440, 443–444
Archiv des öffentlichen Rechts, 167
Arendt, Hannah, 430, 465
Arnaud, André-Jean, 289
Arnold, Matthew, 88
Arntz, Egide, 122, 143
Aron, Raymond, 347, 468
Aryan law, 59
Aryan race, 77, 103–104
Asser, Tobias, 12, 13, 17, 57, 66
assimilation, 372–374, 375, 411
Association for International Conciliation (German), 218
Association internationale Africain (AIA), 121, 136, 145
Association internationale du Congo (AIC), 136, 156
Association internationale pour le progrès des sciences sociales, 12
Austin, John, 34, 46, 48, 92
Austro-German Customs Union case, 222
authoritarianism, 269, 308–309, 313–314, 325–326

balance of power, 23, 29, 189, 192, 311–312, 420, 437, 440, 458, 460, 471, 473
Bar, Ludwig von, 216
Barrès, Maurice, 269, 308, 320
Basdevant, Jules, 312–313
Bechuanaland, 125
Benda, Julien, 317–318, 319, 415
Benjamin, Walter, 392
Bentham, Jeremy, 14
Bergbohm, Carl, 27, 185–186, 189
Bergson, Henri, 318
Berle, Adolf, 497–501
Berlin Act (1885), 62, 65, 125, 126, 416
Berlin Conference (1884–1885), 106, 107, 117, 121–127, 149, 272

559

Index

Bernard, Montague, 33
Berthélemy, Henri, 317
Bildung, 85
biology, 327–331, 339
Bismarck, 64, 91, 109, 110, 118, 123, 189, 194, 207, 256
Bloch, Ernst, 486
Blum, Léon, 313
Bluntschli, Johann Caspar, 40, 46–47, 48, 49, 52, 53, 58, 68–69, 72, 80–81, 84–85, 86–87, 92, 127, 128, 146, 188, 222, 280
and correspondence with von Moltke, 84–85
and nationalism, 64
and organic theory, 46–47, 50–51, 80–81
and the founding of the *Institut*, 42–43, 45
as politician, 90–91
as proponent of "Aryan Law," 59, 103–104
Bodin, Jean, 258
Boer War, 64–65
Bonfils, Henri, 73, 280, 291
Bonnecase, Julien, 318
Bouglé, Charles, 329
Bourgeois, Léon, 153, 267, 284–291, 300, 310, 314, 318, 330, 333, 346
Brazza, Pierre Savorgnan de, 107, 136–137, 143, 145, 272
Brentano, Lujo, 234
Briand, Aristide, 342, 343, 347
Brierly, James, 172–173, 390
Bristler, Edouard (John H. Herz), 256
British Association for the Promotion of Social Science, 59, 72
British North Borneo Company, 117, 122
British South Africa Company (BSAC), 120
British Year Book of International Law, 375
Brockdorff-Rantzau, Ulrich, 236, 293
Brougham, (Lord) Henry, 28
Brunet, René, 270
Bruns, Viktor, 233
Bull, Hedley, 473
Bulmerincq, August, 102–103
Bund neues Vaterland, 218
Burritt, Elihu, 40
Burton, Richard, 147
Bülow, Bernard, 212

Calvo, Carlos, 40
Canning, George, 384
Canon law, 22
"Cape to Cairo plan," 152, 153
capitalism, 60
Carr, Edwin Hallett, 361, 409, 410, 473
Carré de Malberg, Raymond, 269
Casablanca case, 287
Casement, Roger, 158
Castonnet des Fossés, Henri, 167
Catellani, Enrico, 98–99, 168

Catholicism, 37, 91, 247, 315, 322, 323, 326, 334, 339, 351, 425
Cathrein, Viktor, 229–231
Cattier, Félicien, 158–159, 160
Cauchy, Eugène, 275–276
Charter of the United Nations
Article 2(7), 394
Article 55, 394
chartered companies, 109, 117–120, 143–147
Chayes, Abram, 478
China, 132, 134, 414
chronique de droit international, 17
Churchill, Winston, 439
civil law, 280
civilization, 53, 55, 56, 75–76, 76–88, 102–103, 131–132, 132–136, 223, 228–229, 416–417, 500
Clausewitz, Karl, 83
Clemenceau, Georges, 137, 285, 293
Cobden, Richard, 83
Code Civil, 30, 43, 275, 282, 289
codification, 42–43, 45, 47, 307, 306–397
Cold War, 338, 438, 465, 469, 512, 513
collective security, 358, 377–379, 381, 417, 487
collectivism, 69
French 268–269, 289, 298–302
colonialism, 9, 62, 74, 98–178, 359–360
Belgian 168
British 108, 111–112
French 110, 117, 137, 142, 164, 167–168, 271, 272–274, 279, 291
German 109, 110, 118, 119–120, 137, 145, 146
internationalization of, 121–126, 166–178
Italian 168
Commission on Human Rights, 394
Comité des Etudes du Haut-Congo, 136, 143
communism, 67, 68, 318, 329, 339–340, 341, 413, 469, 497, 480, 500–507
comparative law, 13
Comparative Method, 101, 103
competencies, theory of, 332–333, 335
Comte, Auguste, 23, 29, 267, 268, 301, 336, 347
Concept of the Political, The (Der Begriff des Politischen), 436, 440, 442
concrete
order, 416–417, 440, 465
reality (theory of), 182, 251–255
conflict of laws, 66
Congo
Independent State of, 62 108, 121, 155–166, 177, 416
King Léopold's rule over, 155–166
transfer to Belgium, 164–165, 416
Congo Reform Association, 158, 164
Congress of Vienna (1815), 21, 28
conquest, 137

560

Index

Conrad, Joseph, 155
conscience-consciousness (*conscience*), 3, 41, 47–49, 51–54, 71, 80, 91, 177, 189, 489, 511
conservatism, 26, 212, 229–230, 261, 503
   Kaufmann's, 249–261
   Le Fur's, 317–327
Constant, Benjamin, 27, 285
constitutional law, 9, 428–430
   international law as, 330, 333
   League Covenant as, 378–379, 425, 426
consular jurisdiction, 96, 114–115, 133, 134
co-ordination law 32–33, 38, 179, 187, 228, 254
Corfu Channel case, 400
corporatism (syndicalism), 267, 301–302, 329
cosmopolitanism, 37, 44, 50, 53, 55–56, 63, 66–67, 183, 245–248, 267, 356–359, 371, 373–374, 390, 399, 405, 411, 515–516
   Kelsen's, 246–249
   Lauterpacht's, 406–412
   Scelle's, 331–336
   Schmitt's critique of, 424–426
Covenant of the League of Nations, 425, 459
   Article 10, 239, 333, 352
   Article 11, 340
   Article 15, 353
   Article 16, 340, 353, 378, 379, 425
   Article 19, 324, 238, 335–338, 382
   Article 20, 376
   as constitution, 376, 379, 426
   French draft of, 294–295
   German draft of, 220–221, 235–236
   negotiations, 294–295, 333
Crimean War (1854–1856), 11–12, 35
Crisis of Parliamentary Democracy (Die geistesgeschichtliche Lage des heutigen Parlamentarimsus), 429–430
Crowe, Sheryl, 127
Cuba, 413, 481
cultural consciousness, 70–88, 101–105, 107–110, 214–215, 223, 270–274, 295–296
culture
   as character, 75–88
   of formalism, 500–509
customary law in the Orient (project of the *Institut*), 132–133
cynicism, 491–492

Darwinism, 36, 38, 70, 74–76, 104
decisionism in Schmitt and Morgenthau, 427–429, 462, 463, 468–469, 486, 488
decolonization, 175–178, 512–513
dédoublement fonctionnel, 333, 338
deformalized law, 479, 489
Delcassé, Théophile, 153, 155,

Delpech, Joseph, 271
democracy, 31, 60, 178, 313, 319, 363, 407, 429–430, 504, 508
depoliticization, 426–432, 461–462, 485–486
Descamps, Baron Edouard, 141, 160, 161–163, 286
desire principle (*Lustprincip*), 448–449, 469
Despagnet, Frantz, 164, 272–274, 284, 291
Deutsch, Karl, 467
Deutsche Gesellschaft für Völkerrecht, 220, 232, 234–235, 237
Deutsche Ostafrikanische Gesellschaft (DOAG), 119
Development of International Law by the International Court, 403–406, 412
Diderot, Denis, 115, 116
Die internationale Rechtspflege, ihr Wesen und ihre Grenzen, 436, 440–444
difference (logic of) 142, 506–507
division of labor, 269–270, 297
Dominican Republic
   US intervention in, 413, 480, 481, 497–501
drive theory, 444, 448–452, 469, 493
Droit public de l'Europe, 31, 112–115, 415–417
Droun de Lhuys, Edmund, 40
Drummond, Eric, 346
Duguit, Léon, 267, 298–301, 305, 319
Dupuis, Charles, 311, 313, 314
Dupuy, René-Jean, 348, 350
Durkheim, Emile, 267, 268, 297, 302, 315, 331, 336, 347
dynamism in law, 43, 303–304, 443, 444, 459–460, 480, 488, 496

economic policy, 416, 418, 421, 461
   French 329, 342
effective occupation, as basis of title, 109, 123–124, 129, 140–142, 148, 402
effectiveness, 397, 485
Egypt, 120–121, 152, 273
empiricism, 299
Engelhardt, Edouard, 107, 131, 150
Engels, Friedrich, 195
Entente cordiale 154
esprit d'internationalité, 13, 20, 27, 57, 69, 92, 170, 211, 515
ethics, 188, 459, 482, 487, 489, 494
Eurocentrism, 9, 305
European Coal and Steel Community (ECSC), 345, 348
European community ("European civilization"), 22, 25–26, 44, 49, 51, 52–54, 56–57, 66–67, 70–97, 189, 280–281, 316, 416–418
European Economic Community (EEC) 345
European Journal of International Law, 8
European Union, 316
   in Le Fur and Scelle, 342–345, 347–348

561

Index

evolutionism, 74–76, 99, 100, 101–110, 142, 308
exclusion–inclusion logic, 127–130, 141, 175
extradition, 50, 68–69

Falk, Richard, 476, 478, 483
Fashoda crisis, 152–155, 279
Fauchille, Paul, 73, 223, 279–281, 302
federalism, 3, 20, 61, 62, 129, 308, 315–316, 319, 326–327, 354, 355, 357–358, 373–374, 382, 390–391, 424–425, 426
   Lauterpacht's, 376–379
   Le Fur's, 324–327
   Scelle's, 266–267, 269, 331–336
   Schücking's, 216–222
federations (Jellinek on), 202
Fenwick, Charles, 477
Ferry, Jules, 107
Fichte, Johan Gottlieb, 23
Field, David Dudley, 40
Fiore, Pasquale, 54–57, 63, 128
Fischer Williams, John, 173
formalism, 79, 80, 183–185, 228, 247, 258, 262, 303, 312, 341, 349, 365, 395, 417, 425, 459–465, 473–474, 475, 488, 494, 500–509
Foucault, Michel, 9
Fouillée, Alfred, 286
Franco, Francisco, 339, 340
Franco-Prussian War (1870–1871), 36, 39, 84, 182–183
free trade, 27, 35, 58, 111, 123, 335, 417, 418–419, 461
freedom
   of navigation, 122, 123,
   of religion, 53, 60, 65, 79
French Congo, 166
Fried, Alfred, 216, 228, 450, 477
Friedmann, Wolfgang, 414, 420, 477, 478, 480, 497–501
Funck-Brentano, Théophile, 276
Function of Law in the International Community, 368–369, 372, 376, 383, 390, 401, 402, 405, 411
functionalism, 239, 282–285, 476
fundamental
   change (*rebus sic stantibus*) 179–180, 254, 324, 336–338
   rights of States, 282

Galicia, 369, 370
Gallagher, John, 116
gaps in law, 362, 366–367, 441
Geffcken, Friedrich, 109, 146, 147
Geffcken, Heinrich, 226–227
General Act for the Pacific Settlement of International Disputes (1928), 381, 378, 379

general principles of law, 364, 369, 403–404
Geneva Convention for the Amelioration of the Condition of the Wounded of the Armies in the Field (1864), 15, 39
Geneva Protocol for the Pacific Settlement of International Disputes (1924), 306
Gény, Francois, 281
Gerber, Carl Friedrich von, 46, 183–184, 189, 195
German Confederation, 21, 31, 64
German East Africa Company (*Deutsche Ostafrikanische Gesellschaft, DOAG*), 119
German League of Nations Union (*Deutsche Liga für Völkerbund*), 209
German public law theory, 183–185, 187–188, 208–213
German South West Africa, 166
Gide, André, 318
Gierke, Otto, 184, 227
Giraud, Charles, 31, 274
Gladstone, William, 120–121
Goethe, Johann Wolfgang, 10
Goldie, George, 117, 118–119, 126
Grey, Edward, 153
Grossraum doctrine, 251, 414, 415, 420–422, 435, 480
Grotian tradition, 356, 406–411, 473
Grotius, Hugo, 4, 17, 33, 46, 116, 131, 362, 392
Grundnorm, 241, 366
Gumplowicz, Ludwig, 196

Hague Academy of International Law, 193, 214, 251, 319, 331, 474
Hague Conferences (1899 and 1907), 87, 134, 211, 217–218, 275, 284–286, 288
Hall, William E., 81–83, 108
Hamilton, Alexander, 439
Hanotaux, Gabriel, 153
Harcourt, William, 33, 86
Hardenberg, Karl-August, 21
harmony of interests, 461–462, 487
Hautefeuille, Laurent-Basile, 30, 86
Hegel, Georg Wilhelm Friedrich, 23, 32, 180, 182, 195, 197, 198, 260, 262–264, 320
Heidegger, Martin, 264, 295
Heilborn, Paul, 109, 129, 187, 192, 227
Heimburger, Karl, 109, 141, 144
Heller, Hermann, 239–240
Henderson, Arthur, 381, 382
Henkin, Louis, 477
Herz, John J., 467, 471
Herzl, Theodor, 407
Hinsley, F. H., 472
Hinterland, 151
historical school of law, 25, 43, 44–47, 48, 51, 72, 114, 131, 277, 435

Index

Hobbes, Thomas, 359
Hoffmann, Stanley, 465, 469
Holocaust, 388–389, 393, 411
Holtzendorff, Franz, 40, 63, 65, 72–73, 132, 222–223, 263, 280
Holy Alliance, 15, 27–28, 35
Hornung, Joseph, 105, 109, 129–130, 170
Huber, Max, 227–228
Hughes, Charles Evans, 466
Hughes, Thomas, 76
Hull, Cordell, 439
human rights, 3, 50, 52, 99, 104, 128, 130, 199, 356, 514
  Fiore on, 54–57
  Lauterpacht on, 391–399
humanitarianism, 15, 70, 83–86, 129, 130, 265, 424, 436
humanity, as political subject, 433–435
Hurst, Cecil, 390

idea of France, 272, 274, 350, 351
ideal types, 202
idealism (German) 182, 195, 214–215, 257–260
identity (logic of) 142, 515
Imperial British East Africa Company (IBEAC), 119
imperialism, 5, 99, 240, 480, 482, 489–494
  Anglo-American, 238
  German, 207–208
  US, 418, 419, 480–481, 483, 487
In Defense of the National Interest, 437
independence, 21, 175, 177,
Indian Mutiny (1857) 146
individualism, 269, 282, 298–302, 306, 314, 318, 324, 330, 332, 334, 365, 409, 410
  in Kaufmann, 180, 252–253
  in Kelsen, 244
  in Lauterpacht, 357
  in Le Fur, 324–325
  in Scelle, 330, 332, 334
industrialism, 11, 36, 58, 194, 288–289
informal empire, 110–112, 116–121, 144
Institut de droit international, 2, 19, 41, 42, 47–48, 54, 58, 60, 61, 62, 75, 79, 88–89, 92–97, 98, 103, 121, 127, 129, 130, 132–133, 140, 143, 149–151, 157, 163, 170, 173, 179, 181, 188, 193, 210, 211, 216, 223, 237, 258, 276, 278, 280, 293, 302, 313, 511
Institut des hautes études internationales (Paris), 279, 309–311, 314, 315
Institut für auswärtige Politik (Hamburg), 232–233
Institut für Sozialforschung (Frankfurt), 447
institutionalism, 176–178, 396–398, 477, 487
instrumentalism, 435, 485–487

interdependence, 27, 93, 96, 192, 207–208, 222–228, 229, 231, 260, 270, 282, 297–298, 299, 301, 304, 305, 325, 363, 477, 479, 487
interdisciplinarity, 459–460, 464, 476–478, 478–480, 483, 484–485, 488–494
interests, theory of 226–227, 228
International Bill of Rights, 394–395, 398
International Court of Justice, 398–402
International Labour Organization (ILO), 332, 338
International Law and Human Rights, 392–399
International Law Association, 61, 232
International Law Commission, 399–400
international relations as a discipline, 393, 465–474, 482–489, 493, 494
internationalism, 4, 63–67, 222–228, 371–372, 513–516
  in France 270–274, 284, 325
  in Germany 189, 190, 208, 213, 216, 222–228, 233–234, 237, 239, 250, 262–263
interpretation
  Kelsen on, 248
  Lauterpacht on, 357, 368–369, 378, 383, 385–387, 400–401
intervention, 22, 34, 55, 94–95, 238, 271, 332, 335, 339–342, 419, 480–482, 514
irrationalism, 196–197, 229, 256, 356, 360, 407
Israel, 396, 407
ius publicum Europaeum, 415, 417, 420, 426, 432, 438
ius publicum universale, 31

Jameson raid (1895), 120
Japan, 133, 135
Jellinek, Georg, 21, 188, 198–208, 212, 242, 250, 251, 322, 406, 452
  defense of international law, 200–201
  theory of federations, 202
  theory of state, 202–206
  views on war, 207
Jellinek, Walter, 234
Jenks, Wilfried, 408, 477
Jèze, Gaston, 106–107, 132, 137–138, 140, 317, 329
Jhering, Rudolf, 36, 322
Johnson, Lyndon, B., 413
Joseph-Barthélemy, 313, 318
Journal of the History of International Law, 9
judicial legislation, 402–406
just war, 334, 425–426
Jünger, Ernst, 431, 450–451

Kaiser-Wilhelm-Instutut für Völkerrecht (Berlin), 233

563

Index

Kaltenborn von Stachau, Karl Baron, 24–28, 31, 92
Kant, Immanuel, 15, 113, 189, 191, 194, 197, 198, 204, 249, 249, 262–264, 268, 320, 357, 489, 501, 514
Kantorowicz, Hermann, 195–196, 486
Kasson, John A., 138
Katchenowski, D. I., 40
Kaufmann, Erich, 179–181, 189, 233, 249–261, 442, 511
   critique of neo-Kantianism, 251–255
   on the Versailles settlement, 181, 249–250
   on natural law, 258, 260–261
   theory of state, 252–253
Kellogg–Briand Pact (Pact of Paris, 1928), 377, 384, 418, 419, 433
Kelsen, Hans, 182, 238–249, 213, 250–251, 255, 306, 321, 356, 357, 360, 366, 371, 406, 409, 410, 428, 435, 441, 452, 455, 456–458, 471, 494, 495, 496
   as left-liberal, 245–246, 247
   as relativist, 247–248, 409
   theory of state, 243, 244
   theory of validity, 241
Kennan, George, 469, 471
Kiel Institute of International Law, 231–232
Kissinger, Henry, 468, 469
Kitchener, (Lord) Herbert, 153
Klüber, Johann Ludwig, 21–24, 25, 26, 30, 71, 92, 112–116, 131
Kohler, Josef, 213–215, 229
Krabbe, Hugo, 330
Kunz, Joseph, 474

La notion du politique et la théorie des différends internationaux, 453–455
La réalité des normes: En particulier des normes du droit international, 455–457
Laband, Paul, 46, 184–185, 195, 213, 228, 240
Laclau, Ernesto, 504
L'affaire Scelle (1925), 316–317
laissez-faire, 144, 269, 288
Lapradelle (La Pradelle), Albert Geouffre de, 154, 309, 310, 312, 343, 350
Larnaude, Ferdinand, 293, 295
Las Casas, Bartolomé de, 78, 142, 147
Lasson, Adolf, 32–33, 37–38, 63, 92, 182–183, 186, 189, 223, 262
Lasswell, Harold, 468, 475
Lauterpacht, Elihu, 370
Lauterpacht, Hersch, 1, 2, 8, 353–412, 511
   and human rights, 392–399
   as liberal, 360–361, 365, 373, 406–411
   as practitioner, 399–401
   as Zionist, 370–372
   critique of positivism, 355–357, 364
   in Nuremberg, 388–390
   on collective security, 377–381
   on colonialism, 359–360
   on neutrality, 379–381
   on recognition, 382–388
   on self-judgment, 358, 366–367, 377–380, 397, 401, 408
   theory of law as "complete system," 361–369
Laveleye, Emile de, 36, 60–61, 71, 121, 149, 156, 170
Le Bon, Gustave, 196–197, 360
Le Fur, Louis, 315–316, 317–318, 328, 330–334, 339–345, 349, 351
   appointment as Professor in Paris, 316–317
   critique of "German theory," 320–322
   on the European Union, 342–345
   on natural law, 318–319, 323–324
   on Spanish Civil War, 338–342
League of Nations, 7–8, 170–172, 181, 209, 235–236, 236–238, 239, 249–250, 267, 270, 294–295, 306, 307, 311, 312, 320, 330, 342–345, 353–354, 355, 358, 376–382, 393, 411, 445, 461
League of Nations as universal federation, 426
League of Nations' Codification Conference (1930), 265, 466
legal process school, 477–478, 487
legal realism, 475–6, 479, 483
legal system
   completeness of, 366–368, 372, 375, 383, 401–404
Leibnitz, Gottfried Wilhelm, 198–199
Léopold II, 108, 122, 123, 136–137, 153, 156–162
   recognition as the Head of State of the Congo, 155, 156
Lévi-Strauss, Claude, 351
Lévy-Bruhl, Lucien, 329
liberal activism, 26, 35, 57–67
liberal humanitarianism, 51, 53, 54–57
liberalism, 11–19, 27–28, 29, 38, 67–97
   Austrian, 359, 370, 406–407
   Belgian, 16, 90
   British, 59–60, 90, 372–373, 392
   French, 281, 288–291, 301–302
   German, 91 215–222, 252–253, 261
   Morgenthau's critique of, 461–463
   Schmitt's critique of, 426–436
Lieber, Francis, 39, 42, 49, 59, 67, 68, 69, 77, 87, 96
Liszt, Franz, 102, 195, 209, 225–226, 229, 231
Lithuania, 328–329
Livingstone, David, 146
Locarno Treaty (1925), 237, 238, 250, 377, 459

564

Index

Lorimer, James, 33, 34, 62, 66, 68, 69, 70, 77, 104, 129, 131
Lotus principle, 402
Lüderitz, Adolf, 118

Machiavelli, Niccolo, 359
Mackinnon, William, 117, 119
Mahdi, The, 155
Maine, Henry Sumner, 36, 46, 48, 75, 85–86, 100
Maistre, Joseph de, 27
Manchuria,
 Japan's attack on (1931), 239, 353, 377, 378–379
Mancini, Pasquale, 14, 41, 61, 62, 66
Mandates under the League Covenant, 171–172, 360, 375
Marchand, Jean-Baptiste, 153–155
Marcuse, Herbert, 465
Martens, Fedor, 68, 157
Martens, Georg Friedrich, 4, 25, 26, 27, 30, 71, 92, 112–116, 131
Martitz, Ferdinand, 134, 138, 150
Marx, Karl, 88, 195
materialism, 37,
McDougal, Myres S., 474–475, 476, 477–479, 481, 482, 483, 487, 489
McNair, Arnold, 356, 376
Meeker, L. C., 413
Meinecke, Friedrich, 234
Mendelssohn-Bartholdy, Albrecht, 232, 234
Mendlowitz, Saul, 478
Menelik, Emperor of Abyssinia, 108
Mérignhac, Alexandre, 140, 284
Merriam, Charles, 468
Miles, James B., 40
militarism, 35, 48,
Mill, John Stuart, 23, 73
Millot, Albert, 172
Mohl, Robert, 32, 50
Moltke, Count Helmuth von, 83, 84–85
Monnet, Jean, 345–346
Monroe Doctrine, 415, 418, 421
Montesquieu, Charles Secondat, Baron de, 14, 29, 73, 100, 105, 113
"moralism" in foreign policy, 438, 462, 469
morality, 89–97, 299–230, 418, 487–494, 499
 in Durkheim and Scelle, 297–298, 334
 in Lauterpacht, 404, 406–411
 in Le Fur 318–319, 325, 343
 in Politis, 308, 310
Morant Bay Rebellion, 147
Morel, Edmund, 158
Morgenthau, Hans, 436–471, 480–483, 486, 489, 493
 and liberalism, 459–465
 as founder of "international relations," 465–468

 critique of American foreign policy, 437–440
 on national interest, 469, 480–481
 on statesmanship, 463–464, 468–469, 471, 482, 487–488
 on total war, 437
 psychological theory of power, 448–449, 454, 455–456, 468, 469
 theory of sanctions, 455–459
 traditionalism of, 471–472
Mosul Boundary case, 417
Moye, Marcel, 167,
Moynier, Gustave, 39, 121, 12, 149, 156, 163, 170
Munich accords (1938) 353–355

Nachtigal, Gustav, 137
national honor, 441
national socialism, 261–262, 414, 422, 471
nationalism, 37, 58, 62–67, 180, 211–213, 215, 216, 221, 224, 230–231, 256–258, 271, 309, 317–318, 320, 321, 325, 334–335, 355–356, 359, 370
native
 citizenship, 128
 consent, 138, 139, 140–142
 sovereignty, 113–114
 treaties, 109, 128, 136–143
natural law, 4, 20–24, 28–29, 30, 73, 79, 91, 92, 94–95, 96, 100, 105, 115–116, 128, 131, 229–230, 289, 274, 299, 300, 312, 315–316, 318, 319, 322, 323, 334, 337, 346, 356, 357, 365, 373, 392, 396, 466, 476–477
Nazism, 261–262
Nelson, Leonard, 255
neo-colonialism, 175
Neumeyer, Karl, 447
neutrality, 85, 86, 291, 306–307, 379–381, 471, 419
neutralization (of the Congo) 121–122
New International Economic Order, 175, 512
Niemeyer, Theodor, 232–234, 239, 477
Nietzsche, Friedrich, 79, 192, 196, 205, 254, 320, 448, 450
Nippold, Otfried, 192–193
Nobel Peace Prize
 given to Bourgeois 295
 given to Renault, 278
Noble Savage, 74, 101
nominalism (Lauterpacht's), 368–369
nomos, 415, 416, 419, 423, 439, 460, 480
non-intervention, 313–314, 340, 341, 499–500
normative force of facts, 205
normativism, 417, 428–429
Notrecht, 254, 443
Nottebohm case, 400

Index

Nuremberg Trial (1946), 388–390, 418, 422
Nys, Ernest, 160–161

occupation, 148–155, 432
Oncken, Hermann, 234
Oppenheim, Lassa, 8, 92
organic
   solidarity, 297–298, 331
   theory, 31–32, 43, 44, 45, 46, 49, 50, 63, 91, 183–184, 186, 321
Organization of American States (OAS), 413, 497
Orwell, George, 414, 420

pacifism, 35, 209, 210, 211, 213–214, 215–222, 240, 257, 450–451, 458
Pact of Paris (*see* Kellogg–Briand Pact)
Parieu, F. Esquireu de, 40
particularism, 504–509
Peace Act (1933), 381
peaceful change (cf. Covenant of the League of Nations, Article 19)
pedigree history, 101–103
Permanent Court of Arbitration, 212, 217, 275, 286
Permanent Court of International Justice, 193, 215, 221–222, 246
Perrinjaquet, Jean, 151
Peters, Carl, 107, 119, 138
Phillimore, Robert, 34
Pillet, Antoine, 271, 281–284, 300, 302, 311, 349
   as "functionalist," 282–284
   critic of the Versailles settlement, 292–293
Piloty, Robert, 213
Poincaré, Raymond, 296, 346
political
   concept of, 430–437, 440–445, 448–449, 452–455, 468
   disputes, 367–368, 440–445
Political Romanticism (Politische Romantik), 427
Political Theology. Four Concepts on the Concept of Sovereignty (Politische Theologie. Vier Kapitel zur Lehre von der Souveränität), 427–428, 442
Politics among Nations. The Struggle for Power and for Peace, 437
Politis, Nicolas, 305–309, 314, 330
positive freedom 264
positivism, 4, 29, 46, 48, 82, 91, 96, 130–131, 186–188, 257–259, 355, 363, 364, 393–394, 407
Pound, Roscoe, 194
pragmatism, 369, 479, 502, 516
   French, 275, 347, 348–352
   Lauterpacht's 387–388, 399–412
primitive law
   international law as, 361–362

private international law, 43–44, 57, 66, 293
Private Law Sources and Analogies, 366–367, 374–375, 376, 383
privatism, 269, 275–276, 288
progress, 29, 27–28, 29, 46, 48, 57–58, 59, 74–75, 82, 91, 93, 96, 233–234, 302–305, 358–359, 365, 373, 397, 399, 406, 511, 512
property, right of, 104, 113–114, 127–128, 300
protectorates, 109, 117, 118, 119, 124–125, 126, 129, 151–152, 169, 432
Protestantism, 42, 54, 65, 79, 91, 415
Proudhon, Pierre-Joseph, 35, 285
psychological theory, 200–201, 206, 225–226, 242–243, 448–449, 454, 455, 459, 470
public opinion, 15–16, 28, 51, 54–55, 57, 72, 302, 319, 363, 458
Puchta, Georg Friedrich, 45
Pufendorff, Samuel, 73

quasi-contract, 290, 300

racism, 58, 70–71, 96, 103–104, 107, 321, 322–323
radicalism (French), 288–289, 296, 329
rational will (theory of), 190–192, 208
rationalism, 13, 20–24, 24–25, 31, 43, 44, 45, 47, 71, 91, 92–94, 96, 208, 250, 251–252, 275–277, 330, 356, 358–359, 370, 489–490
Rawls, John, 290, 493
Rayneval, Gérard de, 28, 29, 113
realism, 8, 26, 38,195–198, 311, 313–314, 360, 368, 373, 376, 384, 393, 404, 409
   legal, 475–476
"Realism" in international relations, 446, 460, 479
reasonableness, 402–403
rebus sic stantibus, 363, 368, 442 (*see also* fundamental change)
Rechtsstaat, 20, 32, 191, 196, 197, 198–208, 247, 249, 268, 502
recognition, 419, 507, 508
   Lauterpacht on 384–386
   Lorimer's theory of, 70–71
Recognition in International Law, 382–388
Red Cross, 39, 122
Reddie, James, 23, 33, 71, 72
Redslob, Robert, 271, 274
Reeves, Jesse, 164, 165
reform
   advocated by *Institut* founders, 14–19, 57–67
regime theory, 479–480
Reine Rechtslehre, 241, 248
Renan, Ernst, 269
Renault, Louis, 105–106, 274–278, 284, 291, 302, 305, 312

566

Index

Renner, Karl, 246
republicanism (French), 267, 269, 273–274, 288–291, 346
respublica Christiana, 416
Reuter, Paul, 345–346, 347
revolution, 35, 269, 273–274, 288, 289, 301, 374
Revue de droit international et de législation comparée, 4, 12–19, 60, 121, 127, 143, 166, 361
Revue générale de droit international public, 278–279, 362
Rhodes, Cecil, 117, 120
Rivier, Alphonse, 31, 39, 52–53, 67–68, 135, 160, 223
Robinson, Ronald, 116, 126
Rolin, Albéric, 69, 229
Rolin, Henri (1874–1946), 171, 511
Rolin, Henri (1891–1973), 511–512, 513
Rolin-Jaequemyns, Gustave, 12–19, 20, 39–41, 48, 49, 51–52, 60, 61, 63, 65, 67, 76–77, 79, 80, 81, 89, 90, 92, 127, 133, 144, 156, 166, 502, 511, 516
Roman law, 100, 22, 24, 31, 93, 420
romanticism, 47, 427
Roosevelt, F. D., 467
Root, Elihu, 466
Rousseau, Charles, 348
Rousseau, Jean-Jacques, 86, 115, 116, 315, 330
Royer-Collard, Pierre Paul, 31
Rule of Law, 178, 361, 381, 450, 503
rule-skepticism, 463, 475–476
Russell, Lord, 107–108
Russia, 35, 272, 284, 344

Saalfeld, Friedrich, 113
sacred trust of civilization, 171
Salomon, Charles, 106, 130, 132, 137, 144
sanctions, 244, 311, 455–459
Savigny, Friedrich Carl, 32, 36, 43–45, 46, 77, 100, 114, 183, 421, 435
Scelle, Georges, 266–267, 316–317, 319, 327–338, 342–347, 349, 351, 424–426, 471, 511
  and sociological monism, 331–334
  on European Union, 342–345
  on nationalism and self-determination, 334–335
  on Spanish Civil War, 338–342
  political alignments, 329–330
  theory of state, 330
  theory of treaty revision, 336–338
Schachter, Oscar, 477
Schmitt, Carl, 238, 239, 415–437, 453–454, 459–465, 480, 481, 486, 496
  and "total State", 430
  and antisemitism, 424, 426
  and liberalism, 422–423, 426–432
  on democracy, 429
  on friend–enemy opposition, 431–435, 453–454
  on humanitarian war, 434, 451
  on humanitarianism, 434–436
  on Lauterpacht, 424–426
  on Scelle, 424–426, 471
  on sovereignty, 428
Schopenhauer, Arthur, 198–199
Schücking, Walther, 209, 215–222, 232, 239, 306, 450
Schuman Declaration (1950), 338, 345
Schwarzenberger, Georg, 472
science
  international law as, 23, 24–28, 32, 40, 41, 56–57, 95–97, 105, 188–189, 193, 210, 214, 240–249, 289, 297–302, 331, 334, 335–336, 346, 357, 363–364, 384–385, 447, 476
  international relations as, 470–471, 472
Scientific Man vs. Power Politics, 437, 468
scientism, 468
Scott, James Brown, 425
Security Council, 350, 391, 516
security dilemma, 467
Selbstverpflichtung, 201, 205, 206
self-determination, 64, 191, 193, 271, 321, 328, 334
self-legislation (theory of), 186, 192, 201, 204, 208, 321
Shawcross, Hartley, 388, 389
Siam, 16, 133, 134
Sibert, M, 350
Sidgwick, Henry, 74
Simons, Walter, 220, 221, 235
Sinzheimer, Hugo, 447, 449
slave trade, 94
Sloterdijk, Peter, 352
Smend, Rudolf, 233, 452
Smith, Adam, 60
Smyrniadis, Bion, 350,
social solidarity, 298–301, 318, 319, 331
socialism, 58, 60–61, 67, 68–69, 281, 301
Société française pour le droit international, 349
sociology, 23, 72, 97, 99, 188, 195–196, 199, 200, 202–203, 204, 206, 222–228, 233–234, 242–243, 262, 266 *et seq.* 277, 281, 289, 299–302, 322, 327–338, 346, 349, 350, 397, 459, 467–468, 470–471, 486, 488, 494
solidarism, 192, 285–291, 295–297
  in Alvarez, 302–305, 309
  in Politis, 305–308, 309
  in Scelle, 331–338
Sorel, Albert, 276
sovereignty, 3, 4, 20, 21, 25–26, 31, 48, 109–110, 121, 125–126, 127, 128, 134, 137–138, 139, 140–143, 143–152, 156,

Index

sovereignty (*cont.*)
168, 170–177, 204, 239–240, 242, 244, 302, 303, 306–307, 324, 330, 335, 346–347, 355, 358, 359, 365, 389, 393, 407, 428, 514
Soviet Union, 414
Spanish Civil War (1936–1939), 313, 338–342
Speke, John, 147
Spencer, Herbert, 38, 70, 71, 75, 308
Spengler, Oswald, 414, 420, 451
spheres of interest, 125, 154–155, 169
spying, 85–86
Stahl, Friedrich Julius, 180
Stalin, Josef, 439
standard of civilization, 132–136
Stanley, Henry M., 107, 121, 136–137, 138–140, 143, 147
state theory
French, 269, 298–301, 324
German 277, 299, 321–322, 452–453
German theory of, 197–198, 198–208, 244–245, 252–253
States as persons 80–83
Stengel, Carl von, 208, 211–212
Stone, Julius, 361
Strauss, Leo, 465
Stresemann, Gustav, 237, 445
structuralism, 5, 6
struggle for power
Morgenthau's theory, 448–450, 493
nineteenth-century theory, 32–33, 36–38
Strupp, Karl, 238, 265, 445–446
Störk, F., 213
Suarez, Francisco, 78
subjective right, 184, 187
"subjectivism," 320

terra nullius, 129, 134, 154
Third Republic, French, 281, 285, 288–289, 296
Thomas, A. J., 497–501
Torres Campos, Manuel, 168
tradition
in Lauterpacht, 373, 392
in Le Fur 317–327
in Morgenthau, 471–472, 499
treaties, 52, 71–72, 185, 186, 193, 211, 331–332
Triepel, Heinrich, 190, 210, 211, 233, 322
Truyol y Serra, Antonio, 351
Tunisia, 117, 142, 273
Turkey (Ottoman Empire), 62, 73, 104, 129, 133, 134, 135, 272, 273, 344
Twiss, Travers, 33, 78, 108, 122, 132–133, 143, 280

Tylor, E. B., 131
Tönnies, Ferdinand, 227, 234, 235

Ullmann, Emanuel, 224–225, 263
United Nations, 434, 487
Anglo-American plans for, 389–391
United Nations Charter, 391, 392, 394
Article 51, 414
Universal Declaration of Human Rights (Lauterpacht's critique), 395–397
universal
federation, 325–326, 464
norms, 489–494, 499–500
universalism, 71, 100–101, 102–105, 130–131, 141–142, 210, 245–246, 253, 416, 417, 423, 426, 433, 489–494, 500–509
French, 270, 271, 294, 295–296, 307, 318, 322
utilitarianism, 13, 29, 34, 86

Vattel, Emmerich (Emer), 4, 21, 29, 33, 46, 131
Verdross, Alfred, 246–247, 306, 366
Vergé, Charles, 27–28
Verne, Jules, 41
Versailles Peace Conference (1918–1919), 219–221, 236
Versailles Treaty (1919), 181, 236–238, 249, 292, 293, 296–297, 311, 417–418, 442, 445
Vilna, 328,
Vinogradoff, Paul, 75
virtue, 80
vital interests, 441
Vitoria, Francisco de, 78, 142, 147
Volksgeist, 32, 43
Voltaire, François Marie Arouet, 115
voluntarism (will theory of law), 180, 186, 189–190, 192–193, 200–201, 204–206, 256, 258, 275, 320, 321

Walker, T. A., 155
Waltz, Kenneth, 472
war, 29, 35–36, 38, 39, 88–88, 207, 215
as police action, 325, 425
as social ideal, 179–180, 182, 183
discriminatory concept of, 418, 419, 425–426, 433–435, 437–439, 462
formal, 432–433, 437
guilt, 236, 237, 293, 324
total, 419, 462
Weber, Max, 80, 88, 195, 196, 201, 268, 347, 447, 486, 487
Webster, K. C., 473
Wehberg, Hans, 215, 221
Weimar Republic (1919–1933), 248, 250–251, 426–432, 449–450, 459, 495

Index

Wesen des Völkerrechts und die Clausula rebus sic stantibus, 179, 251
Westlake, John, 12, 13, 17, 48, 49, 52, 59–60, 63, 64–65, 70, 76, 80, 85–86, 90, 92, 93, 108, 127, 128, 130, 131, 134, 138, 149–150, 163–164, 166–167, 278, 372–373
Wheaton, Henry, 17, 30, 50, 114–115
White, Hayden, 103
Wight, Martin, 466, 473
Wildman, Richard, 48, 94
William II, 418, 426
Wilson, Woodrow, 171, 220, 235, 294–295, 321, 356, 469
Wimbledon case, 173

Windelband, Wilhelm, 199
Woolsey, Theodor, 100
World Federation of Jewish Students, 370, 371
World Trade Organization (WTO), 177, 513

Xhosa Rebellion (1857), 147

Yalta agreement, 439, 462

Zanzibar, 125
Zimmern, Alfred, 473
Zionism, 369–372, 407
Zitelmann, Ernst, 230
Zorn, Philipp, 208, 211–212, 236
Zouche, Richard, 327